To Finlay

— MS

To Robin, Chloé and Annabelle

— TV

Michael Schaper

Michael Schaper (BA, MComm, PhD) is Head of the School of Business at Bond University, and was previously Small Business Commissioner for the Australian Capital Territory. A past president of the Small Enterprise Association of Australia and New Zealand, Michael is currently a member of the board of directors of the International Council for Small Business. Between 2003 and 2005, he held the foundation professorial chair in Entrepreneurship and Small Business within the University of Newcastle — the first dedicated chair in small business in Australia.

Before his academic career, Michael worked for several years as a professional small business adviser in Australia. In addition, he ran his own business and was involved in numerous other start-up projects.

He holds a PhD and a Master of Commerce degree from Curtin University of Technology, as well as a Bachelor of Arts from the University of Western Australia. Michael has been Visiting Professor at the École de Management de Lyon, France, and at the University of St Gallen, Switzerland.

Michael is the author or co-author of eight books, all in the field of business management, and has been an occasional columnist in *The Australian Financial Review*, *The Australian* and *Business Review Weekly*. He has published over 40 refereed articles in academic journals and numerous pieces in the general media.

Thierry Volery

Thierry Volery is Professor of Entrepreneurship and Director of the Swiss Institute for Entrepreneurship and Small Business at the University of St Gallen, Switzerland. He is also the Managing Director of the Graduate Diploma in SME Management — an executive course offered at the University of St Gallen for owner–managers of small and medium-sized businesses.

From September 1999 until 2002, he was Professor of Entrepreneurship and Management at the École de Management de Lyon, France. He was previously a senior lecturer in entrepreneurship and international business at Curtin University of Technology in Perth, Western Australia.

Thierry was a visiting professor at the China Europe International Business School (CEIBS) in Shanghai and at the Graduate School of Management, University of Western Australia. He has served on several editorial boards, including the *Journal of Small Business Management*, the *International Small Business Journal*, the *Journal of Enterprising Culture* and the *International Journal of Educational Management*. He holds a doctorate in business economics and social sciences from the University of Fribourg, Switzerland. His research interests include entrepreneurship in the Asia–Pacific region, corporate entrepreneurship and strategic alliances.

Entrepreneurship
and Small Business

2nd Pacific Rim Edition

Michael **Schaper**
SCHOOL OF BUSINESS, BOND UNIVERSITY

Thierry **Volery**
UNIVERSITY OF ST GALLEN, SWITZERLAND

John Wiley & Sons Australia, Ltd

Second edition published 2007 by
John Wiley & Sons Australia, Ltd
42 McDougall Street, Milton Qld 4064
Offices also in Sydney and Melbourne

First edition published 2004

Typeset in 10/12.5 Giovanni Light

© Michael Schaper and Thierry Volery, 2004, 2007

The moral rights of the authors have been asserted.

National Library of Australia
Cataloguing-in-Publication data

Schaper, Michael.
  Entrepreneurship and small business: a Pacific Rim
  perspective

  2nd ed.
  Bibliography.
  Includes index.
  For tertiary students.
  ISBN 9780 4708 1082 8.

  1. Small business — Pacific Area. 2.
  Entrepreneurship — Pacific Area. 3. New business
  enterprises. I. Volery, Thierry. II. Title.

658.022

Cover and internal design images: © Digital Vision (main image);
© Photodisc (top image and bottom images)
Wiley Bicentennial Logo: Richard J. Pacifico

Printed in Singapore by
CMO Image Printing Enterprise

10 9 8 7 6 5 4 3 2 1

CONTENTS

PREFACE

Although there are many different career options in business, few offer as much potential for personal achievement and independent wealth creation as starting or running your own business.

Entrepreneurs are people who conceive of new business opportunities, take the risks, and then turn their ideas into successfully functioning enterprises. Small business owner–managers are the people who are responsible for the day-to-day organisation and operation of small firms. Both groups are at the forefront of many of the new ideas, new markets, new jobs and new wealth-generating activities taking place all over the world.

Like any area of potentially high reward, there are many risks involved in new projects. Failure rates are often much higher than for established firms, and operating systems, human resources and financing options are often much more limited than in larger organisations. For these reasons, intending entrepreneurs and small business owner–managers need to carefully prepare themselves before starting out on their venture.

There are many textbooks available on these subjects, but most continue to focus solely on a particular country. Even today, the majority of the English-language books available are British, Australian or American, and often ignore or downplay the important legal, marketing and operational variations that occur between different countries in the region.

For this reason, we have written *Entrepreneurship and Small Business: 2nd Pacific Rim Edition*, a comprehensive, multinational textbook that focuses on a number of different jurisdictions and countries in the region: Australia, New Zealand, Singapore, Malaysia and Hong Kong. New business ventures and established small businesses are key driving elements in each of these economies and, because of their shared British colonial heritage, many of these nations also share a common legal and governmental framework.

The book also incorporates many useful teaching aids and practical information for effective learning:

- **Learning objectives:** A set of clear outcomes is provided at the beginning of each chapter, explaining what students should know by the end of their reading and study.
- **Key words:** Major terms and concepts are highlighted and defined as they occur.
- **Profiles:** Contemporary entrepreneurs and small business owner–managers from the Pacific Rim region are profiled in each chapter.
- **Web addresses:** Useful websites point students in the right direction for further details about particular issues.
- **What would you do?:** Short cases allow students to solve an ethical issue or problem relevant to the chapter.
- **Chapter summary:** A brief review of the major learning points and issues is provided at the end of each chapter.

- **Review and discussion questions:** These are designed to help students become familiar with the learning objectives and major concepts introduced in each chapter.
- **Case studies:** At the end of each chapter, an applied problem requiring the use of both analytical and technical skills is provided for students.
- **End-of-book case studies:** Four comprehensive cases feature at the end of this second edition. These profile entrepreneurs from Malaysia, Singapore, Australia and New Zealand, and offer real-world success stories for students to draw inspiration from.

In addition to these textbook teaching aids, *Entrepreneurship and Small Business: 2nd Pacific Rim Edition* has an accompanying website that includes:

- an Instructor's Resource Guide containing teaching notes and solutions
- PowerPoint presentations for each chapter
- an additional textbook chapter, Information Systems and Technology, for lecturers wanting to cover this area in more depth.

Finally, a word about terminology. As we explain in chapter 4, we recognise that the terms *small business* and *entrepreneurship* are not synonymous. Entrepreneurship is mainly about the creation and growth of a business venture, whereas small business management covers the daily control of a small firm. However, there is often considerable overlap between the two sets of activities (many entrepreneurs start off by creating a small firm that subsequently grows into a larger enterprise). Both entrepreneurs and small business owner–managers are required to be familiar with many of the same technical skills and business concepts. Therefore, in the parts of this book that apply to both entrepreneurs and small business operators, we have used the terms *entrepreneur* and *small business owner–manager* interchangeably.

Whether you want to build an entrepreneurial success story or just a profitable small local enterprise, or are simply seeking to better understand these types of businesses, this book will provide the information you need. We hope you find it useful.

Michael Schaper
Thierry Volery

ACKNOWLEDGEMENTS

No book is ever solely the work of its authors. Many other people play an important part in preparing a textbook of this magnitude, and without them it is doubtful our project could have been completed in time. In particular, we would like to acknowledge the help of Kirstin Miffling (research and editing), Clive Jones (video shooting and editing), Curtin Business School (who provided financial and logistical support for much of the project in its early days), and Nina Crisp and Dan Logovik (John Wiley & Sons Australia). We also acknowledge the contribution of Louise Maufette Leenders and Michiel Leenders for the development of the four comprehensive cases, and to Daryll Cahill, RMIT University, for the additional cases on the website.

We are also indebted to the practitioners who provided access to companies as well as information and suggestions on profile and case drafts. Our special thanks go to Wong Ngit Liong (Venture Corporation), Robert Boyd and Ashley Salisbury (Pure Bliss Foods), Francis Yeoh (YTL Corporation), Simon Sze (Vision Care Eye Centre), Olivia Lum (Hyflux), Michael Whittaker (Atlantis Group), Damon Gorrie (Communicator), Anna Kluczewska (AION Diagnostics), Sam Morgan (TradeMe), Camus Leung (Hildebrand International Travel Service), Carolyn Cresswell (Carman's Fine Foods), Kirsty Harrison and Graeme Wood (Wotif.com), Richard Sheppard (Macquarie Bank), Mohshin Aziz (AirAsia), Phillip Mills and Jill Tattersall (Les Mills International), Nina Quinn and Peter Hanley (Neuromonics), Juanna Tan, Terence Swee and Philip Morgan (muvee Technologies), Henry and Kenny Goh (Macrokiosk).

Finally, our thanks also to the peer reviewers: Barry Hutton, RMIT University; Jayanath Ananda, LaTrobe University; John Gray, University of Western Sydney; Stephane Tywoniak, Queensland University of Technology; Lindsay Cowling, Holmesglen TAFE; Val Morrison, Southern Cross University; Charles Hollis, Australian Catholic University; Les Kirchmajer, University of Wollongong; Donald Geyer, Charles Sturt University; Colin Jones, University of Tasmania; and Rodney Farr-Wharton, University of Sunshine Coast, all of whose comments on the drafts of the second edition have been invaluable.

The authors and publisher would also like to thank the following copyright holders, organisations and individuals for their assistance and for permission to reproduce copyright material in this book.

Images
- © Digital Vision, front cover (main image)
- © Photodisc, front cover (top image and bottom images)
- © PhotoDisc, internal design images (woman with laptop, harbour city)
- © Digital Vision, internal design image (meeting)
- Pearson Education UK, fig. **1.1**, p. 5
- Elsevier, fig **2.1**, p. 31; fig. **2.3**, p. 44
- Marc J. Dollinger, fig. **3.2**, p. 73
- John Wiley & Sons, Inc, fig. **5.1**, p. 111

- Professor Richard Artley, fig. **6.1**, p. 134
- Simon & Schuster, Inc., fig. **6.2**, p. 140
- Blackwell Publishers, fig. **16.1**, p. 401
- Corporate Executive Board, fig. **16.2**, p. 405
- Booz Allen Hamilton, fig. **16.3**, p. 406

Text
- Pure Bliss, case study pages **24–7**/Reproduced with the permission of Robert Boyd
- Harvard Business School Publishing, table 3.5, page 65; table 15.2, page **383**
- Michael Whittaker, case study pages **76–7**
- Basil Lenzo, entrepreneur profile pages **88–9**
- Zach Hitchcock, entrepreneur profile pages **95–6**
- Michael à Campo, case study pages **103–4**
- Carolyn Cresswell, entrepreneur profile page **117**
- Professor Richard Artley, pages **133–7**
- Damon Gorrie, case study pages **156–9**
- Dr Daryll Cahill, case studies pages **171** & **338–9**/Prepared by the Small Business staff, School of Accounting and Law, RMIT University
- Jude Alfeld, entrepreneur profile page **172**
- Kristy Andruszko, entrepreneur profile page **214**
- Infego Communications <http://unlimited.co.nz>, case study pages **219–20**, entrepreneur profile page **237**
- Dr Anna Kluczewska, case study pages **242–4**
- Peter Gordon, entrepreneur profile pages **252–3**
- Leighton Jay, table 10.3, page **254**
- Allen and Unwin, www.allen-unwin.com.au, table 11.3, page **284**
- Kathy Kingston, entrepreneur profile pages **304–5**
- Professor Michael Schaper, pages **322–3**
- Camus Leung, entrepreneur profile page **329**
- Goh Ai Yat, entrepreneur profile pages **352–3**
- Wotif.com, case study pages **393–6**
- AirAsia, case study pages **421–3**/Reproduced with the permission of Mohshin Aziz
- Blackwell Publishers, table 17.3, page **433**
- Kevin Fong, entrepreneur profile page **434**
- Taylor & Khoo, entrepreneur profile page **439**
- Reproduced with the permission of the authors, Professor Emeritus Michiel R. Leenders and Louise A. Mauffette-Leenders, case study pages **448–52**/Les Mills International (LMI); case study pages **453–7**/Dr Peter Hanley of Neuromonics Pty Ltd; case study pages **458–61**/Henry and Kenny Goh of Macrokiosk; case study pages **462–6**/Terence Swee of muvee Technologies

Every effort has been made to trace the ownership of copyright material. Information that will enable the publisher to rectify any error or omission in subsequent reprints will be welcome. In such cases, please contact the Permissions Section at John Wiley & Sons Australia, who will arrange for the payment of the usual fee.

Part 1

The nature of small business and entrepreneurship

Chapter 1

Entrepreneurship: definition and evolution

LEARNING OBJECTIVES

After reading this chapter, you should be able to:

- provide a definition of entrepreneurship
- state the key elements of entrepreneurship
- explain the process of new venture creation
- explain the role of entrepreneurship in economic growth
- discuss the common features of entrepreneurship in the Pacific Rim region.

Entrepreneurship takes a variety of forms in both small and large firms, in new firms and established ones, in the formal and informal economy, in legal and illegal activities, in innovative and more conventional business ventures, and in all regions and economic sub-sectors. Today it is widely claimed that entrepreneurship is a vital component in the process of economic growth and development. As the Organisation for Economic Cooperation and Development (OECD) has stated:

> Entrepreneurship is central to the functioning of market economies. Entrepreneurs are agents of change and growth in a market economy and they can act to accelerate the generation, dissemination and application of innovative ideas. In doing so, they not only ensure that efficient use is made of resources, but also expand the boundaries of economic activity.[1]

The importance of entrepreneurship is perhaps best illustrated in South-East Asia. The transformation of this region and the emergence in the 1980s and 1990s of the newly industrialised economies, or so-called tigers, such as Hong Kong, Singapore, South Korea, Malaysia and Thailand, are largely due to entrepreneurial activities. During the same period, the Australian and New Zealand economies were significantly liberalised, introducing new opportunities for entrepreneurs that contributed to sustained economic growth. For example, the Australian economy has experienced one of its longest uninterrupted growth periods in history. Growth was hardly affected by the 1997 Asian economic crisis or by the dotcom downturn at the turn of the new millennium. Unsurprisingly, Australians are in love with entrepreneurs and entrepreneurship. Memories of the financial shenanigans of the late 1980s and early 1990s, dressed up as entrepreneurship, have faded — to the point where the average consumer cannot get enough of the entrepreneurial spirit.[2] Across the Asia–Pacific region today, entrepreneurs and the brands they stand behind are being embraced by consumers who, in contrast with a decade ago, see big companies as the bad guys.

This chapter focuses on defining the notion of entrepreneurship and examines the role of entrepreneurship as a catalyst for economic growth. The nature of entrepreneurship within the Pacific Rim region is discussed.

Defining entrepreneurship

Industrial Revolution: The term used to describe the changes brought about by the introduction of technology and methods of mass production in the eighteenth and nineteenth centuries.

Entrepreneurship stems from the French word *entreprendre* meaning 'to undertake' or 'to take in one's own hands'. During the **Industrial Revolution**, the term *entrepreneur* was used to describe the new phenomenon of the individual who had formulated a venture idea, developed it, assembled resources and created a new business venture.[3] The entrepreneur has thus emerged as a pivotal figure who operates within a market.

Entrepreneurs such as John Rockefeller (who formed Standard Oil), Andrew Carnegie (who advanced the mass production of steel and lowered its cost), James Watt (who improved on existing ideas and made a workable steam engine), Thomas Edison (who brought the benefits of electricity through new appliances), and William Jardine and James Matheson (who founded Jardine Matheson and sent the first private shipments of tea to England) all contributed to the Industrial Revolution. Entrepreneurs are risk-taking people who react to opportunities, bear uncertainty and serve to bring about a balance between supply and demand in specific markets. Since the Industrial Revolution, many economists have directed their attention to entrepreneurship and contributed to the understanding of the concept.

Towards a definition of entrepreneurship

Entrepreneurship remains difficult to define because it is a multi-faceted phenomenon that spans many disciplinary boundaries. Different studies of entrepreneurship have adopted different theoretical perspectives, units of analyses and methodologies. For example, topics in entrepreneurship have been researched by psychologists, sociologists, historians, finance experts and organisation scholars. The focus of research has varied greatly: the entrepreneur, the social network of the entrepreneur, the new organisation, the new product or service offering, and sometimes the framework conditions of a whole country have been examined.

Therefore, it is not surprising that there is no agreed definition of entrepreneurship, and uncertainty exists regarding what constitutes entrepreneurship as a field of study. One of the main obstacles to building a definition of entrepreneurship stems perhaps from the fact that until the late 1990s, most researchers defined the field solely in terms of who the entrepreneur was and what he or she did. The problem with this approach is that entrepreneurship involves the linking of two conditions: the presence of lucrative opportunities and the presence of enterprising individuals.[4] By defining the field in terms of the individual alone, early research in entrepreneurship generated incomplete definitions that do not withstand scrutiny.

Entrepreneurship: The process, brought about by individuals, of identifying new opportunities and converting them into marketable products or services.

Consequently, we define **entrepreneurship** as the process, brought about by individuals, of identifying new entrepreneurial opportunities and converting them into marketable products or services. Therefore, as suggested by Shane and Vankataraman,[5] the field of entrepreneurship involves the study of *sources* of opportunities; the *processes* of discovery, evaluation and exploitation of opportunities; and the set of *individuals* who discover, evaluate and exploit those opportunities.

The key elements of entrepreneurship

Much of the argument over the definition of entrepreneurship revolves around the factors considered necessary for entrepreneurship to occur. As depicted in figure 1.1, five factors have been commonly cited for entrepreneurship to take place: an individual (the entrepreneur), a market opportunity, adequate resources, a business organisation and a favourable environment. These five factors are considered contingencies — something that must be present in the phenomenon but that can materialise in many different ways.[6] The entrepreneur is responsible for bringing these contingencies together to create new value.

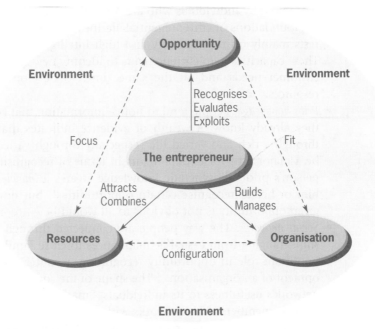

Figure 1.1: The key elements of entrepreneurship

Source: Adapted from P.A. Wickham, *Strategic Entrepreneurship*, Prentice Hall, Harlow, 2004, p. 134.

The entrepreneur

Entrepreneurship requires at least one motivated person. The entrepreneur is the cornerstone of the entrepreneurial process — the chief conductor who perceives an opportunity, marshals the resources to pursue this opportunity and builds an organisation which combines the resources necessary to exploit the opportunity. Researchers have hypothesised a number of factors that influence the way opportunities are recognised and exploited by entrepreneurs. Among these, four have been identified as especially important: active search of opportunities, entrepreneurial alertness, prior knowledge and social networks.

- *Active search of opportunities:* Many of the erstwhile studies in entrepreneurship implicitly assumed that recognition of an opportunity is preceded by a systematic search for available opportunities.[7] Similarly, entrepreneurs are more likely than managers to engage in an active search for opportunities and potentially untapped sources of profit.[8] These findings indicate that actively searching for information is an important factor in the recognition of many opportunities by entrepreneurs, although such searches must be carefully directed in order to succeed.

- *Entrepreneurial alertness:* Kirzner was the first to use this term to explain the recognition of entrepreneurial opportunities.[9] He defined alertness as a propensity to notice and be sensitive to information about objects, incidents and patterns of behaviour. Individuals with high alertness show a special sensitivity to maker and user problems, unmet needs and novel combinations of resources. Therefore, alertness emphasises the fact that opportunities can sometimes be recognised by individuals who are not actively searching for them. But what are the foundations of entrepreneurial alertness? It has been suggested that alertness rests mainly on the creativity and high intelligence capacities of individuals.[10] These capacities help entrepreneurs to identify new solutions for the market and customer needs and, at the same time, to develop creative ways to attract resources.

• *Prior knowledge:* People tend to notice information that is related to information they already know. A wealth of evidence indicates that information gathered through a rich and varied life (especially through varied work experience) can be a major plus for entrepreneurs in terms of recognising opportunities. Each person's prior idiosyncratic knowledge creates a *knowledge corridor* that allows him or her to recognise certain opportunities[11] but not others. Therefore, any given opportunity is not obvious to all would-be entrepreneurs.

• *Social networks:* The way people are connected through various social relationships, ranging from casual acquaintances to close familial bonds, also plays an important role in opportunity recognition, resource acquisition and the development of an organisation.[12] The shape of the social network helps determine a network's usefulness to its individuals. Small, tight networks can be less useful to their members than networks with lots of loose connections (weak ties) to individuals outside the main network. More 'open' networks, with many weak ties and social connections, are more likely to introduce new ideas and opportunities to their members than closed networks with many redundant ties.[13] In other words, a group of friends who do things only with each other already share the same knowledge and opportunities. A group of individuals with connections to other social networks is likely to have access to a wider range of information and resources. To achieve individual success, it is better to have connections to a variety of networks rather than many connections within a single network.

These four factors characterising entrepreneurs have been studied separately and viewed as largely independent aspects of opportunity recognition and resource acquisition. Recently, however, an integrative framework has been proposed, drawing on the research in cognitive science — the study of human intelligence that embraces various academic disciplines such as psychology, linguistics, neuroscience and economics. This approach suggests that entrepreneurs use cognitive frameworks they possess to 'connect the dots' between changes in technology, demographics, markets, government policies and other factors. The pattern they then perceive in these events or trends suggests ideas for new products or services — ideas that can potentially serve as the basis for new ventures.[14]

Opportunity

Opportunity: A situation in which a new product, service or process can be introduced and sold at greater than its cost of production.

In broad terms, an **opportunity** can be defined as a situation in which a new product, service or process can be introduced and sold at greater than its cost of production.[15] But opportunity describes a range of phenomena that begin unformed and become more developed through time.

In its most elemental form, what may later be called an opportunity may appear as 'imprecisely defined market needs, or unemployed resources or capacities'.[16]

Imprecisely defined market needs are the source of *market-pulled opportunities*. Prospective customers may or may not be able to articulate their needs, interests and problems. Even if customers cannot do so, the role of the entrepreneur is to recognise these needs and to develop an offer in which customers will perceive some value.

Under-utilised or unemployed resources, as well as new technologies or capabilities, may also offer possibilities to create new value for customers. In this case, entrepreneurs first identify resources that are not optimally used and then seek a better use or combination of these in a specific market. This type of opportunity can be called *market-pushed opportunities*. For example, the technology for making a material with the combined properties of metal and glass may be developed before there are any known applications. Similarly, new medical compounds may be created without knowledge of their potential applications in the field of medicine.[17]

Resources

Having distilled an opportunity, would-be entrepreneurs must be willing and able to marshal resources in order to pursue the opportunity and transform their idea into an organisation. A resource is any thing or quality that is useful. As detailed in chapter 3, the resource-based theory recognises six types of resources: financial, physical, human, technological, social and organisational.

For the entrepreneur, constructing an initial resource base is an exceptional challenge. The venture's lack of a reputation and a track record creates a heightened perception of risk on the part of potential resource providers. In the majority of new ventures, initial resource endowments are incomplete; entrepreneurs therefore act as if they are trustworthy in order to gain access to other resources. They may use time-relevant language or symbols (e.g. polished business plans, stories, or stylish offices) to create an image of success that will encourage providers to commit resources to the venture. In this way, some resources (social, for example) are leveraged to obtain others (financial, for example). If social capital is favourable, it can be converted into tangible and intangible benefits, including increased cooperation and trust from others, finance, or assets and equipment purchased at less expensive prices.[18]

Organisation

Many different types of organisational arrangement exist for the exploitation of entrepreneurial opportunities. Although most media attention and research in entrepreneurship has focused on new independent start-ups, other possible types of organisational structure include corporate ventures, franchises, joint ventures and business acquisitions. This indicates that entrepreneurship can take place in diverse environments and that there are many ways to become an entrepreneur. The creation of corporate ventures or start-ups inside a corporation, in order to develop, produce and market a new product or service, is an illustration of this point. The new entity can be either a new internal division or a new subsidiary in the established corporation. Joint ventures, licences, franchises and spin-offs (business operations derived as secondary developments of a larger enterprise, which become separate legal entities) are other examples of possible organisational arrangements.

Sometimes it is not necessary to build an organisation from scratch to exploit new opportunities and to combine resources. For example, the acquisition of a business can be an alternative to a start-up if the entrepreneur wants to use an existing vehicle to 'hit the ground running'. In this case, the buyer can introduce substantial innovation along the lines of new products or new processes to give the business a boost. The takeover of a family business by the next generation and the redeployment of its resources according to a new business model are another example.

Many believe that for a venture to be deemed entrepreneurial it is not sufficient for the owner to launch an organisation; the venture must also represent innovation. However, everyday evidence shows that starting a business venture does not always demand much originality or power of invention. The fresh, new firm may be a mere clone of another one in a neighbouring town. As will be explained in chapter 3, the extent of innovation can vary greatly, and the extension, duplication or synthesis of existing products, services or processes can also be considered innovation.

Environment

The environment plays a critical role in entrepreneurship. Entrepreneurs operate in an environment that can be more or less rich in opportunities and where several conditions influence the pursuit of these opportunities. For example, opportunities can emerge because of market inefficiencies that result from information asymmetry across time and place, or as a result of political, regulatory, social or demographic changes.

There are two levels of the environment which exert an influence on the emergence of a business venture: the community level and the broader societal level. At the community level, both the number of organisations in an industry (also called population density) and the strength of the relationship between these organisations are important to entrepreneurs. Individuals trying to create business ventures in a population with high density will find more opportunities for acquiring effective knowledge and creating extensive social networks, but they will also encounter more intensive competition.

At the societal level, at least two aspects shape the environment for organisation: cultural norms and values, and government activities and policies. Changing norms and values alter entrepreneurial intentions and the willingness of resource providers to support new ventures. Government actions and political events create new institutional structure for entrepreneurial action, encouraging some activities and impeding others.[19]

There is abundant evidence that regulatory and administrative burdens can negatively affect entrepreneurial activity. For example, excessively stringent product and labour market regulations have implications for firm entry and exit.

Entrepreneur profile

Wong Ngit Liong — Venture Corporation

Wong Ngit Liong is the founder and CEO of Venture Corporation Limited (Venture), a leading global electronics services provider based in Singapore. Founded in 1984, the Venture group comprises about 30 companies with global clusters of excellence world-wide, and it employs more than 13 000 people. Venture is among the world's top 10 contract manufacturing companies that design, make and deliver products for brand-name electronic icons such Agilent, HP, Motorola and Siemens.

Over the years, Venture group sales have grown exponentially, from S$25.4 million in 1989 to S$3.2 billion in 2005. This represents a compounded annual growth rate of over 40 per cent. These outstanding results are quite remarkable in light of the soft market conditions. With excellent track records and strong engineering expertise and experience, Venture is indisputably a first-class electronics services provider and is widely seen as Singapore's best tech-sector story. Venture has received numerous awards and accolades over the last ten years, with inclusion in Asia's Best Companies by *Finance Asia* in 2001 and Best Managed Companies in Singapore by *AsiaMoney* in 2002. As for Mr Wong, he received the inaugural Entrepreneur of the Year award from Ernst & Young Singapore in 2002.

How did to the company achieve such great success? Mr Wong believes it all boils down to two main reasons: resilience and motivation. He learned very early how to deal with adversity. The youngest of a family of nine siblings, his father died in the war when he was only two months old, leaving his mother and brothers and sisters to look after him. Mr Wong recognises that his mother was a role model: 'She was a great entre-preneur. She started a business, a small fleet of taxis, to make a living for her family.' The young Wong excelled academically. After high school, he was awarded a Fulbright Scholarship to study electrical engineering at the University of California at Berkeley, where he graduated with First Class Honours. He went on to obtain an MBA from McGill University under the Canadian Commonwealth Fellowship program. After a short stint with the Economic Development Board, he joined Hewlett-Packard (HP) and helped to establish HP operations in Singapore and Malaysia. He rose through the ranks to become the first General Manager of HP in Malaysia.

It was at HP that he received his grounding in manufacturing and had the opportunity to work with and learn from Bill Hewlett, the co-founder of the company. Mr Wong credits the legendary entrepreneur as the person who has influenced him the most. He remembers Bill as a man who inspired people and who brought diverse talents together to work towards a common goal. This concept of empowerment and inspiring employees to achieve new heights would one day become the cornerstone from which Venture is built.

After a successful 12-year career with HP, Mr Wong decided to trade in his stable, comfortable job for another that was fraught with uncertainty and risk. He chose to be an entrepreneur. In 1984 he started Venture Manufacturing Singapore and Multitech Systems, which later merged to form Venture Corporation Limited. Things were difficult in the beginning, as it was hard to convince multinationals such as Sony, Apple and HP to award contracts to a start-up with no track record. However, through much per-severance and his knowledge of the industry, the company was able to gain the

The process of new venture creation

Not everyone has the potential to launch a business venture, and not all those with such a capacity will necessarily attempt to do so. Of those who do attempt it, not all will succeed in creating a new venture. The model of new venture creation proposed in figure 1.2 explains these observations. Yet we know that each venture is different, and no single complete model exists to explain how a venture gets off the ground. Entrepreneurs have different personalities and backgrounds as well as different goals; all have a different time frame and aspire to launch their ventures in various industries. Thus, the model presented in figure 1.2 allows for this diversity, rather than specifying a particular path.

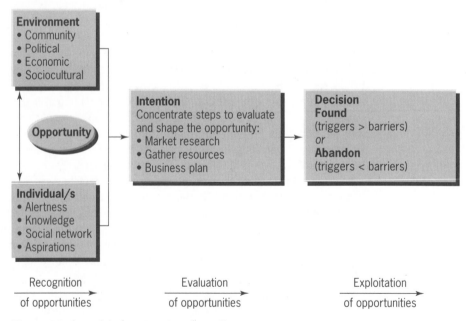

Figure 1.2: A model of new venture formation

Central to the process of new venture formation is the founding individual. Whether the entrepreneur is perceived as a hard-headed risk-bearer or a visionary, he or she is perceived to be different in important ways from the non-entrepreneur (such as the manager), and many believe these differences lie in the psychological traits and background of the entrepreneur. There have been many attempts to develop a psychological profile of the entrepreneur. The need for achievement, the level of confidence and a risk-taking propensity are the three psychological traits that have been used in many studies and shown a high degree of validity in differentiating among types of entrepreneur.[20] Another approach has been to study the background, experience and aspirations of entrepreneurs.

Entrepreneurs do not operate in a vacuum; they respond to their environments. At the opportunity recognition stage, the entrepreneur perceives market needs and/or underemployed resources and recognises a 'fit' between particular market needs and specified resources. A favourable political, economic, social and infrastructure environment facilitates the emergence of new business ventures. Figure 1.2 shows that the initiation of new ventures requires the combination of the right person in the right place. The typical would-be entrepreneur is constantly attuned to environmental changes that may suggest an opportunity.

People may have the propensity to found and develop a business in an environment conducive to entrepreneurship. They may even have identified a promising opportunity, but the actual decision to launch the venture arises from a clear intention, and this implies action. In new venture formation, intention is a conscious state of mind that directs attention towards the goal of establishing the new organisation.[21] With the expression of intent ('I intend trying to start a business'), the hopeful entrepreneur takes some concrete steps towards evaluating the business opportunity and gathering resources for launching the venture. Such steps can include the formulation of strategy, the development of a prototype, market research, the identification of potential partners, and the drafting of a business plan.

Just as the would-be entrepreneur must decide to attempt to establish a business, he or she must finally decide whether to proceed with or abandon the attempt. The decision may be triggered by a specific event or simply by the accumulated weight of confirmatory or contradictory information. Although some precipitating events (such as a dismissal, job frustration, graduation, inheritance) may trigger the launch of the business venture, it is often the passion of the individual — sustained ultimately by motivation — that pushes the entrepreneur to 'take the plunge'. If the venture is launched, the triggers have prevailed over the perceived barriers to start-up. Alternatively, if the person decides to abandon the attempt, then the hurdles are perceived to be greater than the advantages.[22]

Creative destruction: The process of simultaneous emergence and disappearance of technologies, products and firms in the marketplace as a result of innovation.

The role of entrepreneurship in economic growth and development

At a macro level, entrepreneurship is a process of **creative destruction**. By this, Schumpeter[23] referred to the simultaneously destructive and constructive consequences of innovation. The new destroys the old. Entrepreneurs are central to the process of creative destruction; they identify opportunities and bring the new technologies and new concepts into active commercial use. By studying economic history, we can learn valuable lessons about the conditions that allow entrepreneurs and growth to flourish.

Values, politics and economic institutions

Science and technology, in a given culture, can sometimes progress rapidly and then suddenly stop. Consider China's dazzling supremacy in science and technology at the start of the fifteenth century. Curiosity, the instinct for exploration and the drive to build had created in China all the technologies necessary for launching the Industrial Revolution — something that would not occur for another 400 years. China had the blast furnace and piston bellows for making steel; gunpowder and cannon for military conquest; the compass and the rudder for exploration; paper and moveable type for printing; the iron plough, the horse collar and various natural and artificial fertilisers to generate agricultural surpluses; and in mathematics, the decimal system, negative numbers, and the concept of zero. All of these put the Chinese far ahead of Europeans. Yet the Industrial Revolution took place in Britain and Europe in the eighteenth and nineteenth centuries, and the Chinese rejected and ultimately forgot the technologies that could have given them world dominance. Essentially, this was due to a lack of entrepreneurship in China, caused by three broad, overlapping factors: values, politics and economic institutions.[24]

Values

Entrepreneurship is a process of economic change. So a readiness for change, or at least the willingness to live with it, is essential if a society is to get richer (except by conquest). This helps to account for China's falling behind. Chinese civilisation came under the domination of a bureaucratic elite, the mandarins, who gave continuity and stability to Chinese life but were also a conservative influence on innovation, resisting the introduction of new techniques unless they provided a clear benefit to the bureaucracy.[25] As a result, the mandarins often blocked change; at the end of the fifteenth century they ended long-standing sea-trade ventures, choking off commerce and shipbuilding alike.

Acquisitiveness is another value that sustains growth. As change agents in a society, entrepreneurs have a regard for the material and they are willing to exploit nature for human benefit. Yet naked greed is no use. Growth is based on sustainable development; it requires investment, and investment is deferred gratification. The enlightened self-interest praised by economist Adam Smith combines the desire for wealth with prudence and patience.

Politics

Values are a powerful entrepreneurial catalyst at the individual level. At a macro level, politics provides a framework for entrepreneurship. Economic institutions are the tools used by entrepreneurs to capitalise on opportunities and convert those opportunities into marketable products or services.

Once again, China provides a good example of the influence of politics over entrepreneurship. The Ming dynasty (1368–1644) was one of the most stable

Chinese dynasties but also one of the most autocratic. The sprawling bureaucracy needed by the highly centralised government was continued by the subsequent Qing dynasty which lasted until the imperial institution was abolished in 1911. What was chiefly lacking in China for the further development of capitalism was not mechanical skill, scientific aptitude or sufficient accumulation of wealth, but scope for individual enterprise. There was no individual freedom, no security for private enterprise, no legal foundation for rights other than those of the state, and no guarantee against arbitrary extortion by officials or intervention by the state.

If too much order (as in China) impedes entrepreneurship, conversely too much chaos is just as bad. Consider Russia in the 75 years before the Russian Revolution of 1917. Creativity flourished in the chaos of the dying empire. Great authors such as Tolstoy, Dostoevski, Chekhov, Turgenev and Gogol emerged during this period. Likewise, in the world of music, many Russian artists of that period are still played in concert halls. In science, Russia was a leader and produced several Nobel laureates. However, without some degree of order it was impossible for the Russians to use that creativity to develop a successful economy. Chaos led to more chaos and ultimately to the Russian Revolution. Order was reimposed and creativity died.[26] Successful societies create and manage a tension between order and chaos without letting either of them get out of hand. New ideas are easily frustrated if societies are not receptive to the chaos that comes from change, yet societies have to maintain an appropriate degree of order to take advantage of creative breakthroughs.

Economic institutions

Economic institutions are part of the framework conditions influencing entrepreneurship. In the West, where the state was, and is, a central institution, the economic sphere came to be separated from political control under a variety of pressures. This led to a spawning of other institutions such as property rights, stock exchanges, banks, courts, laws of contract and so on.[27] With time, these allow a flourishing of many different types of economic enterprise that are different in size, ownership and organisation. Here was yet another form of pluralism that existed in Europe but not in China or in Japan before the Industrial Revolution — just as governments competed, so did the entrepreneurs and the different forms of organisation.

A model of entrepreneurial process and economic growth

It is the quality of entrepreneurs' performances that determines whether capital grows rapidly or slowly and whether this growth involves innovation and change, that is, the development of new products and new production techniques. Differences in growth rates between countries and between different periods in any one country can therefore be traced back largely to the quality of entrepreneurship. This idea is depicted in figure 1.3, which shows a model of entrepreneurial processes affecting national economic growth.

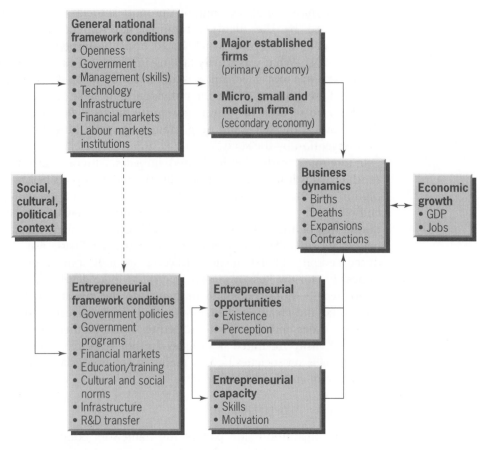

Figure 1.3: Entrepreneurship and economic growth

Source: Adapted from P.D. Reynolds, S.M. Camp, W.D. Bygrave, E. Autio & M. Hay, *Global Entrepreneurship Monitor, 2001, Executive Report*, Kauffman Center for Entrepreneurial Leadership, 2001, p. 53.

Fundamentally, economic growth occurs not because of broad improvements in technology, productivity and available resources, but because entrepreneurs (a) improve their technology, organisation and processes, (b) become more productive and innovative and (c) force other firms out of business. As this ongoing creative destruction occurs, new and better jobs than the lost ones are created, the overall level of productivity rises, and economic wellbeing increases.

One indicator of creative destruction is the **business dynamics** taking place within the national economy.[28] This is the extent to which firms enter an industry, grow, decline and exit an industry. Despite the recognition that business dynamics are a necessary feature of economic growth, it is often hard for public opinion and government to accept the destructive dimension of entrepreneurship. It is illusory to think that society can benefit from the growth and progress generated by entrepreneurial activities (new products and services, job and wealth creation) without incurring enterprise restructuring and bankruptcies and their inevitable consequences (removal of products from the marketplace, staff retrenchments, losses by

Business dynamics: Also called business churning; the extent to which firms enter an industry, grow, decline and exit an industry.

investors). Creation and destruction are two sides of the same coin in entrepreneurship.

The level of entrepreneurial activity is a function of the degree to which people recognise the opportunities available and their capacity (motivation and skills) to exploit them. Entrepreneurial activity is, in turn, shaped by a variety of factors (referred to as entrepreneurial framework conditions) that help to foster start-ups. Such factors include the availability of start-up financing, education and training in entrepreneurship, 'incubator' facilities, government policies, and programs targeting the development of entrepreneurship.

At a broader level, there is a relationship between national conditions (such as legal institutions, general infrastructure, labour and financial markets) and the performance of established firms. History shows that the process of innovation and entrepreneurship consists of an accumulation of numerous institutional, resource and proprietary events involving many actors from the public and private sectors.[29] Finally, social values, politics and institutions shape the macro context within which entrepreneurial processes occur. It is important to recognise, however, that although government agencies and educational institutions can create conditions in which entrepreneurship can prosper, it is ultimately up to individuals and firms to take up the challenge of launching new activities.

Measuring entrepreneurial activity

Given the fact that there are many different institutional ways of exploiting opportunities, measuring entrepreneurial activity in the economy is a difficult task. Substantial attention has been given recently to fast-growing new firms in expanding industry sectors, and this has provided anecdotal evidence that some countries are more entrepreneurial than others. The Global Entrepreneurship Monitor (GEM)[30] is an international research consortium that aims to go beyond such impressionistic evidence and to systematically assess two things: (1) the level of start-up activity, or the prevalence of embryonic firms and (2) the prevalence of those that have survived the start-up phase.

First, start-up activity is measured by the proportion of the adult population in each country currently engaged in the process of creating a business. Second, the prevalence of new firms is measured by the proportion of adults in each country involved in operating a business that is less than 42 months old when the survey is completed. For both measures, the research focus is on entrepreneurial activity in which the individuals involved have a direct, but not necessarily full, ownership interest in the business. Combining these measures provides an excellent index of the total level of entrepreneurial activity.

How entrepreneurial are the people of different countries?

The overall level of entrepreneurial activity for a selection of countries participating in the GEM project is presented in figure 1.4. The vertical bars represent the precision of each estimate based on the size of the sample in each country at the 95 per cent confidence interval. The range in prevalence rates shows a tenfold difference, from a low of 2.4 per cent in Hungary to 22.5 per cent in Thailand. When countries are grouped according to a global region, it appears that entrepreneurial efforts are not uniformly distributed around the world. Without question, entrepreneurial activity is quite low and uniform across most developed European countries. Anglo-Saxon countries have a relatively high level of activity compared with European countries. Latin America has among the highest and most uniform levels of activity. The situation in Asia is contrasted: while Japan has a low rate of entrepreneurial activity (2.9 per cent), Singapore appears in the middle of the pack (8.1 per cent), and China and Thailand are the most entrepreneurial countries in the region.

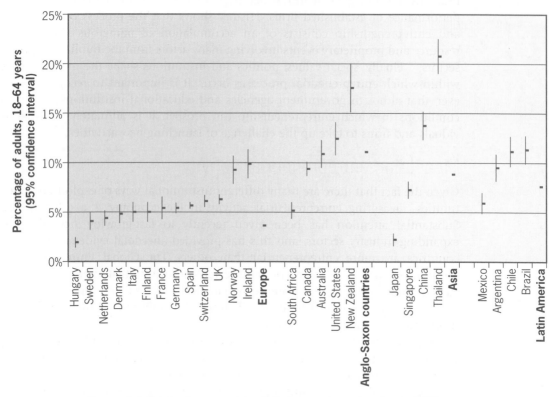

Figure 1.4: Total entrepreneurial activity by country and region in 2005

Source: GEM Consortium <www.gemconsortium.org>.

The GEM study uncovered a dynamic dimension to entrepreneurial activity. Respondents were asked to indicate whether they were starting and growing their business to take advantage of a unique market opportunity (opportunity entrepreneurship) or because it was the best option available (necessity entrepreneurship). In the case of necessity entrepreneurship, people launch a business venture not so much to pursue a unique opportunity but because they have no other way of making a living. Cross-national comparisons indicate that from 1.8 per cent of adults in Japan to over 16 per cent in New Zealand are engaged as opportunity entrepreneurs. The level of necessity entrepreneurs had an even greater variation, from virtually none in Denmark and The Netherlands to 5 per cent or more in Thailand and China. The analysis indicated that developing countries generally have a higher prevalence rate for necessity entrepreneurship.

Common features of entrepreneurship in the Pacific Rim region

Entrepreneurship styles, habits and environments vary significantly across the Pacific Rim region. At first glance, there appears to be little in common in setting up a business in Australia, Malaysia or Hong Kong. Despite the differences, there are some key features in Pacific Rim entrepreneurship that distinguish it from European and American entrepreneurship, for example. A common characteristic is the key role played by the state in the development of entrepreneurship. Another common denominator is the presence of ethnic entrepreneurs. For instance, Chinese people living outside the current administration of the People's Republic of China have been at the heart of the region's economic boom.

Most ethnic Chinese who left the mainland (known as *huaqiao*) did so with little wealth and could not rely on the governments of other South-East Asian countries for assistance. Often battling prejudice and discrimination, these families created their own businesses and, in the process, developed much of the modern private sector throughout South-East Asia. Wary of their new local governments, the ethnic Chinese discovered that a common background provided a basis for mutual trust and, therefore, presented an opportunity for business and trade throughout the Pacific Rim. Language, culture and ethnicity served as common ground, but family provided the most reliable and secure assurances in an area where formal business agreements were difficult to enforce. Today, companies owned by ethnic Chinese families in Singapore, Malaysia, Thailand, Indonesia and the Philippines make up about 70 per cent of the private business sector in those countries and are rising influences in Vietnam, Australia and New Zealand.[31]

Ethnic Indians constitute another sizeable segment of the immigrants of diverse nationalities in the Pacific Rim. In terms of sheer numbers, they are the third largest group behind the British and the Chinese. Over 15 million people of Indian origin have settled in 70 countries, and they constitute more than 40 per cent of the population in Fiji and Mauritius.[32] They are significant minorities in Malaysia, Singapore and Sri Lanka. They have also made important contributions to the development of entrepreneurship across the Pacific Rim. For example, one of the main reasons behind the emergence of Silicon Valley as the world hub of high-tech industries has been the presence of ethnic Indian entrepreneurs. The following sections examine the development of entrepreneurship of ethnic Chinese and ethnic Indians in more detail.

Sociocultural features of ethnic Chinese

Redding[33] suggested that the impact of Chinese culture has worked through the two main determinants of social structures, which in turn affect the workings of organisations. These are (1) the rules that govern the stabilisation and legitimisation of authority, that is, the vertical dimension of order and (2) the rules that govern the stabilisation of cooperation, that is, the horizontal dimension of order. The insecurity experienced by ethnic Chinese also influences social behaviour.

Vertical dimensions of order and Confucian ethics

The norms for vertical relationships are taught via Confucian concepts. The Confucian ethical system regulating social behaviour has three principal ideas: benevolence (*ren*), righteousness or justice (*yi*) and propriety or courtesy (*li*). Regulation is certainly the appropriate term. Confucianism is a secular system developed at a time of chaos to allow harmony to coexist with rigid hierarchy. This worked by providing a set of principles for action, most of which surround the role of the father as the pivot of the social system.

As a result, the style of leadership adopted commonly has a paternalistic flavour, and the adoption of such a style by the business owner sets the tone for other managers to echo it with their subordinates. This style can also bring with it nepotism and autocracy, as social interaction in the Confucian system is very much a tradition. Organisation charts and job descriptions are replaced by social deference. People come into the organisation pre-programmed to understand hierarchy instinctively.

Horizontal dimensions of order in relationships and networks

Similar considerations apply to the rules for horizontal order, particularly in the development and handling of relationships. This begins with a clear distinction between in-group members or insiders (*zijiren*) and out-group members or outsiders (*wairen*). Chinese people typically maintain expressive ties with close family members, mixed ties with friends and other kin, and instrumental ties with strangers or out-group members with whom there is no lasting relationship.[34] Social interaction expectations, norms and behaviours differ among these three kinds of ties.

Western and Eastern entrepreneurs and firms have a different approach to relationships. To most Western firms, relationships are secondary — a company tends to decide which business or projects it is interested in and then cultivates the necessary connections. Asian companies believe that relationships come first and that investment opportunities flow from them. This philosophy finds its root in the historic uncertainty and separateness felt by expatriate Chinese. Many local firms in the Pacific Rim were established by Chinese migrants and their offspring in not-so-friendly environments, away from their country of origin, in countries with rules-based, yet weak, systems. Consequently, expatriate Chinese tended to rely mainly on relationships with extended families and clans to build up the business and reduce risk. The interlocking relationships soon extended to local officials keen to benefit from Chinese entrepreneurial skills. This web of connections, or *guanxi*, is still paramount with most ethnic Chinese groups in the Pacific Rim.

Pragmatism, work ethic and thriftiness

The initial hardship of migration cultivated values that promoted economic survival — values such as pragmatism, a work ethic and materialism — and these corresponded with traditional Chinese values. Since the majority of Chinese migrants left their mother land for similar reasons (to escape turmoil and poverty), three sets of values became dominant in their struggle for survival:[35]

- The Confucian value of family was greatly strengthened as the immigrant family became central to the life of its members, providing a safe haven and welfare.
- The survival of individuals and their families entailed hard work, which also embodied individual members' obligations to their families and friends. Those who were considered lazy and selfish or made little contribution were regarded as outcasts and were slighted and isolated by their families.
- The prospects of long-term insecurity promoted the value of chasing and accumulating material wealth and money.

This work ethic, however, is not unique to the ethnic Chinese. The Protestant ethic, for example, is a code of morals based on the principles of thrift, discipline, hard work and individualism. The adjective 'Protestant' is explained by the fact that these qualities were seen to have been especially encouraged by the Protestant churches, especially those denominations based on the tenets of Calvinism. The major formulator of the concept of the Protestant ethic was the political philosopher and sociologist Max Weber[36] who saw a close relationship between the Protestant ethic and the rise of capitalism.

Ethnic Indians

Although expatriate Indians are often described as a fractionalised community from diverse Indian regions, castes and religions, they nevertheless have unity in their diversity. The vast majority adhere to some form of the caste system, and Hindu mythology pervades their culture. India has also instituted an exceptional education system that has trained a ready core of highly skilled and highly educated professionals and entrepreneurs who are familiar with the English language and Western ways. As a result, most of the recent migrants to Australia, New Zealand, Singapore and the United States are capable of quickly stepping into middle- and upper-level jobs.

Like their less educated counterparts, most high-tech Indian immigrants rely on ethnic strategies to enhance entrepreneurial opportunities. Seeing themselves as outsiders to the mainstream technology community, foreign-born engineers and scientists in Silicon Valley have created social and professional networks to mobilise the information, know-how, skill and capital to start technology firms. Combining elements of traditional immigrant culture with distinctly high-tech practices, these organisations simultaneously create ethnic identities within the region and aid professional networking and information exchange.

Whatever their ethnicity, all these associations tend to mix socialising (whether at Chinese banquets, Indian dinners or family-centred social events) with support for professional and technical advancement. Either explicitly or informally, they offer first-generation immigrants professional contacts and networks within the local technology community. They serve as recruitment channels and provide role models of successful immigrant entrepreneurs and managers. Older engineers and entrepreneurs in both the Chinese and the Indian communities now help finance and mentor younger coethnic entrepreneurs. Within these networks, 'angel' investors often invest individually or jointly in promising new ventures. The IndUS Entrepreneur group, for example, aims to 'foster entrepreneurship by providing mentorship and resources' within the South Asian technology community.

The role of the state

Over the past decades, the state has played a ubiquitous role in entrepreneurship in virtually all Pacific Rim countries. Encouraging entrepreneurship has been increasingly recognised by governments across the region as an effective means of creating jobs, increasing productivity and competitiveness, alleviating poverty, and achieving societal goals. It is therefore not surprising that the state has been a strong promoter of entrepreneurship to the extent that it has even become an entrepreneur itself — hence the term 'state entrepreneurship'.

Promotion of entrepreneurship and SMEs

Every country in the region has engaged in some sort of promotion of entrepreneurship and of small and medium-sized enterprises (SMEs). Singapore showed the earliest interest in promoting entrepreneurship and developed a comprehensive policy in this area. The SME Master Plan formulated in 1989 provided a comprehensive package to encourage entrepreneurship and help SMEs in critical areas such as tax incentives and financial assistance, technology adaptation, business development and international marketing. These schemes have been implemented through a multi-agency network that includes major statutory boards and government agencies.

A comprehensive network of small business agencies has also been set up by the various states in Australia. Likewise, Malaysia has taken a dynamic approach to the promotion of entrepreneurship by creating a ministry totally dedicated to entrepreneurial issues. The Ministry of Entrepreneur Development was set up in 1995 to assume full responsibility for all the functions of the Ministry of Public Enterprise, which was abolished.

State entrepreneurship

Governments have traditionally played an important role in a few 'sensitive' sectors in all Pacific Rim countries. Those sectors include telecommunications, media, real estate, natural resources and banking. Even in countries labelled 'free market economies' such as Australia and Singapore, the government still owns companies in those sectors, although the telecommunications sector has recently been deregulated and government icons such as Telstra in Australia and SingTel in Singapore have been partially privatised.

Singapore is certainly the champion of state entrepreneurship. In the 1960s and 1970s, the government initiated many enterprises in key sectors, including manufacturing, shipping, air transport, international trade and long-term finance. The main vehicle for state entrepreneurship in Singapore is government-linked companies (GLCs). These enterprises are formed under holding companies, which in turn depend on a ministry.[37] Examples of GLCs are Sambawang (infrastructure, marine engineering, information technology and leisure activities), Development Bank of Singapore (banking), Neptune Orient Lines (shipping) and Singapore Airlines (air transport). Consequently, public servants have often played the role of entrepreneurs in Singapore. As Minister Mentor Lee Kuan Yew remarked:

> Because we did not have enough entrepreneurs, and those we had lacked the capital or interest, ministers of finance like Goh Keng Swee, Hon Sui Sen and Lim Kim San launched new enterprises. For example, Goh started a shipping line with government officers and a Pakistani shipping expert to guide them. When Malaysia–Singapore Airlines was broken up, we started Singapore Airlines headed by some outstanding civil servants.[38]

Similarly, the Malaysian government controls companies in various industries, including printing (e.g. Percetakan Nasional Malaysia Berhad, or PNMB), banking (e.g. Bumiputra-Commerce Bank, Danamodal Nasional Berhad), oil and gas (e.g. Petronas), air transport (Malaysia Airlines) and conglomerates such as UDA Holdings Berhad with activities in property development, hospitality and retail. The picture was very much the same in Indonesia until 1999, when the Wahid government, under International Monetary Fund pressure, was forced to privatise and dismantle state monopolies.

Emerging trends

The new millennium brought profound changes that have affected entrepreneurship in the Pacific Rim region. The main force behind those changes lies in the rise and supremacy of the free-market economy as a framework for entrepreneurship. This trend has its roots in the collapse of the communist system (1989); trade liberalisation through the Uruguay round of negotiations (1986–94) under the General Agreement on Tariffs and Trade (GATT — later renamed the World Trade Organization in 1995); and the Asian financial crisis (1997–98). Four major factors — the after-effects of the spread of the free market — are having a huge impact on entrepreneurship and small businesses in the region:
- deregulation and privatisation
- adoption of Western ideas
- emergence of rules-based systems
- increased disclosure and the employment of outsiders.

Deregulation and privatisation

All countries in the Pacific Rim embarked on some program of deregulation and privatisation in the 1990s. Some countries moved towards deregulation on their own initiative, such as New Zealand, Australia, Singapore and Vietnam. Others, such as Thailand and Indonesia, were more or less forced to follow after the Asian financial crisis. Many laws restricting entrepreneurial endeavours, particularly for ethnic Chinese and foreign nationals, have been scrapped or watered down.

Furthermore, several state-owned companies were totally or partially privatised in the 1990s. This change has created new opportunities for would-be entrepreneurs and considerably improved the environment for entrepreneurship.

Adoption of Western ideas

Western ideas have spread quickly into South-East Asia through different channels, such as films, television, advertising, Internet and education systems. For example, many of the ethnic Chinese entrepreneurs who built huge conglomerates are now preparing to hand over those companies to members of the next generation, who have often been educated in American, British or Australian universities where they learned Western ways of doing business. Buzan and Segal[39] suggested that we are moving into a 'Westernistic age' marked by the fusion of Western and other cultures. The power of the West has been, and still is, based on forms of social, economic and political organisation that allow individuals to make more of their human potential than had been possible before. Some parts of Western ideology still encounter strong resistance in South-East Asia, notably democracy, civil society and human rights. But, as Japan, Korea, Singapore and Taiwan demonstrate, 'Westernisation' does not mean becoming identical to the West or losing one's own culture.

Emergence of rules-based systems

South-East Asian economies have traditionally been based on relationships. Business transactions were made on the strength of personal agreements rather than on contracts. Transactions in the Chinese *guanxi* system are still mainly private. They are neither verifiable nor enforceable in the public sphere. After the 1997–98 financial crisis, Asia's governments made a big effort to clean up their financial and regulatory regimes. Stronger rules-based systems were introduced, with stricter insider-trading and contract laws and more rigorous competition policies. Consequently, the usefulness of *guanxi* in gathering information and providing finance and personal favours has begun to decline. As Asia's markets become more rules-based, its entrepreneurs are increasingly prepared to deal with contracts outside the traditional network.

Much has changed in South-East Asian politics as well. The 1997 crisis overturned the established political order altogether in Indonesia and Thailand and shook it to the core in Malaysia. Since then, relatively young, popular, new leaders have come to power in Indonesia, Malaysia and Thailand — not amid protests and putsches, but by normal democratic means.

Increased disclosure and the employment of outsiders

The Asian financial crisis devastated the balance sheets not only of most Asian companies but also of their banks. This meant that firms have had to rely in large part on equity injections from Western banks and capital markets to recapitalise themselves. Typical adaptations have been detailed disclosure in public accounts, the search for an image of good management, and the employment of 'outsiders' in key positions to deal with Western sources of capital and technology.

Summary

Entrepreneurship is the process of people identifying new opportunities and converting them into marketable products or services. Therefore, the field of entrepreneurship involves the study of (1) sources of opportunities; (2) the processes of discovery, evaluation and exploitation of opportunities; and (3) the set of individuals who discover, evaluate and exploit those opportunities. Five factors have been commonly cited for entrepreneurship to take place: an individual (the entrepreneur), a market opportunity, adequate resources, a business organisation and a favourable environment. These five factors are considered contingencies — something that must be present in the phenomenon of entrepreneurship but that can materialise in many different ways. The entrepreneur is responsible for bringing these contingencies together to create new value.

At a macro level, entrepreneurship has been referred to as a process of creative destruction and a catalyst for economic growth. Entrepreneurs identify opportunities and bring the new technologies and concepts into active commercial use. In doing so, they create new business ventures, jobs and wealth, but they also force out of the marketplace the enterprises which failed to innovate. However, measuring entrepreneurial activity in the economy is a difficult task because there are many different institutional forms for exploiting opportunities. The Global Entrepreneurship Monitor, an international research consortium, showed that the level of entrepreneurial activity differed significantly between countries. This difference reflects major variations in the degree to which the opportunities are perceived to exist, rather than differences in opportunities themselves.

While studying entrepreneurship styles, habits and environments across the Pacific Rim region, we can identify two common features: (1) the key role played by the state in the promotion and development of entrepreneurship and (2) the presence of ethnic Chinese and ethnic Indian entrepreneurs who have been at the heart of the region's economic boom. The ethnic Chinese entrepreneurs share common social and cultural features, such as Confucian ethics; a relationship and network-centred approach in conducting business; pragmatism; and thriftiness values.

Following the 1997 Asian financial crisis and the spread of the free market, the region has undergone major changes. Among these, the movement for privatisation and deregulation, the adoption of Western ideas, the emergence of rules-based systems, and the increased pressure for disclosure are likely to have profound effects on entrepreneurship and small businesses.

REVIEW QUESTIONS

1. What are the key elements of entrepreneurship?

2. What are the critical stages in the process of new venture formation?

3. What are the central factors necessary for entrepreneurship to thrive in a country?

4. What are the common features of entrepreneurship in the Pacific Rim region?

5. What are the emerging trends affecting entrepreneurship in the Pacific Rim region?

DISCUSSION QUESTIONS

1. Why is it often said that entrepreneurship is a complex phenomenon? Identify different dimensions of or approaches to this phenomenon.

2. Why does only a small proportion of the population set up new business ventures and become independent entrepreneurs?

3. Are state entrepreneurship and the position of some public servants as entrepreneurs likely to diminish in the near future? Why or why not?

4. Can entrepreneurship be taught and learned?

SUGGESTED READING

Bain, I., *The Dick Smith Way*, McGraw-Hill, North Ryde, 2003.

Dana, L.P., *Asian Models of Entrepreneurship*, World Scientific Publishing, Singapore, 2006.

Shane, S., *A General Theory of Entrepreneurship: The Individual–Opportunity Nexus*, Edward Elgar, Aldershot, 2003.

CASE STUDY

Pure Bliss Foods

At the beginning of 2006, Robert Boyd and Ashley Salisbury, founders of the Melbourne health bar manufacturer Pure Bliss Foods, were reviewing strategies to consolidate their business. The company had managed to obtain a foothold in the highly competitive health snack market and had just reached its break-even point. This was achieved in part by the clever marketing strategies adopted by the company. A couple of years earlier, Pure Bliss Foods established a joint venture with the Collingwood Football Club to develop and market a new range of products. In 2006, they began talks with the New Zealand rugby team, the All Blacks, and began to consider what approach they should follow in pursuing this new opportunity.

The initial business idea

Pure Bliss Foods was established in 2003 when Ashley discovered that she had a winning health bar recipe. Originally from America, she had been working for more than 10 years in hospitality management and ended up advising large hospitality companies about health and nutrition. Ashley had not been able to find in Australia the sort of products that she liked from America, especially in terms of their health and nutrition profiles. Thus she started making her own products and sharing them with friends and business associates. Soon after, a food company offered to buy her recipe. She turned down the offer eventually, as she thought this could be an opportunity to start her own business.

The first partner to come on board was Sharon Pollock, a long-term friend of Ashley and one of the first people to taste the bars. As a mother, Sharon was very interested in the development of these products because she recognised the potential to sell muesli/health bars for children. Sharon helped to finance the company and owns part of the equity. As operations manager, she is responsible for overseeing relations with suppliers and for administrative duties. The second partner to join the company was Robert Boyd. Robert had extensive marketing experience in the food industry and worked for food giant Nestlé for five years. He also had a two-year stint with the Australian Football League (AFL). When Ashley decided that she was going to launch her own business venture, she started to look for a consultant to assist with the development of a marketing strategy. Robert was referred to Ashley by a former colleague from Nestlé, who was working for the company that wanted to buy Ashley's recipe. Robert worked initially as a consultant for Pure Bliss Foods but it soon became his primary activity and he decided to join the company and bought a stake in the business.

The opportunity: an innovative health bar

The founders of Pure Bliss Foods identified an opportunity to meet the growing demand in the wellness industry. This industry encompasses all products and services that help to make people feel healthier, look better, slow the effects of ageing or prevent diseases from developing in the first place. Examples of such products and services include vitamins and food supplements (a $2.4 billion industry in Australia) and weight loss centres (a $400 million industry). Several trends in society — an ageing population, higher standards of education, and increases in snacking and obesity — suggest that the wellness industry will experience double-digit growth over the next few years. Early market research conducted by Robert indicated that seven million Australians were considered obese due to factors such as a lack of exercise and poor nutrition. Furthermore, the modern diet means more snacking, which accounts for 25 per cent of daily energy intake — up from 18 per cent in the 1980s.

Food manufacturers know there is a market for healthy snack products but they find it difficult to produce healthy snacks that also taste good. This is because decreasing the levels of fat and sugar in a bar achieves better nutritional value but the product does not taste as good. Pure Bliss Foods introduced a breakthrough innovation called K'Snap to overcome this dilemma. K'snap uses freeze-dried fruit, which retains up to 95 per cent of the original nutrients, size, shape, colour and flavour of the fruit. Adding freeze-dried fruit delivers a nutritionally superior product with an intense fruit flavour but without added fat and sugars.

In addition, Pure Bliss Foods combined a range of natural ingredients that are widely used in America but not often employed in Australia. For example, they use soy protein, whereas most other companies use whey protein. Soy protein provides a crunchier texture and is easier to digest. Other selected ingredients such as sugar-free syrups and natural fruits and flavours also helped to develop a product that tastes sweet but has low sugar levels. As a result, the first bar launched,

Ki (meaning 'vital energy' in Chinese), has 60 per cent less sugar, 100 per cent more protein and three times less saturated fat than other bars. Initially, the company recruited the Melbourne manufacturing company Future Bake to produce their bars on a large scale.

The joint venture with Collingwood

A turning point for Pure Bliss Foods was in 2004. At that time, the company had launched its first bar and the founders knew their product was probably superior to what was already on the market. However, it was very difficult to attract the mainstream consumer and to get some interest from major retailers such as Woolworths and Coles. Although some retailers would show interest in the product, they were reluctant to take on another supplier and wanted to know the size of Pure Bliss Foods' advertising budget. Getting the venture off the ground was tough. As Robert explains, 'We couldn't offer a million-dollar advertising campaign and we didn't have a track record, so we had to work out a way to make us attractive to major retailers, but also to convince them that we were the sort of supplier that they want to deal with.'

A breakthrough came in April 2004 in the form of a joint venture with the Collingwood Football Club, which promised to boost the presence of Pure Bliss Foods. Collingwood is one of the major sporting brands in Australia and has a business division that manages sponsorship programs and licensing agreements for merchandise. Robert had initiated contact with Collingwood through the marketing manager, Matthew Usher, whom he knew from his time at the AFL. The Collingwood players liked the health bars, and the club saw the product's potential. Pure Bliss Foods and Collingwood established a new company with shared ownership, called Winners Sports Nutrition. The purpose of this joint venture was to develop and commercialise a new range of sports bars for the club's players. To date, this joint venture has successfully launched two products: the Winners Gym bars for the sports market and the Winners Bunyip bars for children.

Collingwood stays away from product development and focuses on marketing the product to generate awareness. The relationship with the club was important in providing access to decision makers in the retail industry and giving credibility to the business venture. It also played a critical role in promoting the brand, through signage at football venues and in the numerous media interviews with players. Another way of increasing awareness has been through the Collingwood community program. For instance, the club organises a football competition for 2000 primary schools in Victoria. Because the major target market for Winners Bunyip bars is primary-school children, Winners can reach these potential consumers through Collingwood's access.

A new opportunity with the All Blacks?

In April 2005, Winners Sports Nutrition convinced Coles to undertake a test market in 30 of their stores with its Winners bars. The bars ended up being in the top three sellers based on units sold per store. Based on this success, the retailer has put the Winners bars into 480 stores across Australia for a period of at least 12 months. From an initial turnover of $500 000 (350 000 bars) in 2004, Pure Bliss Foods reached a turnover of $700 000 (400 000 bars) in 2005. The company anticipates a turnover of $1.8 million (1 million bars) in 2006. Currently, the joint venture generates about 80 per cent of revenue for Pure Bliss Foods.

During 2006, Robert has been discussing the possibility of launching a new range of bars with the New Zealand rugby team, the All Blacks. This opportunity came about through the Collingwood connection: Adidas is a sponsor of both sporting teams. Robert was thinking of launching a 'Winners All Blacks Bar' for the New Zealand market. However, he was not sure of the best business model. Should he establish another joint venture or just buy a licence from the All Blacks? Was it preferable to produce in Australia and export to New Zealand? Wouldn't this new sub-brand dilute the overall brand awareness?

Source: Based on author's interview with Robert Boyd and Ashley Salisbury.

Questions

1. What is the nature of the opportunity identified by the founders of Pure Bliss Foods? How did this opportunity emerge?

2. What sort of organisation/s did the entrepreneurs establish to exploit the opportunity?

3. How should Robert proceed with the All Blacks?

ENDNOTES

1. Organisation for Economic Cooperation and Development (OECD), *Fostering Entrepreneurship*, OECD, Paris, 1998, p. 12.
2. S. Lloyd, 'Heroes rise again', *BRW*, May 5–11, 2005, pp. 40–4.
3. R. Cantillon, *Essay on the Nature of Commerce* (1755), trans. H. Higgs, Macmillan, London, 1931.
4. S. Vankataraman, 'The distinctive domain of entrepreneurship research', in J. Katz (ed.), *Advances in Entrepreneurship, Firm Emergence and Growth*, JAI Press, Greenwich, Conn., 1997, pp. 119–38.
5. S. Shane & S. Vankataraman, 'The promise of entrepreneurship as a field of research', *Academy of Management Review*, vol. 25, no. 1, 2000, pp. 217–26.
6. P. Wickham, *Strategic Entrepreneurship*, Prentice Hall, Harlow, 2004.
7. S. Shane, *A General Theory of Entrepreneurship: The Individual–Opportunity Nexus*, Edward Elgar, Aldershot, 2003.
8. B. Gilad, S. Kaish & J. Ronen, 'The entrepreneurial way with information', in S. Maital (ed.), *Applied Behavioural Economics*, vol. II, Wheatsheaf Books, Brighton, 1989, pp. 480–503.
9. I. Kirzner, *Competition and Entrepreneurship*, University of Chicago Press, Chicago, 1973.
10. S. Shane, *see* note 7.
11. S. Shane, 'Prior knowledge and the discovery of entrepreneurial opportunities', *Organization Science*, vol. 11, no. 4, pp. 448–69.
12. R.P. Singh, G. Hills, R. Hybels & G. Lumpkin, 'Opportunity recognition through social networks of entrepreneurs', *Frontiers of Entrepreneurship Research*, Babson College, Wellesley, 1999, pp. 228–41.
13. M. Granovetter, 'The strength of weak ties', *American Journal of Sociology*, vol. 78, no. 6, 1973, pp. 1360–80.
14. R. Baron, 'Opportunity recognition as pattern recognition: how entrepreneurs "connect the dots" to identify new business opportunities', *Academy of Management Perspectives*, February 2006, pp. 104–19.

15. M. Casson, *The Entrepreneur: An Economic Theory*, Barnes & Noble Books, Totowa, NJ, 1982.

16. I. Kirzner, 'Entrepreneurial discovery and the competitive market process: an Austrian approach', *Journal of Economic Literature*, vol. 35, 1997, pp. 60–85.

17. A. Ardichvili, R. Cardozo & S. Ray, 'A theory of entrepreneurial opportunity identification and development', *Journal of Business Venturing*, vol. 18, no. 1, 2003, pp. 105–23.

18. C. Brush, P. Greene & M. Hart, 'From initial idea to unique advantage: the entrepreneurial challenge of constructing a resource base', *The Academy of Management Executive*, vol. 15, no. 1, February 2001, pp. 64–78.

19. H. Aldrich & M. Martinez, 'Many are called, but few are chosen: an evolutionary perspective for the study of entrepreneurship', *Entrepreneurship Theory & Practice*, vol. 25, no. 4, 2001, pp. 41–56.

20. W.B. Gartner, 'A conceptual framework for describing the phenomenon of new venture creation', *Academy of Management Review*, vol. 10, no. 4, 1985, pp. 696–706.

21. B.J. Bird, *Entrepreneurial Behavior*, Scott, Foresman & Co., Glenview, Ill., 1989.

22. T. Volery, N. Doss, T. Mazzarol & V. Thein, 'Triggers and barriers affecting entrepreneurial intentionality: the case of Western Australian nascent entrepreneurs', *Journal of Enterprising Culture*, vol. 5, no. 3, 1997, pp. 273–91.

23. J.A. Schumpeter, *The Theory of Economic Development*, Harvard University Press, Cambridge, Mass., 1934.

24. L.C. Thurow, *Building Wealth: The New Rules for Individuals, Companies and Nations*, HarperCollins, New York, 1999.

25. R. Marsh, *The Mandarins: The Circulation of Elites in China, 1600–1900*, Free Press, Glencoe, Ill., 1961.

26. L. Thurow, *Building Wealth*, Harper Business, New York, 2000.

27. W.E. Williamson, *The Economic Institutions of Capitalism*, Free Press, New York, 1985.

28. Z.J. Acs, B. Carlsson & C. Karlsson (eds), 'The linkages among entrepreneurship, SMEs and the macroeconomy', in *Entrepreneurship, Small and Medium-Sized Enterprises and the Macroeconomy*, Cambridge University Press, Cambridge, Mass., 1999, p. 16.

29. A. Van de Ven, 'The development of an infrastructure for entrepreneurship', *Journal of Business Venturing*, vol. 8, no. 4, 1993, pp. 211–30.

30. More information on the Global Entrepreneurship Monitor is available at <www.gemconsortium.org>.

31. M. Weidenbaum & S. Hughes, *The Bamboo Network: How Expatriate Chinese Entrepreneurs are Creating a New Economic Superpower in Asia*, Free Press, New York, 1996.

32. J. Kotkin, *Tribes: How Race, Religion and Identity Determine Success in the New Global Economy*, Random House, New York, 1993.

33. G.S. Redding, *The Spirit of Chinese Capitalism*, de Gruyter, New York, 1990.

34. W.K. Gabrenya & K.K. Hwang, 'Chinese social interaction: harmony and hierarchy on the good hearth', in M.H. Bond (ed.), *The Handbook of Chinese Psychology*, Oxford University Press, Hong Kong, 1996, pp. 309–21.

35. M. Chen, *Asian Management Systems: Chinese, Japanese and Korean Styles of Business*, 2nd edn, International Thomson Business Press, London, 2004.

36. P. Baehr & G.C. Wells (eds and trans), *Max Weber: The Protestant Ethic and the Spirit of Capitalism and other Writings*, Penguin Books, London, 2002. [Weber's work was first published in 1904.]

37. S. Choo, 'Developing an entrepreneurial culture in Singapore: dream or reality', *Asian Affairs*, vol. 36, no. 3, Nov. 2005, pp. 361–73.

38. Lee Kuan Yew, 'An entrepreneurial culture of Singapore', *Business Times*, 6 February 2002, p. 10.

39. B. Buzan & G. Segal, *Anticipating the Future*, Simon & Schuster, New York, 2000.

The personality of entrepreneurs

Chapter 2

LEARNING OBJECTIVES

After reading this chapter, you should be able to:

- explain the relationship between the entrepreneur and new value creation

- explain why and how entrepreneurs discover and exploit opportunities

- list the roles and characteristics of entrepreneurs

- identify the relevant performance measures for an entrepreneur

- define the risks of a career in entrepreneurship

- explain entrepreneurial behaviour in a social context.

The individual entrepreneur plays a central role in new venture formation. This chapter identifies and discusses the personal dimensions that can explain or affect the entrepreneurial process. Firstly, it is essential to understand the relationship between individuals and opportunities. We show that entrepreneurs can be understood only in relation to their project, and that individual differences matter in the discovery and exploitation of opportunities. Secondly, the roles and characteristics of entrepreneurs are examined from an economic and psychological perspective. Thirdly, the chapter identifies the social contexts that affect the situations in which entrepreneurial opportunities emerge and are pursued. Three features of a person's social context are reviewed: the stage of life, the role and importance of social networks, and ethnicity.

Individuals and opportunities

The entrepreneur is the central actor in the creation of a new venture. Economic circumstances, social networks, marketing, planning, finance and even public agency assistance are all important. But none of these alone will create a new venture. For that we need someone who can pull all the possibilities together, who identifies and shapes a business opportunity, and who has the motivation to persist until the job is done. The entrepreneur is responsible for creating new value (an innovation and/or an organisation). This section shows how entrepreneurs are intricately related to their project. We explain why some opportunities are discovered and exploited by certain individuals and not by others. Then we outline how the exploitation of opportunities is organised in the economy.

The relationship between the individual and the opportunity

Initially, an opportunity is generally recognised by a single individual who may decide to pursue it alone or with others. That opportunity becomes an entrepreneurial project, and a process of new value creation is initiated. At this stage, budding entrepreneurs clearly express their entrepreneurial intention. As a project matures, it gradually places constraints on the entrepreneur. Frequently, the project also influences the entrepreneurs, as they define themselves to a large extent by the relative success of the venture. The project occupies a large part of the person's life (activities, goals, means, interest) and usually influences the person's social network.[1] For example, emerging entrepreneurs are always alert to resources (information, finance, contacts) that could help them to evaluate and shape the project they pursue. A business seminar, an alumni meeting or even a holiday can bring forward valuable information and contacts for would-be entrepreneurs. In short, many aspects of life, usually seen as independent of a person's business venture, will be seen by the entrepreneur as another arena in which to foster the new enterprise.

Dialogic:
A system with a circular causality process.

Defining the concept of dialogic

Bruyat and Julien[2] see the relationship between the individual and opportunity as a **dialogic**, or a system with a circular causality process. This means that two or more elements are combined into a single unit without losing their individual aspects. Dialogic relationships must be studied as a whole to be understood. (The symbol ⇔ is used to represent a dialogic relationship.) In terms of entrepreneurship, this dialogic means that the individual can be called an entrepreneur only because he or she is pursuing a project to commercialise a new product or service and, in turn, that this entrepreneurial project exists only because there is an individual who has identified this opportunity and is pursuing it.

Entrepreneurship is concerned mainly with a process of change, emergence and creation, for the individual as well as a business opportunity. Figure 2.1 shows the dialogic relationship between the individual and opportunity. The amount of value creation can vary a great deal. In fact, many entrepreneurs create little value — they set up business ventures that merely adapt or improve an existing business concept and, as a consequence, commercialise products and services that are largely identical to what is already available in the marketplace. The importance of change in the individual can also vary a great deal. The changes may affect the entrepreneur's knowledge, relationships or social status and require the person to engage in learning new skills.[3] As a consequence, becoming an entrepreneur can trigger some profound changes for both the entrepreneur and the environment or industry in which he or she evolves. Figure 2.1 shows four types of entrepreneurial outcome built on individual ⇔ opportunity dialogics.

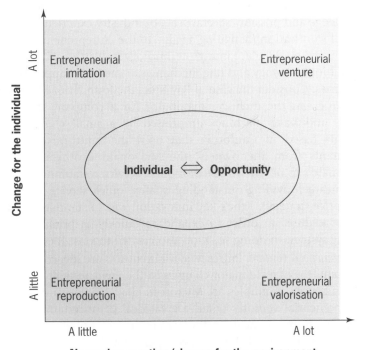

Figure 2.1: Typology of entrepreneurial outcomes

Source: Adapted from C. Bruyat & P.A. Julien, 'Defining the field of research in entrepreneurship', *Journal of Business Venturing*, no. 16, 2000, p. 174.

- *Entrepreneurial reproduction.* This entrepreneurial outcome implies very little new value creation (innovation) and very few changes for the individual. For example, suppose that a chef employed in a restaurant decided to open his own restaurant in a promising location. The competitive advantage of this restaurant might be the location, a specific type of cuisine, or the services offered (high-standard service, live music, home delivery, long opening hours). The entrepreneur chef becomes self-employed by performing an activity that he is already good at. So, in the case of entrepreneurial reproduction, entrepreneurs often concentrate their activities on an aspect of operational efficiency — that is, doing things better or more efficiently and thus adding value to the products or services.

- *Entrepreneurial imitation.* In this outcome, entrepreneurs make great changes in their knowledge, relationships and habits but there is little significant new value creation. In such projects there is usually a great deal of uncertainty, lengthy learning processes and possibly costly mistakes. Urban professionals who set up or buy a 'lifestyle business' in the countryside (such as a bed-and-breakfast, restaurant or winery) are typical examples of entrepreneurial imitations. These people can have a variety of backgrounds (lawyer, clerk, engineer) and venture into a totally new industry for which they have to learn new skills. However, the level of innovation in the new venture is often marginal.

- *Entrepreneurial valorisation.* In this outcome, the entrepreneur sets up an innovative business in his or her field of expertise, hence capitalising on in-depth knowledge and possibly several years of industry experience. Although entrepreneurial valorisation (assigning a value to the entrepreneur's specific qualities) is most likely to take place in high-technology industries such as software development, biotechnology and fine mechanics, it can also happen in more traditional industries. Consider the case of Ray Kroc, the founder of McDonald's. At age 52, Ray Kroc was the exclusive distributor for a company that produced 'multi-mixer' milkshake machines. Impressed by a small chain of hamburger restaurants based in California that used the multi-mixers, Kroc bought the restaurants from the owners, the McDonald brothers. His vision was for McDonald's to be the world's best quick-service restaurant experience. Being the best meant providing outstanding quality, quick service, cleanliness and value (low-price strategy). Kroc's key innovation was to standardise products, services and procedures in order to expand as quickly as possible through the franchising system. In doing so, Kroc also created the fast-food industry.

- *Entrepreneurial venture.* Entrepreneurial ventures are less common, but if they are successful they create major changes in the environment and sometimes create new industries; examples are Microsoft, eBay, Google and Creative Technology. Entrepreneurial ventures entail a great deal of uncertainty because they result from significant changes for the entrepreneur coupled with radical innovation. Because the results of the process depend on the entrepreneur's ability to pick up skills quickly and the speed with which the market takes up the innovation, the results of these projects are less predictable.[4]

Figure 2.1 can be used to chart a specific case, which would be shown by a pathway within the matrix. An entrepreneur can, for example, start a business along the lines of entrepreneurial reproduction and later introduce a significant innovation into the market, thereby moving towards entrepreneurial valorisation. In some cases, the entrepreneurial phase may be destroyed by the cessation of new value creation once the business has been established. This often happens with entrepreneurial reproduction and entrepreneurial imitation. In such cases, the entrepreneur may introduce an innovation at the time the business venture is launched. But once the business is successfully established in the market, there is hardly any innovation or growth taking place.

The discovery and evaluation of entrepreneurial opportunities

It was suggested in chapter 1 that the initiation of new ventures requires the combination of the right individual in the right place. In other words, it is necessary to have both an environment rich in opportunities and people who are able and motivated to pursue those opportunities. Drucker[5] identified three different categories of opportunity:

- inefficiencies within existing markets due to either information asymmetries or the limitations in technology in terms of satisfying certain known but unfulfilled market demands
- the emergence of significant changes in social, political, demographic and economic forces
- inventions and discoveries that produce new knowledge.

It is one thing for opportunities to exist, but an entirely different matter for them to be discovered and exploited. Opportunities rarely present themselves in neat packages. They almost always have to be discovered and shaped. Why are these opportunities discovered and exploited by certain people and not by others? Essentially, it is because people are different and these differences matter.[6] There are four main differences to consider: psychological characteristics, information and knowledge availability, creative processing and cognitive **heuristics**.

Heuristics:
Simplifying strategies that can be used to make judgements quickly and efficiently. Heuristics result from cognition, i.e. the intellectual processes through which information is obtained, transformed, stored, retrieved and used.

Psychological characteristics

Among the almost endless list of entrepreneurial traits suggested, the need for achievement, the ability to control events in one's life and a risk-taking propensity have received wide attention in the literature and show a high level of validity. Entrepreneurs are typically those people who relentlessly pursue their project, feel that they can control their life, and are able to take risks. These characteristics are discussed later in this chapter.

Information and knowledge availability

Specific knowledge and 'knowledge corridors' play a critical role in motivating the search for opportunities. Opportunities can be identified and exploited by people who have the ability to obtain information not possessed by others and can therefore build knowledge about, say, a specific industry or market. Specific knowledge by itself may be sufficient for the launch of a successful enterprise, but networks and social relationships can be a crucial source of information and resources for identifying and shaping ongoing opportunities. Networking allows entrepreneurs to enlarge their knowledge of opportunities, increase their sphere of action, gain access to critical resources (e.g. customers, suppliers, finance, premises) and acquire knowledge that allows them to avoid and deal with business development obstacles.

Creative processing

The ability to make the connection between specific knowledge and a commercial opportunity requires skills, aptitudes, insight and circumstances that are neither uniformly nor widely distributed. Creative processing refers to the way people approach problems and solutions — their capacity to put existing things together in new combinations. It has often been suggested that entrepreneurs see how to put resources and information together in different ways; they have the knack of looking at the usual and seeing the unusual. Consequently, they can spot opportunities that turn the commonplace into the unique and unexpected.[7] People have different creative processing abilities because they use different schemas — that is, mental structures which we use to organise our knowledge of the social world according to theme or subject.

Cognitive heuristics

Heuristics are simplifying strategies that can be used to make judgements quickly and efficiently. In business, this decision process is often referred to as trial and error — a mostly unconscious journey from one event to another, picking up pieces of knowledge and experience both positive and negative. People then filter these data through their own mental set and establish a pattern of behaviour. Since individuals have different business and social experiences, they will make different judgements about a specific situation. Some will consider this situation to be an opportunity and decide to pursue it.

Entrepreneurs appear to differ from other types of people in the use of cognitive mechanisms. For example, it has been suggested that entrepreneurs are more likely than non-entrepreneurs to experience regret over previously missed opportunities. Previous entrepreneurial experience also provides a framework for processing information and allows informed, experienced entrepreneurs to identify and take advantage of opportunities.[8]

The decision to exploit entrepreneurial opportunities

Although the discovery of an opportunity is a necessary condition for entrepreneurship, there is more to it than that. After having identified and assessed an opportunity, potential entrepreneurs must decide whether they want to *exploit* it. Why, when and how do some people and not others exploit the opportunities they discover? The answer again appears to depend on the joint characteristics of the individual and the nature of the opportunity.[9] Entrepreneurs tend to exploit opportunities that have a high expected value. Such opportunities are likely to generate a profit large enough to compensate for the opportunity cost of other alternatives, the time and money invested in the development of the project, and the risk associated with the project. In particular, exploitation is more common when expected demand is large, industry margins are high, the technology life cycle is young, and the level of competition in the industry is low.

Individual differences matter too. Firstly, individuals have different opportunity costs. The **opportunity cost** principle states the cost of one good in terms of the next best alternative. For example, suppose a public servant decides to launch a business venture. The opportunity cost of the entrepreneurial profit is the alternative income that he or she might receive by remaining a government employee. Since people have different incomes and wages, they are likely to make different decisions about whether or not to exploit any given opportunity. Secondly, the decision to exploit entrepreneurial opportunities is also influenced by individual differences in risk perception, optimism, tolerance for ambiguity and need for achievement. The different psychological characteristics of the entrepreneur will be discussed in detail later in this chapter.

Opportunity cost:
The cost of passing up one investment in favour of another.

Triggers and barriers to start-ups

So far, little research has focused on would-be entrepreneurs and the factors likely to influence their decision to launch a new venture. However, certain triggers and barriers often appear to play a role in the decision to exploit an opportunity.[10] For example, the following triggers have been identified:

- *Material rewards.* Many entrepreneurs launch their own business venture because they want to be rewarded according to their effort and because of the anticipated financial gains. For example, 40 per cent of the Fast 100 owners — BRW's list of Australia's fastest growing companies — draw a salary in the first year in business and, for the majority of them, this salary is over $100 000 per year.[11] Launching or buying a business can also represent an interesting investment option for those who have savings.
- *Creativity.* When asked about the variables that motivate the launch of a new venture, many entrepreneurs mention: 'To take advantage of my own talents', 'To create something new' and 'To realise my dreams'. Altogether, these variables translate the desire and the ability to bring something new into existence.
- *Desire for autonomy.* Entrepreneurs want to be independent, and they express the desire to work at a location of their choice, set their own hours of work and be their own boss.

The launch of a new business venture can be a long and difficult process, and entrepreneurs can face all sorts of hurdles while trying to realise their dreams. If these barriers are too high, entrepreneurs may eventually abandon the opportunity. The following barriers appear to play an important role in the start-up process:

- *Lack of resources.* Would-be entrepreneurs often think that they do not possess the necessary marketing and management skills. These personal deficiencies are often worsened by a lack of information on start-ups and the difficulty of finding sufficient finance.

- *Compliance costs.* High taxes and the cost of complying with government legislation are perceived as a major hurdle. Such compliance costs are often referred to as 'red tape'.
- *Hard reality.* Setting up a business venture is often harder and riskier than initially expected. The future is perceived as very uncertain and, as a result, a certain fear of failure emerges while the would-be entrepreneur gathers resources and processes information to launch the venture.

Some precipitating events (such as dismissal, job frustration, graduation or an inheritance) may also trigger the launch of the business venture. However, when the importance of each trigger is examined, it is often the desire to create something new — sustained ultimately by the passion and motivation of the individual — that pushes the entrepreneur to 'take the plunge'.

Modes of exploitation

Another critical question concerns how the exploitation of entrepreneurial opportunities is organised in the economy. Two major institutional arrangements exist — the creation of new firms (hierarchies) and the sale of opportunities to existing firms (markets) — but the common assumption is that most entrepreneurial activity occurs through new independent start-ups. However, people within organisations who discover opportunities sometimes pursue those opportunities on behalf of their current employer. In contrast, independent actors sometimes sell their opportunities to existing enterprises and sometimes establish new businesses to pursue the opportunities. Other institutional forms such as joint ventures or franchises are also possible.

Understanding the profile of an entrepreneur

It is difficult to identify and find entrepreneurs and to determine what they do. Is the artisan, the small business owner–manager or even the manager of a large corporation an entrepreneur? Are entrepreneurs found in private businesses only, or can they be in government and not-for-profit organisations as well? This section reviews the two basic schools of thought on the profile of the entrepreneur: the economists who consider the entrepreneur as an agent who specialises in certain roles, and the behaviourists who concentrate on the creative and intuitive characteristics of entrepreneurs. Later sections present the different risks associated with a career as an entrepreneur, and discuss the relevant performance measures to be considered in entrepreneurship.

The roles of entrepreneurs: an economic perspective

From an economic point of view, entrepreneurship is considered as a function, so entrepreneurs have been all but banished from the theory of the firm and the market. Microeconomics instead gives pride of place to prices. Guided by the wages and interest rates they must pay, businessmen choose from different techniques of production (labour-intensive when workers are cheap, capital-intensive when they are scarce) but they do not reinvent or revolutionise them. Guided by the price their wares will fetch, they decide to make more goods or fewer. In other words, as Casson noted, 'The entrepreneur is what the entrepreneur does'.[12] The status of the entrepreneur can then be analysed in terms of a division of labour that explains this function based on certain roles, such as risk bearer, arbitrageur, innovator, and coordinator of scarce resources.

Risk bearer

Cantillon[13] described an entrepreneur as a person who pays a certain price for a product to resell it at an uncertain price, thereby making decisions about obtaining and using resources while assuming the risk of enterprise. According to this view, merchants, for example, are specialised bearers of risk. Manufacturers can also be bearers of risk in that they purchase the labour of workers before the product of that labour is sold. Consequently, entrepreneurs should be regarded as calculated risk takers.

Risk exists when uncertain outcomes can be predicted with some degree of probability. An entrepreneur is prepared to accept the remaining risk that cannot be transferred through insurance. It was Knight who first developed the distinction between risk, which is insurable, and uncertainty, which insurers will not touch because they have no way of typing and calibrating it. Knight's thesis is that an entrepreneur's new business venture is in some aspects unique, and the relative frequencies of past events are not sufficient to estimate the probabilities of future returns of the venture. Uncertainty, which cannot be eliminated or insured against, is therefore the source of profit:

> Profit arises out of the inherent, absolute unpredictability of things, out of the sheer brute fact that the results of human activity cannot be anticipated and then only in so far as even a probability calculation in regard to them is impossible and meaningless.[14]

Faced with uncertainty, people must rely on their own judgement, because they have no outside information to refer to. It is on this resource, good judgement, that entrepreneurs earn a profit.

Arbitrageur

Arbitrage: The action of taking advantage of a discrepancy in value that exists in the marketplace. Those who ferret out such discrepancies in value and realise profits by acting on them are called arbitrageurs.

For other economists,[15] the entrepreneur is the key figure in the market economy. In a continually changing environment, entrepreneurs move the economy towards equilibrium through speculation and **arbitrage**. The main function of the entrepreneur in this context is one of price discovery. The motivation for price discovery is the prospect of a temporary monopoly gain if the entrepreneur can benefit from being the first to exploit the price differences. Profit is the reward for recognising a market opportunity and providing the intermediary function. Freedom of entry ensures that the entrepreneur receives only a normal profit once the costs of discovery are allowed for.

Innovator

Schumpeter[16] broke with traditional economics because it sought (and still seeks) to optimise resources within a stable environment. He suggested that dynamic disequilibrium brought on by the innovating entrepreneur, rather than equilibrium and optimisation, is the norm of a healthy economy. According to this perspective, the entrepreneur is an innovator who carries out new combinations: introducing a new technology or product, discovering a new export market or developing new business organisations. Schumpeter added that innovations are, as a rule, embodied in new firms. Thus the agent of change is the entrepreneur who, hitting upon the prospective profitability of some unnoticed commercial application, undertakes a new venture by implementing an innovative idea. Banks — the venture capitalists of Schumpeter's era — selected the investment projects to finance.

Coordinator of scarce resources

Another economist, Say,[17] described the entrepreneur as a coordinator and supervisor of production. Most entrepreneurs have the initial insight into an opportunity and know how to explain and describe it. However, they may not have all the resources (e.g. money, labour, premises, technology) necessary to launch a business venture. A critical role of the entrepreneur consists, therefore, in convincing resource holders to commit some resource to the new venture and in coordinating these scarce resources.[18] To achieve this, the entrepreneur must have judgement, perseverance and knowledge of the world of business.

The characteristics of entrepreneurs: a behaviourist approach

The second category of researchers who study entrepreneurs are the behaviourists, including psychologists and sociologists. Early studies in entrepreneurship typically focused on the psychological characteristics and the personality of the individual as determinants of entrepreneurial behaviour. The most common characteristics are shown in figure 2.2.

Figure 2.2: Characteristics of successful entrepreneurs

Self-confidence	Tolerance of ambiguity
Risk-taking propensity	Responsiveness to suggestions
Flexibility	Dynamic leadership qualities
Independence of mind	Initiative
Energy and diligence	Resourcefulness
Hard-work ethic	Good communication skills
Creativity	Perseverance
The need for achievement	Profit-orientation
Internal locus of control	Perception with foresight

Among the almost endless list of entrepreneurial traits suggested, only three have received wide attention in the literature and show a high level of validity:[19] the need for achievement, internal locus of control and a risk-taking propensity.

The need for achievement

Of all the psychological measures presumed to be associated with the creation of new ventures, the need for achievement has the longest history. The **need for achievement** — a person's desire either for excellence or to succeed in competitive situations — is a key personal attribute of successful entrepreneurs.[20] Successful entrepreneurs are highly motivated in what they do. They are typically self-starters and appear internally driven to compete against their own self-imposed standards. High achievers take responsibility for attaining their goals, set moderately difficult goals and want immediate feedback on how well they have performed.

Internal locus of control

Locus of control refers to the extent to which people believe they can control events that affect them. People with a high internal locus of control believe that events result mainly from their own behaviour and actions. Those with a high external locus of control believe that powerful others, fate, or chance mainly determine events. Effective entrepreneurs believe in themselves and have a perception that they can control the events in their lives and can therefore guide their own destiny. This attribute is consistent with a high-achievement motivational drive and a need for autonomy.

What seems to underlie the internal locus of control is the concept of 'self as agent'. This means that individuals' thoughts control their actions and that when they realise this executive function of thinking, they can positively affect their beliefs, motivation, and to a certain extent their performance. As a result, the degree to which they choose to be self-determining is a function of their realisation of the source of agency and personal control.[21] In other words, we can say to ourselves, 'I choose to direct my thoughts and energies towards accomplishment. I choose not to be daunted by my anxieties or feelings of inadequacy.'

Risk-taking propensity

Although entrepreneurs are not gamblers, they are characterised by a propensity to take calculated risks. In a world of change, risk and ambiguity, successful entrepreneurs are those who learn to manage the risk, in part by transferring a portion of the risk to others (investors, bankers, partners, customers, employees and so on). Risk-taking propensity is, however, strongly influenced by cognitive heuristics. Entrepreneurs may not think of themselves as being any more likely to take risks than non-entrepreneurs but, nonetheless, they are predisposed to categorise business situations more positively.[22] Entrepreneurs may thus view some situations as opportunities, even though others perceive those same situations as having little potential.

The characteristics approach eventually reached a dead end, as it could only partially answer the question: 'What makes people set up new ventures?' The study of the demographic background of entrepreneurs (age, gender, previous employment) was another attempt to understand these people and uncover a pattern. Demographic studies generally confirmed that entrepreneurs tend to be better educated; to come from families where the parents owned a business; to start ventures related to their previous work; and to locate their ventures where they are already living and working. Overall, these studies provided mixed results.[23] This is not surprising — being innovators and idiosyncratic, entrepreneurs tend to defy stereotyping.

Entrepreneur profile

Francis Yeoh — YTL Corporation

YTL Corporation managing director Francis Yeoh has a lot to celebrate. He was recently listed in 'People at the Peak — the Who's Who of Malaysia' and, in December 2005, he could preside over the celebration of the company's fiftieth anniversary. In the mid 1990s, the title of *Tan Sri* was conferred upon him; this is the equivalent of a knighthood in Malaysia and one of the country's highest honours. But it is also for his entrepreneurial achievements that Mr Yeoh has won much praise. YTL (the initials stand for Yeoh Tiong Lay, Mr Yeoh's father and the company's founder) has been a consistent money-spinner since it was listed on the Kuala Lumpur Stock Exchange. Today YTL is one of the largest companies listed, and together with its four subsidiaries has a combined market capitalisation of over RM20 billion (A$7 billion).

The journey from humble beginnings in Kuala Selangor to the diversified conglomerate YTL is today took bold vision, perseverance and some divine intervention. 'It all goes back to my grandfather, who came over here from China and started a modest timber business,' says Yeoh. 'My father, with typical entrepreneurial initiative, founded the YTL Construction Company. The migrant tradition produces intellectual risk takers and then as migrants they only found their security in a foreign land through material wealth.'

Mr Yeoh started to work in the business at an early age. He remembers spending his holidays on construction sites with his father at the age of eighteen. In 1973, YTL was severely affected by the oil crisis and Mr Yeoh was so eager to help his father he announced that he would quit school and join the company. Seeing the value of education, his father persuaded him to pursue further studies. The young Yeoh went on to Kingston University in the United Kingdom, where he graduated in civil engineering in 1978. At the age of 25, he took over his father's company and did more than just tag on their power-producing arm (YTL being the first independent Malaysian power supplier), acquire international outfits, or successfully rebrand one of the oldest parts of town.

His efforts have been interpreted by observers as a classic case study of putting your house in order during down time so as to be ready when the economy bounces back, which was exactly what happened. In the 1980s and the early 1990s, he was ready for the opportunities. YTL has been streamlined, the administration and procedures made more efficient, and the collection of data scrutinised. 'We're still builders, but we never stop thinking about how our building improves the quality of life for Malaysians and those who come here,' says Mr Yeoh. The company was listed on the Kuala Lumpur Stock Exchange in 1985 and had a secondary listing on the Tokyo Stock Exchange in 1996. The group is now a major player in construction, utilities, cement production, property development and hotel operations.

Over the past two decades, YTL has established a solid reputation as a building company that can design and complete a project on time, within budget, and with the quality required. 'Once we had a good reputation, we began to win many contracts and we attracted talented people to work in the company,' boasts Mr Yeoh. YTL's strategy of offering 'world class products and services at third world prices' extends across the range of its business activities, and is perhaps the single most important factor underpinning its success today. This policy has ensured that the group is able to offer attractive, high-quality products and services to its customers at competitive prices. One example of this strategy is the 'KLIA Ekspres' rail link connecting downtown Kuala Lumpur to the international airport. The high-speed train travels about 57 kilometres in 28 minutes, for the equivalent of only RM35 (about A$12). This is the cheapest fare per kilometre in the world for rapid rail transit.

The self-assured Mr Yeoh thinks that he owes his success not only to bold vision and hard work, but also to his ability to make good judgements. He does not believe that luck has much influence in entrepreneurship. When asked about his advice to would-be entrepreneurs, he replies: 'Don't read these books about being lucky. If you want to do something better for humanity, it's a very good start. If you want to make it because you want to be rich, I guess you will make it one day, but you are likely to be unhappy.'

Source: Based on author's interview with Tan Sri Francis Yeoh

The risks of a career in entrepreneurship

There are four types of risk to be considered before embracing a career in entrepreneurship: (1) financial risks, (2) career risks, (3) social risks and (4) health risks. All would-be entrepreneurs must ask themselves if they are prepared to live with these risks, and they should prepare strategies to minimise them.

Financial risks

Collateral: Property used as security for a loan. If the debt is not paid, the lender has the right to sell the collateral to recover the value of the loan.

Entrepreneurs usually invest large amounts of their own money to launch a new business venture. They have to commit part or all of their own savings to the venture and offer some **collateral** to raise finance. After start-up, most of the profits are usually reinvested in the business to expand the activities. Entrepreneurs risk losing all or part of the money invested in their business if they go bankrupt, for example.

There are different ways for entrepreneurs to reduce financial risks. In order to set up the business, one strategy is to borrow funds from bankers, venture capitalists or partners. Another strategy is to place personal assets in the spouse's name so that these assets cannot be seized if the firm goes bankrupt. The legal structure of the business can also help to minimise financial risks. For example, entrepreneurs who operate a business as a sole proprietorship or as a partnership face unlimited liability, whereas for a company the liability of the owners is limited to the unpaid value of the shares they hold.

Career risks

A question often asked by would-be entrepreneurs is whether they will be able to find a job or go back to their old job if their venture fails. This is a major concern, especially for well-paid professionals and people close to retirement age. Such people must ask themselves whether they are prepared to accept a lower paid job, not necessarily in their field of expertise, if they have to go back to being an employee. One way to minimise career risk is to launch a business on a part-time basis while still retaining the current job. Should the attempt fail, the person will have a fall-back position and income.

Social risks

Starting a new venture uses much of the entrepreneur's energy and time. Consequently, family and social commitments may suffer. To minimise subsequent reproaches and disappointments, any decision to set up a new business venture should involve the family. This might help would-be entrepreneurs to identify potential family problems that can arise from long working hours, reduced holidays and stress. Discussing the entrepreneurial project also helps to build commitment within a family. Successful entrepreneurs almost invariably recognise the support of their spouses and/or family in their career.

Another type of social risk is linked to the image of the failed entrepreneur. Some societies have little tolerance for failure. A typical example is the *kia su*, or 'afraid to lose' attitude that is pervasive in Singaporean culture. This typifies a mentality where failure is perceived to be a disgrace and to bring shame on the individual and the family.

Health risks

Entrepreneurship is a rigorous activity, not only physically but also mentally. In many instances, work and its demands dominate the lives of entrepreneurs. A clear separation of work and non-work is generally hard to achieve, and a normal work day can extend to 10 or 12 hours. There is evidence that entrepreneurs experience higher job stress and psychosomatic health problems than people who are not self-employed.[24] Would-be entrepreneurs should make sure that their health can cope with the demands and challenges of starting and running a business.

The source of many health problems is stress, which stems from the discrepancies between a person's expectations and their ability to meet demands. One of the solutions for reducing stress is to create an environment that discourages it, for example by having a place where everything can be kept organised.

Relevant performance measures

Entrepreneurship is concerned with the discovery and exploitation of profitable opportunities for private wealth and, consequently, for social wealth as well. There may be many motives for starting a business, such as acquiring higher social status or a new lifestyle, but the financial dimension cannot be ignored. After all, a business must generate a profit to stay in the marketplace, and entrepreneurs must be able to use a simple standard measure — a monetary unit — to assess their performance. The relevant benchmarks in entrepreneurship are: (1) the absolute level of economic performance that provides a return for enterprising effort and (2) the social contribution of the individual effort.

Superior performance relative to other enterprises is not a sufficient measure of success in the case of entrepreneurship because profit must exceed some minimum threshold in order to compensate opportunity seekers for their efforts. Just to break even, profits must compensate for bypassed alternatives (opportunity cost) and for the cash, effort and time invested in the venture (liquidity premium), as well as covering a premium for risk and a premium for uncertainty.

- *Opportunity cost.* Economists use this term to refer to what is given up when a certain course of action is chosen. For example, when choosing to set up a business and become self-employed, entrepreneurs must give up a regular salary and holidays (if they are employees). Opportunity costs are particularly high for well-paid professionals and executives.
- *Liquidity premium.* The entrepreneurial process generally requires substantial investments in order to evaluate and exploit opportunities. Most would-be entrepreneurs invest their own money in pre-start-up activities such as building a prototype, paying a consultant to conduct professional market research, and registering a patent or trademark. In addition, they spend a considerable amount of their own time and effort in fine-tuning the business concept and convincing various resource holders (such as venture capitalists, suppliers, clients and potential employees) to take part in the enterprise.
- *Risk premium.* In economics, risk denotes the possibility of a loss. Risk is present when future events occur with measurable probability. It is measurable because it relates to situations that have many precedents and where, as a consequence, the odds of success can be calculated. The risk premium depends on the outcome probability of the business venture. For example, if the odds of success are relatively high because the entrepreneur has developed a promising product (good trial tests) which can be protected (by a patent or registered trademark) and for which there is a familiar market, then the risk premium is relatively low.
- *Uncertainty premium.* Uncertainty is not measurable, and so cannot be quantified and handled through insurance or other arrangements. Uncertainty occurs in circumstances that cannot be analysed either on rational grounds, because they are too irregular, or through empirical observation, because they are unique. Uncertainty is therefore present when the likelihood of future events is indefinite or incalculable. The uncertainty premium is particularly high if the entrepreneur has no previous experience of the industry in which the business venture is to be established, and if the venture is based on radical innovation implying emerging technology.

As depicted in figure 2.3, results that fall below the sum of the above four components represent an economic loss for the entrepreneur, even if the sum is far above the performance of rival firms. Only the surplus above this minimum can be counted as the entrepreneur's reward.

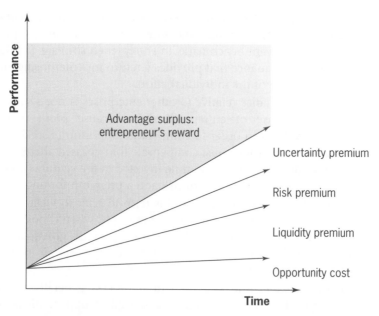

Figure 2.3: Relevant performance measures for entrepreneurs

Source: Adapted from S. Venkataraman, 'The distinctive domain of entrepreneurship research', in J. Katz (ed.), *Advances in Entrepreneurship, Firm Emergence and Growth*, vol. 3, Jai Press, Greenwich, Conn., 1997, p. 134.

What would you do?

The promise of stem cells

Joe Smith is a professor of obstetrics and gynaecology and has spent most of his career in Australia, where he was born. He has published over 100 research papers throughout a long and distinguished career in the embryology and stem cell field. He is a pioneer of in-vitro infertility treatments and is a board member of a prominent US IVF facility. Recently, he joined the Institute of Molecular and Cell Biology, one of the five research centres set up in 2000 by the Singapore government as part of a S$3-billion attempt to turn the city into a world-class centre for biomedical sciences. At the Institute he is leading a team of scientists pioneering human embryonic stem cell research. Stem cells have the ability to act as a repair system for the body, because they can divide and differentiate, replenishing other cells as long as the host organism is alive. As a result, they have been credited with almost miraculous healing potential, offering the possibility of treating disorders from diabetes to cancer.

Professor Smith has enjoyed a significantly higher standard of living since moving to Singapore. He now earns S$200 000 a year, and part of his remuneration package is a four-bedroom apartment in Holland Village, a high-class area of the city-state. The main drawcard for high-calibre researchers such as Professor Smith is the fact that the Singaporean government actively encourages work on stem cells.

This environment and a generous research budget have already produced some promising results. Professor Smith has successfully directed human embryonic stem cells into transplantable brain cell precursors. The research findings offer hope for the treatment of neurodegenerative disorders, including Parkinson's disease. In the future, stem cells could replace those lost by the disease. The findings are so promising that Professor Smith has worked more than 200 hours overtime in the last 6 months to prepare the clinical trials, and he is seriously considering the possibility of resigning and launching his own enterprise in order to exploit this opportunity. A month ago, he was approached by a venture capitalist who would like to take a minority investment in the start-up should he wish to go ahead. Professor Smith is thinking of setting up the company in a new industrial and research park in Singapore. He thinks that he could convince some of his brightest colleagues to join the company.

If successful, Professor Smith's company could capture a significant share of the market for the treatment of neurodegenerative disorders, estimated at US$300 million in industrialised countries. But is all the stem-cell media frenzy justified? 'Scientists are still divided as to whether embryonic stem cells will eventually produce the medical miracles promised by biotech entrepreneurs, but the stock market certainly knows what it likes — and that's government handouts,' one biotech commentator observed.

Questions

1. From a personal perspective, what performance measures should Professor Smith take into account when assessing whether this is a profitable opportunity?
2. What other issues does Professor Smith need to consider before conducting further discussion with the venture capitalist?

Entrepreneurs in a social context

The social context is crucial to understanding the situations in which entrepreneurial opportunities will emerge and be pursued.[25] Three features of a person's social context are important to the perception of entrepreneurial opportunities and the decision to seize them: (1) the stage of life, (2) position in social networks and (3) ethnicity.

Stage of life and entrepreneurial behaviour

Most societies have developed stable and widespread expectations about the appropriate times for major life events. Societal institutions are often organised around these social conventions, such as the age at which schooling should begin, the age at which marriage is appropriate, the age of retirement and so on. One critical life event is starting a job, which usually occurs immediately after completing an educational program. If the decision to become an entrepreneur was a common event for members of society, it would not be surprising to find major regularities in its relation to a stage of life. In reality, however, that is not the case. Entrepreneurial activity involves a minority of the population, and there is no general theory indicating the stage of life that is best for launching a business venture.

However, empirical research has shown that those people most likely to pursue entrepreneurial opportunities are men (women's participation rate being about half that of men across all countries in the Global Entrepreneurship Monitor) with post-secondary education, aged between the ages of 25 and 44, and with an established career record. Although not everyone with these characteristics starts new firms, this set of features is to some extent unique and predictable. Other aspects of the social context may also be associated with the decision to pursue entrepreneurial activities — the significance of the start-up team's background is now being explored, and recent studies indicate that a strong team is critical for new venture growth.[26]

Social networks and entrepreneurial behaviour

Humans are social animals, which means that we relate to others; we all have a **social network**. A person's self-image determines what connections are made and the person's identity is shaped by his or her network. Every tie is unique. The networks that entrepreneurs build for themselves and their ventures stand out in a number of respects:

Social network: The sum of relationships that a person maintains with other people as a result of social activity.

- The networks are genuinely personal, intertwining business concerns and social commitments in individual ties. By way of personal networking, entrepreneurs make their planned venturing career into a way of life. Personal resources (e.g. information, money, labour) are mobilised to set up new ventures that are alien to the market.[27]
- The spatial dimension is relevant. For historical, practical and symbolic reasons, many entrepreneurs and their firms are attached to a place. This means that the local and regional socioeconomic environment is both a major determinant and a major outcome of entrepreneurial activity.

Although networks are important in both Western and Eastern cultures, they are central to many Eastern cultures and particularly to the Chinese. The Chinese navigate complex networks of connections (*guanxi*) which expand throughout their lives. Each person is born into a social network of family members, and as the person grows up, group memberships involving education, occupation and residence provide new opportunities for expanding this network. The *guanxi* philosophy has deep roots. Many South-East Asian firms were established by migrant Chinese or their offspring, who built up networks in which extended families and clans did business in order to reduce risk. The relative permanence of such social networks contributes to the importance and enforceability of the Chinese conception of reciprocity (*bao*).

But how can entrepreneurs build an effective network? In fact, networks have to be carefully constructed through relatively high-stake activities that bring the entrepreneur into contact with a diverse group of people. Most personal networks are highly clustered — that is, your friends are likely to be friends with one another as well. And, if you made those friends by introducing yourself to them, the chances are high that their experiences and perspectives echo your own. However, because ideas generated within this type of network circulate among people with shared views, a potential winner can wither away and die if no-one in the group has what it takes to bring it to fruition. But what if someone within that cluster knows someone else who belongs to a whole different group? That connection, formed by an information broker, can expose the entrepreneur's idea to a new world, filled with fresh perspectives and resources for success. Diversity makes the difference.[28]

Ethnicity and entrepreneurship

Ethnic and religious affiliations have historically played an important role in entrepreneurship, and there is substantial information about the extent to which various ethnic groups or new immigrants engage in entrepreneurial behaviour in the Pacific Rim region. The main explanation of ethnic entrepreneurship is that it is a response to the lack of opportunities in the dominant culture. In this situation, entrepreneurship is very often a necessity triggered by a variety of push factors such as ethnic discrimination in the host society; lack of recognition of qualifications; poor use of local language; and limited opportunities. However, entrepreneurship can also be a first choice between different career alternatives, and this might result from different pull factors such as the presence in the family of entrepreneurs who act as role models; high social status given to the entrepreneur in the culture of the immigrant; perception of good entrepreneurial opportunities in the family and ethnic network; and availability of resources in the ethnic network.

Ethnic Chinese entrepreneurs in South-East Asia

In South-East Asia, there is substantial evidence that entrepreneurship, which is a crucial factor in development, has been steadily supplied by an ethnic minority — the expatriate Chinese. Historical evidence shows how domestic economies in the region faltered when ethnic Chinese entrepreneurs were not allowed to operate.[29] Usually, both push and pull factors have influenced ethnic Chinese entrepreneurship. Ethnic Chinese have often been discriminated against, having, for example, been barred from public service positions and land ownership, and allowed only limited access to tertiary education. As a consequence, they have often had no alternative but to become self-employed. At the same time, *guanxi* has provided ethnic Chinese privileged access to entrepreneurial opportunities and to resources. Initially, ethnic Chinese entrepreneurs fulfilled an intermediation function, particularly in their role as traders. They filled a gap in the existing market by providing goods and services that were not available. Today, although many are still engaged in trading and entrepreneurship, considerable numbers of ethnic Chinese have moved to banking and finance, transport, real estate, property development and hotel and travel services.

The situation in Australasia

In multicultural Australia and New Zealand, the growth of self-employment among ethnic minorities has been a conspicuous feature of entrepreneurial activities. In Australia, research has shown that ethnic business creation is positively related to pull and push motivations.[30] However, it was found that first-generation ethnic entrepreneurs were more influenced by push motivation, whereas third-generation ethnic entrepreneurs were more influenced by pull motivation. The first-generation ethnic entrepreneurs placed significantly greater importance on economic necessity and unemployment — both push motivators. The second-generation ethnic entrepreneurs gave greater importance to opportunities in Australia for doing business and making links to the country of origin — both pull motivators. The third-generation ethnic entrepreneurs went into business largely due to pull motivators such as opportunities in Australia, links for doing business in the country of origin and ethnic networks. Thus, the current trend reveals that ethnic business operators do not enter business activity as a last resort but as a positive choice.

Summary

The entrepreneur and opportunities are the essence of the entrepreneurial process. Entrepreneurs are intricately related to the opportunity they pursue, and together they form a system called a 'dialogic': a system with a circular causality process. It is one thing for opportunities to exist, but an entirely different matter for them to be discovered and exploited. Four types of person-related difference (psychological traits, information availability, creative processing and cognitive heuristics) can explain why some opportunities are discovered and exploited by certain individuals and not by others. Although the discovery of an opportunity is a necessary condition for entrepreneurship, it involves more than that. After having identified and assessed an opportunity, potential entrepreneurs must decide whether they want to *exploit* the opportunity. This decision again appears to be a function of the joint characteristics of the opportunity and of the nature of the individual. There are two schools of thought on the entrepreneurial perspective in individuals: the economic perspective considers that the entrepreneur is an agent who specialises in certain roles, such as risk-bearing, arbitrage, innovation and coordination of scarce resources; the behaviourist approach, on the other hand, has identified three recurrent entrepreneurial traits — the need for achievement, the internal locus of control, and risk-taking propensity.

When considering a career in entrepreneurship, people should also consider the four types of risk (financial risk, career risk, social risk and health risk) and prepare strategies to avoid or minimise them. Similarly, would-be entrepreneurs must be careful to have the correct performance measures in mind. Just to break even, profits must compensate for bypassed alternatives (opportunity cost) and for the cash, effort and time invested in the venture (liquidity premium), and they must cover a premium for risk and for uncertainty.

The social context is crucial to understanding the situations in which entrepreneurial opportunities will emerge and be pursued. Three features of a person's social context appear to play a role in relation to the perception of entrepreneurial opportunities and the decision to seize them: the stage of life, social networks and ethnicity.

REVIEW QUESTIONS

1. Drawing on the individual⇔opportunity relationship (or dialogic), what are the four different types of entrepreneurial outcome possible?

2. Why are existing entrepreneurial opportunities discovered and exploited by certain individuals and not by others?

3. Which entrepreneurial traits suggested from the behaviourist approach have received wide attention in the literature and show a high level of validity?

4. What types of risk should be considered before embracing a career in entrepreneurship?

5. To what extent does the social context play a role in entrepreneurship? What are the key features of a person's social context to consider?

DISCUSSION QUESTIONS

1. Identify major changes that create opportunities for entrepreneurs.

2. Why is there a wide variation in entrepreneurial activity among countries worldwide?

3. Are entrepreneurs born or made?

4. If a would-be entrepreneur evaluates all the potential risks before starting a business, does it mean that the business venture will not fail?

5. Social networks are recognised as important elements for ethnic Chinese entrepreneurs. Are these networks equally important for entrepreneurs of other ethnic origins?

SUGGESTED READING

Aldrich, H. & Ruef, M., *Organizations Evolving*, Sage, Thousand Oaks, CA, 2006.

Bolton, B. & Thompson, J., *The Entrepreneur in Focus*, Thomson Learning, London, 2003.

Ericksen, G., *The Ernst & Young Entrepreneur of Year Award: Insights from the Winner's Circle*, Dearborn Trade Publishing, Chicago, 2002.

CASE STUDY

Vision Eye Care Centre

Optic shops in Hong Kong have traditionally offered free vision tests. Once a customer sits down, the optician will use their computerised machine to test vision and establish a diagnosis. The whole process only takes a few minutes. This service is offered free of charge, even if the visitor does not buy anything in the shop. People have to pay for an examination only if it is done by an eye doctor or ophthalmologist. However, ophthalmologists specialise in curing eye disease, not in optometry — the specialty that focuses on the diagnosis and non-surgical treatment of disorders of the eye and vision care. In 1997, the government introduced a new regulation for optometrists and the Asian crisis made rent more affordable for entrepreneurs. These are some of the reasons that pushed Simon Sze to launch Vision Eye Care Centre, which would aim to provide a recognised service in optometry. The market positioning is between eye clinic and optical shop.

The inception of the business

Simon obtained his Bachelor of Science (optometry) from Hong Kong Polytechnic University in 1992. Upon his graduation, he joined an optical shop. After five years with the same employer, he became dissatisfied with his job and the working environment. The long working hours and limited use of knowledge acquired during his studies made the job unattractive. Simon disagreed with the strategy pursued by his employer, which aimed to sell spectacles, but did not bother about providing customers with eye care service and professional consultation.

At the same time, the government introduced a new regulation that divided the profession into four categories. The first category of optometrists, called Part I, had to hold a BSc Degree in Optometry from Hong Kong Polytechnic University or an equivalent degree. These optometrists were trained to diagnose, manage and treat a multitude of visual concerns including, but not limited to, fitting and prescribing spectacles and contact lenses; treating minor ocular injuries; diagnosing and treating diseases such as glaucoma; and diagnosing others such as diabetic retinopathy. The second category of optometrists had to hold a Higher Certificate in Optometry. They could also prescribe refraction and contact lenses. However, they were not allowed to use diagnostic agents, except for so-called staining agents. The third category included experienced practitioners who could only prescribe refraction and contact lenses. The fourth category included all employees who did not have proper training and had limited experience in the field of optometry. They were usually employed as junior staff and could only examine the client's eyes for short-sightedness, far-sightedness and the fitting of contact lenses.

When the new regulation was introduced, fewer than a hundred optometrists qualified for the top category, recalls Simon. The bulk of optometrists who operated a business belonged to the second and third categories. For these optometrists, selling glasses was the main revenue generator and the cornerstone of their business strategy. They provided a free examination to their clients in order to motivate them to purchase glasses. This created wrong incentives. Simon thought that clients would pay for a professional, accurate examination if they recognised the value of this service. Conducting such an examination and establishing a diagnosis requires highly specialised skills. 'A good optometrist does not rely solely on the machine for the examination because there can be some inaccuracies, especially with children. So accuracy is our strength and one of the major selling points.'

Simon thought it was a good time to launch a business as a registered optometrist, Part I, since there were few similar businesses operating at this top category. With his work experience, the money he had saved since graduation, and the recognition of an unmet market need for professional service, Simon teamed up with his friend Marco to launch Vision Eye Care Centre. The Asian financial crisis, which had hardly hit Hong Kong at that time, brought at least one bit of good news: rents fell dramatically in 1997. It therefore became easier to find a commercial surface and cheaper to launch a business venture. Simon and his partner rented a 300-square-foot commercial surface in the Argyle Centre on Nathan Road, Mongkok, to establish their business.

Trial and error

Traditional optical shops and specialist eye clinics were the main competitors for Vision Eye Care Centre. Simon realised very early that he needed to boost his marketing skills to differentiate his business offering, so he attended several courses to enhance his capabilities. It was difficult to win new customers. Since the centre was located on the nineteenth floor of a commercial building, it relied on word of mouth and referrals. Simon tried to improve services and expand his network to attract new customers. For example, he initiated an agreement with a couple of eye doctors so that both parties would refer their patients or clients to the other whenever necessary. He also kept abreast with technology by maintaining a relationship with professional bodies such as the Hong Kong Association of Private Practice Optometrists and the academic community.

The most important challenges for Simon and his partner were their lack of management and marketing experience and a lack of guidance and counselling. Simon admitted that during the start-up time, they ran the business by trial and error. At the beginning, he estimated they would have a small customer base comprising mainly friends and relatives. However, this could only last for the first three months. Luckily, they were able to attract new customers — mainly students — during the summer holidays, and the business broke even in its first year of operation.

Setting up the business and steering it through the start-up stage put a lot of pressure on Simon. He describes this period as like walking into a black tunnel where he could not see a bright future. He had no free time to participate in social activities and subsequently suffered from insomnia. His relationships with family were affected, as he became impatient and was too occupied by the business. It was not easy to 'get away' from the business. 'When you own a business, you think about it all the time. It is very hard to switch on the knob when you want to work and to switch it off as you leave your business,' says Simon.

Another type of stress emerged as he had to deal with people problems. Marco, Simon's partner, acted only as a silent partner. It was Simon who managed most of the operations. After four years together, they decided to dissolve the partnership because of diverging opinions about business strategies and management. Dealing with staff was not an easy task either. In the beginning, there was only one shop assistant and a high turnover rate. The shop had few customers and, as Simon was focusing on doing his own work, he did not think of communicating effectively with his staff. He thought that everyone could work independently, as he did. This turned out to be wrong; the lack of social interaction made the assistants bored and they left the business. After a while, Simon realised that he needed to talk to and coach his staff. He also hired additional staff as sales took off, and these actions significantly improved staff morale.

Breakthrough and expansion

In 2005, Simon recognised that the Mongkok market was becoming saturated and decided to open a second centre in Causeway Bay. The new 400-square-foot premises allowed him to expand the range of products and gain economies of scale with the existing centre. This forced Simon to improve his leadership skills.

In particular, he learned to delegate tasks and manage his time better, avoiding a tendency to get 'snowed under a plethora of things to do'. He delegated a qualified optometrist and a shop assistant to run the Causeway Bay centre. A part-time trainee was also recruited to share the workload during peak periods in the winter and summer holidays. Now, he does not have to do everything himself and spends more time coaching, monitoring and talking to his staff.

Reflecting on his experience as an entrepreneur, Simon says that setting up his own business brought him a great deal of satisfaction. It is not so much about monetary rewards but rather about freedom and personal satisfaction. As Simon remarks: 'Some people never have enough but, in my view, I think that I earn enough to make a decent living. I don't earn a lot more since I started my business, but I have a lot more freedom and I am more satisfied with my life.' This is his secret for happiness.

Source: Based on Joe Wan, Sally Lam, Sharie Pun and Winnie Yip's interview with Simon Sze.

Questions

1. Drawing on the individual⇔opportunity dialogic, what type of entrepreneurial outcome represents Vision Eye Care Centre?

2. Among the four major risks associated with a career in entrepreneurship, which one/s seem to have affected Simon the most? Why?

3. How can Simon attract more clients and convince them that a vision test is a valuable service that should be paid for?

ENDNOTES

1. C. Bruyat & P.A. Julien, 'Defining the field of research in entrepreneurship', *Journal of Business Venturing*, no. 16, 2000, pp. 155–80.
2. ibid.
3. ibid.
4. ibid.
5. P. Drucker, *Innovation and Entrepreneurship*, Harper & Row, New York, 1985.
6. S. Vankataraman, 'The distinctive domain of entrepreneurship research', in J. Katz (ed.), *Advances in Entrepreneurship, Firm Emergence, and Growth*, Jai Press, Greenwich, CT, 1997.
7. D.G. Mitton, 'The complete entrepreneur', *Entrepreneurship Theory and Practice*, vol. 13, no. 3, 1989, pp. 9–20.
8. S. Kaish & B. Gilad, 'Characteristics of opportunities search of entrepreneurs versus executives: Sources, interests, general alertness', *Journal of Business Venturing*, no. 6, 1991, pp. 45–61.
9. S. Shane & S. Vankataraman, 'The promise of entrepreneurship as a field of research', *Academy of Management Review*, vol. 25, no. 1, 2000, pp. 217–26.
10. T. Volery, N. Doss, T. Mazzarol & V. Thein, 'Triggers and barriers affecting entrepreneurial intentionality: The case of Western Australian nascent entrepreneurs', *Journal of Enterprising Culture*, vol. 5, no. 3, 1997, pp. 273–91.
11. R. Skeffington, 'Follow that Ferrari', *Business Review Weekly*, October 13–19, 2005, pp. 111–12.
12. M. Casson, *The Entrepreneur: An Economic Theory*, 2nd edn, Edward Elgar, Cheltenham, 2005.

13. R. Cantillon, *Essai sur la Nature du Commerce en Général* (1755), trans. H. Higgs, Macmillan, London, 1931.
14. F. Knight, *Risk, Uncertainty and Profit*, Houghton Mifflin, Boston, 1921.
15. Mainly the Austrian economists like F.A. Hayek, *Individualism and Economic Order*, Routledge, London, 1959; I.M. Kirzner, *Competition and Entrepreneurship*, Chicago University Press, Chicago, 1973.
16. J.A. Schumpeter, *The Theory of Economic Development*, Harvard University Press, Cambridge, MA., 1934.
17. J.B. Say, *A Treatise on Political Economy* (1803), trans. C.R. Prinsep, Grigg & Elliot, Philadelphia, 1855.
18. M. Casson, *see* note 12.
19. W.B. Gartner, 'A conceptual framework for describing the phenomenon of new venture creation', *Academy of Management Review*, vol. 10, no. 4, 1985, pp. 696–706.
20. D.C. McClelland, *The Achieving Society*, Free Press, New York, 1967.
21. B.L. McCombs, 'Motivation and lifelong learning', *Educational Psychologist*, vol. 26, no. 2, 1991, pp. 117–27.
22. L.E. Palich & D.R. Bagby, 'Using cognitive theory to explain entrepreneurial risk-taking: Challenging conventional wisdom', *Journal of Business Venturing*, no. 10, 1995, pp. 425–38.
23. T. Mazzarol, T. Volery, N. Doss & V. Thein, 'Factors influencing small business start-ups: A comparison with previous research', *International Journal of Entrepreneurial Behaviour and Research*, vol. 5, no. 5, 1999, pp. 48–63.
24. M. Jamal, 'Job stress, satisfaction and mental health: An empirical examination of self-employed and non-self-employed Canadians', *Journal of Small Business Management*, vol. 35, no. 4, 1997, pp. 48–57.
25. P.D. Reynolds, 'Sociology and entrepreneurship: Concepts and contributions', *Entrepreneurship Theory and Practice*, vol. 16, no. 2, 1991, pp. 47–70.
26. K.M. Eisenhardt & C.B. Schoonhoven, 'Organisational growth: Linking founding team, strategy, environment and growth among US semiconductor ventures, 1978–1988', *Administrative Science Quarterly*, no. 35, 1990, pp. 504–29.
27. B. Johannisson, 'Paradigms and entrepreneurial networks — some methodological challenges', *Entrepreneurship and Regional Development*, vol. 7, no. 3, 1995, pp. 215–31.
28. B. Uzzi & S. Dunlap, 'How to build your network', *Harvard Business Review*, December 2005, pp. 53–60.
29. A.R. Gambe, *Overseas Chinese Entrepreneurship and Capitalist Development in Southeast Asia*, LIT Verlag, Hamburg, 1999.
30. M.S. Chavan, 'The changing role of ethnic entrepreneurs in Australia', *The International Journal of Entrepreneurship and Innovation*, vol. 3, no. 3, 2002, pp. 175–82.

Chapter 3

Creativity, innovation and entrepreneurship

LEARNING OBJECTIVES

After reading this chapter, you should be able to:

- list the three components of creativity

- use a series of creativity techniques

- define and explain the sources of innovation

- discuss the different innovation types

- explain the link between creativity, innovation and entrepreneurship

- define the types and attributes of resources within a resource-based view of entrepreneurship.

reativity and innovation are an integral part of entrepreneurship. Drucker remarked: 'Innovation is the specific instrument of entrepreneurship.'[1] Just as entrepreneurship is crucial for the economy in general, innovation has become an important tool for managers who want to adopt an entrepreneurial approach. Promoting creativity and innovation is important for small and medium enterprises that want to maintain their competitive advantage. Research has shown that, over the past 15 years, the top 20 per cent of firms in an annual innovation poll by *Fortune* magazine achieved double the shareholder returns of their peers.[2] Recently, the search for innovation has also led to a craze for corporate entrepreneurship — fostering entrepreneurial projects inside large companies.

This chapter explains the role of creativity and innovation in the entrepreneurial process. It details the three components of creativity, explains different creativity techniques and discusses the factors influencing creativity. The different sources and categories of innovation are then presented. It is shown that creativity, innovation and entrepreneurship can be approached as a flow of knowledge, which is developed and transmitted mainly by social networks. The roles and attributes of strategic resources are also discussed.

Creativity

Creativity:
The production of new and useful ideas.

Creativity is the point of origination for innovation and entrepreneurship. In business, it can be defined as the production of new and useful ideas.[3] Creativity is the process through which invention occurs — the enabling process by which something new comes into existence. Reaping the fruits of innovation begins with creative ideas. It is therefore not surprising that successful, innovative companies systematically encourage the development of ideas. Those ideas are then screened to see whether they lead to a potential innovation. Experience shows that entrepreneurial companies need to generate hundreds of ideas to end up with four plausible programs for developing new products, and four development programs are the minimum to obtain just one winner. Therefore, it is crucial to create a corporate culture that allows ideas to blossom. 'You have to kiss a lot of frogs to find a prince,' said Art Fry,[4] the inventor of Post-It notes at 3M. 'But remember, one prince can pay for a lot of frogs.'

The three components of creativity

Creativity is usually associated with the arts and is seen as the expression of highly original ideas. In business, originality is not enough. To be creative, an idea must also be appropriate — that is, useful and actionable. In the end, it must fulfil a need in the marketplace and generate profit. To most people, creativity refers to the way people think — how inventively they approach problems, for instance. Indeed, thinking imaginatively is one part of creativity, but knowledge and motivation are also essential.[5]

Creative thinking skills

Creative thinking refers to how people approach problems and solutions — their capacity to put existing ideas and knowledge together in new combinations. The skill itself depends on personality as well as on how a person thinks and works. People are more creative if they feel comfortable disagreeing with others, i.e. if they try out solutions that depart from the status quo. As for working style, people are more likely to achieve creative success if they persevere with a difficult problem. Indeed, plodding through long dry spells of tedious experimentation increases the probability of truly creative breakthroughs. So, too, does a work style that uses 'incubation', which is the ability to set aside difficult problems temporarily, work on something else, and then return later with a fresh perspective.

Further, personality is strongly influenced by cognition, the mental activity by which an individual is aware of and knows about his or her environment, including such processes as perceiving, remembering, reasoning, judging and problem solving. Creative thinking is based on the same kinds of cognitive processes that we use in ordinary, everyday thought — retrieving memories, forming mental images, and using concepts.[6]

Knowledge

Expertise or knowledge encompasses everything a person knows and can do. This knowledge can be acquired in different ways: through formal education, practical experience or interaction with other people. Knowledge constitutes what Simon called his 'network of possible wanderings',[7] the intellectual space that he uses to explore and solve problems. The larger this space, the better.

Motivation

Knowledge and creative skills are a person's raw material — the person's natural resources. But a third factor — motivation — determines what people will actually do. Scientists can have outstanding educational credentials and a great ability to generate new perspectives on old problems. But if they lack the motivation to do a particular job, they simply will not do it; their expertise and creative thinking will either go untapped or be applied to something else. However, all forms of motivation do not have the same impact on creativity.[8] In fact, there are two types of motivation — extrinsic and intrinsic.

Extrinsic motivation comes from outside a person, whether the motivation is a 'carrot' or a 'stick'. If the manager promises to reward employees financially if a project succeeds, or threatens to fire them if it fails, employees will certainly be motivated to find a solution. However, this sort of motivation 'makes' employees do their jobs in order to get something desirable and to avoid something painful. The most common extrinsic motivation that managers use is money, which does not necessarily stop people from being creative. But in many situations it does not help either, especially when it makes people feel they are being bribed or controlled. More importantly, money by itself does not make employees passionate about their jobs.

Conversely, passion and interest — a person's internal desire to do something — are what intrinsic motivation is all about. When people are intrinsically motivated, they work for the challenge and enjoyment of it. The work itself is motivating. Consequently, people will be most creative when they feel motivated mainly by the interest, satisfaction and challenge of the task itself and not by external pressure.

Creativity techniques

Several techniques can be used to get the initial 'creative spark', and most can also be used to fine-tune an entrepreneurial opportunity during the innovation stage. Among the most popular creativity techniques are problem reversal, forced analogy, attribute listing, mind maps and brainstorming.

Problem reversal

Problem reversal:
The action of viewing a problem from an opposite angle by asking questions such as 'What if we did the opposite?' and 'What is everyone else not doing?'

The **problem reversal** technique is based on the premise that the world is full of opposites.[9] Any attribute, concept or idea is meaningless without its opposite. The great Chinese thinker Lao Tzu stressed the need for the successful leader to see opposites all around. For example, he noted the importance of action through inaction (*wu wei*), of letting go and not resisting nature's way of achieving balance. As a result, his philosophy maxims were often expressed as opposites: 'Be upright without being punctilious. Be brilliant without being showy.' All behaviour consists of opposites. To stimulate our creativity, we have to learn to see things backwards, inside out and upside down.

- State the problem in reverse. Change a positive statement into a negative one. For example, if you are trying to improve customer service, list all the ways one could make customer service *bad*. People are often pleasantly surprised at some of the ideas they come up with.
- Figure out what everybody else is *not* doing. For example, Apple Computer did what IBM did not — it was the first computer manufacturer to provide a graphical user interface. Japanese car manufacturers made small, fuel-efficient cars, whereas American car manufacturers focused on large cars.
- Change the direction or location of perspective. For example, examine a particular problem or question from the perspectives of the producer, distributor and client. Similarly, the problem may be different if people are city dwellers or country dwellers or from different nations.
- Turn defeat into victory. If something turns out badly, think about the positive aspects of the situation. One of the most popular products ever developed by 3M, the Post-It note, came about because a 3M engineer took some glue that did not stick properly and put it on small, colourful pieces of paper. This glue was originally considered an innovation failure.

Forced analogy

Forced analogy:
Also called forced relationship; the action of making an association between two unlike things in order to obtain new insights.

Forced analogy is a useful and fun method of generating ideas. This technique takes a fixed element, such as the product or some idea related to the product, and forces it to take on the attributes of another unrelated element. This forms the basis of a free flow of associations from which new ideas may emerge. As before, one should judge the value of the ideas after the process is complete.

Forcing relationships is one of the most powerful ways of developing new insights and new solutions. A useful way of developing the relationships is to have a selection of objects or cards with pictures to help you generate ideas. Choose objects or cards at random and see what relationships you can force. Use mind-mapping or a matrix to record the attributes and then explore aspects of the problem at hand. For example, Olson[10] described the problem of examining a corporate organisational structure by comparing it with a matchbox. This comparison is summarised in table 3.1.

Table 3.1: Forced analogy between a matchbox and a corporation

Attributes of a matchbox	Analogy with the corporation
Striking surface on two sides	The protection an organisation needs against strikes
Six sides	Six essential organisational divisions
Sliding centre section	The heart of the organisation should be 'slidable' or flexible
Made of cardboard	Inexpensive method of structure, disposable

Attribute listing

Attribute listing ensures that all possible aspects of a problem have been examined. List all the major characteristics or attributes of a product, object or idea. Then, for each attribute, list ways each of the attributes could be changed. Consider the following situation: a person in the business of making torches is under pressure from competitors and needs to improve the quality of the product. As table 3.2 shows, by breaking down the torch into its component parts — casing, switch, battery, bulb and weight — and by studying the attributes of each component, it is possible to develop ideas on how to improve each one.

Table 3.2: Attribute listing — improving a torch

Feature	Attribute	Ideas for improvement
Casing	Plastic	Metal
Switch	On/off	On/off low beam
Battery	Power	Rechargeable
Bulb	Glass	Plastic
Weight	Heavy	Light

Attribute listing is a very useful technique for quality improvement of complicated products, procedures or services. It can be used in conjunction with some other creative techniques, especially idea-generating ones such as brainstorming. This allows the entrepreneur to focus on one specific part of a product or process before generating ideas.

Mind maps

The human brain is very different from a computer. Whereas a computer works in a linear fashion, the brain works *associatively* as well as linearly — comparing, integrating and synthesising as it goes. Association plays a dominant role in nearly every mental function, and words themselves are no exception. Every word and idea has numerous links attaching it to other ideas and concepts. **Mind maps** are an effective method of note-taking and useful for the generation of ideas by association.[11] Mind mapping (or concept mapping) involves writing down a central idea and thinking up new and related ideas that radiate out from the centre. By focusing on key ideas written down in your own words, and then looking for branches out and connections between the ideas, knowledge is mapped in a manner that helps you understand and remember new information.

To make a mind map, start in the centre of a page with the main idea and work outwards in all directions, producing a growing and organised structure composed of key words and key images. Mind maps are a way of representing associated thoughts with symbols rather than with extraneous words — the mind forms associations almost instantaneously, and 'mapping' allows us to record ideas more quickly than if we were expressing them using only words or phrases. Because of the large amount of association involved, mind maps can be very creative, tending to generate new ideas and associations that have not been thought of before. Every item in a map is, in effect, the centre of another map.

The creative potential of a mind map is useful in brainstorming sessions. Start with the basic problem as the centre, and generate associations and ideas from it in order to arrive at a large number of possible approaches. By presenting thoughts and perceptions in a spatial manner and by using colour and pictures, a better overview is gained and new connections can be seen.

Brainstorming

The term **brainstorming** has become a commonly used generic term for creative thinking. More concisely, brainstorming is the generation of ideas in a group based on the principle of suspending judgement — a principle that has proved to be highly productive in individual effort as well as group effort. The 'generation' phase is separate from the 'judgement' phase of thinking.

Brainstorming works best when a group of people follows four rules:

- *Suspend judgement.* When ideas are suggested, no critical comments are allowed. All ideas are written down. Evaluation is reserved for later — people have usually been trained to be so instantly analytical and practical in their thinking that this is very difficult to do, but it is crucial. To create and criticise at the same time is like watering seedlings while pouring weedkiller onto them at the same time.
- *Think freely.* Every idea is accepted and recorded. Freewheeling, wild thoughts are fine, as are impossible and unthinkable ideas. In fact, in every session, there should be several ideas so bizarre that they make the group laugh. Remember that practical ideas often come from silly, impractical, impossible ones. By allowing people to think outside the boundaries of ordinary, normal thought, brilliant new solutions can arise. Some wild ideas turn out to be practical too.
- *Encourage people to build on the ideas of others.* Improve, modify, build on the ideas of others. What's good about the idea just suggested? How can it be made to work? What changes would make it better or even wilder? This is sometimes called tagging on, piggybacking or hitchhiking.

- *Quantity of ideas is important.* Concentrate on generating a large stock of ideas so that they can be sifted through later on. There are two reasons for wanting a lot of ideas: (1) the obvious, usual, stale, unworkable ideas tend to come to mind first, so the first ten or so ideas probably won't be fresh and creative; (2) the larger your list of possibilities, the more you will have to choose from, adapt or combine. Some brainstormers aim for a fixed number, such as 20 or 30 ideas, before quitting the session.

Factors influencing creativity

The traditional psychological approach, which focuses on the characteristics of creative people, contends that the social environment can influence both the level and the frequency of creative behaviour.[12] The encouragement of creativity, autonomy, resource availability, workload pressures and mental blocks are important factors to consider in this respect. Since creativity, innovation and entrepreneurship can also take place in an established organisation, these factors should be of prime interest to managers who want to promote an entrepreneurial spirit.

Encouragement of creativity

Encouragement of the generation and development of ideas appears to operate at three major levels within organisations:

- Organisational encouragement plays an important role, and several aspects are perceived as operating broadly across the organisation — such as encouragement of risk-taking and of idea generation, valuing innovation from the highest to the lowest level of management, and fair, supportive evaluation of new ideas.
- Encouragement from supervisors indicates that project managers or direct supervisors can promote creativity. Open supervisory interactions and perceived supervisory support operate on creativity largely through the same mechanisms that are associated with fair, supportive evaluation; under these circumstances, people are less likely to experience the fear of negative criticism that can undermine intrinsic motivation.
- Encouragement of creativity can occur within a group itself, through diversity in team members' backgrounds, mutual openness to ideas, constructive challenging of ideas, and shared commitment to the project.

Autonomy

Creativity is fostered when individuals and teams have relatively high autonomy in the day-to-day conduct of work and a sense of ownership and control over their own work and their own ideas. In addition, people produce more creative work when they perceive themselves as having a choice in how to go about accomplishing the tasks they are given.

Resources

It is generally admitted that resource allocation on a project is directly related to the project's creativity levels. Apart from the obvious practical limitations that extreme resource restrictions place on what can be accomplished, perceptions of the adequacy of resources may affect people psychologically by affecting their beliefs about the intrinsic value of the projects they have undertaken.

Pressures

The evidence that exists about pressures suggests seemingly paradoxical influences. Some research has found that, although extreme workload pressures can undermine creativity, some degree of pressure can have a positive influence if it is perceived as arising from the urgent, intellectual, challenging nature of the problem itself.[13] Similarly, time pressure is generally associated with high creativity in scientists involved in research and development, except when that pressure reaches an undesirably high level. Thus, two distinct forms of pressure can be identified: excessive workload pressure and the pressure of challenge. The former is likely to have a negative influence on creativity, whereas the latter will have a positive influence.

Mental blocks

In addition to organisational constraints, creativity can be impeded at the individual level because of various mental blocks. Prejudice and functional fixation are two examples of mental blocks.

Prejudice stems from the preconceived ideas we have about things. These preconceptions often prevent us from seeing beyond what we already know or believe to be possible, and thus inhibit the acceptance of change and progress. Consider the problem of how to connect sections of aeroplanes with more ease and strength than by using rivets. A modern solution is to glue the sections together. Most people would probably not think of this solution because of the prejudice about the word and idea of glue. But there are many kinds of glue, and the kind used to stick plane parts together makes a bond stronger than the metal of the parts themselves.

Sometimes we see an object only in terms of its name rather than in terms of what it can do. This type of mental block is a *functional fixation*. Consider the case of shopping centres. Traditionally, these were considered to be places where people went to buy something specific, until it was discovered in the mid-1990s that many people go shopping for entertainment. Borders books and music recognised this new trend. Its shop on Orchard Road in Singapore offers a huge selection of books and compact discs, a cafe and a bistro. The revolutionary thing about Borders is that, with its cosy armchairs and well-informed staff, it actually encourages shoppers to browse.

There is also a functional fixation when it comes to people's roles. Think how most people would react if they saw their dentist mowing their lawn, or their car mechanic on a television show promoting a book. In Switzerland, the newly privatised postal service uses its dense logistics network throughout the country to deliver products other than mail — in remote regions of the country, the service also delivers groceries that have been ordered online.

Home alone

Like many middle-aged people these days, Justine Craig, who lives in Sydney, often finds herself worrying about an ageing parent. Her father, Henry, is 85 years old and lives by himself on the Gold Coast, hundreds of kilometres away. 'He's a very independent soul,' she says. Many people in Justine's position feel torn; they want their parents to continue living in their own homes and pursuing their own lives, but are concerned about their parents' increasing frailty. Unlike others, however, Justine can at least feel she is doing something to help resolve this dilemma. As a partner at Knight & Moss, a leading Australian venture capital firm, she is planning to invest in business ventures that will develop new technologies that make life easier, less stressful and even healthier for older people who want to continue living at home.

Demand for such technologies could be enormous, since baby boomers are on the cusp of retirement. About ten per cent of the world's population was 60 years or older in 2000, but that figure will more than double to 22 per cent by 2050. Some countries will be especially hard hit by this factor: 28 per cent of the population in Italy and Japan will be over 65 years by 2030. In the developed world, there will be two old people for every child by 2050.[14] After talking to a specialist in geriatrics — the branch of medicine concerned with the diagnosis, treatment, and prevention of disease in older people and the problems specific to ageing — Justine realises that elderly people living on their own are facing many challenges. As people age, their sensory and cognitive functions, physical endurance and mobility may become impaired. Older adults may also experience depression and multiple chronic conditions that require complicated treatment regimens. Improper use of medications, inadequate food and fluid intake, lack of exercise, and urinary incontinence can make it increasingly difficult for the elderly to care for themselves, which increases the risk of hospitalisation.

To date, Justine has been very disappointed by the number and quality of project submissions that aim to help older adults remain as independent as possible for as long as possible. Justine has approached you to generate new business ideas.

Questions

1. What creativity techniques could you use to generate new ideas for submission to Justine?
2. What are the main areas of assistive technology? Give some concrete ideas in different areas.
3. What are the key challenges linked to the adoption of assistive technology by the elderly?

Innovation

Ideas are not enough for innovation, let alone entrepreneurship, to occur. Many people who are full of ideas simply do not understand how an organisation operates in order to get things done, especially new things. Too often there is an assumption that creativity automatically leads to actual innovation, but this is not true. Once a business opportunity or idea has been identified, it needs to be shaped and assessed, and eventually it has to materialise in a prototype, formula, patent or business plan.

Entrepreneurship can occur with little, if any, innovation. Most of the 'new' products and services launched in the marketplace, and the business ventures set up to produce them, are more or less copycats. Thus, the presence of innovation is viewed as a *sufficient* condition for entrepreneurship but not a *necessary* one. Moreover, newness or uniqueness of innovation is a matter of degree in terms of the tangible characteristics and the relevant market.

It is therefore important to understand that innovation is a multidimensional concept and that it is not necessary to reinvent the wheel to become an entrepreneur. For example, it is possible to innovate along several dimensions — product, service and process. In addition, the extent of innovation can vary greatly. For example, technological product innovation can be accompanied by additional managerial and organisational changes. This section discusses the various categories and sources of innovation.

Incremental versus disruptive innovation

When defined as an outcome, innovation is the tangible product, service or process that is adaptable or diffusable, meaning it can be used in various contexts by different individuals. More broadly, however, the change in condition, outcome or relationship which results from the innovation process itself may be either *incremental* or *disruptive*. The characteristics of incremental versus radical innovations are presented in table 3.3.

Table 3.3: Characteristics of incremental and disruptive innovation

Incremental innovation	Disruptive innovation
• Steady improvements	• Fundamental rethink
• Based on sustaining technologies	• Based on disruptive technologies
• Obedience to cultural routines and norms	• Experimentation and play/make-believe
• Can be rapidly implemented	• Need to be nurtured for long periods
• Immediate gains	• Worse initial performance, potential big gains
• Develop customer loyalty	• Create new markets

Incremental innovation

Incremental innovations are improvements of existing products that enhance performance in dimensions traditionally valued by mainstream customers. They make existing products and services better. Such innovations include, for example, bigger, more powerful mainframe computers. They usually come from tweaking existing designs and listening to big clients, who usually just want steady improvements that yield higher margins. Incremental innovations use established technologies and can be easily and rapidly implemented. Such innovations are a strong suit for established companies that continuously improve their products. But they almost inevitably hit a point at which they offer more quality or features than customers need, want or can afford. In pursuing higher margin business from demanding customers, established firms sacrifice the low end. This creates openings for disruptive innovations, which usually debut at the bottom of the market, among new customers.

Whatever the type of innovation, it remains fundamentally an application of knowledge. This notion lies at the heart of all types of innovation, be they product-, service- or process-oriented and disruptive or incremental. Table 3.4 lists some examples of incremental innovations with this central characteristic (application of knowledge) in mind.

Table 3.4: Types of incremental innovation

Type of innovation	Principle and example
Extension	Improvement or new use of an existing product, service or process, such as the development of desktop, notebook and laptop computers based on the mainframe
Duplication	Creative replication or adaptation of an existing product, service or concept. Duplication can take place across different markets or industries, e.g. fast-food chicken outlets such as Chicken Treat or Red Rooster in Australia were adapted from the Kentucky Fried Chicken model from the USA; or the franchise may be adapted to suit a variety of sectors such as petrol stations, cleaning and childcare, with the concept having originated in the fast-food industry.
Synthesis	Combination of an existing product, service or process into a new formulation or use, such as the fax (telephone + photocopier) or the multi-purpose mobile phone (telephone + camera + organiser + music player)

Disruptive innovation

Conversely, disruptive innovations change the value proposition. Disruptive innovations, such as personal computers, underperform existing products but they are also simpler, less expensive, more convenient, adequate and easier to use. They cause fundamental changes in the marketplace. Such innovations are based on new technologies and often present teething troubles that spoil the clients' bottom line. Invariably, breakthrough innovations require a fundamental rethink. Sometimes they come from dusting off ideas that failed to make it in the past, but more often they stem from the sheer stubbornness of would-be entrepreneurs who refuse to abandon their pet ideas.

Coming up with mould-breaking innovations is very different from making incremental improvements. Important as they are, steady improvements to a company's product range do not conquer new markets. Existing corporations therefore face the difficulty of choosing between sustaining technologies, which deliver improved product performance, and disruptive ones, which may initially result in a worse performance. This is what Christensen called the 'innovator's dilemma'.[15] Truly important breakthrough innovations built on disruptive technologies are initially rejected by clients who cannot currently use them. This rejection can lead firms with a strong client focus to allow their most important innovations to languish. The fatal flaw in these firms is their failure to create new markets and find new customers for these products of the future. As they unwittingly bypass opportunities, they open the door for more nimble, entrepreneurial companies to catch the next great wave of industry growth. The transistor was a disruptive technology for the vacuum-tube industry in the 1950s, just as the personal computer disrupted the typewriter industry in the 1980s.

As shown in table 3.5, entrepreneurs seeking to create value through disruptive innovations can take one of three basic approaches, each of which is suited to certain circumstances.

Table 3.5: Disruptive approaches

---

1. The back-scratcher: scratch an unscratched itch

What it is: Makes it easier and simpler for people to get an important job done

When it works best: When customers are frustrated by their inability to get a job done and competitors are either fragmented or have a disability that prevents them from responding

Historical examples: Federal Express, mobile phones

Current examples: Procter & Gamble Swiffer products, instant messaging technology

---

2. The extreme makeover: make an ugly business attractive

What it is: Find a way to prosper at the low end of established markets by giving people good enough solutions at low prices

When it works best: When target customers don't need and don't value all the performance that can be packed into products and when existing competitors don't focus on low-end customers

Historical examples: Nucor's mini-mill, backpacker accommodation

Current examples: Budget airlines such as Air Asia, Jetstar Asia, Virgin Blue

---

3. The bottleneck buster: democratise a limited market

What it is: Expand a market by removing a barrier to consumption

When it works best: When some customers are locked out of a market because they lack skills, access or wealth. Competitors ignore initial developments because they take place in seemingly unpromising markets.

Historical examples: Personal computers, Sony Walkman, eBay

Current examples: Blogs, home diagnostics, discount broking services such as ComSec and Boom.com

---

Source: Adapted from S. D. Anthony & L. Gibson, 'Mapping your innovation strategy', *Harvard Business Review*, May 2006, p. 107. Copyright © 2006 by the Harvard Business School Publishing Corporation; all rights reserved. Reprinted by permission of Harvard Business Review.

Sources of innovation

Most innovations result from methodically analysing seven areas of opportunity, some of which lie within particular companies or industries, and some of which lie in broader social or demographic trends.

Sources of innovation within companies or industries

Drucker[16] identified four such areas of opportunity within a company or an industry:

- *Unexpected occurrences.* Unexpected successes and failures are productive sources of innovation because most people and businesses dismiss them, disregard them and even resent them. Many innovations are the result of unexpected successes, particularly in the pharmaceutical industry. For example, the antibacterial effect of penicillin was discovered accidentally by Alexander Fleming in 1928. The discovery of the Pfizer blockbuster Viagra was also an accident. In 1991, a group of scientists at Pfizer, led by Andrew Bell, David Brown and Nicholas Terrett, discovered a series of chemical compounds that were useful in treating heart problems such as angina. The compounds were patented as Sildenafil. In 1994, Terrett discovered during the trial studies of Sildenafil as a heart medicine that it also allowed men to reverse erectile dysfunction. The drug acts by enhancing the smooth muscle relaxant effects of nitric oxide, a chemical that is normally released in response to sexual stimulation.

- *Incongruities.* These occur whenever a gap exists between expectations and reality. For example, in 1971, when Fred Smith proposed overnight mail delivery, he was told: 'If it were profitable, the US Postal Office would be doing it.'[17] It turned out Smith was right. An incongruity existed between what Smith felt was needed and the way business was currently conducted — and Federal Express, the world's first overnight delivery network, was born in the United States.

- *Process needs.* These exist whenever a demand arises for the entrepreneur to innovate as a way of answering a particular need. For example, eye surgeons long knew how to perform cataract surgery. An enzyme that made the process easier had been known for decades but was not usable because it was too hard to preserve. In the 1950s an entrepreneur named William Conner figured out how to preserve the enzyme. He and a colleague set up the Alcon Prescription Laboratory (now Alcon Laboratories Inc.) to manufacture and market this new product.

- *Industry and market changes.* There are continual shifts in the marketplace, which are caused by changes in consumer attitudes, advances in technology and industry growth. Industries and markets undergo changes in structure, design and definition. Indeed, when market or industry structures change, traditional industry leaders often neglect the fastest growing market segments. New opportunities rarely fit the way the industry has always approached the market, defined it or organised to serve it. An example is found in the healthcare industry in South-East Asia, where private medical centres are imitating five-star hotels to win a share of wealthy sick customers.

Sources of innovation in the social environment

Three additional sources of opportunity exist outside a company in its social and intellectual environment:

- *Demographic changes.* Of the external sources of innovation opportunity, demographics are the most reliable. Census data, for instance, provide a precise picture of the actual demographic structure of a country, and from these data it is relatively easy to extrapolate the future age structure. In Australia and New

Zealand, two countries which have integrated a large number of migrants over the past decades, 'ethnic food' is one of the fastest growing market opportunities for entrepreneurs. Another demographic trend in the industrialised countries is the ageing population. This creates many opportunities in the field of assistive technology (see What Would You Do? on page 62).

- *Perceptual changes.* Sometimes the members of a community can change their interpretation of facts and concepts, and thereby open up new opportunities. What determines whether people see a glass as half full or half empty is mood rather than fact, and a change in mood often defies quantification. But it is not esoteric. It is concrete and it can be tested and exploited for innovation opportunity. Perceptual changes can particularly affect dimensions such as acceptability, beauty, time and distance. For example, commuters living in suburbs of big cities often perceive a 50-kilometre or one-hour journey to their workplace as acceptable, whereas residents in small towns would not.

New knowledge. Among history-making innovations, those based on new knowledge — whether scientific, technical or social — rank high. Knowledge-based innovations differ from all others in the time they take, in their casualty rates, and in their predictability, as well as in the challenges they pose to entrepreneurs. They have, for instance, the longest lead time of all innovations. To become effective, innovation of this sort usually demands not one kind of knowledge but many. Innovations in bioscience are a case in point. In recent innovations awards organised by *The Economist*, the category receiving the largest number of nominations was bioscience.[18] Interestingly, many of these could just as easily have been classified under nanotechnology. Clearly, innovations in bioscience are built on the combination of new knowledge from several fields.

Entrepreneur profile

Olivia Lum — Hyflux Ltd

Olivia Lum, founder and CEO of the fast-growing water treatment company Hyflux, has never known her biological parents. At birth, she was adopted by a woman she later called 'Grandma', who raised her in Kampar, a poor Malaysian mining town.[19] In 1978, Ms Lum took her primary school vice principal's advice and left Kampar for Singapore, where she would have access to more opportunities and a greater chance of bettering herself. She took with her the blessings of her Grandma and just $10 in her pocket.[20]

In the city-state, she won a place at one of the nation's top junior colleges and later attended the National University of Singapore. After completing her studies in chemistry, she was hired by the multinational corporation Glaxo to develop a water treatment system. During her three-year stint at Glaxo, Ms Lum saw the immense potential of a water treatment business.

In 1989, Ms Lum decided to sell her car and condominium to launch Hydrochem, a company selling water treatment systems in Singapore, Malaysia and Indonesia. During that time, she rode a motorbike from Jurong to Batu Pahat, knocking on factory doors to sell water softeners and filters.[21] Ms Lum ploughed whatever profits she made back

(continued)

into her business, which was later renamed Hyflux. In 2001, the company was listed on the SESDAQ, and in 2003 it was upgraded to the Singapore Exchange's main board.

Just as Singapore was searching for long-term viable options to reduce the country's dependence on external sources of water, Ms Lum appeared on the scene with three commerically feasible solutions: the generation of water from recycled waste water (the product is known as Newater), from sea water (produced at the S$200 million Tuas desalination plant), and from water vapour in the air. Hyflux has also won many overseas contracts. These include desalination plants in China and the Middle East. This series of deals signalled her entrance into the big league. Today Ms Lum's company continues to break new ground as one of the most innovative and impressive water treatment companies in the region.[22]

A series of research and development breakthroughs have secured Hyflux's lead position in water treatment. In the 1990s, Hyflux developed an ultra-fine membrane filter that the company uses in all its major products. In association with a US group, it more recently started manufacturing the 'Dragonfly' condensing system. This device produces potable water by extracting moisture from air. However, this latest technology has some disadvantages: the surrounding air must have at least 40 per cent humidity; it requires a fair amount of electricity to run; and each device costs about S$1000. However, Ms Lum insists that unit prices will fall as her team refines the design, and says the Dragonfly may soon be found in refrigerators and even cars.[23]

Today, Hyflux is one of Asia's leading membrane companies, specialising in water treatment and recycling systems and turnkey plant design. The company, which employs 600 staff in Singapore and China, achieved a pre-tax profit of S$30 million on sales of S$88 million last year. Ms Lum has won many accolades for her achievements. In 2005, she received *Asiamoney*'s Corporate Executive of the Year award in Singapore. Ms Lum was also named Businesswoman of the Year 2004 at the Singapore Business Awards.

Ms Lum attributes her positive outlook on life to her loving grandmother. As a youngster, she declared she wanted to grow up to be a 'big businesswoman'. Always supportive, her grandmother would laugh — but she never dashed Ms Lum's dreams with the pragmatic sense of an adult. The affirmation her Grandma gave served as fodder to her soul in pushing further in everything she did.[24]

The role of knowledge, social networks and strategic resources

While still oversimplified, figure 3.1 is a representation of the links between creativity, innovation and entrepreneurship as a process model. It can be regarded as a logically sequential (though not necessarily continuous) process that can be divided into a series of interdependent stages. The overall process can be thought of as a complex set of communication paths over which knowledge is transferred. These paths include internal and external linkages. At the centre of the model, innovation represents the firm's capabilities and its linkages with both the marketplace and the science base. As shown in figure 3.1, the entrepreneurial process is influenced by two main factors. On the one hand, the unsatisfied needs in the marketplace are one source of opportunity for developing and commercialising new products or new services (pull factors). On the other hand, technological progress, such as powerful computers, microscopes, digital networks and scanners, combined with the advance of science produce knowledge at an exponential rate (push factors). New knowledge can be a formidable source of opportunity for people who are able to use this knowledge to answer needs that are often unformulated.

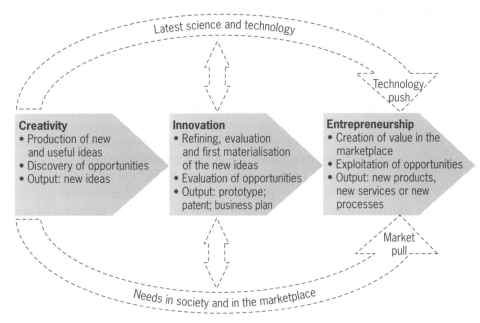

Figure 3.1: A process model of creativity, innovation and entrepreneurship

Many people see the successive stages of ideas generation (creativity), ideas evaluation (innovation) and ideas implementation (entrepreneurship) as being distinct and separate. In fact, these stages can overlap, and entrepreneurship is not necessarily a linear process. Three important concepts are developed in this section:

- It is shown that these three stages essentially consist of creating new knowledge.
- It is suggested that this knowledge is developed and formulated through different types of social network.
- Drawing on the resource-based theory, we discuss the critical role played by strategic resources in securing a sustained competitive advantage.

Knowledge development during the entrepreneurial process

What creativity, innovation and entrepreneurship all have in common is that they are concerned with knowledge development. In other words, the creativity–innovation–entrepreneurship process is like an assembly line of knowledge and ideas. Knowledge is an intangible commodity, but it lies at the core of the three stages.

During the creativity stage, knowledge is present in a very raw form. It might just consist of ideas and sketches drawn on a piece of paper. During the innovation stage, knowledge is further refined and the initial idea should pass the 'feasibility test'. At this stage, knowledge is often codified, for instance in the form of a formula or patent. However, the best patent does not constitute a finished product. For this we need an entrepreneur who is able to organise and coordinate resources to manufacture and market the product that integrates the patented technology. During the entrepreneurship stage, knowledge is embedded in the product or service marketed. It is the extent to which the entrepreneur can generate, explain and protect this knowledge that will ensure the firm has a competitive advantage.

Therefore, the development and deployment of unique resources and distinctive skills are necessary for achieving organisational survival, profitability and growth. Such resources and skills are also referred to as competencies, which must be sustained by continuous learning. Knowledge constitutes the essence of competencies, and the way organisations create new knowledge is intrinsically related to the creativity–innovation–entrepreneurship process.

In the case of established organisations, the crucial role that corporate entrepreneurship activities play in the creation of knowledge has been recognised.[25] Formal and informal corporate entrepreneurship activities can enrich a company's performance by creating new knowledge that becomes the basis for building new capabilities or revitalising existing ones. Indeed, some of the most important contributions of corporate entrepreneurship may lie in the development of critical capabilities that are much needed for the creation and commercialisation of new knowledge-intensive products, processes or services.

Developing and disseminating knowledge through social networks

Social networks are the catalyst for the development and dissemination of knowledge, both for emerging and established organisations. Would-be entrepreneurs' personal networks — the set of people to whom they are directly linked — affect their access to social, emotional and material support. Network relationships and contacts are basic to (1) identifying opportunities and (2) obtaining the knowledge and resources required to exploit opportunities. Regardless of their abilities, would-be entrepreneurs who are low on the socioeconomic scale and who possess poor networking skills may find themselves cut off from emerging opportunities and critical resources.

Social networks can be characterised by three main features: their diversity, their affective or emotional strength, and their structural equivalence — that is, the degree to which actors in the network have similar/dissimilar social relationships. Diversity arises from the various characteristics (in terms of age, gender, ethnicity, education and occupation) of the people forming the network. Diversity in network ties, for example, is essential for would-be entrepreneurs, as it widens the scope of information about potential innovations, business locations, assistance schemes and sources of capital. Therefore, a network of uniform or similar ties will be of limited value to an entrepreneur.[26]

The relationships between the people in the network can be strong, weak, indeterminate/fluctuating.[27] The most durable and reliable relationships in personal networks are strong ties, which are usually of long duration. Strong ties are built on mutual trust and are not governed by short-term calculations of self-interest. Weak ties, on the other hand, are superficial or casual and normally involve little emotional investment. Weak relationships are typically of shorter duration and contact is less frequent. The loosest ties — fluctuating ties — can best be described as contacts. This type of network relationship is created for pragmatic purposes with strangers with whom the individual has generally had no previous contact.

A resource-based theory of entrepreneurship

The most creative ideas and cutting-edge innovations are not sufficient for setting up a business venture. Without resources to exploit an opportunity, even the best opportunity cannot create an entrepreneur.

Principles of resource-based theory

The resource-based theory considers that firms have different starting points for resources (called *resource heterogeneity*) and that other firms cannot get them (called *resource immobility*). New firms emerge to pursue an attractive opportunity as the result of a combination of resources under the leadership of an entrepreneur. Firms usually begin with a relatively small amount of strategically relevant resources and skills, and each company's uniqueness shows how these resources are expected to perform in the marketplace.

According to the resource-based theory, in order to be successful, entrepreneurs must exploit market imperfections based on imperfect information or variations in expectations about prices while adhering to the following simple formula:
1. Buy (or acquire) resources and skills cheaply.
2. Transform the resources into a product or service (production).
3. Deploy and implement (strategy).
4. Sell dearly (for more than you paid — value creation).

However, this is possible only if cheap or undervalued resources and skills exist. Their availability depends on market imperfections and differences of opinion about prices and events. These are not limitations, because perfect agreement seldom exists, and the key to an entrepreneur's vision is insight into the future.[28]

Resource types

Resource:
Any thing or quality that is useful.

A **resource** is any thing or quality that is useful. The resource-based theory recognises six types of resource: financial, physical, human, technological, reputation and organisational. These six types are broadly drawn and include all assets, capabilities, organisational processes, firm attributes, information and knowledge.
* *Financial resources.* Financial resources represent money, shares and other assets. Financial resources are generally the firm's borrowing capacity, the ability to raise new equity, and the amount of internal fund generation. Financial resources are seldom the source of sustainable competitive advantage. These resources are valuable, but they are seldom rare, they are fairly easy to copy, and substitutes do

exist. However, while the actual financial resources may not provide a sustainable competitive advantage, the management of these resources can provide it.

- *Physical resources.* These resources are the tangible property the firm uses in production and administration (e.g. location, equipment, office space). Complex physical technology cannot provide a basis for a sustainable competitive advantage, as it can be duplicated and reproduced. However, if the method for exploiting the technology is not easy to copy (assuming it is rare and difficult to substitute), the other resources can augment technology to provide a sustainable competitive advantage.
- *Human resources.* Human resources include the knowledge, training and experience of the entrepreneur and his or her team of employees and managers. Human capital includes relationship capital (who the organisation's members know and what information these people possess) or social capital. Social capital is important because it allows individuals to obtain resources that are otherwise unavailable to them, such knowledge, capital, clients and access to suppliers.
- *Technological resources.* These resources are embodied in a process, system or physical transformation. They constitute physical or legal entities that are owned by a corporation, for example patents, unique software products and tailored information-system architecture. Technological capital is different from intellectual capital in that intellectual capital is embodied in people and is mobile.
- *Reputation.* Reputation encompasses the perceptions that people in the firm's environment have of the firm. Reputational capital can exist at the product or corporate level, and it may be relatively long-lived. The most important aspects of reputation are product quality, management integrity and financial soundness. Even a start-up business can quickly acquire a reputation, for example by cooperating with a well-established business.
- *Organisational resources.* These resources include the firm's structure, routines and systems. The organisation's structure is an intangible resource that can differentiate it from its competitors. A structure that promotes speed can be the entrepreneur's most valuable resource. Collective remembered history (myth) and recorded history (files and archives) may also be considered organisational resources. The capabilities of a firm — what it can do as a result of teams of resources working together — are also part of organisational resources.

Attributes of strategic resources

Strategic resources: Resources which provide a sustained competitive advantage to a firm.

Not all resources are strategically relevant for the entrepreneur. **Strategic resources** create competitive advantage, whereas common resources are necessary for carrying out the firm's usual activities but provide no specific advantage. Strategic resources matter because they are the basis of the firm's competitive advantage, which in turn determines its ability to earn a profit. Competitive advantage occurs when the entrepreneur implements a value-creating (above normal profit) strategy that is not simultaneously being implemented by any current or potential competitors.[29] Sustained competitive advantage is competitive advantage with an important addition: current and potential firms are unable to duplicate the benefits of the strategy.

The resource-based view of entrepreneurship holds that sustainable competitive advantage is created when firms possess and use resources that are:

- *valuable* — resources are valuable when they help the organisation implement its strategy effectively and efficiently by exploiting opportunities or minimising threats in the firm's environment
- *rare* — these are resources that are not widely available to all competitors
- *non-substitutable* — when common resources are not equivalent to the rare and valuable resources of another firm, the rare and valuable resources are said to be non-substitutable; for example, top-management teams cannot be a source of sustained competitive advantage because, even though these teams are valuable, rare and hard to copy, a substitute exists and can be used
- *hard to copy* — if a resource cannot be duplicated at a price sufficiently low to leave profits, the resource is said to be imperfectly imitable (hard to copy). Imperfect imitability can stem from:
  - *historical conditions* — the initial assets and resources used in the firm's start-up are unique for that place and time; firms founded at a different time in another place cannot obtain these resources, so the resources cannot be duplicated
  - *ambiguous causes and effects* — the relationship between the organisation's resources and its success is not well understood or it is ambiguous, sometimes even to the firm using the high-performing resource
  - *complex social relationships* — as long as a firm uses human and organisational resources, social complexity may serve as a barrier to imitation. The most complex social phenomenon is organisational culture, which is a complex combination of the founder's values, habits and beliefs and the interaction of these elements with the newly created organisation and the market.

As figure 3.2 shows, when a firm possesses and controls resources that are valuable, rare, non-substitutable and hard to copy, and it can protect these resources and maintain these four qualities, it will have a competitive advantage in the long term. If a firm has all these qualities but not in full measure and without protection, competitive advantage will be short-lived because competitors will copy and imitate them.

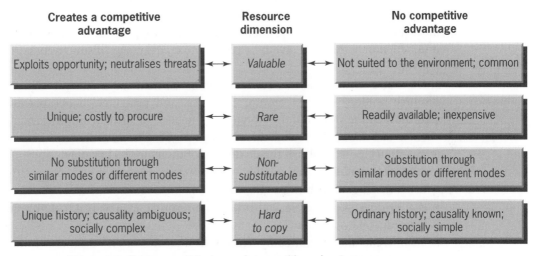

Figure 3.2: Resource attributes and competitive advantage

Source: Adapted from M. Dollinger, *Entrepreneurship: Strategies and Resources*, 2nd edn, Prentice Hall, Upper Saddle River, NJ, 1999, p. 31.

The role of stories in attracting resources

Because of the novelty and uniqueness of their ventures, entrepreneurs confront problems associated with lack of legitimacy of external validation. Given that most start-ups lack proven track records, obvious asset value and profitability, stories can provide accounts that explain, rationalise and promote a new venture, thereby reducing the uncertainty typically associated with entrepreneurship. Lounsbury and Glynn propose that stories play a critical role in the processes that enable new business to emerge. Stories that are told by or about entrepreneurs define a new venture in ways that may encourage positive assessments of the venture's wealth-creating potential and thus create resource flows for the new venture.[30]

Stories are important organisational symbols that use verbal expression and written language. They are structured, having a beginning, middle and end, and they include plotline and twists.[31] A well-crafted story about entrepreneurial resources encapsulates the strategic goals and management of the new venture and indicates why it merits investment. Once an entrepreneurial story is articulated, understood and repeated, it becomes an institutionalised account that provides both an explanation of and rationale for entrepreneurial activity. Thus, entrepreneurial tales aim to suggest plausibility and to build confidence in the idea that the enterprise can succeed.[32]

There are two basic means by which the content of entrepreneurial stories shape and legitimate the identity of the new business venture: (1) by emphasising the distinctiveness of the new venture and explaining its unique characteristics; and (2) by stressing the congruence and similarity with existing enterprises and business models. Entrepreneurs seeking to shape the identity of their enterprise must therefore be able to astutely assess whether (and to what degree) stressing distinctiveness or sameness will lead to the acquisition of resources and wealth creation. You might hear them saying: 'This is a booming industry...The demand has exploded and there are many businesses that have recently been established to meet the growing demand [sameness]. However, we propose a new product with unique features that will give us a competitive advantage [distinctiveness] in this market.'

Of course, entrepreneurial stories must be constructed in such a way that the resource holders, such as venture capitalists and potential clients, perceive the credibility of the story and the storyteller. The basis of such credibility is fidelity, or whether it fits with the beliefs of the target audiences. Entrepreneurs can use different strategies to establish the credibility of their story. They may:

- 'borrow reputation' by relating the business venture to a social structure, network of relationships or elite ties
- give evidence of tangible and intangible resource capital (e.g. patents, credentials, ideas, key personnel)
- detail credentials obtained by neutral third parties or endorsements from reputable third parties
- emphasise the entrepreneur's successful track record or prior performance history.

Summary

This chapter has explained the role of creativity and innovation in the entrepreneurial process. Creativity is the point of origination for innovation and entrepreneurship. It can be defined as the production of new and useful ideas in any domain. Within every individual, creativity is a function of three components: creative thinking skills, knowledge and motivation. Several techniques can be used to obtain the initial 'creative spark'. Among the most popular creativity techniques are problem reversal, forced analogy, attribute listing, metaphorical thinking, mind maps and brainstorming. At the same time, several factors can influence creativity. Encouragement, autonomy, resource availability and workload pressures are important factors in this respect.

Innovation is the successful implementation of creative ideas within an organisation. Most innovative business ideas come from methodically analysing several areas of opportunity, some of which lie within particular companies or industries, and some of which lie in broader social or demographic trends. Innovation is a multidimensional concept. When considering the extent of innovation, it is possible to distinguish between disruptive and incremental innovation. Innovation can also concern different elements, such as a product, a service, a process or a combination of these.

The successive stages of ideas generation (creativity), ideas evaluation (innovation) and ideas implementation (entrepreneurship) can overlap and are not necessarily a linear process. These three stages essentially consist of creating new knowledge, which is developed and formulated through different types of social network. However, a good idea is not enough to start up a business venture. Without resources to exploit an opportunity, even the best opportunity does not create an entrepreneur. A resource is any thing or quality that is useful. The resource-based theory recognises six types of resource: financial, physical, human, technological, reputation and organisational. When a firm possesses and controls resources that are valuable, rare, non-substitutable and hard to copy, and it can protect these resources and maintain these four qualities, it will have a competitive advantage in the long term. Stories that are told by or about entrepreneurs can play a critical role in the acquisition of resources. Entrepreneurial stories can provide accounts that explain, rationalise, and promote a new venture and therefore reduce uncertainty.

REVIEW QUESTIONS

1. What are the different components of creativity?

2. What are the factors that can affect creativity?

3. What are the different sources of innovation?

4. What do creativity, innovation and entrepreneurship have in common?

5. What are the principles of the resource-based theory of entrepreneurship?

DISCUSSION QUESTIONS

1. Can everyone learn to be creative?

2. How is it that one often meets a lot of creative people with business ideas but that only a very small proportion of these people will actually become entrepreneurs?

3. Why do seasoned entrepreneurs often say: 'You don't need to reinvent the wheel to become an entrepreneur'?

4. How do each of the four attributes of resources contribute to sustainable competitive advantage?

5. How can an organisation's culture be a source of sustainable competitive advantage?

SUGGESTED READING

Christensen, C.M., *Seeing What's Next*, Harvard Business Press, Boston, 2004.

Drucker, P.F., *Innovation and Entrepreneurship: Practice and Principles*, Harper & Row, New York, 1985.

Haour, G., *Resolving the Innovation Paradox — Enhancing Growth in Technology Companies*, Palgrave, London, 2005.

< http://inventors.about.com> (website about famous inventions with A-to-Z lists, timelines and history essays).

CASE STUDY

The Atlantis Group

If you haven't met a serial entrepreneur yet, consider the story of Michael Whittaker. During his time at high school, he made money propagating plants and running his own small nursery. While studying towards a bachelor of business at Massey University, he would fly between New Zealand and South-East Asia, importing leather goods and ceramics.[33] Upon graduation, Mr Whittaker and a partner were given the opportunity to start an ice-cream parlour in Queenstown, which later led to the launch of Killinchy Gold ice-cream. A few years later, during a holiday in Hawaii, he would discuss new business opportunities by holding brainstorming sessions by the pool with his friends. A consensus emerged that there would be a market in New Zealand for a superior database marketing service. So in 1996, Mr Whittaker and two friends established the Atlantis Group.

Visible results

'We saw an opportunity in New Zealand for an integrated direct marketing service group,' recalls Mr Whittaker. The industry at that time was fragmented; there were a lot of small local players and a couple of multinationals, which did not really see marketing services as their core business. 'Supplier elimination at that point was quite a popular buzzword for companies to deal with fewer vendors, so we thought that there was an opportunity to get in front of the competition and win it all together,' he says.

Atlantis first offered data input, data management and data analysis services. Then the group started conducting customer service operations on behalf of its clients via telephone calls, letters and emails. Atlantis could now take on all of these mundane, daily operations that bedevil and distract companies — operations such as the analysis of customer spending habits or the mail-out of promotional letters to customers. This contributed to the establishment of Visible Results in 1997, as the customer relationship management (CRM) arm of the Atlantis Group. Today, Visible Results provides innovative CRM solutions for retailers, offering a full range of services and technology applications for managing cards, point of sales (POS) integration and back-end operational processes.

Mr Whittaker does not see the Atlantis Group as a technology company, although innovative and unique technology supports the company's operation. 'Our skills really consist in making that technology work from our client's point of view. The services we provide are designed to provide our clients with meaningful and actionable consumer insights to better understand — and better service — their customers. In the crude sense of the retail business, this means how to influence consumer behaviour, and how do we get customers to come in more frequently and spend more money.' Many retailers with established brands have already turned to Visible Results to implement CRM programs, successfully using the company's approach across multiple retail segments and national boundaries. Visible Results has clients ranging from ANZ Bank in New Zealand; petroleum/convenience store players such as Caltex in Singapore; Dymocks Booksellers in Australia, New Zealand and Hong Kong; and fashion retailers Pumpkin Patch in the UK, Australia and New Zealand.

Smart card technology

Shortly after its inception, the Atlantis Group bought the Graphicard™ distribution rights for the Asia–Pacific region. In 2001, it bought the American company that owned the technology, acquiring all of the related global patents. 'Loyalty cards were an extension of the services we were providing and we came across the thermo-chromic card through our business dealings with various clients. 'We are always looking for new concepts and ideas,' says Mr Whittaker. The Graphicard™ is the company's unique 'smart' card, and it has become a cornerstone of the Visible Results solution. What makes it unique is that the card face is re-writeable — that is, it can be updated with loyalty points gained from the latest purchase, the balance of new points, advertising messages, and upcoming sales and product specials. The face of the card can also provide media space for vendor advertising. Specific programs are designed to target each client's customer base, and the changing look of the card gives it unparalleled consumer appeal.

This makes the card a self-contained database. Consequently, the Graphicard™ may be used throughout a retail network without extensive network communication expenses and POS integration on the retailer's part. The card essentially enables retailers to communicate directly with customers every time they shop.

Retailers also save on costs and time because they are not required to send out hundreds of thousands of statements regarding loyalty points.

The business structure

The unique organisation of the Atlantis Group is one of the factors that led the company to its growth path. To maintain and enhance global responsiveness, the Atlantis Group has centralised all back-end operations such as data management and technical development in New Zealand. 'So when we run a program, for example for The Body Shop in Indonesia, all data comes back in Bahasa to us here in New Zealand every night,' comments Mr Whittaker. This structure prevents infrastructure components from being duplicated and, in turn, enables the company to achieve cost efficiencies that are passed on to its clients. In addition, customer data, internal call centres, data entry and standard document systems are all web-based, resulting in further cost and resource savings.

Although he keeps in close contact with the company's overseas offices and clients, travelling an average of 20 days per month, Mr Whittaker is determined to keep the Atlantis Group's headquarters in Auckland. New Zealand's technical infrastructure is as good as anywhere, and the company can recruit qualified staff at a reasonable price. 'New Zealand is an important base because all our key talent wants to stay here and they have no intention — apart from secondments — to go anywhere else,' he says. The country's remoteness can lead people to find creative solutions. 'It goes right back to our very beginning philosophy of complete solutions, rather than a single part of the offering. I guess that we're a little bit different; we take a New Zealand perspective over four million people and 44 million sheep, and there is a lot of wool between us and anywhere else,' laughs the entrepreneur.

Source: Based on author's interview with Michael Whittaker.

Questions

1. Which of the three components of creativity seem prevalent in Michael Whittaker's case?

2. What type of innovation did the Atlantis Group introduce in the marketplace?

3. What are the strategic resources that gave the Atlantis Group a competitive advantage?

ENDNOTES

1. P.F. Drucker, *Innovation and Entrepreneurship*, Harper & Row, New York, 1985, p. 30.
2. R. Jonash & T. Sommerlatte, *The Innovation Premium*, Perseus Books, New York, 1999.
3. R.W. Woodman, J.E. Sawyer & R.W. Griffin, 'Toward a theory of organizational creativity', *Academy of Management Review*, vol. 18, no. 2, 1993, pp. 293–321.
4. 'Leaps of faith: A survey of innovation in industry', *The Economist*, 20 February 1999, pp. 12–16.
5. T. Amabile, 'How to kill creativity', *Harvard Business Review*, September–October 1998, pp. 77–87.
6. T. Ward, R. Finke & S. Smith, *Creativity and the Mind*, Plenum Press, New York, 1995.
7. H. Simon, *Administrative Behavior*, Free Press, New York, 1997.

8. T. Amabile, *Creativity in Context: Update to the Social Psychology of Creativity*, Westview, Boulder, CO, 1996.

9. C. Thompson, *What a Great Idea!*, Harper Perennial, New York, 1992.

10. R. Olson, *The Art of Creative Thinking*, Harper Collins, New York, 1986.

11. T. Buzan, *The Mind Map Book*, Penguin, New York, 1991.

12. T. Amabile, R. Conti, H. Coon, J. Lazenby & M. Herron, 'Assessing the work environment for creativity', *Academy of Management Journal*, vol. 39, no. 5, 1996, pp. 1154–84.

13. T. Amabile, C.N. Hadley & S.J. Kramer, 'Creativity under the gun', *Harvard Business Review*, Special Issue, August 2002, pp. 52–63.

14. 'Home alone', *The Economist Science Technology Quarterly*, 11 June 2005, pp. 8–9.

15. C.M. Christensen, *The Innovator's Dilemma*, Harvard Business Press, Boston, 1997.

16. Drucker, see note 1.

17. D.F. Kuratko & R.M. Hodgetts, *Entrepreneurship: A Contemporary Approach*, Dryden Press, Fort Worth, 1998.

18. 'Comeback kid?' *The Economist Science Technology Quarterly*, 21 September 2002, p. 3.

19. J. Lloyd-Smith, 'The moisture merchant; Dealing in liquid assets', <www.time.com>, 5 April 2004.

20. 'Olivia Lum', *Caltex Crossings*, Discovery Networks Asia, <http://seasia.discovery.com.>.

21. J. Koh, 'Tale of true grit', *Business Times*, <http://justwomen.asiaone.com.sg.>, 31 March 2005.

22. 'Olivia Lum', *see* note 20.

23. J. Lloyd-Smith, *see* note 19.

24. The Singapore Council of Women's Organisations, 'Conversations with uncommon women — Ms Olivia Lum', <www.scwo.org.sg.>, 16 December 2004.

25. S. Zahra, A. Nielsen & W.C. Bogner, 'Corporate entrepreneurship, knowledge and competence development', *Entrepreneurship Theory and Practice*, vol. 23, no. 3, 1999, pp. 169–89.

26. M. Granovetter, *Getting a Job: A Study of Contacts and Careers*, Harvard University Press, Cambridge, MA, 1974.

27. H.E. Aldrich, *Organizations Evolving*, Sage Publications, London, 1999.

28. M. Dollinger, *Entrepreneurship: Strategy and Resources*, Prentice Hall, Upper Saddle River, NJ, 1999.

29. J. Barney, 'Firm resources and sustained competitive advantage', *Journal of Management*, no. 17, 1991, pp. 99–120.

30. M. Lounsbury & M.A. Glynn, 'Cultural entrepreneurship: Stories, legitimacy, and the acquisition of resources', *Strategic Management Journal*, vol. 22, 2001, p. 546.

31. H.M. Trice & J.M. Beyer, *The Cultures of Work Organizations*, Prentice Hall, Englewood Cliffs, NJ.

32. M. Lounsbury & M.A. Glynn, *see* note 30, p. 551.

33. Massey University, 'The man from Atlantis', *Massey: The Magazine for Alumni and Friends of Massey University*, no. 2, 2002.

Chapter 4

The nature of small business

LEARNING OBJECTIVES

After reading this chapter, you should be able to:

- define what constitutes a small business

- identify the key characteristics that make small businesses different from other types of business organisation

- list the advantages and disadvantages of starting and operating a small business

- outline the importance of small business in the economy

- explain the difference between small business management and entrepreneurship.

W hat is a 'small business'? Small firms are now recognised as a vital and significant part of the economy in the Pacific Rim region and as one of the keys to national goals such as wealth creation and employment growth. In this respect, it is often claimed that 'small business is big business'. But what constitutes a small enterprise? How does it differ from a large one? Are there any characteristics of a small business that are unique?

This chapter examines and explains the essence of small business. It is necessary to understand how the concept of a small business can be defined and to explain the intrinsic characteristics of such firms: how they operate, the way they differ from larger enterprises, the advantages and drawbacks of owning and managing a small business, and the factors that contribute to their success and failure. We examine the importance of the small business sector in different Pacific Rim economies and conclude by looking at the differences between entrepreneurs and small business owner–managers.

Defining small business

Small businesses are the most common form of business worldwide but researchers have always had difficulty in satisfactorily defining them and separating them from larger firms. As most small business researchers would argue, a small firm is not just one that is smaller than a larger organisation; it is also a business that is often managed and run in ways fundamentally different from a large corporation.[1] In this section, we examine the different ways that business organisations can be classified.

Generic definitions

There are essentially two broad ways in which to define a business. The first approach is to focus on the *qualitative* or *intangible characteristics of the firm* — in other words, the way in which it does things and is managed.[2] This is a useful mechanism for understanding how a small firm is organised, how it operates and who runs (or manages) it on a day-to-day basis.

During the last 30 years, a number of qualitative criteria have been suggested as key defining features of a small firm. In a general sense, a business has been regarded as small if it has the following characteristics:

- It is independently owned and operated. The business is not part of a larger corporation nor effectively controlled by another firm. In other words, the owners of the business are not answerable to anyone else for the decisions they make.
- The owners contribute most, if not all, of the operating capital. They take the responsibility of funding the business idea, bear the risk (such as potential bankruptcy) if the project fails, and are entitled to most of the profits if it succeeds.[3]
- The main decision-making functions rest with the owners, who usually also work full time in the firm; thus, they are often referred to as owner–managers. Most of the critical decisions are made by one or two people, since the firm is rarely big enough to support a group of professional specialists in areas such as marketing, administration, finance or logistics.[4]

- The business has only a small share of the market in which it operates. Typically, the firm does not dominate its industry; rather, it is just one of many businesses competing for a limited pool of customers.[5]

Qualitative definitions are very useful in helping to understand the nature of the business, the role of the owner, and the way the business is run, since such explanations focus on the people who work within the firm and control the firm, and the way they behave. However, it can be extremely difficult to measure and analyse these characteristics, since such qualitative definitions are often based on subjective concepts.

The alternative is to look at some *quantitative aspects of the business*. These are empirical measures that are relatively easy to define and measure. Some common quantitative variables used to categorise and sort businesses include:[6]

- the number of staff (if any) that work in the firm
- annual wages and salaries expenditure
- legal structure of the firm
- the total annual turnover (sales revenue) that the business generates
- the dollar value of the assets (such as office equipment, factory machinery and/ or property) that the business owns
- the share of ownership that is held by the owner–manager/s.

As simple as these indicators might appear, they are still not perfect. All statistical measures are subject to interpretation and can have their own problems of definition. For example, if the number of employees is to be used as the yardstick, then what constitutes an 'employee'? Does it mean only permanent employees, or should part-time and casual staff be included as well? If assets are the indicator of size, how is it possible to compare two businesses that have similar asset bases if one leases all its equipment and the other purchases its equipment?

With so many issues to consider, it is clear that striking a balance between all these different qualitative and quantitative criteria can sometimes be very difficult. The task is made even more complicated by the fact that small businesses are found in every country in the world and in every industry, and they take many different organisational, legal and operating forms. Few areas of business studies have to deal with a subject that is as heterogeneous, diverse and challenging as small enterprise research.[7] However, as a general definition, a **small business** can be defined as an independent firm that is usually managed, funded and operated by its owners, and whose staff size, financial resources and assets are comparatively small in scale.

As at least one researcher has pointed out, no classification system will ever be complete enough to cover all types of small business; every firm is unique in one way or another.[8] Indeed, it is not surprising that there is no universally agreed-upon definition of what exactly a small business is. However, the above typologies do provide a method of understanding the basic ways in which small firms operate: independently, with limited resources, and with one or two key individuals taking most of the responsibility, risk and rewards in the project. It is these characteristics which set small enterprises apart from all other types of business organisation.

Small business:
A small-scale, independent firm usually managed, funded and operated by its owners, and whose staff size, financial resources and assets are comparatively limited in scale.

National definitions of small business

Given the lack of a common set of definitions, it is not unusual to find that throughout the Pacific Rim region widely varying terms are used to define and categorise a small business (see table 4.1).

In Australia, the most commonly cited definition is that provided by the Australian Bureau of Statistics (ABS), which uses a combination of both qualitative and quantitative measures. The ABS describes a small firm as, first of all, having a number of qualitative characteristics: it must be independently owned (not part of a larger organisation) and managed by an individual or a small number of persons. Once these criteria are met, then a quantitative value, the number of staff, is used as an additional measuring tool.[9]

According to the ABS, there are four main categories of business:

- *micro-enterprises*, which employ fewer than five staff — this includes self-employed people who work on their own.
- *small businesses*, which have between five and 19 staff
- *medium-sized businesses*, consisting of firms employing 20–199 people
- *large firms*, consisting of businesses with more than 200 staff.

Table 4.1: Summary of the various definitions of small businesses

Country	Criteria
Australia	Micro-enterprise: <5 employees Small business: 5–19 employees Medium-sized enterprise: 20–199 employees Large firm: 200+ employees
New Zealand	Small firm: <6 full-time employees Medium-sized firm: 6–19 full-time employees Large firm: 20 or more full-time employees
Singapore	At least 30% local equity Fixed assets (defined as net book value of factory building, machinery and equipment) not exceeding $15 million Employment size not exceeding 200 workers for non-manufacturing/ services companies
Malaysia	Manufacturing, large-scale agricultural and related industries: <150 full-time employees *or* annual sales turnover <RM25 million (Malaysian ringgit) Services, primary agriculture and information communications technology industries: <50 full-time employees *or* annual sales turnover <RM5 million
Hong Kong	<100 employees in manufacturing <50 employees in other sectors

Sources: OECD, *Globalisation and SMEs*, vol. 2, 1997; Australian Bureau of Statistics, *Small Business in Australia 2001*, 2002; NZ Ministry of Economic Development, *SMEs in New Zealand: Structure and Dynamics*, 2003; 'FAQs on SMEs and Domestic Sector', 2006, <www.spring.gov.sg>; Small and Medium Industries Development Corporation, Malaysia, *Definition of SMEs*, 2003, <www.smidec.gov.my>. For full source details see endnotes.[10]

Collectively, micro-enterprises, small businesses and medium-sized firms are referred to as SMEs (small and medium-sized enterprises). The terms *small business* and *SME* are sometimes used interchangeably by academic researchers, since medium-sized firms share many of the characteristics of their smaller counterparts. As a result, some of the data about small firms are usually embedded among results covering the whole SME sector. Likewise, the term *small business* usually includes micro-enterprises as well, unless the two have been specifically separated. (In this book, when referring to Australian firms, the term *small business* includes both micro-enterprises and small businesses as defined by the ABS.)

In previous years, Australian researchers and the ABS also made a distinction between manufacturing and non-manufacturing industries, but this defining criterion has since been abolished.[11] In the agricultural sector, an employment-based definition is not used, due to difficulties in defining employment and in the common use of temporary labour. Agricultural businesses can have large-scale operations with relatively few permanent employees, often using large numbers of seasonal itinerant workers to overcome short-term labour needs. The ABS has therefore developed a measure of small agricultural firms based on the estimated value of agricultural operations. However, the agricultural category is generally excluded from most ABS small business publications.[12]

A somewhat similar definition is used in New Zealand, where the Ministry of Economic Development labels a small business as an independent business entity personally managed by the owner and employing 0–5 persons, and a medium-sized enterprise as one that has 6–19 employees. Using this measure, it is estimated that SMEs account for 96 per cent of all business enterprises in that country.[13]

Definitions for Hong Kong, Singapore and Malaysia are based on a number of categories, which usually include both the number of employees and another quantitative variable. In these countries, the term *SME* is frequently employed instead of *small business.*

In recent years there have been some attempts to introduce common international definitions, so that SME distributions can be studied and compared from one country to another. However, there are numerous problems involved in developing such a data set. For example, some countries collect information based only on surveys, while others rely on taxation information; likewise, some nations exclude the self-employed but others do not. Thus, international comparative data remains very limited at present.[14]

Characteristic features of a small business

Apart from formal definitions, there are several other characteristics that separate small firms from other types of business. Many of these also indicate that the art of establishing and managing a successful small firm is often quite different from the skills required in managing larger firms, government agencies or not-for-profit organisations. In this section, we examine the general or typical characteristics of small businesses, before comparing small businesses with larger corporations. The advantages and disadvantages of operating a small firm are examined and spelt out, and we look at the factors that contribute to success and failure among small business owner–managers.

General aspects

As the qualitative definitions at the start of this chapter have shown, a number of features are typical of most small enterprises:

- *Owned by just one or two individuals.* These key people are usually responsible for almost all of the critical events in the life of the business: they conceived the original idea, founded the venture, oversee its daily activities, employ other staff, decide what will be sold, and ultimately are often responsible for ceasing activities.[15]
- *Financing provided by the owner.* Capital from external investors is often hard to come by, so most start-up funding and working capital is provided by the owner and from retained profits within the enterprise.[16]
- *Limited market share.* Most small enterprises can cater to only a relatively limited number of customers; their size and resources preclude them from being the dominant player in their industry.[17]
- *Limited life span.* Few small firms remain in existence for more than 10–15 years.[18] Although there are clearly exceptions to this rule, the life of a small enterprise is often marked by a relatively high business-closure rate, the cumulative effect of which is that most go out of operation after a decade.
- *Sometimes run on a part-time basis.* Many firms, especially ones run from home, are in fact part-time ventures. They may be run by someone as a form of casual income supplement, or constructed as part of a 'portfolio career' that combines self-employment with part-time work for another organisation.
- *A low level of net profit.* Although the opportunity to make a windfall gain always exists, the reality is that many firms report a low level of net profit. This relatively poor financial return often results in owner–managers earning an income well below average annual salaries for wage-earners.[19]
- *Limited product or service offering.* Rather than trying to be a comprehensive provider, most small firms tend to specialise in one or two things that they do best. By concentrating on their core areas of strength, they can maintain a competitive advantage that helps them survive against larger rivals.
- *Often home-based.* As is discussed in chapter 17, in some countries such as Australia the majority of small firms are located in the owner's personal residence. However, in some other parts of the Pacific Rim region, this is not the case. In Singapore, for example, business owners have until recently been prevented from working at home.
- *Geographically limited to one or two locations.* Even when a small firm is located in commercial premises, it usually has only one or possibly two outlets; the existence of a multi-branch operation is usually restricted to a limited number of aggressively growing firms.
- *Often a family-based business.* Often, ownership and managerial control is vested in the members of the founder's family. Although outsiders may work in the

enterprise, they rarely reach the position of chief executive officer. (Note, however, that not all small businesses are family businesses, or vice versa: several notable large firms, such as the Lowy or Murdoch family empires, are also effectively controlled by just one family.)

- *Located only in the private sector.* All economies consist of three essential sectors: the public sector (which represents government agencies, trading entities and departments); the private sector (business organisations principally owned by private individuals and groups); and the not-for-profit sector (non-government organisations that deliver services in the welfare, conservation, education, health and related areas). Although enterprises in all three sectors carry out commercial activities, genuine small firms are found only in the private sector.

A profile of a 'typical' small business owner

Is it possible to construct a picture of what might be termed a 'typical' owner–manager? As any statistician will point out, the concept of 'average' is rarely a valid way of constructing an image of a group of people. A more accurate way is to look at the mode: the most frequently occurring event within a given set of descriptors. Based on recent research publications by the Australian Bureau of Statistics,[20] it is possible to list the most common modal features of small business owners in Australia. The typical business owner–manager in Australia:

- is male (most small businesses are owned by men)
- was born in Australia
- works as a tradesperson or professional (these are the two largest occupational groups that owners come from)
- is aged between 30 and 50 years
- has completed a secondary school education or trade qualification
- has been trading for between one and five years
- used personal financial resources to start and fund the enterprise
- has not undertaken any formal management training
- does not use a business plan.

Differences between small and large businesses

Small organisations are not just 'shrunken' large enterprises. As the previous section of this chapter implies, there are often substantial differences between large and small firms. These variations are not just about the size of the firm. They also relate to many aspects of the organisation's activities, operations and management methods. Some of the major differences have been statistically measured,[21] and the following are features of small business:

- *More female owner–managers.* There are more women who are the owner–managers of small businesses than there are women who are chief executives or owners of large corporations.

- *Managers have fewer qualifications.* In general, fewer small business owner–managers hold formal tertiary or technical degrees and diplomas, either in business or in their particular area of expertise, than do executives in large corporations.
- *Fewer union employees.* Due to the informal nature of the workplace, employment relationships and job contracts tend to be negotiated directly between the manager and the staff member rather than through the agency of a trade union.
- *Fewer hours of operation each week.* Although one might expect small firms to operate for longer hours than large ones, in some countries (such as Australia) the large number of part-time, home-based operations skews the results towards a low average number of operating hours.
- *Less likely to use formal management improvement and planning techniques.* Whereas large organisations have adopted many systems and procedures to enhance performance, such as quality assurance, total quality management, or just-in-time delivery systems, smaller firms are much less likely to do so. Many more large corporations have a business plan than do small firms.
- *Less likely to access government assistance.* Although governments often provide services specifically designed to help small businesses in areas such as planning, marketing and human resources, uptake of such programs tends to be limited.
- *Less likely to export.* Trading overseas is an important means of expanding a business, and is especially important for nations with small domestic markets, such as New Zealand and Singapore. Despite this, most small and medium-sized enterprises tend to focus on their local market, and do not export.
- *Less external financing.* Most funding to start the venture comes from the owner; finance for subsequent growth is usually met by reinvesting profits and/or additional capital contributions from the owners.
- *Less likely to want to grow bigger.* For many small business owners, the goal is to have a successful business, not to constantly grow larger. This is a key difference in separating genuine growth-oriented entrepreneurs from conventional small-firm owner–managers.
- *More likely to fail.* As Storey[22] has noted, one of the fundamental characteristics of small businesses is their higher failure rate. Although the overall level of business exits is quite low, there is nevertheless a clear link between firm size and business exit rates. This issue is discussed in more detail later in this chapter.
- *Differences in managerial perspectives.* This issue is harder to quantify and measure, but just as important. Small businesses rely heavily on their owner–managers, but have very limited physical and financial resources. Their managers often think, plan and implement decisions with a very different perspective from that of their counterparts in large corporations. The way in which small-firm owner–managers operate their businesses, the way they market their firm, the level of personal risk they face, and their degree of sophistication differs significantly from the approach of professional corporate managers. Compared with their counterparts in large firms, small-firm owner–managers plan for shorter time frames, use less formal communication forms, and are more personally involved in more areas of the firm.[23]

The advantages and disadvantages of operating a small business

Another critical issue to examine in any analysis of small business is the reason people choose to work in a small business. Small business owners must face a number of challenges, and success is rarely guaranteed. Why, then, do people choose either to start a new small-scale business venture or to buy an existing firm?

The key factor that often drives people to start their own business enterprise is a desire to be independent. The dream of 'being your own boss' is very attractive to people who want to have more direct control over their own working life, their personal income and their capacity to make decisions.

A second factor is the ability to fulfil personal goals and interests. Running a business can allow people to follow a dream or an opportunity that they have long been interested in. It can also let them apply their energies and enthusiasm to a field in which they already have a personal interest and talent (see the Entrepreneur Profile of Basil Lenzo, founder of Instyle Shoes). It is not unusual, for example, for owner–managers to turn their hobby interests into a full-time business.

Entrepreneur profile

Basil Lenzo — from fishing to footwear

Small business operators can be found in all sorts of industries, and often take their inspiration from many different sources, as the career of Basil Lenzo exemplifies.

In 1982, after finishing high school, Basil enrolled in a Bachelor of Science degree at the University of Western Australia, but shortly afterwards decided instead to work with his father. Guiseppe Lenzo, a migrant from Sicily, had been fishing in Western Australia since 1952. For the last century, the western rock lobster has been arguably regarded as one of the most prized lobster ('crayfish') in the world, and is found in abundance along the coastline north and south of Fremantle. In 1986 Basil took over full time as the skipper of the family boat.

Today, fishing for rock lobsters is a highly sophisticated, capital-intensive industry. Each vessel typically consists of two deckhands and an owner–captain, and represents a major financial investment. In addition to the substantial cost of the boat itself, there are large expenses for engine maintenance and running costs such as fuel, insurance, boat pens and crew wages. Using high-tech sonar and global positioning satellite systems, boats fish for a limited annual season, starting in November and finishing in the following June. The catch is usually processed on land the same day and is either consumed domestically or exported live to the key Asian markets of China, Taiwan and Japan. It is a highly regulated industry, with strict limitations on the number of fishing pots that can be deployed.

Basil's decision to work for himself was the most logical career option, right from the beginning. 'It's all I've ever known. My father had a lot to do with it; working alongside him helped prime and prepare me. But I think it's fundamentally part of my nature. You've got to value your independence and be self-motivated.'

While many owner–managers are content to skipper their own boat, Basil was not. 'I'm very conscious of the risks that small business owners face when they rely on just one form of income, so in 1997 I purchased part ownership of another boat. This allowed me to diversify: I no longer had to totally rely on my own labour for my regular income.'

A few years later, Basil and his wife, Jenny, decided to diversify again. As part of a small consortium, they purchased an existing shoe shop in South Fremantle, and a year later established a brand-new retail operation, Instyle Shoes. These two operations now have a total of nine employees.

The decision to branch out into another industry might surprise some, but made perfect sense to Basil. 'I did it because any industry always has its ups and downs. You get the good and then the bad. I needed something to flatten out the periodic downturns.'

'Small business is like fishing. You don't know what's coming next. That's what gets me excited: tomorrow I might make $500 or $5000. That's part of the excitement and danger in working for yourself. And there's also a great sense of satisfaction when you can operate a business and succeed.'

Source: Based on the author's interview with Basil Lenzo.

If properly managed, there are also potential financial opportunities. A well-run business can be a highly profitable one, producing a better income for the owner than would be earned as an employee for someone else. A business can also become an asset that produces ongoing (residual) income or that can be sold at a later stage for a substantial capital gain.

Finally, there may be family benefits from establishing a firm, especially if it is managed with a long-term vision. A successful business can provide opportunities for children to inherit wealth and income that their parents could not otherwise hope to provide.

On the other hand, the disadvantages of going into small business for oneself are relatively clear. A main consideration is uncertainty. There are few, if any, guaranteed outcomes in being a business owner–manager. For many firms, ambiguity and constant change are almost a given. There can be major fluctuations in sales income, profitability, government regulations, competitors and market dynamics from one year to another.

A second variable is the potential for financial loss. If the business fails to make a profit, then the owner will usually be out of pocket. Even if a profit is made, it may be lower than expected, which will in turn produce a lower return on investment. Finally, if the business collapses, then the owner may lose all the original investment and possibly even personal assets (such as the family home) if these have been used to help guarantee a bank loan.

There are increased responsibilities that come with being an owner–manager. As 'the boss', the small business owner must make decisions about hiring and firing staff, dealing with customer complaints, day-to-day problems, financial control of the enterprise, and legal responsibility for compliance with government rules. This often substantially increases the pressure on the owner, which may be hard to avoid or overcome. Personal stress is very common for business owner–managers.

What would you do?

Time to motor on?

After three years working for yourself as a freelance self-employed courier, delivering parcels and packages around the city from one business to another, you have been able to earn enough to pay off your motorbike, meet all your living expenses and still accumulate a modest amount of money (A$13 000) for the future. However, the hours are very long, it's a competitive game (with many rival couriers and fickle customers), and there doesn't seem to be much opportunity to grow the business further. You already have a university Bachelor's degree (a double major in languages and marketing) and feel that the long-term prospects could be better elsewhere.

A recent tempting thought has been to give it all away and get a job with a big local marketing corporation. There is heavy demand for graduates in the local employment market at present, so your chances of gaining an entry-level position would be strong. However, there is some gossip that the corporation is thinking of splitting up and selling off the local branch, which could lead to job losses in the future.

You recently applied for a scholarship to a prestigious private university in Hawaii, with a view to studying for a two-year Master's degree in Japanese. Estimated tuition fees, boarding and travel expenses would be A$13 500 for the first year, plus food and living costs. A letter arrives one day stating that you've been accepted to the university but, on the same day, one of your fellow couriers suggests that you join forces and establish a courier company together. She says there are plenty of opportunities around town and that a A$10 000 initial capital investment each should pay off handsomely within two or three years.

Questions

1. List the different options that you have for the next 12 months, and the advantages and disadvantages of each course of action.
2. What would an entrepreneur do in a situation like this?

Factors leading to success and failure

The process of small business formation and development is a hazardous one, and it seems logical to conclude that the risk of failure will be high, especially in the early years of a business's existence. At the macro (economy-wide) level, the turnover of firms is a natural and inevitable phenomenon in any market-based economy, which has a number of beneficial effects. The emergence of new enterprises often indicates the creation of new, innovative products and services, and it also provides new job opportunities within the community. The demise of a business can also be positive, in that it frees up finance, managers and personnel for new businesses.[24] At the individual level, however, there can be a high cost from business turnovers, including unemployment and the loss of personal financial assets and self-esteem. It is important, therefore, to understand the factors that lead to business success and failure.

The causes of failure have been more extensively discussed and researched than the reasons for success. Theoretically, almost every aspect of business can potentially cause a business to fail if not dealt with properly. However, there are a number of general trends that appear to indicate the most common areas of likely failure (see table 4.2). For example, Cromie[25] found that problems could be grouped into four functional areas: finance, marketing, production and personnel. In addition to these specific organisational problems, a fifth critical area was identified: personal factors, such as a lack of time, having to perform too many different duties, being unable to sell oneself, being too conservative, and having difficulty in generating ideas.

Table 4.2: Some potential problems facing small business managers — findings of researchers in three countries

Problem type	Cromie (UK)	Soh-Wee (Singapore)	Rashid (Malaysia)
Finance	Lack of funds, cash flow, getting paid	Cash flow	Lack of working capital
Marketing	Obtaining sufficient sales, pricing, distribution, competition	Pricing, lack of marketing knowledge	Lack of marketing skills
Production	Premises, quality, obtaining supplies, over-expansion	Low-quality product/service	
Personnel	Getting good staff, laying staff off	Difficulty in hiring personnel, interpersonal problems (conflict with partners/employees)	
Personal	Stress, immersion in the business, long hours	Stress, no family support, social problems (e.g. prejudice and distrust towards women)	Lack of respect, tension between personal life and career (particularly for women)

Sources: S. Cromie, 'The problems experienced by young firms', *International Small Business Journal*; A. Rashid & M. Zabid, and C.W.L. Soh-Wee, in Low Aik Meng & Tan Wee Liang (eds), *Entrepreneurs, Entrepreneurship and Enterprising Culture*, 1996. For full source details see endnotes.[26]

Abdul Rashid's Malaysian research found that the problems of the business owner vary depending on the stage of business development. At the initial level, finance and marketing issues were a key concern, whereas in slightly older firms personal and family matters seem to be more important, especially for women.[27]

In Singapore, Soh-Wee studied start-up and early development problems confronting young small business owner–managers. Her findings show that the rising costs of doing business and the difficulty of obtaining finance are the most pressing problems facing young business owner–managers. The loss of control over one's workforce is the next most important problem. Inadequate technical and managerial knowledge, as well as strong competition, however, were perceived to be less important.[28]

Another way of analysing the causes of failure is to break possible contributing factors down into two groups: problems within the organisation itself and external variables. The former group includes bad management practices, poor product/service quality, employing the wrong staff, a lack of sufficient capital and cash flow (liquidity), and personal shortcomings of the owner, such as a tendency to autocratic decision making or poor time management.[29] External causes of business failure can include the activities of competitors, change in market demand, economic recession, change to government policies and laws, and the introduction of new technologies or processes. Research studies in Singapore showed that internal factors are the predominant cause of business failures in that country.[30]

Just how high is the rate of small business failure? This is a difficult issue to measure. So-called failures can occur when a business goes into bankruptcy, is sold to another owner, is merged with another firm or is liquidated by the owners,[31] although even in these cases it is not always possible to determine the causes of such events. In fact, there is no single definition of business failure. For example, financial failure can mean anything from making a trading loss each year to simply not making a satisfactory level of profit or sufficient return on capital invested. In terms of the firm's marketing performance, a business could be considered a failure if its product recognition is low, its market share declines or its original market ceases to exist, even if it still trades at a profit. In addition, a firm may have gone out of existence for other reasons, such as the owner's wish to retire, ill health of the owner, or even a merger with another firm to create a bigger enterprise. For these reasons, the use of the word *failure* is often inappropriate.

Business exit:
Any situation in which a business ceases to exist, through closure, liquidation, bankruptcy, sale or transfer to another owner, or merger.

The concept of **business exits** may be more appropriate. An exit refers to any situation in which a business ceases to exist, and can include closure, liquidation, bankruptcy, sale or transfer to another owner, or merger. A study of exits in Australia during the late 1990s indicated that approximately 7.5 per cent of all businesses exit each year. Rates for small firms tended to be slightly higher than the norm for all firms.[32] This has been confirmed by more recent evaluations, which have shown that about 8 per cent of businesses exit after their first year of trading. Almost all of these were small or micro-businesses.[33] The cumulative effect of this is that about two-thirds of all businesses still exist after five years, half are still trading after 10 years, and about one-third remain after 15 years.[34]

Research in New Zealand indicates slightly different exit rates, although it also shows that smaller firms are far more likely to exit than larger enterprises.[35] A comparative examination of 1500 SMEs operating in New Zealand between 1997 and 2004 found that the survival rate for firms is perhaps higher than popularly believed. It revealed that 76 per cent of the original population were still operating in 2004, indicating that the survival rate of small firms is much higher than previously thought.[36]

Survival rates have not been studied in as much detail in Singapore, but analysis of existing data by the government agency Statistics Singapore indicates that about half of all business enterprises are still in existence after five years of trading.[37]

The important point to note is that few firms 'fail' as such. Most businesses will still be in existence after several years, and (in Australia and New Zealand at least) they have quite good chances of surviving for about 10 years. Even those that do cease operating usually do so for reasons other than actual failure.

Just like the measurement of failure, evaluating success rates and the factors that contribute to them can be difficult. There have been various suggestions about how 'success' in small business can be measured. Kelmar,[38] in his review of several studies published in this field, noted that most authors indicated that marketing characteristics are particularly important. For example, success is often deemed to occur when a business shows that it can profitably sell its goods or services in the marketplace. This is followed by financial considerations (such as a growing level of profit), whereas measures of management rank third. If one looks more closely at the characteristics indicated under these generic headings, it appears that growth constitutes the predominant indicator of success. This classification is rather broad in its interpretation and includes business growth, employment growth, productivity growth, profit growth and sales growth. Other important indicators of success may be more subjective: the amount of income the owner earns, the amount of free time he or she has, or the level of personal satisfaction regarding business achievements. Interestingly, a small business can be both a success and a failure simultaneously. It is possible, for example, for a firm to have a very poor financial return and yet at the same time provide the owner with a feeling of satisfaction because some personal psychological needs (such as feelings of independence) are being met by the firm.

Given the wide range of possible ways of measuring success and the difficulties of doing so, it is not surprising that the number of studies in this area is relatively limited. Interestingly, most small business operators tend to regard themselves as a success, despite what others might think of their performance. The Australian Bureau of Statistics, for example, found that 90 per cent of small-firm owners regarded themselves as successful.[39]

The economic significance of the small business sector

Small firms are more than just an interesting phenomenon; they are also a critical component in the structure of any economy. Although the economic basis of countries in the Pacific Rim region varies substantially, ranging from agricultural-based production in Indonesia and mass-scale manufacturing in China through to high-tech service industries in Singapore and Hong Kong, all of them possess one common factor: a sizeable small business sector.

General importance

More specifically, small firms are important to all national economies because they provide:

- *employment opportunities for people*. This includes the self-employment of the business owner–manager and the conventional jobs provided to the staff who work for the owner. Although there are no hard and fast rules, generally speaking small businesses account for about half of all the jobs in the private sector of most countries.

- *the next generation of large firms.* Large organisations are not permanent; they too are born, exist and eventually exit the marketplace. Many of the large corporations that dominated the stock exchanges of Australia and New Zealand at the start of the 1900s, for example, are no longer in existence. They have been replaced by other firms that started out as small-scale ventures and have since grown in size to join the ranks of large enterprises. Although it is difficult to predict which small businesses will succeed and become the leviathans of the future, one thing is clear: without an ample supply of small firms, there can be no 'next generation' of large ones.

- *competition.* When a market is dominated by only one or two firms, then customers can often suffer from high prices, low-quality products and poor service. In contrast, the existence of a number of competitors serves to keep businesses responsive to the needs of their clients and ensures that customers have a choice in what they buy, where, and for how much. If such competition were removed from the marketplace, the range of offerings available would be much smaller.

- *innovation.* The existence of small firms not only acts as a catalyst for competition but also serves as a spur for innovation. Competition encourages firms to constantly seek new and better ways of providing improved goods and services; to find more efficient and effective ways of managing the business; and to adopt new production methods. In addition, small firms can also be used as a vehicle for launching an innovation if no large firm or government agency is willing to take the risk.

- *an outlet for entrepreneurial activity.* As mentioned in chapter 1, entrepreneurs often use a small business as their vehicle for launching a new business idea or for experimenting with an innovative product or service. If small firms did not exist, or could not be started easily by enthusiastic entrepreneurs, there would be few opportunities in which to test ideas and offer them in the marketplace.

- *exports.* To survive, some small firms also have to seek markets beyond their own national boundaries. In Singapore, for example, a small national market imposes substantial limits on the opportunities for future growth. Many Singaporean firms have chosen to expand by offering their products to the neighbouring nations of Malaysia and Indonesia. A similar situation applies to small firms in New Zealand, many of which have found new markets in Australia and the Pacific islands.

- *specialised products and services.* Because of their limited size and resources, small businesses are often better able to survive by focusing on a specific range of activities. Many of these products or services appeal to a small niche market, but not to a large group of customers. For example, stamp-collecting shops or horse-drawn caravan holidays will appeal to small groups of people interested in buying such goods or services, and this demand will be enough to support one or two people in a full-time occupation at a modest level of profitability. However, the scope is so limited that no large corporation would be interested in such offerings.

- *support to big business.* Many large corporations actually rely on small businesses for their own survival. They use such firms to provide them with materials, support and ideas. Big businesses (such as manufacturers) often source many of their component parts, casual labour and consultancy services from smaller firms, as well as relying on small retail shops to sell their products to the public. Although it tends to be overlooked, large and small firms often have a symbiotic (mutually beneficial) relationship rather than a competitive one. For example, the technical solutions supplied by Zach Hitchcock's Feedback Sport (see Entrepreneur Profile below) provide specialist support for elite teams in popular sports.

- *decentralisation.* Most economic activity takes place in large cities, where the population is highly concentrated, infrastructure is reliable, transport costs are lower, there is ready access to skilled labour and most resources, and marketing to a concentrated cluster of consumers is more cost-effective. However, many people live outside major cities, often in small towns, villages and isolated communities. It can be difficult for them to attract large corporations to their region, mainly because the consumer base is so small. For these people, small firms are the main means of purchasing goods and finding employment.

- *distribution of economic resources, wealth and opportunities.* When an economy is dominated by a relatively limited number of large enterprises, the imbalance can restrict wealth, financial assets and opportunities to a small clique of highly influential business owners and senior managers. In contrast, a nation with a flourishing small business sector is one that provides numerous opportunities for many people to build wealth and create their own economic future.

- *flexibility in the overall economy.* Finally, a society with a large number of small firms is one with a higher capacity to withstand economic upheaval and change. A diverse range of firms, in many sizes and industries, can act as a buffer and increase flexibility in responding to adverse change.

Entrepreneur profile

Zach Hitchcock — Feedback Sport

'Even while I was at university, I always thought one day it would be good to own my business. I guess it's just my personality. I don't like taking orders from others or being bottom of the food chain!' There lies the explanation behind Zach Hitchcock's decision (at only 27 years of age) to start up his own limited liability company, Feedback Sport. Based in Christchurch, New Zealand, the firm develops technical solutions for elite sports teams and individual athletes. Currently the core products of the company are Feedback Cricket (which captures ball-by-ball match footage) and Feedback Football (which has the capability to capture a similar sort of video and data for individual matches). Feedback cricket has been in use by the New Zealand cricket team since 2001 and by the English cricket team. Others using the product include English county teams (such as Somerset and Leicestershire) and New Zealand provincial sides (including Auckland and Canterbury). Feedback Football, launched in 2005, is a relatively new venture that Zach developed in partnership with Chris Cairns. *(continued)*

With pre-start-up work experience in the same industry, a Bachelor of Information Science, and a willingness to improve his business skills, Zach's future as a young entrepreneur looks promising. Even though the company is currently of a small scale (employing only contractors, and only when needed), Zach has big ambitions. He has a strong desire to grow the business to a global status, and wants his firm to be 'the world leader in terms of the provision of sports technology'. To do so will mean a lot of hard work expanding market share and revenue streams and increasing the reputation and presence of the products globally — something Zach is committed to doing.

Another important consideration has been the ability to set and control his own agenda. 'I think one of the best things for me is to be able to take the work that I am doing in the direction that I want, and I get the full benefit of that effort.'

For more information on Zach and his firm, visit his website at <www.feedback sport.com>.

Profile prepared by Kate Lewis, Massey University, New Zealand.

National and regional economic significance

Given the general importance of small enterprises as outlined above, it is not surprising to find most data show, collectively, that small businesses are a major economic force in the Pacific Rim and around the world.

An evaluation of their importance throughout the Pacific Rim region is regularly conducted by the Asia–Pacific Economic Cooperation forum (APEC), which represents 21 nations throughout the region. APEC examines both small and medium-sized firms, although the vast majority of these are small businesses. There are about 45 million SMEs in APEC[40] and, as figure 4.1 shows, the size and employment impact of the SME sector varies from country to country. Small and medium-sized enterprises represent over 95 per cent of all firms, employ over 60 per cent of the workforce,[41] contribute between 30 and 60 per cent of the GDP of APEC economies, and account for 35 per cent of exports in the region.[42] An earlier study, by the Australian Department of Foreign Affairs and Trade, estimated that small businesses make up 98 per cent of all enterprises in the APEC grouping, provide 60 per cent of all private sector employment, and generate 30 per cent of the region's direct exports.[43]

Figure 4.1 also highlights the fact that the impact of small and medium-sized firms can vary substantially from one country to another in terms of both proportion of firms and employment share. When the very different population levels in each country are also taken into account, the data reveal that there are major international differences in the level of SME intensity or penetration into the general population. Some countries have relatively high numbers of small firms for their population size, and others have quite low ratios. As Hall[44] has shown, there is usually about one SME for every 20 people in the population of a developed country (see figure 4.2 on page 97). Using this rule of thumb, it can be seen that some countries in the Pacific Rim (such as Australia, New Zealand and Hong Kong) have very high proportions of SMEs while others (including Singapore, China, Brunei and the Philippines) are quite low; this would seem to indicate that the latter nations have much more capacity to expand their SME sectors.

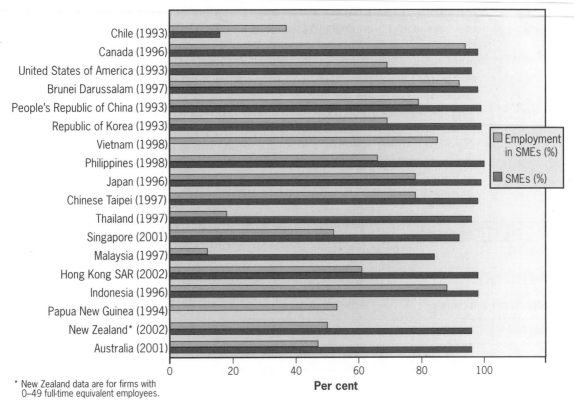

Figure 4.1: The role of SMEs in APEC member economies

Source: Data from APEC SME Working Group, *APEC SME Guidebook*, 2000, p. 3; HK Trade and Industry Department, *What Are SMEs?* 2002; NZ Ministry of Economic Development, *SMEs in New Zealand: Structure and Dynamics*, 2002; Australian Bureau of Statistics, *Small Business in Australia 2001*, 2002. For full source details see endnotes.[45]

Figure 4.2: APEC economies: number of people in the adult population per SME, 1997–98

Source: Data from C. Hall, 'Entrepreneurship densities in APEC and Europe: How many entrepreneurs *should* there be in China, or other developing countries?' *Small Enterprise Research*, vol. 10, no. 1, p. 7, 2002.

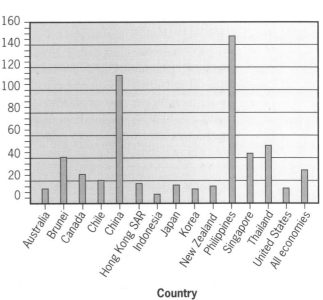

Globally, though, SMEs seem to share a number of common features with firms in Australia and New Zealand (see table 4.3). For example, in most countries SMEs usually account for at least 95 per cent of firms in existence, or 19 out of 20. In other words, large firms rarely exceed a 1-in-20 distribution rule. In addition, micro-sized firms predominate, giving rise to a pyramid-type structure in which micro-enterprises are the biggest single group of enterprises, followed by small ones, then medium-sized enterprises, and capped off by a limited number of large firms. Although it is not shown here, recent research also appears to show that these proportions and distributions have not changed much over the last 20 years. In other words, the pattern of firm distribution appears to be relatively fixed and enduring.[46]

Table 4.3: Distribution of firms by size in selected nations and geographic regions

	Western Europe, 2003	UK, 2002	USA, 2000
Micro-enterprises	17 820 000 (92.28%)	2 600 000 (68.42%)	19 988 000 (94.18%)
Small businesses	1 260 000 (6.53%)	1 170 000 (30.79%)	1 009 000 (4.75%)
Medium-sized enterprises	180 000 (0.93%)	27 000 (0.71%)	167 000 (0.79%)
Large firms	40 000 (0.21%)	7 000 (0.18%)	59 000 (0.28%)
Total	19 310 000 (100%)	3 804 000 (100%)	21 223 000 (100%)

Figures are rounded.

Sources: European Commission, *SMEs in Europe 2003*, 2004; United Kingdom Department of Trade and Industry, *Statistical Press Release: Small and Medium-Sized Enterprise Statistics for the UK 2002*, 2003. For full source details see endnotes.[47]

The following are brief snapshots of small business (or, in some cases, SME) performance in the countries that are the main focus of this book.

Australia

In 2001 there were just over 1.26 million non-agricultural small private sector businesses.[48] (As mentioned previously, most Australian statistics usually exclude agricultural firms from their calculations.) Overall, small enterprises constituted more than 96 per cent of all firms in the country, and employed some 3.2 million people (which represented about 47 per cent of all jobs provided by private sector businesses in Australia).[49] In mid 2002, the introduction of the Australian Business Register (a database of all businesses that apply for an Australian business number, or ABN) enabled the ABS to substantially revise the database from which it sources business information. The ABS also amended its method of counting employee numbers, included agricultural firms in its count, and altered its collection data on the overall business population (to include business trusts, non-trading firms and those with an uncertain level of business activity). Using this revised framework, in June 2004 there were approximately 3.015 million private sector business organisations in existence, 97.2 per cent of which had fewer than 20 employees.[50] More detail on the breakdown by firm size is provided in table 4.4.

Table 4.4: Number of private sector firms in Australia in 2004, by size

Small and micro (0–19 staff; includes self-employed)	2 932 000 (97.2%)
Medium-sized (20–199 employees)	78 000 (2.6%)
Large (200+ staff)	5 000 (0.2%)
Total	**3 015 000 (100%)**

Figures include agricultural enterprises; totals are rounded.

Source: Australian Bureau of Statistics, *ABS Business Register — Counts of Businesses*, cat. no. 8161.0.55.001, ABS, Canberra, p. 11, 2005.

As in New Zealand, the biggest group is the self-employed, and there is a strong concentration in the health and community services, education, property and business services sectors.[51] The majority of firms are also home-based (a phenomenon which is discussed in more detail in chapter 17).

New Zealand

In New Zealand in 2004 there were 324 000 small and medium-sized businesses, representing 96 per cent of all firms in the country.[52] Together, these enterprises employed 480 000 people (about 30 per cent of all employment in the country) and generated approximately 37 per cent of national economic output, even though the typical small firm in New Zealand employs only five people. The majority of small firms are found in the services and related areas, including such fields as personal services, finance and insurance, construction, property and business services, the cultural and recreational industries, and communications services.[53]

Hong Kong

Statistics gathered in the Hong Kong Special Administrative Region cover both small and medium-sized firms. In June 2005, there were approximately 285 000 SMEs in the Hong Kong SAR, representing 98 per cent of all business enterprises. In aggregate, they employed about 1.34 million people — roughly 60 per cent of the private sector workforce.[54] In Hong Kong's SME sector, the majority of employees are usually family members, and most firms employ fewer than 10 people. About 98 per cent of all manufacturing firms are SMEs. In relative terms, such firms are typically smaller than European or American small businesses.[55]

Singapore

In 2006 there were an estimated 130 000 small and medium-sized enterprises in Singapore. These made up 99 per cent of all firms in the republic, and they employed about 62 per cent of the workforce (more than 770 000 people). Although many multinational corporations in the Pacific Rim are based in Singapore, it is clear that most of the country's economic activity is still generated by SMEs: small and medium-sized firms account for 47 per cent of the total value added in the manufacturing and services sectors.[56]

Malaysia

SMEs are sometimes also referred to as small and medium industries (SMIs) in Malaysia. In 2004 it was estimated that there were some 205 000 SMEs in the country, representing 96.1 per cent of all business establishments. They are primarily concentrated in the wholesale and retail trade sector (some 170 000 firms); manufacturing (20 000 enterprises); and in service fields such as health, education and others.[57] Another study from 2003 indicated that SMEs employed some 375 000 people.[58]

Entrepreneur or small business owner–manager?

A final but very important issue when examining the nature of small firms is the difference between small business management and entrepreneurship. Among the general community and even in parts of the business world, the small business owner–manager is often regarded as an entrepreneur and vice versa. This is not surprising, since the two roles are closely related and even overlap in many respects. But the two concepts, although similar, are not synonymous.

How do small business owner–managers differ from entrepreneurs? Entrepreneurs discover, evaluate and exploit new business opportunities. Although they may start up new small businesses as their vehicles for doing this, they may equally operate through the forum of an existing large firm, a government agency or a not-for-profit organisation. In contrast, a small business owner–manager is a person who runs an existing small business; there may be little innovation, idea-generation or risk involved in such a project.

The term *entrepreneur*, as mentioned in chapter 1, best describes a person who develops new ideas, starts an enterprise based on these ideas, and provides added value to society based on independent initiative. Not all small business owners fit this category, since many small firms do not actively seek out new ideas or business opportunities. For example, people who leave a job with a large corporation or government agency and simply recreate the same job on an outsourced basis with a separate legal business entity are really just small business operators, rather than true entrepreneurs. They are not developing any innovative ideas or taking substantial risks, but recreating their old job under a different format.

The distinction between the two terms is often subtle, but still important. The person who establishes a fast-food franchise chain is called an entrepreneur, but the local owner–manager of a solitary, long-established restaurant is best called a small business operator. Distinguishing factors are that entrepreneurs have a vision for growth, a commitment to innovation, persistence in gathering the necessary resources, and an overriding need to achieve. The small business operator does not always exhibit these characteristics, and they are not always necessary for the successful management of a small-scale firm[59] (see table 4.5).

Table 4.5: Differences between entrepreneurship and small business management

	Entrepreneurship	Small business management
Definition of the field	The process whereby an individual discovers, evaluates and exploits an opportunity independently	The administration of a small independent business venture
Firm size	Large, medium or small	Small
Degree of risk involved	Very variable	Generally lower risk
Number of people involved in the business	Can range from very small to very large	Small
Economic sector	Found in private, government and not-for-profit sectors	Found only in private sector
Growth focus	High	Variable
Key individual	Entrepreneur	Owner–manager
Key attributes of the individual	High need for achievement (set up a business to realise a dream); high internal locus of control; high risk-taking propensity; creative and innovative; growth-oriented	Moderate need for achievement (run a business to make a living); good organisational skills to manage efficiently; no/little innovation; moderate growth

People can also hold these different titles at different points in their working lives. For example, some people start out as entrepreneurs (creators of a new, innovative business) but can then be called a small business owner–manager once the business venture has been established and they no longer have any ambition for innovation and growth. Conversely, a small business manager can also become an entrepreneur — for example, a person may buy an existing business with the initial purpose of running a 'lifestyle business', but may subsequently take up various opportunities to expand the business (such as introducing new product lines, developing new markets, or providing additional services to clients).

Summary

There is no single definition of what constitutes a small business, and a variety of both qualitative and quantitative factors can be used to separate small firms from other businesses. From a qualitative perspective, the business has to be independently owned and operated, closely controlled and funded by the owner, and the principal decision-making functions must rest with the owner–manager. In addition, the small business can be defined using a variety of quantitative indicators, such as number of employees, value of assets, turnover, and share of ownership retained by the owner–manager. Small businesses form the backbone of the economy in Australia, New Zealand and the Pacific Rim region.

Small firms share a number of typical characteristics that separate them from other types of business organisation. Some of these differences include a smaller market share, a small ownership base, a limited life span and limited net profit. Compared with larger firms, small businesses are more likely to be operated from home, to be run by a family and to have female managers. There are few formal planning procedures, less access to outside capital, less government support and a greater likelihood of 'failure'.

The advantage of owning a small business includes flexibility, personal achievement and the freedom to pursue one's own goals. The disadvantages include an increased exposure to uncertainty and risk, financial loss and personal stress.

Most small businesses face a series of generic problems in the first years of operation. These difficulties fall into four main functional areas — finance, marketing, production and personnel — plus personal difficulties that are caused by running the business. These problems may eventually lead to the failure of the business. Some studies show that internal problems, such as poor management within the firm, are usually the underlying causes of failure; other research points to external circumstances (such as recession or the lack of available capital) as a key determinant of small business failure. Measuring success in a small firm is also difficult.

Small businesses are a major economic force throughout the Pacific Rim region. They provide many of the jobs and a good proportion of GDP in each country, as well as support to large firms, flexibility in the overall economy, and the more equitable distribution of economic resources, wealth and opportunities.

The concept of small business management differs from the concept of entrepreneurship. Whereas small business management is concerned mainly with the art of managing a small-scale commercial firm, entrepreneurship can be viewed as the process of identifying new market opportunities and converting them into a marketable product or service.

REVIEW QUESTIONS

1. List the main qualitative and quantitative criteria used to define a small business.

2. Outline the economic significance of SMEs in the Pacific Rim region.

3. How does a small business differ from a large one?

4. What is a business exit and how does it differ from the concept of business failure?

5. List the general characteristics of a small business.

DISCUSSION QUESTIONS

1. Is there any meaningful difference in the definitions of small business and entrepreneurship?

2. In your opinion, what are the three most important causes of business failure?

3. Spell out the advantages and disadvantages of developing a standard international definition of an SME.

SUGGESTED READING

Australian Bureau of Statistics, *Characteristics of Small Business, Australia*, ABS, Canberra, 2004.

Hashim, M.K. & Wafa, S.A., *Small & Medium-Sized Enterprises in Malaysia: Development Issues*, Prentice Hall, Kuala Lumpur, 2002.

Ministry of Economic Development, New Zealand, *SMEs in New Zealand: Structure and Dynamics*, Ministry of Economic Development, Wellington, 2005.

Storey, D.J., *Understanding the Small Business Sector*, Routledge, London, 1994.

CASE STUDY

Vanust — a tale of two perspectives

In 2001 John and Mia purchased the Vanust Restaurant in Melbourne. Although the site had previously been a restaurant for a number of years, it had lately been closed for some months. Both Mia and John were in their early thirties and had previously each operated their own restaurants, where they enjoyed the sense of freedom and control that comes with being the decision maker, so they were keen to become business owners again.

There was no goodwill included in the purchase price, and the acquisition cost was relatively low. By using their own funds, getting some help from their families, and utilising finance leasing for kitchen equipment, restaurant tables and chairs, they were able to self-finance the full amount of capital needed to establish the business. Neither owner had wanted to be indebted to the banks. Although a small overdraft had been set up with the purchase of the business, trade credit was used in preference to the overdraft for any short-term cash flow issues. This was easily obtained because of the good relationship fostered by John and Mia with their suppliers.

The new owners refurbished the premises so that it could seat approximately 40 customers at a time, and they opened for breakfast, lunch and dinner, seven days a week. After a short while, and contrary to their business plan, they decided that breakfast and lunch were not going to be profitable so they stopped providing these. However, evening meals were quickly becoming popular. The restaurant was soon taking an average of 90 diners per night.

Vanust served traditional Italian food, made with local ingredients at a very affordable price. Patrons came largely from the local area and neighbouring suburbs, and many guests were dining there more than once a week.

In the early years of Vanust, John and Mia wanted to create a restaurant with an atmosphere, service and cuisine that would communicate their personality but also provide them with a comfortable income. Vanust soon gained a reputation for providing great food at very reasonable prices. Since many restaurants often lose sales when patrons cancel, the owners made the decision not to take bookings, and a customer waiting list formed each night. On busy nights customers sometimes waited for over an hour before being seated. They would either wait at the small bar inside the premises or else go to a nearby hotel for a pre-dinner drink and wait to be called by the restaurant when a table became free.

Three floor staff, including Mia, were needed to wait on tables. Mia had completed one year of a university commerce degree, so initially she looked after the bookkeeping side of the restaurant as well. Mia also compiled the wine list and ordered wine, managed staff rosters and dealt with hiring, firing and paying staff. John worked principally as the head chef, in charge of a small team that consisted of a second chef, an apprentice chef and a kitchen hand. Both Mia and John were now working quite long hours — about fifty a week — but were taking home an income slightly above the average wage.

In early 2006, the two partners brought in a third business owner. The workload was becoming too great for them to manage, so they decided to invite a 'friend of a friend' to buy into the partnership. Jennifer had strong management and financial experience, and took on the financial responsibilities of the business, as well as staffing and marketing. She also computerised what had previously been a manual accounting system.

Jennifer noticed that some enquiring customers would not wait for a table, often moving to other nearby restaurants where they could get a table straight away. With Vanust at capacity, and prices very low, net profit had stabilised at approximately five per cent. Jennifer believed that by increasing prices and renegotiating trade terms, she could more than double the net profit margin without reducing the number of diners seated each night. However, John and Mia felt uncomfortable with this change in direction. They took great pride in the fact that it was difficult to get a seat at their restaurant and were unwilling to tamper with a 'successful' formula.

In addition to increasing profitability, Jennifer wanted to grow the business by increasing the seating capacity, and possibly even opening further restaurants. Although in principle each of the owners agreed with this new strategy, tensions soon developed. Mia and John liked the way things had traditionally been done and the stability associated with the past. They were becomingly increasingly uncomfortable with Jennifer's new systems and the more formal procedures needed for her proposed growth strategy.

Case study prepared by Michael à Campo, The University of Newcastle, Australia.

Questions

1. What are the qualitative and quantitative points that may define Vanust as a small business?

2. Are all three owners entrepreneurs? Justify your answer.

3. Compared to a large business, why are the management perspectives different for a small business?

ENDNOTES

1. J.A. Welsh & J.F. White, 'A small business is not a big business', *Harvard Business Review*, vol. 59, no. 4, 1981, pp. 18–32.
2. G.G. Meredith, *Small Business Management in Australia*, 4th edn, McGraw-Hill, Sydney, 1993.
3. Government of the United Kingdom, *Committee of Inquiry on Small Firms* (Bolton Report), HMSO, London, 1971.

4. Department of Trade and Industry, *Report of the Committee on Small Business* (Wiltshire Report), AGPS, Canberra, 1971.

5. G. Meredith, *A National Policy for Small Enterprise Development*, University of New England, Armidale, 1975.

6. Australian Bureau of Statistics, 'Defining businesses by size', *Small Business in Australia 1999*, ABS, Canberra, 2000, pp. 135–50.

7. P.A. Julien, *The State of the Art in Small Business and Entrepreneurship*, Ashgate, Aldershot, 1998, p. 3.

8. ibid., p. 133.

9. ABS, *see* note 6, p. 149.

10. OECD, *Globalisation and SMEs*, vol. 2, OECD, Paris, 1997, pp. 119–21; Australian Bureau of Statistics, *Small Business in Australia 2001*, ABS, Canberra, 2002; NZ Ministry of Economic Development, *SMEs in New Zealand: Structure and Dynamics*, Ministry of Economic Development, Wellington, 2000; Singapore Standards, Productivity and Innovation Board, 'FAQs on SMEs and Domestic Sector', 2003 <www.spring.gov.sg>; Small and Medium Industries Development Corporation, Malaysia, *Definition of SMEs*, 2003, <www.smidec.gov.my>.

11. ABS, *see* note 6, p. 149.

12. Australian Bureau of Statistics, *Small Business in Australia*, ABS, Canberra, 1998.

13. Ministry of Economic Development, New Zealand, *SMEs in New Zealand: Structure and Dynamics*, Ministry of Economic Development, Wellington, 2005, p5.

14. P.E. Atkinson, 'Strengths and Weaknesses of SME Statistics Systems: The Users' Perspective' OECD presentation of identified key issues, Special Workshop on 'SME Statistics: Towards a More Systematic Statistical Measurement of SME Behaviour', 2nd OECD Conference of Ministers responsible for SMEs, Istanbul, 3–5 June 2004, <www.oecd.org>; Ministry of Economic Development, New Zealand, *SMEs in New Zealand: Structure and Dynamics*, Ministry of Economic Development, Wellington, 2005, p. 4.

15. Department of Trade and Industry, *see* note 4.

16. Government of the United Kingdom, *see* note 3.

17. G. Meredith, *see* note 5.

18. I. Bickerdyke, R. Lattimore & A. Madge, *Business Failure and Change: An Australian Perspective*, Productivity Commission, Canberra, 2000.

19. Department of Employment, Workplace Relations and Small Business, *A Portrait of Australian Business: Results of the 1996 Business Longitudinal Survey*, AGPS, Canberra, 1998, p. 38.

20. Department of Industry, Science and Tourism, *The 1995 Business Longitudinal Survey*, AGPS, Canberra, 1997; Australian Bureau of Statistics, *Characteristics of Small Business, Australia*, ABS, Canberra, 2004.

21. ibid.

22. D.J. Storey, *Understanding the Small Business Sector*, Routledge, London, 1994.

23. S. Carter, 'Small business marketing', in M. Warner (ed.), *International Encyclopedia of Business and Management*, Routledge, London, 1996, pp. 140–56.

24. I. Bickerdyke, R. Lattimore & A. Madge, *see* note 18.

25. S. Cromie, 'The problems experienced by young firms', *International Small Business Journal*, vol. 9, no. 3, 1991, pp. 43–61.

26. S. Cromie, 'The problems experienced by young firms', *International Small Business Journal*, vol. 9, no. 3, 1991, pp. 43–61; A. Rashid & M. Zabid, pp. 290–8, and C.W.L. Soh-Wee, pp. 345–66, in Low Aik Meng and Tan Wee Liang (eds), *Entrepreneurs, Entrepreneurship and Enterprising Culture*, Addison-Wesley, Singapore, 1996.

27. A. Rashid & M. Zabid, 'Management practices, motivations and problems of successful women entrepreneurs in Malaysia', in Low Aik Meng & Tan Wee Liang (eds),

Entrepreneurs, Entrepreneurship and Enterprising Culture, Addison-Wesley Publishing, Singapore, 1996, pp. 290–8.

28. C.W.L. Soh-Wee, 'Start-up and early business development challenges confronting young entrepreneurs in Singapore', in Low Aik Meng and Tan Wee Liang (eds), *Entrepreneurs, Entrepreneurship and Enterprising Culture*, Addison-Wesley Publishing, Singapore, 1996, pp. 345–66.

29. J.C. Collins & C.I. William, *Managing the Small to Mid-Sized Company — Concepts and Costs*, Irwin, Chicago, 1995.

30. C.M. Siew, *Corporate Turnaround: A Review and Case Study*, National University of Singapore, Singapore, 1990.

31. J. Watson & J. Everett, 'Defining small business failure', *International Small Business Journal*, vol. 11, no. 3, 1993, pp. 35–48.

32. Australian Bureau of Statistics, *Business Exits in Australia*, cat. no. 8144.0, ABS, Canberra, 1997.

33. Australian Bureau of Statistics, *Experimental Estimates, Entries and Exits of Business Entities, Australia*, cat. no. 8160.0.55.001, ABS, Canberra, 2005, p. 5.

34. I. Bickerdyke, R. Lattimore & A. Madge, *see* note 18, p. xviii.

35. Ministry of Economic Development, New Zealand, *SMEs in New Zealand: Structure and Dynamics*, Ministry of Economic Development, Wellington, 2005, p. 21.

36. D. Tweed, 'Eighty percent do not fail: exploding an SME myth,' paper presented to the 3rd Annual Research Symposium of the New Zealand Centre for SME Research at Massey University, Wednesday 16 February 2005, Wellington.

37. Statistics Singapore, 'Survival rates of enterprises', *Statistics Singapore Newsletter*, September 2003, p. 17.

38. J.H. Kelmar, 'Measurement of success and failure in small business: A two-factor approach', *Journal of Enterprising Culture*, vol. 1, no. 3, 1994, pp. 421–36.

39. Australian Bureau of Statistics, *Characteristics of Small Business, Australia*, ABS, Canberra, 2002.

40. C. Hall, 'Entrepreneurship densities in APEC and Europe: How many entrepreneurs *should* there be in China, or other developing countries?', *Small Enterprise Research*, vol. 10, no. 1, 2002, p. 5.

41. Address by Ambassador Choi Seok-Tyoung, APEC Secretariat Executive Director, to the 12th APEC SME Ministerial Meeting, 1 September 2005, Daegu, South Korea, <www.apec.org>.

42. APEC SME Working Group, *APEC SME Guidebook*, 2000, p. 3, <www.apecsec.org.sg>.

43. Department of Foreign Affairs and Trade, *Small Business and Trade in APEC*, Department of Foreign Affairs and Trade, Canberra, 2002.

44. Hall, *see* note 40, pp. 3–14.

45. Data from APEC SME Working Group, *APEC SME Guidebook*, 2000, p. 3, <www.apecsec.org.sg>; data for Hong Kong updated from HK Trade and Industry Department, *What Are SMEs?*, 2002, <www.sme.gcn.gov.hk>; data for New Zealand updated from NZ Ministry of Economic Development, *SMEs in New Zealand: Structure and Dynamics*, Ministry of Economic Development, Wellington, 2002; data for Australia updated from Australian Bureau of Statistics, *Small Business in Australia 2001*, ABS, Canberra, 2002.

46. M. Schaper, 'Distribution patterns of small firms in developed economies: Is there an emergent global pattern?' *International Journal of Entrepreneurship and Small Business*, vol.3, no.2, 2006, pp. 183–9.

47. European Commission, *SMEs in Europe 2003*, Observatory of European SMEs Report No. 2003/7 submitted to the Enterprise Directorate-General of the European Commission by KPMG Special Services, EIM Business & Policy Research, and European Network for SME Research, Luxembourg: Office for Official Publications of the

European Communities, 2004; United Kingdom Department of Trade and Industry, *Statistical Press Release: Small and Medium-Sized Enterprise Statistics for the UK 2002*, Department of Trade and Industry, Sheffield, 28 August 2003.

48. Australian Bureau of Statistics, *Characteristics of Small Business 2004*, ABS, Canberra, 2005, p. 31.

49. ibid., pp. 8, 11.

50. Australian Bureau of Statistics, *ABS Business Register: Counts of Businesses*, cat. no. 8161.0.55.001, ABS, Canberra, 2005, p. 17.

51. ibid., pp. 13, 27.

52. It should be noted that these figures exclude agricultural enterprises.

53. Ministry of Economic Development, New Zealand, *SMEs in New Zealand: Structure and Dynamics*, Ministry of Economic Development, Wellington, 2005, pp. 3, 7, 9, 14–15.

54. Trade and Industry Department, Hong Kong Special Administrative Region, *What Are SMEs?*, 2005, <www.sme.gcn.gov.hk>; Trade and Industry Department, Hong Kong Special Administrative Region, <www.success.tid.gov.hk>.

55. T. Fu-Lai Yu, *Entrepreneurship and Economic Development in Hong Kong*, Routledge, London, 1997.

56. Opening Address by Mr Willie Cheng, Board Member of SPRING Singapore at the Standards and Accreditation Partners' Day on 19 October 2006, <www.spring.gov.sg>.

57. Small and Medium Industries Development Corporation, Malaysia, *SME Performance 2003*, SMIDEC, Kuala Lumpur, 2004, pp. 12–14.

58. Small and Medium Industries Corporation, Malaysia, *Output, Added Value and Employment of SMIs, 2003 and 2002*, 2005, <www.smidec.gov.my>.

59. D.H. Holt, *Entrepreneurship: New Venture Creation*, Prentice Hall, Englewood Cliffs, NJ, 1992, p. 11.

Part 2
Getting into business

Chapter 5

Options for going into business

LEARNING OBJECTIVES

After reading this chapter, you should be able to:

- explain the three major issues that all prospective entrepreneurs and small business owners must consider before going into business
- compare and contrast the advantages and disadvantages of starting a new business
- outline the factors to take into account when assessing a business for purchase
- explain the different ways of calculating a business purchase price
- describe how a franchise operates
- use the '6 step' process to organise your strategy for going into business.

Entering into the business world as the owner–manager of a firm is a complicated, time-consuming activity. It is a decision that should not be taken lightly, and involves a careful weighing up of both the advantages and disadvantages of going into business.

Several different options are available to people intending to go into business. Although starting a new firm is often the most popular choice, it is not always the most appropriate one. Sometimes it may be more beneficial to purchase an existing enterprise, with its own established production processes and customer base. Another avenue to consider is that of franchising, where a person buys the right to use a pre-existing operating and selling system. In this chapter, each of these options is considered in detail, and different methods of calculating purchase prices and costs are examined. Also, the steps involved in deciding on a business start-up, a purchase or a franchise are explained. This knowledge can help prospective entrepreneurs and small business owners to make a more informed and accurate decision about the most appropriate way for them to go into business.

Issues to consider before going into business

Before examining each of the various business options available, it is best to understand the framework in which new, small entrepreneurial ventures begin. As discussed in the previous chapters, any business venture is driven by three forces: the entrepreneur or small business owner; the resources that he or she has; and the nature of the business opportunity itself (see figure 5.1). Each of these has a major bearing on the methods and strategy used when going into business.[1]

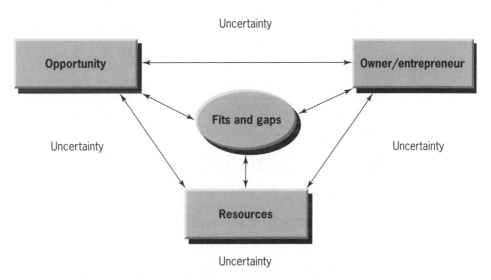

Figure 5.1: Three issues to consider before going into business

Source: W.D. Bygrave, 'The entrepreneurial process', in *The Portable MBA in Entrepreneurship*, 2nd edn, John Wiley & Sons, New York, 1997, p. 11.

The entrepreneur/small business owner: personal goals and abilities

Personal self-awareness is important for a successful business venture. Effective owners or entrepreneurs have a thorough and honest understanding of their own personal strengths and weaknesses and a clear idea of their own (as opposed to their prospective business's) goals before they commit themselves to the business.

The amount of prior knowledge and enthusiasm they have for the industry sector they wish to work in is important. Most business owners find that their chances of success are greater if they are involved in an industry in which they already have some experience and in which they enjoy working.

Business owners should also have a clear idea about why they are going into business and what they hope to achieve. Such personal goals may include:
- a certain level of personal income each year ('to make $X per year')
- a specified (percentage) return on investment for funds invested in the project
- personal freedom ('being my own boss')
- providing job opportunities for other family members
- making the business grow into a larger enterprise within a certain time period.

The prospective business owner's personal risk profile also needs to be considered. No business is ever guaranteed. There will always be uncertainty about whether a firm will succeed. Going into business inevitably involves risking a certain amount of one's own money, credibility, time and enthusiasm. Just how much risk a person is willing to take is an important determinant in assessing business options.

Individual business owners, like other members of the community, can usually be classified into one of at least three different categories of risk-related behaviour. *Risk-averse people* are usually unwilling to bet much, if anything, on their new venture. For these people, business operations with a proven track record (such as a franchise or well-established existing business) are a preferred option. *Moderate risk takers* will usually be willing to invest up to, but not beyond, a predetermined amount of resources. They will usually choose to buy an established firm or a new business that has been soundly researched and whose viability is reasonably self-evident. *High risk takers*, who often put up most of their own personal resources, are usually people who start up new businesses, especially in 'cutting-edge' and capital-intensive markets, where the chances of failure are much higher, although the potential return on investment is also more lucrative.

Resource availability

Entry cost: The price of starting up or buying a business enterprise.

Exit cost: The price involved in liquidating or closing a business enterprise.

Access to resources can be a key determinant of the business option chosen. Business ventures require the owner/entrepreneur to have or obtain numerous resources.

The most obvious of these resources is finance. Prospective small business owners or entrepreneurs who do not have a great deal of money will be limited in their choices, and they will usually opt for a new business in a field where both **entry costs** (the price involved in starting the firm) and **exit costs** (the price involved in liquidating the enterprise if it does not prove to be viable) are low. For example, service-sector businesses generally have low entry and exit costs, whereas the reverse is true for manufacturing and retail firms.

Almost as important is a supply of personnel for the venture. A committed team of employees can allow a business project to be much larger in scale and ambition than a solo venture; on the other hand, difficulties in employing appropriately trained staff can cripple otherwise viable projects.

Another important resource is time. Some business ideas can take a long time to reach fruition, and this may not always coincide with the desires of the entrepreneur. Some people are prepared to spend a lengthy period of time getting their idea right, whereas others may have a more pressing need or desire to realise an immediate financial return on their investments. Starting a new business may prove to be a useful option in the former case, but not in the latter.

The opportunity

Different business opportunities also impose implicit constraints on the type of business chosen. If a person wants to run a McDonald's store, for example, then there is only one option: enter into a franchise arrangement with the parent company. Alternatively, if an entrepreneur has a unique product idea that has not been previously tested in the market, then a start-up operation is probably most appropriate, since it will allow the owner–manager to structure the venture in a way that best suits the unique circumstances.

Starting a new business

Once personal goals have been set, available resources determined and the business opportunities examined, the choice of business option can be made. The first option that usually springs to mind for most budding small business owners or entrepreneurs is starting their own business operation as a totally new venture.

The advantages of starting a new business

Sometimes intending business operators find that they have to start their own enterprise simply because there is no existing business available for purchase. Alternatively, they may find that the only firms available for sale on the open market are too expensive, or the asking price is, in some other way, considered unreasonable. However, starting a new business venture does provide a number of opportunities that other forms of business management do not offer; these are outlined as follows.

Ability to determine business direction

Ideally, a new business start-up allows the owner of the venture to exert near-total control over the enterprise. The products to be sold, the target customer base, the organisational culture of the enterprise, and the financial strategy of the business can all be determined by the entrepreneur, since he or she will be personally responsible for building each of these elements. In contrast, the purchase of an existing business usually means that the new owner has to assume responsibility for many unfamiliar operating procedures that may take some time to change, if they can be altered at all.

Flexibility

Because a new business is a 'blank slate' at its inception, it can be moulded and shaped to fit the needs of both the owner and the market. In contrast, an existing business has established systems, strongly held organisational procedures, and defined ways of operating, all of which preclude rapid change. From this perspective, a new business is seen to be more flexible and to have a greater capacity to innovate than its established counterpart. In addition, the start-up business owner is able to build up the project slowly over time, and get it right as it progresses.

Cost minimisation

Properly handled, many new small businesses (especially micro-enterprises) can start trading with a lower cost base than established businesses, since they do not have the ongoing costs of their established competitors or any of the inefficiencies that may have built up over time. While a new business can sometimes be successfully commenced with lower fixed costs, purchasing an existing business may result in the new owner paying for several additional unwanted items, such as the purchase of goodwill, existing assets or stock on hand, regardless of whether the new owner wishes to use them or not.

New lifestyle goals

A new business allows the owner to develop a particular desired lifestyle. For example, many people seek self-employment because they no longer wish to have a 'boss' to whom they are answerable. For others, a new business may bring with it the opportunity to work more convenient hours, to spend more time with friends and members of their family, to work from home, to build an asset they can pass on to their children, or to avoid a stressful environment in their current workplace.

What would you do?

Food for thought

You are a business broker who advertises and sells businesses. This morning a mother and son arrived at your office. Alex is 25, has a communications degree, and has been working for the last three years as the personal assistant to the chief executive of a large public corporation. Alex plans to put all his savings into buying a business for himself. His mother, Elaina, is 48 and has just inherited a sizeable amount from her husband, who died two months ago. Elaina worked for a few years in a television studio, but has spent most of her life as a stay-at-home mother. The two want to go into business together and have come to ask about two fast-food shops you have advertised for sale.

One is a well-established stand-alone enterprise that's been selling hamburgers, fries and salads for the last seven years, but the owner wants to retire. The existing staff plan to stay on, and the price includes all fixtures, fittings and trading stock. The premises are rented on a secure long-term lease.

The other is a take-away noodle franchise controlled and run by a large US firm that also owns the premises where the business is located. The price covers not only all fixtures and trading stock but also a franchise entry fee. The new franchisee will be able to sign a five-year agreement with the franchisor.

The two shops operate across the road from each other in a middle-class suburb where they have been fierce rivals since the franchise opened five years ago.

The entry price for both businesses is the same. Although the price is high, your clients have just enough funds to cover it and associated legal fees. However, the commission you will receive for selling the franchise business is much larger.

Your clients are keen to buy, but they are unsure which business is the best for them, so they have come to you for your expert professional opinion. Under both the code of ethics of your profession and the law of the land, you are required to give your clients a balanced assessment of each course of action and your recommendation as to what they should do.

Questions

1. What advice will you give your clients?
2. Are there any other options that they should consider if they want to go into business?

The disadvantages of starting a new business

Despite the benefits outlined above, starting a new business can also be very risky. There are several limitations and drawbacks that can potentially destroy or weaken the viability of a new business venture.

Raising capital

Because a new business does not have any established financial history or resources to draw on, financing the business venture can be difficult. Many financial institutions are reluctant to extend credit to unknown and unproven enterprises, and the business owners may find that they have to provide much (if not all) of the initial capital themselves. If the intending business owner does not have the necessary access to finance, the business may quickly fail from a lack of sufficient start-up funds or working capital.

Lack of an established customer base

By definition, the formation of a new business means that the entity does not yet have any customers of its own. Although the owner may be in a position to attract customers through personal networks and previous industry experience, there are rarely enough to immediately create a viable business. Instead, the business owner will need to invest a considerable amount of time, energy and money in researching and marketing to a defined target market base.

Cash flow shortages

Lack of capital and a shortage of customers may mean that the business's cash flow will be under severe stress during the early days of its existence. This cash flow shortage is common in new businesses, and may exist for a few months or even several years. When cash flow is tight, a sudden unexpected change in the business environment (such as an interest rate increase, a currency devaluation or additional unplanned expenses) may mean that the business can no longer pay its bills on time.

Learning curve expenses

Because a new enterprise is one in which nobody has previously done the work required, there will be a considerable number of one-off events where the owner will have to invest time, effort and money to get the business working effectively (frequently referred to as a *learning curve*). For example, the operator of a new business must develop a name and brand, decide on suitable premises, recruit and train staff, devise an initial marketing campaign, and make the firm known in the marketplace. Much of this will not result in the direct generation of customer sales, but it is still necessary. However, because this is a new activity, it is likely to take far longer than would be the case in an established business.

Costs of a start-up venture

Regardless of the type of business venture being explored, some costs are common to all new enterprises. Any starting business will need to meet the following costs:
- licences and permits required to operate the business
- working capital
- communications equipment (such as telephones, computers and fax machines)
- operating plant and equipment
- staff recruitment expenses
- insurance
- raw materials (or trading stock)
- rental of premises (unless working from the owner's home)
- stationery.

These are just the most basic of all expenses, but they will still typically run to several thousand dollars for even the simplest and most budget-conscious enterprise.

Purchasing an existing business

Sometimes commercial goals and ambitions are best fulfilled by the acquisition of a firm that is already operating — sometimes also referred to as a *going concern*.

The main advantage of purchasing an existing business is that it allows a proprietor to begin trading immediately, since an established business operation, cash flow, staff, product range and customer base already exist. It is also easier to arrange finance for the venture, and the established track record of the firm allows the prospective owner to make a more objective evaluation of likely future performance than would be the case if starting a new enterprise. In many respects, the advantages of buying an existing firm are the mirror opposite of the disadvantages of starting a new firm, as mentioned above.

Potential businesses can be found in a variety of ways. They may be advertised for sale by a business broker (an agent who specialises in listing and selling businesses, and who may often focus on one or two particular industries); listed by the current owner in a newspaper or online advertisement; sold through accountancy firms; or, in the case of very troubled businesses, disposed of via insolvency or bankruptcy trustees. Another option is to cold canvass existing owners to see if they are willing to sell. This was the case with Carolyn Cresswell, whose story appears in the Entrepreneur Profile below.

Although accurate market research and an honest appraisal of business opportunities are critical to the launch of a brand-new firm, the issues involved in the purchase of a going trading concern are more complex. In addition to such market analysis, the prospective purchaser must also be able to correctly calculate a purchase price, and know the appropriate issues to investigate before making an offer.

Entrepreneur profile

Carolyn Creswell, Carman's Fine Foods

In 1992, at the age of eighteen, Carolyn Creswell was studying for her Bachelor of Arts degree while also working one day a week in a bakery making muesli. Nine months after starting work, she was told that the business was to be put up for sale and she would lose her job. So she bought it herself.

'It was a very small, very basic business at the time. There was no registered business, no bank account, about 80 clients, and just a few people working to a recipe in space sub-let from a Melbourne baker.'

Rather than lose her job, Carolyn decided to confront the challenge head on. Together with a workmate, they bought the tiny business for $1000 each.

Carman's (a synthesis of the two purchasers' names) was born. In 1994, Carolyn bought out her partner, and today still directly manages the firm herself. The product range now includes muesli, muesli bars and organic honey, which are distributed to thousands of outlets Australia-wide. She has recently started successfully exporting into Hong Kong, Malaysia, Singapore, the Philippines and several Pacific island nations. Once a casual worker at Coles supermarkets, Carolyn has now come full circle to be a supplier of this major Australian supermarket chain.

The business also operates on an interesting model. 'We contract everything out. The manufacturing of muesli is contracted out; someone else does sales; and someone else does our accounting. We have fewer than half a dozen staff, who mainly process orders and oversee our business contracts. Contracting out has given us tremendous leverage that we couldn't achieve otherwise.'

Turnover in first year was $80 000, but by last year it had risen to over $6 million. In 2005, Carolyn's work was also recognised when her firm was listed on the prestigious *BRW* Fast 100 — a list of the nation's 100 fastest growing firms.

'Lots of people think about starting up but get scared. Don't. Just give it a go. You don't need a huge amount of money or a fancy setup. You can work from your bedroom. It doesn't have to be a big deal. But if you want it, then you've got to commit and start somewhere.'

The initial investment of $1000, along with the bare basics provided by the existing business concept, have enabled Carolyn to create a highly successful business.

For more information, see <www.carmansfinefoods.com.au>.

Source: Based on author's interview with Carolyn Cresswell.

Establishing a purchase price

How much is a business worth? As more than one economist has noted, an item is worth whatever someone is prepared to pay for it. Such a refrain may be of little consolation to a buyer who is trying to negotiate a complex deal and who needs to have some realistic understanding of what constitutes a 'fair' price.[2]

The methods for establishing a reasonable purchase price tend to fluctuate, and can be prone to trends and fads among advisers as to what is the 'best' method. The definition of what constitutes a best price also depends on whether one is a purchaser (to whom a lower price is preferable) or a vendor (to whom the highest possible selling price is critical). Finally, different industries also tend to favour different valuation methods, which can make the task even more complicated.

Generally speaking, there are several different ways in which the price of an existing business can be set. Purchase prices can be broken down into three broad categories — market-based valuations, asset-based valuations and earnings-based valuations.[3]

Market-based valuations

In an efficient and open marketplace, the price of a business should be easily determined by reference to previous sales. If a similar business has been sold in the past, then that price can be seen as an accurate reflection of what the current business is worth. According to this school of thought, the open marketplace is the best judge of a firm's worth.

There are two main types of market-based valuation:

- *The going market rate method.* As its name suggests, this is simply the 'current market' price for a particular type of firm. It is usually established by reference to recent selling prices for other firms of a similar size and industry type. For example, if a small IT firm in a particular city was recently sold for $350 000, then the next such firm put up for sale will be priced at about the same amount.

Selling price = Selling price of similar firms

  Although such a technique may not fully reflect a firm's own particular strengths or weaknesses, it is a useful starting point in working out a final price. Current market rates can often be determined by studying similar businesses advertised for sale online, in newspapers or via a business broker.

- *Revenue multiplier method.* A slightly more sophisticated approach is to adopt one of a number of 'rules of thumb' (informal guidelines) on pricing. The most common of these is the use of a revenue multiplier. This technique is often used in the purchase of professional practices, such as businesses run by doctors, dentists and accountants. In most such industries, there is a common 'industry multiple' that is used to estimate the most likely purchase price of the practice. The selling price is established by multiplying the annual turnover of the business by this multiple.

Selling price = Turnover × Standard industry multiple

  For example, an accountancy practice may use an established industry multiple of 0.7 or 1.0. If the annual turnover of the firm is $225 000, and the multiple applied is 0.7, then the asking price would be $157 500.

Whether one uses the going market rate or the revenue multiplier method, such approaches avoid the need to undertake detailed calculations or complex financial analysis. The techniques are simple and easy to understand, especially for entrepreneurs and small business owners who are not familiar with valuation methodologies. However, such methods have a number of serious weaknesses. The price reached is largely dependent on broader sales trends, and may not fully recognise the special circumstances of the individual business being considered. If prices in the market as a whole become overinflated, then the purchaser will pay more for the business than it would otherwise be worth. Moreover, these methods do not take into account the future earnings potential of the business or the value of the assets in hand. Finally, it can often be difficult to collect accurate information about market prices, since few small businesses are sold by public tender or share floats, or in other public forums.

Asset-based valuations

An alternative to relying on market forces is to set a price after examining the assets and liabilities of the business. This involves examining present and historical data about the business, which is usually found among the financial records ('books') in the balance sheet.

- *Book value.* In this process, the asking price is set by first calculating the worth of all the firm's assets. These may be tangible items (such as stock on hand, equipment, property, vehicles, furniture and fittings) and intangible commodities (such as intellectual property rights and goodwill). The liabilities of the business are then subtracted to produce a final value.

Selling price = Tangible assets + Intangible assets − Liabilities

- *Adjusted book (net asset) value.* In practice, the simple book value method is really only the starting point in price calculations. Relying on the books of accounts means that only historical information is referred to, rather than contemporary information. For example, a building may be shown on the balance sheet at the price paid for it several years ago (less depreciation), but it may actually be worth much more today because of a general increase in property asset prices. To overcome this, valuers often adjust the initial book value in a number of ways. The assets may be revalued to reflect their current worth, as may the liabilities. This is a somewhat subjective measure, which can vary from one valuer to another.

Goodwill:
An intangible commodity; the extra value ascribed to a business, piece of intellectual property, brand name, or other business-related activity.

Similarly, the question of determining exactly what constitutes **goodwill** is extremely problematical. At its simplest, goodwill is simply the extra value a purchaser is prepared to pay because of the firm's unique position. This may be something as simple as a track record of consistent net profits, or it may be something less easily measured but just as important to its success, such as a highly favourable location, a well-known brand name, a good reputation in the local community or a loyal customer base. In many cases, one or two years net profits may be used as a proxy measure for the sum of a firm's goodwill.

- *Liquidation value.* Sometimes a prospective purchaser of a business may plan to break up and sell the various assets of the firm rather than continue to operate it as a going concern. During the 1980s, for example, a number of entrepreneurs made considerable profits by purchasing large corporations and then selling off their assets. When this is a possibility, the book value may have to be adjusted to see what the business is worth when it is liquidated. To do so, the individual assets of the business are valued at the price they are likely to receive if sold quickly. In many respects, a liquidation price represents a floor or bottom price below which the vendor will not go, since he or she could sell the assets as stand-alone items for the same amount.[4]

- *Replacement value.* If a liquidation price represents the lowest price purchasers can offer, then the replacement book value often equals the highest price they will usually want to offer. In this exercise, the cost of replacing all the firm's tangible assets (at current market costs) is calculated. This is the price an entrepreneur or small business owner would have to pay if starting up a similar business rather than buying the current one. Unless there are substantial intangible assets (such as goodwill), this is the maximum price worth paying for the business.

Earnings-based (cash flow) valuations

In contrast to the historical or present-day focus of book valuations, some purchasers are more concerned about the potential of the business they want to buy. From this perspective, future earning power and the ability to produce cash income (which can, in turn, be used to provide working capital, grow the business, reduce debt and reward the owner) are most important.

- *Return on investment.* The capitalised value method — commonly referred to as the return on investment (ROI) technique — is one of the most widely accepted and used valuation tools.[5] It is based on the assumption that the risk and return of a business should be reflected in its selling price. It works on a formula that includes the estimated future profit:

$$\text{Selling price} = \text{Net annual profit} \times (100/\text{ROI})$$

Different industries have different levels of risk, and therefore differing ROI. As in all investment decisions, a higher level of risk is often associated with a higher level of return. In other words, if investors in a business are prepared to be exposed to a high chance that the business will fail and their money will be lost, then they are entitled to a higher ROI. However, because they are riskier enterprises, the selling price of such firms is likely to be low. Future income cannot be guaranteed to the purchaser.

Conversely, industries that are safer tend to produce a lower ROI, but can command a higher price. This is because their level of performance is more predictable; the purchaser of an enterprise in a low-risk field should reasonably expect that the business will be able to consistently produce a profit, year in, year out.

In other words, low risk = low return = high selling price and vice versa. For example, the selling price of a business making $100 000 profit in a high-risk industry with an ROI of 50 per cent will be $100 000 \times (100/50) = $200 000. If that same industry were more stable and secure, and the required ROI consequently was set at the much lower rate of 10 per cent, then the purchase price would be $1 000 000.

- *Discounted cash flows.* A common but more complex analytical tool is the use of discounted cash flow (DCF) models. Originally devised for use in the assessment of capital budgets, this model reduces (discounts) the future cash income generated by the business to its current value. The fundamental principle governing this procedure is the assumption that the valuation of the business is equal to the present value of its estimated future cash flow. In other words, if a business is expected to generate a healthy cash stream for the next 10 years, how much is that prospective cash worth in today's dollars?

This future cash stream usually includes both annual cash flows and the terminal value expected when the business is sold. Such a valuation approach gives a dynamic rather than a static perspective of the firm, since the selling price is based on future cash-creating activities.

A discounted cash flow can be estimated using the following formula:

$$\text{Value} = \sum_{t=1}^{n} \frac{\overline{CF}_t}{(1+r)^t} + \text{Terminal value}$$

CF_t = expected cash flow in period t
r = required rate of return, or discount rate, or opportunity rate
n = number of periods considered in the analysis
Terminal value = value of the business after the forecast period. There are two ways to calculate this value: (1) use the liquidation value of the business expected at the end of the timeframe under consideration, or (2) take the last period's cash flow as a perpetuity and discount it back to present value.

This is a more complex analytical tool, and its effectiveness depends on whether realistic assumptions (such as the required rate of return) are used.

Choosing between valuation methods

In reality, the above valuation methods rarely provide a complete guide to a final purchase price. Indeed, the techniques discussed above are only some of the more common ones used. There is a wide variety of methods that can be used, and many different ways they are calculated and names they are known by.

For these reasons, the approaches described are perhaps best treated as guidelines that can be used to establish a negotiating stance. In theory, if used effectively, the various methods should all produce broadly similar valuations.[6] However, this is rarely the case in practice.

Most entrepreneurs and small business owners tend to place greater reliance on some methods than on others. The arguments that 'cash is king' and that a solid predictable stream of income is central to future success lead some people to favour cash flow (earnings) valuations. However, due to the relative complexity of such calculations and the difficulty of predicting future earnings, some purchasers prefer to use an asset-based method. This has the advantage of being easier to calculate and understand. Market-based prices are the easiest of all for small business owners to use but, since few small firms are publicly traded, information on the purchase price of other similar businesses is usually difficult to obtain.[7]

Questions to ask

Researching information about an existing business for sale usually requires at least as much, if not more, effort than starting up a firm. For example, the purchase will often entail assuming responsibility for debts or liabilities incurred by the previous managers. These may include unpaid tax bills, accrued staff leave entitlements, legal actions outstanding against the firm, or creditors whose accounts are due. It is important to note that in many jurisdictions, such liabilities continue to rest with the business itself, regardless of the change of ownership. These liabilities may not be apparent unless a thorough examination of the business's accounts and records is made before purchase. Less obvious, but still significant, are other potential liabilities such as undesirable or poorly trained staff, products with a poor reputation in the marketplace, or a large base of unsatisfied previous customers — all this comprises **ill-will**. In addition to current or potential liabilities, there is always the risk that a dishonest or negligent vendor has misled the purchaser.

Overcoming this requires the purchaser and advisers to conduct a **due diligence** study. Due diligence is the detailed scrutiny of a business in order to obtain all the information needed to comprehensively evaluate it and determine whether it is a worthwhile investment. Such an investigation is best performed by a team assembled by the prospective purchaser, and should include accountants, legal advisers, a business broker and specialist consultants. Common questions that should be asked include:

- Why is the vendor selling?
- Will existing staff remain if the business is sold?
- What current liabilities does the business have?
- Are there any outstanding taxation debts?
- Is there any outstanding litigation against the firm?
- Can all licences and permits to operate be transferred to the new owner?
- How accurate and honest are the financial accounts that have been provided?
- What is the level of accrued staff leave that will have to be paid?
- What is the likely future state of the industry — is demand increasing or decreasing?
- Is the lease on the premises secure? Is it transferable to a new business purchaser? How long does the existing lease run?
- Will suppliers continue to provide stock, and at the same price, as they have previously?
- What is the condition of the physical assets? Will any need to be replaced in the near future?
- Will customers remain loyal to this business once the current proprietor has departed?

Other issues

When negotiating the purchase of a business, it makes good sense to include a **restraint of trade clause** in the final contract of sale. This prohibits the vendor from establishing a rival business within a reasonable distance of the premises.

Ill-will: Negative perceptions or attitudes towards a firm; an intangible commodity which detracts from the overall value of a business.

Due diligence: A process of detailed scrutiny aimed at obtaining all the information needed to comprehensively evaluate a business for purchase and to establish whether the projected business is a worthwhile investment.

Restraint of trade clause: A contractual restriction on the right of a business vendor to operate a similar business in rivalry with the new purchaser of the firm.

Although such clauses are often limited by the courts, they do prevent the vendor from selling a firm and then using the proceeds to become a competitor.

In addition to the purchase price, buyers should also be aware that they will face ancillary costs. These can include the accountant's fees, for reviewing the books of the business; legal fees, for the contract of sale; valuation costs; government taxes, such as stamp duty, on the sale transfer and contract registration; and bank fees, when loans are established to pay for the business.

Entering a franchise system

Franchising has become an increasingly popular form of business system over the last 30 years.[8] Although franchising has been in existence for well over a century, it is still relatively new in many industries. It provides another avenue through which people can begin their own business, and many franchises now exist in such diverse fields as petrol retailing, motor vehicle distribution, real estate sales, personal services, professional practices, fast food and retail sales.

At its simplest, a **franchise** is an arrangement whereby the originator of a business product or operating system (commonly referred to as the **franchisor**) gives a prospective small business owner (the **franchisee**) the right to sell these goods and/or to use the business operations system on the franchisor's behalf. In 2004, there were approximately 800 franchise systems in operation in Australia, accounting for a total of 50 600 franchised outlets. Most franchise systems in Australia are actually quite small: the typical franchisor has about 26 franchisees. Sixty per cent of all franchise systems have fewer than 30 franchisees, and there are only about 15 per cent who have more than 100 franchisees.[9] Studies in New Zealand indicate that the country has about 300 systems, with about 5000 franchisee outlets.[10]

There are two basic types of franchise. A **product franchise** gives a small business operator the right to sell a particular commodity or set of goods. In this arrangement, the franchisee is used as a distribution mechanism for a good or service, and has a large measure of independence as to how the business will be set up and operated. The franchisor's role is limited to ensuring that sufficient stock is made available and that the franchisee is selling the product at a satisfactory price and providing customers with suitable after-sales service and support. One of the first such franchises was that created to distribute and sell sewing machines; today, many other individual products (including clothing, vehicles and household goods) are sold via this system.

In contrast, a **business system franchise** is a more detailed agreement between the two parties. In this arrangement, the franchisor not only supplies the product but also gives comprehensive guidelines on how the business is to be run. The franchisee is expected to follow a predetermined set of rules about all aspects of managing and operating the business. This will usually include pricing; production processes; marketing; staff recruitment, remuneration, training and evaluation; product offerings and promotional methods; recordkeeping; operating hours; use of different suppliers; store layout and fittings and so on. A well-known example of a business system franchise is that operated by fast-food giant

Franchise: An arrangement whereby the originator of a business product or operating system permits another business owner to sell the goods and/or to use the business operating system on the originator's behalf.

Franchisor: A business or individual who owns the rights to a particular business franchise system or product.

Franchisee: The business/person given contractual permission by the original owner of a system or product to operate a business franchise system or sell a product.

Product franchise: A franchise to sell a particular product or service.

Business system franchise: An arrangement whereby the franchisor supplies the product and gives comprehensive guidelines on how the business is to be run.

McDonald's. The store proprietors (franchisees) are usually expected to follow a comprehensive set of instruction manuals and operating systems written by the franchisor, and they are usually given detailed training in these before starting their own restaurant.

The main benefit of the system franchise is that all aspects of organising and operating the business have already been investigated, pre-tested and successfully implemented by the franchisor, and the viability of the franchise has also usually been assessed in advance. There is little, if any, extra management work or market research that the franchisee has to do, apart from going through the actual process of setting up and then overseeing the particular store. In many ways, this type of franchise represents a compromise between the previous two business options: although franchisees are still technically starting a new firm, they are also buying in a large body of existing knowledge.

Advantages and disadvantages of franchising

There are many benefits to be gained from entering a franchise arrangement, particularly if it is a business system format. The new business owner is spared the task of developing an operating system, which usually represents a large amount of time and energy in most new small firms. There is less 'learning by mistakes', which can often cause many businesses to falter and fail. As a result, most franchises have a lower failure rate than new independent small businesses.

Customers are usually attracted by the presence of an established product or brand name, which is backed up by the franchisor's ongoing marketing efforts. Most franchisors provide continuing training for franchisees, as well as market research into emerging trends and purchasing behaviour. The cost of raw materials and supplies is often lower, as the franchisor can use the combined power of many franchisees to negotiate discounts. All these advantages mean that raising capital can also be easier, since financial institutions are often more willing to lend money to buy a franchise than they are to start a new, unknown enterprise.

However, access to these systems does not come cheaply. The purchase price for entering into a business system franchise is often quite high, and may be beyond the reach of many small-scale entrepreneurs. In addition to this initial outlay, franchisees are usually expected to pay a proportion of their profits to the franchisor, and may also be required to pay a separate marketing levy.

There are other limitations and drawbacks. Many franchises are sold on a geographical basis. Franchisees are often restricted to serving a set market, and may not expand beyond a predetermined boundary. The opportunities for individual store owners to innovate and change the pre-set rules are limited, since the core appeal of many franchises is their uniformity. If the parent company (franchisor) fails or is poorly run, then the dependent franchisees may also be at risk of collapsing.

It is also important to bear in mind that a franchise is essentially a contractual arrangement, and therefore has a limited lifespan. At the end of a set period (which is typically from five to seven years), the franchisee will have to negotiate a new contract with the parent franchisor; renewal of the contract is not always guaranteed.

Franchises can be an attractive option to many intending small business owners, especially those who are risk-averse or who have only limited experience in managing their own enterprise. However, franchises are often not suitable for entrepreneurial personalities who have their own ideas about what products to offer and how to manage a firm, and who wish to aggressively increase their market share. More information about franchises can be obtained from the sources listed in table 5.1.

Table 5.1: Franchise organisations

Country	Entity
Australia	Franchise Council of Australia <www.franchise.org.au>
Hong Kong	Hong Kong Franchise Association <www.franchise.org.hk>
Malaysia	Malaysian Franchise Association <www.mfa.org.my>
Singapore	Franchising and Licensing Association (Singapore) <www.flasingapore.org>
New Zealand	Franchise Association of New Zealand <www.franchise.org.nz>

Comparison of options

As the preceding discussion and table 5.2 show, there is rarely a clear best choice among the three different types of business avenue. Each of the three forms of market entry (start-up, purchase or franchise) has its own respective advantages and disadvantages.

Table 5.2: Differences between businesses

Factor	Start-up	Purchase	Franchise
Market/customer base	Unknown	Defined	Predetermined
Advertising and pricing strategy	Unknown	Defined	Predetermined
Future growth possibilities	Unlimited	Unlimited	Restricted
Staffing flexibility	High	Low	Moderate
Flexibility in managerial decision making	High	Moderate	Low
Risk of failure	High	Moderate	Low
Level of initial financial outlay	At owner's discretion	Substantial	Substantial
Subsequent financial commitments	Nil	Nil	Yes (ongoing levies and royalties)
Goodwill costs	No	Yes	Yes
Ability to raise external funds	Poor	Moderate	Moderate

There is rarely, if ever, a best option that will suit the needs of all entrepreneurs or small business owners. Determining the most suitable mechanism for an entrepreneur or small business owner will usually involve careful consideration of personal goals and financial and other resources, and a clear understanding of the nature of the business opportunity that the prospective owner or entrepreneur wishes to exploit.

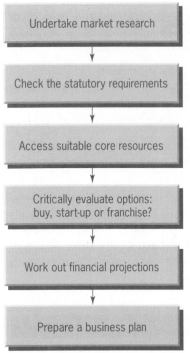

Figure 5.2: The process of going into business

Procedural steps when starting a business venture

Once the decision to start a new business has been made, there are a number of steps which, if followed in a logical manner, provide a useful framework for evaluating and then acting on the intended project (see figure 5.2). They are designed to be conducted in a sequential 'lock-step' manner (i.e. each stage must be largely completed before moving on to the next). In this way, if the idea appears unviable at any stage, it can be aborted before too many resources have been committed to the project.

1. Undertake market research

Before beginning, it is necessary to know whether there really is a demand for the proposed service or product and whether there is room for another business in the market. This stage involves the collection of critical strategic information, such as data on competitors, general industry trends, the intended target customer base, products, pricing, and production/delivery processes. Such information must be collected in an impartial and accurate manner; this is explained in more detail in chapter 6.

2. Check the statutory requirements

There are many laws that cover small business, and it is the responsibility of all owner–managers to comply with the relevant legislation. This can include rules regarding business names, permission to operate in a particular location, health and safety laws, taxation rules and export permits. In many nations there are several different jurisdictions that apply the laws, from national governments to state or provincial governments and local councils. Failure to obtain the necessary approvals will mean that the business cannot trade, so securing such permits is an important early step in the process.

It is also necessary at this stage to obtain an indication of the likely legal structure of the business. This can be as a sole trader, where the owner retains all rights and liabilities; a partnership, where profits and responsibilities are shared; or a company, which is a more complex legal structure that owns the business and takes responsibility for it. These structures are explained in more detail in chapter 8.

3. Access suitable core resources

Any business venture requires a suitable business address and facilities before it begins operating. For a home-based business, this may be a relatively simple issue; it may involve, for example, ensuring that there are enough desks and chairs and adequate space, or that the local authority will allow the business to operate from a residential location. In contrast, if commercial facilities are required, more attention to detail is needed. The intending owner must ensure that the premises are in a good location, suited to the needs of the business, and that a satisfactory lease contract has been negotiated.

The decision to proceed with a new venture also rests on access to suitable equipment and tools. For example, a mobile carpentry service that cannot obtain work tools and an appropriate vehicle is unlikely to succeed, as is a restaurant that does not have sufficient refrigeration or cooking facilities.

An important but often overlooked aspect of any proposed business start-up is the availability of suitable insurance. Although some insurance policies (such as workers compensation and third-party motor vehicle insurance) are compulsory in many countries and easily obtainable, other policies may be discretionary but very important. For example, an abseiling business that cannot obtain sufficient insurance to cover possible injury claims by clients may need to reconsider its plans, since failure to obtain such coverage could cause the business to fail if faced with a large negligence claim.

These operational issues are examined in more detail in chapter 12.

4. Critically evaluate options: buy, start-up or franchise?

The collection of the preliminary information outlined above should now allow the intending business operator to make a more knowledgeable and honest assessment of the chances of success. At this point, it is also preferable to compare the benefits and disadvantages of the start-up venture model with those of buying an existing business or entering into a franchise. Ideally, this analysis should be done in conjunction with an accountant or other qualified business adviser.

5. Work out financial projections

The intending business owner will need to know each of the following financial considerations before going into business:

- the amount of money required to start (for equipment purchases, advertising, wages, insurance, leases, vehicles, and/or other items)
- the amount of money that will need to be borrowed, and whether the money can be obtained (either from funds the owner already has, or through a financial institution); if funding is not available, then the project may not be viable
- the projected cash flow for the next year
- the projected profit and loss for the whole year (which will show whether the business is viable in the long-term).

If purchasing an existing firm, the prospective owner will also need to see a balance sheet.

6. Prepare a business plan

If the decision is made to proceed, the prospective business owner should now develop a more detailed plan for the business, covering as many different aspects of operations, marketing and finance as possible. This provides a blueprint for action and a timeline for implementation, and also helps in the raising of any necessary capital. The contents of a business plan are shown in detail in chapter 7.

Summary

Going into business requires budding small business owners and entrepreneurs to understand the three factors that influence all business ventures: (1) the personal goals, desires, experience and abilities of the owner or entrepreneur; (2) the financial, human and other resources that can be used in the enterprise; and (3) the nature of the business opportunity itself.

There are three very different ways of getting into business: starting a new business, buying an existing operation or entering into a franchise arrangement. Starting a new business involves the wholesale development of a complete business idea, which must cover not only all the issues involved in starting up, but also the task of managing the business on a day-to-day basis once it begins trading. A new business provides maximum flexibility, but also heightens the risk of business failure.

Buying an established enterprise can lower the risk of business failure. It will also provide the owner with an immediate source of cash flow and customers. But this is a more expensive option, and great care must be taken when determining what constitutes a reasonable purchase price. There are three main ways of setting a price: market-based valuations, asset-based valuations, and earnings-based (cash flow) valuations.

Franchises may take the form of either product or business system arrangements. The latter is more comprehensive, and usually has a lower failure rate, but it severely limits the freedom and flexibility of the business owner and can be expensive to enter into.

There are six steps involved in the process of evaluating business options. These start with undertaking market research; understanding the legal requirements pertaining to the proposed business venture; and obtaining all necessary resources required for the business venture. After these first three steps, the intending business owner must critically evaluate which business avenue is the best option. Once this decision has been made, some preliminary financial projections can be made, and then a business plan prepared.

REVIEW QUESTIONS

1. Explain the respective advantages and disadvantages of starting and buying your own business.
2. What are the different formulas used to calculate the selling price of a business?
3. Explain the difference between a product franchise and a business system franchise.
4. What are the six steps to follow when starting a business venture?
5. What are the main differences between the three types of business start-up options?

DISCUSSION QUESTIONS

1. Why is it important to work out one's personal business goals before choosing a business venture option?
2. If you were preparing to sell your own business, what specific management actions could you take to maximise its selling price?
3. What personality types are best suited to the start-up, purchasing and franchising options respectively?

EXERCISES

1. *Using the ROI valuation technique.* Calculate the purchase price for a business with a $250 000 annual profit and a level of risk that commands a 15 per cent return on investment. What would be the purchase price for the same business if the anticipated ROI was 10 per cent?
2. *Altering earnings-based valuation factors.* Repeat the two calculations in exercise 1 above, but with a firm whose net profit is only $30 000.
3. *Using different valuation methods.* A business has tangible assets of $875 000 and liabilities of $50 000, and produces a net profit of $56 000 per annum based on a turnover of $430 000. It is a professional practice (multiple = 2) and has an ROI of 7 per cent. There are no intangible assets. Calculate the purchase price for this firm using each of the book (asset) value, market value (revenue multiplier) and ROI methods. Which of these three methods is the most appropriate one to use? Give reasons for your answer.

SUGGESTED READING

Holmes, S., Hutchinson, P., Forsaith, D., Gibson, B. & McMahon, R., *Small Enterprise Finance*, John Wiley & Sons, Brisbane, 2003.

Sherman, A.J., *Franchising and Licensing: Two Ways to Build Your Business*, American Management Association, New York, 1999.

Small Business Development Corporation, *A Guide to Buying a Small Business*, SBDC, Perth, 1998.

CASE STUDY

Charting a new future?

Megan Chu sat down in the late afternoon Wellington sun, enjoying the view out over Lambton Harbour. She was feeling excited and on the verge of a major new change in her life. Just this afternoon, while browsing through various New Zealand websites, she'd come across an advertisement that caught her eye.

Megan had always wanted to be her own boss, and hated her current job as a cartographer. She'd rung her cousin Andrew, an accountant with a local major firm, and asked him to meet her for coffee as soon as possible. She didn't want to let this chance go by, but she knew that some expert advice would also be critical.

'What do you think?' she asked hopefully, showing him the information she'd downloaded.

Andrew took a quick look and laughed out loud. 'You'd be mad to bid for this. Are you out of your mind?'

Megan's world felt suddenly shattered, and she couldn't understand her cousin's reaction. This seemed like a great opportunity, so why was Andrew so adamant that it would be disastrous? She looked again at the printout of the advertisement, which read as follows:

Name of business: Way To Go Maps & Books

Ownership: Partnership between John & Bradley O'Riordin

Description: Seller of specialised geographical printed resources (books, travel guides, street maps, touring atlases, wall maps and nautical charts) to local residents and industry in Wellington

Asking price: NZ$45 000

Background: This business was formed in 2004 and has operated continuously from the same premises (on a month-by-month tenancy) in Mount Victoria, a suburb of Wellington, since that time. There is no other such specialist business in the city.

Staffing: Operated by the owners and one full-time assistant, Marianne O'Connor

Legal: The firm owns a web address and has registered its business name.

More information: This business is being sold directly by the owners. Any further enquiries should be directed personally to them at the store.

Financial performance:

Profit and Loss (previous financial year)	
Sales revenue	235 000
Less: Cost of goods	120 000
Gross profit	115 000
Less:	
Operating costs	25 500
Administrative costs	23 500
Staffing costs	47 000
Net profit	19 000

Balance Sheet	
Assets	
Cash on hand	2 000
Maps and charts in shop	39 000
Fixtures, fittings	19 500
Accounts receivable	3 500
Total assets	64 000
Liabilities	
Accounts payable	15 500
Inland Revenue Department	6 500
Wages payable to staff	4 500
Total liabilities	26 500
Net equity	37 500

Questions

1. Is Andrew's assessment correct, or should Megan still go ahead and buy the business?

2. What questions does Megan still need to ask before deciding to buy or not?

3. What would be a reasonable asking price for the business?

ENDNOTES

1. J.A. Timmons, *New Venture Creation*, Richard D. Irwin, Homewood, IL, 1990.
2. Small Business Development Corporation, Western Australia, *A Guide to Buying a Small Business*, SBDC, Perth, 1998.
3. S. Holmes, P. Hutchinson, D. Forsaith, B. Gibson & R. McMahon, *Small Enterprise Finance*, John Wiley & Sons, Brisbane, 2003, p. 315.
4. H.H. Stevenson, M.J. Roberts & H.I. Grousbeck, *New Business Ventures and the Entrepreneur*, 3rd edn, Richard D. Irwin, Homewood, IL, 1989.
5. Small Business Development Corporation, *see* note 2.
6. D. Waldron & G.M. Hubbard, 'Valuation methods and estimates in relation to investing versus consulting', *Entrepreneurship Theory and Practice*, no. 16 (Fall), 1991, pp. 43–52.
7. R. McMahon, S. Holmes, P.J. Hutchinson & D.M. Forsaith, *Small Enterprise Financial Management: Theory and Practice*, Harcourt Brace, Sydney, 1993.
8. S. Weaven & L. Frazer, 'Current status of franchising in Australia', *Small Enterprise Research*, vol. 13, no. 2, 2005, pp. 31–45.
9. ibid.
10. National Bank of New Zealand, *Franchising Your Business: The Fundamentals*, Solution Guide, June, 2004, p. 1.

Chapter 6

Analysing opportunities and developing a strategy

LEARNING OBJECTIVES

After reading this chapter, you should be able to:

- explain how to evaluate entrepreneurial opportunities

- list the types of secondary research sources commonly available

- list some common forms of primary market research

- explain the different perspectives on strategy

- list the key steps of strategy formulation for new business ventures.

Y ou have your business idea and you have thought carefully about your own motivations and characteristics. Now you need to demonstrate that your idea represents an opportunity to build a business. Put simply, you need to show that there are people who will buy what you are hoping to produce and sell. This requires that you quantify the opportunity and develop an understanding of how much new value might be created. Obtaining information on the opportunity is viewed as an investment in the business, and must be considered as such. Information collected about the industry and the market, together with the firm-specific variables, will assist the entrepreneur in developing a strategy for the business.

In this chapter, we present a framework for analysing entrepreneurial opportunities. We consider methods of market research that examine how to use both secondary and primary sources of data, and we examine how strategy is formulated in new business ventures. The value of a well-considered and well-defined strategy is advocated.

A framework for analysing opportunities*

There are many different tools available for evaluating entrepreneurial opportunities, most of which have been developed by venture capitalists and business consultants. One such tool has been developed by ETeCH AG, a leading Swiss venture capitalist that provides seed funding to high-tech start-ups. The process used to identify significant commercially viable applications from original inventions is termed the ETeCH Technology Bridge™, because it builds bridges for technology into markets; this is illustrated in figure 6.1. The process consists of a series of strict filters that are first used to screen out technologies that are not viable owing to their lack of novelty or lack of ownership. It then precisely documents potential applications for viable technologies and screens out any that are not commercially viable. This process leaves the technologies that are viable, and these are narrowed down to those that are *significantly* commercially viable. Only upon these can a business plan be developed.[1]

The aim of the exercise is to determine all possible applications for the technology and then, from these, to select those for which there might be sensible buyers for sensible reasons at the right price. In addition, the projected return must be enough to justify the whole development process and give such buyers what they require. Although the process focuses on technology-based opportunities, it is also useful for other types of opportunity (e.g. incremental innovations and innovations in the service industry).

Essentially, the process aims to assess whether the opportunity suffers from one of several fatal flaws that make it impossible for a new business venture to succeed.[2] Just like the ETeCH Technology Bridge™, any tool that aims to assess an opportunity should address three critical issues:

- *Technical feasibility:* Can the product be made or service delivered using currently available, or at least feasible, technology?

* The authors acknowledge the contribution of R. Artley, G. Dobrauz, G. Plasoning & R. Strasser for this section. See R. Artley, G. Dobrauz, G. Plasoning & R. Strasser, *Making Money out of Technology*, Linde International, Vienna, 2003.

- *Marketing feasibility:* Does anyone want it? Has the product any features that someone values and would be ready to pay for?
- *Economic feasibility:* Can the product be developed, manufactured and distributed while generating a profit? Business ventures that are not based on a sound revenue model and cannot generate a profit cannot survive in the long run.

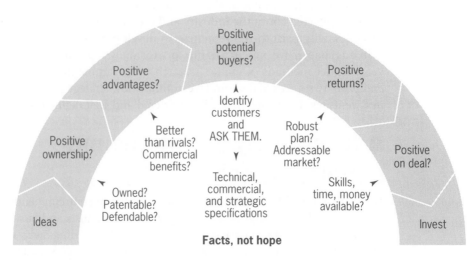

Figure 6.1: A framework for evaluating opportunities

Source: R. Artley, G. Dobrauz, G. Plasoning & R. Strasser, *Making Money out of Technology*, Linde International, Vienna, 2003.

Establishing the novelty, patentability and ownership

The first step of the process consists of determining the novelty, the patentability and the ownership of the innovation. Typically, about 50 per cent of opportunities would not pass this filter because the innovation is not genuinely novel, it cannot be patented or the entrepreneur does not own the technology; someone else, somewhere else, has already disclosed and/or patented it. Thus, even though the entrepreneur may have filed a patent, it could be challenged.

Is it novel?

Quite a few 'inventions' are not novel — findings in one field turn out to be well known in another, a situation not helped by specialist scientific jargon and acronyms. Many would-be entrepreneurs are in fact reinventing the wheel. An initial search on the internet might quickly reveal that an invention is not novel, since most leading scientific groups these days use the internet extensively to post details about themselves and their work. It is also easy to conduct a patent search via the websites of the main patent registration authorities in the world, such as the US Patent and Trade Mark Office (<www.uspto.gov>) and the European Patent Office (<www.european-patent-office.org>).

Is it patentable?

As will be explained in detail in chapter 8, a patent is a right granted for any device, substance, method or process that is new, inventive, and useful. Double-checking that the 'innovation' meets these basic requirements can potentially save a lot of work that would otherwise be wasted. Although commissioning a patent search costs money, it is not a vast amount, and the use of a professional patent lawyer is recommended.

Other new and useful innovations such as artistic creations, mathematical models, plans and schemes are not patentable but can be protected by other intellectual property rights. Trademarks, copyrights, and design rights may therefore have a valuable role and should be included in the search at this stage.

Who owns the technology?

Another key task in this first stage is identifying the owner/s of the technology. Innovations often take place in a variety of organisations and involve several people who may each have a different status within the institution. Three key questions will help in determining the ownership of the technology:

- *Was the innovation made while the inventor was affiliated with an organisation?* Today, most inventions are made in research laboratories located within universities or private companies. These organisations have policies that establish the ownership of inventions in detail.
- *Who was involved in the discovery of the invention?* There may be several individuals involved in the discovery of the invention. These individuals may each have a different status (such as lecturer or student) in the organisation, which can influence the ownership of the invention. This issue is usually covered in the policy of the organisation.
- *Who funded the research?* Research projects can be funded in a variety of ways, from state-funded research grants to industry-association research grants and company research grants. The contract signed with the research grant also covers the ownership of intellectual property resulting from the research project.

Does it work and is it better than existing products?

This is the point at which 30 per cent of 'innovations' fail. Cases of scientific fraud are few but do occur. More frequently there are misinterpreted results or, quite simply, a better product already exists.

Does it work?

How do you find out? One way is to conduct a peer review. Under suitable non-disclosure agreements, opinions should be sought from other leading professional scientists in the relevant technical field. They should also be able to inform you of any rival technologies.

Is it better than rival products?

An internet search should now be conducted using a search engine such as Google. Again, a skilled search will swiftly lead to the discovery of existing products if they are available. Separate searches should be conducted for each application of the technology, and they should be carried out in two ways: first, for the exact product, and second, for products that perform the same function. Which offers commercial benefit? Which is faster, cheaper and easier? Remember that the market is indifferent to how the technology works, instead buying the benefits that technology can provide. Industry reports are of limited value, because the market will have moved, but their web-published contents lists are a good way of checking relevant companies and technologies.

Through close examination of rival technologies, it is possible to determine which technical attributes are advantages. A good rule of thumb is that the new technology should have at least one feature that promises to be ten times better than its rivals, and this should be quantifiable in a definite measure such as dimension, speed, time, range or availability.

What applications?

The next step involves a creative brainstorm to devise potential applications. This process can be structured in such a way that for each of the technical advantages, possible current and future applications are considered. Creating such a list requires considerable ingenuity and insight ('think wide, think deep'), since it is common for a technology to generate many ideas on how it might be applied.

Applications generation can be done by pure brainstorming but, to achieve comprehensive coverage of potential applications, more structured methods are generally advised. This helps to ensure completeness and that each application is considered in isolation. These structured methods, which include attribute listing and mind maps, have been presented in chapter 3.

Are there commercial advantages?

Are the technical advantages relevant? In other words, do they enable commercial advantages for each of the applications? Note that there are only three types of commercial advantage: (1) the saving of time in comparison to existing products (time to market or to money); (2) the saving of money in comparison to existing products; or (3) the enabling of future, valuable products of a type not currently available. Potential applications can be dismissed because the technical advantages do not translate into commercial advantages. 'Smaller is only better if smaller is needed.'

Identify potential buyers

The next filter aims to check that there are indeed potential buyers — whether individuals or companies — willing to adopt and pay for the commercial advantages. Each of the applications with commercial advantages should be examined carefully to identify who the potential buyers might be. These buyers should then be contacted to verify that they would value the offered advantages if the development proved successful, and to determine what they would require in order to make such a decision. There is no greater reassurance of the viability of a novel technology than potential customers who clearly state that they would like to obtain and are willing to pay for the commercial advantages that the technology could offer.

It is not necessary to consider every potential customer at this stage; only a few 'lead buyers' should be contacted. Note that any 'not interested' answer from a potential buyer is only on behalf of that buyer alone — this individual does not speak for the industry as a whole or all existing rivals. Again it is worth checking why an offer has been rejected, as this allows any perceived or actual inadequacies to be addressed. Therefore, it is more effective at this stage to take a qualitative approach that involves contacting key potential customers to seek their opinions and discuss the product offering in detail.

Is there a positive return?

From consulting potential buyers you have an end-point specification; from the current state of the technology you have a starting point. The business plan is the document that links the former to the latter. It involves planning resources and developing a budget, which is then compared with the end-point value (the sales projections derived from a market survey) to ascertain the true market size that can realistically be captured.

What is the market size and attributes?

Would the market size and attributes lead to the advantages actually being paid for? In other words, are the applications viable or would the market either ignore their benefits (as nice but not needed) or wish to absorb the benefits (taking them if offered but not paying for them)? To find this out, questions must be asked about the size of the markets, the openness of the markets to new products or attributes, and the rate and direction of change in the markets. The result of this inquiry helps to identify potential market segments, determine paths to the market and ultimately generate sales projections. Methods of market analysis are discussed in the next section.

Drafting a business plan

The information gathered can be used to determine the commercial viability of a new start-up, product offering or purchase of a business. Usually, the feasibility analysis will be summarised in a business plan — the comprehensive document that serves as a 'roadmap' for new business ventures.

In chapter 7, the specific contents of a business plan are examined in detail. An examination of the plan will show that it essentially involves answering a great many questions, which can only be done effectively if accurate research is conducted beforehand.

Entrepreneur profile

Annah Stretton — Stretton Clothing Ltd

Annah Stretton is the founder and CEO of her own company, Stretton Clothing Ltd, which is based in Morrinsville, New Zealand. The company was founded in 1992, supplying bulk orders for mass-market chain stores. A qualified accountant, Annah saw an opportunity to supply large fashion retailers with well-styled knit garments. She secured regular large orders — up to 20 000 units — despite having no building to work from, no regular staff and no infrastructure.[3] These orders provided the launching pad for the business. As she could see an opening in the rural market for classic-style clothes at an affordable price, she later decided to set up her own boutique-style stores in Havelock North, Cambridge and Taupo.

Today Annah Stretton is one of New Zealand's best known designers with her Annah.S. label, which she re-branded to her full name of Annah Stretton in 2003. She also designs Garb, a label that caters for larger women. Her interest in the styles of many different eras is expressed in a rich combination of fabrics and accessories including safety pins, jewels, pearls and embroidery.

Stretton Clothing has consistently achieved yearly growth, reaching an annual turnover of NZ$8 million. The company has a strong presence in the New Zealand market, with 30 fashion retail sites (21 owned and nine franchised) operating throughout the country, employing more than 100 staff. Over the years, Annah has diversified her business base with the development of nine franchises in New Zealand, successful export markets in Australia, Europe, the UK and USA, plus the development of three fashion labels to maximise retail appeal.

Annah continues to have hands-on involvement in all parts of the business, from daily monitoring of cash flow to PR and the creative development of new collections. No job or opportunity is ever too minor for her to consider. She says: 'Leading by involvement connects me with every member of my team. I am not averse to spending a day in my warehouse, working alongside the team handling thousands of garments or assisting a franchise in organising a fashion show for a local Plunket fundraiser.' When asked whether she perceived herself as an entrepreneur or a designer, she stresses that art alone is not what fashion is about. She says: 'I drive a business as well, so I use a commercial edge to design.' She adds: 'I'm not a purist. I don't struggle like some others in this industry who are more artists.'[4]

In 2005, Annah Stretton ventured into new territory and bought *Her Business*, New Zealand's leading magazine for businesswomen. She sees *Her Business* magazine as a good vehicle for balancing creativity with the business bottom line and, importantly, sharing her success. 'I would like to make *Her Business* into one of the strongest business magazines out there — to produce a real resource that both inspires and empowers women in business,' she says.[5]

The role of market research

One of the most common problems faced by entrepreneurs is a lack of information that relates to their business idea. There is now much evidence to show that a lack of research is a key inhibitor to new venture creation.[6] A lack of effective research can also create less obvious barriers to business survival and growth:

for example, many venture capitalists report that the business plans presented to them by entrepreneurs often do not contain in-depth market information and analysis, thus reducing their prospect of obtaining investment capital.[7]

Market research:
The use of information to identify and define marketing opportunities and problems.

Market research refers to the use of information to identify and define market opportunities and problems. It is used to generate, refine and evaluate marketing-related activities within a small firm or to help determine future marketing strategies and sales forecasts for a new business venture.[8] Typical market research activities include identifying target markets for a new product; surveying members of these markets to understand their purchasing behaviour relevant to such products; and estimating the cost of producing an item and supplying it to the marketplace. The application of research to marketing issues is examined in chapter 11.

What to research?

One of the first issues to be considered is exactly what information should be investigated. As is frequently the case in marketing, a number of alternative frameworks for studying the wider environment are available, the most conventional of which describes it in terms of an 'onion'. This is a useful approach, since it distinguishes between three different degrees of interaction: the market, the industry and the macro-environment.

The market

As suggested in the previous section, the market is the primary concern for the entrepreneur. The market consists of the people or firms who could benefit from the use of the new product, who have the means to buy it and who will be offered the opportunity to do so.[9] Some specific information requirements about the market are:

- *The customer profile/s and segment/s.* What is the typical customer profile in terms of socioeconomic or other relevant dimensions? Are there different needs, requirements and buying behaviours among the customers?
- *The product or service.* How should it be tailored to meet customer needs?
- *Price.* What are competitors charging and what are customers' pricing expectations?
- *Sales and distribution channels.* What is the most appropriate distribution channel to reach the customers?

The industry

The industry is the next category to consider. Porter identifies five forces that determine the attractiveness of an industry, and he regards these as forming the micro-environment, as opposed to the macro-environment. These forces consist of those influences close to a company that affect its ability to serve customers and make a profit. As shown in figure 6.2, the five forces are: the risk of new competitors entering the industry, the threat of potential substitutes, the bargaining power of buyers, the bargaining power of suppliers, and the degree of rivalry between existing competitors. A change in any of the forces normally requires a company to reassess its position in the industry.

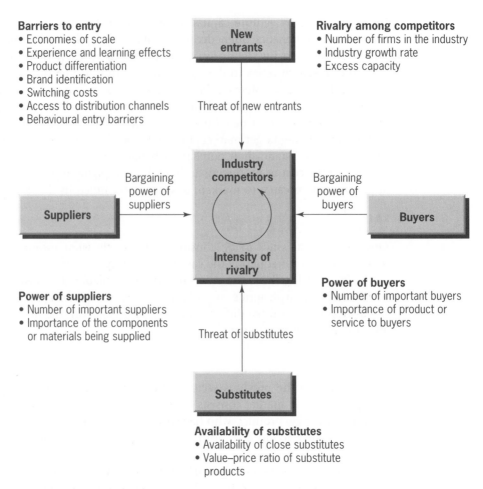

Barriers to entry
• Economies of scale
• Experience and learning effects
• Product differentiation
• Brand identification
• Switching costs
• Access to distribution channels
• Behavioural entry barriers

Rivalry among competitors
• Number of firms in the industry
• Industry growth rate
• Excess capacity

Threat of new entrants

Bargaining power of suppliers

Bargaining power of buyers

Power of suppliers
• Number of important suppliers
• Importance of the components or materials being supplied

Power of buyers
• Number of important buyers
• Importance of product or service to buyers

Threat of substitutes

Availability of substitutes
• Availability of close substitutes
• Value–price ratio of substitute products

Figure 6.2: Porter's five forces

Source: Adapted with the permission of The Free Press, a Division of Simon & Schuster Adult Publishing Group, from M. Porter, *Competitive Advantage: Creating and Sustaining Superior Performance*, Free Press, New York, 1985, p. 6. Copyright © 1985, 1998 by Michael E. Porter. All rights reserved.

The macro-environment

The macro-environment is often not recognised as a force impinging on organisations, and yet it may well contain the major factors that determine the performance of a new business venture. These external factors are most often grouped as the STEP factors (social, technological, economic and political), and they can have dramatic effects on organisations. A political factor such as legislation, for example, determines the boundaries of the actions of most organisations, and yet it is often 'taken as read', going relatively unnoticed in regard to its effect on organisational performance.

Environmental scanning: Analysing and understanding the internal and external forces that may affect a company's products, markets or operating systems.

Environmental scanning enables entrepreneurs to understand both the external environment and the interconnections between its various elements. In other words, environmental scanning is 'a kind of radar to scan the world systematically and signal the new, the unexpected, the major and the minor'.[10] Scanning provides intelligence that is useful in determining organisational strategies, and it helps in fostering understanding of the effects of change on an organisation; forecasting; and bringing expectations of change to bear on decision making.

Constraints on research

The ability to conduct effective research is constrained by several limiting factors. Each of these affects the final results that are available to the firm and the entrepreneur.

Cost

All research has a cost. It consumes not only money but also personal effort by owners or employees. 'Perfect' information, in the sense of data that is easily available, cost free, and fully relevant, is rare. Information is an expense, and costs arise both when the information is originally collected and when it is stored for future use. Entrepreneurs need to know how much this expense is likely to be and how much they are prepared to pay. Can the cost be justified? What is the cost of not collecting data? Which sources are being used? Is there another source of information that is cheaper or easier to use? Does the cost of collection outweigh the benefit of any information derived from it?[11]

Research experience and competency

Firms and individuals familiar with the conduct and analysis of information tend to be better researchers and to produce more meaningful results than novices in the area. On the whole, the generalist nature of small business management (the fact that the owner has to be competent in many different areas of business) and the lack of research experience by many entrepreneurs mean that few of them have well-developed skills in this area. As a result, the data they collect is often limited in scope and, consequently, value.

Reliability of data

What level of confidence can the entrepreneur have in the information collected? Is the data worth relying on or is further investigation needed to verify the claims made? Over-reliance on one or two key information sources can compromise the results of a study and any conclusions drawn. Wherever possible, it is best to use a variety of sources and research methods so as to overcome possible bias arising from the use of a single data source.

Personal prejudices

One common problem in research is the tendency to seek out self-verifying information, that is, seeking information that proves one's own biases or claims without adequately considering other contradictory material. Some entrepreneurs and business owners collect only the evidence that supports their initial biases and perspectives rather than information which provides a fully balanced and objective assessment.[12]

Uniqueness

Some entrepreneurial business ideas are so unusual and so different that there is very little existing research to help assess its viability. This is typically the case with a radical innovation that fundamentally changes the existing way of doing business or that offers a completely new product with which no-one is familiar. When this occurs, it may be very difficult to collect any information that is relevant to the venture idea. However, such occurrences are rare. Most products, services and processes have been trialled previously, and most innovation is in fact built on existing ideas and research.[13]

Time

The amount of time available to properly investigate an issue can vary enormously. Some intending business owners believe that a measured, detailed study over a substantial period of time is necessary to gain all of the required information for their business idea; others want to launch their venture as quickly as possible, even if this means compromising the amount of time spent conducting research.

The above limitations mean that most owner–managers operate in a situation of what has been termed 'bounded rationality'[14] — that is, their ability to make well-informed and logical decisions is often distorted by real-world constraints and restrictions on the actual information collected. Contrary to popular belief, research rarely follows a truly logical and sequential path; despite the best efforts of researchers, it is often affected by personal and organisational constraints.

Most of the existing studies of research-gathering among small business owners and entrepreneurs indicate that data collection and analysis tends to be disorganised, limited in scope, and heavily skewed towards one or two sources. In many cases, very little formal planning and research are done. Instead, owner–managers tend to rely heavily on their instincts and beliefs. Among existing small firms, market research is often limited to feedback from immediate customers.[15] When market research is undertaken, informal information sources such as friends and family members are favoured over more conventional data sources. There is often a strong distrust of formal market studies and methods.[16]

Conducting research

The business researcher has two main avenues when seeking and collecting information. One is to consult existing sources of data (secondary information) that will provide a general picture of the current state of knowledge about a particular problem or factor under investigation. Once this step has been completed, it often becomes necessary to investigate some issues in more detail by undertaking original research from primary data sources. Both are important to the information collecting process, although they have different roles to play.

Although it may be tempting and seemingly convenient to rely solely on just one of these research sources, effective research results can really only be obtained by consulting both types. Used together as twin arms of an integrated research strategy, primary and secondary data can allow the entrepreneur to develop a solid understanding of the business venture and the environment in which it operates.

Secondary information

Secondary data:
Business research
that has been
done previously.

Data that has already been collected, analysed and published by other parties is broadly defined as **secondary data** (sometimes called 'desk research'); that is, the reader receives the information secondhand.[17] Secondary data sources can take many forms, some of which are discussed below.

Publications

There are numerous books, magazines and industry journals relevant to the modern business environment (see table 6.1). General magazines can provide an overview of economic conditions, and feature stories can provide knowledge of competitors and the industry as a whole. Newspapers are also a source of information, both direct and indirect; they contain feature articles, and their advertisements may give a further clue about the marketing activities of competitors.

Although sometimes overlooked, trade magazines are particularly valuable, as they provide direct information about particular industries, product offerings, policy issues and likely future developments. Trade journals rate as one of the most frequently used sources of secondary data for established small businesses.[18]

Similarly, scientific publications, including reports and journals from academic bodies, can also be a good source of established research. Much of this information has been independently reviewed (validated) by other researchers prior to publication, and therefore tends to have a more substantial basis than do popular magazines and business periodicals.

Table 6.1: Major business newspapers and magazines in the Pacific Rim region

Country	Publications
Australia	*The Australian* *The Australian Financial Review* *BRW (Business Review Weekly)*
New Zealand	*The New Zealand Herald* *The National Business Review*
Singapore	*The Business Times* *Singapore Economic Review* *The Straits Times*
Malaysia	*Business Times* *Malaysian Business* *New Straits Times*
Hong Kong	*Asian Wall Street Journal* *Far Eastern Economic Review* *HK Enterprise*

Business directories

Much information is collated and presented on a commercial basis by a number of private sector organisations such as Dun & Bradstreet and Kompass. These directories can offer data on company backgrounds, credit risk, trading activities, business locations, office holders, staff size and history (see table 6.2).

The Yellow Pages and other similar telephone directories provide an often overlooked source of basic and useful information, such as the number of firms working in a particular industry category, their location and their product offerings. This often constitutes one of the first reference points when attempting to compile a list of competitors.

Table 6.2: Directories and general publications

Country	Publications
Australia	Dunn & Bradstreet Australia <www.dnb.com.au> Yellow Pages <www.yellowpages.com.au>
New Zealand	New Zealand Trade Directory <http://nztrades.com> UBD New Zealand Business Directory <www.ubd.co.nz>
Singapore	Times Business Directory <www.timesbusinessdirectory.com.sg> Singapore Business.com <www.singapore-business.com>
Malaysia	Business Directory of Malaysia <www.eguideglobal.com/my> Malaysia Company Directory Index <www.malaysia-index.com>
Hong Kong	Business Directory of Hong Kong <www.business-directory.com.hk> Hong Kong Enterprise Directory <www.hked.com>

Private market researchers and competitive intelligence providers

A variety of commercial researchers compile their own databases of company and industry information, which can be purchased by prospective users. However, such companies sell more than just streams of raw facts and figures (data). Instead, they sell processed and meaningful data (information). Performance benchmarks, industry and sectoral analyses, and company financial critiques are just some of the many different items that such researchers can provide information on.

While there are many small businesses and regional players providing these services, there are also several global companies in this field, such as Kroll, Euromonitor International, the Economist Intelligence Unit and Factiva. Kroll, for example, provides a range of services, including business intelligence, investigation services, and background and screening services. Factiva provides business news and information by sifting and analysing information from many mediums. It gathers information from print sources, newswires, websites and company reports, and it provides powerful filtering and results visualisation. Most university libraries subscribe to Factiva.com.

Government bodies

Government departments and agencies are another good source of information and research, although it may take some time to uncover the government agency with the most relevant data for a particular business project. Useful bodies can include statistical authorities and departments of commerce or trade. In countries with a federal or provincial structure, such as Australia and Malaysia, it may be necessary to contact national agencies and the corresponding state department as well. Table 6.3 lists some important national government and statistical websites.

Table 6.3: National government and statistics websites

Country	Website
Australia	Business Entry Point <www.business.gov.au> Australian Bureau of Statistics <www.abs.gov.au>
New Zealand	New Zealand Government Online <www.govt.nz> Statistics New Zealand <www.stats.govt.nz>
Singapore	Government of Singapore website <www.gov.sg> Department of Statistics <www.singstat.gov.sg>
Malaysia	Government of Malaysia website <www.gov.my> Department of Statistics <www.statistics.gov.my>
Hong Kong	HK Special Administrative Region Census and Statistics Department <www.info.gov.hk>

The internet

The internet is a rich source of information in many different ways. In addition to global search engines such as Google or Yahoo!, there are some specific national search directories (such as Sensis in Australia) that can help find relevant websites quickly. It is important to remember that search terms and concepts need to be relatively detailed to prevent too many irrelevant sites being uncovered, and that the spelling used in many Pacific Rim countries is subtly different from that used by US websites and search engines.

Other electronic sources that are often overlooked are the many chat rooms and virtual communities that exist online. These are forums in which people with a common interest in a particular topic interact electronically to discuss issues, share ideas and pass on information. It may be possible, for example, to access a chat room dedicated to alternative medicines and to brainstorm your ideas for a new herbal remedy you wish to develop. Such feedback is free and can usually be obtained very quickly.

Trade shows

Meetings and conventions that bring together manufacturers, distributors, competitors and regulators are an invaluable means of keeping up to date with developments in many industries. Trade shows are now common in many industries, including the mining sector, healthcare, tourism, sports retailing and manufacturing.[19]

Company annual reports

When looking for information about existing competitors and industry performance, it often pays to consult the annual reports that all publicly listed firms must prepare. Firms on a stock exchange are required to provide shareholders with information about their financial performance, their goals and mission, the composition of their board of directors, details about their key senior staff, and the products or services they offer. It is also common to provide a forecast of future activities and a comment on the general state of the industry (or industries) in which they operate.[20]

Industry associations

Many industrial and professional activities are represented by a trade association, chamber of commerce or related body. These are organisations established by business operators in a particular industry or region to promote the interests of members. To this end, such bodies undertake research, survey their members, publish data and promote a greater public knowledge about their industry and its economic significance. Associations are also helpful sources to consult when trying to gauge likely legislative, social and economic changes in an industry sector.

What would you do?

Pet services

Anna Lee is never short of new ideas. During a recent journey through New York to visit her cousin, she came across a service that every dog in the world could only dream about: a pet chauffeur. Anna's cousin, a successful investment banker on Wall Street, regularly booked a pet chauffeur to take his poodle to the vet. Anna is an overseas student, enrolled in the last year of a bachelor of commerce at a Sydney university. As she owns a dog in Hong Kong, she knows that pet owners need a variety of services for their companions. She loves dogs so much that she is often asked to housesit and take care of dogs belonging to friends who live in the affluent suburbs of Darling Point and Mosman.

Anna has several business ideas in mind. Emulating Pet Chauffeur, she would like to provide a service for the owners to commute with their dogs to work in fancy midtown offices. Another service could be social networking for pets. This would involve picking up the dogs for afternoon 'play dates' with friends or for dog birthday parties.

She also knows that pets can prove expensive if they become sick or are involved in a car accident. Unlike Medicare (the Australian public medical insurance), there is no such thing as bulk billing veterinarian bills for your animals. She recently read in *The Australian* that 'Hollard Insurance reported vet bills of A$4750 for an animal involved in a motor vehicle accident, and A$713 for dog fight lacerations.'[21] Pet insurance could therefore prove a good business opportunity as well.

Anna recently came across some facts and figures that clearly show a potential market. Of the 30 million pets in Australia, 3.9 million are dogs, 2.5 million are cats, 12 million are fish, and the rest comprise horses, rabbits, guinea pigs and other small pets.

Questions
1. What business idea seems more feasible? Why?
2. What sort of data can Anna collect to assess the market potential for her business ideas?

Primary information

Not all information takes the form of previously collected data. Once the process of secondary information collection has been completed, it will usually become apparent that additional input is needed. At this point, new information must be unearthed. **Primary data** refers to information that is collected first-hand for a specific research problem, and this is generally done once the secondary data process is complete. Primary information (which is sometimes also known as field research) is usually meant to 'fill in the gaps' that secondary research cannot answer.[22] As shown in table 6.4, there are four basic primary data collection techniques: observation, experimentation, surveys and interviews.[23]

Table 6.4: Types of primary research

Type of research	Advantage	Disadvantage
Observation	Cheap, convenient	No personal feedback
Experiment	Helps identify causal relationships Key variables can be influenced	Difficult to administer May not replicate actual business situation
Survey: telephone	Quick Can cover wide area	Misses personal cues Not everyone has a phone
Survey: personal	Very rich source of data Can elaborate on issues	Time-consuming, expensive
Survey: mail	Quick Can cover a wide area	Misses personal cues Data usually needs to be manually entered
Survey: email	Quick and cheap Can cover wide area	Misses personal cues Not everyone is online
Focus group	Cost-effective Deep insight into customer views	Time-consuming Difficult to generalise results
In-depth interview	Detailed explanation of an issue Flexible	Time-consuming Difficult to generalise results

Observation

Direct visual evidence of business activities is one of the oldest and most commonly used tools in research. Simply watching consumers in action is a very economical yet powerful way of understanding their behaviour. Observation can help solve many different research questions: What products do customers select from a supermarket shelf? How many people actually pass by the proposed business premises during the course of a working day? What retail floor outlet works best in attracting customers to a particular product display? Relatively simple measurements and recordings can be made while observing people in action.[24]

Experimentation

Experiments involve the comparison of groups or individuals who have been differentially exposed to changes in their environment.[25] At its most basic, the experimental method subjects groups of people to a change and then measures the outcome (dependent variable). At the same time, a second group (the control group) is also monitored to see if their outcomes change. An example of experimentation in action is to select a group of shoppers and see if they buy more products when the price is lowered. A second group of shoppers (the control group) would not be offered a lower price, but the number of items purchased (dependent variable) would still be measured. This approach is designed to determine whether a causal relationship exists between variables. Does lowering the product price lead to greater sales? Experimentation is not as widely performed in business research as observation or surveys.

Surveys

Survey:
A system for collecting information using a questionnaire.

Often the most effective way to collect information is by simply asking someone (a respondent) directly. This process requires a **survey** to be conducted, using the collection instrument known as a questionnaire — a series of predetermined questions for individual respondents to answer. This is a powerful research tool, since it allows investigators to collect much more information, in a potentially richer form, than either observation or experimentation permits.

There are many ways to administer a questionnaire. If there is a need to interact with the respondent, then an interview can prove the most adequate collection method. It is not always necessary to organise a face-to-face meeting in order to administer a questionnaire, as interviews can also be conducted over the phone or via a videoconference. The main advantage of the interview lies precisely in the interaction with the respondent. This can prove useful in rephrasing questions, making interjections and observing the non-verbal behaviour of the respondent. If there is no need to interact with the respondent, the questionnaire can then be administered via mail or email.

Focus group:
A small group of people with an interviewer trained to solicit their views about a particular issue or product.

Interviews

In-depth personal interview:
An interview that encourages respondents to explain their views, and which probes responses to explore an issue in greater detail.

Sometimes it may be more useful to talk to a small group of potential (or actual) consumers together, rather than individually. A **focus group** gathers data relating to the feelings and opinions of people involved in a common situation.[26] It involves a number of people (the best number is between five and 12) having a discussion with a trained interviewer, who solicits their views on a product, service or issue. This allows researchers to more cost-effectively collect data, and it provides a much deeper insight into the nature of consumer preferences and feelings.[27]

In-depth personal interviews encourage respondents to talk and explain their views. They probe ambiguous or interesting responses and generally explore an issue in more detail.[28] Such a personal discussion and question-and-answer session with people can often be a very helpful source of knowledge. Conducting an interview can take a lot of time but may reveal information that would otherwise remain concealed. Detailed discussions with people already working in the industry, retired businesspeople, trade and industry association representatives and academic researchers can help entrepreneurs compile background data for the overall industry analysis.

General issues to consider in primary research

Good primary research is often very hard to conduct. Although it may seem straightforward, there are many factors that can distort the results or give rise to erroneous conclusions:

- Is the *sample* — the group of people studied — representative of the general population or target market about which information is being sought?
- Is the *measuring instrument* used appropriate to the method chosen, especially when conducting interviews or surveys?
- How high is the *response rate*? Are the results of the study based on a large number of respondents or on only a few limited replies?
- Has the test been conducted in a *reliable* manner (that is, could another researcher using the same methods and sample collect the same results)?
- Is the information that is collected truly *valid* (that is, does it measure what the researchers claim it measures)?
- How *generalisable* are the results? Can they really be applied to people other than those in the sample group?[29]

Developing a strategy

The immediate objective of gathering information through market research is to determine the feasibility (commercial viability) of a new start-up business, product offering or purchase of a business. However, this information will also help to forecast likely future events, and it will provide the foundation for developing a strategy for the business venture. Strategy is important because of its role in the direction taken by the firm. Without a strategy, firms' short-term decisions will conflict with their long-term goals, so success is likely to be brought about by chance and thus cannot be reliably sustained or repeated.

Two perspectives on strategy

The strategy concept can be approached and interpreted from several points of view. It can be seen as a plan, a ploy, a pattern, a position or a perspective.[30] A strategy defines the business's direction and scope, and it will seek competitive advantage. Mintzberg[31] suggested that strategy development process should be about 'capturing what the manager learns from all sources (both the soft insights from his or her personal experiences and the experiences of others throughout the organisation and the hard data from market research and the like) and then synthesising that learning into a vision of the direction that the business should pursue'. The strategic fit between the internal aspects of an organisation and the external environment determines competitive advantage.

There are two dominating perspectives that explain how to achieve a strategic fit: the market-led view and the resource-based view. The market-led view proposes that firms gain competitive advantage through identifying external opportunities in new and existing markets and then aligning the firm with these opportunities. This approach is founded in the so-called 'strategy-conduct-performance paradigm'. The basic tenet of this paradigm is that the economic performance of an industry is a function of the conduct (or strategy) of buyers and sellers, which in turn is a function of the industry's structure.[32] In this approach, competitive changes within an industry determine which markets the business venture should enter, stay in or exit. This approach is presented in further detail in this section.

Alternatively, the resource-based view of competitive advantage suggests that, to maximise returns, the business venture should assemble and deploy appropriate resources that provide opportunities for sustainable competitive advantage in the business's chosen market. As explained in chapter 3, competitive advantage is thus created by distinctive, valuable firm-specific resources that competitors are unable to reproduce.

Figure 6.3 combines the market-led and resource-led perspectives to outline a process of strategy development. The model presented recognises that strategy formulation is intimately related to the personality of the entrepreneur. Typically, the entrepreneur and his or her team will consider both internal and external factors when developing a strategy logic — a subjective representation of the thinking of key persons in the business venture. The strategy logic forms a sort of information filter that screens relevant data. The filtered data is then integrated into the strategy, systems, goals and reinforced behaviour of the venture. The realised strategy is the outcome of the strategy formulation and the dominant orientation of the firm. This will in turn influence the performance of the firm.

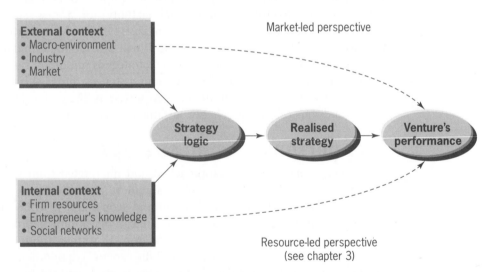

Figure 6.3: The process of strategy development

Market-led perspective on strategy

Chandler, one of the early thinkers in strategic management, considered strategy as 'the determination of basic long-term objectives of an enterprise, the adaptation of course of action, and the allocation of resources necessary for carrying out these objectives.[33] Therefore, strategy is intricately related to the development of a plan, specifying the enterprise's objectives, developing policies and plans for achieving these objectives, and allocating resources in order to implement the plans. Strategic planning is the highest level of managerial activity, usually performed by the entrepreneur and other key associates. It provides overall direction to the whole enterprise. Strategy formulation involves the following steps:

- *Setting objectives* by crafting a vision statement (a long-term view of a possible future), a mission statement (the role that the organisation gives itself in society), objectives (both financial and strategic) and goals.
- *Conducting a situation analysis*, considering both the internal (organisation-specific) and external (micro-environmental and macro-environmental) factors. Such analysis is usually conducted by examining the strengths, weaknesses, opportunities and threats (SWOT analysis) of the business venture.
- *Selecting a strategy* that will provide the enterprise with a competitive advantage.

This three-step strategy formulation process is sometimes referred to as determining where you are now, where you want to go and how you plan to get there. These three questions are the essence of strategic planning. A strategic plan should not be confused with a business plan. The former is likely to be a short document, whereas a business plan is usually a much more substantial and detailed document. A strategic plan can provide the foundation and framework for a business plan. For more information about business plans, refer to chapter 7.

Formulating a vision, a mission, objectives and goals

The preparation of a strategic plan is a multi-step process covering vision, mission, objectives and goals.

The first step is to develop a realistic vision for the business. This should be presented as a picture of the business's likely physical appearance, size and activities in three or more years' time. In order to formulate a vision, consideration must be given to the future products, markets, customers, processes, location and staffing of the business. For example, Macrokiosk, featured in the comprehensive case study on pages 458–61, has the following vision: 'Macrokiosk's vision is to become the leading mobile messaging technology enabler in Asia.'[34]

In the second step, the business attempts to indicate its purpose and nature by means of its mission. In Macrokiosk's case, the mission is 'to provide scaleable mobile messaging solutions to conveniently disseminate services over borderless markets and constantly satisfy customers beyond expectations'. A statement such as this indicates what the business is about and is more specific than saying, for example, 'We're in electronics' or, worse still, 'We are in business to make money'.

The third key step is to explicitly state the objective of the business — what it wants to achieve in the medium to long term. Aside from the need to achieve regular profits (expressed as return on shareholders' funds), objectives should relate to the expectations and requirements of all the major stakeholders, including employees, and should reflect the underlying reasons for running the business. These objectives could cover growth, profitability, technology, offerings and markets.

Next come the goals. These are specific interim or ultimate time-based measurements, and they are achieved by implementing strategies that pursue the company's objectives. For example, a business might aim to achieve sales of $3 million in three years' time. Goals should be SMART: specific, measurable, achievable, realistic and time-bound. They can relate to factors such as market (sizes and shares), products, finances, profitability, utilisation and efficiency.

SWOT analysis

Once objectives have been identified, the existing and perceived strengths, weaknesses, threats and opportunities are discovered and listed. The aim of any SWOT analysis should be to isolate the key issues that will be important to the future of the organisation and that will be addressed by subsequent marketing plans. Typically seen by managers as the most useful planning tool of all, SWOT puts some of the key pieces of information into two main categories of factors, internal and external, which can either help or impede the attainment of objectives. The essence of a SWOT analysis is that it precisely identifies:

- *strengths* — attributes of the organisation that are helpful to the achievement of the objective
- *weaknesses* — attributes of the organisation that are harmful to the achievement of the objective
- *opportunities* — external conditions that are helpful to the achievement of the objective
- *threats* — external conditions that are harmful to the achievement of the objective.

As shown in table 6.5, the results of SWOT analysis are often presented in the form of a matrix. Note, however, that SWOT is just one aid to categorisation. It also has its own weaknesses. It tends to persuade entrepreneurs and owner–managers to compile lists rather than think about what is really important to their business. It also presents the resulting lists uncritically, without clear prioritisation, so that, for example, weak opportunities appear to balance strong threats.

Table 6.5: SWOT analysis matrix

Attributes	Helpful to achieving objectives	Harmful to achieving objectives
Internal (attributes of the organisation)	Strengths	Weaknesses
External (attributes of the environment)	Opportunities	Threats

Selecting a generic strategy

A new business venture positions itself by leveraging its strengths. Porter[35] has argued that a firm's strengths can ultimately be divided into the two categories of cost advantage and differentiation. By applying these strengths in either a broad or narrow scope, three generic strategies result: cost leadership, differentiation and focus. They are called generic strategies because they are not firm- or industry-dependent. The development of generic business strategies is often a function of specific industry structure characteristics. That is, the success of any given strategy relates to the firm's ability to engage in activities that lead to increased concentration and to barriers that hinder the entry of other firms. The height of the barriers determines the extent to which superior profits can be gained.

- *Cost leadership*. This strategy emphasises efficiency. By producing high volumes of standardised products or services, the firm can take advantage of economies of scale and learning-curve effects. The product is often a basic no-frills item that is produced at a relatively low cost and made available to a very large customer base. Maintaining this strategy requires a continuous search for cost reductions in all aspects of the business. The associated distribution strategy is to obtain the most extensive distribution possible. Promotional strategy often involves trying to make a virtue out of low-cost product features.[36]

- *Differentiation*. This strategy involves creating a product that is perceived as unique. If this strategy is to be successful, the unique features or benefits must provide superior value for the customer. When customers see the product as unrivalled and unequalled, the price elasticity of demand tends to be reduced and customers tend to be more loyal. This can provide considerable insulation from competition. However, there are usually additional costs associated with the differentiating product features, and this could require a premium pricing strategy.[37]

- *Focus*. This strategy concentrates on a narrow segment and within that segment it attempts to achieve either a cost advantage or differentiation. The premise is that the need of the targeted segment can be better serviced by focusing entirely on it. A firm pursuing a focus strategy often enjoys a high degree of customer loyalty, and this entrenched loyalty discourages other businesses from competing directly. Firms that succeed in a focus strategy are able to tailor a broad range of product development strengths to a relatively narrow segment of the market that they know very well. The vast majority of start-ups and small businesses pursue a focus strategy.[38]

Towards 'blue ocean' strategies

Traditional business strategies originate from military models. As companies shape their strategies and plot their objectives, warlike metaphors abound: the business must confront its opponents, render them harmless and gain the advantage. Translated into strategy, this language generates a model for competing in a fixed market and gaining advantage over other entrants in the same field. However, bold competition may be essential in entrepreneurship and small business management, but it is not the only corporate strategy.

Blue ocean strategy:
A strategy aiming to develop compelling value innovations that create uncontested market space.

Kim and Mauborgne[39] recently suggested an alternative approach based on their conviction that effective strategies must be differentiated from convention. They argue that the only way to beat the competition is to stop trying to beat the competition. They called this approach **blue ocean strategy**. Blue oceans are 'untapped market space, demand creation, and the opportunity for highly profitable growth. Although some blue oceans are created well beyond existing industry boundaries, most are created by expanding existing industry boundaries...In blue oceans, competition is irrelevant because the rules of the game are waiting to be set.'[40]

The key element of a blue ocean strategy is value innovation: a combination of differentiation and low cost that sets a product line or service apart from its competitors. Examples of value innovation include Starbucks, which made coffee a neighbourhood treat, or The Body Shop, whose natural and affordable cosmetics established a blue ocean in a high-end industry full of pricey competitors. To succeed, a value innovation must demonstrate actual savings and an appreciable benefit that a customer can use immediately.

Yellow Tail is a typical example of value innovation. A wine created explicitly for the US market, Yellow Tail was launched in 2000 by Casella Wines, a small family-owned Australian winery. Casella altered the taste of its wine, making it fruitier and sweeter, and targeted beer and cocktail drinkers by promoting its wine as fun.[41] Breaking with traditional marketing techniques, Casella rejected the idea of relying on wine's elitist tag, with its emphasis on complex taste, ageing and vineyard location. It replaced the wine buff's jargon on the label with a distinctive kangaroo logo (the name and logo come from a small, colorful breed of kangaroo — the yellow-footed rock wallaby — known to roam the Casella vineyards). As a result of this strategy, Yellow Tail became the top-selling 750-ml-bottle red wine in the USA by August 2003. Casella also grew to be one of the largest wineries in Australia.

Entrepreneurs who want to develop a blue ocean strategy are advised to follow six principles:

- *Reconstruct market boundaries.* Entrepreneurs should re-evaluate the premises that form their industry's assumptions and shape their company business model. They must strategically examine their industry's key competitive drivers (such as customer preferences, product qualities, price and industry standards) to create a 'strategy canvas' that visually maps the current industry environment in two dimensions. The horizontal dimension includes the range of factors on which an industry currently competes and those factors in which it invests. The vertical dimension shows levels of performance against each factor, measured qualitatively.

- *Focus on the big picture, not the numbers.* Keep your eye on the overall view and do not get lost in the statistics. Many strategists get bogged down in data, so they often lose sight of where they are heading. To maintain a sense of direction, entrepreneurs can use the strategy canvas to visualise their competitors' products, price and industry position.

- *Reach beyond existing demand.* Businesses naturally focus current customers, a process that invariably leads to greater market segmentation analysis. However, real growth lies beyond existing demand. To reach open water, entrepreneurs must focus on future customers.

- *Get the strategic sequence right.* The strategy should be sequentially executed to achieve 'value innovation'. Simply having fancy new technology is not necessarily value innovation. To be compelling, the technology must provide convenience, safety and entertainment. Entrepreneurs are advised to check, at several stages, the experience they want their buyers to have. Similarly, they should assess their product's usefulness, ease, handiness, safety, entertainment value and environmental friendliness in from the point of view of the customer buying and using it.

- *Overcome key organisational hurdles.* Successful execution demands that the business venture must resolve internal differences. Since building a blue ocean strategy involves uncertainty and risk, creating trust among participants is essential. A successful strategy launch and implementation requires extra effort from a unified team.
- *Build execution into the strategy.* The management risk can be reduced by incorporating blue ocean implementation into the ongoing business process. Managers must link the three Es — engagement, explanation and expectation — with the actual process of developing the strategy and acting upon it at all levels of the organisation.

Summary

There are two important steps that entrepreneurs must consider in analysing opportunities. Firstly, all opportunities have to be screened in order to identify the significant commercially viable ones. Secondly, comprehensive market research has to be conducted to determine the size of the market and potential segments. Information collected about the industry and the market, together with the firm-specific variables, will help the entrepreneur to develop a strategy for the business.

One process used to identify significant commercially viable applications from original inventions is the ETeCH Technology Bridge™. It builds bridges for getting technology into markets. The process consists of a series of strict filters that are first used to screen out technologies which are not viable because they lack novelty or clear ownership. It then precisely documents potential applications for viable technologies and screens out all applications that are not commercially viable. From these commercially viable ones, only significantly viable applications are selected.

As soon as one or several commercially viable applications and lead buyers have been identified, comprehensive market research must be conducted to determine the size of the market and behaviour patterns in the different segments. When conducting the research, it is useful to consider the industry and the macro-environment, as well as the market. Both secondary and primary information have a role to play in the collection of credible research data. Secondary information sources include print publications, tertiary institutions, private market researchers, telephone and business directories, database vendors, government statistics and official reports, the internet, company reports and industry associations. Primary market research can take the form of direct observation, experimentation and surveys. Careful consideration has to be made as to the sample, the type of measuring instrument used, the type of question asked, the response rate, and the reliability, validity and generalisability of the results.

The information gathered during the research process will help forecast likely future events, and it will provide the foundation on which to develop a strategy for the business venture. Strategy is important because of its role in the direction taken by the firm. There are two dominating perspectives on the process of making strategy: the market-led view and the resource-based view. However, a new approach on strategy — blue ocean strategy — has recently emerged. Contrary to most corporate strategies based on military models and direct confrontations, blue ocean strategies build new business where none existed, giving innovative entries clear sailing. The core element of a blue ocean strategy is value innovation — that is, tangible product advancements accompanied by demonstrable savings.

REVIEW QUESTIONS

1. What are the key steps in analysing opportunities to identify commercially viable applications?
2. What are the factors that act as constraints to effective research?
3. List and briefly explain the different types of secondary research sources available.
4. Explain the process of strategy making.
5. What are the essence and the key principles of a blue ocean strategy?

DISCUSSION QUESTIONS

1. Many entrepreneurs rush to set up their business without properly assessing whether the opportunity is feasible. What are the key areas they typically fail to assess?
2. What are the limitations of desk research using secondary data?
3. Identify five simple rules for designing an effective questionnaire.
4. What are the main criticisms of strategic planning?
5. How can a firm create a competitive advantage?

SUGGESTED READING

Kim, W.C. & Mauborgne, R., *Blue Ocean Strategy*, Harvard Business School Press, Boston, 2005.

Lukas, B., Hair, J.F., Bush, R.P. & Ortinau, D.J., *Marketing Research*, McGraw-Hill, Sydney, 2003.

Moore, G.A., *Crossing the Chasm*, HarperCollins, New York, 2002.

CASE STUDY

Communicator

Sydney-based Communicator is a leader in mobile marketing and web development services. It specialises in developing strategies and creative platforms designed to leverage client brands and forge deeper relationships with the consumer. The company was established in 2000 by Damon Gorrie. At the end of the

2005–06 financial year, Communicator employed 27 staff in Sydney and four others in its newly created New York office. Communicator also generated a turnover of A$8 million. Although Communicator has mainly focused on three applications until now, Damon Gorrie is aware that there are other possible applications that should be assessed through market research.

Damon Gorrie became an entrepreneur at a very young age. When he was five, he started selling lemons from the family tree in Perth. His father also established several business ventures that young Damon got to hear about at the dinner table. By the age of 13, Damon was washing cars at a Melbourne radio station and making enough money to have two employees. 'It was a brilliant gig. And I did that for about two years and then got bored with car washing,' he says.[42]

Damon went on to study computer science at Monash University in Melbourne, where he obtained a bachelor of computing. 'I grew up with computers and I always had this sort of fascination for technology. And then I was involved in the dotcom industry and internet advertising, so I sort of had an idea of the potential of technology for marketing purposes,' he confesses. The growth of the mobile phone was just too big an opportunity to miss.

In late 2000, the emergence of internetwork operability provided an additional opportunity. Although short message services (SMS) had been around for a while, it was initially only possible to send same-network text messages; then suddenly people could receive an SMS from someone using another network. 'The idea of mobile marketing came about while I was having a drink with a friend on a Sunday afternoon at a pub in Oxford Street,' says Damon Gorrie. 'We realised we could send text messages to each other from different networks and we were running a lot of parties at the time.' Soon Damon and his technology colleague Jean-Claude Abouchar were texting other friends to let them know about their next event.[43]

The mobile marketing technology

Based on a variety of readily available statistics, Damon Gorrie estimated there were eight or nine million mobile phones in Australia, when the population was around 19 million people. The first numbers published by the telecommunications industry in the first quarter of 2001 indicated that there were 50 billion SMS messages sent globally. But apart from these broad figures, there was a lack of information regarding the industry. 'So we conducted our own research with the aid of Austereo, who had launched a platform because they saw the benefits based on these crude numbers,' comments Damon Gorrie.

He adds: 'We conducted survey information on the demographic profiles of potential consumers and types of use with the Austereo database and ran some promotions with the Austereo network to assess what area and what other applications we should be focusing on.'

The technology has improved too. The emergence of the third generation 'Universal Mobile Telecommunications System' (UMTS) represents an evolution in terms of capacity, data speeds and new service capabilities from second generation mobile networks. Third generations networks (3G) offer mobile operators significant capacity and broadband capabilities, which can support greater numbers of voice and data customers. Such networks now support Multimedia Message Services (MMS) which allow text messages to include longer text, graphics, photos and audio and video clips.

Applications

Marketing is usually defined as the 'process of planning and executing the conception, pricing, promotion, and distribution of goods and services to satisfy individual or organisational need.'[44] This definition implies sequential marketing stages as well as temporal and spatial separation between buyers and sellers. Mobile devices blur these boundaries and distinctions by extending traditional marketing's time-space paradigm. Mobile phones, free from traditional land-based internet connections, amplify the two main arguments of e-commerce — location independence and ubiquity.

To date, the main mobile marketing applications using SMS or MMS developed by Communicator include:

- *Information services.* These advertising-funded information services include news, weather, traffic, market rates and songs just played on the radio. This was one of Communicator's first applications, as Damon Gorrie developed an SMS-based application for Austereo. Listeners would text the radio to receive a return message listing recently played songs.
- *Customer relationship management (CRM).* Text messaging supports customer relationship activities such as free newsletters, pictures, ring tones, bonus points and coupons after joining a customer program. For example, Communicator devised a reverse queuing application to improve customer relations. 'No-one likes being put on hold by a call centre,' says Damon Gorrie. 'But imagine sending an SMS to the call centre. Because your mobile number rides along with the SMS, they can call you back. You don't wait. They serve you!'
- *Entertainment.* Entertainment services can increase customer loyalty and add value for the customer. As most people have a natural playfulness, providing games and prizes via text messaging yields high participation. One of the first applications in this field was designed for Pepsi in 2001. Pepsi consumers could SMS the unique code on a can of Pepsi and win an instant prize. 'With such an impulse-buy product, the SMS technology is more convenient than using the internet or a 1900 phone number dial-in,' says Damon Gorrie.

Other new possible applications include mobile couponing (sending coupons to mobile phones via SMS); branding (conducting a branding campaign via SMS or MMS); and product launches (providing information about new products and services). However, Communicator is not keen to move into push-marketing activities, sending unsolicited messages, 'because there are a lot of people doing emails and spam and that was the first area where people saw SMS as the opportunity,' says Damon Gorrie. 'We stay away from that just because the mobile is such a personal device. So our whole philosophy is getting the individuals to actually want to interact with an application or a brand.'

Business model

Communicator has four different revenue streams. The first revenue stream is the agency model. In this case, the company invoices clients based on the creative concepts and strategic thinking provided to them. The second stream is revenue generated through actual application development and customisation for clients and through setting up technology solutions. The third way of generating revenue is through SMS traffic and premium billing. Finally, the fourth revenue stream comes from licensing services solutions or technology to clients and other agencies (even competitors), allowing them to connect to Communicator's SMS gateways. In doing so, the client connects to the carriers and uses Communicator's applications. This allows smaller agencies to run their own activity.

Based on this model, Communicator can offer a flexible service to a variety of clients. Damon Gorrie says: 'Clients pay us initially for the thinking and the strategy. Then we set up the actual activity, so they pay us for the development of the application. And lastly we get the trailing revenue through the SMS volumes.'

Source: Based on author's interview with Damon Gorrie.

Questions

1. What are the advantages of mobile marketing over traditional marketing and online marketing?

2. What new applications do you think offer the greatest potential for Communicator?

3. What market research would you suggest conducting in order to determine the size of the market for new applications?

ENDNOTES

1. R. Artley, G. Dobrauz, G. Plasoning & R. Strasser, *Making Money out of Technology — Best Practice in Technology Exploitation from Academic Sources*, Linde International, Vienna, 2003.
2. J. Legge & K. Hindle, *Entrepreneurship: Context, Vision and Planning*, Houndmills, Palgrave Macmillan, 2004, p. 94.
3. 'It's the orders you write, sweet pea', *Unlimited: Business with Imagination*, <http://unlimited.co.nz>, 1 December 2005.
4. M. MacKinven, 'Mentoring, making it overseas and women in business: Designer Annah Stretton gets frank', *Business to Business*, 7 February 2006.
5. 'Annah Stretton to re-vitalise her business mag', *Scoop*, no. 20, January 2006.
6. C.G. Brush, 'Marketplace information scanning activities of new manufacturing ventures', *Journal of Small Business Management*, vol. 30, no. 4, October 1992, pp. 41–54.
7. G.E. Hills, 'Market analysis of the business plan: venture capitalists' perceptions', *Journal of Small Business Management*, vol. 23, no. 1, January 1985, pp. 38–47.
8. P. Kotler, S. Adam, L. Brown & G. Armstrong, *Principles of Marketing*, Prentice Hall, Sydney, 2001, p. 93.
9. J. Legge & K. Hindle, *see* note 2, p. 104.
10. J. Pfeffer & G.R. Salancik, *The External Control of Organizations*, Harper & Row, New York, 1978.
11. M. Evans, 'Market information and research', in K. Blois (ed.), *The Oxford Textbook of Marketing*, Oxford University Press, Oxford, 2000, pp. 150–74.
12. W.L. Neuman, *Social Research Methods*, 3rd edn, Allyn & Bacon, Boston, 1997.
13. J.G. Longenecker, C.W. Moore & J.W. Petty, *Small Business Management: An Entrepreneurial Emphasis*, 11th edn, South-Western, Cincinnatti, OH, 2000, p. 154.

14. H.A. Simon, 'Rational choice and the structure of the environment', *Psychological Review*, vol. 63, 1956, pp. 129–38.
15. G.E. Hills & C.L. Narayana, 'Profile characteristics, success factors and marketing in highly successful firms', in R. H. Brockhaus (ed.), *Frontiers of Entrepreneurship Research: Proceedings of the Babson College Conference on Entrepreneurship*, 1989, pp. 354–62.
16. T.J. Calahan & M.D. Cassar, 'Small business owners' assessments of their abilities to perform and interpret formal market studies', *Journal of Small Business Management*, vol. 33, no. 4, October 1995, pp. 1–10.
17. P. Kotler, G. Armstrong, L. Brown & S. Adam, *Marketing*, 4th edn, Pearson, Sydney, 1998, p. 159.
18. C.G. Brush, *see* note 6.
19. J.R. McColl-Kennedy & G.C. Kiel, *Marketing: A Strategic Approach*, Nelson Thomson, Melbourne, 2000, pp. 617–8.
20. J. Dunn, 'The devil's in the details', *Weekend Australian*, 9–10 November 2002, p. 34.
21. G. Bullock, 'Pet project: furry friends bite into your health bill', *The Australian*, 8 October 2003, p. 10.
22. P. Burns, *Entrepreneurship and Small Business*, Palgrave, London, 2001, p. 119.
23. P. Kotler, S. Adam, L. Brown & G. Armstrong, *see* note 8, p. 101.
24. D. Bangs & M. Halliday, *The Australian Market Planning Guide*, 2nd edn, Business & Professional Publishing, Sydney, 1997.
25. W.L. Neuman, *see* note 12, p. 176.
26. J. Hussey & R. Hussey, *Business Research*, Macmillan, London, 1997, p. 155.
27. P. Kotler, G. Armstrong, L. Brown & S. Adam, *see* note 8, p. 166.
28. G.W. Ticehurst & A.J. Veal, *Business Research Methods*, Longman, Sydney, 2000, p. 97.
29. J. Hussey & R. Hussey, *see* note 26, pp. 57–8.
30. H. Mintzberg, 'The strategy concept: five P's for strategy', *California Management Review*, vol. 30, no. 1, pp. 11–24.
31. H. Mintzberg, 'The fall and rise of strategic planning', *Harvard Business Review*, January–February 1994, p. 107.
32. J.S Bain, *Barriers to New Competition*, Harvard University Press, Cambridge, MA, 1956.
33. A. Chandler, *Strategy and Structure*, MIT Press, Cambridge, MA, 1962.
34. Macrokiosk, *Vision*, <www.macrokiosk.com>.
35. M.E. Porter, *Competitive Strategy*, Free Press, New York, 1980.
36. This paragraph is reproduced from Porter Generic Strategies, <www.answers.com>.
37. ibid.
38. ibid.
39. W.C. Kim & R. Mauborgne, *Blue Ocean Strategy*, Harvard Business School Press, Boston, 2005.
40. ibid.
41. 'Blue ocean strategy', <www.getAbstract.com>, p. 4.
42. 'Damon Gorrie: the party boy turned communicator', *Small Business*, <http://smallbusiness.ninemsn.com.au>.
43. ibid.
44. American Marketing Association, 'AMA Board approves new marketing definition', *Marketing News*, vol. 19, no. 1, 1985, p. 1.

Preparing a business plan

LEARNING OBJECTIVES

After reading this chapter, you should be able to:

- explain what a business plan is
- list the advantages and disadvantages of using a business plan
- state the major elements of a business plan
- explain how plans may differ in a number of variables
- explain the business-planning process.

Starting and organising a business venture is a demanding task. Whether one is buying an existing business or beginning a brand-new enterprise, there are always many tasks to do and issues to deal with. One way is simply to deal with each question or problem as it arises. The other strategy, long favoured by business advisers and commentators, is to carefully plan the business venture at the start.

In this chapter, the notion of business planning is defined and explained. We also compare the benefits and disadvantages of planning. The major elements of a plan are discussed, as is the process by which an effective plan is prepared and implemented.

The concept of a business plan

Business plan:
A written document that explains and analyses an existing or proposed business venture.

A **business plan** is a written document that explains and analyses an existing or proposed business venture. It spells out in some detail the business owner's intentions for the future of the firm. As such, it is a forecast, or forward projection, of a business idea. It explains the goals of the firm, how it will operate and the likely outcomes of the business venture.

In some respects, a business plan can be likened to a 'blueprint' that an architect prepares for a new building, or that an engineer drafts for a new piece of machinery. In each case, a document is prepared that gives the reader an overview of what the intended project will look like, how it will work and what activities must take place to reach the final goals.

Business plans can be applied to any type of enterprise, small or large, and can be equally useful to existing firms as well as new businesses. It is an organising tool that helps structure, communicate and sell an entrepreneur's or small business owner's idea and convert it into reality.

Although some research has shown that successful businesses are more likely to use plans than their unsuccessful competitors, the level of business planning undertaken by firms can still be surprisingly low.[1] In Australia, for example, a comprehensive survey of several thousand enterprises revealed that only 16 per cent of businesses had a formal plan and that most of these tended to be large, well-established firms.[2] A more detailed analysis of this study, along with similar research conducted in subsequent years, revealed that large firms tended to plan more than their smaller counterparts.[3] Small firms were, on balance, less likely to have a plan, even though the need for such a document is probably just as strong within these enterprises. A large-scale study of New Zealand business practices and performance found that, although most firms in that country did indeed undertake some sort of planning, most of it was relatively short term in focus, with the most successful firms tending to be the ones more likely to adopt a formal plan.[4]

The advantages and disadvantages of planning

A number of benefits can accrue from the development of a business plan.[5] A well-prepared business plan provides a clear statement of direction and purpose for a firm. It allows management and employees of the firm to work towards a set of clearly defined goals, thus enhancing the likelihood of the goals being reached.

This allows the organisation to take the initiative in determining its fate, rather than just reacting to events that occur in the outside environment.

Planning also provides a suitable yardstick for periodically evaluating the performance of the firm. Different quantifiable targets, such as sales revenue, the number of items sold, market share and profitability, can be compared with the actual results at the end of the plan period.[6] Entrepreneurs need to assess the reasons for substantial discrepancies between the forecast and the actual results and initiate action to overcome the gaps.

Because it is a comprehensive document, a business plan encourages managers and entrepreneurs to effectively review all aspects of their operations, rather than just dealing with day-to-day issues and problems.[7] The review and decision-making processes involved in business plan construction foster the more effective use of scarce resources (such as staff, time and money), improve coordination among staff members and promote greater internal communication. Since an effective plan also demarcates responsibilities, spelling out the roles of key personnel, it helps clarify job expectations and improves the accountability of staff to the owner–manager.

In addition, the very process of collecting information, analysing it and integrating it into a written document can help ensure that the entrepreneur or small business owner has adequately researched the business idea. If properly done, preparation of a business plan will foster skill development in the process of balanced and objective data collection, systematic analysis of the positive and negative results revealed by the research and the development of a comprehensive business response strategy that integrates all activities of the proposed venture with its internal and external environment.

Other people, including professional advisers, accountants, other owners and the firm's staff, can provide feedback on the accuracy of the completed business plan before it is implemented. This can avoid costly mistakes by identifying and eliminating any errors at the start.

However, it is also important to bear in mind that business plans, in themselves, are not a guarantee of success. Although some research indicates that failed firms are less likely to have a business plan than other businesses, the mere possession of a plan does not ensure survival.[8] No plan can promise success, although preparation of such a document does tend to enhance many of the critical and analytical skills that successful entrepreneurs strive for.

Plans on their own cannot eliminate uncertainty for no organisation exists in a completely predictable environment. No forecasts will be completely accurate and no written plan in itself is a guarantee of success, since this will ultimately rely on a combination of both internal and external environmental factors.[9] In addition, many entrepreneurs have often expressed their fear that a high level of planning will reduce their flexibility and room to move, rather than enhance it.[10] In some cases, an inflexible over-reliance on a predetermined plan, even in the face of overwhelming evidence of significant changes taking place in the business environment, can do more damage to the business than might otherwise be the case.

There are several other errors that may reduce the effectiveness of a plan. Common failings can include a lack of sufficient detail in explaining the intentions of the entrepreneur or small business owner; relying on outdated, limited or biased information; failure to undertake detailed market research to validate the sales forecasts, expense estimates and marketing plans of the enterprise; and preparing a document that appears self-evident to the writer, but cannot be understood by other readers.[11]

How effective are plans to the overall success of a business? This is a debatable point. For many years, researchers have tried to quantifiably measure the impact of a business plan on a firm's performance. Intriguingly, studies into this question have failed to conclusively show that planning is beneficial.[12,13] Although many reports show a link between business planning and firm survival or growth, other studies have produced contradictory results.[14] In the absence of clear-cut data to support one side of the argument or the other, it is up to individual business owners to make their own decisions on whether to use a plan and the extent to which formal planning processes should be incorporated into the management of their business ventures.

Elements of a business plan

There is no universal format for a business plan; the structure of individual documents can vary from one writer to another. Despite this, most documents include a common mix of items, since there are universal issues that all business enterprises must deal with.[15]

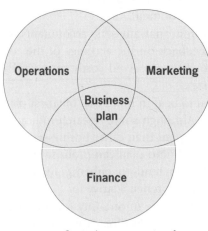

Figure 7.1: Central components of a business plan

The main issues dealt with in all business plans can be broadly grouped into those relating to marketing, operations and finances (see figure 7.1). These three elements are universal. All business owners and entrepreneurs need to research their market, know their customers, understand the state of the industry they operate in and have a comprehensive knowledge of the products or services they sell. They must also be able to structure, manage and operate the business in a logical manner, so that it can work effectively on a day-to-day basis. Finally, they must know how much money is required to start the business, its prospective sales turnover and what returns they are likely to receive from it. The business plan is the point at which these three aspects intersect and align themselves with one another.

One possible format of a plan is discussed below. It covers the three core elements of marketing, operations and finances, and considers additional issues that help round out the business idea and explain it comprehensively. At the end of this chapter, there is an example business plan for a small personal consulting business based in Sydney that follows the same plan structure. As you read through this chapter, it will become apparent that much of this material needs more detailed explanation than is given here; that additional information is provided in other chapters of this book.

Title page

The title page normally shows the name of the business and the owners, and provides contact details (addresses, phone and fax numbers, website URL and email addresses).

Executive summary

An executive summary is an introductory segment briefly summarising the key features that are explained in more detail later in the plan. It is a quick 'snapshot' of the idea and is often critical in influencing a reader's judgement of the whole document. Typically, it discusses the following items.

- *Business ideas and goals.* This section provides an overview of the business project, what product or service is being sold and what the entrepreneur's goals are. It also indicates where the business expects to be in a year's time and later.
- *Marketing.* How will the products or services of the business be sold? Who will be the main target markets (customer groups) and what are the main elements of the proposed advertising and promotional strategy for the firm?
- *Operations.* Where will the business be located? How many staff will there be and how will they be organised? What is the legal structure of the business? How will it be managed?
- *Finances.* What profit is the firm expected to make by the end of the business-plan time period? What finance is required and what will it be used for? Where will such capital be obtained from and what will the repayments be?

Background

In this section, the business owner or entrepreneur sets down the issues driving the business project. These include:

- *Mission statement.* What is the philosophy and overall vision that the owners have for the business? Why do they want to start and run such a venture?
- *Company history.* Many existing businesses already have well-established systems, products and operating processes and a customer base. It is important to briefly outline these before discussing the changes planned for the future. This segment typically explains how long the enterprise has been in existence, what products or services it sells and its achievements (and problems) to date.
- *Business goals.* What are the goals of this business? It is useful to provide both short-term goals (those for the next 12 months) and long-term ones (those covering the next 2 or 3 years, or perhaps even longer). It is always desirable to provide some specific, measurable targets (such as net profit sought, anticipated sales revenue, number of staff employed, product range offered and market share to be held) rather than vague or ambiguous statements (such as 'to be the

best business in our field') that cannot be evaluated or used as a yardstick for subsequent performance appraisal.

An important, but often overlooked, aspect of goal setting is the development of an exit strategy — that is, what the entrepreneur needs to do to get out of the business. As chapter 15 discusses in more detail, many entrepreneurs hope to build their wealth by eventually selling their business. A proposed exit strategy is also important for venture capitalists and other investors who usually want to know how their investment will be returned to them.[16] This segment should cover the method of exiting, timeline for such events and steps needed to bring the business to this point.

Marketing

The marketing segment provides the rationale for the existence of the business. Among other things, it gives the entrepreneur the opportunity to show what market research has been done, the likely level of demand for the firm's products, what exactly will be sold by the firm and the intended customer base.

- *Market research.* What research has been done to prepare the plan? It is a good idea to list the primary and secondary sources consulted. If appropriate, attach the results of any surveys, or other particularly relevant data, as an appendix.
- *Market analysis.* What is the result of the research? It is especially important to cover the following issues:
  - *Industry:* What are the characteristics of the industry in which the firm will operate? This section is especially concerned with providing an overview of the industry as a whole, rather than the individual business. What is the current state of that industry and what are the likely prospects for future growth? A common tool used in such analyses is Porter's five forces model.[17] If deemed appropriate, this or other models can be used at this point.
  - *Seasonality:* Are sales in this industry likely to be affected by changes at different times of the year?
  - *Competitors:* How many competitors are there, both direct and indirect? Who are the main players and what is known about them (such as where they are located, what they sell, what prices they charge, how long they have been in the industry, their after-sales service, staffing and customers' views of them)?
  - *Potential strategic allies:* Are there other firms that the business can work with on joint projects, cross-referral of work or in other ways that provide mutual benefits?
  - *SWOT analysis:* Using the above data, as well as one's own understanding of the business idea, it should be possible to construct a table or list that identifies the various *strengths* and *weaknesses* of the business, as well as the *opportunities* and *threats* that it faces.
- *Marketing plan.* In this section, the four Ps of marketing are dealt with.
  - *Products/services and target market:* Describe or list the main product(s) and/or service(s) to be sold by the business. If making a product, how will it be packaged? What is the target market (who are the main groups of customers for the product/service mix)? Describe the main characteristics of each customer group (such as their age, sex, income level, locality and family structure), their

motives for buying this product and the likely number of purchasers in each group. Does one target market have priority over others?

- *Placement (distribution channel):* How will goods be distributed to customers? What costs and legal issues may be involved?
- *Promotions and advertising:* How will the venture's goods and services be advertised and promoted to consumers? What media will be used? Who is responsible for promotions and what is the cost of each method? It is advisable in this section to map out the advertising and promotions schedule for the course of the whole year.
- *Pricing policy:* What prices will be set? What sort of pricing strategy will be used? Will there be any discounts for bulk purchases or special customer groups? Will credit terms be offered to any clients?
- *Evaluation of marketing.* How will the effectiveness of the marketing program be assessed? What performance indicators will be used to measure success and how often will this be done?

Operations and production

Organisational details, day-to-day operating processes and other issues that do not have a clear marketing or financial role are usually discussed here.

- *Legal and licensing requirements.* Include the business name and the legal structure of the business and the laws and licences that the business operates under or must obtain.
- *Management details.* Provide background details about the owners and/or managers, including full name, residential address, phone number, email address, date of birth, qualifications, special skills and job history. Is there any other information about the proprietors that could be important? Do the proprietors have any outstanding loans, guarantees or other financial exposure? Have they ever been bankrupt or charged with an offence that could affect their ability to operate the business? What previous business experience do they have?
- *Organisational structure and staffing.* Who will do which jobs in the business? If there will be more staff than just the owner–operator, who else will be employed? What skills and qualifications do they need? How will the firm recruit staff and at what rate of pay? What further training will staff need? If possible, include an organisational chart for the firm.
- *Professional advisers.* Provide the names and contact details of all the outside business and technical advisers the business expects to use. This may include an accountant, a bank manager, an insurance broker and management consultants.
- *Insurance and security needs.* What insurance will be required for the business and how much will it cost? Are there any special security precautions that need to be considered for the business's property and equipment?
- *Business premises.* Discuss and explain all the issues related to location. Where will the business be based? How accessible is this to customers? Is it convenient to local roads and transport services? If the proposed site is to be leased, what rent, lease period, payments and conditions apply? Are any special facilities required (that is, does the business need a certain building size, specialised customer access, special lighting, airconditioning or rest rooms)?

- *Plant and equipment required.* What equipment does the business need? Provide a list of likely needs, along with the type and make, cost, life expectancy, running costs and service and maintenance requirements.
- *Production processes.* Briefly explain how the product is made, including the supply of any raw materials or trading stock, production processes in the premises and any related issues.
- *Critical risks and contingency plans.* All businesses face potential problems and threats that can derail the goals outlined in the business plan, or possibly even destroy the firm. Although not all of these can be identified in advance, major ones should be discussed here, along with strategies for dealing with such issues if they arise.

Financial projections

In this section, the financial documents are presented, along with background notes and information that help a reader make sense of the financial forecasts.

- *Basic assumptions and information*
  - Explain the assumptions made in estimating income and expenses and in calculating the various documents. Justify any unusual items, significant omissions or unusual variations in the figures. What estimates have been made about inflation or increases in costs, wages and interest rates?
  - It may be useful to provide details about the bank accounts that the business operates. What financial institution are these with, what type of account is it (savings, cheque or cash management) and what fees are charged? Does the financial institution have the facilities that the business might need (such as credit card access and online or telephone banking)?
  - Does the business currently have any loans or overdrafts outstanding? Provide details about the lender, the amount borrowed, the current balance still outstanding and the terms of the loan.
  - If additional funds are needed by the business, how much and how are they to be raised? If this money is to be borrowed, provide information about the proposed lender, total amount sought, date required, monthly repayments due, interest rate, loan conditions and term (duration) of the loan.
- *Financial forecasts*
  - *Sales mix forecast:* Use market research and/or past performance to determine likely sales revenue for the first 12 months. Estimate the number of items sold each month, sales income from these and cost of goods sold.
  - *Cash flow forecast:* A cash flow statement summarises the monthly amount of cash movements (cash inflows and cash outflows) and the resulting cash balance for a year.
  - *Projected profit and loss statement:* Also known as a 'statement of financial performance', this shows business revenues, expenses and net profit for the forthcoming year.
  - *Balance sheet:* Also known as a 'statement of financial position', the balance sheet reports a business's financial position at a specific time. It provides details about the assets (financial resources owned by the firm), liabilities (claims against these resources) and net worth of the business. A balance

sheet is usually not provided for a new business. (There is no balance sheet in the sample plan in the appendix to this chapter because Blueprints Business Planning Pty Ltd is a new business. However, a sample balance sheet can be found in figure 14.2 on page 350.)

- *Personal expenses, assets and liabilities:* Since much of the capital funding for a new or small business venture is provided by the owner, it is often recommended that the business plan contain details about the owner–manager's personal assets and liabilities. In addition, since the owner usually draws income from the business, it is a good idea to include an estimate of likely personal expenses that will need to be drawn from the business.

- *Analysis of financial forecasts*
  - From the data provided, it may be desirable to conduct ratio analysis or other pertinent calculations. These could include (but are not necessarily limited to) an estimation of break-even point, fixed and variable costs, contribution margins, mark-ups and margins.

Implementation timetable

This section provides a schedule of the activities needed to set up and run the business. It is usually organised on a monthly basis, providing a set of milestones for the owner–manager to work by.

Appendixes

In this section, includes any extra useful information such as résumés of the entrepreneur and key management personnel, credit information, quotes for major capital purchases, leases or buy/sell agreements, other legal documents, competitors' promotional material, maps of the business site, floor plans of the business premises, and reference sources and key statistics collected during the market research process.

Different types of plans

Not all plans follow a common template. There are many different structures and sometimes also a difference in the emphasis that entrepreneurs/owner–managers put on particular issues.[18] One of the key features of a business plan must be its flexibility — that is, its ability to accommodate the changing needs of the business and its owner, and to be adjusted as circumstances dictate. In this section, we briefly examine some of the major causes of variations among different plans.

Specificity

In some enterprises, business plans are highly specific and detailed. This is often the case, for example, in a very small micro-enterprise, where there may be only an owner–operator involved in the firm. When a firm is new, small and focused on a limited target market with a constricted product range, it is relatively easy to prepare a business plan that covers all details. In contrast, larger firms may find that their plans are more generalised, owing to the diverse range of their business operations and product range, and the high staff numbers they must take into consideration.

Length

There is no one 'ideal' length for a business plan. Some are simple documents with no more than 10 pages, and others can be several hundred pages long. For some organisations (especially smaller ones), a short plan is a good plan. A document that is too long is unlikely to be regularly consulted and may be left in a desk drawer where it is soon forgotten. Other business ideas, however, may require much more elaborate explanation and detail. This is especially likely where very large sums of money are being committed, there are numerous parties involved in the business venture, the product or service offering is complex or the organisational requirements are substantial.

Audience

To whom is the business plan addressed? Is it written mainly for the benefit of the organisation's owners and employees, or is it geared towards convincing outsiders (such as financiers) that the firm is a worthwhile venture to invest in? This will affect the level of detail and tone of the finished document, as well as the amount of confidential or commercially sensitive material disclosed.

In some cases, external factors will be the driving force behind the decision to prepare such a blueprint. This can occur, for example, when finance is being sought for a business project. Banks, venture capitalists, other financial institutions and private investors will want to know a great deal of detailed information before committing themselves to a new business venture or to the expansion of an existing one.[19] Government assistance to small business also often depends on the presentation of a suitable business plan. In such cases, it is important to ensure that the completed document is well written, logically argued and puts forward a clear case for support from external parties. However, it is often very difficult for entrepreneurs and business owners to determine how much confidential or commercially sensitive information should be released to outsiders.

In other cases, internal factors will be the main reason for developing a plan. For example, an entrepreneur may wish to draw together all his or her thoughts into a cohesive whole and ensure that no important details have been omitted in the development of the business project. Another reason may be to improve coordination of existing activities within the firm or to clarify the production targets the business is expected to reach.[20] When the document is being prepared largely for use 'in house', it may be easier to commit confidential information to paper. In some cases, the business plan can also identify future staffing needs of the business and help to 'map out' how current or future staffing arrangements will operate. It may also be possible to omit some details that are well known to everyone, since all likely readers of the plan are already involved in the project.

Tangled up at yoga?

Recently, a friend of yours, Kevin, has been considering buying a yoga studio. For the last five years, he has been taking basic yoga lessons every Wednesday evening. Recently the owner, Mr Smythe, has been talking about selling the business.

Kevin is excited about the prospect and has asked Mr Smythe a lot of questions about the operation. Approximately 130 people take lessons each week. Some of these individuals are signed to 10- and 20-lesson contracts, while others come on a casual basis. The current owner could not give any details on the weekly running expenses of the studio, although he did say that he felt the business was very profitable.

Some people pay by credit card and others with cash, but not all of these amounts have been entered in the books. Unfortunately, it isn't possible to pinpoint how many people actually come in for lessons because the instructors sometimes collect the money and pocket their share before giving Mr Smythe the remainder.

Kevin has mentioned that the facilities are 'becoming slightly run down'. Mr Smythe said that he had some major renovations planned but was vague on what these would be, their cost and when they might start.

Mr Smythe runs an advertisement every week in the Sunday edition of the local paper and believes that his own presence has been important to customers because he arrives at the studio every day at midmorning and does not go home until after the last lesson. As a result, Mr Smythe knows all of these people personally and encourages them to keep up their lessons and bring their friends along.

Mr Smythe says he has a business plan but won't let Kevin see it until an agreement to buy the firm has been signed. 'I can't let any competitors see my goals and strategies in advance,' he says.

Questions

1. Evaluate and discuss Mr Smythe's yoga business. What are the major strengths and flaws of this small business?
2. Do you think Kevin should agree to Mr Smythe's request and sign the agreement before examining the business plan? Is there any other way to deal with Smythe's concerns about confidentiality?

Case study prepared by the small business staff, School of Accounting and Law, RMIT University

Time frame

A business plan can be geared for a short time period (anything up to a year) or it may have a longer perspective. Short-term plans can afford to be more detailed, whereas a long-term orientation means that the plan must be more generalised in its contents. Many researchers argue that business planning in small firms tends to be overwhelmingly short term in orientation and that it is unusual to find a small business with plans that extend beyond a 2-year time horizon.[21] Of course, there are always some exceptions to this rule — some firms have been able to successfully use a very long-term time scale to help turn around their business. In general, however, a shorter term focus is used by most small organisations.

Entrepreneur profile

Jude Alfeld, Rivers Café

Jude Alfeld is the founder and owner of Rivers Café, a seasonal business that operates during the New Zealand tourist season (September to May) each year. It is located in Murchison, a small tourist town on the west coast of New Zealand's South Island.

Jude started the business because she felt the need for a challenge. She had previously worked and managed hotels in the United Kingdom, South Africa and in other parts of New Zealand. 'I firmly believed that Murchison had a gap for this type of business, so with a business partner we bought an existing café that was in receivership. We borrowed NZD $15 000 to set up the business, which we were able to completely pay back after the first two seasons.'

'The plan for our first year was to get up and running, market ourselves, buy all the equipment we needed and position ourselves as a supplier of interesting, desirable food.'

After a successful first season, retained profits were reinvested into the business. The café was refurbished, including a new kitchen, a separate bar area, new carpets and more tables and couches. In addition, extra money was spent on advertising the café.

'Unfortunately, we ended the third season with a large overdraft. Our ordering and spending was a bit out of control. Then my business partner wanted to get out, so I bought her out and ran the café myself.'

Now in her fourth year of trading, Jude's planning is focused on running the business at maximum efficiency. 'I keep a very vigilant eye on how things are used and ordered, our staffing rates and opening hours. I've also employed someone to help with the paperwork, which has given me more time to focus on efficiencies.'

'I've learned to plan for the shut-down periods. Although we are closed during the winter months, we still have money going out for power, phone, mortgage and rates. So I have been careful to manage finances to cover these months.'

Jude also has long-term goals firmly in mind. 'I'd like to continue building this business and sell it as a going concern in maybe five years' time. And I want this café to be an interesting and memorable place that guests want to come back to.'

Jude and her husband own the building that houses the café and rent part of it to another business, Ultimate Descents, a rafting and kayaking business. The café can be found on their website: <www.rivers.co.nz/cafe.htm>.

Source: Based on author's interview with Jude Alfeld

Strategic plan:
A plan that sets out the long-term focus of the business, its mission and its vision, and attempts to understand the environment in which the business operates.

Strategic or operational orientation

Business plans should not be mistaken for another common business tool, the strategic plan. A **strategic plan** sets out the long-term focus of the business, its mission and vision, and attempts to understand the environment in which the business operates.[22] In contrast, business plans tend to be more focused on operational issues. As the contents of a typical business plan reveal, such documents focus on putting an idea into action and cover most of the practical day-to-day issues involved in business creation, growth and management. In reality, there is often some overlap between the two: after all, most business plans can be devised only if the owner or entrepreneur has a long-range vision for the venture and an understanding of the external environment in which it will operate.

Preparing the document: the business-planning process

Few business plans are written at one sitting. More typically, a plan is the result of a series of logical steps that most entrepreneurs work through, regardless of whether or not they are conscious of the process involved (see figure 7.2). These steps are often iterative; a person may go through some of them several times before finally developing a plan that all parties feel comfortable with. The following are critical steps in the **business-planning process**.

Business-planning process:
A series of logical steps governing the creation, implementation and revision of a business plan.

Figure 7.2: The planning process

1. Set preliminary goals

All prospective business operators have a vision of what they want to achieve, what business they want to be in and what they want to sell. A useful first point in planning, therefore, is to commit these initial (often vague) goals to paper.[23]

2. Conduct initial secondary research

Using the preliminary goals spelled out above, the entrepreneur/small business owner must now collect information from existing data sources that can provide more details on the current state of the industry and the prospective viability of another entry into the field. At this point, rather than undertaking potentially expensive and time-consuming primary data collection, the entrepreneur may find that secondary data are more useful and easier to gather.

3. Confirm goals

Initial, general research should allow an entrepreneur/small business owner to either confirm or cancel the original goals. Does the business idea now seem viable? If the preliminary research does not clearly indicate that there is room for another market entrant, it may be advisable to abort the business idea at this stage. If the initial idea does seem viable, attention should be turned to developing specific goals and action plans.

4. Conduct subsequent detailed research

Now is the time to collect detailed information from as many different and specific sources as possible. This is the stage at which all the detailed elements of the business plan (such as marketing, operations and finances) must be investigated.

5. Develop draft business plan

Once market research results have been obtained and analysed, the entrepreneur/ small business owner must prepare a first version of the proposed business plan, covering all the subject matter suggested in the business plan outline.

6. Critically assess the proposed plan

Once a first draft is completed, the entrepreneur/small business owner should set the plan aside for a brief time before returning to it with a critical and editorial perspective. Does the document read well? Are all elements integrated? Are there any weaknesses in the argument that must be revised? At this stage, it is often useful to have an outsider evaluate the plan for some unbiased feedback.

7. Implement

Once devised, the business plan must, of course, be put into action. As time unfolds, the entrepreneur/small business owner must adhere to the processes and goals outlined in the original business plan unless there are strong reasons to do otherwise. If a plan is not implemented, the value of preparing the document in the first place is highly questionable.

8. Evaluate the plan

At the end of a year, or another given time frame, it is necessary to review and evaluate the plan and draw up a new set of forecasts for the future. This is also a useful opportunity to reassess the venture's stated goals to see if they are still realistic or whether some modification is warranted.

When business planning is seen by an entrepreneur or small business owner as an event that occurs only once a year, it can produce an inflexible perspective. On the other hand, those owner–managers and entrepreneurs who treat business planning as an ongoing process are more likely to build firms that are highly responsive to their environment. This latter group regard the business plan as a tool that is constantly reviewed; this allows them to respond quickly to any dramatic or rapid changes in their operating environment. Such responsiveness is especially important for new and small firms that operate in highly dynamic conditions.

Summary

A business plan is a written outline of a business. It may be devised for an existing firm or for a new venture that has not yet been launched. The main advantages of business planning include more complete information gathering, balanced decision making and assistance in raising finance. Disadvantages of a plan can include skewed information seeking, incorrect assumptions, inflexibility and unrealistic expectations.

All business plans, whatever their structure, should cover the key issues of marketing, operations and financing. The major elements of a typical plan can include an executive summary, background on the firm (if an existing enterprise), marketing details, operational arrangements, financial projections, a timetable for implementation and other relevant details.

Plans vary from one business to another. Formats and sequence are often quite different, although all of them should cover the basic issues. In addition, written business plans may have different levels of specificity, be written for different audiences, and cover short-term or long-term time frames.

The business-planning process is an ongoing process by which plans are constructed, implemented and evaluated. It includes the steps of preliminary goal setting, initial information gathering, formulation of set goals, detailed research, plan preparation, critical analysis of the proposed plan, implementation and subsequent evaluation and revision.

REVIEW QUESTIONS

1. List the different types of potential audience for a firm's business plan.
2. Summarise the seven major elements of a business plan.
3. What is the difference between a strategic plan and a business plan?
4. 'The disadvantages of preparing a business plan outweigh its advantages.' Do you agree with this statement? Explain your reasons.
5. Outline and briefly explain (in the correct sequence) the eight steps involved in the business-planning process.

DISCUSSION QUESTIONS

1. Read section 3 (Marketing) of the business plan for Blueprints Business Planning Pty Ltd in the appendix to this chapter. In your opinion, has sufficient market research been done to prove that the business is potentially viable?
2. If you were the owner of a business but employed a full-time manager to run your firm, who would be best placed to write up the plan?
3. Why is it necessary to include so much detail in a business plan?

SUGGESTED READING

Bangs, D. & Schaper, M., *The Australian Business Planning Guide*, 2nd edn, Allen & Unwin, Sydney, 2003.

Compton, T., *Preparing a Business Plan*, Wrightbooks, 2002.

Friend, G. & Zehle, S., *The Economist Guide to Business Planning*, The Economist, London, 2004.

CASE STUDY

A blueprint for success?

For several months, three friends had been thinking about starting their own business. Stephen Molloy, Jessie Jones and Andrew St John had talked about running their own business for a long time but nothing had gone much further than a talk over coffee now and then.

Finally, in May 2007, Jessie Jones rang her two friends and decided to take action.

'I have an idea for a business,' she told them. 'We'll call it Blueprints Business Planning. Since I have a lot of business experience, I will run it and I will be the starting point for the venture. If you are prepared to put in some money and a little bit of time serving as directors, I think we can eventually grow this into something bigger.'

Andrew and Stephen were intrigued. 'What do we have to do?,' they asked.

'Not much at present,' Jessie said. 'Let me do a draft proposal and then we can meet to discuss it.'

Two weeks later, they met to discuss the results so far. Jessie had exhausted herself preparing an initial business plan for the other two to read and was quite proud of what she had done in such a short time.

Andrew said, 'I have a few problems with your business plan.' Stephen nodded in agreement.

Jessie was quite hurt. She had put a lot of work into the idea. What should she do now?

Questions

1. Review the sample business plan prepared by Jessie in the appendix to this chapter. What are the strengths and weaknesses of the plan as it currently stands?

2. Should the directors proceed with the project as outlined in the business plan? Why or why not?

3. Why do you think Andrew and Stephen have reservations about the plan? What alternative strategies could Jessie adopt for going into business?

ENDNOTES

1. J.A. Pearce, D.K. Robbins & R.B. Robinson, 'The impact of grand strategy and planning formality on financial performance', *Strategic Management Journal*, vol. 8, no. 2, 1987, pp. 125–34.
2. Department of Industry, Science and Tourism, *The 1995 Business Longitudinal Survey*, AGPS, Canberra, 1997.
3. B. Gibson & G. Cassar, 'Planning behavior variables in small firms', *Journal of Small Business Management*, vol. 40, no. 3, 2002, pp. 171–86.
4. S. Knuckey, H. Johnston, C. Campbell-Hunt, K. Carlew, L. Corbett & C. Massey, *Firm Foundations: A Study of New Zealand Business Practices and Performance*, Ministry of Economic Development, Wellington, 2002, p. 45.

5. M. Schaper, 'Writing the perfect business plan', *My Business*, October, 1996, pp. 26–7.

6. M.P. Stephenson, 'Completing the picture: The business plan', *Fundraising Management*, vol. 22, no. 9, November, 1991, pp. 49–50.

7. A.M. Hormozi, G.S. Sutton, R.D. McMinn & W Lucio, 'Business plans for new or small businesses: Paving the path to success', *Management Decision*, vol. 40, no. 7–8, 2002, pp. 755–64.

8. S.C. Perry, 'The relationship between written business plans and the failure of small businesses in the US', *Journal of Small Business Management*, vol. 39, no. 3, 2001, pp. 301–9.

9. J.M. Bryson, *Strategic Planning for Public and Nonprofit Organisations: A Guide to Strengthening and Sustaining Organisational Achievement*, Jossey-Bass, San Francisco, 1995.

10. A. Gibb & L. Davies, 'In support of frameworks for the development of growth models of the small business', *International Small Business Journal*, vol. 9, no. 1, 1990, pp. 15–31.

11. 'New study shows six critical business plan mistakes,' *Business Horizons*, vol. 46, no. 4, 2003, p.83.

12. T. Mazzarol, 'Do formal business plans really matter? An exploratory study of small business owners in Australia', *Small Enterprise Research*, vol. 9, no. 1, 2001, pp. 32–45.

13. B. Honig & T. Karlsson, 'Institutional forces and the written business plan', *Journal of Management*, vol. 30, no. 1, 2004, p.29.

14. C.R. Schwenk & C.B. Schrader, 'Effects of formal strategic planning on financial performance in small firms: A meta-analysis', *Entrepreneurship Theory and Practice*, vol. 17, no. 3 (Spring), 1993, pp. 53–63.

15. S.R. Rich & D.E. Gumpert, 'How to write a winning business plan', *Harvard Business Review*, vol. 63, no. 3, May–June, 1985, pp. 156–66; W.A. Sahlman, 'How to write a great business plan', *Harvard Business Review*, vol. 75, no. 4, July–August, 1997, pp. 98–108.

16. T. McKaskill, *Finding The Money: How To Raise Venture Capital*, Wilkinson Publishing, Melbourne, 2006, p.71.

17. M.E. Porter, *The Competitive Advantage of Nations*, 2nd edn, Free Press, New York, 1998.

18. P.D. O'Hara, *The Total Business Plan*, 2nd edn, John Wiley, New York, 1995.

19. C. Mason & M. Stark, 'What do investors look for in a business plan? A comparison of the investment criteria of bankers, venture capitalists and business angels', *International Small Business Journal*, vol. 22, no. 3, 2004, p.227.

20. *How to Prepare, Present and Negotiate a Business Plan*, EPB Publishers, Singapore, 1994.

21. W. Glen & J. Weerawardena, 'Strategic planning practices in small enterprises in Queensland', *Small Enterprise Research*, vol. 4, no. 3, 1996, pp. 5–16.

22. C. Sutton, *Strategic Concepts*, Macmillan, London, 1998, p. 16.

23. A.M. Hormozi, G.S. Sutton, R.D. McMinn, & W. Lucio, *see* note 7.

Sample business plan

Note: *The business plan in this appendix is hypothetical and is provided solely for the purposes of illustrating the nature and content of a completed plan. The business name, personal details, statistical data and references are fictional; no link with any actual person or organisation is intended.*

Blueprints Business Planning Pty Ltd

Business plan for the period
July 2007 to June 2008

Blueprints Business Planning Pty Ltd
Australian Business Number (ABN) 99 999 999 999

135 Central Boulevard
Sydney
New South Wales, 2000
Australia

Telephone: +61 2 9999 9999
Facsimile: +61 2 9999 9998
Email: jessie@blueprintsbusinessplanning.com.au
Internet: www.blueprintsbusinessplanning.com.au

Prepared June 2007

Contents

Section 1: Executive summary

1.1 Business idea and goals

The main goal is to establish a small private (proprietary limited) company that specialises in management consulting services for the small and medium-sized enterprise (SME) sector in Sydney and other cities within the state of New South Wales, Australia. The services to be provided will include preparation of business plans, training in small business management skills and book sales.

The owners plan to begin by employing one person full time (Jessie Jones, a major shareholder) and gradually grow to the point where the business employs three or four people within 2 to 3 years of inception. The business intends to generate sales revenue of about $100 000 and to make a $2000 profit by the end of its first year of trading.

1.2 Marketing

Blueprints Business Planning Pty Ltd will have two key target markets: small business managers (for whom it will prepare business plans, feasibility studies and associated services) and SME support agencies (for whom it will provide contract services, principally training in small business management skills). There are approximately 200 000 SMEs in the Sydney metropolitan area. Market research indicates that there is currently unmet demand for the products we plan to offer. We will promote the business using a variety of methods, including direct mail, telephone canvassing, a Yellow Pages listing, networking, a website and testimonials.

1.3 Operations

The business will operate with one employee (Jessie Jones, managing director) at start-up and be based from an office at her home. A minimal outlay of equipment and expenses is envisaged at this stage, as most necessary equipment has already been obtained.

1.4 Finance

The business will be self funding. The directors will provide an initial capital injection of $10 000, and it is envisaged that the company will generate enough funds from subsequent operations to allow it to operate on a 'no borrowing' policy unless there is a major change in focus.

Section 2: Background

2.1 Mission statement

Blueprints Business Planning Pty Ltd exists to provide business planning services, business education (training) programs and management advice to small and medium-sized organisations.

The company intends to become known as one of the best business planners and advisers in the Sydney marketplace. We want to be known as an organisation that emphasises honesty, accuracy and objectivity in the information we provide to clients; that values confidentiality and sensitivity in all its relations with other parties; and that gives tailor-made responses to individual client needs.

In this way, Blueprints Business Planning Pty Ltd seeks to promote the interests of the following.

- *Clients.* By providing the above services, we can help our clients achieve success in the marketplace and realise their own business goals.
- *The wider community.* Helping businesses become more successful ultimately stimulates local economic development, job creation and wealth distribution.
- *Our employees.* A well-paid, motivated and well-educated staff is essential to ongoing success. In return, employees should expect to receive secure employment, to continually expand and improve their business skills, to be encouraged to try new ideas and approaches and to work in a comfortable, encouraging environment.
- *The owners of the company.* Successful achievement of the company mission should allow the company to operate profitably and to provide a fair return on effort and investment by the owners on a long-term basis.

2.2 Company history

This is a new business that springs from the existing work of Jessie Jones as a management consultant (operating as a sole trader) from August 2001 to June 2007. During this time, Jessie provided training programs, mentoring services and a limited amount of business planning to a range of clients.

2.3 Business goals

The business's goals for the short term (next 12 months) are to employ at least one person full time on a salary of approximately $42 000 p.a. (gross), to meet all operating expenses and to generate a net profit of at least $2000 for future investment. The long-term (next 2 or 3 years) goals are to establish a viable consultancy service employing up to five people based in Sydney, delivering services in business planning with its own purchased building.

A future exit strategy has been agreed to by the three foundation shareholders/ directors, should any of them wish to liquidate their interest in the business at a later stage. The directors have agreed that, after the end of the third year of trading, any shareholder will have the right to ask for the business to be independently valued; the remaining directors will then have first option to buy out that person's interest. If they do not wish to exercise this right, the shareholder may sell to an outside party.

Section 3: Marketing

3.1 Market research

The following sources were used to prepare this business plan:
- Australian Bureau of Statistics
- NSW Small Business Advisers' Network

- personal interviews with several business enterprise centres in and around Sydney
- Institute of Management Consultants, Australia
- a brief survey of SMEs that already use outside consultants
- other existing management consultancies
- a search of the relevant management literature.

3.2 Market analysis

After a review of the industry, the following conclusions were drawn.

(a) *Industry analysis*

There is a definite demand for generic management consulting services, although the industry is still unregulated and ill defined (Brown 2005, p. 48). Most services provided are aimed at larger corporations since, at the 'bottom end', micro-enterprises are too small to afford business planning services. Accordingly, niche opportunities to provide these services best exist among small to medium-sized (mid-range) businesses (Ziericki 2004, p. 206). A study of Australian SMEs recently showed that most need more training but are unsure where to find this (Australian Bureau of Statistics 2006, pp. 23–4). This need is especially evident among the 200 000 known SMEs in the Sydney metropolitan region (Sydney Chamber of Commerce 2007).

(b) *Seasonality*

It is estimated that business declines in December and January, which represents the Christmas break and summer holiday period in Australia.

(c) *Competitors*

The business's competitors are very similar to its potential strategic allies. They include:

- other management consultants (especially those who focus on SME training)
- accountancy practices (which also act as advisers to many small firms)
- publicly funded business support agencies (such as business enterprise centres)
- commercial training providers.

The Sydney Yellow Pages lists 123 management consultancies, 3000 accountancy practices, 20 public agencies and 34 commercial training providers in the city. This does not include non-Sydney advisers who are contracted on an 'as needed' basis by firms who wish to use their services.

(d) *Potential strategic alliances*

Potential exists to subcontract work from:

- accountants (that is, those who don't want to do business plans themselves but who do want to offer it as a service to their clients)
- business enterprise centres (such as those who want training courses provided or business plans assessed)
- other management consultants (who may need someone to help if their workload becomes too great).

We intend to focus our efforts on finding a small number of strategic allies (about six) with whom we can form long-term relationships.

(e) *SWOT analysis*

The information above was used to develop a list of potential strengths, weaknesses, opportunities and threats.

Potential strengths	Jessie's substantial SME advisory experience Links to NSW Small Business Advisers Network
Potential weaknesses	One-person operation at present Minimal track record in external consultancies Little skill in preparing tenders
Potential opportunities	Growth in external training programs Growth of ongoing mentoring services Good placement to qualify if sector becomes regulated
Potential threats	Competitors Sensitivity of SMEs to economic downturns

3.3 Marketing plan

3.3.1 Products/services and target market

(a) *Business planning*

Preparation of detailed business plans, covering all parts of a firm's activities

Target markets:

- Small to medium-sized firms (10 to 100 employees)
- Sydney metropolitan area
- Established companies (preferably 2 years or older)
- Approximately 200 000 such firms

Customer buying motives:

- SMEs often need specialist expertise to help in running their firms.
- It is often too difficult to do themselves.
- Such advice is often needed for organisational survival or repositioning.

(b) *Training*

Short, intensive (one- or two-day) courses on marketing, human resources, business planning, basic financial management and record-keeping for SMEs

Target markets:

- New small business owners and existing owners keen to increase their knowledge
- Central Sydney metropolitan area
- Sufficient business income ($200 000+) to be willing to pay for services
- An estimated 5000 new businesses that start trading each year

Customer buying motives:

- Owner–managers of SMEs want short, focused courses that develop their own knowledge base and competencies.

- Such courses allow them to acquire useful skills in different aspects of management.
- The increased knowledge helps them to grow their own business.

(c) *Small business development books*

Sales of various book titles, best done in conjunction with training courses (that is, sell books at the end of a particular course)

Target markets:

- Participants in training courses, as discussed above
- Central Sydney metropolitan areas
- Sufficient business income ($200 000+) to be willing to pay for services

Customer buying motives:

- These books provide more information about materials initially covered in our training courses.

3.3.2 Placement

Since this is a home-based business dealing directly with clients at their premises, no particular distribution arrangements are envisaged as necessary.

3.3.3 Promotions and advertising

To start trading, the business already has a number of secure contracts in place. As such, it is not necessary to actively promote the enterprise to the general community. However, it would be useful to alert other potential clients to its existence, with a view to seeking work from them at a later stage. To this end, the following promotional tools will be used by the business:

- business cards and letterheads
- direct mail followed up by telephone contacts
- listing in the next edition of the Sydney Yellow Pages under 'Management Consultants'
- promotional literature — a series of A4 sheets about the company covering staff of the organisation, services provided, the benefits of using the company and a listing of previous clients
- networking — links to other practising professionals through membership of the Institute of Management Consultants and other local business bodies
- testimonials — a file of positive testimonials from clients that can be used as references for future marketing
- internet — a website and more links to this to be built in over time.

3.3.4 Pricing policy

Charge-out rates for tendered or casual consulting and training services will be $120 per hour, which is the current market rate (Jones 2007, p. 1). The standard price of preparing a basic 10-page business plan will be $2000; this figure is comparable to prices charged by other private sector business planners (both fees exclude GST). Any specific costs (such as travel and accommodation) will be additional. These prices are set towards the higher end of those charged within the commercial training sector but well within the acceptable price range for management consulting services. Terms of payment will be 10 working days (2 calendar weeks) and accounts will be tendered on the day that the services are provided.

3.4 Evaluation of marketing

The effectiveness of our marketing strategy will be assessed on a 6-monthly basis by analysing sales data to see what draws the company's work. For example, if most work is coming from the distribution of promotional brochures, then this source of promotion will be seen to be effective.

Section 4: Operations

4.1 Legal and licensing requirements

(a) *Business name and legal structure*

Blueprints Business Planning Pty Ltd (Australian Business Number 99 999 999 999) is a proprietary limited company. The company structure has already been registered and established with three shareholders:

Stephen Molloy   (40% shareholding)

Jessie Jones   (40% shareholding)

Andrew St John   (20% shareholding)

who also serve as the directors of the entity.

(b) *Operating laws and licences*

After checking with the Small Business Development Corporation's Business Licence Centre, it appears that no specific licences are needed to operate this business except for a home-based business permit from the City of Sydney.

4.2 Management details

The managing director of the company will be:

Jessie Jones

Home address: 135 Central Blvd, Sydney NSW 2000

Ph: (02) 9999 9999 Fax: (02) 9999 9998

Date of birth: 14 August 1970

Qualifications: Bachelor of Business (distinction)

Experience: Owner of cafe, 1992–2001

Management consultant and owner of Jones Consultancies, 2001–07

4.3 Organisational structure and staffing

Initially, the following tasks of the business will be done by the managing director:

- consulting
- training
- servicing board of directors
- marketing and public enquiries
- bookkeeping and administration of the enterprise.

Two casual trainers will be employed to help deliver the training programs, and to help conduct research and write business plans for clients. Both will report directly to the managing director.

The following is an intended final staffing structure as part of the business's long-term (2–3 years) goals:

- *Managing director — business consultancy*
  Duties: Provide business planning, mentoring and occasional training to clients; undertake marketing of the business; provide administrative services and strategic development of the firm
  Salary: Set at approximately $42 000 per annum in year 1, rising to $50 000 by the end of year 2
  This role will be filled by Jessie Jones.
- *Consultant — general business planning*
  Duties: Conduct business planning and general management consultancy work for clients; undertake office management
  Salary: $45 000 per annum
  Qualifications required: Aptitude for dealing with the public; small business background; experience in preparing and evaluating business plans; business degree useful, but not essential
- *Consultant — training activities*
  Duties: Prepare and deliver training courses
  Salary: $45 000 per annum
  Qualifications required: Aptitude for dealing with the public; small business background; training qualifications (or willingness to obtain); proven ability to deliver effective training sessions; formal educational qualifications preferred

More detailed job descriptions, employment contracts and ongoing performance appraisal mechanisms will be needed during the second year of operations, or when the employment of full-time staff other than Jessie is necessary (Anderson & James 2005, p. 2). This information must be compiled and entered into that year's business plan. When the business does reach the stage of employing more than one full-time person, it will also use a team-based approach in dealing with specific projects, with different staff members leading the rest of the team on particular assignments.

Training

A minimum of 20 hours' professional development must be undertaken by each employee each year, as such training is needed to keep abreast of general developments in the field. One area where specific knowledge is needed is in the preparation of tender submissions.

Professional associations

The managing director will seek to join the Institute of Management Consultants of Australia (IMCA).

4.4 Professional advisers

Accountant
Sunshine Street Accountants
4 Sunshine Street, Midland NSW 2050
Ph: (02) 7999 9999 Fax: (02) 2222 9999 Email: info@sunshinestreet.com.au

Lawyer
Moot & Moot Partners
Suite 1, 1 Main St, Sydney NSW 2002
(Postal address: PO Box 1, Sydney NSW 2045)
Ph: (02) 8999 9999 Fax: (02) 3999 9999 Email: reception@moot.net.au

Insurance broker
To be determined

Bank account
MegaBank Australia
5 St Gregory Tce, Sydney NSW 2000
Manager: Janine Gregory
Ph: (02) 2222 3333 Fax: (02) 2222 3334
Email: Janine.Gregory@megabank.com.au

Bookkeeper
To be determined. This will not be sought unless the managing director can no longer provide this service herself.

4.5 Insurance and security issues

The following insurance will be required for the business:
- professional indemnity
- public liability
- workers compensation
- director's liability (possibly).

It is estimated all of these will cost approximately $2500 in year 1 of trading.

Necessary security precautions for the business property and equipment include the provision of a locked filing cabinet for client records. Online security for the website will be needed and electronic data will be backed up regularly and stored off-site.

4.6 Business premises

(a) *Location*

The business will be based at Jessie's home at 135 Central Boulevard, Sydney NSW 2000. A separate room that can be used as a dedicated office is available, with all required furniture and equipment. The property concerned is owned by Jessie and her husband so has security of tenure indefinitely. No rent is payable and no special equipment or fixtures are required.

Training courses will be conducted at specialised venues that can be hired on a daily basis.

(b) *Council and government rules*

A home-based business licence will have to be obtained from the City of Sydney. No other licences apply to the project. Trainers and business planners do not need to be licensed.

(c) *Ability to access target market*

Since most services will be provided on-site at the customer's premises, the office will easily allow the business to access its target markets. The office is located close to most major roads and freeways. Clients will be scattered throughout the metropolitan area so the firm will need to travel to the client's preferred locations.

4.7 Equipment required

The equipment required for the business will be:
- fax machine
- answering machine
- telephone line
- mobile phone
- computer, printer and scanner
- internet access
- filing cabinet
- table
- ergonomic office chair.

Quotes from suppliers indicate that the total cost of these items will be approximately $11 500. All materials required for the proposed training programs (such as TV, video and whiteboard) are provided by commercial training venues.

Likely future needs

If future growth necessitates the use of a fax/modem, the existing home phone line will need to be replaced with a business phone line. Future computing needs will probably include an upgraded system with internet and fax/modem access.

4.8 Production processes

An operations manual, updated every 6 months, will explain procedures and processes within the office. It will also allow the company to apply for quality assurance certification at a later stage, if it wishes to do so.

4.9 Critical risks/contingency plans

The critical risks facing this business and contingencies to deal with them are:
- lack of work — to be covered by a renewed and ongoing focus on marketing
- liability — to be covered by professional indemnity insurance
- injury to the managing director — to be covered by workers compensation
- excessive workload — other directors may take on work or it may be redirected to other consultancies with whom a strategic alliance has been developed.

Section 5: Financial projections

5.1 Basic assumptions and information

(a) *Calculation of income and expenses*

Expenses have been calculated based on market research and the manager's own knowledge of costs. It is assumed that all accounts revenue will be paid within the month issued (so there is no delayed income on a monthly basis). No provision has been made for the impact of inflation or increases in costs.

Pricing and costs for the second year of operations will be reviewed in next year's business plan to take these factors into account.

Depreciation of equipment items purchased in July 2007 is calculated using the straight-line method at 10 per cent per annum of total initial outlay. Book sales assume a gross cost of goods of 60 per cent (that is, a $20 gross profit on sales price of $50). Only 1 year's forecasts have been provided due to the difficulty of forecasting over a longer time period. All figures are in Australian dollars (A$).

(b) *Financing of the business*

The directors will provide an initial capital contribution to the business according to their shareholdings — Stephen Molloy $4000, Jessie Jones $4000, Andrew St John $2000. Sales income for July 2007 is based on commitments or early orders from prospective clients, thus providing initial cash flow and removing the need for short-term debt financing. The overall financing strategy is to operate, wherever possible, with a cash surplus in the bank account at all times. Bank loans will not be required. If necessary, the directors will reduce the wages paid to them during times of cash flow difficulty.

The bank account required for the business is one that:

- has cheque-writing facilities, and telephone and internet banking
- pays interest on sums below $5000
- provides monthly bank statements (for reconciliation with accounts)
- has credit card and electronic funds transfer facilities.

For security reasons, a minimum of two directors will be required to sign all cheques.

(c) *Distribution of profits*

Profits in year 1 will be retained in the business. In future years, annual net profit after tax will be divided in the following manner: three-quarters will be paid to the shareholders at the end of the financial year in accordance with their shareholdings, and the remaining quarter will be kept as retained earnings. The retained capital will be used for reinvestment in the business, mainly to upgrade equipment and to meet unforeseen contingencies. If the business is highly profitable, some of the retained capital may eventually (in 2–3 years' time) be used to help fund the purchase of permanent business premises.

(d) *Goods and services tax*

No GST figures are shown in any of the financial documents; in other words, all forecasts are net of tax.

(e) *Loans*

The firm has no current loans or debts.

5.2 Analysis of financial forecasts

(a) The owners have decided to use net profit margin as the main indicator of the firm's performance. Based on the projections made in this document, it is estimated for year 1 that this will be:

$$\text{Net profit margin } \% = \frac{\text{Net profit before tax}}{\text{Sales turnover}} = \frac{\$2320}{\$103\,750} = 2.24\%$$

This figure is quite low and below industry norms, according to a recent study by Jones (2007), but is not unusual for a business in its first year of trading. We expect margins to increase substantially in years 2 and 3.

In future years, as more data are gathered, it will also be possible to use other ratios to help analyse the financial performance of the firm.

(b) *Break-even point*

Assuming that cost of goods sold is the only variable cost, the contribution margin is equal to the projected gross profit margin (94%).

$$\text{Projected fixed costs} = \$95\,280$$

$$\text{Break-even point in dollars} = \frac{\text{Fixed costs}}{\text{Contribution margin}}$$

$$= \frac{\$95\,280}{0.94}$$

$$= \$101\,362$$

5.2.1 Sales mix forecast

Blueprints Business Planning Pty Ltd
SALES MIX FORECAST
for the period July 2007 to June 2008

	Jul.	Aug.	Sep.	Oct.	Nov.	Dec.	Jan.	Feb.	Mar.	Apr.	May	Jun.	TOTAL
Item: Business planning													
Number sold	2	2	3	3	4	0	1	3	4	5	5	5	37
Selling price	$2000	$2000	$2000	$2000	$2000	$2000	$2000	$2000	$2000	$2000	$2000	$2000	
Total sales income	4000	4000	6000	6000	8000	0	2000	6000	8000	10000	10000	10000	$74000
Cost of goods sold per item	0	0	0	0	0	0	0	0	0	0	0	0	0
Total cost of goods sold	0	0	0	0	0	0	0	0	0	0	0	0	0
Item: Training courses													
Numbers sold (hours delivered)	15	15	15	20	20	10	15	20	25	25	25	20	225
Selling price	$120	$120	$120	$120	$120	$120	$120	$120	$120	$120	$120	$120	
Total sales income	1800	1800	1800	2400	2400	1200	1800	2400	3000	3000	3000	2400	$27000
Cost of goods sold per item	20	20	20	20	20	20	20	20	20	20	20	20	
Total cost of goods sold	300	300	300	400	400	200	300	400	500	500	500	400	4 500
Item: Supplementary books													
Number sold	3	3	3	5	5	2	5	5	6	6	6	6	55
Selling price	$ 50	$ 50	$ 50	$ 50	$ 50	$ 50	$ 0	$ 50	$ 50	$ 50	$ 50	$ 50	
Total sales income	150	150	150	250	250	100	250	250	300	300	300	300	$2750
Cost of goods sold per item	30	30	30	30	30	30	30	30	30	30	30	30	
Total cost of goods sold	90	90	90	150	150	60	150	150	180	180	180	180	1650
Total sales revenue	$5950	$5950	$7950	$8650	$10650	$1300	$4050	$8650	$11300	$13300	$13300	$12700	$103750
Total cost of goods sold	$390	$390	$390	$550	$550	$260	$450	$550	$680	$680	$680	$580	$6150

5.2.2 Cash flow forecast

Blueprints Business Planning Pty Ltd
CASH FLOW FORECAST
for the period July 2007 to June 2008

	Jul.	Aug.	Sep.	Oct.	Nov.	Dec.	Jan.	Feb.	Mar.	Apr.	May	Jun.	TOTAL
Income													
Sales revenue	$5 950	$5 950	$7 950	$8 650	$10 650	$1 300	$4 050	$8 650	$11 300	$13 300	$13 300	$12 700	$103 750
Capital	10 000												10 000
Sundry													
Total income	15 950	5 950	7 950	8 650	10 650	1 300	4 050	8 650	11 300	13 300	13 300	12 700	113 750
Expenses													
Cost of goods sold	390	390	390	550	550	260	450	550	680	680	680	580	6 150
Accounting/legal services	1 500		800					200					2 500
Advertising	2 000	100	100	100	180	100	100	100	100	100	100	100	3 180
Bank fees	15	15	15	15	15	15	15	15	15	15	15	15	180
Equipment purchases	11 500												11 500
Equipment leases													0
Insurance	2 500												2 500
Light & power													0
Loan repayments													0
Motor vehicle — fuel	50	50	50	50	50	50	50	50	50	50	50	50	600
Motor vehicle — other costs													0
Petty cash	25	25	25	25	25	25	25	25	25	25	25	25	300
Postage, printing & stationery	400												400
Rent													0
Repairs & maintenance	100			100			100			100			400
Staff casual wages	2 000	2 000	2 000	2 000	2 000	2 000	2 000	2 000	2 000	2 000	2 000	2 000	24 000
Staff superannuation												6 000	6 000
Staff director's wages	3 400	3 340	4 700	3 220	3 340	3 400	3 220	3 340	3 400	3 220	3 340	3 400	41 320
Telephone	50	50	50	50	50	50	50	50	50	50	50	50	600
Other	100	50	50	50	50	50	50	50	50	50	50	50	650
Total expenses	24 030	6 020	8 180	6 160	6 260	5 950	6 060	6 380	6 370	6 290	6 310	12 270	100 280
Cash surplus/(deficit)	$(8 080)	$(70)	$(230)	$2 490	$4 390	$(4 650)	$(2 010)	$2 270	$4 930	$7 010	$6 990	$430	$13 470
Bank balance													
Start of month	0	(8 080)	(8 150)	(8 380)	(5 890)	(1 500)	(6 150)	(8 160)	(5 890)	(960)	6 050	13 040	
End of month	(8 080)	(8 150)	(8 380)	(5 890)	(1 500)	(6 150)	(8 160)	(5 890)	(960)	6 050	13 040	13 470	

5.2.3 Projected profit and loss statement

Blueprints Business Planning Pty Ltd
PROJECTED PROFIT AND LOSS STATEMENT
for the period July 2007 to June 2008

Revenues	
Sales revenue	$103 750
Less: Cost of goods sold	6 150
Gross profit	97 600
Expenses	
Accounting/legal services	2 500
Advertising	3 180
Bank fees	180
Equipment purchases	11 500
Equipment leases	0
Insurance	2 500
Light & power	0
Loan repayments	0
Motor vehicle — fuel	600
Motor vehicle — other costs	0
Petty cash	300
Postage, printing & stationery	400
Rent	0
Repairs & maintenance	400
Staff wages	24 000
Staff superannuation	6 000
Staff director's wages	41 320
Telephone	600
Other	650
Depreciation	1 150
Total expenses	95 280
Net profit	$ 2 320

5.2.4 Owner's personal expenses

Blueprints Business Planning Pty Ltd
OWNER'S PERSONAL EXPENSES: JESSIE JONES
for the period July 2007 to June 2008

	Jul.	Aug.	Sep.	Oct.	Nov.	Dec.	Jan.	Feb.	Mar.	Apr.	May	Jun.	TOTAL
Monthly commitments													
Food	$ 400	$ 400	$ 400	$ 400	$ 400	$ 400	$ 400	$ 400	$ 400	$ 400	$ 400	$ 400	$ 4 800
Health	100	100	100	100	100	100	100	100	100	100	100	100	1 200
Clothes	80		80			80			80			80	400
Entertainment	200	200	200	200	200	200	200	200	200	200	200	200	2 400
Transport	120	120	120	120	120	120	120	120	120	120	120	120	1 440
Education													0
House payments	1 400	1 400	1 400	1 400	1 400	1 400	1 400	1 400	1 400	1 400	1 400	1 400	16 800
Car payments													0
Other loan repayments													0
Telephone			100			100			100			100	400
Electricity & gas		120			120			120			120		480
Rates			1 300										1 300
Personal income tax	900	900	900	900	900	900	900	900	900	900	900	900	10 800
Credit cards	100												100
Other	100	100	100	100	100	100	100	100	100	100	100	100	1 200
Monthly drawings needed*	$3 400	$3 340	$4 700	$3 220	$3 340	$3 400	$3 220	$3 340	$3 400	$3 220	$3 340	$3 400	$41 320

* Shown as 'Staff — director's wages' in cash flow forecast

5.2.5 Owner's personal assets and liabilities

Blueprints Business Planning Pty Ltd
OWNER'S PERSONAL ASSETS AND LIABILITIES: JESSIE JONES
as at 1 July 2007

Assets

Own house (market value)	$300 000
Other real estate (market value)	0
Motor vehicle (insured value)	15 000
Cash (on hand or in bank)	6 000
Superannuation	84 000
Furniture & personal effects (insured value)	25 000
Other (list if appropriate)	0
Total assets	430 000

Liabilities

Outstanding mortgage (on home)	201 500
Outstanding mortgage (on other real estate)	0
Personal loans	0
Credit cards	100
Current bills	0
Other debts	600
Total liabilities	202 200
Personal worth (total assets minus total liabilities)	$227 800

Section 6: Implementation timetable, 2007–08

2007

July	Apply for home-based business licence
	Open business bank account
	Prepare letterheads, business cards
	Send copy of business plan to accountant and lawyer (for their information)
	Obtain all relevant insurance policies
August	Start direct mail campaign
	Review contents of website
September	Start compiling operations manual
	Visit accountant re: progress to date, record-keeping
	Enquire re: computing equipment required
October	Enquire with Institute of Management Consultants (Australia) re: membership
November	Prepare promotional brochure
December	Print promotional brochure

2008

January	Staff/directors' retreat to review progress to date
	Review business plan
	Review effectiveness of marketing plan and analyse source of sales to date
	Review operations manual
February	Attend Small Business Development Corporation course on managing business growth
March	Implement benchmarking of advertising by outside adviser
April	Update website
May	Visit accountant re: end-of-financial-year returns
June	Write business plan for 2008–09
	Review and write new marketing plan

Section 7: Appendix — Research reference sources

Anderson, F. & James, B., *Small Business Employment Guidebook*, John Wiley & Sons, Brisbane, 2005.

Australian Bureau of Statistics, *Training Needs in Australia*, Cat. No. 1222.8, ABS, Canberra, 2006.

Brown, M., 'An overview of new enterprise opportunities', *Micro-Enterprise Australia*, vol. 2, no. 3, September, 2005, pp. 47–9.

Jones, J., 'Consultancy rates — an overview', *Management Techniques and Issues*, no. 2, January, 2007, pp. 1–5.

Small Business Development Corporation, *Opportunities for New Businesses*, SBDC, Sydney, 2006.

Sydney Chamber of Commerce, *Survey of Small Firm Member Needs for Professional Development*, Sydney Chamber of Commerce & NSW Department of Commerce and Trade, Sydney, 2007.

Ziericki, J.J., *Consulting in the Personal Services Sector: An Overview*, available online at Management Investigation website <www.managementinvest.com>, 2004.

Chapter 8

Legal issues

LEARNING OBJECTIVES

After reading this chapter, you should be able to:

- explain the main types of legal structure under which a business may operate
- discuss the pros and cons of each type of legal structure
- describe the various forms of intellectual property
- explain the main unfair trade practices.

All business activities are, to some extent, regulated by government. Entrepreneurs and new business owners must comply with a variety of regulations and laws that can appear somewhat confusing and arbitrary at first. One way of understanding these requirements is to break them down into four components that take place in the following order: (1) choose a legal structure to operate under; (2) protect any intellectual property the business has; (3) determine which operating permits and licences the industry must comply with; and (4) examine any ancillary issues, such as trade practices law. Each of these is discussed in detail below.

Legal structures

All businesses must assume a legal form during their existence. Although there are many variations on these in different jurisdictions, in essence there are three main legal structures that a business can operate under: a sole proprietorship, a partnership and a company. Another significant structuring option is to use a trust. In Australia, most businesses are sole proprietorships (38 per cent), although proprietary limited companies are also popular (26 per cent). Trusts and partnerships represent respectively 18 per cent and 15 per cent of the business registered, while other structures constitute 3 per cent.[1] Asian businesses differ from their Australian and New Zealand counterparts with respect to the separation of ownership and control. Voting rights (control) often exceed profit rights (ownership) via pyramid structures and cross-holdings.

Sole proprietorship

Sole proprietor or sole trader: A person who wholly owns and operates a business.

A **sole proprietor**, sometimes also known as a **sole trader**, is a business in which the owner is synonymous with the firm. There is no distinction in law between the business and the individual owner. All profits and assets of the firm are the owner's, just as any liabilities or debts are also the responsibility of the owner. Note that the term *sole trader* does not mean 'sole employee'. A sole trader, just like a partnership or company, can employ other people. The most common form of legal structure for new start-ups in Australia, for example, is the sole proprietorship.

Advantages and drawbacks of sole proprietorships

The advantages of the sole proprietorship are as follows:

- *Ease of formation.* There are fewer formalities and restrictions compared with other legal forms. The sole proprietorship may also, at a later stage, be converted into a partnership or a company.
- *Total control over the business.* The owner–manager is able to exercise full control over the operations of the enterprise, and retains all the profits generated by the business.
- *Relatively cheap to set up and maintain.* The laws governing the operations of sole proprietorships are usually less onerous than other legal structures, so administrative costs may be quite low.

- *Few regulations.* There are few formalities involved in running a sole proprietorship, as this form is the least regulated of all the business structures. Those formalities that do exist apply equally to other legal structures.

It is these features that many new business operators find attractive, and many small businesses begin life under this structure. However, the sole proprietorship also has several drawbacks:

- *Unlimited liability.* Since all assets and liabilities belong to the owner, the individual may be faced with a potentially ruinous set of claims if the firm is forced into bankruptcy or is the subject of legal action. In these situations, the personal assets of the owner may be seized to satisfy outstanding claims, since legally they are indistinguishable from other assets of the owner/firm.
- *Limited resources.* Sole proprietorships rely heavily on the owner–manager to finance the business start-up and expansion and may therefore face funding problems. Similarly, this type of business has limited human resources, as the owner–manager largely relies on personal skills to manage the business.
- *Lack of continuity.* A sole proprietorship has no independent existence and is tied to the owner–manager who runs it. Therefore, the business usually ceases to exist if the business owner dies or is otherwise rendered incapable of operating the business.
- *Tax.* In nations with a high marginal tax rate, the inability to separate business income from other personal sources of income may lead to potentially higher rates of personal income tax being paid.

Establishing a sole proprietorship

In Australia, a sole proprietorship may be established by the simple fact of a person trading under his or her own name. If the person operates the business under another name, the business name must be registered with the appropriate state agency. Renewal of registration varies from state to state. Most firms will also require an Australian business number (ABN), which can be obtained online free of charge from the Australian Taxation Office (ATO). Table 8.1 shows the different authorities for registering a sole proprietorship in some countries in the Pacific Rim region.

Table 8.1: Authority and formation for sole traders

Country	Authority
Australia	Individual state agencies and Australian Taxation Office <www.ato.gov.au>
Hong Kong	Business Registration Office, Inland Revenue Department <www.ird.gov.hk>
Malaysia	Companies Commission of Malaysia <www.ssm.com.my>
New Zealand	Ministry of Economic Development, Companies Office <www.companies.govt.nz>
Singapore	Accounting and Corporate Regulatory Authority <www.acra.gov.sg>

Partnership

A sole proprietorship allows only one person to carry on a business. This is a major limitation. When several people are in business together, this business relationship is called a **partnership**. These people pool their resources (such as capital, time and knowledge) and agree to share the profits as well as the liabilities of the venture.[2] Partnerships are common in husband-and-wife teams. This is an arrangement in which mutual cooperation and trust is very important.

Partnership: A relationship that exists between people carrying on a business in common with a view to making a profit.

Advantages and drawbacks of partnerships

The main advantages of partnerships are as follows:

- *Ease of formation.* Legal formalities and expenses are few compared with companies.
- *Ease of operation.* A partnership is usually easier to operate, more flexible for tax purposes and cheaper to run than either the smallest company or trust (in Australia).
- *Distinct existence.* Unlike a sole proprietorship, a partnership can be clearly demarcated as a separate entity for marketing and accounting purposes.
- *Combined resources.* A partnership is often an effective vehicle for pooling members' funds, so it is often more effective than a sole proprietorship when it comes to raising finance. It is also a useful mechanism for bringing together people who have different resources to contribute to a business venture.
- *Direct rewards.* Partners directly share the profits, thus providing a direct link between contribution and remuneration.

However, partnerships suffer from several drawbacks, which include:

- *Unlimited joint liability.* Each partner is responsible for the debts and activities of all others. In some countries, the liability of particular classes of partnership may be limited by legislation; similarly, in some professions in some regions (such as dentists in Western Australia) there are various laws that require operators to act either as sole proprietors or as partners (so assuming direct responsibility for their own work).
- *Potential conflicts.* The decision-making process is split among all the partners. Hence, people with a high need for personal control and autonomy may find this arrangement unsatisfactory. Few people anticipate problems when they first join with others in a business venture. However, this informal relationship can easily break down under stress and, as a result, the business may ultimately fail, creating a potential loss for each partner.
- *Lack of continuity.* Most partnership laws stipulate that the partnership ceases to exist if one of the partners dies, becomes incapacitated or simply withdraws from business. To continue with the business, the remaining partners must usually start a new partnership.

Partnership agreement A written document that covers all matters relating to the partnership.

Establishing a partnership

A **partnership agreement** is usually strongly recommended, although it is rarely compulsory. This is a written document spelling out details of the partners in the business, the share of profits they are entitled to, the liabilities they are accountable for, and the roles and responsibilities of the different partners. It also puts in place a mechanism for winding up the partnership or for selling or transferring partners' interests if they no longer wish to be involved in the enterprise. Partners should determine their own positions with regard to these points and be fully supportive of all the provisions of the proposed agreement.

Although there are many advantages to choosing the partnership form of business, many personal issues need to be considered before entering a partnership with another person. Entrepreneurs must ask themselves:

- Do I like and respect the prospective partner/s?
- Do our skills complement each other?
- Do our visions and goals run parallel?

The regulatory requirements governing partnerships are minimal. In Australia, Malaysia and Singapore, a partnership can be established by a minimum of two people and a maximum of twenty. Partnerships do not pay income tax. The share of profit or loss distributed must be declared by the partners in their individual tax returns and all income is taxed at the personal income rate. The different authorities for registering a partnership structure in the Pacific Rim region are the same as for sole proprietorships, shown in table 8.1 (p. 200).

Company

Neither sole proprietorships nor partnerships are particularly effective entities for entrepreneurs who plan to undertake ventures that may expose them to high levels of liability, who need to raise large amounts of capital, or who have a project that will be funded and owned by a large number of people. When this is the situation, a **company** is a more appropriate legal structure.

Company:
A separate legal entity that has an existence independent of its owners and managers.

In a company, ownership is held by a number of shareholders, who may transfer shares to other people and who elect a number of their own members to serve as the directors of the company. The directors are responsible for setting the broad policies of the firm, selecting and overseeing a chief executive officer or managing director, and ensuring solvency and legal compliance. A written constitution (in some jurisdictions known as the memorandum and the articles of association) spells out the basic rules under which the firm is governed and administered. In Australia, the *Corporations Act* contains replaceable rules governing the internal affairs of a company, but a company can set up its own constitution if it wishes to adopt different rules.

Advantages and drawbacks of companies

Key advantages of a company include the following:[3]

- *Perpetual existence.* A company will continue to exist even if the founder or one of the shareholders dies; rights to their shares are simply transferred to their legal beneficiary.
- *Limited liability.* The liability of the owners of the company (the shareholders) is usually limited to the unpaid value of the shares they hold.
- *Rights of a natural person.* Like an individual, a company may buy, hold and dispose of assets in its own right. It can sue and be sued; can enter into contracts

and transactions in its own name; and has a separate legal identity from the individual shareholders. It has its own registered name, corporate office and address.

On the other hand, a company typically faces the following drawbacks:

- *High set-up and maintenance costs.* The laws regulating the operations of corporations are usually tighter than those which apply to partnerships or sole traders.
- *Spread ownership.* Ownership is spread among several people, which can make decision making more difficult (although in Australia it is possible to have one-person firms, with only one shareholder, who is also the sole director and managing director of the organisation).

When owner–managers run a company, it seems almost automatic that they take on the role of director. Yet many owner–managers in Australia are doing so with little understanding of their financial and legal liabilities. For example, many of them are under the misapprehension that if they set up a company they will be exempt from personal liability, thinking 'my only risk is the capital that I put into the business'. However, company directors can have a personal exposure to the ATO with regard to preference of action. That arises when the company goes into liquidation within six months of having paid its tax. The liquidator then brings a preference action against the ATO, saying that the money was paid at a time when the company was insolvent and that there were reasonable grounds for the ATO to suspect that the company was insolvent when it received the payment of the tax. If the liquidator succeeds against the ATO then it is required to pay the money back to the liquidator. In those circumstances, the ATO can pursue the directors personally for the money.[4]

Establishing a company

Although there are several variations on the types of company allowed in various countries, the main distinction is between *private* companies, in which the number of shareholders is limited (usually to 50), and *public* companies, in which shares can be bought and sold on a stock exchange by anyone. Private companies are often designated by the terms Proprietary Limited (Pty Ltd) in Australia, Private Limited (Pte Ltd) in Singapore, or Sendirian Berhad (Sdn Bhd) in Malaysia.

Table 8.2 provides a list of the authorities with which a private limited company must be registered. In all cases, the following formalities must be completed for the company to come into existence:

- A memorandum and articles of association or a constitution must be drawn up for the purposes of registration (in Australia, a company can adopt the standard replaceable rules of the *Corporations Act* or draw up its own constitution).
- An application must be made for approval of the name of the company; an existing firm's name cannot be used.
- The requisite fee must be paid.
- The company is incorporated when, on registration, a certificate of registration is issued.

In Australia, most small businesses do not have formal company boards, which include independent directors who are registered with the Australian Securities and Investments Commission (ASIC). However, small private companies are increasingly setting up advisory boards that can provide them with the benefits of a directorial board without the expensive salaries. A business venture seeking to establish an advisory board would usually seek out three to five executives and a number of experts who have industry knowledge, access to networks and strategic vision. Unlike the members of a formal board, members of an advisory board just make recommendations rather than decisions.

Table 8.2: Authority for registering private limited companies

Country	Authority
Australia	Australian Securities and Investments Commission <www.asic.gov.au>
Hong Kong	Companies Registry <www.info.gov.hk/cr>
Malaysia	Companies Commission of Malaysia <www.ssm.com.my>
New Zealand	New Zealand Companies Office <www.companies.govt.nz>
Singapore	Accounting and Corporate Regulatory Authority <www.acra.gov.sg>

Trusts

Trust:
An obligation imposed on trustees to deal with the trust property (over which they have control) for the benefit of the beneficiaries.

Trust deed:
A written document that evidences the creation of the trust. It sets out the terms and conditions on which the trust assets are held by the trustees and outlines the rights of the beneficiaries.

A **trust** exists when a person (the trustee) holds property for others (beneficiaries) who are intended to benefit from that property or from the income of that property. The **trust deed** sets out the terms and conditions under which the trust assets are held and outlines the rights of the beneficiaries. In general, a trust is not established until it is 'constituted' meaning both that the trust deed is signed and that money, or something of value, is transferred to the trustee. Trusts are a very popular form of ownership structure, particularly in Australia and New Zealand. One of the main reasons is that trusts offer attractions — tax minimisation and other benefits — for families intent on creating wealth for present and future generations by acquiring and holding onto assets. There is also some appeal in running a family business via a flexible trust structure or developing a family estate to survive intergenerational transfers.

Trust structure

In any trust, there is dual ownership of the trust property. As shown in figure 8.1, the trustee is the legal owner of the trust property, and beneficiaries are the equitable owners. The trustee can be one or more persons or a company. The trustee controls and manages the trust property for and on behalf of the beneficiaries. The duties and powers of the trustee are set out in the trust deed. Any kind of property — real estate, shares or business assets — can be the subject of the trust.

Beneficiaries are the equitable or beneficial owners of the trust property. They are the ultimate owners of the property. If there is a conflict between the trustee and the beneficiary, the interests of the beneficiary always prevail. Figure 8.1 shows a simple trust structure in which a company (X Pty Ltd) is the trustee. (Note that other people can act as joint trustees.) In this case, the business is owned by the trustee company.

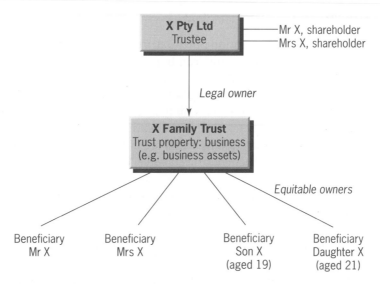

Figure 8.1: Trust structure

In Australia, there are four main types of trust that a family or small business might consider:[5]

- *discretionary*, in which the annual distributions of income and capital profits to beneficiaries are at the discretion of the trustee
- *fixed*, in which the income and profit entitlements of the trust beneficiaries are fixed
- *hybrid*, which is a blend of fixed and discretionary; a common structure gives beneficiaries a fixed entitlement to capital and a discretionary entitlement to income
- *unit*, in which a beneficiary has a fixed entitlement to a trust's assets as well as to a share of trust income in proportion to units held.

Many issues need to be considered before setting up a trust. For example, the current and projected level of income of the entrepreneur is one factor. In essence, the tax treatment of the trust income depends on who is and is not entitled to the income as of 30 June each year. A family with at least one taxpayer who has an income above A$150 000, where the top personal tax rate cuts in, may have good reason to set up a family trust. The sophistication of the entrepreneur's financial affairs is another factor to consider. It is essential, therefore, to do your homework and get good advice.

Once people have established that they need a trust, the next step is working out what is involved in setting up and running it. Establishment costs depend on how complicated a person's financial affairs are and the professional help employed to set up the trust. It is possible to buy an off-the-shelf trust deed for A$1500, but you need to be sure it will cover all circumstances. For example, a person may want to place restrictions on who will be the beneficiaries. Expenses could therefore range from A$1500 for something small and simple to several thousand dollars for a more complex trust.

Advantages and drawbacks of a trust

In addition to tax minimisation potential, trusts offer a number of other advantages:
Income splitting. A family trust can boost family income if the investments held in the family trust are allocated to a spouse and children. Since the income is spread over several family members, each family member's income falls into a lower tax bracket. However, children under 18 are not efficient beneficiaries because of the penalty tax regime that exists for this group.

- *Capital gains tax*. Discretionary trusts are able to pass on the 50 per cent capital gains tax discount to beneficiaries tax-free; companies are not able to do this for their shareholders.
- *Control*. Although the assets are owned by the trust, control remains firmly with the family via the trustees, which could be individuals or a private company with family members as directors.
- *Asset protection*. Trusts can allow private family assets to be isolated from business assets and protected if a business collapses. In a matrimonial conflict, a trust enables assets to be protected from an estranged spouse, although changes have been made in this area via family law amendments.
- *Stability*. Trusts can be very stable structures and last beyond the death of the original trustees. If the shares in the company are transferred to trustees before death, a trust can be used to prevent the unnecessary liquidation of a family company. The terms of the trust will ensure that the individual's wishes are observed. This may be particularly advantageous if the family members have little business experience or if they are unlikely to agree on the correct way to manage the business.

Nevertheless, there are a number of limitations and drawbacks to trusts:

- *Small business capital gains tax (CGT)*. Entrepreneurs establishing a trust need to be aware of the pitfalls concerning the various small business CGT concessions — it may be difficult to qualify for some, and entrepreneurs need to know the rules.
- *Divorce and death*. Potential conflicts can arise involving divorce or partners of beneficiaries who have remarried after a beneficiary's death.
- *Hiding assets*. Entrepreneurs should not expect to be able to hide assets from creditors by setting up a family trust for their personal assets just before their business collapses. Courts can order the repayment of personal or business money directed into a trust within five and a half years of a collapse, especially if legal action has already been taken against the business.
- *Legislative risk*. The tax advantages trusts can offer continue to make them targets for government and regulators. In 2002 the Australian government decided to shelve draft legislation for a new family trust regime, but there is no guarantee regulators will not attempt to make changes in the future.

Comparing legal structures

The choice of legal structure should take into consideration the type and profitability of the business venture and the relationship, family, financial and tax positions of the people going into business. The set-up and running costs of the structure should be considered in relation to perceived benefits. Table 8.3 details some of the differences between the four main legal forms of ownership discussed above. Ideally, the structure chosen should:

- comply with legal requirements
- be simple and cost effective
- maximise protection of assets
- minimise personal liability
- minimise both income and capital gains tax
- allow for admission of new partners or investors
- be flexible.

Table 8.3: Differences between legal structures

Feature	Sole proprietor	Partnership	Company	Trust
Formation cost	Low	Moderate	High	Moderate/high
Personal liability of owner/s	Unlimited	Unlimited	Limited	Limited
Ability to raise external capital	Low	Moderate	Moderate/good	Moderate
Permanence	Limited to owner's lifetime	Usually limited; may be overcome by agreement	Enduring	Enduring
Ongoing cost of compliance	Low	Low	High	Moderate/high
Privacy	High	Moderate	Low	High

There is no single business structure that is right for every business. Every decision involves some trade-offs. At the start-up stage, the focus tends to be on cost and simplicity. Entrepreneurs are looking for a structure that has low set-up and running costs. In many cases, the simpler the structure the better, as this requires less management time, less formalisation and fewer operations. The problem comes, however, when businesses mature beyond start-up stage. Often they have earned their goodwill and developed assets, so the cost of restructuring runs high.

Evolving a business from 'start-up' to 'grown-up' means making structural adjustments. In most cases, high-growth business ventures will choose between companies and trusts or a mix within the structure. Companies and trusts will normally provide a higher level of asset protection and risk management. The objective should be to protect the assets of the owners and shareholders from risks associated with the business. These two structures also separate the operations of the business's assets, so they can be dealt with separately and different risk exposures within the business can be quarantined. It is not uncommon to see the intellectual property of brand goodwill held within a passive entity and then licensed to the operating entities for their use.[6]

Choosing a legal structure for Baik

Patricia Budiyanto and Suzy Elenawati met in Subang Jaya, Malaysia, during their first year at a private college that offers international study programs. Patricia was enrolled in an Australian university bachelor of accounting program. Suzy, who had always been interested in arts and crafts, was enrolled in a design course. Shortly after their arrival at college, both girls joined the Indonesian Students Association and were elected to the board of the association, with Patricia as treasurer and Suzy as events organiser. This meant they often had to collaborate on preparing budgets for various events. They got on so well that they decided to share a flat during their second year of study. This provided them with the opportunity to get to know each other better, and they discovered they had a great deal of admiration and respect for each other.

The two girls are now in the middle of their third and last year of study, and Patricia has suggested that they start a business together in Kuala Lumpur. She has noticed that more and more Malaysians and expatriates are interested in buying Indonesian furniture and wood sculptures. Their business model is straightforward — buy furniture in Bali, import the goods into Malaysia and set up a retail shop in Kuala Lumpur. Suzy is thrilled with the idea. Every piece bought in Bali will be selected for its uniqueness, high quality and functional ability. Working with top designers and craftspeople, Patricia and Suzy plan to bring the finest and rarest Balinese items to Malaysia. The two friends even have a name for their business: Baik — Indonesian for 'fine'. The main hurdle at this stage is funding. They both have about RM30 000 in savings — just enough to organise the first shipment and pay for the lease deposit. However, they are both determined to set up their business as soon as they graduate in four months.

Questions

1. What legal structure would you recommend Patricia and Suzy adopt for their business?
2. What steps must the two friends take in order to set up their business?

The pyramid structures of Asian firms

Although all countries in the Pacific Rim region basically have the same legal structures under which businesses operate, most Asian companies have a distinctive feature. Control of firms is enhanced through 'pyramids' — extraordinarily complex and opaque structures of private holding companies, layer upon layer of subsidiaries, and cross-holdings and informal links with yet more companies. Voting rights consequently exceed formal profit rights, especially in Indonesia and Singapore.[7] Most of these pyramids have been established by overseas Chinese entrepreneurs, and their purpose is to draw outside capital into the family group and retain control over the use of this capital within the family.

To see how this works, picture a pyramid, at the top of which sits a private holding company owned by the patriarch and his family. It owns 51 per cent of subsidiary A, which owns 51 per cent of subsidiary B, which owns 51 per cent of subsidiary C, which owns 30 per cent of company D. Separately, the family has another (wholly owned) vehicle, F, which owns 21 per cent of company D. In terms of voting rights, the patriarch and his family therefore control 51 per cent of company D. At the same time, the family can claim only 25 per cent of company D's profits (51% × 51% × 51% × 30%, + 21% through company F).

This discrepancy between the family's control (voting rights) and ownership (profit rights) creates an opportunity, and indeed an incentive, to expropriate minority shareholders in company D and its parents. How? One way is for the controlling family to make company D pay miserly dividends. Better still, the family could make company D sell an asset to company F at an artificially low price, or make company D buy an asset from F at an inflated price.[8]

Such risks are pervasive in several Asian countries, where more than two-thirds of firms are generally controlled by a single shareholder. Separation of management from ownership is rare, and the top management of about 60 per cent of firms whose shares are not widely held is related to the family of the controlling shareholder. The evidence also suggests that in some countries a significant share of corporate assets rests in the hands of a small number of families. At the extreme, 16.6 per cent and 17.1 per cent of the total value of listed corporate assets in Indonesia and the Philippines respectively can be traced to the ultimate control of a single family. The ten largest families in Indonesia, the Philippines and Thailand control half of the corporate assets listed.[9]

Intellectual property

Intellectual property, in business terms, means proprietary knowledge. This can result from an invention, original design or the practical application of a good idea, and it is a key component of success for business today. It is often the competitive edge that sets successful small businesses apart and, as world markets become increasingly crowded and competitive, protecting a firm's intellectual property is essential.

Intellectual property is often a valuable asset, and it is important to clearly identify and safeguard it. It may be the business's name, a brand logo, a graphic design or an invention. Failure to protect such property can put a key asset of the business at risk.

As shown in table 8.4, specific government bodies deal with intellectual property issues in several countries. These agencies provide information about the latest legislation, costs and procedures in relation to the five main types of intellectual property rights — patents, trademarks, industrial designs, copyrights and trade secrets.

Table 8.4: Intellectual property agencies

Country	Authority
Australia	IP Australia <www.ipaustralia.gov.au>
Hong Kong	Intellectual Property Department <www.ipd.gov.hk>
Malaysia	Intellectual Property Division, Ministry of Domestic Trade and Consumer Affairs <www.mipc.gov.my>
New Zealand	Intellectual Property Office of New Zealand <www.iponz.govt.nz>
Singapore	Intellectual Property Office of Singapore <www.ipos.gov.sg>

Patents

A **patent** is an exclusive right to exploit (produce and sell) a particular product or use a specific process for a certain period of time. Patent laws are intended to encourage inventions and new technology and protect these for a limited period. In most countries, the standard length of protection is 20 years, and the patent can be renewed after this initial period.

A patent can be granted to someone who has created something that is inventive, new and useful. Essentially, the invention must be new and not obvious to people who understand the technology. This means that if an inventor demonstrates, sells or publicly discusses the invention before applying for a patent, the right to protection will be lost. It is also a good idea to do a search of existing inventions before applying for a patent in case the invention is already known. Table 8.5 lists the relevant patent legislation and length of protection.

Table 8.5: Patent legislation and length of protection

Country	Legislation	Length of protection
Australia	*Patents Act 1990*	20 years (standard); 8 years (innovation)
New Zealand	*Patents Act 1953*	20 years
Malaysia	*Patents (Amendment) Act 2000*	20 years
Singapore	*Patents (Amendment) Act 2004*	20 years
Hong Kong	*Patents Ordinance 1997*	20 years (standard); 8 years (short term)

In Australia, there are two types of patent:
- the *standard patent* gives long-term protection and control over an invention for up to 20 years
- the *innovation patent* is a relatively fast, inexpensive protection option that lasts for a maximum of eight years. It provides local industry with a relatively cheap patent right, and it is quick and easy to obtain. This patent system is designed to protect inventions that are not sufficiently inventive to meet the inventive threshold required for standard patents. It is an attractive option for SMEs.

A patent is often referred to as a monopoly granted by the government to an inventor for a limited period in return for the disclosure of the invention so that others may gain the benefit. Hence, the patent may also be viewed as a reward for creative innovation and intellectual advancement, and the exclusive rights give the inventor the incentive to innovate.[10] The patent owner has the right to sue for any infringement, regardless of whether the owner uses, sells or makes any product using the patent. It is up to the owner of a patent to bring an action, usually under the civil law, for any infringement of patent rights.

The process of registering a patent varies slightly from one country to another, but always starts with the completion of an application form stating the applicant's request for the grant of the patent and the names of the inventor/s, plus any other descriptions, claims and drawings. The authority then determines whether the patent lodged supports a genuine invention and conducts a thorough search process. If there are no adverse findings or opposition, the authority publishes the application and makes known its details to the public. The cost involved in filing an application is minimal. However, the process of registration (search, opposition, publication) takes several months and can amount to between S$4500 and S$6000 in Singapore and between A$5000 and A$7000 in Australia. These figures can be substantially higher if the specialist services of a patent attorney are used and if inventors want protection overseas.

Most inventors wanting protection overseas lodge a patent cooperation treaty (PCT) application, which lasts for 18 months and covers 124 countries. Then comes the cumbersome and expensive step: to extend the protection beyond this initial period, inventors must then file individual applications in each country where they want protection. The complexity and cost of filing international patents provides a business opportunity for entrepreneurs. For example, PCTFiler <www.pctfiler.com> is a start-up providing a software system that allows the user to apply for international patent protection at a substantially lower cost than by using the conventional legal channels.

Trademarks

A trademark is a 'sign' used to distinguish the products or services of the trademark owner from those of competitors.[11] A **trademark** can be a letter, number, word, phrase, shape, logo, picture, aspect of packaging or combination of these. One trademark that is known all over the world is the 'golden arches' of McDonald's. The right to use a trademark can be assigned or licensed to someone else for the specified product or service. Registered trademarks are identified with an ®.

A trademark may be a valuable marketing tool, as consumers often associate products or services bearing a particular trademark with a certain quality or image. Whereas a patent protects the function, the trademark protects the look of a business.[12] For this reason, it is recommended that for each new product or service developed and introduced, trademarks should be given an equal amount of consideration. Table 8.6 shows trademark legislation and length of protection.

A combination of good business operations and imaginative intellectual property protection can be used by new businesses to gain a competitive advantage and earn valuable market share. Some people still think of trademarks as the brand name of a product and its logo. However, in 1995 the Australian *Trade Marks Act* expanded the range of items that could be registered. These items, dubbed 'non-traditional trademarks', include shapes, colours, sounds and smells. One company that capitalised on a non-traditional trademark is Eagle Boys Dial-A-Pizza. The company, through trademark registration of their fuchsia lighting and innovative two-tiered pizza boxes, developed valuable assets that have been incorporated into its franchising and earned it very high product recognition. Within months of opening its first outlet in 1986, Eagle Boys had registered a trademark; the company then gained the exclusive right to use the fuchsia glow in its shopfronts, a landmark move in the trademark registration system.[13]

Many small businesses wrongly assume that having a business name registered in Australia gives trademark protection. A recent survey by IP Australia showed that an alarming 85 per cent of small businesses believed that business name

Trademark:
A word, phrase, logo, symbol, colour, sound or smell used by a business to identify a product and distinguish it from those of its competitors.

registration would stop other businesses using the same name. Moreover, 80 per cent of small businesses assumed that registering their business name automatically gave trademark protection.[14] Registering a trademark is therefore essential in protecting the business brand and intellectual property. One solution for small businesses is to register their business name as a trademark.

Table 8.6: Trademark legislation and length of protection

Country	Legislation	Length of protection
Australia	*Trade Marks Act 1995*	10 years, renewable every 10 years thereafter
New Zealand	*Trade Marks Act 2002*	10 years, renewable every 10 years thereafter
Malaysia	*Trade Marks (Amendment) Act 2000*	10 years, renewable every 10 years thereafter
Singapore	*Trade Marks (Amendment) Act 2004*	10 years, renewable every 10 years thereafter
Hong Kong	*Trade Marks Ordinance*	10 years, renewable every 10 years thereafter

Industrial designs

A design refers to any aspect of the shape or configuration of the whole or part of an item.[15] The right provided by a design registration is in many ways similar to that provided by a patent, but the protection is limited to the appearance of the product, such as its shape or pattern. Whereas a patent aims to provide protection for the underlying invention, a registered design protects the visual appearance of a product. For example, the Australian Designs Bill 2002 protects the visual feature in relation to a product, which includes the shape, configuration, pattern and ornamentation of the product.

Despite this narrow form of protection, good industrial design of a product is becoming increasingly important for gaining a marketing edge, and registration does provide a means of protecting the subtleties of a design that might have taken a designer many hours of work and thousands of dollars to achieve.

Designs are protected in Australia, New Zealand, Malaysia, Singapore and the Hong Kong Special Administrative Region (SAR). In a major move to increase the protection of intellectual property, the Hong Kong SAR established its own independent design registry in June 1997. The designs registration system is similar to the patent system, but separate from the system operating in other parts of China.

Copyright:
The exclusive right granted by law to a copyright holder to make and distribute copies of, or otherwise control, their literary, musical, dramatic or artistic work.

Copyright

Copyright covers literary, dramatic, musical or artistic works. It is the exclusive right to produce or reproduce a work by making copies of it or performing it, or to license others to do so.[16] Many copyright laws also contain provisions for the protection of 'works of applied art', such as artistic jewellery, furniture, greetings cards and wallpaper. Originators of copyright material have a number of rights, the most explicit being 'economic rights'. The most important right of the originator is the exclusive right to reproduce. The originator's other rights include performing the work in public, broadcasting it, publishing it and making any adaptation of the copyright work.[17]

Copyright protection is an automatic right that arises when a work is created — the material is protected from the time it is first written down, painted, drawn, filmed or taped. In Australia, for example, copyright protection is provided under the *Copyright Act 1968*. Australian law regards an employer as the owner of copyright if the author was, when the work was created, an employee and was employed for the very purpose of creating the work.

Singapore and Hong Kong have taken important measures to investigate and curb intellectual property piracy problems that are particularly acute in the computer software and entertainment industry (CDs and books being a prime example). Singapore set up a dedicated Intellectual Property Warrant Rights Unit (IPRWU) in 1995. Similarly, the Hong Kong SAR Copyright Ordinance 1997 provides stiff penalties; those who indulge in copyright piracy are liable to a maximum fine of HK$50 000 per infringing article and a term of imprisonment of up to four years.[18] Importing or exporting pirated articles is also a criminal offence.

Trade secrets

Most companies (including start-ups) have a wealth of information that is critical to their success, but does not qualify for patent, trademark or copyright protection. Some of this information is confidential and therefore needs to be kept secret in order to help the business maintain its competitive advantage. Sometimes entrepreneurs also find it too expensive to patent their invention or they do not want to attract the attention of potential competitors. Therefore, before filing for protection, entrepreneurs should consider the market for their product. The Chairman of the Inventors Association of Australia, Stuart Fox, commented: 'If you are short of funds, don't mortgage the house and spend heaps on patents. Look at whether you can get the idea into production and sell it to customers.'[19]

Trade secret: Any idea, formula, pattern, device, process or information that provides a business with a competitive advantage.

A **trade secret** is any idea, formula, pattern, device, process or information that provides the owner with a competitive advantage in the marketplace. Trade secrets include marketing plans, product formulas, financial forecasts, employees' rosters and laboratory notebooks. The medium in which information is stored has no impact on whether it can be protected as a trade secret. As a result, written documents, computer files, videotapes and even the employees' memory of various items can be protected from unauthorised disclosure.[20]

Unlike patents, trademarks and copyright, there is no single government agency or legislation that regulates trade secrets. Therefore, it is the firm's responsibility to protect itself by exercising caution in storing and communicating information. Companies often use confidentiality agreements to prevent employees from revealing their secret or proprietary knowledge during and after employment. If an agreement is breached, the employer will have evidence of the agreed terms and subsequent protection by law.

Entrepreneur profile

Kristy Andruszko

Kristy Andruszko is barking all the way to the bank on the success of her pet care and accessories business Puppy Phat. However, it has not always been a walk in the park. Kristy learned the hard way that without thorough research and preparation, setting up a business can be a very costly experience, both financially and emotionally.

Kristy originally opened her business in 2003 under the name of Lush Puppy. The business was born out of Kristy's desire to fill a niche in the market for funky pet care products, including collars, beds and pet fashion. Kristy started up a wholesale business selling her products to retail outlets before opening her own retail store in Daylesford, Victoria. In 2004, Lush Puppy's retail stores were launched with much fanfare. The Channel 10 small business program *Bread TV* documented Kristy's start-up journey. With this exposure, Lush Puppy had a huge beginning, selling out of many products within the first couple of weeks.

However, success turned into stress. After just ten days of operation, Kristy was sent a letter from the legal advisor of another business to inform her that her business name was infringing the registered trademark of another company. Kristy was warned that legal action would result if she did not cease trading under the Lush Puppy name. 'The irony of the situation was that when I first set up my business I kept thinking to myself, "I'm going to have to trademark the Lush Puppy name so no-one rips me off". Then someone sent me a letter saying that I was trying to rip them off,' Kristy said. She added: 'I didn't know that this company existed, [nor did I] have any intention of ripping them off, so I was devastated when I received the letter.'

Kristy wasn't aware that a business name doesn't provide any protection for a brand name — only a registered trademark can provide that level of protection nation-wide. 'It wasn't until I looked at how I should have set up my business that I saw all the additional checks that I should have done — checks that would have saved me heaps of time, money and stress,' she said. She wasn't aware of IP Australia's Business Name Application Search Service (BASS), which will check out very similar pending or registered trademarks for a small fee.

Kristy sought legal advice immediately, but the news was not good. 'My lawyer told me that I could fight to keep trading as Lush Puppy, but that my chances of winning were slim,' she recalls. So she made the difficult decision to abandon the Lush Puppy business name, which meant destroying all her Lush Puppy stock, closing down her website and deregistering her business name. Kristy also lost her wholesale business and all the goodwill generated from Lush Puppy's exposure on *Bread TV*.

Kristy has learned a lot about intellectual property from her experience, and she admits that it has forced her to make changes for the better. Her advice to others is to be IP smart from the start: 'A business name is a legal requirement which is in place more to protect the consumer than the business owner,' she said. 'Business owners need a business name to operate but, to protect yourself, your business and your brand, a registered trademark is the most important thing.'

Source: IP Australia, 'Beware of the dog', Smart Start Case Studies, Commonwealth of Australia, <www.ipaustralia.gov.au/smartstart/>.

Other legal issues

Once the legal structure of the business has been established and any intellectual property has been protected, the entrepreneur/business owner needs to examine other, more generalised legal matters that may be relevant to the enterprise. Because there are so many, and they depend on the nature of business activity being undertaken, it can be difficult to cover all these in advance. Some of the more common legal matters concern licences and permits; registering for a business number and for the goods and services tax (GST); trade practices; and taxation.

Licences and permits

Regardless of the business structure chosen, each industry has its own set of regulations that participants must comply with. Therefore, in addition to formally registering a business entity, a business owner must ensure that the firm can comply with all necessary permits and licences imposed by government. For example, hairdressers often need to be registered by a board before they can operate. Doctors and dentists need an appropriate degree and professional registration before they can open a practice. Restaurant premises must be approved by health authorities to ensure food is hygienically prepared. In most countries, local government authorities have strict zoning rules about what business activities can take place in particular localities, and whether a business can be operated from home.

Licences take a variety of forms and are administered by a number of different authorities. In some countries, governments have developed 'business licence centres' that contain a centralised database of all required permits. It is important not to underestimate the need to obtain all necessary permits before starting a business venture. In many respects, permits may be regarded as the main indicator of the viability of a proposed business idea; if all necessary permits cannot be obtained, then the business is usually not feasible.

Registering for a business number and the goods and services tax (GST)

In Australia, the Australian business number (ABN) is a single identifier for all business dealings with the Australian Taxation Office (ATO) and for future dealings with other government departments and agencies under the *New Tax System (Australian Business Number) Act 1999*. All companies covered by the *Corporations Act* have an ABN. Other entities, including an individual, partnership or trust, are also entitled to an ABN if they meet the definition of an enterprise — any activity or series of activities undertaken in the form of a business. In general, the ATO encourages businesses to register for an ABN. Business owners can register electronically or obtain a registration application from the ATO. In addition to applying for an ABN, the form also provides the opportunity of applying for a tax file number and registering for GST.[21]

The goods and services tax (GST) is a broad-based tax of 10 per cent on most supplies of goods and services consumed in Australia. It is based on the *supply* of goods or services, including advice, information, real property and certain dealings with rights and obligations. When a business that is registered for GST makes a taxable supply, one-eleventh of the consideration received for that supply is GST. Businesses with an annual turnover of A$50 000 or more and non-profit organisations with an annual turnover of A$100 000 or more must register for GST. Those with a lower turnover are not required to register for GST, although they may do so if they wish and if they meet the definition of an enterprise.

GST (of 12.5 per cent) is also New Zealand's main type of tax apart from income tax. In Singapore, GST was first introduced in 1994, and has increased from four per cent to five per cent. There is no GST in Malaysia, but a tax on sales; the normal rate is 10 per cent. Currently, there is no value-added or sales tax in the Hong Kong SAR.

Trade practices law

All existing and proposed businesses need to be aware that most countries have laws governing what is 'acceptable' business conduct. These laws generally prohibit anti-competitive behaviour such as deliberately misleading customers or suppliers, price-fixing, the formation of cartels, and unfair conduct against competitors. In Australia, there are several federal, state and territory statutes that protect consumers.

Among the various statutes, the *Trade Practices Act 1974* operates as national consumer protection legislation. An independent statutory authority, the Australian Competition and Consumer Commission (ACCC) administers the Act. The broad objective of the Act is to allow each business to compete on its merits, making its own decisions and treating consumers fairly.[22] The Act provides ways of achieving this objective:

- It encourages competition in Australian markets by prohibiting anti-competitive conduct such as illegal price agreements and market-sharing agreements.
- It stops anti-competitive mergers that may result in the further concentration of ownership of the production of goods or the provision of services. Such mergers can reduce the ability of small businesses to shop around for commercially favourable prices and terms when buying goods and services.
- It prohibits unfair trading practices, such as misleading and deceptive conduct (for example, withholding relevant information, making false predictions, exaggerating sales); false representations (false statements made in advertising); and sharp selling practices (for example, bait advertising, which is advertising non-existent or limited quantities of goods and services, and referral selling, whereby a business will not sell its goods to a customer unless the customer gives referrals).
- It protects small business from unconscionable conduct and provides for better disclosure and dispute resolution for small businesses. The unconscionable conduct provision (s. 51AC) prohibits a stronger party dealing with a disadvantaged party in a harsh or oppressive manner. A disadvantage here includes

illiteracy, age, poverty, illness, mental impairment and inequality in bargaining power.

New Zealand's main statute in the area of competition law is the *Commerce Act 1986*, which is very similar to Australian legislation. The *Commerce Act* is enforced by the Commerce Commission. In Singapore, a Consumer Protection (Fair Trading) Bill was passed in 2003. It has been the result of the government recognising the need to give consumers more protection against unscrupulous businesses. In Malaysia, the *Consumer Protection Act 1999* provides greater protection for consumers. Only the Hong Kong SAR government has adopted a piecemeal and sector-specific approach to both consumer protection and competition.

Taxation

Another form of business regulation involves the government imposition of taxes that must be complied with. These can include sales taxes, goods and services taxes, employee payroll deductions and local government levies. In most countries, businesses need to:

- account for income tax
- account for business expenses that are claimed as deductions
- keep business records, and report and pay tax.

Income tax is levied on a person's or a business's taxable income and must generally be paid to the central government. In Australia, sole traders do not need to complete a separate return for their business; they use their personal income tax return to report their business income and deductions. Partnerships must complete a partnership tax return to show the partnership's income and deductions and to show how the profit or loss was shared among the partners. Companies must complete a company tax return to calculate the tax it must pay. A trust must also lodge an annual income tax return under its own income tax file number. All beneficiaries who receive an income from the trust must in turn declare this income in their personal income tax return.

Under income tax law, a person carrying on a business can claim deductions for costs that are necessarily incurred to produce assessable income, provided these expenses are not of a private, domestic or capital nature. Such deductions include motor vehicle expenses; expenses relating to the area occupied by the business in a personal home; travel expenses such as fares, car hire and accommodation; tools; employees' expenses; and interest on borrowed money. In addition to the business books, business owners are advised to keep evidence of transactions (such as invoices and receipts) and evidence of usage (such as motor vehicle logs for vehicle expenses and airline tickets for travel expenses).

Good business records help small business operators to manage their business and make sound business decisions. They are also useful if an owner wants to sell the business. Under tax law, a person carrying on a business must keep records covering all transactions. These records include any documents that are relevant for the purpose of working out the person's income and expenditure. Any books of accounts, records or documents relating to the preparation of the income tax return must be retained for five years. In Australia, other statutory provisions, such as corporate law, require a company to retain records for seven years after completion of the transaction to which they relate.

The best sources of advice on taxation obligations, including recordkeeping requirements, are qualified accountants or the relevant taxation authority. The main taxation authorities in the countries referred to here are listed in table 8.7. These authorities generally provide helpful guidebooks as well as online information about taxation requirements.

Table 8.7: Main taxation authorities

Country	Authority
Australia	Australian Taxation Office <www.ato.gov.au>
Hong Kong	Inland Revenue Department <www.info.gov.hk/ird>
Malaysia	Inland Revenue Board of Malaysia <www.hasil.org.my>
New Zealand	Inland Revenue Department <www.ird.govt.nz>
Singapore	Inland Revenue Authority of Singapore <www.iras.gov.sg>

Summary

There are three basic types of legal structure — sole proprietorship, partnership and company. In Australia and New Zealand, a trust is also a legal structure under which a business may operate. Each of these has varying degrees of complexity and cost, as well as variations in the level of individual control that can be exercised by the business owner. Asian companies often differ from their Australian and New Zealand counterparts in respect to the separation of ownership and control, since in many Asian corporations voting rights (control) often exceed profit rights (ownership) via pyramid structures and cross-holdings.

Intellectual property is another legal issue entrepreneurs must consider. Intellectual property is a valuable asset and it should be clearly identified. It is often the competitive edge that sets successful small businesses apart and, as world markets become increasingly crowded and competitive, a firm's intellectual property must be protected. Once the intellectual property has been identified, appropriate strategies should be put in place to safeguard it. There are five main types of intellectual property rights — patents, trademarks, designs, copyrights and trade secrets — which business owners can use to protect their intellectual property. Failure to protect such ideas, and to do so early, can put a key asset of the business at risk.

The business owner also needs to examine other, more generalised legal matters that may be relevant to the enterprise. Because there is a wide range of legal matters and their relevance depends on the nature of the business activity being undertaken, it can be difficult to cover all these in advance. Some of the more common ones are licences and permits, registering for an Australian business number and the goods and services tax, trade practices and taxation.

REVIEW QUESTIONS

1. What are the different legal structures a business can operate under and how do they differ from one another?
2. What is intellectual property?
3. What is the difference between a patent, a trademark and an industrial design?
4. Why do certain categories of business require a licence or a permit to operate? Give some examples of such businesses in your own country.
5. What are the main duties of a business with regard to taxation?

DISCUSSION QUESTIONS

1. 'A partnership is a lot like a marriage.' How accurate is this statement?
2. What role do patents play in everyday life?
3. A patent registration granted by a national patent office does not necessarily protect an invention worldwide. What can be done to obtain international protection?
4. List and explain the main kinds of anti-competitive practices that a national trade practices law could prohibit.

SUGGESTED READING

Birch, C., *Law for Small Business*, 2nd edn, John Wiley & Sons, Brisbane, 2002.

Birt, I., *Legal Aspects of Your Small Business*, Pearson Education, Sydney, 2002.

Barron M.L. & Fletcher R., *Fundamentals of Business Law*, 4th edn, McGraw-Hill, Sydney, 2003.

CASE STUDY

HGM Design Ltd

'I just wish I could try it on.' How many times does a jewellery retailer hear that wistful lament? Dale Mooney, founder and managing director of HGM Design Ltd, Auckland, heard it too. In fact, he heard it so many times as a manager for Diamond & Time in Auckland and Hamilton, it got him thinking that there must be a way to close a sale in-store. So he came up with Try-On — a simple scanner, touch screen and software package to help sell jewellery. Dale had now fine tuned the technology and manufactured a couple of prototypes. But he was still wondering about the best way to tackle the jewellery retail market and how he should protect his intellectual property.

The business idea

The principle of Try-On is very simple. A customer simply walks into a jewellery store, puts their hand into the scanner, and 90 seconds later their hand appears on the screen. They can then choose a ring to suit their hand and price range from the program's library (currently 200 rings with 70 variations per ring), or design their own using the components in the system. The ring appears on the screen hand in a 3D image, as if the customer was really wearing it. This simple idea can mean the difference between an uncertain customer walking away and a decisive customer buying a ring worth several thousand dollars.

In 2001, Mooney started HGM Design to pursue the idea. He initially had problems finding a software company that could help translate his concept into reality. It cost him around NZ$120 000 to produce a crude prototype that still could not do exactly what he wanted. 'I found very quickly that if you don't know about the technical side, people can easily pull the wool over your eyes.' He had chewed through NZ$60 000 of his own money and a similar amount from an 'angel investor' — his cousin Ross Mackenzie, managing director of successful exporter Old Fashioned Foods, who threw in a business plan along with his cash.

Mooney and Mackenzie decided it would be cheaper to refine the product and easier to retain control with in-house software experts. They enlisted the help of IRL's DeviceWorks, which specialises in developing smart industrial machines. The result was a sophisticated scanner that could do what Mooney had envisioned. Today, the HGM Design Ltd core team comprises Dale, 3D jewellery modellers Jason Mobberley and Phil Hull and computer programmer Alex Lavrinovich. They are now working on Dale's initial thoughts from offices at the Auckland University of Technology building in Penrose.

The first trial

The turning point, at least in Mackenzie's eyes, came about two years ago when they visited the Brisbane headquarters of Michael Hill Jeweller to obtain feedback on their idea. The retail jeweller had been hunting worldwide for such a product, but had yet to find anything that did the job. Michael Hill said that HGM Design's version had the 'wow' factor, recalls Mackenzie. 'That meeting with Michael Hill gave me a lot of confidence that if we could develop the product, there would be a market for it.' Up until then, he'd been investing on blind faith.

In 2004, he entered the inaugural AUT/Unlimited Up-Start competition for start-up companies. Although not a winner, he was invited to join the tech park to help commercialise his product. The one-man band has since grown to eight employees and has just started trialling Try-On with the Auckland Ring Company. 'We're the guinea pigs,' says owner John Crockett. 'It's quite an innovative concept and different to anything anyone else has tried. It could only have been conceived by someone with an intimate knowledge of the jewellery trade and the foibles of its customers.'

Mooney's share in the company has dwindled, with Mackenzie — who has invested around NZ$1 million so far — taking a controlling 51 per cent shareholding. The company has also gained a total of NZ$305 000 from various grants. Mooney admits that losing majority ownership wasn't easy, but says he'd rather see his idea succeed than get personal gain for himself. He also admits to 'feeling a bit tired' after five years of getting the product to this point.

Source: Adapted from F. Rotherham, 'Getting hands on', *Unlimited: Business with imagination*, <http://unlimited.co.nz>, no. 83, 1 June 2006

Questions

1. What are the main advantages and drawbacks of having chosen a company as a legal structure?

2. What legal steps does Dale need to take to protect his business idea?

3. What benefits does Dale's device provide to the jewellers and what business model should he adopt to sell to it to them?

ENDNOTES

1. Australian Bureau of Statistics, *ABS Business Register — Counts of Businesses*, ABS, Canberra, 2005, p.17.
2. M. Soe, *Principles of Singapore Law*, 2nd edn, IBF, Singapore, 1992, p. 502.
3. S. Terry, *Establishing a Company in Hong Kong*, 3rd edn, Pitman, Hong Kong, 1996.
4. H. McCombie, 'Owning your responsibilities', *Company Director*, vol. 22, no. 4, May 2006, pp. 24–6.
5. J. Wasiliev, 'Family values — trusts are back on track', *Weekend Australian Financial Review*, 26–27 October 2002, pp. 29–32.
6. G. Hayes, 'Well begun, half done', *BRW*, 16–22 February 2006, p. 54.
7. S. Claessens, S. Djankov & L. Lang, 'The separation of ownership and control in East Asian corporations', *Journal of Financial Economics*, no. 58, 2000, pp. 81–112.
8. 'In praise of rules — a survey of Asian business', *Economist*, 7 April 2001, p. 6.
9. S. Claessens, S. Djankov & L. Lang, *East Asian Corporations: Heroes Or Villains?*, World Bank Discussion Paper, no. 409, World Bank, Washington, 2000.
10. J. Holyoak, *Intellectual Property Law*, Butterworth, London, 1995.
11. Baker & McKenzie, 'IP issues in Australia', 1997, <www.bakerinfo.com>.
12. P. Mollerup, *Marks of Excellence*, Phaidon Press, London, 1997.
13. 'The eagle has landed', *Inside Business Success*, November 1997.
14. IP Australia, *Registered Business Names Survey*, Commonwealth of Australia, Canberra, October 2005.
15. P.J. Groves, *Intellectual Property Rights and their Valuation*, Woodhead Publishing, London, 1997, p. 35.
16. C.S. Tay, *Copyright and the Protection of Designs*, SNP Corporation, Singapore, 1997.
17. Australian Copyright Council, <www.copyright.org.au>.
18. Intellectual Property Department , <www.houston.com.hk/hkgipd>.
19. K. Le Mesurier, 'Invention has its price', *BRW*, 16–22 June 2005, p. 86.
20. B. Barringer & R.D. Ireland, *Entrepreneurship — Successfully Launching New Ventures*, Prentice Hall, Upper Saddle River, NJ, 2006.
21. Australian Taxation Office, *Tax Basics for Small Business*, ATO, Canberra, July 2002.
22. Australian Competition and Consumer Commission, *Small Business and the Trade Practices Act*, ACCC, Canberra, February 2002.

Chapter 9

Financing new and growing business ventures

LEARNING OBJECTIVES

After reading this chapter, you should be able to:

- distinguish the sources of finance according to provider, term and business life cycle
- discuss the financing options at the different stages of the business life cycle
- identify and explain the various types of debt finance
- identify and explain the various types of equity finance
- list and explain alternative sources of finance.

D ue to the risks involved in entrepreneurial pursuits, the financing of new ventures is often the main obstacle facing many intending business start-ups. An idea, product or service may be great and well researched, supported by sound marketing policies and good management but, without adequate financing, it is doomed to failure.

The struggle to get finance does not stop after the business is set up, and small businesses have traditionally been at a disadvantage in raising finance compared with large corporations.[1] This chapter explains the types of financing option available to entrepreneurs and discusses the sources of such capital. It also explains the factors that financial institutions take into account when assessing applications for finance and looks at alternative sources of finance, such as debt factoring and government-backed schemes.

A typology of financing

There are three main ways to categorise business financing, although these are not mutually exclusive: (1) we can examine financing options from the fund-provider's perspective and establish two categories — debt holders and equity holders; (2) financing options can be tackled from a timeframe perspective, distinguishing between short-term and long-term finance; (3) financing needs and possibilities vary according to the different life stages of the business venture so we can distinguish early-stage finance from expansion finance.

Debt versus equity

Debt finance is money borrowed from an outside party; equity finance is money provided by the owner(s) of a business venture. The main difference between equity and debt is that equity provides a residual ownership interest in the business, whereas debt does not. However, this distinction tends to become blurred in the case of small enterprises because of the highly intertwined relationship between the owner–manager and the business.[2] It is very common for small business owner–managers to invest money that has been raised by means of a loan secured over their personal assets. As a result, the owner–manager is more likely to regard these funds as personal debt rather than equity.

Another difference between debt and equity finance is that debt must be reimbursed on a fixed date, whereas equity is not reimbursed (unless the business goes into liquidation). Debt finance also requires the payment of interest at a fixed and predetermined rate, whereas equity providers receive a variable remuneration in the form of a dividend.

Leverage: The degree to which a business uses borrowed money; what the debt–equity ratio measures.

The underlying factors that determine the options the small business owner chooses for financing operations depends on the business needs and whether the assessment criteria required by each mode of finance can be met. In all cases, it is recommended that owner–managers adopt the best **leverage** possible in their capital structures. However, businesses that are highly leveraged may be at risk of bankruptcy if they are unable to pay their debt; they may also be unable to find new lenders in the future. Leverage can increase shareholders' return on their investments and often there are tax advantages associated with borrowing.

Demand for finance generally follows a 'pecking order' of (1) internal equity, (2) short-term debt, (3) long-term debt and (4) external equity. The pecking order can be readily applied to emerging and small firms because their closely held nature means that their owners prefer not to issue new equity, and there is greater uncertainty in accurately pricing equity and the supply of debt finance.[3] However, direct empirical testing of the pecking order hypothesis is very limited and, as yet, inconclusive.

Short-term versus long-term finance

Business and accounting literature usually considers short-term finance as debts that must be reimbursed within 12 months. Long-term finance encompasses all forms of finance where the term extends beyond 12 months.

Short-term finance usually takes the form of a bank overdraft, trade credit, credit card purchase or cash advance. These finance the day-to-day operations of the business, including wages of employees and purchases of inventory and supplies. Also, **bridging finance** (interim loans with a short fixed term) can be used to finance accounts-receivable contracts, which are relatively risk-free but delayed for one to three months.

Bridging finance: Financing extended to a firm using existing assets as collateral in order to acquire new assets; bridging finance is usually short term.

Money for short-term operations may be secured against (1) any unencumbered physical assets of the business and then (2) additional funds from shareholders or personal guarantees from principals. On occasion, inventories can be used as temporary security for operations loans. Bridging finance is normally secured by assignment of all the receivables and personal guarantees. On the balance sheet, accounts receivable, inventory and supplies are shown in the current assets section, whereas the counterpart loan information is displayed in the current liabilities section.

Long-term finance can, on the other hand, take the form of a long-term loan or a mortgage. Such finance is arranged when the scheduled repayment of the loan and the estimated useful life of the assets purchased (such as building, land, machinery, computers, equipment and shelving) are expected to exceed 12 months. Long-term finance is normally secured (1) by the new asset(s) purchased (up to 65 per cent), then (2) by other unencumbered physical assets of the business (for the remaining 35 per cent) or, failing that, (3) by additional funds from shareholders or personal guarantees from the principals. On the balance sheet, the equipment purchased is shown in the non-current assets section, and the counterpart loan information is shown both in the current liabilities section (for the interest currently payable) and in the non-current liabilities section. The useful life of the assets is directly reflected in their depreciation schedules.

Debt lenders (creditors) make loans to businesses that show strong management ability and steady growth potential. A business plan, including a cash flow projection demonstrating the business's ability to repay the loan principal and interest over the term of the repayment schedule, is required. The lender will expect the entrepreneur to have appropriate insurance to protect the assets.

Early-stage versus expansion finance

The type of funds needed is often also closely related to the stage of development of the firm. It is possible to distinguish between two main categories in relation to the business life cycle: early-stage financing and expansion financing.[4]

Early stage financing covers the following aspects of a new venture's launch and early days of trading:

- *Seed financing.* Seed money is necessary for product development, building a management team or completing a business plan. At this stage, an outline of the strategy is important, as is a research and development action plan identifying key milestones. This is the most difficult and expensive money to raise because it is needed before management can prove that the product will sell or that it can be produced and distributed at a competitive price. The entrepreneur's family, friends, relatives and personal savings are main sources of seed capital.
- *Start-up financing.* This represents the funds needed to facilitate the process of organising the business structure, facilities and relationships of a firm. At this stage, the business has completed testing of the product or service and is now ready to commercialise it. This money costs companies less equity per dollar of funding than seed capital does but more than expansion financing.
- *First-stage financing.* This is the money provided when firms have exhausted their initial capital and require additional funds to initiate full-scale production and marketing.

Much of the early-stage financing relies on boostrap finance — a means of financing start-up through highly creative acquisition and use of resources without raising equity from traditional sources or borrowing money from a bank. Bootstrap finance is further described in the section outlining alternative sources of finance at the end of this chapter.

Expansion financing, on the other hand, applies to firms that have successfully survived the start-up phase and have become established in their industry. For these businesses, the focus is on growth and expansion. Accordingly, their financial needs usually fall into one of the following categories:

- *Second-stage financing.* This refers to funds provided to operating firms that are expanding and that need extra funds to increase their working capital; these firms may not yet be showing a profit.
- *Third-stage (or mezzanine) financing.* Mezzanine financing refers to investment provided to a company already producing and selling a product or service to help the company achieve a critical objective (such as increasing inventories to achieve greater sales) that will enable it to go public. At this stage, the firm is making a profit and the new funds are usually applied to plant expansion, working capital or the development of an enhanced product. Mezzanine funds are typically lent to decrease a company's overall cost of financing by helping the company attract a significantly better price for its shares in a later public offering.
- *Initial public offering (IPO).* This is when a company first offers shares to the public and lists on the stock exchange. The track record of a business and management in seeking an IPO is critical. Historical information and several years'

financial results and forecasts will need to be analysed and explained in a detailed review of the business for a potential investor.

Many investors and especially venture capitalists, when funding new business ventures, adopt a 'stage-financing approach' to reduce their risk. Funding a company in 'stages' means apportioning the committed money as the company meets pre-established goals. If the company fails to meet a goal, investors are relieved of their obligation to provide additional funds. In this way, investors can cut their losses when a company does not meet expectations. At the same time, the company gets a commitment for its full funding, which it can obtain by meeting its goals. Customarily, the company apportions shares to investors as the money is received.

As shown in figure 9.1 (below), financing options depend to a large extent on the business life cycle. For example, during the seed stage, would-be entrepreneurs need to rely on their personal funds, as well as those of family, friends and perhaps 'business angels'. Banks do not provide seed financing; they focus, rather, on established businesses with a track record and a cash flow stream. Similarly, venture capitalists focus on the start-up and expansion stages. They usually sell their equity stakes through an exit mechanism (such as initial public offering, sale to strategic partner or management buyout) before the business venture reaches its maturity.

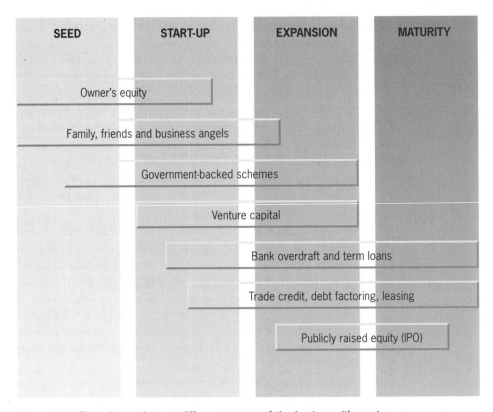

Figure 9.1: Financing options at different stages of the business life cycle

Debt finance

Most small business owners will, at some time or another, find that their own financial resources are insufficient to meet all their needs. When this point is reached, they will need to consider accessing funds from an outside party. This requires going into debt: that is, having an obligation or outstanding liability to an outside party. The main types of debt financing available to businesses include bank overdrafts, trade credit, term loans and leasing.

Banks, which provide overdrafts, term loans and mortgages, are the obvious choice for many entrepreneurs. However, small businesses often fail to obtain finance for three main reasons:

- The security offered by the applicant is considered insufficient to support the bank risk.
- The term requested by the applicant to pay back the loan is considered too long from the bank's point of view.
- The business lacks a track record of performance, so the bank is unable to assess the business's ability to repay the loan.

In studies of the problems faced by bank officers dealing with loans for small businesses, research has shown that proposals submitted for businesses that are unprofitable is the variable that loan officers perceive as the most important in adversely affecting their decisions.[5] The next most important variables are the inability of the applicant to provide collateral as requested, followed by incomplete information on the loan application, the applicant's lack of knowledge of overall business management and the proposed direction of the business. Variables, such as having no account with the bank, lack of knowledge of banking facilities for small businesses and the business being managed by the owners themselves, were not important to loan officers.

Bank overdraft

Overdraft:
The amount by which withdrawals exceed deposits or the extension of credit by a lending institution to allow for such a situation.

An **overdraft** is a credit arrangement permitting a business to draw more funds from a bank than it has in its account. There is an upper limit on how much the business can overdraw its account. New business ventures often use a bank overdraft as a source of finance for working capital, and it often represents a large element of borrowing on the balance sheet of many small businesses.[6]

Overdrafts are highly flexible, so they have several advantages as a short-term funding source. Only the amount needed is drawn on and interest is paid only on the daily balance outstanding, so interest costs may be less than for a long-term standard loan. Interest payments are tax-deductible in many jurisdictions. There is also the ability to link overdrafts with bank cards or credit cards and to use commercial bank branches and automatic teller machines to access needed funds.

However, overdrafts can have expensive administration costs, and the interest rate charged on the overdrawn sums may vary as commercial lending rates change. Moreover, owner–managers must remember that the overdrawn amount is always payable on demand, which means that the bank can recall the funds whenever it wishes.

Trade credit

Trade credit is a company's open account arrangements with its suppliers. In this situation, goods are received from the suppliers before payment is made. Suppliers are an important, but too often ignored, source of finance with no explicit cost (such as interest or dividend) to the entrepreneur who obtains such credit. Terms of trade can influence cash flow favourably by reducing the average collection period of accounts receivable while capitalising on the full duration of accounts payable periods.

Term loan

Offered by banks and finance companies, **term loans** are a source of long-term debt. The borrower of a term loan usually contracts with the lender to repay the loan by regular periodic payments over a specified period (the term). The sum may be borrowed at a fixed interest rate, in which case the repayments will be fixed for the specified term or a variable rate is set that is subject to fluctuation. Often the loan must be secured by assets (either the business's or the owner's). A term loan is most suited to financing major long-term capital requirements such as the purchase of manufacturing equipment or premises.

A term loan is a stable source of financing and the interest payments are often tax-deductible. The bank has no direct involvement with the running of the business and repayment costs are often fixed and predictable for the life of the loan. One problem with term loans is that associated establishment fees and other possible charges may affect the interest cost structure, making it effectively higher than the rate quoted. If the borrower defaults and has used personal assets as security for the loan, these can be seized or the lender can force the business into bankruptcy. Other disadvantages include inflexibility of conditions and variable interest rates.

When examining a loan application, loans officers will often consider the 'five Cs of credit':

- *Character* — willingness of the debtor to meet financial obligations. The morality, integrity, trustworthiness and quality of management are assessed. The applicant's background provides useful indications about these various aspects.
- *Capacity* — the ability to meet financial obligations out of operating cash flows
- *Contribution* — the amount of money the entrepreneur or owner–manager is putting into the project. Few lenders will advance funds if the owner is not contributing a substantial amount of money, since this would leave most of the risk in the hands of the financier, rather than the entrepreneur.
- *Collateral* — assets pledged as security. These can include real estate, bonds, shares, motor vehicles, plant and equipment.
- *Conditions* — general economic conditions related to the applicant's business (such as industry, business cycle, community and financial conditions).

Leasing

A **lease** gives a business access to plant or premises without paying the full cost. Leasing can be defined as an agreement whereby a lessee (the small business owner–manager) undertakes to make lease payments or rentals to the lessor, in return for which the lessor allows the lessee to use the leased property. The lessor is thus both the financier and legal owner of the property.[7]

There are two types of lease: finance leases and operating (or true) leases. The one that business operators choose depends on what they expect to do with the equipment once the lease has expired. Finance leases, also known as capital leases or conditional sales, work best for companies that intend to keep the equipment when the lease expires. The main advantage of this type of lease is that it gives the business owner the option to purchase the equipment for a nominal fee. Payments on finance leases generally represent the full value of the equipment. The lessor retains legal ownership, but all the risks and benefits are effectively transferred from the lessor to the lessee. Thus, all finance leases are required to be capitalised in the lessee's accounts and must appear in the financial statements (this requirement does not apply to operating leases). A finance lease can be a good option if the business owner does not wish to tie up large amounts of cash.

On the other hand, operating lease payments do not cover the full value of the equipment. In an operating lease, the lessor retains substantially all the risks and benefits incidental to ownership of the leased goods. At the end of the lease, the lessee can choose to walk away from the equipment or purchase it at fair market value that, for office equipment, is usually at least 10 per cent of the original purchase price.

Leasing may be a way to gain access to costly capital equipment such as construction and manufacturing equipment, computers, fittings and fixtures, premises and vehicles. One of the advantages of leasing is that it offers fairly minimal up-front costs. Unlike bank loans, which may require a substantial down payment, generally only two payments are required at the beginning of a lease. In addition, leasing protects against equipment obsolescence by forcing the lessor to evaluate the useful life of the equipment and to set lease terms accordingly. Finally, leasing can lessen the business tax burden. Depending on how the lease is structured, the business owner may be able to fully deduct lease payments as a business expense rather than depreciating the value of the equipment as for a capital expenditure.

What would you do?

IsoSing

Melissa Tan has just completed her honours thesis in Chemistry at Nanyang Technology University (NTU) in Singapore. She has been working on isotope technology over the past two years, and the professor who supervises her research has just informed her that she will graduate with first class honours. Similar to DNA fingerprinting, the isotopic composition of substances provides a chemical signature. The power of isotopic analysis is the ability to identify the source of a substance. This type of analysis has recently been used to establish the origin of drugs, explosives, soil, fish and wildlife.

Melissa knows that many more potential applications exist. One area that she investigated in her thesis was the monitoring and testing of environmental applications. She developed two innovative procedures: one to link contaminants to their specific sources; and another for the quantification of the impact of contaminants on the local environment.

(continued)

After watching forensic television series such as *Crime Scene Investigation* (commonly referred to as CSI) and *Law & Order*, she realised that another potential application was criminal forensics. Here the purpose is to establish conclusive links between physical evidence left at a crime scene and physical evidence located at the suspect's address.

When Melissa told her supervisor about these potential applications, he replied: 'Yes, you are right! This is exactly where the field is moving today and I know at least two or three potential buyers for these applications'. Melissa would like to set up her own business, perhaps with some friends from NTU, to exploit this opportunity. However, conducting isotopic analysis requires expensive and sophisticated equipment such as mass spectrometers and distillation apparatus. Buying such equipment would cost S$150 000 to S$200 000. Melissa has only S$20 000 in savings and, although her parents have promised to match this amount, she is now wondering if S$40 000 will be enough to launch the business. Therefore, Melissa would like to find out what other sources of finance are available.

Questions
1. What are the potential sources of finance and resources available to Melissa?
2. If you were Melissa, what steps would you follow from now on?

Equity finance

The alternative to borrowing or using other people's money is to use funds belonging to the owners of the business: that is, either the original founder of the firm or other people who subsequently become part-owners of the enterprise. Sources of equity finance include owner's equity, family and friends, 'business angels', venture capital firms and the public through the initial public offering process.

Owner's equity

This type of equity is usually acquired from the owner's savings or the sale of personal assets. Using personal money means that there are no lending or interest costs payable to an outside party. Funds can be used with maximum flexibility and invested for the long term. There is no chance that an outsider can force the business to be closed for a default of payments. If the founding owner's funds are insufficient, the amount can be increased by broadening ownership of the firm to include other people who are willing to invest their money in it or by reinvesting the profits that the business earns. However, taking in other investors as part-owners can lead to ownership dilemmas or conflicts over the distribution of profits, since such investors may expect a higher return on their investment.

Family and friends

Family members, friends and friends of friends are the best place to start the search for capital. This is the most common avenue for financing start-ups and the most accessible for small enterprises. Entrepreneurs should nevertheless be cautious with this type of financing — many cherished friendships and family relationships have been destroyed through inadequate protection and provision for personal creditor repayment related to a business failure. A common mistake is 'over-valuation', where the total valuation of the company far exceeds the substantiated and potential earnings growth value of the young enterprise.

Business angels

One of the fastest growing sources of equity finance for entrepreneurs comes from people called **business angels**.[8] 'Angel' investors are wealthy people who invest in entrepreneurial ventures, usually at an early stage. Traditionally, the type of person who becomes a business angel is retired but, as news of the concept spreads, executives and portfolio investors are now becoming angels. Like venture capital firms, many business angels provide cash to young businesses and take equity in return. However, angel investors typically invest smaller amounts of money in individual businesses than venture capitalists do, making them a suitable choice for small business owners who have exhausted the resources of family and friends but are not ready to approach venture capitalists.

> **Business angels:** Wealthy people who invest in entrepreneurial firms and contribute their business skills.

Start-up and first-stage finance is the most obvious benefit business angels can offer entrepreneurs, but they can also act as mentors, offering special expertise and business and professional advice. Angels often have a background in business or investment and can provide an extra pair of hands to help run the business. In some cases, they prefer to remain a silent partner. Business angels can also provide specialisation that the business may not otherwise be in a position to acquire. Therefore, the best angel for a start-up is the one who can contribute significant experience, knowledge and networking opportunities, as well as the cash needed for the business venture to grow.

Some business angels are members of angel groups, allowing them to increase their access to investment opportunities and giving them the possibility of investing jointly with other angels to hedge their risk. These angel groups are often called **business introduction services**. Some groups provide or arrange advice services for entrepreneurs to help them become investment-ready. Four examples of business introduction services are Business Angels Pty Ltd in Melbourne, Australian Business Angels in Sydney, the Mentor Investor Networks (MINE) in New Zealand and the Business Angels Network of South East Asia (BANSEA) in Singapore. Both private investors and businesses register with these organisations and, after thorough interviews, the needs of businesses are matched with private investors' criteria.

> **Business introduction service:** A service that arranges or facilitates the meeting of private investors and businesses seeking external capital.

Venture capital

Venture capital (VC) is money provided by professionals who invest alongside owners and management in young, rapidly growing businesses with the potential to generate a high return on investment. There are several types of VC firms, but mainstream firms invest their capital through funds organised as limited partnerships in which the VC firm serves as the general partner. The most common type of VC firms are called 'private, independent VC firms' and have no affiliations with

> **Venture capital (VC):** Independently managed, dedicated pools of capital that focus equity investments in high-growth businesses.

any other financial institutions. Other venture firms may be affiliates or subsidiaries of a commercial bank, investment bank or insurance company and make investments on behalf of the parent firm's clients. A third type may be subsidiaries of industrial corporations making investments on behalf of the parent itself. These latter firms are typically called 'direct investors' or 'corporate venture investors'.[9]

How does venture capital work?

Venture capitalists help businesses grow but they eventually seek to exit the investment in three to seven years. An early-stage investment may take seven to ten years to mature, whereas a later-stage investment may take only three years, so the VC firm must match its investment with its desire for liquidity. The venture investment is neither a short-term nor a liquid investment and must be made carefully. In essence, venture capitalists buy a stake in an entrepreneur's idea, nurture it for a period of time and then sell their investment.[10]

When considering an investment, venture capitalists carefully screen the technical and business merits of the proposed venture. This is very important — it is estimated that, out of every hundred business plans considered by venture capitalists, only six are funded; even then, almost four of those six can be expected to fail in the medium term.[11] With these risks in mind, venture capitalists have to be highly selective in their investments, tolerant of failure and willing to adopt a long-term perspective. To help enhance the prospects of success, they work actively with the venture's management by contributing their experience and business knowledge gained from helping other businesses with similar growth challenges.

There is no standard set of rules VCs use to judge investment propositions — that is why an entrepreneur can be turned down by one VC and be accepted by another. However, the following aspects are always taken into account when evaluating an investment:

- *Team*. Investors back people. If the entrepreneur does not have the track record, there should be someone on the team who does. A team is better than a single person, especially if they have worked together with success.
- *Industry*. Most VC firms back projects in an industry they know and where they have made money before. As a result, they often specialise in a limited number of industries. Entrepreneurs should check out the specific sectors a VC firm has targeted before approaching the firm.
- *Business model and technology*. The VC will ask for evidence that the project has a significant and defensible competitive advantage against existing and potential competitors. The entrepreneur will need a working prototype of the business's technology or product and ownership of key intellectual property rights.
- *Market opportunities*. VC firms focus on opportunities within large, rapidly growing markets and those within highly profitable niches.
- *Exit*. The VC needs to know and believe that there will be a way to sell the shareholding in the business within three to seven years. There are different exit strategies, such as initial public offering, management buyout, and sale to another company.

Table 9.1: Venture capital contact points

Country	Venture capital association and journal
Australia	Australian Venture Capital Association <www.avcal.com.au>
	Australian Venture Capital Journal <www.vcjournal.com.au>
Hong Kong	Hong Kong Venture Capital Association <www.hkvca.com.hk>
Malaysia	Malaysian Venture Capital Association <www.mvca.org.my>
New Zealand	New Zealand Venture Capital Association <www.nzvca.co.nz>
Singapore	Singapore Venture Capital Association <www.svca.org.sg>
Asian region	*Asian Venture Capital Journal* <www.asiaventure.com>

How to approach a venture capitalist

Once the business plan and an executive summary have been completed, the entrepreneur can submit the proposal to the appropriate VC firms. These firms can have different investment criteria, such as:

- the amount invested in a business (for example, $0.5 to $1 million)
- the sector invested in (such as telecommunications, biotechnology and multimedia)
- the geographic focus of the fund (for example, a particular state or country)
- the particular aim of the fund (such as job creation or commercialisation of local research and development).

The best way to approach a VC is through a referral. As venture capital has become increasingly popular and more readily available as a source of equity funding in the last 10 years, there may be someone among the entrepreneur's family and friends who has been through the process. Accountants and solicitors are likely to have experience and should be consulted at an early stage for guidance on who might be the appropriate backer for the deal. If the entrepreneur is not satisfied with, or able to use, personal recommendations, there are a number of directories that can help, such as the national venture capital associations in the Pacific Rim region shown in table 9.1.

The VC firm will then evaluate the proposal and may require exclusivity for the period of the evaluation. Normally, the entrepreneur should ask for a confidentiality agreement to be signed once the investor has read the executive summary and has shown an interest in the proposal. Ideally, the VC should give a provisional response within a week or two — either a definite 'no' or a request for a meeting and further information. If the VC says no, it is useful to find out why the proposal was turned down. Once the VC firm has indicated its interest, the process can take anything between a couple of months and a year. The entrepreneur will need the VC to keep to a timetable and must in turn comply with requests from the VC.

Initial public offering (IPO): Also called *flotation, going public, listing;* refers to a business's initial offer of shares to the public via a stock exchange.

Publicly raised equity

Selling part ownership (shares) of an incorporated company on a public stock exchange is a way of raising finance from the general public. In this case, the business 'goes public' by making an initial offering of ordinary shares or securities to the general community. This process is called an **initial public offering (IPO)**. A large amount of money can be raised in this way and it also serves to increase the public profile of the firm.

This method of financing has become, however, less popular over the past few years in Asia–Pacific. An abundance of private equity money and the improving capital market skills of private company operators mean IPOs are less attractive to expanding companies than in the past. For example, seven years ago, 62 per cent of the companies on BRW's 'Fast 100' list of fast-growing SMEs in Australia said they wanted to list within years; in 2005, only 10 per cent said listing was a corporate goal.[12]

Advantages of going public

Some entrepreneurs consider that going public legitimises their efforts and confirms their success, and they plan long and hard for the opportunity to run a public company. Those who go public believe that the proceeds generated and other benefits of being a public company are worth the effort and expense required to complete a public offering. But going public is not the right decision for every business and does not ensure future success. Seeking funds from private investors or from traditional lending sources may make more sense. At times, going public may be impossible because of market conditions unrelated to a prospective candidate's strength.

Determining whether going public makes sense requires consideration of a number of factors including timing, business history, prospects for future growth and management's personality. The advantages and disadvantages of going public should be weighed carefully before a decision is made to seek funds in public markets.[13] Some of the advantages are:

- *capital for continued growth.* Perhaps the most obvious benefit of going public is the proceeds (cash) of the offering. This money can be used for a variety of company purposes as long as they are disclosed in the company's offering documents. Typical uses are to increase working capital, to acquire new divisions or technologies, to increase marketing efforts, to pay for research or plant modernisation or to repay debt.
- *lower cost of capital.* Going public is often triggered by management's belief that it can raise more money and get a better price for its shares by selling to the public than to a venture capitalist or other private investor. When this is true, a public offering can raise money at lower cost and with less dilution of management's shareholdings.
- *increased shareholder liquidity.* Going public makes it easier for company shareholders to sell their shares by creating a public market for the company's shares. Shareholders who register their shares in the company's offering hold freely tradable shares once the offering is completed. Even the shares that are not registered in the offering become more liquid.
- *improved company image.* Going public, with all the financial disclosure and investor relations planning it requires, usually attracts the attention of the business and financial press. Free publicity, coupled with the perception that going public is a significant milestone of success, enhances a company's image.

Disadvantages of going public

The advantages of going public can be substantial but they can be outweighed by the disadvantages, depending on management's goals and the circumstances of the company. Among the disadvantages that should always be considered are:

Underwriter:
An intermediary between an issuer of a security and the investing public, usually an investment bank.

- *expense.* Going public is expensive. The **underwriter's** discounts alone can amount to as much as four to eight per cent of the total proceeds of the offering.[14] Other expenses include filing fees, transfer agent fee, legal fees, printing fees and accounting fees. Most of these expenses must be paid at the close of the offering.

- *loss of confidentiality.* Going public forces a company to prepare and distribute to potential investors a complete description of the company, its history, its strengths, its weaknesses and its future plans. Detailed disclosures of financial information are required. Once information is filed, it becomes readily available to competitors, employees, customers, suppliers, union organisers and others.

- *periodic reporting.* Going public subjects a company to a number of periodic reporting requirements with the national regulatory agency. For most companies, these and other reporting requirements, which force the company to maintain audited financial statements, increase the company's cost of doing business by imposing more stringent accounting practices and by making additional demands on management's time.

- *reduced control.* A public offering can reduce management's control over a company if outsiders obtain enough shares to elect a majority of the company's board of directors. Thus outside shareholders can remove members of the management team. Public companies are also more susceptible to unfriendly takeovers because their shares are easy to accumulate.

- *shareholder pressures.* Even entrepreneurs or owner–managers who retain voting control over their companies find that going public subjects them to pressures that can affect the way they run their businesses. Many entrepreneurs find that shareholder expectations and the reporting requirements of the national regulatory agency combine to create significant pressures on a company to continually improve its performance every year.

There are many complex factors that should be considered when contemplating an initial public offering. This discussion does not cover them all. Entrepreneurs should consult their accountants, solicitors, investment bankers and other advisers before taking their businesses public.

Overview of the IPO process

An IPO starts long before the first day of trading. An issuer must undergo numerous procedures from the decision to proceed with an IPO through to listing. Figure 9.2 (p. 236) shows the four main phases in an IPO.[15]

Assuming a company has attracted the interest of underwriting investment banks, the first step requires managers to choose an underwriter. Most public securities offerings are sold (or underwritten) by underwriters who specialise in such transactions. The managing (or lead) underwriter in the syndicate selects the right combination of underwriters to achieve a distribution of the company's shares among private individuals and institutional purchasers that will ensure a good price and adequate trading in the shares after it is completed. The managing underwriter usually supports the company in the financial community after the offering by making a market in the company's shares, providing research and analysis on the company for investors, organising communications with potential investors and generally helping the company create a following in the investment community.

1. Planning and preparation
- Selecting the underwriter and advisers (solicitor, accountant)
- Strategic discussion
- Preparing the schedule

2. Structuring
- Preparing the prospectus
- Due diligence
- Enterprise valuation

3. Realisation and marketing
- Publishing the prospectus
- Briefing analysts
- Contacting investors

4. Price determination and secondary market
- Price determination
- Method of allocation
- First trading day

Figure 9.2: The four main stages of an initial public offering

In the second phase (structuring), the company will ask external auditors to conduct a due diligence. The aim of due diligence is to identify problems within the business, particularly any issues that may give rise to unexpected liabilities in the future. The due diligence will also help management determine the value of the company and prepare a prospectus for potential investors. A proper due diligence is not confined to looking at the historical and prospective financial position; it also closely examines a number of areas of the business including:

- the financial statements — to ensure their accuracy
- the assets — to confirm their existence, value, condition and legal title
- the employees — to identify and evaluate key employees
- the systems — to confirm their efficiency
- company contracts and leases — to identify the risks and obligations.

On completion of the due diligence, the company produces a prospectus with its underwriter and registers it with the national regulatory agency (such as Australian Securities and Investments Commission, Securities Commission of Malaysia, Securities Commission of New Zealand or Registry of Companies and Business in Singapore). This document must contain all the information potential investors need to make an informed investment decision about the company — it must explain the offer, including the terms, issuer, planned use of the money, historical financial statements and other information that could help a potential investor decide whether the investment is appropriate. The underwriter then distributes the prospectus to potential investors.

Once the national regulatory agency has approved the prospectus and the application to float, the company can move to the third phase (realisation and marketing). The company is ready for a series of meetings with potential investors. Following each investor presentation, the lead underwriter records indications of interest in an order book. Final decisions on price and quantity are based on this order book. But entrepreneurs have to keep in mind that pricing an IPO is more of an art than a science. If the company has a bright future and it is an exuberant time in the market, it is not uncommon for its shares to be oversubscribed many times.

Entrepreneur profile

The Optima Corporation

Auckland-based Optimal Decision Technologies was formed in 1998 and changed its name to The Optima Corporation in 2006. Optima specialises in providing easy-to-use visually appealing interfaces, that conceal complex mathematics to solve a number of resourcing problems concurrently. One of its products is a software system developed specifically for emergency services, particularly ambulance services. Siren — Simulation for Improved Response for Emergency Networks — as the software is known, has its roots in operations research, the science of using sophisticated mathematical algorithms. It helps organisations schedule staff and resources in the most efficient way possible. Today, Siren is being used by ambulance services in Perth, Toronto, West Yorkshire and Melbourne. Chief Operating Officer Andrew Goldie says the company is also on the brink of signing another NZ$1 million worth of sales to three ambulance services in the US.

Overseas sales have kept Optima marginally profitable since day one. Its turnover to 31 March 2006, will be NZ$1.2 million, with a modest profit of NZ$300 000. It has also doubled its staff base from 15 to 30 in a year. CEO Cory Williams estimates a turnover increase to NZ$2.9 million in the coming year.

To fund all of this expansion, Optima has raised NZ$1.3 million to date through Ice Angels, the investor network of the University of Auckland Business School's business incubator Icehouse. Williams, the former head of Ice Angels, was so taken with the company that he joined them and was key to the raising of venture capital. Goldie says the attraction of the Ice Angels funding was that investors didn't just come with money; they came with contacts. The new shareholder representative on the Optima board is Ian McCrae, CEO of Orion Systems — a technology company that sells to the health sector worldwide. Optima is now out of the Icehouse incubator and going it alone.

Marketing offshore is now the key to success. Optima has recently secured a NZ$100 000 market development grant from New Zealand Trade and Enterprise. Andrew Goldie says one way forward is finding implementation partners in future markets. To that end, Optima is talking with the Centre for Traffic and Transport in Denmark, which consults to ambulance services in that country. The centre is sending a technical person to New Zealand to learn about Siren so the organisation can resell the system in Scandinavia.

Source: Adapted from M. Slide, 'The siren call', *Unlimited: Business with imagination*, no. 81, April 2006.

Alternative sources of finance

Bootstrap finance: Creative financing methods of meeting the need for resources without relying on debt or equity finance.

In addition to the traditional debt and equity finance already presented, there are other sources that are categorised separately because they are 'off-balance-sheet financing' or because of the specific nature and purpose of the funds that can be obtained. These alternative sources of finance are often referred to as 'bootstrapping'. **Bootstrap finance** refers to the use of methods of meeting the need for resources without relying on long-term external finance from debt holders or new owners.[16] It offers many advantages for entrepreneurs; aside from getting money from friends and family, it is probably the best way of getting a business venture operating and well positioned to seek debt financing from banks or equity finance from outside investors later. Bootstrapping relies greatly on networks, trust, cooperation and wise use of the firm's existing resources, rather than going into debt or giving away equity.[17]

The main sources of boostrap finance are:

- *debt factoring*. This is a financing method where the firm sells its accounts receivable to a buyer at a discount. This method is described further in the following section.
- *customers*. One way to use your customers to obtain financing is by having them write you a letter of credit. Another way is to obtain prepaid licences, royalties or advances from customers.
- *real estate and equipment*. For example, entrepreneurs can simply lease a facility. This reduces start-up costs because it costs less to lease a facility than it does to buy one.
- *government and industry partners*. Local, regional and federal government entities can provide various types of seed funding, such as grants and interest-free loans. Similarly, it is often possible to obtain seed funding from various industry partners such as enterprises, universities and industry associations.

Debt factoring and discounting

Factoring:
The selling of a firm's accounts receivable to a financier who assumes the credit risk and receives cash as the debtors settle their accounts.

Factoring involves selling or exchanging a business's debts for cash at a discount. This is a financing system whereby an invoice is sold to a 'factor' who pays 80–90 per cent of the invoice and assumes responsibility for the control and administration of receivables and bears the risk of non-collection. Many new and growing businesses have trouble obtaining traditional bank financing because of the length of time in business, profitability and financial strength. By factoring, they can raise cash from approved invoices in as little as 24 hours. Debt **discounting** is similar to factoring; the business sells its invoice to the financier but keeps responsibility for collecting monies owing. This is ideal if the business wants to maintain a relationship with its customers and keep track of what is happening in the industry.

Discounting:
The selling of a firm's accounts receivable to a financier while the firm keeps responsibility for collecting monies owing.

Debt factoring and discounting are commonly used to meet short-term seasonal funding requirements but in some cases it may be an ongoing working capital facility. In situations where a bank may be unwilling to provide or extend an overdraft, debt factoring or discounting may be the most effective way to enhance the liquidity and cash flow of a firm. A key advantage is that they provide immediate cash inflow, although the firm loses collection control with debt factoring. This type of financing does not appear in the balance sheet, so it is often referred to as *off-balance-sheet financing*.

Factoring and discounting are forms of financing that do not suit all businesses. For example, they would not be suitable for retailers, contractors receiving progress payments or a business sector with a high level of trade disputes. Factoring is suitable for an SME with the following attributes:

- credit sales (not cash)
- manufacturing or wholesaling with continuous trading with established customers

- no unusual selling terms (such as consignment sales or guarantees)
- sound management and profitable trading.

Government-backed schemes

Many governments have recognised the importance of start-ups and SMEs to their national economy. As a result, they have established a variety of schemes to provide finance to new firms and fast-growing SMEs (see table 9.2). These schemes can be a valuable source of both debt and equity funding if the applicant meets the specified criteria. In general, government-backed schemes have the following criteria:

- Schemes focus on a specific stage of the firm's development. Consequently, funding can target the seed, start-up or expansion stage of a business venture.
- Schemes mostly aim to support SMEs. The size to qualify for funding can be determined in different ways: yearly sales, number of employees, assets under management or a combination of these.
- Schemes usually target specific industries. In most cases, governments tend to back firms from various high-tech sectors, such as biotechnology, biochemistry, electronics, telecommunications, software and fine mechanics. Similarly, schemes often focus on research and development (R&D) and the commercialisation of innovation.

Would-be entrepreneurs and SME owner–managers need to be aware of these features when applying to a government-backed scheme and be prepared to go through the tedious application process.

Table 9.2: Government-backed schemes in selected countries

Scheme or fund	Amount	Objective	Agency/website
Australia			
Innovation Investment Fund (IIF)	A$220 million invested by the federal government, matched by A$138 million from private sector investors	To promote the commercialisation of R&D through the provision of venture capital to small, high-tech businesses	AusIndustry <www.ausindustry.gov.au>
Commercialising Emerging Technologies (COMET)	A$170 million until 2011; offers grants from A$5000 to A$120 000 for up to two years	To increase the commercialisation of innovative products and services	AusIndustry <www.ausindustry.gov.au>
New Enterprise Initiative Scheme (NEIS)	Variable; several A$ million per year	To help unemployed people establish a business by providing income support and business advice	Department of Employment and Workplace Relations <www.workplace.gov.au> Provided through a network of private, community and government organisations known as NEIS providers
Hong Kong			
SME Loan Guarantee Scheme (SGS)	Maximum guarantee: HK$2 million for business installations and equipment; HK$1 million for working capital needs	To assist SMEs secure loans when acquiring equipment and meeting their working capital needs	Administered by the Trade and Industry Department <www.smefund.tid.gov.hk> Offered through 44 Participating Lending Institutions (PLIs)

(continued)

Scheme or fund	Amount	Objective	Agency/website
SME Export Marketing Fund (EMF)	Grant equivalent to 50% of the total approved expenditures or HK$30 000 (whichever is less)	To help SMEs expand their businesses through active participation in export promotion activities	Trade and Industry Department <www.smefund.tid.gov.hk>
Malaysia			
Bumiputera Entrepreneurs Project Fund	RM300 million; maximum funding per enterprise: 60% of the contract value or RM3 million (whichever is less)	To provide financing to indigenous Malay entrepreneurs who have been awarded projects by government agencies and private companies	ERF Sdn Bhd Banka Negara Malaysia <www.bnm.gov.my> Offered through Participating Financial Institutions
New Entrepreneurs Fund 2	RM2350 million; maximum funding per SME: RM5 million	To help stimulate the growth of indigenous Malay SMEs	Banka Negara Malaysia <www.bnm.gov.my> Offered through Participating Financial Institutions
Fund for Small and Medium Industries 2	RM4750 million; maximum funding per customer: RM3 million	To promote SME activities in both the export and domestic sectors	Banka Negara Malaysia <www.bnm.gov.my> Offered through Participating Financial Institutions
Small Entrepreneur Guarantee Scheme (SEGS)	Maximum loan amount per SME: RM50 000	To provide bank overdrafts and term loans to Malaysian-owned and controlled companies	Banka Negara Malaysia <www.bnm.gov.my> Offered through the Credit Guarantee Corporation <www.iguarantee.com.my>
New Zealand			
Venture Investment Fund (VIF)	Investing up to NZ$100 million with private investors on a 1:2 basis in a series of privately managed funds	To increase the supply of seed, start-up and expansion capital to innovative young enterprises	New Zealand Venture Investment Fund Limited <www.nzvif.com>
Seed Co-Investment Fund	Total NZ$40 million Investment up to NZ$250 000 per SME with at least a 50:50 matching from private investors	To provide seed funding for early stage businesses with strong growth potential	New Zealand Venture Investment Fund Limited <www.nzvif.com>
Grants for Private Sector R&D (GPSRD)	NZ$10 000 to NZ$100 000 per SME	To provide funding up to a third of increased R&D costs for SMEs	Administered by the Foundation for Research Science and Technology and Technology New Zealand <www.frst.govt.nz>
Singapore			
Enterprise Investment Incentive Scheme (EII)	Issue certificates to investors for investments of up to S$3 million	To ease the difficulty faced by high-tech start-ups in obtaining capital by providing investors with a loss insurance for their investments	Economic Development Board <www.edb.gov.sg>
SPRING SEEDS	Variable; in 2005, private investments in SEEDS companies was S$45.3 million	To provide equity financing for start-ups; matches, dollar for dollar, every third-party private sector investment, up to S$300 000	SPRING <www.spring.gov.sg>

| Venture Investment Support for Start-ups (VISS) | S$50 million | To support young local start-ups and to attract foreign start-up companies through co-investments in the seed and early stages | TIF Ventures Pte Ltd <www.tifventures.com> |
| Micro Loan Program | Loan of up to S$50 000 per enterprise | To provide fixed interest loans to very small local enterprises | Administered by SPRING <www.spring.gov.sg>; offered through 16 participating financial institutions |

Summary

Obtaining finance is one of the major difficulties in establishing and running a small enterprise. There are three major issues to consider when seeking financing: (1) whether the venture should be funded through debt, equity or a combination of both; (2) whether the funding is needed on a short-term or long-term basis; and (3) what point in the business life cycle the firm is at (early stage or expansion).

The first type of finance is debt, which includes short-term options such as a bank overdraft and trade credit, as well as long-term products such as leasing, term loans and loan capital. The second type of finance is equity in the form of owner's equity, retained profits, funding by family and friends, business angels' investments, venture capital and publicly raised equity through an initial public offering. Internal sources of finance are particularly important to small businesses. The major source of finance for many small firms, particularly at inception, is the owner/s.

In addition to the traditional debt and equity finance, entrepreneurs often rely on alternative sources of funding or bootstrapping. There are two main alternative sources: debt factoring and government-backed schemes. Debt factoring involves selling a business's debts for cash at a discount, often referred to as 'off-balance-sheet financing'. Many governments in the Pacific Rim region have established a variety of schemes to provide finance to new firms and fast-growing SMEs. These schemes can be a valuable source of both debt and equity funding if the applicant meets the specified criteria.

REVIEW QUESTIONS

1. What are the three main ways to categorise business financing?

2. What are the specific features of debt finance? Give some examples of debt finance.

3. What is venture capital and how does it work?

4. What are the advantages and disadvantages an owner–manager should consider before seeking funds in the public market?

5. What are some alternative sources of finance for entrepreneurs?

DISCUSSION QUESTIONS

1. Why are start-ups and small firms viewed as being more risky than large enterprises?
2. Which is better — debt or equity funding? Give reasons for your answer.
3. Why does the character of a loan applicant matter to a lender, even when the loan has been guaranteed by sufficient collateral?
4. What are the similarities and differences between business angels and venture capital financiers?
5. Why might entrepreneurs and small business owner–managers face difficulties in accessing government-backed schemes?

SUGGESTED READING

Gollis, C., *Enterprise and Venture Capital*, 4th edn, Allen & Unwin, Sydney, 2002.

Holmes, S.et al., *Small Enterprise Finance*, John Wiley & Sons, Brisbane, 2003.

McKaskill, T., *Finding the Money: How to Raise Venture Capital*, Wilkinson Publishing, Melbourne, 2006.

CASE STUDY

AION Diagnostics

Nanotechnology — technology that relates to the manufacture of microscopic objects which are then used to create products such as paint, textiles and drugs — offers formidable potential and is transforming the future of medicine, materials and manufacturing. AION Diagnostics is one of many companies recently established to exploit the unique properties of this technology. In April 2006, Dr Anna Kluczewska was facing one of her first major challenges as Managing Director of the company: the seed money provided by the parent company, pSivida, would run out in a few months and A$20 million was needed to develop the prototypes and run the first clinical trials.

The unique technology

Subiaco, a western suburb of Perth, Western Australia, is best known for Subiaco Oval — the home ground of the West Coast Eagles and Fremantle Dockers Australian Football League (AFL) teams. It is not where you would expect to find the headquarters of a global nanotechnology company. Yet it is from this location that pSivida and its spin-off, AION Diagnostics, are coordinating their worldwide operations. pSivida focuses on the development and commercialisation of BioSilicon™ — silicon that is nanostructured to create nanopores within the material. 'In other words, we take silicon from the electronics industry as we know it, but in a very pure form, and we engineer it to contain tiny pores at the nano level,' explains Dr Kluczewska. The pores can be loaded with drugs including small molecules, peptides, proteins and vaccines.

As a new and exciting biocompatible material, BioSilicon™ offers numerous potential applications across the high-growth healthcare sector. These potential applications include controlled release drug delivery, targeted cancer therapies (including brachytherapy — the delivery of radioisotopes directly into a tumour), tissue engineering and orthopedics. pSivida owns the intellectual property pertaining to BioSilicon™ for use in or on humans and animals.

BioSilicon™ has key advantages over other material, as it is both biodegradable and biocompatible. Pre-clinical studies have shown that it dissolves in body fluids into silicic acid, which is commonly found in everyday foods. In addition, it is abundant and low cost — silicon makes up approximately 28 per cent of the Earth's crust and is freely available. As 40 years in the electronics industry has demonstrated, it can be easily manufactured.

The launch of AION Diagnostics

In September 2004, pSivida decided to incorporate a spin-off, AION Diagnostics, to create a product portfolio for BioSilicon™ in the healthcare diagnostics sector. pSivida provided the seed funding for AION Diagnostics through an investment of A$1.2 million and licensed the use of BioSilicon™ in diagnostics to AION. It was up to AION to invent a product portfolio based on the nanotechnology. Within a year, AION had two divisions — Imaging and Biosensors — with a portfolio of 15 products, and it made a seminal discovery in the application of BioSilicon™. With proof of concept completed, the company was ready to raise the next round of funding to take the product portfolio through clinical trials. pSivida owns 80 per cent of the shares in AION Diagnostics. To spearhead the new company, pSivida appointed Dr Kluczewska as Managing Director. Prior to her appointment, she was pSivida's Head of Diagnostics. Dr Kluczewska obtained a degree in dental surgery from the University of Western Australia and then completed Primary Examinations with the Royal Australasian College of Dental Surgeons. Upon graduation she joined Baxter Healthcare, where she progressed into managing Baxter's global product portfolio for the BioSurgery division. pSivida owns 80 per cent of the shares in AION Diagnostics; the remaining are owned by the management of AION Diagnostics. To spearhead the new company, pSivida appointed Dr Kluczewska as Managing Director. Prior to her appointment, she was pSivida's Head of Diagnostics. Born and raised in Perth, Dr Kluczewska obtained a degree in dental surgery from the University of Western Australia and then completed her fellowship at the University of Michigan. Upon graduation she joined Baxter and spent three years there, where she managed a global product portfolio for the Healthcare's BioSurgery division.

Through the adoption of the biocompatible and biodegradable properties of BioSilicon™, AION Diagnostics aims to develop and commercialise diagnostic products that will provide real-time continuous measurement of important diagnostic markers. The basic principle of imaging involves the presence of a specific molecule embedded in the BioSilicon™ that can be activated and seen on a scanner, thereby signalling the presence or absence of a tumour in a patient. 'We believe this technology represents a milestone in preventive medicine, enabling improved diagnostics before disease impacts on the body, rather than after,' says Dr Kluczewska.

According to research group Clinica, the worldwide market for in-vitro diagnostic products totalled over US$20 billion in 2005. The market is undergoing a significant transition, driven by the advent of new analytical technologies that are beginning to expand the scope of diagnostics testing and its role in healthcare. For example, direct-access testing has emerged as a new trend in the industry and an increasing range of tests are now available for patients to use in the home. Traditional laboratory diagnosis and spot monitoring of chronic conditions is evolving to meet the need for real-time, accurate testing that provides on-the-spot or continual information to patient and physician on the status and health of the individual.

The need for a second round of financing

Today, AION Diagnostics certainly has the skills and product potential to create a strong market presence in the diagnostics sector. However, there is a need for a second round of financing to run the clinical trials and initiate commercialisation of the products. Although the company will not conduct all of the research and trials on its own (several partnerships with Australian and American universities have been initiated to this effect), Dr Kluczewska has calculated that A$20 million is needed to successfully develop the first series of marketable products.

You would expect that, with a buoyant stock market, such a high-potential start-up would have little trouble attracting funding in Australia. However, along with a handful of companies in the biotechnology sector, pSivida continues to wage a frustrating battle to convince investors that Australia needs to look beyond mining to secure its future. Mr Gavin Rezos, CEO of pSivida and Chairman of AION Diagnostics, recently declared in *The West Australian*: 'One would expect that most people realise uranium takes a long time to get out of the ground; in fact it takes longer than it does to get a drug approved.'[18] The other problems are the small size of the biotechnology sector in Australia, and the lack of investors financing projects in this sector. 'Most investors don't understand how value is created in this sector,' says Dr Kluczewska.

Frustrated by the lack of support in Australia, pSivida has been looking overseas for funding. Listed on the Australian Stock Exchange and on the NASDAQ, the company has turned to the rich equity market in the US and Europe. Should AION Diagnostics follow in the steps of its parent company? Is there further funding potential to be explored through the universities' partnerships in Australia? These are the immediate issues that Dr Kluczewska needs to address, and most entrepreneurs would perceive this as a challenge — but not the young and dynamic Dr Kluczewska. 'I don't see any challenges; I see only opportunities', she says.

Source: Based on author's interview with Dr Anna Kluczewska.

Questions

1. What are the different financing alternatives that you would recommend Dr Kluczewska consider?

2. What measures in terms of structure and organisation does AION Diagnostics need to take to obtain funding from a US venture capital firm?

3. What is the likely effect of ownership dilution on the current shareholders of AION Diagnostics?

ENDNOTES

1. G.N. Robson, *Financing Techniques for Growing Small and Medium Sized Enterprises*, Small and Medium Enterprise Research Centre, Edith Cowan University, Perth, 1996.

2. S. Holmes, P.J. Hutchinson, D.M. Forsaith, B. Gibson & R. McMahon, *Small Enterprise Finance*, John Wiley & Sons, Brisbane 2003.

3. A. Cosh & A. Hughes, 'Size, financial structure and profitability in UK companies in the 1980s', in A. Hughes & D. Storey (eds), *Finance and the Small Firm*, Routledge, London, 1994.

4. J.S. Osteryoung, D.L. Newman & L.G. Davies, *Small Firm Finance: An Entrepreneurial Perspective*, The Dryden Press, Fort Worth, TX, 1997.

5. S. Harron, 'Lending to small business in Australia', *Small Enterprise Research*, vol. 4, no. 1, 1996, pp. 17–26.

6. J. English, *How to Organise and Operate a Small Business in Australia*, 6th edn, Allen & Unwin, Sydney, 1995; L. Bland, 'Invoice finance v. bank overdraft', *Secured Lender*, vol. 53, no. 1, 1997, pp. 62–4.

7. J. Petty, R. Peacock, M. Burrow, A. Keown, D. Scott & J. Martin, *Basic Financial Management*, Prentice Hall, Sydney, 1996.

8. Industry Commission, *Informal Equity Investment*, Information Paper, AGPS, Canberra, 1997.

9. C. Gollis, *Enterprise and Venture Capital*, 4th edn, Allen & Unwin, Sydney, 2002.

10. B. Zider, 'How venture capital works', *Harvard Business Review*, November–December 1998, pp. 131–9.

11. J.L. Nesheim, *High Tech Start-Up*, 2nd edn, Free Press, New York, 2000.

12. C. Roberts, 'Listing loses its appeal', *BRW*, 11–17 August 2005, p. 48.

13. J.B. Arkebauer & R. Schultz, *Going Public: Everything You Need to Know to Take Your Company Public*, 3rd edn, Dearborn Financial Publishing, New York, 1998.

14. M. Horvath, 'An insider guide to going public', *Financial Times*, Mastering Management, part 8, 20 November 2000, pp. 2–4.

15. Ernst & Young, *The Ernst & Young LLP Guide to the IPO Value Journey*, John Wiley & Sons, New York, 1999.

16. J.Winborg & H. Landström, 'Financial bootstrapping in small businesses: Examining small business managers' resource acquisition behaviors', *Journal of Business Venturing*, vol. 16, no. 3, 2001, pp. 235–54.

17. H. Frederick, *Sources of Funding for New Zealand Entrepreneurs*, Ten3, Auckland, p. 4.

18. C. Low, 'Big biotech potential ignored', *The West Australian*, 6 April 2006, p. 54.

Chapter 10

Accessing business advice and assistance

LEARNING OBJECTIVES

After reading this chapter, you should be able to:

- identify the benefits of using a professional adviser

- list the different types of adviser styles available to entrepreneurs and small business owners

- explain the three different types of advisory style

- list the issues involved in choosing an adviser

- describe the main categories of government and private sector assistance available

- explain how a business incubator works.

Successful small business managers and entrepreneurs are expected to develop a broad range of skills and competencies in many different areas. Apart from technical knowledge related to the field in which their businesses operate, entrepreneurs must learn to deal with many other issues that arise in the daily process of managing an enterprise. It is not always possible for one person to keep abreast of all these areas or to be particularly effective in all of them. For this reason, most owner–managers eventually find that they must turn to a business adviser for help.

A number of government and private sector assistance schemes are designed to encourage new business formation and expansion. Many of these can provide practical advice, planning services and financial support. Using these services can help a business get started or grow more quickly than would otherwise be the case.

This chapter provides an overview of the different types of business adviser available, the issues important in the development of an effective working relationship with them, and sources of external financial and management assistance. We explain the concept of an 'adviser' — what the term means, the different types of service that advisers offer, and their varying approaches. The factors to take into account when selecting an adviser are discussed, and the range of government and private services provided to firms is explained.

The business adviser

Business adviser:
Someone who works with client businesses to provide specialised skill and knowledge in one or more particular aspects of business operations.

A **business adviser** is someone who works with client businesses to provide specialised skill and knowledge in one or more aspects of business operations. Such a person has developed a considerable body of knowledge and experience that can be used to help solve the problems of clients.

Many different terms are used to describe a person who works with a business in this manner. The label 'adviser' is commonly used, but there are other terms (sometimes used interchangeably): consultant, counsellor, facilitator, mentor, business coach. The difference between these is explained later in this chapter. Professional business advisers can be found in the private sector (and charge for their services), as well as in government-funded programs (many of which are free for small business owners and entrepreneurs who wish to use them).

The main benefit of an adviser is the application of particular skills and abilities to help improve the business performance of clients. Entrepreneurs and small business owners must, by virtue of the many different demands placed on them, be generalists, and so cannot usually hope to acquire the same level of specialist skill as advisers.

In many respects, using a professional adviser is a more effective use of resources than the alternative approach of entrepreneurs trying to master the topic themselves. This is because it takes a considerable amount of time, effort and money for the owner–manager to acquire as much knowledge as the specialist adviser already has. Even though such services may be expensive when charged at an hourly rate, they may still be cheaper than trying to spend time mastering the topic privately.

Employing an adviser can also be more convenient, because the service can be contracted for a specific task or time period. This removes the problem of the business having to permanently dedicate one or more staff members to acquiring a particular body of knowledge. Business advisers also play an important role in bringing new ideas, information and techniques to existing businesses. Good advisers will be aware of new developments and techniques, and can suggest when these tools might be usefully employed by a business. Advisers often know from their own previous experience what works and what does not, thus allowing the entrepreneur to minimise mistakes and avoid errors.

Finally, an outside adviser can often provide an alternative point of view to that of the business owner. In this way, the merits and problems of different approaches can be discussed, debated and evaluated, and the chances of adopting a successful final solution are increased. Good advisers can provide a dispassionate, objective evaluation of business ventures — something that owners may not be able to achieve because they are too caught up in the daily management of their enterprise.

What would you do?

Cooking up a storm

You are a full-time professional private business adviser. You do not have a specialist area of interest, but work as a general consultant on an hourly fee-for-service basis.

On Monday morning, a new client comes into your city office. She is a middle-aged woman who runs her own business, an Italian restaurant in the heart of the central business district.

She explains that she is having some financial problems — more money is going out than is coming in. This is having an impact on her ability to meet liabilities and to pay staff on time. Three casual employees have already quit over the lateness of their pay; another is threatening legal action.

You explain to her that this is probably a cash flow problem, and you discuss ways in which she can better manage her liquidity. You are just about to close the interview when you ask if these money matters are having any effect on her own drawings.

She explains that much of the money is being spent in a divorce settlement. 'It is much more than I need to pay, but I feel guilty. My ex-husband worked hard to build this business up, and now that he has left I feel that I need to repay him.' She explains that she spends a lot of time on the phone talking to him about these issues, and that she still relies on him to advise her on daily management matters.

The ex-husband has started another restaurant down the road, in partnership with a much younger cook who was recently voted Best Female Chef of the Year.

Staff are leaving your client's business, there is not enough cash, and there is a rising number of customer complaints in the restaurant. Last week the Health Department served notice that several improvements had to be made or else the business would be closed immediately.

What should an adviser do?

Questions
1. Identify the problems facing the firm and list them in order of priority.
2. What advice would you give this client? Why?

The evolution of business advisory services

The level of business advice and assistance available today in the Pacific Rim is the result of many years of evolving responses to the needs of business operators. Although small businesses and entrepreneurs have been around for as long as commerce has existed, the provision of formal government assistance and support for small and new firms is a relatively new phenomenon. In the period after World War II, many countries adopted national policy frameworks and created formal specialised agencies to promote entrepreneurial activity and the small-firm sector. The United States, for example, created its Small Business Administration in 1953, and Japan adopted a national small-enterprise development strategy in 1947.[1] The role of these programs was to conduct research, develop policies and provide practical assistance to entrepreneurs and small-scale business ventures. This trend gathered strength and eventually resulted in similar bodies being formed throughout much of the world.

In Australia, however, government-sponsored support for small enterprises and new business ventures is a relatively recent development. It was not until the early 1970s that the federal government conducted its first review of the sector.[2] The Wiltshire Committee's report suggested that government could do much more to promote an effective small business sector; as a result, the federal government established the National Small Business Bureau in 1973.[3] This was followed in the 1980s by the creation of various small business development agencies or bureaus within each state and territory. Today, both state and federal governments provide funding to small business advisory agencies, as well as a wide variety of specific programs that offer grants, technical advice, infrastructure assistance and educational and developmental support to small firms. Many local governments also provide assistance to new and small ventures within their municipalities.

This development has been mirrored by an increased emphasis on public assistance schemes in other countries in the Pacific Rim region. Singapore, for example, has produced a number of 'master plans' since the 1990s, each designed to map out the future development of the sector and provide tangible assistance schemes.[4] A similar approach has been used in Malaysia, which has created specific government agencies and its own master plan.[5] In New Zealand, both government agencies and private organisations offer an extensive range of state-run assistance and advisory centres, although the nature and duration of these has changed from time to time.

In contrast, private sector business advisers have been in existence for much longer than publicly funded agencies. Local private industry groups, such as chambers of commerce and chambers of manufacturers, were formed during the early years of European settlement in Australia, Singapore, Hong Kong, Malaysia and New Zealand. These networks of business owners provided both formal and informal support to their members. Private sector firms such as accountancy practices, law firms and banks have also provided advice and financial access to small and new entrepreneurial firms. Indeed, in many cases the growth of such professions has been accelerated by the existence of small firms, which usually form the bulk of their clients.

Types of professional adviser

Many different people, professions and occupations represent a source of possible beneficial advice to the business owner or entrepreneur. Some of the more important ones are discussed below.

Accountants

Accountants provide a number of useful functions. In many cases, their main role is to ensure that sound financial records are being kept, but this is only one aspect of the range of services they offer. A business accountant can also help to ensure compliance with relevant taxation laws, prepare tax returns, compile future financial projections, determine the future funding needs of the business and sources of such capital, and help the business owner make effective use of personal income. A recent study of how and why Australian SMEs use accountants for advice has shown that while they are mainly consulted for financial matters, accountants are also used for issues such as operational performance reviews. Accountants are often seen as the 'most trustworthy' and reliable form of external advisor.[6] They are usually required to be registered members of a state or national professional institute, such as CPA Australia or the New Zealand Institute of Chartered Accountants (see table 10.1). They must also have completed a tertiary qualification in their field.

Table 10.1: Accounting institutes

Country	Institute
Australia	Institute of Chartered Accountants in Australia <www.icaa.org.au> CPA Australia (the society of certified practising accountants) <www.cpaaustralia.com.au> National Institute of Accountants <www.nia.org.au>
Hong Kong	Hong Kong Institute of Certified Public Accountants <www.hkicpa.org.hk>
Malaysia	Malaysian Institute of Accountants <www.mia.org.my> Malaysian Institute of Certified Public Accountants <www.micpa.com.my>
New Zealand	New Zealand Institute of Chartered Accountants <www.nzica.com>
Singapore	Institute of Certified Public Accountants of Singapore <www.accountants.org.sg>
General	Confederation of Asian and Pacific Accountants <www.capa.com.my> International Federation of Accountants <www.ifac.org>

Lawyers

Knowledge of legal processes and consequences is important for small businesses whenever a contract has to be negotiated with an outside party, a lease is being signed, a dispute occurs over non-payment or non-performance between the business and a client, or litigation is initiated against the business. For entrepreneurs, legal advice is often needed when dealing with issues such as the registration of intellectual property.

Lawyers should be members of their relevant professional association, hold a degree in law, and have been admitted to practise at the Bar in their state, provincial or national jurisdiction (see table 10.2). In some countries, this role is split into two different jobs — the *barrister* (who represents clients in court) and the *solicitor* (who advises clients and prepares cases for barristers).

Table 10.2: Law societies

Country	Pertinent body
Australia	Law Council of Australia <www.lawcouncil.asn.au>
Hong Kong	Law Society of Hong Kong <www.hklawsoc.org.hk >
Malaysia	Malaysian Bar Council <www.malaysianbar.org.my>
New Zealand	New Zealand Law Society <www.nz-lawsoc.org.nz>
Singapore	Law Society of Singapore <www.lawsoc.org.sg>

Management consultants

'Consultant' is a widely used term with a number of meanings, and it is often applied indiscriminately to many different occupations. However, a properly qualified management consultant is usually taken to mean someone with extensive practical experience in a particular aspect of business. Typical management consulting roles may include human resource management advisers (consultants who advise on recruiting, employment relations, salaries and benefits, or staff terminations); trainers (who develop and implement business skills courses for clients); marketing advisers (who advise on market research, product branding, or integrated advertising and promotional campaigns); and production advisers (who examine workplace processes, quality control, error reduction, retooling, production techniques and equipment use). There is usually no mandatory requirement for a management consultant to be a member of a professional association or to have any particular level of education.

Bank managers

At first glance, it may seem that bank managers simply have a vested interest in ensuring that their clients can meet their financial obligations (such as payments on an outstanding loan) when these fall due. However, more astute managers also realise that by helping businesses to grow, they may generate more sales of banking products and services. To this end, they can represent a useful source of financial advice, money management ideas and investment options.

Financial planners

Many business owners realise that wealth generation and protection should not focus solely on the business enterprise. In many cases, it makes sound sense to diversify personal assets and income sources, so that in the event of business failure the entrepreneur's wealth is not lost. Financial planners can help with the development of an integrated personal financial strategy, tax planning and investment advice.

Publicly funded small business agencies

Government-supported small business development agencies exist in a number of countries. In many cases, staff in these organisations provide ideas, information and advice to small business managers. Many of these people will have their own direct experience of owning or managing a small business. These agencies usually have a good working knowledge of other government programs that can help new and small firms, and so constitute an additional source of outside knowledge. An example of a publicly funded agency is provided in the Entrepreneur Profile below.

Mentors

Other successful business operators can be a source of assistance to entrepreneurs. Learning from others is a highly effective way of transferring experience, building personal networks, exchanging ideas and identifying new opportunities. **Mentoring** is the process of transferring advice and ideas from one business owner to another, and is usually provided on a voluntary no-cost basis. Because it is peer-based, it often has more credibility and resonance than external advice provided by paid 'experts'. Mentors can include retired businesspeople (who often provide their advice free of charge to new start-ups) and venture capitalists who have taken an equity position in an entrepreneur's business.[7]

Mentoring: The process of transferring advice and ideas from one businessperson to another on a voluntary no-cost basis.

Entrepreneur profile

Peter Gordon

Not all business advisers work exclusively in either the public or private sector. Some of them actually operate in both spheres, and so bring a slightly different perspective to the role of business consulting.

Peter Gordon is such a person. He's the sole director of Something Ventured Pty Ltd, a Canberra-based company that has been trading since 1999. Something Ventured provides private coaching and consulting services for firms in southern New South Wales and the Australian Capital Territory on a fee-for-usage basis, and it delivers free advice and information under contract to various government agencies. Since 2001, Peter's firm has operated the Canberra Business Advisory Service on behalf of the ACT government. In this role, it provides free support directly to local entrepreneurs starting a new business or operating an existing one — a role similar to the Business Advisory Services in some other Australian states. Peter also delivers services to indigenous entrepreneurs on behalf of the Commonwealth government agency Indigenous Business Australia.

Peter has a long history of business experience, having run his own petrol stations and gift shops, and has worked with a government small business centre in country New South Wales. This has been crucial to working effectively as an adviser. 'It's much easier to empathise with clients, because I've experienced many of the same ups and downs that they're going through.'

Overall, Peter believes very much in the role of the adviser as facilitator. 'I don't tell people what to do, unless it's blatantly wrong or illegal. I can't judge outcomes. I've seen people with an ordinary idea succeed, while those with brilliant concepts have sometimes folded. It's hard to predict what will and won't work, so individuals have to decide that for themselves — not advisers.'

Is there a difference between publicly funded and user-pays business advice? 'Definitely. Some people, such as micro-business owners, are more willing to use a service if it's free. People just going into business for the first time also tend to rely on free government-sponsored assistance schemes, since they don't have a lot of money to spend in this area. Private advisers see a different type of client, typically larger firms with more financial capacity. They also have more competition, such as professional coaches and accountants who also charge to give out management advice.'

For more information, visit <www.canbas.com.au> or <www.somethingventured.com.au>.

Personal coaches

Business coach:
A person who works with entrepreneurs, business owners or senior managers to help them deal with problems in their work and private life.

More expensive than many other advisers, but growing in popularity, are so-called **business coaches**. These are people who work with entrepreneurs, business owners or senior managers to help them deal with problems in their work and private life. The goal is to enhance the performance of the firm by improving the psychological environment in which a firm's key decision maker operates. A mixture of counsellor, psychologist and business adviser, the coach helps a person solve personal and work-related issues.[8]

Family and friends

In addition to professional consultants, budding entrepreneurs and existing small business operators often turn to their own range of personal contacts (such as family members and friends) for support, counselling, advice and ideas.

Other business operators

One of the most common sources of advice is other entrepreneurs. Although this may seem surprising (after all, businesspeople may also represent a competitive threat to the firm), such people will have had many similar experiences. Like mentoring, the common background and informal transmission of acquired knowledge is often valued by small-firm owners as being more credible than that of 'the professionals'.[9]

External directors and equity investors

If an entrepreneur has raised capital from outside investors, such individuals can provide valuable ongoing feedback about business performance and management of the enterprise. Venture capitalists and 'business angels', for example, often provide such services to entrepreneurs, and may also serve as directors of the business. There has also been an increasing trend among the owner–managers of growth-oriented firms to appoint a number of outside directors to the board of their company in order to tap into their networks and gain their counsel on business problems.

How much are advisory services used?

Unfortunately, many small businesses do not fully avail themselves of the many services available to them. In many cases, new and emerging firms are often unaware of what help is available, are more reluctant to ask for advice than established firms are, and are often sceptical of the benefits of such assistance.[10] When they do decide to seek information, it is often limited to matters such as taxation and accounting; they do not access the full range of services available to help them improve the business and increase their profitability.

To date, there is some evidence to suggest that small business owners have a preference for particular types of service, and are more likely to use some advisers than others. The most substantive data from the Pacific Rim in support of this contention arises from the results of the Business Longitudinal Survey,[11] an Australian study that examined the use of external advisory services. It found that some advisers (especially accountants, banks, family and friends, and fellow business owners) were clearly preferred above others, including government agencies and professional consultants. Similar results were found by Jay and Schaper, who examined the services used by the owner–managers of micro-businesses in Western Australia[12] (see table 10.3).

Table 10.3: Use of business advisory services by home-based businesses

Type of business adviser	Proportion of owners using adviser	Mean number of visits per year
Accountants	94%	1.56
Banks	90%	1.32
Other business operators	72%	1.16
Family or friends	68%	0.99
Lawyers	31%	0.40
Other government agency	29%	0.35
Industry association/chamber of commerce	24%	0.28
Business consultant	19%	0.22
Small business development corporation	19%	0.21
Business enterprise centre	12%	0.12
Other	9%	0.12

Source: L. Jay & M. Schaper, 'The utilisation of business advisory services by home-based businesses in Western Australia', paper presented to the 15th annual Small Enterprise Association of Australia and New Zealand (SEAANZ) conference, Adelaide, 22–24 September 2002.

As can be seen from table 10.3, there are marked differences in the types of adviser used. Accountants are the most highly used service, usually because their skills are necessary to comply with legal requirements such as tax returns and record keeping.[13] Personal contacts, local bank branches and colleagues in the same industry are also extensively used. These sources are usually free and easily accessible, and they are trusted because of the personal links the business owner has with the provider of advice. It may also reflect a limited knowledge of what services are available, or indicate a predilection, when confronted with a problem, to turn to 'those you already know'.[14] These results are not unusual. In New Zealand, a national survey of business practices also found that banks, accountants and other business operators were among the most widely used sources of assistance and that government bodies and universities were the least used. Many firms were either unaware of the services provided by government, or else perceived them to be too bureaucratic and difficult to access.[15] Similar results have also been noted in numerous surveys in nations such as the United Kingdom.[16]

These studies indicate that the market for small business assistance seems to operate inefficiently. There is an over-reliance on a limited number of sources, while the services of many other advisory bodies are not extensively used. Furthermore, many business owners still report that their specific needs are not met by the advisers they do use.[17]

A separate but equally important issue to consider is the effectiveness of such advisers. Just how much difference does an adviser make to a small business owner or a budding entrepreneur? Some researchers have shown that the use of external advice can improve the survival of start-up firms or the performance of existing and growing ones.[18] However, several other authors have questioned whether advisers make any substantive difference to the actual performance of client firms, or indeed whether they can truly add value to a small firm's operations at all.[19] This issue is compounded by the difficulty of measuring an adviser's impact. Should an adviser's performance be measured quantitatively (such as in the amount of extra revenue they help their clients make), or are intangible results (such as boosting a client's confidence or helping them comply with the law) more important? Finally, is an adviser creating a successful outcome or not when he or she counsels a client to stop trading because the business is failing and likely to go further into debt if it continues?

Advisory styles

There are a number of different approaches to dealing with business problems, each of which reflects a different way of working with clients and helping to solve their problems. Although it can be difficult to accurately categorise all the ways that advisers work with clients, several researchers have developed typologies that try to explain these different perspectives.[20] Schein argues that there are three fundamentally different types (or modes) of advisory style: the expert consultant, the hired 'pair of hands' and the process facilitator.[21]

Expert consultant mode

Expert consultant: A business adviser with highly developed skills in a specific area.

This is the classic popular idea of the **expert consultant** or business adviser. An expert is seen here as someone with a high degree of business skill in a specific area. This person is usually contracted to come into an organisation and deal with either company-wide issues or a specific problem. Just as a doctor uses acquired medical knowledge to diagnose and treat a patient's condition, the expert consultant is expected to identify what is wrong and prescribe potential solutions for the organisation. Management consulting firms, lawyers and accountants typically fall into this category.

Although often time-efficient and effective for businesses with clearly identifiable problems, this mode has some problems. Entrepreneurs, owners and employees ('the patients') may be reluctant to reveal their problems or weaknesses to the consultant. Moreover, such outside experts often may not ask the right questions and therefore do not uncover the full picture of what is occurring in and around the firm. They do not usually know the background of the firm and the owner/entrepreneur very well, and may prescribe solutions that are wrong because they do not take into account all the issues involved. Similarly, there is no ownership of the solutions proposed by the consultant. The owner or firm is told what to do and how to do it. Thus, the next problem that emerges will also have to be dealt with by another outside expert.

'Pair of hands' mode

Another option is to 'buy in' advice for a limited period. The **'pair of hands' adviser** is a person whose expert services or skills are purchased for a defined length of time. An example is the use of information technology (IT) specialists who come into a company for six months to write and set up a computer program specific to the organisation's needs. Once the assigned task is completed, the adviser leaves.

This approach does provide some longer term benefit for the small firm. It allows the business to employ staff to solve specific problems without taking on the long-term obligation of a permanent employment contract. There is also the possibility of knowledge being transferred from the adviser to in-house staff during this period. However, it still requires the entrepreneur/owner or senior staff members to be able to accurately diagnose what the problem is before making the decision to bring in a 'pair of hands'. Moreover, once the consultant departs, the firm may once again find itself lacking the skills that it needs.

Facilitator or process mode

A **facilitator** is a person who works alongside entrepreneurs and their staff to help them identify and solve their own problems. The facilitator does not need to be an expert in multiple fields, but rather must possess the ability to help people help themselves. The major role of the facilitator is to help business owners reflect on the processes occurring in the firm. They help business owners to become aware of their own strengths and weaknesses, to identify the problems in their business, and to develop their own solutions to those problems.

This style of advice is based on a number of assumptions. Facilitators (or, as they are sometimes referred to, counsellors) argue that understanding and learning comes about only when small business clients realise for themselves what the problem is.[22] If they are simply told 'the correct answers' by an outside expert, no learning has taken place. Equally importantly, facilitators believe that true change within a business can take place only when owner–managers take responsibility for implementing changes themselves. To bring in an 'expert' or a 'hired pair of hands' who simply deals with a particular issue and then moves out of the firm is solving only a specific issue. Organisational change and development is much more enduring if entrepreneurs can be taught to recognise problems, identify their own possible solutions, and make the necessary reforms themselves.

One of the strongest advocates of the facilitative approach is Ernesto Sirolli,[23] who was responsible for the establishment of the Business Enterprise Centre network (now known as Small Business Centres) in Western Australia. Sirolli has argued that only facilitation can make a real difference to entrepreneurs, since such people naturally tend to want to take responsibility for their own lives and their own business. Self-learning gives enterprising business operators the ability to continually learn and adapt to changing circumstances. In contrast, encouraging them to rely on an outside expert or 'pair of hands' simply creates a perpetual dependency situation — clients never learn to fix their own problems, and so constantly have to find someone else who can.[24]

The three different advisory styles broadly represent a continuum of approaches (see figure 10.1). At one extreme, the expert consultant is highly authoritative, making judgements and prescribing solutions; most of the decision making about the problem and how to treat it is left to the expert. At the other extreme, facilitation essentially relies on the business owner taking responsibility for dealing with the issue. The differences between the three approaches are summarised in table 10.4.

| Expert consultant | 'Pair of hands' adviser | Facilitator/counsellor |
| Problem-focused, e.g. accountant, lawyer; identifies symptoms of business problems and suggests cure | Short-term contractor, e.g. IT consultant; completes an assigned task and then leaves | Client-focused, e.g. business enterprise centre; helps businesses help themselves |

Figure 10.1: The three types of adviser

Table 10.4: Differences in advisory style

	Expert consultant	'Pair of hands' adviser	Facilitator
Level of specialist business knowledge	Highly specialised	Highly specialised	Generalist; broadly familiar with many different business fields
Problem identification	Consultant identifies	Client identifies	Client identifies
Solution implementation	Either consultant or client implements	Adviser implements	Client implements

Sourcing advisers

In addition to knowing what types of advice are available in the marketplace, entrepreneurs must also know how to access such assistance. There are a variety of different avenues that can help identify potential advisers, such as the following:

- *Professional bodies.* Organisations such as law societies and accounting institutes are often the first and most logical source to turn to for names of potential advisers. Generally, it is not difficult to obtain a list of their members in the same locality as the business. The benefit of such an approach is that it ensures the advisers are properly qualified and comply with all the relevant professional codes of conduct. However, professional bodies will usually not recommend specific individuals or firms on the list, either from fear of future liability or to avoid the impression of favouritism. The owner or entrepreneur must still make the final choice of adviser.
- *Advertisements.* Although some professional associations may limit the amount and type of self-promotion that their members may engage in, most advisers will undertake some advertising of their services. Telephone directories, professional industry journals, websites and public advertising are therefore all likely sources for names of advisers.
- *Personal recommendations.* In many cases, initial information about the relative merits of a particular adviser will be supplied by people the entrepreneur knows personally. Friends, relatives and business colleagues will usually have their own advisers, and so may be able to provide recommendations.
- *Small business agencies.* Such bodies will often provide details of local advisers, and may be able to provide first-hand assessments of their costs and quality of service. However, to avoid claims of bias, they may be reluctant or unable to recommend specific individuals.

Choosing a professional adviser

Several commercial and personal factors should be taken into account by the owner–manager or entrepreneur when selecting an adviser (see figure 10.2, p. 259).[25] Some of these issues include the following:

- *Qualifications.* Does the adviser have a recognised tertiary qualification in the professed field of expertise? Has the person undertaken any continuing education courses since graduation? Is the adviser a member of a professional body? If not, does the adviser qualify for membership? It is wise to think twice before engaging the services of anyone without such professional/peer recognition.
- *Experience and industry knowledge.* What first-hand experience does the adviser have in the entrepreneur's particular industry? Is this sufficient? If the adviser does not have relevant experience, will he or she still be able to provide an appropriate level of service? Generally, consultants who operate in the 'expert' or 'pair of hands' mode discussed previously will be highly technically proficient in a defined area, whereas facilitators will tend to have a much broader, generalised knowledge base.

- *Friendliness/personal rapport.* Can the owner–manager or entrepreneur relate to the adviser? Ideally, the business manager and the consultant will develop a relationship over a considerable period of time, so it is important that they are able to work well together.[26] In some situations, a client can be made to feel uneasy, awkward or uncomfortable when dealing with a particular professional adviser. If this is the case, then it is probably better to find someone else.
- *Networking ability.* It is rare to find one adviser who has the answers to all of a client's questions. Often an array of different skills and knowledge bases is required. This is often the case during the launch of a new entrepreneurial venture, when a team of advisers, each with particular abilities, must be put together if the project is to be successfully launched. To this end, a good adviser will often have an extensive body of contacts and personal contacts who can be used as needed to help the client.[27]
- *Services provided.* What exactly will the client receive for the money? Can the adviser provide the full range of facilities and knowledge that the business owner requires? For example, an effective accountant must not be just a glorified bookkeeper. The accountant should also be able to advise on taxation law, prepare financial documents and have a good working knowledge of accounting principles.
- *Price.* How much will the adviser charge? Is this figure set at an hourly rate, or is the charge fixed, regardless of the amount of time taken? Are there likely to be any additional or hidden costs (for consumables, telephone calls and on-site visits, for example)?
- *Conflicts of interest.* Are there any situations in which the adviser may have conflicting loyalties or should not be involved in the business? Trust is an important issue for many owner–managers when selecting an adviser.[28] For example, it would not be appropriate to engage a management consultant to develop a business plan for a particular venture if that consultant were also preparing one for a rival enterprise, as information may be transferred between the two businesses.

Figure 10.2: Adviser selection criteria

Forms of support for new and small firms
Government assistance

In recognition of the importance of entrepreneurship and small business to overall economic growth, many governments have attempted to stimulate business start-ups and growth by providing financial and informational assistance to businesses within their jurisdictions.[29] These forms of help include:

- *Business start-up assistance.* Programs include grants to start a business, training schemes for prospective business start-ups, access to low-cost or free business advisers, help in preparing a business plan, and general information provision.

- *Business development and improvement.* For existing businesses that seek to improve their performance or expand, government grants or subsidies may be provided to employ consultants to advise on different aspects of business management. These can include the areas of business planning, improved production processes, quality assurance certification, human resource management, business networking programs, the use of new information technology, and marketing campaigns. In some cases, governments may wholly subsidise these activities.

- *Infrastructure support.* Another common avenue of practical government support is the provision of key services to help a particular industry. For example, governments may meet the cost of improving road and rail links to a port to encourage the growth of industries that export by sea. Business incubators (discussed below) are another form of small-scale infrastructure assistance.

- *Tax concessions.* In some jurisdictions it is possible to claim tax reductions for costs related to business start-ups, growth and expansion. Some regional authorities even offer 'tax holidays' for firms that start trading in or relocate to a specific area. This is a form of subsidy that reduces the overall tax liability of the business.

- *Trade assistance.* Export credits, foreign market intelligence, trade missions and training courses have all been provided by various countries keen to enhance the level of exports undertaken by their small businesses.

Generally, government assistance is not confined to a particular department or agency. Often different forms of help are available from different government departments, so it may be necessary to make enquiries with all relevant arms of government. However, entrepreneurs and small business owners do not always have enough time or knowledge of government systems to access all these bodies. As a result, most countries now provide an agency that can act as a 'gateway' to other arms of government. Bodies such as enterprise centres, small business development corporations, or SME first-stop shops act as integrated facilities where businesspeople can receive advice about their business project, suggestions for improvement, and referrals to other government schemes or departments that might be of help.

Different countries have adopted different approaches to small business and new venture development. Some regions, such as Hong Kong, have traditionally been quite minimalist in their approach. Other nations, such as Australia, have focused on information provision rather than just financial aid. One of the countries with a sophisticated national strategy for small firms is Singapore, which has developed an SME Master Plan that covers many different issues related to small

manager experienced in working with new and growing entrepreneurial ventures. The focus is on helping businesses to successfully enter the marketplace and then to consolidate and secure their existence. Firms can rent space on a weekly or monthly basis, but do not have to commit themselves to long-term leases. As the term *incubator* might suggest, tenants are typically expected to 'leave the nest' within two or three years of start-up, by which time it is assumed they will either be viable, and able to operate on their own, or not feasible.[31]

The typical services offered in an incubator are:[32]

- *Convenient, reasonably priced tenancies.* Incubator rentals do not have many of the onerous conditions or long-term lease obligations found in many commercially run shopping precincts.
- *In-house business services.* These include receptionists, secretarial services, conference and meeting rooms, photocopiers, fax and postage services, and access to bookkeeping and word-processing professionals.
- *Business advisory services.* The manager of the centre will usually work alongside tenants to help them solve specific business problems or develop their range of generic business skills.
- *Business support.* Operating alongside other entrepreneurs gives owner–managers an immediate network of fellow businesspeople, providing mutual support, sharing ideas and knowledge, and forging business collaborations.

There are three common types of business incubator. *Embedded incubators* are often part of, or share premises with, another organisation. One of the most common such alliances in Australia is with Business Enterprise Centres (BEC). The BEC manager acts as the incubator manager, providing tenants with continuous access to up-to-date business knowledge. In return, the BEC supplements its income by collecting a management fee. *Independent incubators* are 'stand-alone' facilities that operate on their own. The management of the incubator is separate from any other small business support services, and dedicated solely to dealing with incubator clients. *Specific-purpose incubators* provide support to a particular industry or trade. Common types of single-purpose incubator are technology parks and incubators dedicated to arts and crafts, biotechnology and environmentally sustainable industries.[33]

Incubators often represent a mix of public and private support. In many cases, the initial funding for the establishment of an incubator is provided by government, but ongoing management of the centre is contracted to a private sector adviser or community organisation.[34]

Summary

This chapter examined the importance of seeking assistance from individuals and agencies outside the business itself. Advisers can be of benefit to small and entrepreneurial firms because they bring in new ideas, provide a more effective use of resources, and act as an objective source of information and analysis. Business advisory services have been in existence for a long time; however, most publicly funded services in the Pacific Rim region have emerged only in the last 20 years.

Advice may come from a number of different sources, including accountants, lawyers, management consultants, bank managers, financial planners, small business development agencies, industry mentors, business coaches, family and friends, and other business entrepreneurs. There are marked differences in the frequency with which such services are used.

There are essentially three different working styles an adviser can adopt. In the expert consultant mode, the adviser analyses, diagnoses problems, and suggests change. The 'pair of hands' mode occurs when an adviser is bought in to work within the firm for a temporary period. Finally, the facilitative process mode encourages owners and entrepreneurs to take responsibility for their own situation; the adviser's main goal is to help businesspeople learn how to help themselves.

Issues to take into account when choosing an adviser include qualifications, experience, industry knowledge, level of personal rapport, networking abilities, the range of services provided, price, and the presence or absence of any conflict of interests.

Government and private sector assistance to entrepreneurs and small businesses can take many forms. This may include start-up help, business development and improvement for existing firms, provision of infrastructure, tax concessions and trade support. Business incubators represent a hybrid of public and private assistance. They provide convenient tenancies, in-house business services and advice, and the opportunity to build links with kindred business operators.

REVIEW QUESTIONS

1. Briefly list and explain the function of each type of business adviser.

2. What are the issues to take into account when choosing an adviser?

3. Explain the four types of service offered by a business incubator, and the three different types of incubator.

4. Where can entrepreneurs go to find the names of potential advisers for their businesses?

5. What types of business adviser do new and small firms most commonly use?

DISCUSSION QUESTIONS

1. In your opinion, which business adviser style is most important to an entrepreneur/business owner? Why?

2. Is there any particular advantage or disadvantage in seeking financial assistance or information from a private sector agency instead of a government body?

3. What are the limitations of using family and friends as your main source of business advice?

SUGGESTED READING

Agar, J. & Witzel, M., *Developing Better Business Advisers: A Study of What Excellent Business Advisers Do*, Agar Associates, London, 1997.

Bacon, T.R. & Spear, K., *Adaptive Coaching: The Art and Practice of a Client-Centered Approach to Performance Improvement*, Davies-Black Publishing, Mountain View, CA, 2003.

Sirolli, E., *Ripples in the Zambezi: Passion, Predictability and Economic Development*, Institute for Science and Technology Policy, Murdoch University, Western Australia, 1995.

CASE STUDY

Hatchlings

Three years ago, Amelia and Rod Coppings came up with a bright new idea for the New Zealand tourism market: helping young children, the sick and those with disabilities who were travelling on their own. After a year of thinking about the idea, talking to their friends, investing $25 000 of their own money in start-up costs, and attending a six-week 'business planning' course during evenings at their local technical institute, they launched Hatchlings.

For a daily fee, staff from Hatchlings will accompany young children travelling abroad or interstate to meet up with their parents. Hatchlings staff act as surrogate parents for the trip, ensuring the child's safety and security until arrival at their destination, where they are met by their parents or legal guardian. A similar service is now also offered for adults with a physical illness or disability who want to undertake independent travel.

Rod, 45, was previously a high-school language teacher and principal who had grown tired of the education sector. He now fills the role of office manager, bookkeeper and salesperson, while Amelia, 38, a nurse, spends much of her time on the road with the actual travelling clients. Six other employees work on a casual 'as needs' basis for the firm, assisting when Amelia cannot do all the travel herself. Although they spent the first year working from a leased office, for the last year they have been based in the suburbs of Auckland at a business incubator with a free, on-site business advisory service. In the last two years, they turned over $150 000 and $160 000, but this left them with a net profit of only $55 000 and $52 000 respectively.

Rod and Amelia have been married for five years. All their assets are tied up in the business. They do not have any substantial private savings left, nor do they own any other financial assets such as real estate.

In light of the relatively low turnover and profits, Amelia has recently suggested that they expand into other tourism areas by organising children's holidays to national parks in the north island of New Zealand and to popular tourist destinations such as Akaroa in the south island. She estimates that it would cost about $20 000 in additional marketing expenses to branch out.

Rod disagrees strongly with his wife, as he believes that they should stay focused on their original core business until it becomes more established and profitable, so they spoke to the manager of the incubator. He was enthusiastic about the proposal. 'I think expanding into other areas could work wonders for you, although I'm concerned that you haven't done any market research, developed any financial projections or put together a written business plan. And I don't know if children's tourism is the best market. What about other areas, like providing personalised tours for the numerous German and other European tourists who come to New Zealand each year?'

Because the business is structured as a partnership, Amelia and Rod also spoke to their accountant, Eva Jones. She was more sceptical about the idea, and suggested that perhaps the most profitable option would be to close the firm and find full-time employment instead.

'You're not making much, and you probably never will. We have a shortage of skilled teachers and nurses at present, so why not take advantage of your real competitive advantage?' Eva said. But that certainly wasn't what Amelia wanted to hear — she still had her heart set on the children's tourism venture.

Questions

1. List the five most important problems facing this business at present.

2. What information would a business adviser need in order to best help Rod and Amelia?

3. Which solution would you chose? Why?

ENDNOTES

1. I. Campbell, *Perspectives on Small Business Assistance*, Law Foundation of New South Wales, Sydney, 1975.
2. Department of Trade and Industry, Commonwealth of Australia, *Report of the Committee on Small Business* (the Wiltshire Report), Government Publisher, Canberra, 1971.
3. G.G. Meredith, *Small Business Management in Australia*, 4th edn, McGraw-Hill, Sydney, 1993.
4. Singapore Standards, Productivity and Innovation for Growth (SPRING), *SME 21*, <www.spring.gov.sg>.
5. Small and Medium Industries Development Corporation, Malaysia, *SMI Development Plan 2001–2005*, <www.smidec.gov.my>, p. 5.
6. P. Carey, R. Simnett & G. Tanewski, *Providing Business Advice for Small To Medium Enterprises*, CPA Australia, Melbourne, 2005.
7. D. Leonard & W. Swap, 'Gurus in the garage', *Harvard Business Review*, vol. 78, no. 6, November–December 2000, pp. 71–82.
8. S. Berglas, 'The very real dangers of executive coaching', *Harvard Business Review*, vol. 80, no. 6, June 2002, pp. 86–93.
9. R.W. Peacock, *Home Business, Tip of the Iceberg*, Bookshelf Pubnet, Adelaide, 2000.
10. S. Holmes & S. Smith, 'The impact of subsidised business advice upon aspects of non-financial performance in small firms', *Small Enterprise Research*, vol. 5, no. 1, 1997, pp. 56–67.

11. Department of Employment, Workplace Relations and Small Business, *A Portrait of Australian Business: Results of the 1996 Business Longitudinal Survey*, Department of Employment, Workplace Relations and Small Business, Canberra, 1998.

12. L. Jay & M. Schaper, 'The utilisation of business advisory services by home-based businesses in Western Australia', paper presented to the 15th annual Small Enterprise Association of Australia and New Zealand (SEAANZ) conference, 22–24 September 2002, Adelaide, South Australia.

13. K. Mole, 'Business advisers' impact on SMEs: An agency theory approach', *International Small Business Journal*, vol. 20, no. 2, 2002, pp. 139–62.

14. R.W. Peacock, *see* note 9.

15. S. Knuckey, H. Johnston, C. Campbell-Hunt, K. Carlew, L. Corbett & C. Massey, *Firm Foundations: A Study of New Zealand Business Practices and Performance*, Ministry of Economic Development, Wellington, 2002, pp. 192–3.

16. R.J. Bennett & P. Robson, 'The use of external business advice by SMEs in Britain', *Entrepreneurship and Regional Development*, vol. 11, no. 2, 1999, pp. 155–80.

17. J. Breen & S. Bergin-Seers, 'The small business assistance dilemma: Is the disparity between the offerings of support agencies and the needs of businesses irreconcilable?', *Small Enterprise Research*, vol. 10, no. 1, 2002, pp. 49–58.

18. *See*, for example, J.J. Chrisman & W.E. McMullan, 'Outsider knowledge as a knowledge resource for new venture survival', *Journal of Small Business Management*, vol. 42, no. 3, 2004, pp. 229–44.

19. A. Gibb, 'SME policy, academic research and the growth of ignorance: Mythical concepts, myths, assumptions, rituals and confusions', *International Small Business Journal*, vol. 18, no. 3, 2002, pp. 13–35; J. Watson, J. Everett & R. Newby, 'Improving the odds of success: The effect of screening and professional advice', *Proceedings of the 45th International Council for Small Business World Conference*, 7–10 June 2000, Brisbane.

20. *See*, for example, P. Moran, *Clarifying and Enhancing the Role of Business Counsellors in Relation to Small Enterprise Development*, Durham University Business School, Durham, 1995.

21. E. Schein, Process *Consultation: Its Role in Organization Development*, 2nd edn, Addison-Wesley, Reading, Mass., 1988; E. Schein, *Process Consultation: Lessons for Managers and Consultants*, 2nd edn, Addison-Wesley, Reading, MA, 1987.

22. A.A. Gibb, 'Developing the role and capability of the small business adviser', *Leadership and Organization Development Journal*, vol. 5, no. 2, 1984, pp. 19–27.

23. E. Sirolli, *Ripples in the Zambezi: Passion, Unpredictability and Economic Development*, Institute for Science and Technology Policy, Murdoch University, Western Australia, 1995.

24. C.F. Hogan, *Understanding Facilitation*, Kogan Page, London, 2002.

25. C. Massey, 'Capturing the outcomes of enterprise agencies: A changing approach to measuring effectiveness', *Small Enterprise Research*, vol. 3, nos 1–2, 1995, pp. 57–64; Small Business Development Corporation, Western Australia, *Working with Your Business Adviser*, Small Business Development Corporation, Perth, 1997.

26. J. Agar & M. Witzel, *Developing Better Business Advisers: A Study of What Excellent Business Advisers Do*, Agar Associates Ltd, London, 1997.

27. A.A. Gibb, *see* note 19.

28. M. Schaper & C. Dunn, 'The field of service provision' in van der R. Horst, S. King-Kauanui & S. Duffy (eds.) *Keystones of Entrepreneurship Knowledge*, Blackwell, Oxford, pp. 355–6, 2005.

29. T.Y. Lee & L. Low, *Local Entrepreneurship in Singapore — Private and State*, Times Academic Press, Singapore, 1990.

30. Singapore Standards, Productivity and Innovation for Growth (SPRING), *see* note 4.

31. United Nations Industrial Development Organisation, *Business Incubators,* <www.unido.org>, 2000.
32. P. Dowling, *Business Incubation in Australia: Best Practice Standards and an Industry Profile,* Australia and New Zealand Association of Business Incubators, Wollongong, 1997, pp. 4–5.
33. ibid., pp. 8–9.
34. Australia and New Zealand Association of Business Incubators, *Incubation Works: Case Studies of Australian Small Business Incubators and Their Impact,* ANZABI, 2004.

Part 3

Managing key functions

Chapter 11

Marketing

LEARNING OBJECTIVES

After reading this chapter, you should be able to:

- define the concept of marketing and its importance to entrepreneurs and small business owners

- explain the six steps involved in the marketing process for new and small firms

- list the 'four Ps' that make up the marketing mix, and discuss the major elements of each

- calculate a break-even point, contribution margin, mark-up and margin for pricing purposes

- discuss how to evaluate the effectiveness of a firm's marketing efforts.

I n essence, a business exists to make a profit by identifying a market opportunity and successfully delivering goods and/or services to customers who are willing to pay a price for them. However, achieving this is often easier said than done.

Many firms fail because they do not know how to satisfactorily market their products. Indeed, marketing problems are often nominated by small business researchers, and by entrepreneurs themselves, as one of the most common causes of difficulties and failure.[1] Even today, many business owners think that marketing is simply about advertising; they fail to recognise that it covers many more issues.[2]

In this chapter, we discuss marketing in the context of the entire business venture. The concept of marketing and the different philosophies that can be adopted are examined. The marketing process is explained, followed by a detailed examination of the 'four Ps' that are found in every marketing plan. Special attention is paid to price setting, since this is an issue many entrepreneurs have difficulty dealing with. The chapter concludes with some suggestions about how to evaluate the effectiveness of a firm's marketing plan.

The concept of marketing

Marketing:
The process of planning and executing the conception, pricing, promotion and distribution of ideas, goods or services to create exchanges that satisfy individual and organisational goals.

Modern marketing theory can be a somewhat complex concept, although in essence the notion is relatively simple: it is a process through which individuals and businesses exchange products with one another.[3] The term *marketing* has its origins in the traditional medieval marketplace, where producers and consumers gathered to trade. Today, it is recognised that successful marketing must take into account many different issues. Accordingly, a contemporary definition of **marketing** is 'the process of planning and executing the conception, pricing, promotion and distribution of ideas, goods or services to create exchanges that satisfy individual and organisational goals'.[4]

Marketing is a multistage process involving a number of different activities that must all be successfully integrated if the business venture is to succeed. Identifying a group of potential customers, understanding the reasons why they purchase, developing a strategy for communicating with those customers, and delivering a product or service to them are all part of an effective marketing plan. Marketing is one of the core activities of all firms, and is closely linked to the financial and operational management of an enterprise.

The research evidence to date suggests that there are some differences in marketing approaches between large firms, small businesses, and growth-oriented entrepreneurs. For example, smaller enterprises have less sophisticated marketing resources available to them, and often tend to rely substantially on a niche focus, identifying markets that larger competitors overlook[5] or using so-called guerilla marketing techniques. In recent years increased attention has been paid to the concept of 'entrepreneurial marketing'[6] — the study of how entrepreneurs undertake marketing. Compared to more established competitors, entrepreneurs tend to place a greater focus on creating value-adding innovations for their customers and servicing new customer groups in dynamic and emerging markets, and they are often highly opportunistic in deciding what is the best way to reach and meet a customer's needs.[7]

An overview of the marketing process

As figure 11.1 shows, effective marketing requires prospective entrepreneurs and small business owners to carefully develop a plan through a series of considered, logical and sequential steps. It begins with a clear vision of business goals, followed by market research to better understand the likely acceptance of the product/service offering in the market and to develop priority target markets. The marketing mix (product, price, placement and promotion) must then be developed and implemented, after which the effectiveness of the marketing effort should be assessed.[8]

Goal setting

The first thing to consider in any marketing plan is how the firm wants or needs to market itself, since this will have a major impact on what strategy is adopted and whether it is successful.[9] This is often closely linked with the life cycle of the business venture, the stage in the life cycle of the product, the personal goals of the business owner, and the owner's own marketing philosophy.[10]

Different marketing strategies are often linked to the age and life cycle of the enterprise. The priority for new, small firms is to make themselves known in the marketplace. This often means that an initial heavy investment in research, marketing expenditure and effort is needed to help ensure that the firm starts getting customers through the door as quickly as possible. On the other hand, existing businesses with an established market presence, well-known products and a stable customer base may not need to put as much thought into their annual marketing plans. Older firms that are in decline, however, often need to re-evaluate their whole marketing strategy and may need to radically alter their target customer groups and even the products they offer. More information about business life cycles is provided in chapter 15.

The second issue to consider is whether the product is completely new to the market (at the beginning stages of the *product* life cycle). When the product that is being sold is totally original, much of the marketing effort must be devoted to alerting potential customers to the existence of the product, educating them about its features and benefits, and encouraging them to buy something new. This requires a long-term, often expensive approach that may take some time to pay off. On the other hand, if the firm intends to sell a product that is already known to consumers (already well into its life cycle), then the business does not need to focus on educating buyers about what the item *is* — the firm can, instead, concentrate on explaining why people should buy from this business rather than from a competitor.

Figure 11.1: The marketing process

A third factor concerns the goals of the business owner. Why is he or she in business in the first place? If the owner's goals are to aggressively grow and expand the business, then the marketing approach will often concentrate on issues such as achieving high levels of turnover, increasing market share, competing on price, and reaching out to as many potential customers as possible. This is the typical focus of many entrepreneurs. On the other hand, if lifestyle goals are the owner's priority, then it may make more sense to focus on a narrow **niche market** that can be easily served, where only a low level of marketing is needed, and where a price can be charged that maximises returns while minimising individual effort. This approach is commonly found among many small business owners, especially those who are not entrepreneurially minded.

Niche market:
A narrowly focused target market for goods and/or services.

All businesses tend to adopt, either consciously or by default, a particular marketing approach. A *production-oriented philosophy* places the main focus on what is made by the business — an item is produced as efficiently as possible, and it is then the role of the marketer to sell that finished item to consumers. This approach is typical of small business owners who are convinced of the inherent attraction and value of their offering and whose competitive advantage lies in efficient operating and production systems. A *sales-oriented philosophy* is concerned more with generating sales, regardless of what is made or what the consumer wants. Typical of this approach are the salespeople who believe they can sell anything to anyone, given the right circumstances. The third perspective, a *consumer-oriented approach*, concentrates on understanding and meeting customer needs and desires. Here the marketer focuses on understanding what the client wants and then works backwards to ensure that the firm can deliver it.[11]

Understanding the market

The next step is to research the market and clearly spell out the core customers the business intends to sell to.

Marketing and market research are closely intertwined. In chapter 6, the role and importance of market research were examined, and the tools that can be used to investigate a business idea were analysed. Such research is needed to understand several issues. Good market analysis can help identify exactly who the target market is, customers' perceptions about the product or service being offered, expenses of production, likely sales price, and the factors that will induce customers to purchase or not.

Target market:
A core group of customers that a business intends to focus its marketing efforts on.

A key issue here is to define the group of customers who are likely to purchase. A **target market** is the core group of customers a business intends to focus on. Although it may be theoretically possible to sell products to almost anyone (potential customers), in reality no business sells everything to everyone. Successfully identifying one or more target markets allows the small firm to make the most of its limited advertising and promotions budget and to ensure that the efforts of the staff are concentrated on those customers deemed most likely to want what the firm has to offer. This does not necessarily mean that the business will sell only to members of such a target group; it simply means that the business intends to devote its efforts to these key groups. Any other sales will, of course, be a pleasant addition.[12]

Markets can be segmented and targeted on the basis of several criteria:[13]

- *Geography.* Many small businesses make a conscious decision to sell in a particular area only. For example, a lawnmowing business may concentrate on one or two suburbs of a city, since the owner can achieve the greatest return if customers are located near one another. An internet service provider may focus on servicing a key city, state or province rather than a whole country.
- *Demographic characteristics.* Many consumers can be categorised on the basis of their age, gender, education, ethnicity, income or other features. For example, dividing markets in Singapore into Tamil-, Bahasa-, Chinese- and English-speaking groups can help entrepreneurs better develop specific strategies for each group of potential clients.
- *Psychographic features.* Lifestyle, socioeconomic status and attitudinal characteristics are another way of distinguishing consumers. University students, for example, tend to have different needs and wants (and less ready cash) than corporate executives. It rarely makes sense to try to sell to both groups using the same strategy.
- *Individual or business?* It is also worth remembering that, for many firms, their main customers are not members of the public (business-to-consumer), but rather another business or group of businesses. These are sometimes referred to as business-to-business (B2B) transactions. Secretarial services, for example, usually find that their customers are other small businesses, and an electrician may act as a subcontractor to one or more large business firms.

Many firms do not necessarily have just one target group of customers; they may, in fact, have as many as three or four. When this is the case, it is important to rank the relative significance of each group. Although it is often a very useful strategy to diversify and have more than one client base, the business owner must carefully assess how much effort to devote to each. If all client groups generate roughly equal levels of sales and profits, then it makes sense to spread the marketing effort among all groups. However, if one group is responsible for the vast majority of all turnover, then efforts should focus on retaining their loyalty and custom.

Another issue to consider at this point is the difference between potential and actual customer sales. Although the number of *potential* customers in a particular target group may be large, it is very rare for all these to become *actual* customers. Indeed, the number of actual customers may turn out to be only a very small proportion of the total available population. This needs to be taken into account when estimating future sales from each target group. It is often difficult to estimate the final number of paying customers, but some industries tend to have market averages or 'rules of thumb' that can be used as a guideline when calculating the conversion rate between potential and actual purchasers. A common (but by no means universal) rule is the *Pareto principle* — the argument that 80 per cent of all results is attributable to 20 per cent of participants.[14] In other words, most sales tend to come from a very small group of active customers rather than a large number. If this is true, then it makes sense to accurately target those key customers.

The marketing mix

Some business owners think of marketing as being synonymous with advertising — as if getting the latter right will automatically mean the former is also being done correctly. However, there are many other issues that need to be considered in the development of a comprehensive marketing strategy. Marketing is perhaps best implemented in terms of the 'four Ps' of the marketing mix — product, promotion, price and placement. This is a convenient model that helps ensure that all the critical sub-elements are integrated and work cohesively.[15]

The product or service

Having developed some clear goals about what needs to be achieved and to whom the business intends to market itself, the business owner can then prepare each of the items in the marketing mix. The first of these is usually the product itself. What are the advantages and strengths of the product? How do these compare with other products already in the marketplace? What are the weaknesses of the service or good? (This last is important to know, so that the firm can respond to criticisms of its offerings.)

One thing that many small business owners fail to appreciate is the difference between **product features** and **benefits**. The features of a product or service are a statement of what the offering is or does, whereas the benefits refer to the advantage that a consumer can receive by purchasing the good or service (see table 11.1). Marketing a good or service on the basis of its features (what it actually is) is very different from a benefit-based approach (which promotes a good on the basis of what the customer will gain from it).[16] Firms with a strong consumer-oriented marketing philosophy tend to have a clear idea of the benefits of their offerings, whereas many production- and sales-oriented businesses concentrate more on the features.

Product feature: What a product or service is or does.

Product benefit: The advantage that a consumer can receive by purchasing a good or service.

Table 11.1: Examples of product features and benefits

Product	Feature	Benefit
Fast food	Quick, mass-produced	Convenience
Dog wash	Pet regularly washed by professional dog handler	Saves time and mess
Email	Fast, computer-based communication	More regular contact with friends and relatives

Promotional tools

The promotional strategy focuses on the way the firm communicates with customers — how it informs, persuades and reminds potential buyers about its products and services, with a view to generating a decision by the customer to buy that item.[17]

How will the business promote its product and let the marketplace know that it is available? There are several tools available to most businesses:[18]

- *Personal canvassing.* This involves personally contacting people and making them aware of what is for sale. Time-consuming and expensive, this method is best suited to firms selling high-cost items that have a very limited market or to those conducting business-to- business transactions.

- *Electronic tools.* A large number of customers throughout the Pacific Rim region now use the internet as a tool for finding and purchasing products, so an interesting and easy-to-find website can substantially help firms boost product sales from this cohort. Other electronic tools can also be helpful. Emails, for example, can be used to alert customers to sales and special offerings, while online banner advertisements and links from other sites or search engines can increase customer awareness.
- *Print media advertising.* Newspapers, general magazines and special-interest journals are a traditional format for advertising and are still widely used today. Advertisements can be placed in particular sections of a paper or in special-interest journals to target certain categories of reader; for example, a sports store may advertise in the sports results pages.
- *Telephone directories.* Phone listings are still an important means of customer access. Especially useful is a prominent listing in the Yellow Pages (commercial) telephone directory in most cities.
- *Signage.* Signs are one of the few forms of advertising that, once erected, work continuously for a business. Provided they are placed at the correct visible point, the one-off investment in a sign can result in substantial long-term exposure. Suitable positions can include above or at the front of the premises, outside one's home (if the business is home-based and such signs are permitted by the relevant authority), along major customer traffic flow areas, and on the owner's and/or business's vehicles.
- *Logos and business names.* A good business name can clearly explain to a prospective customer exactly what the business does and can help it to stand out from its competitors. In contrast, names that are obscure or easily misspelt can create problems. The name can be accompanied by a simple visual graphic device (a logo) to reinforce the image.
- *Pamphlets.* Printed leaflets or flyers are a cheaper way of distributing information, usually through handouts or letterbox drops. However, most pamphlets have a low impact rate, since they are quickly discarded by readers.
- *Business cards.* Cards are a simple means of ensuring that customers, suppliers and other key stakeholders retain information about how to contact the firm.
- *Television and radio advertising.* These are broadcast (wide-ranging) media with the capacity to reach many customers at once. However, such advertisements are also expensive and require professional production to maximise their impact.
- *Sponsorship.* Donating goods, money or services to a local community activity or association can also help promote the firm. Many small business owners provide sponsorship in return for having their business name prominently displayed in any related promotion of the community group or event.
- *Word of mouth.* Hardest of all to measure and maintain, personal recommendations are still one of the most effective ways of promoting a firm. However, such publicity usually comes about only if the firm has a high level of customer service and a good reputation for solving client problems or complaints.
- *Trade shows.* Industry conventions where manufacturers, suppliers and distributors (and sometimes the public) come together are a good opportunity to

Understanding the mechanics of price setting

Price setting involves more than just dealing with customers' perceptions of a product and their willingness to spend. It is also closely related to the firm's capacity to meet its own costs and to generate a reasonable return for the owner (and investors, if any). An understanding of the principles that govern the mechanics of pricing will help astute business owners find a price which not only is acceptable in the marketplace, but also meets their own financial goals.

The nature of costs

The first step in developing an understanding of the pricing process is the ability to discriminate between different types of expense. The costs involved in running any business operation can be broken down into two basic categories: fixed costs and variable costs.

Fixed costs are those expenses that remain the same, regardless of the level of activity or sales turnover a business generates. Many of the day-to-day expenses of being in business (rent, administration, legal and accounting fees, insurance, electricity costs and so on) fall into this category. Such overheads are the cost of being in business. They are relatively unchanging, and must be paid for each year, regardless of how many sales the business makes.

Variable costs refer to expenditure items that increase or decrease as sales volume moves correspondingly. As more items are sold, the level of variable expenses will rise, usually in a direct relationship (so a 10 per cent increase in sales will be met with a matching 10 per cent increase in variable cost outlays). Conversely, a decline in sales is often matched by a drop in variable expenses. For a manufacturer, the main variable expense will be the raw materials used to produce a finished product; other expenses may include energy consumption and labour costs if these are directly proportionate to product output. In a retail shop, the main variable expense is the trading stock (inventory) purchased for resale to customers. In contrast, service operations are largely based on personal endeavours rather than on the sale of goods; as a consequence, such firms tend to have very few, if any, direct variable expenses.

In the rest of this chapter, the term *cost of goods sold* (COGS) is used when discussing both raw materials and trading stock. This is the major variable cost for most businesses; in fact, in many cases it is the *only* variable expense worthy of note (see table 11.2).

> **Fixed costs:** Expenses that remain the same, regardless of the level of activity or sales turnover a business generates.
>
> **Variable costs:** Expenditure items that increase or decrease as sales volume changes.

Table 11.2: Some common fixed and variable costs

Fixed costs	Variable costs
Electricity, gas and water	Cost of goods sold — raw materials, trading stock
Wages	Wages of factory staff (if a manufacturing firm)
Equipment	Wages of sales and other staff (if paid on a commission basis)
Rent of premises	
Use of professional advisers	
Insurance	

A good starting point in analysing a firm's fixed and variable costs is to examine its profit and loss statement (also called a statement of financial performance). Most items can be easily divided into one or other category, although some items will appear to be partly fixed and partly variable (for example, most firms have a fixed minimum amount of advertising that they undertake each year, although it would also be reasonable to expect this cost to directly increase if the firm wished to increase sales). In general, however, it is preferable to keep the analysis simple and to regard as variable only those items which inevitably move with the level of sales. In these situations, many firms will end up with cost of goods sold as the only variable cost.

Having completed the initial breakdown into fixed and variable costs, the business owner should next consider the role of business income. Every dollar of revenue received by a business has at least three components:

- Any price established must, first and foremost, cover the direct variable cost of producing the particular item which is sold. In other words, a certain portion of the product price or service fee must pay for the cost of the goods actually sold.
- There must also be sufficient to help defray the fixed costs (overheads) of the business.
- If anything is left over once fixed costs and variable expenses have been paid for, this represents profit for the owner. Profit is used to pay a fair return to the owner/s of the enterprise for time, effort and risk-taking in establishing and running the enterprise. Some of it must also be retained for reinvestment in the firm for future growth; and a final portion of the profit will also usually be taken away as a tax on business profits by government. (This is not the same as a compulsory sales tax, VAT or GST, which must also be levied on the final sales price of the item. The impact of such consumption taxes is explained separately at the end of this section.)

Break-even point

Each time a product is sold, it should be priced at a level that at least covers the variable expenses (cost of goods sold) and yet has enough left over to make a contribution to recovering the fixed annual costs of the enterprise. At what point have enough items been sold to fully cover all those fixed costs (and, by definition, all the variable expenses to date)? This level of sales is referred to as the **break-even point**. At break-even point, net profit is nil, but all expenses have been met.[25]

Break-even analysis allows the owner to calculate the point at which a business generates enough sales to meet all its costs. Beyond that level, any more items that are sold will provide a certain amount of profit. However, if sales fall below that point, then the business will run at a loss.

One conventional formula for calculating a break-even point is:

$$\text{Break-even point in units} = \frac{\text{Total fixed costs}}{\text{Unit sales price} - \text{Variable cost per unit}}$$

This equation calculates the total number of *unit sales* needed to reach the break-even point. (If the actual dollar amount is needed, this can be calculated by multiplying the total number of units by their individual selling price.) The break-even point in units can be easily calculated by using a profit and loss statement, along with a knowledge of the selling price and variable cost of the individual item.

Break-even point:
The level of sales where all expenses have been met, but no profit has been made.

With a little variation, the formula can also be used to calculate the level of sales needed to produce a specific level of profit:

$$\text{Number of items needed} = \frac{\text{Net profit} + \text{Total fixed costs}}{\text{Unit sales price} - \text{Variable cost per unit}}$$

Example 1

Killer Kiwi Stationery is a small part-time venture that buys and sells only one item — marker pens — which it retails for $2 each to schools. The proprietor of the store buys the pens for $1.20. The only variable expense is the cost of goods sold. The fixed costs are all the operating expenses (overheads). Last year, the firm sold 50 000 pens, and its profit and loss statement was as follows:

Sales revenue	$100 000
Less: Cost of goods sold	60 000
Gross profit	40 000
Less: Operating expenses	30 000
Net profit	$ 10 000

To calculate the break-even point, the following formula can be used:

$$\text{Break-even point in units} = \frac{\text{Total fixed costs}}{\text{Unit sales price} - \text{Variable cost per unit}}$$

$$= \frac{\$30\,000}{\$2.00 - \$1.20}$$

$$= 37\,500 \text{ pens (which is actually } \$75\,000 \text{ worth of sales)}$$

If the owner wanted to make a net profit of $20 000 this year, she could use the following formula:

$$\text{Break-even point in units} = \frac{\text{Net profit} + \text{Total fixed costs}}{\text{Unit sales price} - \text{Variable cost per unit}}$$

$$= \frac{\$20\,000 + \$30\,000}{\$2.00 - \$1.20}$$

$$= 62\,500 \text{ pens } (\$125\,000 \text{ worth of sales)}$$

Contribution margin: The proportion of money left in each dollar of sales after variable costs have been met, and which is available to cover fixed costs and contribute to profits.

Contribution margin

Calculating the break-even point using the above formula is useful but can be quite cumbersome and slow. In many cases, it would be easier if a more concise equation could be developed for such simple calculations. This is the role of the contribution margin.[26]

The **contribution margin** represents the proportion of money left in each dollar of sales after variable costs have been met, and which is available to cover fixed costs and contribute to profits. In other words, it answers the following question: For every dollar that the business earns, how much is left over after variable costs (cost of goods sold) have been paid for? This is the amount that the owner can use to pay for fixed costs and then help generate a profit.

A contribution margin can be calculated using the formula:

$$\text{Contribution margin} = \frac{\text{Total sales} - \text{Total variable costs}}{\text{Total sales}}$$

Just like the break-even point, the information on a profit and loss statement can be used to perform this calculation. However, where the only variable cost in a business is the cost of goods sold, then the calculation of a break-even point becomes much easier, because the contribution margin will equal the gross profit margin shown on the profit and loss statement.

Once known and expressed as a percentage, the contribution margin can then be used to calculate break-even point. (Note that this figure is expressed as a dollar value, not number of items sold.)

$$\text{Break-even point in dollars} = \frac{\text{Fixed costs}}{\text{Contribution margin}}$$

It can also be used to estimate the dollar value of sales needed for a particular net profit:

$$\text{Dollar value of sales needed} = \frac{\text{Net profit} + \text{Total fixed costs}}{\text{Contribution margin}}$$

Understanding how to establish fixed and variable costs, and then using this information to calculate a contribution margin, can allow a business owner to work out whether the proposed break-even point is realistic (can the firm really make that many sales in a year at that price?) and whether a particular profit target is also achievable.

The analysis of pricing mechanisms discussed above works best with a firm that offers a single product or service. Where a number of different products at very different prices are sold, then analysis becomes somewhat more difficult.

Example 2

Using the information provided in example 1, Killer Kiwi Stationery's contribution margin can be calculated in the following manner:

$$\text{Contribution margin} = \frac{\text{Total sales} - \text{Total variable costs}}{\text{Total sales}}$$

$$= \frac{\$100\,000 - \$60\,000}{\$100\,000}$$

$$= 0.4$$

$$= 40\%$$

This could also have been found by referring to the profit and loss statement. Since the only variable expense is the cost of goods sold, the resulting gross profit margin is the same as the contribution margin of 40 per cent.

The contribution margin can then be used to calculate the break-even point and sales needed to make a net profit of $20 000, as in the previous example, but using the simpler formula:

$$\text{Break-even point in dollars} = \frac{\text{Fixed costs}}{\text{Contribution margin}}$$

$$= \frac{\$30\,000}{0.4}$$

$$= \$75\,000 \text{ worth of sales}$$

$$\text{Dollar value of sales needed} = \frac{\text{Net profit} + \text{Total fixed costs}}{\text{Contribution margin}}$$

$$= \frac{\$20\,000 + \$30\,000}{0.4}$$

$$= \$125\,000 \text{ worth of sales}$$

Mark-ups and margins

Mark-up:
The extent to which the price of a product is increased from its original cost of goods sold to its final selling price.

A **mark-up** is the extent to which the price of a product is increased from its original cost of goods sold to its final selling price. It shows the percentage increase from cost price to sales price. Mark-ups are always measured in relation to the cost price, and are calculated thus:

If measuring the whole of the business:

$$\text{Mark-up} = \frac{\text{Gross profit}}{\text{Cost of goods sold}}$$

If analysing an individual product:

$$\text{Mark-up} = \frac{\text{Profit}}{\text{Cost price}}$$

The first formula can be applied if the firm's profit and loss statement is known, and the second applies when only individual product information is available.

Margin:
A measure of how much of the final sales price is gross profit.

A **margin**, on the other hand, is a measure of how much of the final sales price is gross profit. Sometimes also referred to as a gross margin, it indicates the proportion or percentage of the sales price that is gross profit (thus it is always related to the selling price):

If measuring the whole of the business:

$$\text{Margin} = \frac{\text{Gross profit}}{\text{Sales}}$$

If analysing an individual product:

$$\text{Margin} = \frac{\text{Profit}}{\text{Selling price}}$$

Example 3

Since there is only one product on offer at Killer Kiwi Stationery, analysis of a mark-up and margin is relatively straightforward, and can be calculated using either the profit and loss statement or the individual product information provided previously.

If measuring the whole of the business:

$$\text{Mark-up} = \frac{\text{Gross profit}}{\text{Cost of goods sold}}$$

$$= \frac{\$40\,000}{\$60\,000}$$

$$= 0.67$$

$$= 67\%$$

If analysing an individual product:

$$\text{Mark-up} = \frac{\text{Profit}}{\text{Cost price}}$$

$$= \frac{\$0.80}{\$1.20}$$

$$= 0.67$$

$$= 67\%$$

If measuring the whole of the business:

$$\text{Margin} = \frac{\text{Gross profit}}{\text{Sales}}$$

$$= \frac{\$40\,000}{\$100\,000}$$

$$= 0.4$$

$$= 40\%$$

If analysing an individual product:

$$\text{Margin} = \frac{\text{Profit}}{\text{Selling price}}$$

$$= \frac{\$0.80}{\$2.00}$$

$$= 0.4$$

$$= 40\%$$

Also worth noting at this point is that the final gross profit margin is *always* less than the initial mark-up, since the amount by which the product has to be increased from its original base cost of goods is always more than the resulting profit margin (see table 11.3).

Table 11.3: The relationship between mark-ups and margins

Mark-up on cost	... results in the following gross profit margin on sales
10.0%	9.09%
20.0%	16.67%
25.0%	20.00%
33.3%	25.00%
50.0%	33.30%
100.0%	50.00%

Source: J. English, *How to Organise and Operate a Small Business in Australia*, 7th edn, Allen & Unwin, Sydney, 1998, p. 165.

What is the relevance of mark-ups and margins? Firstly, where the only variable cost in the business is the cost of goods sold, then the gross margin will, as mentioned before, be the same as the contribution margin. This information can then be applied to calculate break-even point, or sales needed for a particular level of net profit, as discussed previously.

Secondly, in many retail businesses, the selling price of a product is set by taking the cost price (cost of goods sold) and adding a set mark-up.

Thirdly, an understanding of mark-ups and margins can help business owners understand the significance of discounting on their final profit. In general, there is an almost exponential relationship between an increase or decrease in mark-up and the resultant effect on profitability. For example, a 10 per cent discount in sales price for Killer Kiwi Stationery would result in its net profit reducing to nil, whereas a 10 per cent increase in sales price would double its net annual profit to $20 000.

Example 4

If Killer Kiwi Stationery reduces the sales price of its marker pens ($2.00 in example 1) by 10 per cent, then its sales revenue will also decline by 10 per cent and the resultant profit and loss statement will be:

Sales revenue	$90 000
Less: Cost of goods sold	60 000
Gross profit	30 000
Less: Operating expenses	30 000
Net profit	$ nil

Note that even though the price reduction leads to decreased sales revenue, the cost of goods sold and operating expenses remain the same. Accordingly, profit is reduced to zero.

On the other hand, a 10 per cent increase in sales price from the original will produce the following result:

Sales revenue	$110 000
Less: Cost of goods sold	60 000
Gross profit	50 000
Less: Operating expenses	30 000
Net profit	$ 20 000

In this case, a 10 per cent price increase has led to a 100 per cent improvement in net profit compared with the original forecast.

Setting an hourly rate

For many small firms in the services sector, the above tools are of limited value, since service businesses have little, if any, cost of goods. Unlike firms that deal in tangible commodities and can evaluate their profitability and break-even point by the number of items they sell, service-based organisations often calculate their financial break-even points on a time-based process. This is especially important for self-employed business owners. Accordingly, an alternative costing method is required.

If the main or only cost of a business is the time and labour of the owner–manager, then a simple method of calculating a price is on the following basis:

$$\text{Hourly charge rate} = \frac{\text{Total funds required}}{\text{Hours available}}$$

The total funds required consist of the fixed operating costs of the business and the personal income the owner needs.

Note that the number of hours available here is not necessarily the hours a business owner is available to work, but the number of hours that can be charged out to customers — time spent working but not earning income does not count. As exercise 3 on page 291 shows, most people can charge out only about 1100 to 1400 hours a year.

If the resulting rate is at or below the going market rate, the business is clearly viable. However, if the hourly rate is substantially above the market rate, then the owner will need to find enough customers willing to pay at this higher rate if the business is to succeed.

Example 5: Amy's hourly rate

Amy Delzon is currently working as a self-employed interior design consultant. She wants to earn a gross personal income roughly similar to what she earned in her last paid employment (about $55 000 per annum). It also costs her $10 000 a year to run her business (phone calls, travel, insurance, internet costs and so on).

Amy believes that she will be able to generate about 1200 to 1400 hours of chargeable work each year. Conservatively, she assumes only 1200 hours of work annually.

Therefore, her rate will be:

$$\frac{\$65\,000}{1200\text{ hours}} = \$54.166$$

Amy can round up her rate to produce a final figure of $55 per hour.

If you are setting an hourly rate for a business with more than one person, it is necessary to increase both the number of chargeable hours available and the net income required.

Dealing with a goods and services tax

Many regions now have a value-added tax (VAT) or goods and services tax (GST), which requires merchants and service providers to add a set percentage rate of tax to their asking price (see table 11.4). Sometimes, especially in retail businesses, manufacturers and wholesalers may provide vendors with a recommended price that already includes the tax.

Table 11.4: Goods and services tax rates

Country	GST levy
Australia	10.0%
New Zealand	12.5%
Singapore	5.0%

For the examples and exercises in this chapter, however, GST has been excluded from all calculations. If GST had been included, then the final prices and fees would have been different — in example 5, Amy's final hourly rate in Australia would be $55 + 10 per cent, or $60.50. For Killer Kiwi Stationery in New Zealand, the pens would have to increase in price from $2 to $2.25. (For the sake of simplicity, it is often preferable to calculate fixed and variable costs, break-even point, contribution margins, mark-ups, margins and hourly rates exclusive of GST and then simply add GST to the final charge.)

Placement

Placement:
The exchange of goods or services between buyers and sellers.

The final element in the marketing mix is **placement**: how will the exchange of goods or services between buyers and sellers occur?[27] It is not enough simply to produce an offering that customers want to buy; it is also important that customers have the opportunity to buy it. To ensure this occurs, the business owner must plan how to get products or services to a point where customers can purchase them. To achieve this, a placement strategy must include a distribution mechanism as well as deal with storage and transport issues.

Distribution channels

There are a number of ways in which a business owner can sell to a consumer. One is to do so directly. This is convenient, simple and often done by many small firms. Examples are farmers who sell their produce direct to the public in farmers' markets, and people who sell their crafts or products in local markets. Other options involve the use of intermediaries — third parties in the distribution channel that help facilitate the sale of a product or service.[28]

Brokers can bring together the buyer (consumer) and the seller (business) to help the two parties negotiate a deal. Such an arrangement tends to be a one-off affair. However, agents (also known variously as manufacturers' agents or sales agents) act as permanent intermediaries. They market the product to consumers for a fee. Agents and brokers tend to be found in industries where there are many small product producers and retailers who lack the capacity to find one another.[29]

Wholesalers provide a more comprehensive suite of services than agents or brokers. They purchase goods from the producer and then sell them directly to retailers. In the process, they take responsibility for storing, delivering and promoting the product. They have their own sales staff, and often provide product servicing and credit terms to purchasers. Confectionery and magazines are often sold in this way.

Retailers are the most common public face of a distribution channel. A retailer sells goods or services directly to the ultimate consumer (often the general public). They usually have a storefront, although some operate through party-plan, mail order, telephone or electronic means. Many retailers are also franchisees.[30]

Issues to consider

The selection of a suitable distribution channel depends on a number of factors:
- *Comparative advantage.* In many cases, it makes more sense to use an intermediary than to directly sell items from the business itself. Each party has a

specialised skill that they are particularly good at and which they can perform better than the other. For example, a small-scale manufacturing plant will typically not have many salespeople on its staff; its core competency is the efficient production of physical goods. Such a firm would be well advised to sell through a wholesaler or retailer and focus its own energies on remaining an effective manufacturer.

- *Industry norms.* In some business sectors, there are conventions about how items are sold. When this is the case, it is usually easier for a new firm to follow the industry trend rather than try to redesign the distribution process.
- *Pricing.* Prices have to be set so that all parties in the transactional process receive a reasonable return on their investment while still making the final sales price attractive to customers. If a distribution channel contains several intermediaries, each party's ability to charge a maximum price is usually limited.
- *Packaging and handling of goods.* Goods must be securely packaged and stored. Damage to goods in transit (en route between the supplier and retailer) can result in lost income and customer inconvenience.
- *Payment.* Entrepreneurs need to carefully work out how payment will be made for goods that are being distributed through another firm. In some industries, an invoice is issued and payment is expected within a certain time after the goods have been delivered. In other sectors, receiving firms may be required to pay for goods in advance or at the time of their receipt. Another option is consignment, where payment is expected only if the goods in question are successfully sold to the end consumer.
- *Contractual and legal issues.* It is generally recommended that a brief written contract sets out the rights and responsibilities of all parties involved in the distribution process.

What would you do?

E-fish takes flight

Despite the often limited living space, the people of Hong Kong have long had a passion for keeping small pets such as goldfish and birds.

You have just bought a small business that specialises in selling fish and birds to local residents in the New Territories region of Hong Kong, and you have decided that the business needs to grow. One of your objectives is to encourage sales from other HK residents and, if possible, to export your products to nearby Macau and Taiwan. However, to do this you need to have a web-based presence. You've done a bit of research on how to maximise the web, and you've been especially intrigued by the results of a recent academic study which show that although increased interactivity is often appreciated by potential clients, simply attracting more site visitors is rarely sufficient to make the website a success.[31] You also need to be able to convert visits to sales, and not everyone who visits a website will automatically also buy from it.

To help address this problem, you've engaged the services of a local web design firm to create a site, since the business did not already have one. Since then, you've made the site known to your existing customers, encouraged them to visit it, and asked them when they next visit your store to let you know what they thought of it. Typical responses from the dozen clients who have given you feedback run along the following lines:

- 'Distracting ...'
- 'Too long to load.'
- 'The graphics were great but my friend's machine couldn't load it.'
- 'Doesn't have all the information that I want.'

The designers assure you that the site is, in their view, best practice, and have actually shown you the websites of other aquaria. They're correct — the site is as useful as anyone else's. But somehow that doesn't seem to be encouraging your customers. It may be time to start the web design process all over again or else drop the electronic marketing strategy altogether.

Questions

1. Who should you ask to design your website?
2. Construct your own homepage for this business. What content would you have on it?

Evaluation of marketing

Marketing is not, in itself, sufficient to guarantee the success of any business project. There are many firms that have developed comprehensive and sophisticated marketing strategies which have not been effective. To ensure that the strategy adopted is the correct one, the entrepreneur must be satisfied that the stated goals of the original marketing process are being met. This is the purpose of marketing evaluation.

One common evaluation technique is to *compare marketing expenditure with sales revenue*. In this technique, the amount of money spent on a particular marketing mechanism is compared with the level of sales or enquiries that this has generated. If an increase in marketing investment has resulted in a corresponding or greater level of sales, then the process is usually deemed a success.

Another way is to *trace the sources of sales*; in other words, how did customers find out about the business — was it via the Yellow Pages, the local newspaper, word of mouth or some other avenue. This may be as simple as asking customers at the point of sale where they found out about the business, or it may be by more detailed means, such as a survey.[32] This is especially important when evaluating the effectiveness of the promotional strategy used in the marketing mix.

The business owner may also wish to gauge the *satisfaction of existing or previous customers*. To do this, the firm may initiate a customer feedback program using surveys, personal contacts from a member of the business, or indirect feedback from the firm's sales representatives or agents in the field.

Another evaluation tool can be *customer complaints*. These provide an interesting body of data about possible problems in the firm's marketing strategy. Continual complaints about poor delivery, for example, can indicate a problem with distribution channels. Feedback indicating that the firm's products are too expensive may mean that pricing mechanisms have to be reviewed.

Summary

Marketing is the process of planning and executing the conception, pricing, promotion and distribution of ideas, goods or services to create exchanges that satisfy individual and organisational goals. There are six steps to the marketing process: goal setting, market research, target market definition, establishment of an appropriate marketing mix, implementation of the marketing mix strategy, and subsequent evaluation of its performance.

Target markets of customers are either potential or actual. They can also be segmented on the basis of geographical, demographic and psychographic features or classified as business-to-consumer or business-to-business (B2B) sales.

The marketing mix centres on the four Ps: the product/service, promotion, price and placement (distribution).

Understanding the product or service requires business owners to know the product's relative strengths and weaknesses compared with other offerings, its features, and the benefits customers can derive from its use.

Promotional tools that can be used by new and small business ventures include canvassing, the internet and email, printed publications (newspapers, magazines, trade journals), telephone directories, signs, logos and business names, pamphlets, business cards, television and radio advertising, sponsorship, word-of-mouth recommendations and trade show exhibits.

Pricing strategies can include charging the going rate, cost-plus pricing, charging the maximum possible, pricing to a perceived level of value, skimming, discounting and using loss leaders. To effectively set a price, a business owner must also understand the mechanics of price setting, including how to distinguish between fixed and variable costs, and how to calculate contribution margin, break-even point, mark-up and margin.

Placement issues cover the distribution of goods to the final customer. Matters that must be considered at this point include whether to use a direct or indirect method of distribution; the issue of comparative advantage; industry norms; the establishment of a price that gives all parties a financial interest in the sale; packaging and transport of goods; payment for sales made; and legal and contractual issues.

The final part of the marketing process is an evaluation of the marketing effort. Evaluation can be done in various ways: by comparing marketing expenditure with sales revenue generated; by tracing the sources of sales; by measuring the level of satisfaction of customers; and by analysing customer complaints.

REVIEW QUESTIONS

1. Outline and briefly explain the issues that determine the marketing goals set by a business owner.

2. What are the advantages and disadvantages of the various promotional tools?

3. What are the different types of pricing strategy that can be used by a firm?

4. How are a break-even point and a contribution margin calculated?

5. Explain the different types of intermediary that exist in the placement component of the marketing mix.

DISCUSSION QUESTIONS

1. Which firm is more able to market its products/services effectively: a new, small entrepreneurial venture or an established large corporation?

2. What are the advantages and disadvantages of marketing goods on the internet?

3. How does the creation of target market groups help the overall marketing process?

EXERCISES

For all exercises, exclude the impact of GST in your calculations.

1. *Calculating margins and mark-ups.* A retailer buys cloth for $4 per metre and sells it at $5 per metre. What are the mark-up and margin on the cloth?

2. *More margins and mark-ups.* Imported olives can be bought from Spain for $6.50 per kilo; they retail at $8 per kilo. What are the mark-up and margin on this item?

3. *Establishing an hourly rate.* Jim is a potential lawnmower start-up in New Zealand who wants to earn $35 000 a year. His total fixed costs are $8000, and he wants two weeks annual leave plus another two weeks up his sleeve for unforeseen problems. He will work six days a week, and estimates that he will actually be mowing lawns for five hours on each of those days. He presumes there are no direct costs of goods.

   Calculate the hourly rate required. If the going rate is $35 per hour, is this business viable?

SUGGESTED READING

Bjerke, B. & Hultman, C.M., *Entrepreneurial Marketing: The Growth of Small Firms in the New Economic Era*, Edward Elgar, Cheltenham UK, 2002.

Gaujers, R., Harper, J-A. & Browne, J., *Smart Marketing for Small Business*, McGraw-Hill, Sydney, 2001.

Smith, K., *Marketing for Small Business*, Wrightbooks, Milton, Qld, 2002.

CASE STUDY

Higham's Hardware

Harriet Higham returned home when her father fell seriously ill and needed someone to take over the store. The business, which had been going for six years, sold hardware to local residents and small building businesses. Its main competition was a chain of nationally known hardware and timber-supply stores.

Harriet was concerned that pricing of items was not being done correctly. She decided to check out the latest financial returns of the firm.

HIGHAM'S HARDWARE SHOP
Profit and Loss Statement
for financial year 1 July to 30 June

Sales revenue	$450 000
Less: Cost of goods sold	337 500
Gross profit	112 500
Less: Operating expenses	92 700
Net profit	$ 19 800

'Of the $92 700 in expenses, $79 200 are fixed costs and the remainder are variable costs,' the accountant explained. 'There is no advertising, so that helps keep expenses low. Anyway, at least you're making money.' Nevertheless, Harriet thought this was a poor return.

Questions

1. Calculate the break-even point of this business, using the contribution margin.

2. If Higham's Hardware wanted to make a net profit of $35 000, use the contribution margin to calculate the total dollar value of sales needed.

3. Harriet needs to develop a marketing plan to increase sales. How should she do this?

ENDNOTES

1. Australian Bureau of Statistics, *Small Business in Australia*, ABS, Canberra, 1998.
2. H. Assael, P. Reed & M. Patton, *Marketing Principles and Strategy*, Australian edn, Harcourt Brace, Sydney, 1995.
3. P. Kotler, S. Adam, L. Brown & G. Armstrong, *Principles of Marketing*, Prentice Hall, Sydney, 2001, p. 5.
4. J. Summers, M. Gardiner, C.W. Lamb, J.F. Hair & C. McDaniel, *Essentials of Marketing*, Thomson, Melbourne, 2001, p. 6.
5. K.S. Lee, G.H. Lim, S.J. Tan & H.W. Chow, 'Generic marketing strategies for small and medium-sized enterprises: A conceptual framework and examples from Asia', *Journal of Strategic Marketing*, no. 9, 2001, pp. 145–62.
6. E. Collinson & E. Shaw, 'Entrepreneurial marketing — a historical perspective on development and practice', *Management Decision*, vol. 39, no. 9, 2001, pp. 761–6.
7. M.H. Morris, M. Schindehutte & R.W. LaForge, 'Entrepreneurial marketing: A construct for integrating emerging entrepreneurship and marketing perspectives', *Journal of Marketing Theory and Practice*, Fall, 2002, pp. 1–19.
8. ibid., p. 17.
9. D. Bangs & M. Halliday, *The Australian Market Planning Guide*, 2nd edn, Business & Professional Publishing, Sydney, 1997.
10. D. Carson & A. Gilmore, 'Marketing at the interface: Not "what" but "how"', *Journal of Marketing Theory and Practice*, vol. 8, no. 2, 2000, pp. 1–8.

11. J.R. McColl-Kennedy & G.C. Kiel, *Marketing: A Strategic Approach*, Nelson Thomson, Melbourne, 2000, p. 16.
12. L. Hailey, *Kickstart Marketing*, Allen & Unwin, Sydney, 2001, pp. 63–5.
13. P. Kotler, G. Armstrong, L. Brown & S. Adam, *Marketing*, 4th edn, Pearson, Sydney, 1998, pp. 308–9.
14. D.F. Kuratko & R.M. Hodgetts, *Entrepreneurship: A Contemporary Approach*, 5th edn, Harcourt Brace, Fort Worth, TX, 2001, p. 650.
15. P. Burns, *Entrepreneurship and Small Business*, Palgrave, London, 2001, p. 100.
16. ibid., p. 99.
17. J. Summers et al., *see* note 4, p. 313.
18. M. Ali, *Practical Marketing and PR for the Small Business*, Kogan Page, London, 1998.
19. J.R. McColl-Kennedy & G.C. Kiel, *see* note 11, pp. 617–8.
20. I. Chaston & T. Mangles, *Small Business Marketing Management*, Palgrave, London, 2002; D. Carson, 'Marketing in small firms', in K. Blois (ed.), *The Oxford Textbook of Marketing*, Oxford University Press, Oxford, 2000, pp. 570–89.
21. T.S. Hatten, *Small Business: Entrepreneurship and Beyond*, Prentice Hall, Upper Saddle River, NJ, 1997.
22. P. Thorpe, *Small Business Street Smarts*, rev. edn, The Advertising Department, Sydney, 1994.
23. S. Burton, 'eBay's chink, Sam's chance', *The Sydney Morning Herald*, 7 March 2006.
24. V. Walker, 'Morgan reluctantly trades up to a life in the spotlight', *The Australian*, 9 March 2006.
25. P. Burns, *see* note 15, pp. 104–5.
26. J.W. English, *How to Organise and Operate a Small Business in Australia*, 7th edn, Allen & Unwin, Sydney 1998, p. 229.
27. W. Reynolds, A. Williams & W. Savage, *Your Own Business*, 3rd edn, Nelson Thomson, Melbourne, 2000, p. 287.
28. W.L. Megginson, M.J. Byrd & L.C. Megginson, *Small Business Management: An Entrepreneur's Guidebook*, 3rd edn, Irwin McGraw-Hill, Boston, MA, 2000, pp. 190–3.
29. J. Summers et al., *see* note 4, p. 232.
30. L. Hailey, *see* note 12, pp. 100–1.
31. P. Auger, 'The impact of interactivity and design sophistication on the performance of commercial websites for small businesses', *Journal of Small Business Management*, vol. 43 no. 2 April 2005, pp. 119–37.
32. M. Ali, *see* note 18, p. 195.

Chapter 12

Operations management

LEARNING OBJECTIVES

After reading this chapter, you should be able to:

- define the concept of operations management and the three basic steps in the operations process

- outline the main types of business premises

- explain the different types of physical site factors to be considered when structuring operations

- list the differences between batching and continuous production arrangements

- discuss the issues relevant to effective inventory and supply management

- state the factors to consider when purchasing operating equipment

- explain the ways in which an entrepreneur can evaluate, protect and improve operational performance.

All businesses produce a product of some sort, be it a physical commodity (goods) or an intangible service for a client. To do this, the production activities of the business must be organised in a logical way that allows the firm to generate products in an efficient and effective manner.

In this chapter, the practical issues involved in establishing and maintaining these operational aspects are examined in detail. The concept of operations management is defined and explained, and the three elements that constitute the operations management process are discussed. We then cover how firms can achieve operational efficiency by paying careful attention to physical site factors, production processes and control mechanisms.

Operations as a management process

Operations management:
The control of the process by which a firm makes a product.

Operations management refers to the control of the process by which a firm makes a product. The operations process consists of three elements:

- *Inputs* are the raw materials or stock from which the final product will ultimately be made.
- Processing involves the *transformation* of inputs into final products. This is a conversion phase in which staff, plant and equipment combine to change the raw materials into a product.
- The end result of the transformation process is the *output*: that is, the products made by the firm that are intended for consumption by its customers.[1]

Figure 12.1 illustrates an operations process — the production of a daily newspaper. The inputs consist of the stories filed by journalists, advertising lodged by different firms and the raw newsprint paper that is used for the published edition. The transformation process involves editing and formatting the stories, laying out pages to accommodate text and advertisements, printing the newspaper, and bundling and distributing it to the many vendors located at different shops throughout the city and its surrounding hinterland. The output is the completed newspaper that is bought by members of the public, who are usually unaware of the extraordinarily complex and detailed planning required to deliver their morning paper on time every day.

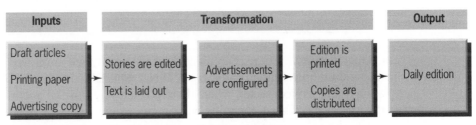

Figure 12.1: The operations process for a newspaper

Contemporary research into operations management has shown that effective control of these activities is an important factor in the overall success of the business venture, since it enables a firm to produce a reliable, quality product at a competitive price. However, most operations management tends to focus on micro-management of particular issues, rather than on all the issues as a coherent and interlocked system.[2] Moreover, small business managers frequently tend to overlook the importance of managing their operational workflow and underestimate the importance of this function in achieving commercial viability for their enterprise.[3]

To achieve successful operations management, three main components must be considered by entrepreneurs when planning a new business venture: (1) the choice of an appropriate business premises, (2) the structuring of the production process itself, and (3) the ongoing task of improving operations over time.[4]

These factors are discussed in more detail throughout this chapter. However, many other variables contribute to the effective management of a small firm's operations. These include the human resources of the business, the management team, pricing and distribution strategies and a coherent business plan that links operations management with other parts of the firm's activities.[5] These are discussed in more detail in other chapters and drawn together in the sample business plan in chapter 7.

Physical site factors

One of the first operational tasks to consider in the development of a new business venture is the physical infrastructure: that is, the site on which the firm will operate and the way in which the premises will be configured.

Premises

Firstly, the type of business premises must be determined. There are several different facilities available for new and start-up firms (see table 12.1). These give business owners a wide choice and a certain measure of flexibility when planning the business.

Table 12.1: Premises options for new and small firms

	Cost	Flexibility	Tenure
Home-based business	Low	High	Long term
Serviced office	Low	Low	Short term
Business incubator	Low–medium	Medium	Short–medium term
Rented premises	Medium	Medium	Medium–long term
Purchased site	High	High	Permanent

Operating from home is an ideal choice for many self-employed people and for micro-sized firms in their early stages. This is especially the case for businesses operating in the services sector, where there is often very little (if anything) required in the way of specialised operating equipment, storage space or street-front visibility. A *home-based business* allows the business owner to keep rental costs low, if not eliminate them entirely. It also means the business can be run as a sideline or part-time venture if needed. Home-based businesses are very popular — in Australia and New Zealand, about two-thirds of all small firms are based at the owner's home.[6]

Serviced offices are, in some respects, one step up from a home-based business. In this arrangement, the firm temporarily rents an office suite in a complex specifically established for this purpose. Such offices allow the business owners to use rooms on a casual or ongoing basis, so they can work at home most of the time and use the more sophisticated premises when it is necessary to impress a client or when a centralised meeting location is required. Serviced offices typically provide customised telephone answering facilities and mail collection points, and can allow a small business to have an expensive office address without all the overheads usually associated with such a location.

Similarly, *business incubators* provide specialised offices for small firms. An incubator is usually a non-profit facility that provides cost-price accommodation for new businesses. The incubator itself usually consists of a collection of premises housing many different businesses, overseen by a professional manager with experience in mentoring and advising start-up ventures. These arrangements allow new and small ventures to be located in an environment shared with other start-up firms, reducing the isolation and loneliness that can often be found when working on a new venture.[7] Lease commitments are usually run on a month-by-month basis. Incubators are discussed in more detail in chapter 10.

Renting a commercial facility or industrial site is another option for new businesses. This arrangement gives starting business owners maximum choice of a location and site best suited to their needs. Entering into a lease arrangement with a property owner usually requires the tenant to be bound by a long-term lease that may run for a number of years, which can be expensive if the business venture fails and the property cannot be re-let.

Purchasing a property is another option for some business operators, but it requires a large capital outlay. Purchasing maximises the owner's ability to reconfigure the premises and gives the most freedom to operate it in the chosen manner. It also eliminates monthly rental fees and may provide a sound investment option if property prices increase. However, few starting businesses have the additional capital required for this option.

Location

Once the type of premises has been determined, the location that best suits the needs of the firm must be assessed. In the first place, the owner must be aware of the relevant zoning, licensing and statutory requirements that limit business placements. Many local, state and federal agencies have the power to restrict the operations of different enterprises to specific geographical locations. For example, heavily polluting manufacturing plants are restricted to specified 'heavy industry' zones, and the placement of retail firms is usually limited by local governments to shopping centres and designated strip-shopping locations.

Transport to and from the premises is also critical. The ease with which customers can get to the business will affect retail operations, which usually require high public visibility and easy access via public transport (such as buses or trains) or by private vehicle. Such positioning can drive up the price of rented premises. For manufacturing, industrial and wholesaling enterprises, an important consideration is access to reliable transport facilities that allow raw materials and goods to be moved quickly and cost-effectively. They can be based in less central (and, therefore, cheaper) localities, so long as there is ready access to road, rail, air and/or sea transport links.

Competitors also influence the location decision. For some businesses, it is an advantage to be physically separate from competitors. On the other hand, sometimes it is useful to be based near competitors when customers want a range of options before making a choice. Restaurant or coffee shop precincts are an example of this type of successful co-location of similar businesses. Similar complementary effects can arise from a manufacturer or wholesaler situated close to suppliers, thus reducing transport time and costs.

The personal preferences of the owner may be important, especially if the business is being set up with lifestyle goals as a high priority. In this case, higher profitability or reduced costs may be willingly sacrificed for reduced commuting time or proximity to a desirable residential address.

Internal layout

Having acquired suitable premises, the business owner must consider how the space within the given facilities will be used to maximum advantage. This is referred to as the layout or **floor plan** of the business. Firms in certain industry sectors can enhance their productivity and lower their costs by adopting particular configurations within their premises.

Retail operations tend to take one of three basic forms: a standard grid, an open plan or a boutique (shop) layout. *Grid formats* are best suited to large numbers of independent customers who wish to guide themselves through the premises (figure 12.2). The store is arranged in a straightforward, easily understood manner that facilitates the rapid movement of people through the premises. Typically, there is a series of aisles with each section devoted to a common theme or related range of products.

Floor plan:
The arrangement of operational activities within a business premises.

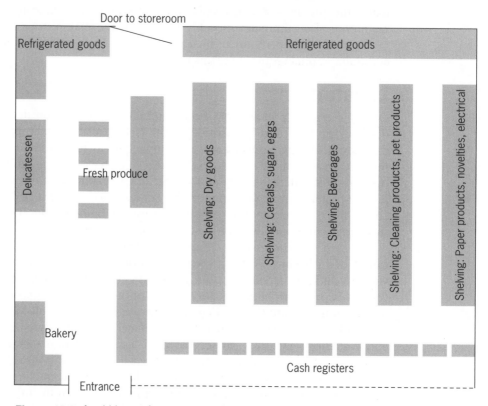

Figure 12.2: A grid layout for a supermarket

An *open-plan arrangement* (figure 12.3) is a layout whereby products are displayed in a manner that allows customers to move easily from one area to another. Products may be displayed in any number of different ways and need not be confined to an aisle setup.

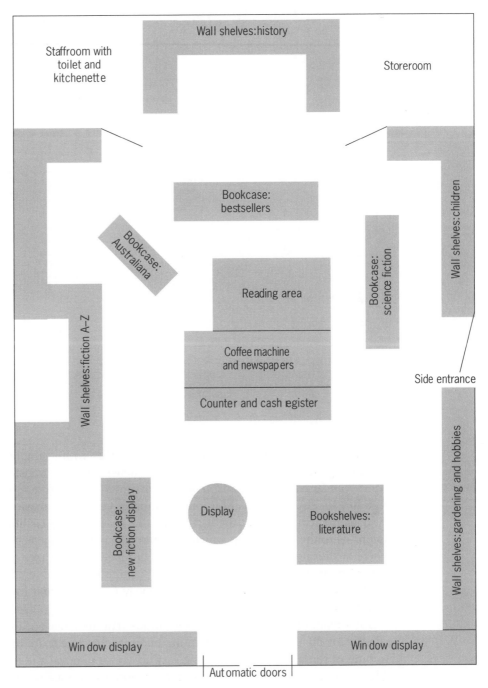

Figure 12.3: An open-plan layout of a bookshop

A *boutique (shop) layout* places different groups (or types) of goods together thematically, allowing customers to browse through related products (figure 12.4).

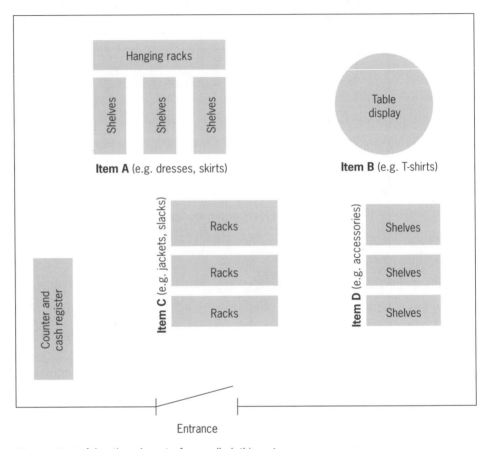

Figure 12.4: A boutique layout of a small clothing store

Manufacturing firms emphasise an internal design with a simple layout — one in which goods can be easily and quickly (hence cheaply) transferred in at one point, processed in the most efficient manner and then removed from the premises for storage or distribution via another outlet. Two basic layout options for a manufacturing plant are a *product-based layout*, where facilities are situated according to the sequence in which activities take place, and a *process-based format*, where facilities related to similar tasks are grouped together (see figure 12.5). An important issue for manufacturers is the organisation of operating equipment within the site, since much equipment is likely to be fixed and cannot be moved quickly from one place to another.[8]

Other types of firms have their own unique requirements. For example, wholesalers focus on arranging the maximum amount of storage space in the minimum amount of room, while still allowing easy access for removal and storage of items. Priority is given to storage volume and economies of scale when designing the floor plan for a wholesale business.

Service businesses face a more variable set of requirements. They may find their workspace configurations determined by the internal structure of the business, by production requirements or by customer needs. For example, a law firm may find that it operates best by arranging staff together in areas of activity, giving only minimal concern to customer traffic, since most clients have very little contact with the internal operations of the firm. On the other hand, a veterinary practice will need to ensure that operating rooms are located near animal accommodation for convenient access. A restaurant's priorities will be customers' easy access to seating and proximity of the kitchen to ensure food is delivered hot.

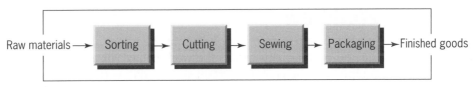

(a) Product-based layout — garment manufacturer

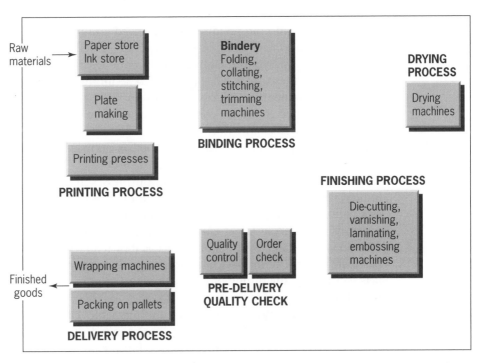

(b) Process-based layout — book printer

Figure 12.5: Manufacturing floor plans

Each industry tends to have its own norms about what constitutes 'best practice' in an effective layout. The floor plan adopted by a business will affect the way staff, equipment, supplies and work timetables are organised to make the most effective use of resources.

Production processes

In addition to the physical structure within the business premises, other issues are integral to a sound operations management system:

- The working processes of staff must be structured in a logical manner.
- The supply of raw materials and distribution of finished products need to be organised so that inputs and outputs can flow freely.
- The correct operating equipment must be selected to allow the transformation process to proceed.

Workflow

In every business premises, there must be a logical system for organising the production process. This guides the work behaviour and activities of the people and equipment. The goal is to establish a workflow that sees inventory (inputs) move through the transformation process and emerge as completed goods or services (outputs) as quickly and economically as possible.

One approach is to adopt *continuous production*, a system wherein the firm manufactures a fixed array of goods in a standardised format. In this process, raw materials move into the premises, are arranged and processed in a number of set steps and then emerge completed in a series of activities that is invariably the same. The factory layout, equipment set-up and operating times are all geared to ensuring that these steps take place with a minimum amount of disruption. Staffing arrangements emphasise employees with a fixed, finite range of skills, since most of their duties are confined to work of an essentially repetitive and predictable nature. Assembly-line work has traditionally been built around such an approach and applied to industries as varied as car manufacturing, cattle abattoirs, biscuit bakeries and timber mill sawing.

Continuous production is suitable for businesses that manufacture or process a limited range of standardised goods. The economies of scale can be considerable, especially when large numbers of the same items are produced. As a result, this system is common in larger enterprises. However, delays at any point of the production system can have a major impact as they tend to affect all other parts of the processing line. The introduction of new equipment, operating systems or products will change the timing of production and require production processes to be reconfigured.

A different strategy is to focus on a more flexible, customer-oriented system of production. When small-scale orders are required, *batch production* (sometimes called *jobbing*) is used. This involves altering the work system for each different item or small group of items produced. As a result, batch production is more labour intensive and costly per item since different arrangements of equipment, operating systems and staff need to be ordered for each task. In addition, the operating process manager needs to put more work into ensuring that the right specifications are adhered to and clearly detailing the individual tasks.

Batching allows small firms to more efficiently deal with the special needs of a particular client. It is often used as a competitive tool against larger enterprises that have structured their entire manufacturing or production process on the basis of a production line (continuous production) strategy. Batching also tends to require more multiskilled staff and to provide employees with more autonomy and discretion in their work. The development of new technology, although very capital intensive, can allow firms to use machines that can be pre-programmed and, therefore, quickly reconfigured to deal with individual orders. However, the unit cost of production tends to be much higher.

The layout and the production system of the business are closely integrated. Most firms that have a continuous production workflow system also adopt a product-based layout, such as the classic assembly-line form of production, which may be set up in a straight-line layout or in an L, a U or an S shape (see figure 12.6). On the other hand, a process-based floor plan is often associated with batch production. Many firms have hidden inefficiencies and costs because their floor plan is not aligned to their production processes. Ensuring that the two factors are aligned is a simple, but often overlooked, way of improving operational effectiveness.

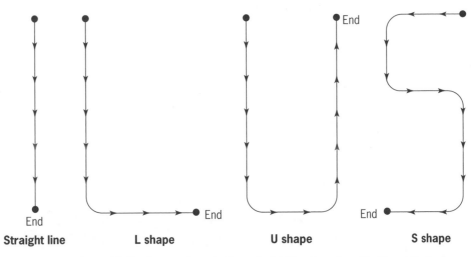

Figure 12.6: Assembly-line forms of production: straight-line layout and L, U and S shapes

Inventory and supply management

Economic order quantity (EOQ): The amount of goods that minimises the total purchase and storage costs while still being sufficient to meet the production requirements of the business.

Another aspect of operations management is the handling of raw materials or trading stock ('inventory'). One issue is the amount of stock that should be held by the firm. At any given time, a firm will have stock tied up in the form of finished goods, raw materials, batches of goods awaiting further processing or delivery and items being repaired. Too much stock on hand can be expensive, since a large amount of capital is tied up in the purchase price and in the cost of actually storing the goods. Too little stock can mean that the firm may be unable to meet client orders as they come in.[9] To balance these conflicting demands, firms usually seek to establish an **economic order quantity (EOQ)**: that is, the amount of goods that minimises the total purchase and storage costs while still being sufficient to meet the production requirements of the business.[10]

Just-in-time delivery: An inventory management system where materials are delivered to the firm at the time needed for production.

One approach that some firms have adopted is the **just-in-time delivery** method, in which materials are delivered to the firm at the time needed for production. This can help in significantly reducing holding costs and quantities and can free up additional working capital, especially for firms that regularly deal with large quantities of physical stock. However, it requires careful attention to scheduling and ordering, both of which must be executed at the right time if the flow of inventory is to be maintained.[11]

The establishment of a satisfactory supply source for inventory is important. Manufacturers and retailers are heavily dependent on the successful maintenance of an effective supply chain. Issues to consider in the selection of a supplier include cost, frequency of delivery, product range and ability to provide a satisfactory standard of materials or product. Other important aspects include intangible measures such as the supplier's reputation in the industry, reliability, ability to deal flexibly with any changes in orders and willingness to meet any special or urgent requirements that the business may have from time to time.

In some industries, the range and number of suppliers is strictly limited, and the new business owner has little opportunity to negotiate price and the conditions under which the supplier will deliver. However, where there is a range of different supplying firms competing with one another for the small firm's trade, there is considerable room for negotiation that may lead to lower prices, bulk discounting or more flexible delivery arrangements.

Both inventory and supply management constitute input elements into the operations process. Without an adequate input arrangement, the other parts of the operations process (transformation and outputs) cannot take place.

Once transformation into the final product has occurred, another supply and inventory matter arises: how will the completed products (output) be distributed to the clients of the firm? Distribution channels are discussed in chapter 11 as they form part of the firm's marketing strategy.

Entrepreneur profile

Kathy Kingston

One of the most challenging logistical and distributional projects for small business is the distribution of fresh food to consumers. High standards of hygiene, tight deadlines and sophisticated coordination are all needed to ensure that an item arrives at the right price and in the right condition on the dining room table.

One of the most sensitive products are oysters, and one of the best-known importers in Hong Kong is Kathy Kingston, the founder of both Kathy's Oysters and Ocean Brand Ltd. Kathy began Ocean Brand in 1994 when she was asked to find some items for a new oyster bar opening near The Peak on Hong Kong island. Business took off quickly; by 1995 the *South China Morning Post* newspaper had labelled her the 'Oyster Queen of HK.'[12]

The business specialises in importing live shellfish. All of her oysters are sourced live, which means that they have to be taken out of the water in oyster farms from different locations around the world, cleared by local health authorities, packed and airborne within a day.

Her firm brings in over 15 000 kilograms of live shellfish to Hong Kong each and every week. The produce comes from right across the globe — North America, France, Australia, Ireland and New Zealand. The vast bulk of this is oysters, and the main customers are catering firms, restaurants, hotels and private organisations. So far, Kathy's systems seem to be working. The loss of oysters from spoilage is quite low — about 1 per cent.

In the Hong Kong market, the major competitors are the importers of frozen oysters, which are significantly cheaper. Part of Kathy's job, therefore, has been to convince clients that live is best. This focus on fresh products has been a key competitive advantage and also a reason why there are no plans to export into China, where logistic management is much more complicated and quality control is harder to maintain.

Today, the business is based in Kwai Chung in the New Territories region of Hong Kong with a very small number of full-time staff. By sharing resources with another company, the firm can access transport and modern warehouses without having to meet all of the costs itself.

Kathy is also attempting to diversify her business activities, especially after the SARS crisis saw sales drop by 90% for a while.[13] She has also created Kathy's Oysters, which provides in-house catering for both private dinner parties and corporate events. She'll send along the shuckers (service staff) and even provide a full bar featuring Kingston Coast wine from her private South Australian label.

For more information, visit <www.kathysoysters.com>.

Source: Based on author's interview with Kathy Kingston.

Operating equipment

For a new or intending firm, the equipment needed is also an important concern. Almost all businesses, regardless of the size or nature of the enterprise, will need an essential core of equipment. This will probably include communications equipment (telephones, facsimile, online access), a computer, a workroom, tables, chairs and filing cabinets. Beyond this, the equipment required depends on the type of business.

Retail operations usually require equipment for displaying and transporting stock. Manufacturing firms typically have the highest expenditure tied up in equipment that transforms inputs into completed outputs. Operating equipment for wholesalers includes storage apparatus and devices to move products around within warehouses. The increasing use of information technology as a business tool has generally meant that, over time, equipment needs have become more sophisticated for many businesses and, so, more expensive.

When costing a firm's equipment needs, the business owner must factor in the associated expenses of maintenance and service costs (especially for computing technology and industrial processing equipment), the expected life span of the item and the training that staff will need to operate the equipment.

Once a list of equipment has been compiled, the business owner can determine what should be purchased immediately and what purchases can be held off until later. If finance is a problem, one option is to use a 'phased purchase' strategy where only the minimum requisite tools are obtained at the start, with other equipment being purchased as future cash inflows allow. However, this limits the ability to offer a wide product range at the time of business launch and is rarely suitable for manufacturers in particular. It may also be possible to purchase second-hand equipment if it is still suitable for the task required. An alternative approach is to hire or lease equipment. This has the benefit of providing immediate use of the necessary items while still minimising initial capital outlays and smoothing subsequent cash outlays.

Evaluating, improving and securing operational activities

The third challenge in operational management lies in evaluating, controlling, enhancing and securing production-related activities. The entrepreneur or owner–manager and the team of senior managers must ensure that there are sound systems in place to handle all the basic tasks so that they can free themselves to focus on business strategy, growth and new opportunity identification. Thus there should be systems to measure and assess the level of performance, tools that can be used to improve processes and satisfactory safeguards in place to ensure that the firm is not critically damaged by unforeseen events or risks.

Assessing and controlling current operations

Different industry sectors face different types of control and evaluation problems. Retail operations, for example, need to keep control of their level of stock on hand, customer complaints and damaged or lost inventory. Service firms are more concerned with the efficient use of time per employee, since they often charge out their services on an hourly basis. Manufacturing firms need to focus on maximising usage of raw materials (inputs) and minimising rejected goods (outputs). However, all face one common issue — control of the firm's operations is an ongoing task.[14]

Effective evaluation and control in operations management requires four basic steps:[15]

- *Set expected standards of performance.* Clearly communicate the production standards that the firm and its employees are expected to achieve.
- *Measure actual performance.* Understand what is being done.
- *Compare the results with the desired standards.* Identify any substantial discrepancies.
- *Make corrections.* Introduce changes as needed to bring actual performance up to standard.

The evaluation and management of current activities can be performed by several different measuring techniques and tools: (1) scheduling, (2) inspection of products and (3) measurement of firm productivity.

Scheduling:
Setting a time frame and sequence of events to perform an activity.

Scheduling mechanisms

Scheduling is setting a time frame and sequence of events required to perform a certain activity. It establishes the timelines for production and is a useful framework around which the different parts of the operation process can be organised. One of the most common scheduling tools is a timeline, which simply states what events will occur and when. Slightly more sophisticated, but visually much easier to follow, is the Gantt chart, which shows how long each part of the production process should take and tracks activities using a bar chart (see figure 12.7).[16]

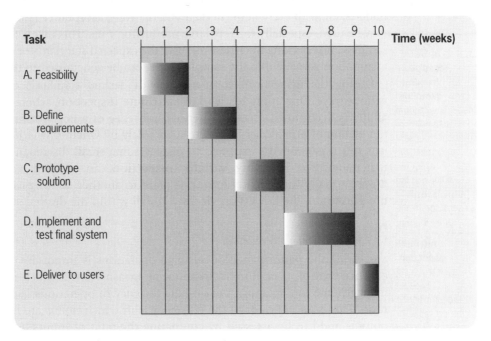

Figure 12.7: A Gantt chart

A variation on the Gantt chart is a PERT (performance evaluation and review technique) chart, which shows a sequential list of activities and the estimated time for the completion of each. Also known as the critical path method, it maps out the steps that culminate in the achievement of a designated outcome; however, it cannot be compiled until all events in the production process have been identified and their time requirements gauged. This encourages managers to carefully plan operating activities in advance and allows them to monitor progress.[17] Gantt charts are more useful for routine production, whereas PERT charts can be most helpful for complicated production arrangements.

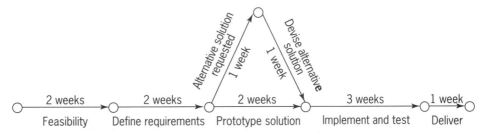

Figure 12.8: A PERT chart

Inspection regimes

Inspection of items being produced is another important evaluation mechanism. During the operations process, inspections may be carried out before the start of the transformation process, at key points within it, and usually also at the completion of work (the output phase). In some production systems, **100% inspection** is undertaken, with every item checked. Alternatively, **acceptance (random) sampling** may be used, especially for very large production runs. This involves taking random samples and checking that these all meet the expected standards of performance; an assumption is made that the sample results can be generalised to the entire output.

During the inspection, comparison with desired standards can be done in various ways. One approach is to use **attribute inspection**, where product acceptability is determined on the presence or absence of a key attribute. For example, the quality of a pen may be determined solely by whether it writes. Where products can reasonably be expected to display some small discrepancies that do not materially affect its utility, **variable inspection** can be used. For example, cut flowers usually vary slightly from one plant to another; as long as the variation is not significant, the flowers are deemed to fall within the desired standard.

Productivity indicators

Measuring the performance of business operations is important for maintaining effective control. If performance cannot be measured, it is much more difficult to manage. One tool to gauge the overall efficiency of operations is the **productivity ratio**. This is an indicator of the efficiency with which inputs are transformed into outputs and can be assessed by comparing the ratio of inputs used with outputs produced.[18] The higher the ratio, the greater the efficiency of the firm. Productivity ratios can be estimated either for the whole firm, for part of it or for individuals, using the basic formula:[19]

$$\text{Productivity} = \frac{\text{Outputs}}{\text{Inputs}}$$

For example, total productivity for a whole firm would be:[20]

$$\text{Total productivity} = \frac{\text{Value of outputs (products or services produced)}}{\text{Inputs (labour costs + capital + raw materials + other inputs)}}$$

If a firm spent $3 million in inputs and generated some $10 million in sales, its productivitiy ratio would be 3.33. The challenge for the managers of the business would be to ensure that this ratio did not decrease from year to year but, rather, continued to increase.

Timing of evaluation

Control and evaluation techniques can all take place at different points in the operations process.[21] **Feedforward control** mechanisms are anticipatory evaluations or controlling measures undertaken in advance of actual performance.

100% inspection: When all items produced are inspected.

Acceptance (random) sampling: Inspecting random samples of product to ensure they meet the expected standard; the sample result is generalised to the entire output.

Attribute inspection: Determining product acceptability on the presence or absence of a key attribute.

Variable inspection: Determining product acceptability by results falling within predetermined boundaries.

Productivity ratio: A comparison of inputs used with outputs produced.

Feedforward control: Control measures taken in advance of actual performance.

Gantt and PERT charts operate in this manner. A quality assurance system can also be used for feedforward control; this procedure is discussed later in the chapter.

Sometimes it is also necessary to evaluate work-in-progress. **Concurrent control** tools include methods such as the use of real-time computer-based statistical analysis, on-site personal monitoring of business activities and inspection of production work-in-progress.

Feedback control measures evaluate performance after it has taken place. Typical examples of post-event indicators include the productivity ratio, rejection rate (number of unusable goods produced), number of customer complaints or waste emissions produced by the firm. Financial documents and ratios (which are discussed elsewhere in this book) are other examples of such monitoring tools. These compare the financial performance of the firm (such as its annual profit or loss, and the various analytical ratios) with industry standards or with the business's own previous results. However, such tools often suffer from a significant time lag, since the documents in question may be compiled several weeks or even some months after a financial reporting period ends.

Procedural systems and quality assurance

One way to effectively organise the operating activities of any firm larger than a single-person enterprise is to compile a procedures manual. This document explains how certain activities are done, sets out the sequence of steps involved in any particular task and who is responsible for each step, and provides any other relevant information needed to ensure the task can be done correctly.

In time, a procedures manual can act as a body of 'corporate knowledge' that exists independently of the people in the firm. This frees the business owner and senior staff from having to closely supervise the activities of subordinates, since most standard operating procedures are in a printed format that employees can consult when and as needed. Such procedures also ensure uniformity, since the steps involved are clearly spelled out. If an employee leaves the firm, the manual can ensure that much of the employee's practical knowledge is still retained.

In a practical sense, a procedures manual can also form the basis of the next step in developing an effective business operation — the implementation of a quality scheme. A **quality assurance system** is a set of processes and principles designed to ensure the production of a set of consistent activities, goods or services. It is a compilation of internal rules that the business follows so that its products always conform to a predetermined standard. In this sense, 'quality' means a system that meets required standards — if the firm promises to produce goods to a certain benchmark for its customers, an effective quality system will ensure that it always does. It may not be 'quality' in the popular understanding of the word (that is, the very best type of product in its range), but it will consistently provide customers with what they have come to expect.[22] The term **total quality management (TQM)** refers to the adoption of a quality system and philosophy throughout the entire firm, not just in its operations.[23]

Concurrent control: Control measures performed on work in progress.

Feedback control: Control measures instituted after an event has taken place.

Quality assurance system: A set of processes and principles designed to ensure the production of a set of consistent activities, goods or services.

Total quality management (TQM): The adoption of a quality-based philosophy throughout a firm.

One common set of standards is the International Organization for Standardization (ISO) quality system series (the ISO 9000 family of standards), which provides guidelines on formalising, documenting and implementing the procedure systems by which firms supply their goods and services. Participants in an accredited quality assurance (QA) system are required to have their system audited and verified by an external assessor on a regular basis, thus ensuring that their commitment to the system is upheld. QA certification is often an important prerequisite in successfully tendering for government work or in obtaining contracts with larger firms. Moreover, some businesses also find that quality certification can be an important and useful marketing tool.[24]

The adoption of a QA system usually results in the development of a comprehensive set of detailed manuals that document almost all aspects of the firm's operations and processes. These manuals provide a very clear set of guidelines for staff to follow and help reduce the scope for errors throughout the production process. However, in some cases, the expenses can be substantial (especially for micro-businesses) and firms may become overly reliant on 'following the rules' rather than remaining flexible and innovative.

An interesting variation on this theme has been suggested by Gerber who argues that small firms can use some of the advantages of 'systemisation' to improve operational efficiencies, reduce their traditional over-reliance on the business owner as the key decision maker in the firm and provide scope for future growth.[25] He suggests that entrepreneurial small firms should adopt standard operating systems to establish and maintain routine day-to-day activities, freeing up the energies of the lead entrepreneur and senior management to concentrate on identifying and exploiting new growth opportunities. Such a system need not be as formal as a QA system, but it should allow routine activities to be governed by simple, easy-to-understand rules and operating procedures.

Risk management

It is not possible for a business owner to know what will happen to the business in the future. However, it is reasonable to assume that from time to time difficulties will emerge. Many of these have the potential to create serious problems for the firm, and it is prudent to have some contingency plan for these events whenever possible.

Risk:
The possibility that a situation may end with a negative outcome for the firm.

Risk refers to the possibility that a situation may end with a negative outcome for the firm, such as a loss of sales, a loss of money or even the collapse of the business itself.[26] All entrepreneurial ventures are risky, since they involve starting a new or untried idea in a competitive marketplace where success is not guaranteed.

Risk management:
The process of identifying risks in advance, assessing their likely occurrence and taking steps to reduce or eliminate them.

Risk management is the process of identifying risks in advance, assessing their likely possibility of occurrence and then taking steps to reduce or eliminate the risk. Conducting market research into likely consumer demand for a product is a simple risk-management tool. This activity is designed to eliminate or at least reduce the risk that a product cannot be sold once it is produced. A quality assurance system is also a risk management tool, since it seeks to eliminate the possibility of faulty goods or services reaching the customer. At the macro level, the process of environment scanning, where a business owner develops a comprehensive picture of all the different external forces likely to affect the entrepreneurial venture (see

Contingency plan:
How a firm will respond to a threatened risk.

chapter 6),[27] is another risk-management tool. Good risk management usually contains a **contingency plan** — a plan of how to respond should a threatened risk actually occur. Collectively, these steps are now recognised as a specific operational task and are often described as the technique of 'enterprise risk management.'[28]

What would you do?

Should quality cost?

You run a small housing-related business that has now just finished its second year of activity. Launched by yourself and two silent partners, the business specialises in manufacturing high-quality brass fittings for plumbing products. These are very popular with many new residential housing and unit developments in your city, where they adorn the bathrooms of wealthy professionals and other high-income earners.

You currently employ seven people. Business has been good, but, like so many other new small businesses, your strength lies more in making sales and designing new products than it does in organising the business.

You are concerned that some aspects of the business are not doing too well. The error rate (defined as the number of items returned due to defective manufacture) has moved from 6.4 per 1000 in the last quarter to 7.2 during the current 3-month period. Although no formal records are kept, you seem to be getting a few more customer complaints as well.

Last year your business inputs cost $12 750 000 and generated total sales of $13 400 000. This year, the corresponding figures have been $13 100 000 and $13 700 000. The extra costs are largely attributable to the expense of employing a team of QA consultants to prepare the firm's first-ever quality manual. Sales are up slightly, but it's hard to tell if this is due to extra revenue because you are QA certified or just general economic growth.

Recently, one of your employees approached you with an innovative idea. He had substantial experience working in this industry before being recruited by your firm and has been benchmarking the performance of the business against competitors. He is convinced that the firm does not need to spend over $250 000 each year on a formal quality system. He believes that there are a number of simple performance indicators at all three points of the operations management process that will be sufficient to keep the firm on track. Better still, these can be monitored by the staff themselves.

What should you do?

Questions
1. Should you maintain the QA system or move to a self-run system?
2. Does the feedback you have received so far indicate that there is a genuine production problem?

Security:
The protection of equipment and ideas from the risk of theft, loss or unauthorised use.

Security

Risk management at the operations level is concerned with a wide variety of threats and dangers. **Security** relates to the protection of equipment and ideas from the risks of theft, loss or unauthorised use. The protection of the physical business premises can involve the installation of movement detection alarms, patrols by contracted guards and/or the installation of suitable locks and grills. Managing security leaks or thefts by staff can be more difficult, but personal references should be thoroughly vetted before employment begins. Where intellectual property is an important asset of the firm, staff and other people granted access to the relevant idea may be required to sign a confidentiality agreement that prevents them from disclosing details to another party without authorisation. Many items of intellectual property can also be protected by trademark, patent or design registrations.

Insurance

Insurance:
A contract to provide compensation for any damage or loss suffered by the firm if a specified act occurs.

Another element in any risk management strategy is insurance. **Insurance** is a contract to provide compensation for any damage or loss suffered by the firm if a specified act occurs. It is a safeguard against risk that provides financial compensation when an untoward event happens. The insurance contract is commonly called a policy, and the payment the firm makes to the insurer for cover is known as a premium. A common form of insurance is workers' compensation, which meets the cost of rehabilitating employees if they are injured at work.

Different forms of insurance cover different types of risks (see the box on 'Insurance products' below). However, the cost of fully insuring a business venture against *all* possible risks would be prohibitive. Where the likelihood of an event occurring is quite low, the business owner may decide that the minimal risk does not justify payment of the premium. In other situations, an insurer may be willing to provide a policy only to established businesses — new firms may not able to obtain insurance until they have an established track record that allows the insurer to confidently assess the likelihood of risk.

Insurance can be acquired by purchasing the relevant policy directly from an insurance company or through a broker who will find the most suitable policy at the best premium from a range of different insurers.

Insurance products

- The following list of business product offerings provided by most Australian insurance companies indicates the many different types of insurance cover available:
- motor vehicle insurance — protects against the loss or damage of company cars
- professional indemnity – covers liability from claims arising due to breach of professional duty
- general property — protects against loss arising from flood, earthquake, fire, burglary or explosion
- business interruption — protects against costs and lost profits arising

from damage to the premises by a fire or other defined event
- burglary — covers replacement of contents stolen from the business premises
- fire and other defined events — compensates for damage to buildings, contents, or customers' goods and trading stock
- money — covers funds stolen from the business site or in transit
- fraud or dishonesty — protects against loss of money or goods due to a fraudulent or dishonest act by a staff member
- machinery — compensates for breakdown of equipment

- electronic equipment — protects against physical loss, destruction or damage (including breakdown)
- negligence liability — covers claims made against the firm for damaged property or personal injury
- multiple risks — provides cover for business property against accidental damage
- personal accident and illness — provides the proprietor with funds to cover the loss of income if injured or sick
- tax audit — covers accountants' expenses incurred when a detailed investigation is made by the tax office.

Source: Adapted from NSW Department of State and Regional Development, 'Insurance and your industry,' available online at <www.smallbiz.nsw.gov.au> (accessed 9 May 2006).

Summary

Operations management covers many different aspects of a firm. Its core focus is on ensuring maximum efficiency in the operations process, which includes the gathering of inputs, their transformation into a final product and the delivery of that output (completed product) to the firm's customers.

Physical site factors are a basic element in a firm's operational management. Several different types of business premises can be used. These include home offices, serviced offices, a business incubator site, rented premises and purchased locations. Once the appropriate site has been selected, the internal layout must be organised. Retail firms can choose between the grid, open-plan and boutique formats, whereas manufacturing premises use either a product-based or process-based layout.

Production processes deal with the issues of workflow, inventory and supply management, and operating equipment. The sequence in which work is performed is an important issue and often determines matters such as layout, staffing needs and site location. Continuous production is commonly found in large-scale manufacturing, whereas job (batch) production methods predominate in firms with a small-scale and customer-driven focus. Inventory and supply management deal with the raw materials and trading stock held by the organisation. All firms strive to reach an inventory level that approximates an economic order quantity; many firms now use a just-in-time focus to minimise the costs of holding excessive stock. A related issue is the supply of raw materials. Firms must decide which suppliers to use and the terms of supply. Business owners must also take into account the type of equipment they will need, and its cost, durability and role.

The final part of operations management is concerned with evaluating, improving and maintaining operational performance. Evaluation and control are usually performed by examining schedules, conducting inspections and measuring productivity ratios. Improvements to operational performance can be made by instituting formal procedures and by the adoption of a quality system. Risk management (protection of the existing assets of the firm) is usually done through security procedures designed to protect people, equipment and ideas, and by taking out suitable insurance policies that will provide financial compensation if a specified risk occurs.

REVIEW QUESTIONS

1. Summarise the different location options available to a new business venture. What factors should be taken into account when assessing the suitability of a particular site?

2. Explain the two basic types of workflow structures and the advantages and disadvantages of each.

3. When choosing a supplier for a new business, what issues should the owner or entrepreneur investigate?

4. Compare and contrast the benefits of using new or second-hand equipment for a start-up business venture.

5. Explain the meaning of the term 'quality system' and its significance to the operations of a firm.

DISCUSSION QUESTIONS

1. What inventory and supply issues would a dental practice need to manage?

2. In your opinion, what are the three most common risks that most businesses face? How can these be prevented or reduced?

3. Outline and briefly explain the stages of the operations evaluation and control cycle. Give an example of how this could be applied to a university course.

SUGGESTED READING

Gerber, M.E., *The E-Myth: Why Most Businesses Don't Work and What to Do About It*, Harper Business, New York, 1995.

Gulati, M.L., *Management of Production Systems*, Amexcel Publishers, New Delhi, 1999.

Sutherland, J. & Canwell, D., *Key Concepts in Operations Management*, Palgrave Macmillan, Basingstoke UK, 2004.

CASE STUDY

Pineapple Palace

When Peta Green decided to open up her own business in northern Queensland, she had no idea just how many different tasks she would have to plan for. After conducting an initial feasibility study, doing some primary research and preparing a business plan, she decided to proceed with her idea for the Pineapple Palace.

As she explained to her bank manager, who was providing 50 per cent of the total cost of the project: 'Tourists to far north Queensland just love seeing and doing things that they would never do at home. This will probably be the only chance many city dwellers get to see how their fruit comes to their table each day'.

Under her ambitious proposal, the Palace will be a one-stop shop for both tourists and food wholesalers. Local pineapple growers will deliver their product to the site each afternoon and the fruit will be processed and packaged there. Then the pineapples will be sold to tourists from a shop at the front of the Palace, and to fruit and vegetable stores in the nearby city of Cairns. The Palace will be located on the major highway that runs between Cairns and the city of Townsville.

Some pineapples will be sold whole, but most will be transformed at the Palace into pre-cut pineapple pieces that Cairns supermarkets, restaurants and health food shops can use as ingredients for fruit salads, desserts and snack foods. This transformation involves sorting the fruit into those that will stay whole and the ones that will be cut, and then slicing the fruit. The pre-cut pineapples are wrapped in plastic and placed in styrofoam boxes, which hold about thirty pre-cut pineapples. About one hundred of these styrofoam boxes form a whole crate.

Trucks from Cairns will arrive in the morning and collect crates of the pineapple pieces. Only two crates can fit onto each truck, and Peta estimates that she will produce ten truckloads a day. Tourists will be able to view the food processing activities by walking around a small viewing platform, which she plans to install high above the factory floor.

Questions

1. Prepare a floor plan for this business. Make sure that it provides room for all the facilities and functions that Peta has in mind.

2. What are the four most important insurance policies Peta needs?

3. What equipment will she need?

ENDNOTES

1. J. Corman & R.N. Lussier, *Small Business Management: A Planning Approach*, Irwin, Chicago, 1996, p. 217.
2. J.N. Pearson, J.S. Bracker & R.E. White, 'Operations management activities of small, high growth electronics firms', *Journal of Small Business Management*, vol. 28, no. 1, January 1990, pp. 20–9.
3. B.A. Saladin & R.R. Nelson, 'How small businesses view productivity and its relationship to operations management', *Journal of Small Business Management*, vol. 22, no. 1, January 1984, pp. 16–22.
4. W.L. Megginson, M.J. Byrd & L.C. Megginson, *Small Business Management: An Entrepreneur's Guidebook*, 3rd edn, Irwin McGraw-Hill, Boston, 2000, pp. 276–94.
5. J.N. Pearson et al., *see* note 2.
6. Australian Bureau of Statistics, *Characteristics of Small Business, Australia*, ABS, Canberra, 2002.
7. United Nations Industrial Development Organisation, *Business Incubators*, available online at <www.unido.org> (accessed 25 September 2002), 2000.
8. J.W. English, *How to Organise and Operate a Small Business in Australia*, 7th edn, Allen & Unwin, Sydney, 1998, p. 275.
9. T. Hill, *Small Business Production/Operations Management*, Macmillan, London, 1987, p. 140.
10. J.H. Blackstone & J.F. Cox, 'Inventory management techniques', *Journal of Small Business Management*, vol. 23, no. 2, April 1985, pp. 27–34.

11. M.L. Gulati, *Management of Production Systems*, Amexcel Publishers, New Delhi, 1999, pp. 157–64.
12. A. Fenton, '"Mother shucker" finds goldmine in imported oysters', *South China Morning Post*, 22 Jan 2005, p. B4.
13. J. Sharp, 'Hong Kong's Mother Shucker, Kathy Kingston', *The Correspondent*, <www.fcchk.org>, June–July 2004.
14. L. Galloway, *Operations Management: The Basics*, Thomson, London, 1996.
15. W.L. Megginson et al., *see* note 4, p. 312.
16. T.S. Hatten, *Small Business: Entrepreneurship and Beyond*, Prentice Hall, Upper Saddle River, 1997.
17. J. Corman & R.N. Lussier, *see* note 1, pp. 230–1.
18. J.G. Longenecker, C.W. Moore & J.W. Petty, *Small Business Management: An Entrepreneurial Emphasis*, 11th edn, South-Western, Cincinnati, 2000, p. 441.
19. T. Hill, *see* note 9, p. 151.
20. T.S. Hatten, *see* note 16, p. 408.
21. W.H. Newman, *Constructive Control: Design and Use of Control Systems*, Prentice Hall, Englewood Cliffs, 1975.
22. T. Wilde, 'A commitment to quality', in B. Whitford & R. Andrew (eds), *The Pursuit of Quality*, Beaumont Publishing, Perth, 1994, pp. 3–7.
23. D. Stringfellow, 'Challenge for Australian quality — achieving best practice', in B. Whitford & R. Andrew, ibid., pp. 8–13.
24. P.S. Wilton, *The Quality System Development Handbook*, Prentice Hall, Singapore, 1994.
25. M.E. Gerber, *The E-Myth: Why Most Businesses Don't Work and What to Do about It*, Harper Business, New York, 1995.
26. J.G. Longenecker et al., *see* note 18, p. 544.
27. D.F. Kuratko & R.M. Hodgetts, *Entrepreneurship: A Contemporary Approach*, 5th edn, Harcourt, Fort Worth, 2001, p. 190.
28. Fagg, S. 'Has ERM earned its stripes?' *Risk Management*, April 2006, pp. 14–15.

Human resource issues in new and small firms

LEARNING OBJECTIVES

After reading this chapter, you should be able to:

- define and explain the concept of human resource management

- explain the importance of human resource management as a strategic business tool

- outline the major steps in acquiring, maintaining and terminating human resources

- list the main legal obligations of an employer

- explain the key differences in employment practices between large and small firms

- state how human resource management varies among countries in the Pacific Rim region.

A part from the single-person enterprise, all businesses will sooner or later employ other people. Additional staff increase the firm's capacity to produce goods or services, allow it to deal with an expanded client base, and free up the entrepreneur/business owner to concentrate on the management and growth of the business. Some businesses employ staff at the start of operations; other small firms wait until the business has established itself. Regardless of the point at which staff are employed, there must be a consistent and logical approach to dealing with them. This involves many different issues: How will the people be recruited? On what basis will they be selected? How much should they be paid? How will the workplace be structured? What tasks will be done? What is the best way to evaluate their workplace performance? How does a manager arrange for the termination of employment at a later stage?

Bear in mind that many jobs in the Pacific Rim region are in the small business sector. The Asia–Pacific Economic Cooperation forum estimates that SMEs provide more than 60 per cent of private sector jobs in the APEC region (and more than 30 per cent of all employment once workers in the government and non-profit sector are also taken into account). Micro-firms account for about 30 per cent of all the private sector jobs, small-sized enterprises about 10 per cent, medium-sized firms 20 per cent, and large firms the remaining 40 per cent.[1]

This chapter gives an overview of the practical steps involved in employing people in new ventures and small firms, explains how to maximise performance from staff, and briefly examines the differences in employment practices between small and large firms, and among some countries in the Pacific Rim region.

Concept and functions of human resource management

Human resource management (HRM): A firm's approach to managing its employees.

The term **human resource management (HRM)** can have a number of different meanings. At its simplest, HRM is simply a generic term '... denoting any approach to employment management'.[2] This covers all the aspects related to dealing with people in the workplace, and includes the tasks of recruiting, organising, paying, supervising, disciplining and monitoring them. Since no firm, not even the most sophisticated internet-based enterprise, operates without the input of its employees, HRM is a crucial function in all business entities. Indeed, staff wages and associated expenses are typically one of the largest single-cost items for most small firms,[3] so it makes sense to manage this resource as effectively as possible. Since there are many different ways a firm can structure its HRM activities, and these all directly or indirectly affect its success in other fields, a more accurate description of HRM might be:

> ...competitive advantage through the strategic deployment of a highly committed and capable workforce, using an array of cultural, structural and personnel techniques.[4]

As this definition emphasises, the most crucial aspect of successful HRM focuses on the efficient use of staff to achieve the entrepreneur's goals.

There are many different theories and perspectives on how HRM does — or should — operate within the workplace. At its simplest, however, effective HRM in all organisations revolves around three main issues (see figure 13.1):[5]

- *Acquisition.* How are employees to be found and their services secured for the use of the entrepreneurial business venture?
- *Maintenance.* How can the firm ensure the effective management of its staff once they are working within the enterprise?
- *Termination.* How are people to be let go once their services are no longer required within the firm?

These functions will be explored in further detail in the remainder of this chapter.

Acquisition	Maintenance	Termination
• Decide to employ or not • Undertake job analysis • Set remuneration and reward structure • Choose recruitment source • Negotiate employment contracts • Select employee	• Undertake orientation and introduction • Provide training • Conduct regular appraisal	• Offer voluntary termination • Enforce dismissal

Figure 13.1: The three main components of human resource management

HRM as a business strategy

An essential element to bear in mind is that effective HRM involves a large element of strategic decision making by the entrepreneur or small business owner–manager. Although there are mandatory legal requirements that all firms have to adhere to, many other staff issues are determined by the business owner and senior staff. Owners, senior managers and entrepreneurs effectively have a large amount of choice in how they deal with their employees.[6]

Each strategic choice will have an impact on many other aspects of the business. For example, a participative **organisational culture** that promotes shared decision making can often make it difficult to execute decisions when market demands shift dramatically, since it will be expected that most or all employees will have a say in the final response the firm makes. In contrast, a small business run in an autocratic manner by its owner may be able to change direction quickly once the owner makes a decision, but the owner will often be shouldering a large amount of responsibility and stress because there is no delegation of command.

Organisational culture:
The shared values, attitudes and behaviour of employees in a firm.

The particular type of HRM strategy adopted can have major implications for business survival. For example, it has long been argued that particular types of organisational features are more conducive to successful entrepreneurship than others. Successful entrepreneurial firms typically contain senior managers who have a clear vision of the business, are strongly supportive of their staff, and operate in a 'blame-free' culture where mistakes and risk-taking (even if unsuccessful) are seen as a necessary part of organisational and individual learning. These firms tend to encourage teamwork and the sharing of credit for success. They offer managers 'prescribed limits' within which experimentation, change and alternative approaches are encouraged. Feedback on ideas and performance is openly given.[7]

However, many large organisations have traditionally adopted strategies that are an active impediment to entrepreneurship. Formal hierarchies, a heavy emphasis on following due procedures and rules, staff specialisation in narrow areas, and the division of employees into separate divisions or departments (which often leads to rivalry and mutually destructive conflict) are anathema to the concept of a flexible, adaptive organisation. However, bureaucratic structures are still essential when dealing with very large workforces or when accountability and procedural equity are important policy issues.

Whether an entrepreneurial or a traditional strategy is adopted, both benefits and costs arise. For example, the entrepreneurial structure may be quite flexible and open to innovation, but it is much more difficult to manage than an organisation with clearly defined rules and standard operating procedures. Similarly, the decision to encourage innovation and risk-taking may be laudable, but the firm must also be willing to tolerate the financial and resource costs that arise each time a mistake is made. On the other hand, a traditional structure with rigid standard procedures means that operations can be run like clockwork, but it discourages innovation and initiative. In each case, there is a trade off — between innovation and efficiency, and between flexibility and predictability. Ultimately, only the business owner can decide what constitutes an acceptable HRM trade-off of costs against benefits.

Acquisition of staff

The initial phase of the HRM model covers several activities. In the first place, the firm must make a decision to employ someone. The business owner must consider the implications this will have on the organisational structure of the firm, how the job will be structured, and the methods that will be used to recruit and select an appropriate person. Issues relating to the level of remuneration (pay) and the employment contract must also be resolved.

To employ or not?

A new or existing firm becomes an employing business when the owner or entrepreneur makes the decision to recruit staff members. Before beginning the search for a new employee, the owner must make a realistic assessment of why someone is needed, and take a number of issues into account.

Growth goals

How will the employment of another person fit into the overall goals of the business? Will the new employee help achieve targets? Does the new job fit into the objectives set out in the business plan or will that document need to be revised? What staff needs are foreseen for the next few years of the business?

(This issue may be extremely hard to estimate for a start-up or rapidly growing business, since future survival and organisational activities are difficult to reliably gauge in advance.)

Personal issues for the business owner

How comfortable will the owner be with the addition of another staff member? This is especially important for entrepreneurs taking on their first employee. Not all personality types are well suited to dealing with staff. Some business owners find it hard to 'let go' and effectively delegate work to another person; others may feel threatened if another person suddenly takes responsibility for part of the business. Alternatively, if an entrepreneur already has several employees, a more important recruitment issue might be whether any new staff member fits in comfortably with the existing internal culture and goals of the business that the owner–manager has created.

Marketing issues

Many human resource issues in a small enterprise are related to the overall successful marketing of the firm. If a business has built up much of its customer base on the founder's personal relationship with clients, how will a new employee taking over client relations affect that relationship? Will it be possible to guarantee the same level of customer service once the owner disengages from the marketing role? (On the other hand, recruiting new staff may have a positive outcome if the business owner is deficient in such skills.)

Operations and facilities

If a decision is made to bring in new staff members, what facilities will be required? An extra person will often mean additional expenditure on equipment and extra working space; and there will be increased administrative responsibilities and legal issues relating to employment of other people (this is discussed in more detail later in the chapter).

Financial issues

Employment of another person will have a direct impact on the financial resources of the firm. Expenditure on wages, on-costs and facilities will have an immediate impact on the cash flow of the firm and, ultimately, on the overall profitability of the enterprise. Does the firm have enough liquidity to cover the increased cash expenditure? Will the new employee ultimately generate enough revenue to cover the cost of being employed? See the box (p. 322) on calculating employee costs and benefits.

Alternatives to employment

It is important to determine whether staff employment is, in fact, the best option for the firm. There may be alternative ways of dealing with increased demands on the firm. If the perceived employment need arises due to the need to correct a specialised problem, it may be more cost effective to bring in an expert consultant or 'pair of hands' adviser to deal with the issue (the function of these advisers is discussed in more detail in chapter 10). Alternatively, can the work arrangements of existing staff be reorganised to accommodate the demand for extra help? Could they be asked to work overtime? Can the task be outsourced to another firm?

Calculating employee costs and benefits

One way of determining the cost-effectiveness of an employee is to do the following calculations. (All businesses should be able to fill in the 'Annual expenses' item, but it may not be possible to complete the 'Annual revenue' and 'Surplus/deficit' items if the job is administrative or the employee's revenue productivity is hard to measure.)

Annual expenses

Calculate the true annual cost of an additional staff member. Itemise the estimated expenditure for each of the following items (leave blank if not relevant):

Category	Cost
Yearly wage or salary	
Holiday leave loading	
Replacement of staff during their leave	
Superannuation	
Fringe benefits	
Fringe benefits tax	
Payroll tax	
Workers compensation insurance	
Other insurance premiums	
Office furniture	
Phone lines/calls	
Vehicle expenses	
Training and education	
Stationery	
Bank fees	
Administration	
Other equipment	
Total annual employee expenses	

Annual revenue

Calculate the total income the new employee is expected to generate during the year. If the firm is a retail or manufacturing operation, deduct the cost of goods sold in order to estimate the net additional income the employee will create.

Total sales income by employee	
Less: Cost of goods sold	
Net revenue produced by employee	

Organisational structure

Every business has a mechanism for structuring and organising the behaviour of its employees. The organisational design of a firm refers to the way in which people are allocated tasks, the way their activities are coordinated, the way information flows and decisions are made, and the way units of people work together.[8] An **organisational structure chart** shows these relationships diagrammatically. Such a chart should not only cover existing employees, but also provide a map as to how any future staff will fit into the overall business.

Organisational structure chart: A diagrammatic representation of the way in which employee work relationships are structured within a business.

Although there are many different ways of structuring a business, one key issue for entrepreneurial and small firms is the choice between a traditional (hierarchical) structure and an organic one. The classic hierarchical structure, which is often best exemplified by a bureaucracy, has a strict division of labour into different units, multiple layers of command, and an emphasis on hierarchical information and decision making (figure 13.2).

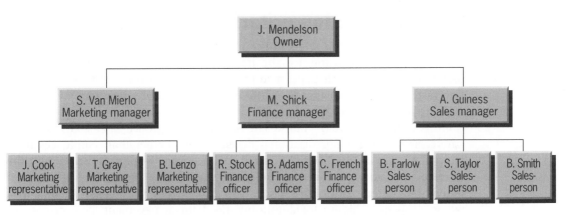

Figure 13.2: Simple hierarchical organisational structure

In contrast, organic structures are often found in new small firms, and they emphasise small groups sharing information, ideas and tasks; there is a flat management structure and considerable flexibility. This structure is typically associated with successful micro-firms and truly entrepreneurial large ones.

When planning the introduction of a new staff member, the organisational structure chart should be consulted to determine where the individual will fit into the business. This helps the entrepreneur determine who will be responsible for overseeing the new employee.

Job analysis

What, exactly, will the new employee be required to do, and what sort of person best fits the requirements? To answer these questions, a **job analysis** must be performed to determine the duties and skill requirements of a job and the sort of person who might fit these demands. A job analysis contains two main components: a job description and a job specification.[9]

A **job description** is a written statement of what a job entails, how it is done, and under what conditions. Typical issues covered here include:

- the job title
- who to report to (name of immediate supervisor)
- work tasks and responsibilities (whether performed daily, weekly, monthly or irregularly)
- the hours of work expected.

A **job specification** details the personal traits and experience required to do the job effectively. In other words, what kind of person, with what kind of qualities, will do this job best? It includes criteria such as:

- the level of education or training a person should have
- how much previous experience (if any) is required for the job
- ability to work as part of a team (if relevant)
- communication skills
- special physical attributes (if required).

These are the elements on which job advertisements are constructed, selection criteria are devised and the suitability of applicants is assessed.

Job analysis: The process of determining the duties and skill requirements of a job, and the sort of person who might fit these demands.

Job description: A written statement of what a job entails, how it is done, and under what conditions.

Job specification: The personal traits and experience required from a prospective employee.

Setting selection criteria

The term *selection criteria* refers to the set of factors by which the business owner judges potential applicants for the new position, and these factors are largely based on the job analysis performed previously. Establishing a simple set of selection factors helps the owner to clarify expectations of the new employee and to evaluate potential job applicants more accurately.

Firms seeking to develop a more entrepreneurial approach can also use selection criteria as a tool for organisational development. Rather than employees being selected simply on the basis of formal qualifications, work experience and other external indicators, prospective candidates may also be assessed on the basis of individual characteristics. This assessment can include an analysis of their risk-taking propensity, desire for autonomy, need for achievement, goal orientation and internal locus of control.

Remuneration and rewards

How much to pay is another important issue in attracting suitable candidates. While remuneration rates for many jobs were once set by regulations or industrial bodies (such as the Australian Conciliation and Arbitration Commission), today the majority of job pay rates are determined by market mechanisms. This means that entrepreneurs have to decide for themselves the most appropriate level of pay. Some owners have strong preconceived ideas about what an employee should be worth. In almost all countries, however, there are legal minimum levels below which pay cannot fall. Setting a pay rate too low may result in a shortage of acceptable applicants, whereas setting a pay rate too high may mean that the firm is paying more for the employee than the employee is generating for the firm.

Another issue to consider is what form the remuneration will take. One common form is a **wage payment**, in which employees are paid a base rate for working a set number of hours per week; this may be topped up by extra payments for additional work (overtime). Another form is a **salary**, which gives employees a 'total pay' package regardless of the number of hours worked; there is no provision for extra payment if additional work is required. Remuneration in some occupations, such as sales work, is often performance-based, with most of the person's income based on the number of items sold, regardless of the hours worked.

> **Wage:** System of remuneration in which employees are paid at a set hourly rate.

> **Salary:** Remuneration in which employees receive a fixed 'total pay' package, regardless of the number of hours worked.

The total cost of an employee is usually much more than just the nominal rate of pay shown as wages or salary. There are numerous ancillary costs which must also be taken into account. These 'on-costs' include superannuation or pension (provident fund) contributions, insurance expenses, the provision of equipment and facilities, and fringe benefits for employees (see 'How to compensate employees' below). In many Asian countries, it is standard practice to provide an annual bonus to employees. On-costs typically run to an extra 20–40 per cent on top of the actual wage or salary paid.

A final element to consider when structuring a compensation package is how to provide a positive incentive for creative, innovative work performance. Successful entrepreneurial firms ensure that employees receive more than just a wage or salary. They also make an effort to provide a reward system that encourages individual enterprise, reward for effort and calculated risk-taking. For example, some large corporations now remunerate in-house entrepreneurs (intrapreneurs) by offering them part-ownership (equity) in the business if their idea generates a new enterprise.

How to compensate employees

When negotiating an employment contract, there are many possible ways of rewarding staff. Cash and legally required benefits are simply the starting point. Some compensation packages may also include:

- additional retirement funds (over and above the minimum required by superannuation or provident fund laws)
- profit sharing
- equity involvement (employee share ownership schemes)
- flexible time schedules
- unpaid time off
- personal use of company equipment or facilities
- education expenses
- motor vehicles or transport
- recreation services (health club memberships; in-store gymnasium or massage)
- company trips

Recruitment sources

Once selection criteria and remuneration have been settled, the employee/s must be found. Many business owners are unaware of the full range of options available to them or of the issues that need to be considered when deciding on the correct recruitment medium. The most common sources of job candidates include:

- *Newspapers and websites.* Job advertisements in the print media have traditionally been one of the most common methods of recruiting applicants. It is relatively cost-effective (reaching a wide market for a fixed cost) and can sometimes be targeted at particular industries. Web-based job recruitment is the electronic version of the traditional generic newspaper advertisement. However, both tools are targeted only towards candidates who are actively looking for a new job. Other prospective employees who are already in jobs, but who could be lured away to work for the business if the right offer was made, are unlikely to be reading the situations vacant section or browsing job websites each week.

- *Unsolicited approaches.* Some interested jobseekers may have previously approached the firm seeking employment, and their applications should be kept on file for future reference. These people are obviously aware that the business exists, are keen to find a job and are interested in the work the firm performs.

- *Government employment agencies.* In some nations, government agencies provide (or fund) employment-placement organisations. They often focus on helping the unemployed or those in career transition. Such organisations can offer a cheap, relatively easy way to fill staff vacancies, but the calibre of the job applicants should be carefully assessed.

- *Competitors.* Poaching a valued employee from another business is another option. This can provide the firm with a trained, experienced person familiar with the industry and with the activities of the firm's competitors.

- *Friends and family.* The employment of family members is well documented, especially in small-scale enterprises.[10] Employing family members usually provides a common sense of purpose, a greater commitment to the long-term survival of the firm, and a sense of security that arises from working among people the owner or entrepreneur already knows and trusts. Similar considerations often apply in the recruitment of friends. However, not all family members have the necessary skills needed for particular jobs, and it can often be difficult to disentangle personal and emotional issues from workplace performance.

- *Educational and special-interest organisations.* Secondary schools, industry groups (employer associations), trade unions and universities often have a database of prospective jobseekers with specialist qualifications. This option is often valuable when a firm requires applicants to have a degree, a particular training qualification or specialist industry experience.

- *Recruitment agencies.* These consultants specialise in conducting the recruitment and selection process for client firms, and they are often engaged to 'headhunt' or seek out particular people. They use their databases of interested jobseekers, market research, personal contacts and industry sources to locate and assess potential applicants.

Once a pool of potential employees has been collated, the business owner needs to decide which seems most suitable. Jobseekers can be evaluated in a number of ways. The most common is by conducting an interview, which is usually done face-to-face. If candidates are applying from another city or country, telephone or videoconference interviews can also be held. Interview data can be supplemented by other information, such as a portfolio of previous work (useful in the creative industries), realistic job previews (where candidates spend time in the actual workplace), role-playing activities, and referees' reports.[11]

The employment contract

An employment contract needs to be negotiated between the business owner and the employee; this document spells out pay rates, additional benefits, holiday and leave entitlements, probation periods and termination issues. In all cases, there are still minimum conditions (such as basic rates of pay, annual leave entitlements, illness and maternity leave) that must be observed, regardless of the final form the contract takes.

Employment relationships can be constructed in various ways:

- *Industrial awards.* These are prescribed minimum conditions of employment set out for particular industries by the Australian Industrial Relations Commission or similar regulatory entities. Employers can pay above the award, but generally may not go below these conditions. These were once common in Australia, but are increasingly being replaced by other types of employment agreement.
- *Individual written contracts.* In many cases it is possible for the employer and employee to directly negotiate most of the terms of employment, such as working hours, pay rates and fringe benefits, and then settle on a formal written contract that spells out the rights and obligations of each party and the terms on which the contract may be ended. These are sometimes referred to as workplace agreements in Australia and New Zealand, and many employment arrangements take this form of contract. In some circumstances, employee unions may negotiate the contract collectively on behalf of union members at a worksite, thus removing the need for an employer to negotiate directly with each staff member.
- *Informal contracts.* In many situations, employees work on the basis of an unwritten agreement. Pay, conditions and benefits are usually set at about the norm for a particular industry. These common law contracts are often based on the assumption by both parties that they conform to established industrial precedents. However, in the event of a dispute, it may be difficult to determine the true rights and responsibilities of both employer and employee.

Maintenance

Once a suitable employee has been found and engaged, the task of the business owner is not over. The next HRM function involves retaining people in the firm and ensuring that they work as effectively as possible. This task is sometimes more demanding than the acquisition phase.

Although it may sound like a cliché, the expression 'people are our most important asset' still holds true in many cases. Many small business owners complain that a lack of suitable staff is a key barrier to further growth, and that a lack of confidence in the ability of current employees often prevents them from letting go and allowing others to manage the firm on their behalf. This is often compounded by the entrepreneurial personality, which can find it hard to delegate work.

Orientation and induction

Once the new employee has been signed on, the business owner needs to introduce the firm's existing employees, explain current work procedures and operating processes, arrange for any necessary additional training, and perhaps also introduce the employee to customers, suppliers and other owners of the business (if any). This ensures that the new employee is fully aware of the working environment, and minimises mistakes or lost time. It is also common to have a probation period at the start of employment, during which time the employee may be dismissed for breaches of requirements or an inability to satisfactorily perform the work.

Motivation mechanisms

Motivation:
The willingness of employees to exert effort to achieve business goals.

Motivation is the willingness of employees to exert effort to achieve business goals.[12] Motivating people to perform to the best of their ability and in ways that benefit the business organisation has always been an important issue for managers at all levels of a firm. For example, just one poorly motivated employee in a restaurant can generate many customer complaints and the loss of future customers. There is no single measure which can guarantee continued high levels of motivation, although human resource theorists have put forward a number of theoretical frameworks that might help.[13]

In a practical sense, however, there are a number of ways a business owner can enhance motivation and performance. At a basic level, a satisfactory level of pay is necessary. As the proponents of 'equity theory' point out, employees who believe they are underpaid will cut back on their efforts or seek a new job if the gap between their remuneration and those of others is too great.[14] In many industries, performance-based pay is used as a motivating tool, via mechanisms such as piece-rate pay (payment per item produced), commission-based sales, wage incentive schemes and profit-sharing plans. Although the evidence is far from clear, such programs also appear to provide improved financial returns for firms as well.[15]

Other actions that are believed to improve employee motivation include allowing employees to work flexible hours; including them in decision making about critical business goals; providing them with an opportunity to purchase shares (equity) in the firm; and ensuring that reward systems match individual needs. For employees with a high need for personal achievement, the opportunity for advancement or for assuming a higher level of responsibility can be an important incentive.[16] Such measures are also conducive to the development of an entrepreneurial culture within the firm.

Entrepreneur profile

Camus Leung

Camus Leung is the proprietor of Hildebrand International Travel Service Limited, a small agency based in Tsim Sha Tsui, Hong Kong. Ms Leung began her business in 1991, operating the business on her own. Since that time, however, the business has grown and she now employs six other staff as well as herself.

Camus began her working life in sales and then worked in numerous fields, including the hospitality and television industries and as an office secretary, before she eventually began working as a tour guide. However, she was not content to simply remain an employee.

'I'm quite an ambitious and energetic person, and I felt that these jobs were not suitable for me,' she explains, 'so finally, I ended up starting up a very small travel business on my own.' Although a degree might have helped, 'life is more than just about theory ... practical experience is more important. I had worked in tourism, so I knew the industry quite well.'

Her first staff member was employed within a year of start-up after Camus discovered there was too much work for just her to handle.

At first, she found employees by placing advertisements in newspapers such as the *South China Morning Post*. More recently, though, she has begun using online advertising. 'Internet recruitment has been effective in finding the sort of people that I need,' she says. 'It also helps demonstrate that applicants have some form of computer literacy.'

At first, employee pay rates were set by reference to the going rate. 'There was no real science, just what seemed to be the market standard.' Since then, Ms Leung has set rates based on her own perception of what is both reasonable and yet affordable for the business. 'If applicants are not satisfied with this, they don't need to apply for a job here.' Once staff prove themselves and she is satisfied with them, the option of additional remuneration is used as an incentive to encourage higher performance.

Human resources management is split within the office. Camus manages the development, mentoring and training of staff personally, but the administrative tasks (such as payroll) are shared by Ms Leung and another long-standing staff member.

Camus has also noted a major attitudinal difference in her firm between being an entrepreneur and being an employee. 'When I first started employing, I expected my staff to work with the same vigour and energy. But I have since come to the conclusion that most do not have the same level of passion as I have.'

Nevertheless, she continues to nurture willing staff with guidance and mentoring. She intends to encourage her staff to take up more responsibilities within the firm, but is always conscious of the fact that it is more her business than theirs.

For more information, see the Hildebrand website at <www.hildebrandtravel.com>.
Profile contributed by Andrew Wong, Hong Kong

Training

Another way to improve performance at work is to ensure that staff have the appropriate sets of skills to perform their tasks. Almost all industries operate in a dynamic and changing environment, and it is unlikely that employees will always come fully equipped with complete knowledge and the ability to perform their work role perfectly. Training removes or reduces shortfalls and gives the business a greater set of skills than it can productively use.

Training needs analysis: An evaluation of the skills and knowledge employees need, what they currently hold, and what gap exists.

A **training needs analysis** is an evaluation of the skills and knowledge employees need, what they currently hold, and what (if any) gap exists between these two conditions. Such an analysis is usually made with reference to the firm's goals and its staffing (organisational) chart, and this helps the owner set out a course of future action to remedy the skills and knowledge shortfall. Ideally, such training will not only equip staff to do their current jobs more effectively but will also allow them to further their careers within the organisation, thereby equipping the firm to better deal with future business challenges.

If managed correctly, effective training can result in direct tangible benefits for the business, including a more efficient use of staff time; reduced errors and waste within the workplace; higher sales; a greater adoption of new ideas and technologies; improved communication; enhanced customer satisfaction; and a better ability to deal with change and competition.[17] Some common training areas include:

- generic management skills
- customer service skills
- use of existing or new technology
- production processes
- business planning
- refresher courses in current business processes
- legal compliance issues
- quality systems
- environmental, health and safety issues.

Training can be undertaken in a variety of ways. Within the workplace, training can involve mentoring by other, more experienced staff; job rotation among different duties; or informal advice from work colleagues. Outside the workplace, training can be accessed via formal enrolment in a technical college or tertiary institution; participation in short-term professional development courses by accredited trainers; or development programs offered by small business agencies, private organisations and government departments.

Performance appraisal

Evaluating the performance of employees at work is also important. An employer needs to know if new recruits are achieving what they set out to do for the firm and, if not, why this is so. Some of the many appraisal mechanisms that exist include:

- *interviews* — personal, direct evaluation of employees in a formal context
- *management by objectives* — providing a set of discrete goals that employees should achieve within a given time frame; employee performance is subsequently judged on capacity to meet these goals
- *rating scales* — questionnaires that ask supervisors to rank employees on a number of different work-related dimensions
- *on-the-job assessment* — direct observation of employees while in their usual work environment.

There are some more subjective, informal mechanisms that are also used. These are more common in small firms, where there is limited time or inclination to undertake formal procedures, and the owner often personally knows or directly supervises the employee. These mechanisms are:

- *stakeholder feedback* — input from immediate supervisors, the employee's workplace peers, and other key people with an involvement in the firm (such as other owners of the business)
- *external feedback* — judging performance on the basis of feedback from outside parties, for example the number and type of customer complaints or compliments about an employee
- *owner/entrepreneur's assessment* — informal, subjective assessment made largely on the owner/entrepreneur's personal impressions of a worker's performance to date.

It is also possible to make some evaluations about staff management on a firm-wide basis. One common indicator is the level of **staff turnover**; that is, the number of employees who leave the business. This is often the ultimate indicator of staff dissatisfaction with the working conditions in the business, and can be due to a wide combination of factors: low pay, poor in-house facilities and equipment, bad management practices or inadequate training and induction. Where a firm has a higher turnover than the industry norm, or the rate has increased over time, it is often indicative of poor employee management practices.[18]

Staff turnover:
The number of employees who leave the business.

Termination

The final component of any employment relationship occurs when the firm and employee part company.

A *voluntary termination* occurs when an employee leaves of his or her own free choice, and this situation is relatively easily handled. A staff member may be dissatisfied working in the firm or may decide to retire or pursue a new career; they may have plans to move away from the geographical area where the business is based, or else want to leave the paid workforce for a period of time.

An *enforced dismissal* is more difficult. Employees may be dismissed because the firm can no longer afford their services; there is no longer demand for the tasks they perform (they have become redundant to the business's needs); there has been a restructure of the organisation; they have a history of poor work performance; or they have broken the law or employment contract. In many small firms and entrepreneurial business ventures, where failure rates are usually much higher than in established large corporations, dismissal will also occur when the business venture itself collapses.

Termination of a worker's employment has a number of consequences for the business as a whole. Consideration must be given to the financial payouts the firm may have to make (such as payment in lieu of notice or payment of accrued leave owing) and to the effect a dismissal will have on other employees in the firm: Will it affect morale? Who will do the job of the dismissed person? In some cases, it may be necessary to ensure that a disgruntled employee does not sabotage relationships with the firm's existing suppliers or customers, or pass on valuable intellectual property to a competitor.

Sometimes there is an alternative to outright termination, such as shifting employees from full-time to part-time work (useful when there is a temporary short-term fall in demand); providing training and mentoring (to help overcome any skill deficiencies); or finding the employee work with one of the firm's strategic allies.

Given the complexities and difficulties inherent in any termination decision, voluntary or not, small business owners are strongly encouraged to seek advice from a lawyer or an employer association before dismissing an employee.

What would you do?

On the wings of a dilemma

You are the managing director of a small aviation firm that has a contract to fly mining personnel into and out of the Indonesian province of Papua (Irian Jaya) for a large Australian resource firm based in Darwin. Your firm has three aircraft and a pool of six pilots, as well as several support staff, aviation mechanics and technicians. Safety is a critical issue in this industry. All the pilots have extensive experience and are periodically tested for alcohol and drug use, and the mechanics rigorously crosscheck their work to ensure that the firm's blemish-free accident record is maintained.

Lately, one of the pilots has begun to behave erratically. At age 30, Miles O'Connor should be one of the most competent pilots in the industry. He has had a wealth of flying experience throughout the Middle East and South-East Asia, and has been with your business for the last two years. He has a young family and has often expressed his desire to find and keep a 'safe, comfortable, secure job'.

However, two weeks ago he turned his plane around on the tarmac, just before take-off, and ordered one miner off the aircraft after she had made a joke that he found offensive. On the return flight, he turned up late, thus causing departure to be delayed for an hour.

Last Monday, Miles had a screaming argument with one of his fellow pilots, his best friend, over a trivial incident in the coffee room. This is not like him; Miles is usually a quietly spoken person. You suspect he may be suffering from anxiety, depression or family problems.

He has become increasingly sullen and moody, and his actions are beginning to affect the rest of the firm. Already one of the other pilots has intimated that she may look around for another job if such threatening behaviour becomes the norm.

Miles is on a lucrative employment contract which has another two years to run. To dismiss him would require you to pay out the remainder of the contract or else risk an unfair dismissal court action. There is also the chance that another pilot, who is a close friend of Miles, will leave with him, rendering the firm unable to honour its fly-in fly-out contract. Unfortunately, it is becoming increasingly hard to find pilots willing to work in Papua, given the volatile security environment there.

You have asked Miles to come into your office this afternoon and discuss the matter with you. He is already 15 minutes late and it is time for you to decide how to handle the issue.

Questions
1. Should Miles be dismissed? What alternatives can you suggest?
2. If Miles's employment is to be terminated, how should it be done?

Governmental and regulatory requirements

Employers have to meet a wide range of legal obligations when taking on any new staff.[19]

Occupational health and safety

Employers have a general duty of care to ensure that the workplace they provide, and the conditions they expect their employees to operate in, are reasonably safe and that all possible steps are taken to eliminate or at least minimise the risk of work-related death or injury. Most governments have specific legislation that lays down the employer's duties in this respect, and there are also agencies that police the level of workplace health and safety.[20]

Workers compensation insurance

This is insurance that is taken out to meet the cost of treating, rehabilitating or compensating any injured staff members who have been hurt in a work-related event. Premiums for this type of insurance will vary, depending on the level of risk for each industry. Workers compensation is an employer, not an employee, obligation.

Taxation

Employers must give details of their employees to taxation authorities and, in most countries, deduct tax from their wages or salaries and forward this tax to the tax office. In some cases, there may also be additional taxes or levies that firms have to deduct from employees' pay and forward to tax authorities; in Australia, such deductions include Higher Education Contribution Scheme (HECS) debts and childcare support payments.

Equal employment opportunity

In many jurisdictions, it is illegal to discriminate against job applicants on the grounds of age, sex, physical disability, ethnicity or marital status. Unless these are directly relevant to the job, such specifications must be kept out of job advertisements, selection criteria or job specification forms.

Retirement and superannuation funds

In several Pacific Rim countries, firms are required to make payments towards their employees' retirement schemes. This is the case, for example, with the Central Provident Fund system in Singapore, the Mandatory Provident Fund in Hong Kong and the Superannuation Guarantee Levy in Australia. Firms must arrange for the required money to be forwarded to the relevant retirement or superannuation fund at predetermined intervals.

Table 13.1: Retirement/pension/superannuation information

Country	Authority
Australia	Superannuation Guarantee Levy, Australian Taxation Office <www.ato.gov.au>
Hong Kong	Mandatory Provident Fund Schemes Authority <www.mpfahk.org>
Malaysia	Employees Provident Fund <www.kwsp.gov.my>
Singapore	Central Provident Fund Board <www.cpf.gov.sg>

Suitable records

To supplement other recordkeeping requirements, statutes in many countries require employers to keep adequate records of the time worked by employees, the payments made to them, leave accrued and/or used, fringe benefits, and related payments made for tax, retirement or workers compensation purposes.

Information on these employer responsibilities is usually available from professional business advisers, small business assistance agencies or accountancy practices, government departments concerned with labour or employment (see table 13.2), and the various taxation authorities (listed in chapter 8).

Table 13.2: Main government agencies dealing with labour or employment issues

Country	Authority
Australia	Department of Employment and Workplace Relations <www.dewr.gov.au>
Hong Kong	Labour Department <www.labour.gov.hk>
Malaysia	Ministry of Human Resources <www.mohr.gov.my>
New Zealand	Department of Labour <www.dol.govt.nz>
Singapore	Ministry of Manpower <www.mom.gov.sg>

Differences in employment practices between large and small firms

The evidence to date suggests that there are a number of ways in which human resource management in small firms is different from that in large corporations and public bodies.

Firstly, HRM methods in small businesses tend to be more informal.[21] There is less reliance on standardised procedures and regulations, and more emphasis on specific judgements and solutions that attempt to deal with the issue or problem at hand.[22] For example, whereas a government department or multinational corporation might have well-established rules about how to handle leave requests or temporary recruitment of staff, in a small firm the owner or another senior manager is more likely to make a decision on the spot based on current needs and the situation. It is only as new small firms grow larger that HRM practices tend to change, become more formalised and place more emphasis on hierarchy, documentation and administrative processes.[23]

Secondly, in small businesses, managerial decision making tends to be more closely concentrated at the top of the organisational apex (that is, in the hands of the owner) rather than diffused among different members of the firm.[24] This means that the owner or entrepreneur is more likely to be personally responsible for HRM decisions than would be the case in a large business.

Thirdly, structure and composition of the workforce are different. Several researchers have shown that small businesses tend to have a smaller proportion of union members in their workforce, more members of the owner's family working in the firm, a higher proportion of part-time workers, and staff with lower-level formal qualifications.[25] Smaller enterprises are also less likely to adopt explicit training and human resource development programs.[26]

Fourthly, there are subjective (or perceived) differences. A large problem that many small firms face is the perception among employees that a job in a new or small business is a second-rate option compared with employment in a large public corporation or government body. Although the recent history of large-scale retrenchments from corporations and government agencies has changed this view somewhat, it is still strongly held by many people. It is often assumed that career prospects are limited in small firms; that they do not have sufficient capacity to pay high wages, salaries and benefits; and, in the case of family-based businesses, that owners will always give preference to family members over talented outsiders.[27]

Taking these factors into account, it appears that small and new firms have more difficulty than larger organisations in attracting and retaining suitable staff. However, this overlooks the fact that small firms do offer some competitive advantages. They can often provide a more intimate, family-like atmosphere in which all employees know one another and people are on first-name terms. Small business owner–managers can also provide more flexibility for their staff, since the absence of formal human resource policies or strict rules allows them scope to accommodate staff needs. Also, it is often easier for employees to advance to the top of a small business than it is in a large corporation. In many situations, it is not uncommon for a valued staff member to eventually buy out the original owner or to become a part-owner. These opportunities rarely come to employees in a large corporation. In fact, recent evidence seems to support these conclusions: small firms often record lower total employee turnover rates than their larger counterparts, which appears to confirm the view that small companies are often the preferred workplace for many employees.[28]

HRM variations across the Pacific Rim

There are some substantial differences in HRM policies and practices among nations in the Pacific Rim region. For example, the use of fairly comprehensive recruitment and selection procedures is common in Singapore, Malaysia, Australia and New Zealand, but less so in Hong Kong. Many South-East Asian countries offer substantial supplementary benefits to their employees (such as medical services, housing subsidies and 'thirteenth month' bonuses), whereas such compensation is not usually found in Australia or New Zealand.[29]

National variations can also be seen in the regulatory framework that governments in each country have established for employers. Australia and New Zealand have traditionally had a high level of union involvement in the workplace, although this has declined substantially in recent years. As a result, both countries have fairly extensive rules to protect employees. Singapore has a substantial body of employment legislation, but it focuses more on productivity and economic development than on employee protection. Malaysia has a wide variety of employment laws, but these are not as extensive as those in Australia or New Zealand. In Hong Kong, the Special Administrative Region government, like its colonial predecessors, has adopted a minimalist approach, with only limited regulation of the labour market.[30]

Another way that Pacific Rim countries differ is in the use of family members within the firm. Although there has always been a large overlap between family-based businesses and small firms throughout the world, many of Asia's largest and most aggressive firms have continued to be family-run even as they have grown. Many Chinese-owned businesses are strongly centralised and dominated by the family patriarch. Preference in employment is often given to family members, and outsourcing, rather than recruiting new staff, is often a preferred means of entrepreneurial growth.[31] In contrast, few large entrepreneurial firms in Australia or New Zealand have remained completely in the hands of the originating family — their interests often become diluted by equity investors, and as the firm grows it is more likely to be run by a professional manager drawn from outside the family. The characteristics of Chinese-run businesses are discussed in more detail in chapter 15.

Summary

Human resource management plays a crucial role in starting a new entrepreneurial business venture and in the successful operation of existing small firms. Although there are prescribed minimum legal standards that firms must follow, there is also considerable scope for business owners to exercise their own judgement when establishing the firm's HRM activities. Successful entrepreneurial firms tend to avoid conventional hierarchical structures and prefer more flexible working systems that place an emphasis on risk-taking, information sharing, management support and an enterprising organisational culture.

The HRM function of acquisition begins when the entrepreneur decides to employ a new staff member. Issues to take into account at this point are the growth goals of the firm, marketing and operational factors, financial implications, alternatives to employing another person and the owner's willingness to give up some responsibility and power.

Once a decision has been made to employ someone, the organisational structure chart must be reassessed, a job analysis carried out, selection criteria established, suitable compensation determined and the appropriate recruitment source chosen. When a candidate has been selected, an employment contract must be organised.

The maintenance HRM function centres around retaining and developing employees to maximise their effectiveness within the organisation. These aspects include orientation and induction, motivational mechanisms, training, and performance appraisal.

The final HRM function is that of termination. People may leave the business voluntarily or they may be dismissed, in which case there are a number of complexities that must be considered.

All governments impose a number of regulatory and legislative requirements on employing organisations. These include issues relating to occupational health and safety, workers compensation, taxation, equal employment opportunity, retirement funding and the maintenance of employment records.

There are some significant differences in employment practices between small and large firms. Small businesses tend to have more informal employment practices and may find it harder to recruit staff. To counter this, small enterprises need to emphasise that they can provide greater flexibility in their staffing arrangements and career advancement opportunities.

Differences also exist between nations in the Pacific Rim region. Legal frameworks vary, as do the types of remuneration and benefits paid to staff. Compared with many other business models, enterprises owned by ethnic Chinese entrepreneurs tend to remain in family control and to give preference to kin, even when the enterprises grow larger.

REVIEW QUESTIONS

1. How can HRM be used as a strategic tool by business owners and entrepreneurs?
2. What issues does an owner or entrepreneur need to consider before deciding whether to employ another staff member?
3. What are the major components of the HRM maintenance function?
4. Outline and briefly explain the major legal obligations of employers.
5. List the major differences in employment practices between small and large firms.

DISCUSSION QUESTIONS

1. What is the most effective source for recruitment? Why?
2. What steps need to be taken in order to construct an organisational structure chart? What is the use of such a chart once completed?
3. A self-employed signwriter working from a small suburban business incubator realises that he can no longer manage his workload alone, and he resolves to recruit an assistant to help him with his painting work. Such a move will mean additional equipment and outlays (estimated expense: $20 000), and the market wage rate for such a position is about $55 000 per annum. The signwriter also estimates that on-costs will be another 30 per cent. An assistant

should help boost firm revenue by \$350 000 during his or her first year at work, with a cost of goods sold of 75 per cent. With these outlays, is employing a new person a worthwhile investment of time and money? Why?

SUGGESTED READING

Grensing-Pophal, L., *Employee Management for Small Business*, Self Counsel Press, Bellingham, Washington, 2005.

Kotey, B. & Slade, P., 'Formal human resource management practices in small growing firms', *Journal of Small Business Management*, vol.43, no.1, January 2005, pp. 16–40.

Nankervis, A., Compton, R. & Baird, M., *Strategic Human Resource Management*, 4th edn, Nelson Thomson, Melbourne, 2002.

Schaper, M., *The Australian Small Business Guide to Hiring New Staff*, Business and Professional Publishing, Sydney, 2000.

CASE STUDY

DotHot Fashions

DotHot Fashions is a small fashion design company, established 15 years ago by Dorothy ('Dot') Ho. Initially, Dot opened her female clothing design and retail store with only three employees: herself, her aunt Kay and her niece Kim. Both Kim and Kay contributed a small amount of the start-up capital and held a small proportion of the firm's shares. Sales were slow, and the three women were more than able to handle all of the chores. However, over the years, as the store's reputation grew and sales increased, Dot realised that she would have to hire more people. She then employed two designers, Anna and Simon, to help her with that side of the firm. This left the aunt and the niece to do the in-store retail sales and other day-to-day operational tasks.

While on a fashion tour five years ago, Dot met a young designer, Yvette Walenski, whose work she had seen previously in a show and to which she had taken an immediate liking. Although DotHot Fashions already employed two designers, Dot felt that Yvette, with her different approach to design, would appeal to a much larger and younger clientele, and so she decided to ask her to join the company. The additional salary meant an increase in operating costs, but Yvette worked hard and enthusiastically.

During the first three years of her employment, Yvette's designs sold well and the company's sales increased dramatically. She was not, however, too happy about being treated as the most junior designer, especially as Dot, Anna and Simon travelled extensively and she was often left behind. Last year, Simon had a car accident and, after recovering, did not return to work. Yvette felt that the time had now come for her to be made chief designer.

However, Dot decided that both Anna and Yvette should stay in their current positions with an increase in salary, while Dot took on the extra duties. This news disappointed Yvette enormously, to the extent that she even considered looking for a new job. However, her friends pointed out that she was receiving a top salary and would soon enjoy the benefits that Anna already received.

With the extra work and increased family commitments, Dot spent the next nine months in a constant rush to meet deadlines. She vaguely noticed that Yvette was not quite herself and that the standard of her work dropped markedly. Yvette's recent designs lacked the flair and instant marketability that had previously been her hallmark.

To overcome her tight workload, Dot concluded that it would be best to hire people to help with the in-store sales and allow her aunt and niece to handle the non-selling activities. 'It's easier to train someone to sell than it is to teach them how to handle stock, payroll and administrative work. If I lose one of the new people and am short of a salesperson, I can always call on Aunty Kay or Kim to help out. However, if I hire a woman to take care of stock or purchasing and she leaves, the burden will fall directly on my shoulders,' she told her relatives.

Four new people have since been brought on board in the last eight weeks to do the sales tasks, and Dot has also decided to further increase the salaries of both designers, mainly to address Yvette's obvious unhappiness.

Unfortunately, things have not worked out as well as Dot had hoped. The new staff do not seem to know how to sell. Additionally, one of them has already asked for a pay rise. When Dot replied that she would have to think about it, the woman pointed out that all other retail stores in the area were paying 20 per cent more for equivalent jobs than DotHot Fashions. And, just as worrying, Yvette is not producing any new designs.

Questions

1. Is an increase in salary likely to restore Yvette's motivation and work performance?

2. Evaluate Dot's performance as a human resources manager. What are her weaknesses?

3. Potentially, there is at least one other major human resources issue in this case that Dot appears to have overlooked. Review this case and outline what you think the undiscussed issue is.

Case study prepared by the small business staff, School of Accounting and Law, RMIT University.

ENDNOTES

1. APEC SME Working Group, *Profile of SMEs and SME Issues in APEC 1990–2000*, World Scientific Publishing, Singapore, p.1.
2. J. Storey, *Human Resource Management: A Critical Text*, 2nd edn, Thomson Learning, London, 2001, p. 5.
3. J.G. Longenecker, C.W. Moore & J.W. Petty, *Small Business Management: An Entrepreneurial Emphasis*, 11th edn, South-Western, Cincinnati, 2000.
4. J. Storey, *see* note 2, p. 6.

5. S.P. Robbins, P.S. Low & M.P. Mourell, *Managing Human Resources*, Prentice Hall, Sydney, 1986, pp. 9–10; A. Nankervis, R. Compton & M. Baird, *Strategic Human Resource Management*, 4th edn, Nelson Thomson, Melbourne, 2002.

6. A. Nankervis et al., *see* note 5.

7. J.B. Quinn, 'Managing innovation: Controlled chaos', *Harvard Business Review*, May–June 1985, pp. 73–84.

8. K. Bartol, D. Martin, M. Tein & G. Matthews, *Management: A Pacific Rim Focus*, 3rd edn, McGraw-Hill, Sydney, 2001.

9. G. Dessler, J. Griffiths, B. Lloyd-Walker & A. Williams, *Human Resource Management*, Prentice Hall, Melbourne, 1999, pp. 157–8.

10. CPA Australia, *Small Business Survey Program: Employment Issues*, CPA Australia, Melbourne, 2002, p. 4.

11. M. Schaper, *The Australian Small Business Guide to Hiring New Staff*, Business and Professional Publishing, Sydney, 2000, p. 72.

12. K. Bartol et al., *see* note 8.

13. S.P. Robbins, R. Bergman, I. Stagg & M. Coulter, *Management*, 2nd edn, Prentice Hall, Sydney, 2000.

14. J.E. Dittrich & M.R. Carrell, 'Organisational equity perceptions, employee job satisfaction, and departmental absence and turnover rates', *Organisation Behavior and Human Performance*, August 1979, pp. 29–40.

15. H. Rheem, 'Performance management programs', *Harvard Business Review*, September–October 1996, pp. 8–9.

16. S.P. Robbins et al., *see* note 13.

17. D.H. Bangs, *The Personnel Planning Guide: Successful Management of Your Most Important Asset*, 3rd edn, Upstart Publishing, Dover, NH, 1986.

18. J. English, *How to Organise and Operate a Small Business in Australia*, 7th edn, Allen & Unwin, Sydney, 1998, p. 299.

19. Australian Government, 'Employing people', <www.business.gov.au> 2006.

20. Department of Productivity and Labour Relations Western Australia, *Everything You've Always Wanted to Know about Employing Someone . . .*, Government of Western Australia, Perth, 1998.

21. J.M.P. De Kok, L.M. Uhlaner & A.R. Thurik, *Human Resource Management within Small and Medium-sized Firms: Facts and Explanations*, EIM Business and Policy Research, Zotermeer, The Netherlands, 2002; T. Bartram, 'Small firms, big ideas: The adoption of human resource management in Australian small firms', *Asia–Pacific Journal of Human Resources*, vol. 43, no. 1, April 2005, pp. 137–54.

22. J. Gilbert & G. Jones, 'Managing human resources in New Zealand small businesses', *Asia–Pacific Journal of Human Resources*, vol. 38, no. 2, Summer 2000, pp. 55–69.

23. B. Kotey & A. Sheridan, 'Changing HRM practices with firm growth', *Journal of Small Business and Enterprise Development*, vol. 11 no. 4, 2004, pp. 474–85.

24. Department of Industry, Science and Tourism, *The 1995 Business Longitudinal Survey*, AGPS, Canberra, 1997.

25. D. Lee-Ross, *HRM in Tourism and Hospitality: International Perspectives on Small to Medium-sized Enterprises*, Cassell, London, 1999, p. xvi.

26. Department of Industry, Science and Tourism, *see* note 24.

27. M. Schaper, *see* note 11.

28. Australian Institute of Management, *National Salary Survey*, Australian Institute of Management, Brisbane, 2005.

29. A. Nankervis & S. Chatterjee, *Understanding Asian Management: Transition and Transformation*, Vineyard Press, Perth, 2002, pp. 16–17.

30. ibid., pp. 9, 14.

31. G. Redding, *The Spirit of Chinese Capitalism*, de Gruyter, Berlin, 1990.

Financial information and management

LEARNING OBJECTIVES

After reading this chapter, you should be able to:

- define the purposes for which financial information is collected

- prepare a sales mix forecast, a cash flow statement and a profit and loss statement

- list the main types of financial documents and explain their purpose

- explain the ways in which financial information can be analysed

- list the different financial records used in most businesses.

A ccurate financial information is important in the successful development of new business ventures, as well as in the management of existing firms.[1] Although profits may not be the sole consideration for starting or running a business, most entrepreneurs and business owners understandably develop a keen interest in the financial performance of their business. Financial information plays an important role in providing a more complete picture of the operations of a business and its current status, and it helps determine whether future projects are viable.

However, to properly understand and analyse such data, business owners and entrepreneurs must be familiar with the way key financial documents operate and the way they are constructed: documents such as cash flow statements, profit and loss statements (now also referred to as *statements of financial performance*) and balance sheets (also termed *statements of financial position*).

In this chapter, the different types of financial information are described and explained. The basic documents common to all businesses (new or established, small or large) are explained. In addition, since most small and new ventures are often funded by the owner, some ways of documenting and analysing personal finances are also examined. Ratios for analysing financial data are then examined. Finally, an overview is provided of financial recordkeeping systems, so that entrepreneurs and owner–managers understand how to establish and maintain accurate data sources.

The purpose of financial information

Financial data are more than just a set of books or interesting sets of figures. When carefully collected, presented and analysed, the data represent an important source of management information.

Objectivity

Financial statements are practical documents. They represent data that have been measured and quantified, so they are objective indicators of business performance. In contrast, many of the other assessment methods used to gauge operational and managerial effectiveness (such as employee performance appraisal, the nature of customer complaints or compliments, and owner's opinions) are more likely to be based on subjective criteria such as personal assessments, 'gut feeling' and internal comparisons, and are therefore less reliable.

Financiers' expectations

If business owners want to borrow funds from a bank, or entrepreneurs need the support of venture capitalists, then they need to provide such lenders with a clear financial picture. They need to explain how the money will be used and to convince the lender that the business can repay its debts as they fall due. Other additional financial information, such as the ability of the owner to provide security for the loan, or any other current borrowings incurred by the entrepreneur, may also be required.[2]

Statutory requirements

Governments require businesses to keep accurate financial records, both for the purposes of collecting statistical information and, more importantly, for taxation compliance. In many cases there are legal requirements, and these cannot be avoided. For example, in both Australia and New Zealand there are statutory requirements concerning the collection of the goods and services tax and its periodical remittance to the Australian Taxation Office and NZ Inland Revenue department respectively.

Viability

For any proposed new business venture, entrepreneurs need to assure investors and themselves that the idea is, in fact, financially viable. To do this, documentation must be prepared that shows the firm can generate sufficient sales, has enough cash flow, and can ultimately be financially rewarding enough to make the project worthwhile. Start-up firms often use projections of financial information, along with other data such as prices, to work out their break-even point (discussed in more detail in chapter 6). Other questions are also important. Is sufficient return on investment being generated? Are all assets being used productively? What will the business investment be worth in two years' time? Is there enough profit? Only financial information can answer these questions.

Profitability

For many business owners, one of the main goals of being in business is to generate a profit. As will be shown later in this chapter, *profit* does not necessarily mean funds available as cash. Many firms have access to large amounts of money (and are therefore seen as having sufficient liquidity) yet they can still fail to generate a profit. In order to determine whether a profit has been made, appropriate returns must be collected.

Goal setting

Many small business owner–managers have established other goals for themselves, apart from profitability, which they are seeking from their enterprise. These may include a satisfactory return on investment, a comfortable level of owner's drawings, or the development of a strong asset base. Financial returns can help evaluate whether such goals are realistic and are being achieved or whether the firm is failing to meet the owner's expectations.

Purchase or sale of a business

If the sale of an existing small business is being contemplated, then astute purchasers will want to carefully scrutinise the performance of the firm to date, and will require access to a comprehensive set of financial records. Vendors who wish to enhance the asking price of their firm realise that a set of accurate, verifiable documents can sometimes help improve their final selling price.

Performance appraisal

Assessing a business can take many different forms, and financial figures form an integral part of any comprehensive monitoring program. Items as diverse as the level of sales generated (sales revenue), operating costs, sales per employee, and profitability from one year to the next can all help determine business performance if appropriate financial data are collected. In many cases, such data can also be compared with industry benchmarks to determine the firm's performance relative to its competitors.

Differences between small and large firms

Is entrepreneurial and small business financial analysis similar to that undertaken by corporate entities? In many respects, the answer is 'yes', in that the documents serve largely the same purposes and take similar formats in all businesses. However, there are some differences.

It is much more difficult to prepare financial forecasts for entrepreneurial firms than for existing large firms, because the former are usually geared to a new business concept and are thus extremely hard to quantify accurately. An entrepreneur is usually making a 'best informed guess' when estimating financial projections for a new venture, since nothing can be guaranteed in advance of actual operations.

In addition, small business owners typically have to take personal responsibility for collating and presenting their own financial information, whereas in a large firm this duty is the responsibility of a specialised department with full-time experts, such as in-house accounting staff. Within a small firm, even when the task is handed over to someone else, such as a bookkeeper, the owner–manager must still be able to understand the documents and make decisions based on them. Not surprisingly, most research into financial management indicates that firms tend to become better organised and more sophisticated in their handling of financial information as they grow larger.[3]

Small firms are also less willing or able to make their financial data available to external parties. This can occur for a variety of reasons: in part, it is because their recordkeeping is frequently not as sophisticated as that of larger enterprises; however, another reason is that many business owners prefer not to divulge such information in case it is used by their competitors.[4]

Finally, both small business owners and entrepreneurs tend to take more personal financial risks than staff in a large business. Much of the business funding is drawn from their own finances. Many small business ventures operate under a sole proprietorship or partnership legal structure in which the owners are personally responsible for the debts of the firm. (In contrast, a company is a legal entity in itself, and debts and liabilities belong to the company, not the owners or shareholders.)

For all these reasons, financial control is very important to small-scale firms. However, because entrepreneurs and small business owner–managers have to be skilled in so many different areas of business activity (such as marketing, human resources, operations, logistics and sales), most tend to have only a general understanding of financial issues.[5] For this reason, this chapter focuses on getting the basics of such documents correct, rather than on providing a detailed accounting-based method.

Types of financial information

The most common financial forecasting and reporting documents used by small businesses are the sales mix forecast, cash flow statement, profit and loss statement, and balance sheet. For a new business, these financial documents will be forecasts only. In addition, information about the owner's personal expenses and personal assets and liabilities may also be required. For a completed example of these for a new business (except the balance sheet), refer to the sample business plan in the appendix to chapter 7 (p. 178).

Sales mix forecast

Sales mix forecast:
An estimate of sales of each major product or service, the revenue generated by each of these, and the resulting cost of goods sold.

A **sales mix forecast** is an estimate of the likely sales of each major product or service, the revenue generated by each of these, and the resulting cost of goods sold. It is typically prepared on a month-by-month basis. This projection helps the business owner to accurately gauge the level of sales revenue that will be generated during a year of trading.

Once the business owner has decided what products will be sold and at what price, collected market research should be used to estimate how many items of each commodity will be sold each month. This will provide an estimate of total revenue for a month.

For many items, there will also be a cost of goods sold, which represents the raw materials or trading stock (also known as *inventory*) consumed in order to generate the sales. For example, retail businesses have a very large cost of goods sold (represented by the stock they buy to sell to the purchasing public), as do manufacturers. Conversely, service-based industries typically have a very low cost of goods sold — if any at all.

Blueprints Business Planning Pty Ltd has a relatively simple sales mix forecast (see p. 191). There are only three key sales items outlined in its business plan: business plan preparation, training courses and the books sold during the training courses. Each of these is accorded a separate entry in the sales mix, and the number of sales for each month is estimated. For example, in July it is anticipated that there will be two sales of business plans, each worth $2000, along with the delivery of 15 hours of training courses at $120 per hour, and three book sales, producing a total income of $5950. The training courses also have a small cost of goods sold (representing items such as training room hire, course materials and food for participants) of $20 per hour of training, and the cost of goods sold for books is $30 each, all of which produces a total cost of goods sold of $390. This format is then replicated for the other months across the trading year, providing a total estimated monthly and annual sales revenue.

Although not foolproof, this method is more concise and sophisticated than simply making up a total sales revenue figure for the year. It can also be reviewed by outside advisers or other staff to help the business owner refine and improve the original forecast figures.

A useful additional step is to determine whether any goods will be offered for sale on credit (buy now, pay later). If so, the business owner must calculate when this money will actually be collected. In the example of Blueprints Business Planning Pty Ltd, there are no credit sales. However, it is worthwhile to look at the forecasts and determine what the impact on sales revenue would be if 10 or 20 per cent of each month's sales were made on a 30-day credit basis instead.

Cash flow statement (or forecast)

Cash flow statement (or forecast): A document that shows the movement of all cash into and out of a business during a given time frame.

A **cash flow statement (or forecast)** shows the movement of all cash into and out of the business in a given time frame. It can be used to predict the amount of funds immediately available to a business at any given moment. Although different time frames can be used, the most common reporting period is on a month-by-month basis.

A cash flow document shows how much money the business actually receives each month and how much it spends. In this way, it outlines the pattern of revenue generation and expenditure, and the amount of cash left to meet unforeseen emergencies, to fund expansion programs, to provide additional personal drawings to the owner or to meet any other contingencies. Note that, in this context, 'cash' does not literally mean just coins or banknotes; it refers to any easily convertible commodity, such as currency, cheques, credit card sales, bank orders, electronic funds transfers and internet transactions. For a cash flow document to be accurate, it is assumed that all cash funds are deposited into the business's bank account.

A cash flow forecast is worked out in the following way:

- Estimate the sales to be made over the course of a year. The sales mix is the preferred source for estimating these data. Determine not only the level of sales to be made, but also when the revenue is likely to be received. Goods sold on credit, for example, will often not be realised as cash until one or two months after the actual transfer of goods has taken place and an invoice has been issued to the customer.
- It is then necessary to calculate any other revenue that may be added to the business bank account in each month, such as additional capital contributions, bank interest earned or loans made to the business. This is important, because the cash flow forecast tries to accurately show *all* money moving in and out of the business account — not just sales revenue.
- From market research and previous experience, estimate what expenses are likely to fall due each month. Again, this must include both business and non-business expenditure that is drawn from the business's bank account. Owner's drawings for personal use, for example, should be included in this figure.
- Subtract revenue from expenses to calculate a monthly surplus or deficit.
- Note the actual bank balance the business has at the start of the trading period. This is recorded as the 'Bank balance: Start of month' amount.
- Add the first month's surplus (or deficit) to this figure to arrive at the 'Bank balance: End of month' figure.

Look again at the business plan in the appendix to chapter 7, where the entrepreneur, Jessie Jones, has decided to start a new venture, Blueprints Business Planning Pty Ltd. In the first month of trading, Blueprints Business Planning will generate $5950 in sales and receive $10 000 in the form of the owner's capital contribution. During the course of the month, a total of $24 030 will be spent on various expenses, leaving a cash shortfall for the first month of $8080. The business will begin trading in July with nothing in the bank (meaning that the entry 'Bank balance: Start of month' equals zero), and at 31 July the 'Bank balance: End of month' will be overdrawn by $8080.

Calculating the second month's income and expenditure follows the same format, except that the opening bank balance ('start of month') is exactly the same as the closing bank balance ('end of month') of the preceding month. This is because whatever funds the business has in its account at midnight on the last day of July will be exactly the same as it has on the first day of August. In the case of Blueprints Business Planning Pty Ltd, trading will begin in August with an overdraft of $8080. Over the course of the year, the closing bank balance will change significantly each month, and although it will be overdrawn for most of the year, the firm will end with a substantial cash surplus at the close of June.

For many businesses, cash flow management is a more important issue than profitability. This is because even though a business may turn out to be profitable over the course of a year, if it does not have enough funds in its bank account to meet its debts as and when they fall due, its survival may be at risk. For example, a temporary mid-year cash flow problem may result in the business being unable to pay its rent by the due date, leading to eviction from the premises. In this case, a profitable figure on the profit and loss statement at the end of the first trading year will be meaningless, because the business no longer has any premises from which to trade.

Central to understanding this process is the concept of the cash flow cycle, or the manner in which money moves through a typical small business. In many cases the payment for raw materials, labour and other costs will precede the actual sale of the finished product to the customer, which means there is a time lag between expenditure and revenue collection. This gap must be funded in some way, so a business must have sufficient **working capital** on hand to ensure that cash flow remains positive. If the customer does not pay immediately for the goods, but instead is invoiced for them and asked to pay at a later stage, then the gap between payment for expenses and cash collection is even greater, and this, in turn, will require a commensurately greater amount of working capital.

Working capital: Funds used in operating a business on a daily basis.

Cash flow can be improved in a number of ways (see the box 'Eight ways to improve cash flow' on p. 348). For example, if the owner believes that the business account will be overdrawn for a long period of time, he or she might have to provide more capital or raise a long-term loan to pay for some of the start-up costs. The owner could also seek to defer the payment of some items or spread payments over a longer period of time. What other steps could the owners of Blueprints Business Planning Pty Ltd do to reduce its substantial cash overdraft?

Finally, a cash flow document is useful for quickly evaluating performance. It shows what expenditure is being made and when; it can also help show the amount of personal drawings the owner is taking from the business (cash flow shortages often occur because the owner takes excessive amounts of money from the business). If the projection also shows that the business is likely to end up with a negative 'Bank balance: End of month' figure, then the business will either need to arrange an overdraft facility or to raise more working capital and deposit it in the account before the bank balance becomes overdrawn.

> **Eight ways to improve cash flow**
> 1. Wherever possible, collect payment in cash at the time of the sale.
> 2. Where credit is offered, always issue invoices immediately on completion of a job or sale.
> 3. Offer clients incentives or discounts to pay promptly (but note that this may have an impact on eventual net profit).
> 4. To make payment easier, allow customers to pay by credit card or online.
> 5. Chase up outstanding debtors on a regular basis.
> 6. Smooth out expenses by leasing rather than buying capital items.
> 7. Pay large bills (such as insurance premiums) monthly rather than yearly.
> 8. Minimise expenditure by reducing owner's personal drawings from the firm.

Look at Blueprints Business Planning's cash flow forecast, in which Jesse has failed to provide any estimates of bank overdraft fees and interest charges. What would such additional expenses do to the cash flow of the firm?

Profit and loss statement

Profit and loss statement:
A document that shows business-related revenues and expenses and the resulting profit or loss.

A profit is the difference between revenue earned and expenses incurred. Sometimes also known as a *statement of financial performance, revenue statement* or *income and expenses statement*, the **profit and loss statement** is a summary of the business's trading activities over a specific time frame (usually one year). It shows the total revenue generated by the business during the period, and sets out all the expenses associated with that period's activities. An example of a profit and loss statement is shown in figure 14.1 (opposite).

Depreciation:
The diminution of the value of an item through use.

Note that because the profit and loss statement is meant to accurately account for both business revenue and the expenses associated with the creation of that revenue, and to match these for a given period of time, it differs in several respects from the cash flow document. For example, it does not include revenue generated by bank loans or owner's capital contributions (since these are not sales revenue), and it also takes into account non-cash expenditure items such as **depreciation** (the diminution of the value of an item through use). Depreciation is not a cash expense, since the business owner does not actually write a cheque to cover the wearing down of the equipment. Nevertheless, it must be taken into account when determining total business costs for a period. Similarly, sales revenue generated during this period, but not yet collected, is still brought to account in this document. In a sole proprietorship or partnership, owner's drawings are not considered standard business expenses, but rather an advance on the profits eventually earned, and so are not included in the 'operating expenses' category. Finally, expenditure on capital items is usually not included in the profit and loss statement, since these constitute one-off or irregular purchases, rather than an ongoing cost of being in business.

ABC Company Pty Ltd
PROFIT AND LOSS STATEMENT
for the period 1 July 2007 to 30 June 2008

Revenues

Sales revenue	$150 000	
Less: Cost of goods sold	50 000	
Gross profit		$100 000

Operating and administrative expenses

Accounting and legal fees	3 000	
Advertising and marketing	8 000	
Depreciation	5 250	
Insurance	750	
Premises rental	12 500	
Stationery	500	
Staff wages	27 350	
Phone, electricity	1 400	
Travel	1 250	
Total expenses		60 000
Net profit		40 000
Less: Tax on profit		13 000
Net profit after tax		**$27 000**

Figure 14.1: Format of a profit and loss statement

As a result, the link between the profit and loss statement and the cash flow document is not always clear-cut or obvious. In fact, it is unusual for total figures in a cash flow document to exactly equal those in the profit and loss statement.

It can be quite difficult for an individual small business owner to take all these items and variations into account, and most entrepreneurs and small business owners are not well informed about the finer points of accounting principles. Therefore, it is usually preferable for the business owner to prepare a basic profit and loss statement that simply lays out sales revenue and expenditures in the conventional format, and to leave the accountant to make any necessary revisions.

Balance sheet:
A document that details the assets, liabilities and net worth (owner's equity) of the business.

Owner's equity (or net worth): The difference between the assets and liabilities of a business; the value of the business to the owner if all its assets were sold and all liabilities were paid.

Balance sheet

Also sometimes known as a *statement of financial position*, the **balance sheet** is a snapshot of the worth of a business at a given moment in time. It shows the value of all items owned by the business, the debts it has, and the resultant **owner's equity (or net worth)**. These three aspects are related to each other by means of a fundamental accounting equation, which can be found in all balance sheets:

$$\text{Assets} = \text{Liabilities} + \text{Owner's Equity}$$

Assets:
Items of worth
owned by the
business.

Liabilities:
Debts or financial
obligations of the
business.

Assets are items of worth owned by a business, and can be divided into two broad groups: those that are easily converted into cash if necessary (current assets) and those which cannot be quickly converted (non-current assets). Another key component is the **liabilities** (debts or financial obligations) of the firm, which can also be divided in a similar manner into current and non-current items. Finally, the difference between the total assets and total liabilities represents the owner's equity (or net worth). Theoretically, this is the value of the business to the owner if all its assets were sold and all liabilities were paid. Owner's equity is also frequently divided into two sections: the *owner's capital contribution* represents the funds the owner has put into the business to start or expand the venture, and the *retained profits* are the profit subsequently kept within the business to fund growth or bolster firm value.

A balance sheet is typically compiled at a particular moment in time, such as at the close of business on the last trading day in the financial year. Subsequent balance sheets can then be compiled at the end of the following financial years, thereby allowing a comparison of the growth and composition of business assets and liabilities over time.

Balance sheets are difficult to prepare for start-up ventures, since it is difficult to estimate in advance the firm's net worth at the close of the next financial year. However, they are important for existing enterprises, whose owners will be keen to know if the worth of their business has increased over the last year.

No balance sheet is included for Blueprints Business Planning in its business plan, since it is a start-up venture. However, figure 14.2 shows the standard format of a balance sheet for another hypothetical firm.

XYZ Trading Solutions Pty Ltd
BALANCE SHEET
as at 1 July 2007

Assets

Current assets:	
Cash at bank	$ 10 000
Accounts receivable	12 000
Work in progress	22 000
Prepaid expenses	14 000
Non-current assets:	
Property	50 000
Less: Depreciation	(10 000)
Equipment	132 000
Less: Depreciation	(11 000)
Goodwill	12 000
Total assets	$231 000

Liabilities

Current liabilities:	
Overdraft	$ 3 000
Accounts payable	18 000
Provision for taxes	5 000
Non-currrent liabilities	
Long-term loans	98 000
	$124 000

Owner's equity (net worth)

Owner's capital contribution	$ 70 000
Retained profits	37 000
Total owner's equity	$107 000

Figure 14.2: Format of a balance sheet

A word about the goods and services tax

Some nations, such as Australia, Singapore and New Zealand, operate a broad-based consumption tax that requires businesses to levy and collect a tax when selling goods or services (see table 11.4, p. 286, for these countries' GST rates). This is most commonly referred to as a goods and services tax (GST). Similar systems apply in the United States, Europe and the United Kingdom (where it operates as a value-added tax, or VAT). What impact do these tax systems have on a firm's financial statements?

In the first place, it affects both the sales mix and the cash flow documents. Adding a 10 per cent GST to the price of goods or services in Australia, for example, will cause the sales price to increase accordingly. The cash flow will also need to reflect the outflow of GST payments to the tax office (which may occur monthly, quarterly or annually).

However, this inflated price is not shown in the profit and loss statement — only the GST-free sales revenue is given. Why? Because the GST is not revenue earned by the firm — it is money held in trust, so to speak, for a government tax authority. For example, a firm's sales of $1100 in goods ($1000 + 10 per cent GST) would show only $1000 as sales revenue and no GST expense in the profit and loss statement. But the $100 does show up on the balance sheet as a liability if it is due and has not yet been forwarded to the tax authority. (In the business plan in the appendix to chapter 7, these figures have been excluded to help simplify the explanation of the document construction process.)

Personal expenses

Sometimes it is necessary to know the level of the business owner's personal expenditure. If the firm operates as a sole proprietorship or partnership, then money taken out of the business is referred to as the owner's **drawings**. (In a company structure, an owner–manager who works in the business is regarded as an employee of the business, and so such payments are treated as part of the overall wages and salaries bill.) Compiling this figure on a month-by-month basis makes it possible to determine whether the business can afford to pay this amount to the owner on a regular basis. The amount and type of spending made by the owner can usually be broken down into a number of different categories (such as expenditure on food, clothing, housing, medical care and recreation).

Drawings: The income the business owner takes out of the business.

This amount is then fed into the cash flow forecast to see whether the level of drawings can be maintained by the business. If not, the business owner must either reduce the level of personal expenditure or generate additional sales revenue.

For example, our entrepreneur, Jessie Jones of Blueprints Business Planning, requires a total of $41 320 per annum to live. This amount is shown as the 'Staff — director's wages' line item in both the cash flow forecast and the projected profit and loss statement in the firm's business plan (in the appendix to chapter 7). Since both documents show that the firm can accommodate this expenditure and still remain both liquid and profitable, Jessie has been able to demonstrate that the business is a viable full-time income source for her.

Owner's assets and liabilities

It may be necessary for the business owner to provide information on the composition and level of personal worth. This is often required by financiers, who will typically lend funds to small businesses only if the funds can be secured against the owner's personal assets. Many entrepreneurs seeking to launch new ventures face similar hurdles. This **owner's assets and liabilities** document is similar to a business balance sheet, in that both documents present a statement of assets and liabilities, and the resulting difference between them (net worth).

Owner's assets and liabilities: A document that shows the private assets, liabilities and net worth of a business owner.

Jessie Jones's personal assets are included in Blueprints Business Planning's business plan. They show a person with considerable assets ($430 000) and substantial net personal worth ($227 800). Therefore, in financial terms, it seems that Jessie would be a successful applicant for bank finance should it be required.

Forecasts or historical documents?

All the documents discussed can be prepared either as estimates of likely future performance or as historical records (that is, a chronicle of what has actually happened). Tax returns, for example, are a form of historical profit and loss statement, whereas a sales revenue budget for the next year is essentially a forecast of the next year's sales mix. New business ventures are based heavily on future estimates, whereas existing firms use both historical (actual) data and trend projections when preparing forecasts. In many cases, it pays to compare the two sets of documents, since original forecasts can often be substantially different from what is finally achieved, and they need to be examined to find out where the discrepancies lie and how they can be corrected in the future.

Entrepreneur profile

Goh Ai Yat

Financial information is not only a useful tool for internal control but also a valuable means of market and competitor analysis. An enterprising Malaysian has been able to use the demand for up-to-date business and financial information to build her own successful business.

Ms Goh Ai Yat and her team from SBF.com Sdn Bhd have been data-mining publicly available economic, industry and financial information in the country since 2001. The information, processed and collated for easy reference and use, is sold online on a subscription basis as well as on a piecemeal basis via its website (<www.creditassess.com>) to organisations that need it. The website boasts a databank that contains comprehensive financial data and information on all the companies listed on the Malaysian Stock Exchange.

'Making the right decisions quickly requires timely, up-to-date and reliable data and information,' Ms Goh explains. 'Gathering, collating and processing such data and information, however, can be a very time-consuming and costly process. It can often be so resource-intensive that organisations find it too difficult to do so, which in turn means a lower quality of decision making by managers.

'It was with this in mind that creditassess.com was conceived and developed as an alternative. It allows organisations to quickly find and access corporate data at minimal cost.'

Ms Goh is the Chief Executive Officer of sbf.com Sdn Bhd, as well as a management trainer and consultant who has worked in Singapore, Malaysia and Indonesia. Prior to setting out on her own several years ago, she was attached to Sogelease (M) Sdn Bhd as its Deputy General Manager, and held various management positions at Hong Leong Finance (M) Bhd, United Orix Leasing Bhd and Supreme Finance (M) Bhd. She is also actively involved in advising and helping local businesspeople in structuring their financing needs, preparing feasibility reports, and developing new markets and business tie-ups.

The company operates from offices in Kuala Lumpur with a team of 20 staff. It is now poised for its next phase of growth through working with strategic alliance partners to provide value added information to investors in Malaysia and Singapore.

Analysing financial data

The collection of financial information is not an end in itself. Once compiled, the figures in a profit and loss statement or balance sheet can be used to assess the performance of the business. One simple way of doing this is to compare one year's figures with another's. However, this may not always be effective, since total (absolute) amounts may vary greatly from one time to the next. In addition, simply using dollar value figures makes it difficult to compare performances between firms, since the turnover of other businesses may be higher or lower than the owner's firm.

To this end, business analysts have developed a number of useful ratios to measure performance. Ratios have the benefit of converting absolute figures into meaningful proportions, so allowing for differences in firm size or turnover. Moreover, most industries have evolved general indicator ratios that are commonly used as benchmarks by firms within that sector. These are handy 'rules of thumb' which can be used to assess the performance of one's own business against industry standards. Ratios can also be used internally, to compare the firm's performance on a particular dimension over the years.[6]

Profitability ratios

A key issue in financial management is the creation of sufficient profit. How much profit is the business making for each dollar of goods or services that it sells? The higher the profit margin, the better. Two key profitability indicators are derived from the profit and loss statement, and they analyse the profit generated in relation to the sales performance of the business:

$$\text{Gross profit margin \%} = \frac{\text{Gross profit}}{\text{Sales turnover}}$$

$$\text{Net profit margin \%} = \frac{\text{Net profit before tax}}{\text{Sales turnover}}$$

Both the gross profit and net profit margins can be compared with industry-wide benchmarks. A low gross profit margin compared with industry norms indicates a relatively high cost of goods (raw materials or trading stock) expense item, whereas a high percentage result indicates that the manager is keeping raw materials costs down. Net profit is the bottom line for most businesses — how much is available for the owner? The average net profit margin of all Australian firms is approximately nine per cent, although some industries (such as the services sector) usually produce much higher margins, and other industries (such as retail traders and hospitality firms) underperform.[7]

There are two other useful profitability ratios that assess how effectively the existing assets of the enterprise are being used to help create a profit. These are return on equity and return on assets.

$$\text{Return on equity} = \frac{\text{Net profit before tax}}{\text{Owner's equity}}$$

What sort of return is the owner receiving for the funds he or she has invested in the business? This formula estimates the return on the investment that has been made by the owner of the business to establish and fund the venture. A high return on equity is indicative of a very productive use of one's own capital contribution; a low figure is generally regarded as a poor performance.[8]

$$\text{Return on assets} = \frac{\text{Net profit before tax}}{\text{Total assets}}$$

How well is the firm using the assets (not just the owner's contribution) under its control? Again, a higher level of return is more desirable. A declining ratio usually indicates that expenses are rising faster than sales or that increases in the firm's total asset base are occurring more rapidly than any increase in its net profit.

Liquidity ratios

These indicators are essentially measures of the business's ability to survive. A common cause of failure among small firms and new business ventures is short-term cash flow problems, such as an inability to meet the demands of creditors. Liquidity ratios are designed to evaluate how well the firm's cash flow is being managed.

$$\text{Current ratio} = \frac{\text{Current assets}}{\text{Current liabilities}}$$

This ratio is drawn from the business's balance sheet, and indicates the firm's ability to repay its short-term debts.[9] A desirable result for an established firm in many industries is a figure of about 2. Firms embarking on a period of rapid growth may have a lower figure, whereas those with a long operating cycle (such as firms that take a long time to collect debts) may have a higher figure.

$$\text{Liquid ('quick') ratio} = \frac{\text{Current assets} - \text{Trading stock}}{\text{Current liabilities}}$$

A variant of the current ratio, the liquid ratio determines how quickly a firm could meet its short-term debts if payment was required in a short period of time. Because trading stock typically takes some time to be sold, it is removed from the equation. A satisfactory ratio level here for many different types of firm is about 1, although this may vary from one industry to another.

Efficiency ratios

A number of other ratios are used to monitor particular aspects of business operations.

How efficiently are the total assets of the business being used to generate sales? A high level of asset turnover indicates that the business's asset base is being well used in order to maximise sales revenue. A declining turnover rate can be a cause for concern, since it indicates some inefficiencies in the deployment of the firm's assets and possibly also in its marketing strategy.

$$\text{Asset turnover} = \frac{\text{Sales}}{\text{Total assets}}$$

An indication of the financial structure of the business, the ownership ratio measures the proportion of the business owned by the owner–manager. When the ratio drops below 50 per cent, it indicates that financiers and creditors have more involvement in the firm than is probably desirable.

$$\text{Ownership ratio} = \frac{\text{Owner's equity}}{\text{Total assets}}$$

The debt-to-equity ratio is another way of measuring the financial structure and risk distribution in the firm. This formula measures the extent of a firm's debt burden. A high debt ratio (say, over 1) can be a cause for concern, since it indicates the business has a high risk profile caused by excess debt.[10]

$$\text{Debt-to-equity ratio} = \frac{\text{External debts}}{\text{Owner's equity}}$$

The stock turnover ratio evaluates how many times a year the business sells, or turns over, its trading stock. The higher the resulting figure, the quicker the business is 'churning' through sales. Generally a high stock turnover rate is desirable, as a relatively quick turn around between obtaining goods and reselling them helps improve the firm's cash flow and reduces the risk of potential losses from holding outdated stock.

$$\text{Stock turnover} = \frac{\text{Annual cost of goods}}{\text{Average stock on hand}}$$

Keeping records of financial information

When a business begins to operate, there needs to be a system that allows for the systematic collection, summary and preservation of the financial transactions that take place. This recordkeeping process is an essential step for the construction of historical financial documents, and is often required by law.

Such records must usually be kept for several years after the financial year in question has ended, and must be stored in either a hard format (written documentary) or electronic format accessible to statutory bodies such as taxation authorities. In many countries, records must be maintained in a particular language (such as English in Australia).

What would you do?

Rolling in money?

As a way of raising some extra cash income, you've recently gone into business with two of your fellow students, running a hot dog stall on weekends at the local community markets. These markets attract a wide range of both local residents and tourists, and you've agreed to share the workload between you. After three weeks of trading, all three of you sit down together one night to work out exactly how much your little venture has made.

'I've kept a list of our expenditure to date, and I've been putting the money we made into a drawer at my parents' place for safekeeping,' says Kelly proudly. 'I took all of our accounts that we've been keeping in this pile of papers, and looked through them. The first week, we earned $150 and spent $120. Week two, we collected $240 but only spent $80. And last weekend our revenue was $230 and our expenses were $130.'

'Great,' states Jane. 'We've got $100 in the bank, so it all seems okay. Why don't we split the profits three ways? That would give us $33 each.'

However, Kelly isn't particularly happy with this idea. 'I did put in $50 of my own money at the start so we could buy our first lot of sauce, buns and sausages. I need to be reimbursed before anything else. I've got the receipt to prove it, too — it's at home with my own bank statements.'

Questions

1. What problems are evident in the current financial information management procedures of this business?
2. Which financial information management tool would you introduce into this business first — a cash flow statement or a profit and loss statement? Why?

Most businesses generate a wide range of documents that need to be recorded. These can include duplicate receipts (documentary proof of money received from clients), cash till dockets, expense receipts when purchasing items from other parties, wages records, bank statements, credit card merchant transaction records, cheque books, petty cash vouchers, copies of any contracts involving financial responsibilities (such as equipment leases, rent agreements and employment contracts), vehicle log books and invoices. (Invoices are primary documents sent to clients, billing them for work performed for which payment has not yet been received; a sample is shown in figure 14.3, opposite.) It is also becoming increasingly important for businesses to maintain an accurate record of all online and electronic transactions.

CAMDEN & CLARKE DESIGN. PTY LTD
ABN 99 555 666 777
27 Wells Lane • Melbourne • Vic 3000
Phone: (03) 4141 4242
E-mail: rob@camdenclarke.com.au
Website: www.camdenclarke.com.au

TAX INVOICE		No. 001

Date: 10 July 2007
To: Super Corporation Pty Ltd
     PO Box Y6E
     St Kilda Vic 3182
Customer order no. 25/X14

For preparation of corporate design including logo, stationery, building plaques	$1650
Plus 10% GST	165
Total due	$1815

Terms: 10 working days
Contact for queries: Robert Marks

Figure 14.3: A sample invoice for a small firm

Records must be kept of the day-to-day financial activities of a business. Some of the more common types of records are the following:[11]

- A *sales journal* is used to record the sales made by the business, either on a daily or weekly basis.
- A *purchases journal* provides information about purchases made for business-related activities. This can include the purchase of trading stock, equipment, services and any other goods.
- A *petty cash book* is a record of minor cash expenses such as newspapers or a carton of milk, reimbursing a taxi fare for a staff member, or the occasional small unexpected expense that must be paid immediately in cash.
- An *accounts receivable ledger* is a record of outstanding debtors (people who owe the business money). This occurs when a business sells items on credit to customers, sends out an invoice, and has to wait for the payment to be made. If most sales are made in this way and the money is not collected quickly enough, then a cash flow problem can emerge. An *ageing schedule* is often used to analyse how long various accounts have been outstanding, and to determine whether the number of debtors and the outstanding amounts are increasing.
- An *accounts payable ledger* shows the outstanding bills the business must still pay to its creditors. It is a list of purchases the firm has made on credit and not yet paid for.
- An *asset register* is a list of the capital equipment purchased for the business — what items were bought, when, and for what price. This information is very useful for calculating depreciation expenses in the profit and loss statement (via

a *depreciation schedule*). It can also help if an insurance claim has to be made for lost, stolen or damaged assets.

Generally, all these records are brought together and consolidated in a *general ledger*. However, such a ledger can sometimes be quite complex and time consuming for a small firm to manage, especially if staff do not have experience in bookkeeping systems. For this reason, many small business advisers recommend that firms focus on maintaining effective cash books or cash journals.[12]

Cash journals are records of all the revenue collected and expenses incurred by the business each month. They record each item of revenue and expense as and when the relevant cash or cash equivalent is paid (similar to the way in which a cash flow document is prepared). The journals provide summary details of all money spent and received, whether by hard currency, cheque, electronic transaction, credit card or money order.

As figure 14.4 (p. 359) shows, a cash receipts journal records all cash receipts, detailing the date collected, the source of the funds, the invoice number (to cover accounts receivable as they are collected) and the amount received. Additional columns help analyse the business activity that generated the revenue (in this example, we have used a hypothetical document for Camden & Clarke Design Pty Ltd, whose main activities are consulting, corporate designing and stationery sales). A final 'sundries' column is used to account for unusual or one-off items. A similar format applies to the cash payments journal in figure 14.5 (p. 359), except that the columns analyse expense categories instead of revenue. As figure 14.6 (p. 360) shows, this information can then be used to help prepare a cash flow statement.

A more detailed and comprehensive system of recordkeeping is desirable for larger businesses or for complicated dealings in smaller businesses. It is usually more time- and cost-effective for the business owner to delegate this duty to another staff member or to outsource it to an accountant or bookkeeper. There are many computerised accounting packages available today, such as MYOB and QuickBooks, which are tailored to the needs of a business according its size, nature and number of employees. MYOB, for example, is widely used in small to medium-sized businesses in Australia.

Simple steps to improve recordkeeping
- Open a bank account in the name of the business.
- Keep all personal expenses of the business owner separate from business expenses, if possible.
- Ensure all business expenses are paid from a business account.
- Keep a 'paper trail' to help justify all expenses.
- File all documents in an organised manner.
- Ensure the business bank account has cheque-writing and electronic funds transfer facilities.
- Talk to an accountant before the start of trading, to ensure the firm's recordkeeping system meets the accountant's needs as well.

Figure 14.4: Format of a simple cash receipts journal for Camden & Clarke Design Pty Ltd

Date	Received from	Inv. no.	Total amount	Consulting	Corporate designing	Stationery sales	Sundries	Notes
1 July	R Marks	nil	1000.00				1000.00	Capital owner's contribution
18 July	Super Corp.	001	1650.00		1650.00			
27 July	Bronze Bros	003	3000.00		3000.00			
29 July	Sunshine Pty Ltd	002	200.00	200.00				
Total			5850.00	200.00	4650.00		1000.00	

Figure 14.5: Format of a simple cash payments journal for Camden & Clarke Design Pty Ltd

Date	Payment method	Paid to	Total amount	Accounting and legal	Advertising	Bank fees	Salaries	Materials	Sundries	Notes
2 July	chq. 02	Tax solutions	100.00	100.00						Advice
3 July	chq. 03	Chronicle newspaper	25.50		25.50					
3 July	chq. 04	BP Petrol	50.00						50.00	
15 July	chq. 05	F Smith	200.00				200.00			
18 July	Visa	FE Books	38.00					38.00		Research
28 July	Direct debit	NewBank	13.50			13.50				Account fees
Total			427.00	100.00	25.50	13.50	200.00	38.00	50.00	

Camden & Clarke Design Pty Ltd
CASH FLOW STATEMENT
for the period 1 July to 31 July

Revenues	
Consulting	$ 200.00
Corporate designing	4650.00
Sundries	1000.00
Total revenues	$5850.00
Expenses	
Accounting and legal fees	100.00
Advertising	25.50
Bank fees	13.50
Salaries	200.00
Materials	38.00
Sundries	50.00
Total expenses	427.00
Cash surplus (deficit)	$5423.00

Figure 14.6: Format of a completed cash flow statement, based on the cash journals of Camden & Clarke Design Pty Ltd

Summary

Financial information management collates objective data that can be used to create and operate business enterprises efficiently. This information can be used to evaluate the business, help raise finance, meet legal recordkeeping obligations, assess the viability and profitability of a new entrepreneurial venture, help in the sale of an existing firm, and help measure goal achievements and operational performance in existing firms.

Financial documents usually required in a new or small business include the sales mix forecast, cash flow forecast/statement, profit and loss statement and balance sheet. In addition, because most new and small firms typically are funded by the owners and must pay for their upkeep, two other documents are also useful: a statement of the owner's personal assets and liabilities, and an estimate of the owner's personal drawings from the business.

Common analytical ratios used to analyse the profit and loss statement and/or balance sheet include profitability ratios (gross profit, net profit, return on equity, return on assets); liquidity ratios (current, quick); and efficiency ratios (asset turnover, ownership, debt-to-equity, stock turnover).

Financial information is collected by recording information from all invoices, receipts and documentation relating to financial transactions in journals. For a very small firm, the most important of these are the cash payments and cash receipts journals, which record all revenue and expenditure. These journals are then used by an accountant to prepare other financial documents. Computerised accounting packages are available, tailored to the needs of small and medium-sized businesses.

REVIEW QUESTIONS

1. Why is it necessary to maintain accurate financial information?

2. Explain the four basic business financial documents and two personal financial documents discussed in this chapter.

3. What are the different types of ratios that can be used to analyse the financial information provided by a small firm? How are they calculated?

4. What are the different types of financial record found in most businesses?

5. How can cash journals be used to compile a cash flow document?

DISCUSSION QUESTIONS

1. What impact would a 10 per cent GST have on the financial documents in the Blueprints Business Planning Pty Ltd business plan shown in the appendix to chapter 7?

2. If you were an entrepreneur planning a new business venture, would you prepare the financial forecasts yourself, or use an accountant? Why?

3. How can you increase the gross profit margin in a retail business?

EXERCISES

1. *The Canberra Surf Shop — start-up costs and budget*
   This exercise will give you practice in developing a cash flow document. Read through the description and then complete the cash flow statement for the Canberra Surf Shop, using the blank pro forma provided on page 363.

   Part 1: The first month
   In the first month of business (January), the Canberra Surf Shop is largely pre-occupied with setting up. As a result, it earns only $1000 in sales. These are cash sales and not credit — the owner, Maxine Gold, hasn't yet made arrangements to provide credit facilities. She has borrowed $12 000 in a long-term loan from the bank. No other money is used to fund the shop's operations.

   However, there have been plenty of start-up costs. The accountant charged $900 for advice on establishing a bookkeeping system; $450 was spent on advertising; Eastern Power Corporation required a prepayment of $300 for the electricity supply; the insurance broker asked for the first insurance premium payment of $100; and a video display unit was leased for two months, with a monthly payback fee of $200. No loan repayments were due to the bank yet, but running the car to the coast to examine the surf tour possibilities cost $500 in repairs and fuel. A good lease was negotiated on the shop, but two months payment (at a cost of $400 per month) was required in advance. The new logo on the stationery looks good; it cost $400 to design and print. However, while preparing to open, Maxine's only staff member, John, put a ladder through an uninsured $1200 plate glass window that had to be replaced immediately. Despite this, Maxine still paid him his $460 weekly wage (gross — it includes $60 a week in tax, which must be remitted to the taxation authorities immediately).

Getting started meant that the firm charged up a telephone bill of $360. Finally, the Canberra Surf Shop spent $6800 to purchase new clothing stock, and another $3000 to buy some surfboards, skateboards and a windsurfer to sell.

Required:

(a) Prepare a cash flow projection for the first month of operations of the Canberra Surf Shop (using the pro forma provided on page 363). Make sure it also includes the owner's drawings of $500 for all her hard work to date. What is the cash position at the end of January? Is there a surplus or shortfall and how much is it? (Assume that the first month equals four weeks exactly, and that all figures are exclusive of GST.)

Part 2: Second month of operations

Things are moving! February has been good to the shop. Maxine earned $16 500 in sales this month (all cash — still no credit card facilities). Better still, some additional clothing stock cost only $6850 to buy.

Of course, there were expenses. Advertising, John's wages, the phone, insurance and video leasing expenses all cost as much as last month. In addition, there was an electricity bill of $150, bank charges of $6, and the first instalment on the loan repayments of $644. The business was also charged $20 in bank interest for the overdraft caused by last month's cash shortfall.

Despite this, Maxine paid herself only $500 again this month. This is a smart move — Maxine is looking after her cash flow!

Required:

(b) Complete the cash flow statement (p. 363) for the Canberra Surf Shop's second month of operations. How is the cash flow looking now? How much cash (if any) will the owner have on hand at the start of the third month?

(c) Add the columns and thus create the company's profit and loss statement for the two-month period.

2. *Preparing some financial records for Blueprints Business Planning Pty Ltd*

Jessie Jones finds that running a full-time business alone can be more complicated than originally expected. During the course of the first month (July), she makes four sales totalling $3000 (one for training and the others for business planning), but also spends up considerably: $500 is paid to Aherns Ltd for office furniture on 2 July, and $1000 is paid to OfficeWorks for stationery three days later. On 15 July, Jessie pays herself $800, and a fortnight later another $400. The cost of company formation ($1200) was paid to the Australian Securities and Investments Commission on 1 July.

On the first day of the month, she managed to secure $4500 of the original capital contribution forecast in the business plan (all from herself), and the promise of another $1500 if she needs it. She paid $600 to Telstra Corporation on 25 July for phone line installation.

Of her clients, the first job (worth $900 from Newrise Computing for a business plan) is paid for as soon as it is completed on 12 July. The second job worth $500 (for a one-day training course for Squirrel Health Shops) is paid for on 25 July. The other clients — Mercury Energy ($1500) and Indifferent Enterprises ($100) — have not paid by the end of July.

Canberra Surf Shop CASH FLOW STATEMENT For the period 1 January to 28 February		
Item	**January**	**February**

All expenses are paid by cheque, and in sequential order. The business starts activities with no money in the bank.

Devise cash receipts and cash payments journals, a cash flow statement and a profit and loss statement for the firm's first month of trading. What is the total cash revenue and expenses? What is the closing bank balance in the cash flow? What profit (or loss) has the firm recorded? How do these compare with the forecasts in the original business plan?

Use the blank pro forma sheets on pages 364 and 365 to do your calculations.

Blueprints Business Planning Pty Ltd
CASH RECEIPTS JOURNAL
for the month of July

Blueprints Business Planning Pty Ltd
CASH PAYMENTS JOURNAL
for the month of July

Blueprints Business Planning Pty Ltd		
FINANCIAL STATEMENTS		
for the month of July		
Item	Cash flow	Profit and loss

SUGGESTED READING

Harvard Business School Press, *Finance for Managers*, Harvard Business School Press, Cambridge, MA, 2002.

Holmes, S., Hutchinson, P., Forsaith, D., Gibson, B. & McMahon, R., *Small Enterprise Finance*, John Wiley & Sons, Brisbane, 2003.

Williams, A., *Keeping the Score: Record Keeping, Financial Planning and Management for Small Business*, McGraw-Hill, Sydney, 2001.

CASE STUDY

House As Art Pty Ltd

Alicia and Andrew decided to set up their own business. They had studied architecture together at Melbourne University, and shared a house in the early years when they were working for different, large architecture practices.

With her flair for bold colours and contemporary fashions, Alicia was the extrovert of the pair. Vivacious, well spoken and a keen networker, she was a natural marketer and promoter. On the other hand, Andrew was quiet and sedate. He worked hard, made sure that all the administration was done, and got back to the drawing board only when he was satisfied that all necessary compliance and paperwork had been completed.

Initially they had planned to work in the field they had trained for, but they quickly dropped their interest in architecture when it became apparent that there were many more opportunities available in the design field. Using Alicia's extensive contacts, and networking with the many art students they had met while at university, the duo found that the real demand was for interior and exterior design of new houses and commercial buildings.

Many architectural practices simply designed the outside of the buildings they were planning for clients; they usually did not attempt to devise a 'whole-of-building' plan that also covered the interior. Using their architectural skills, Alicia and Andrew were able to provide customers with innovative, exciting house designs and furniture that fitted in neatly with the architect's plans.

After a year working under a partnership structure, they realised that they couldn't do all the work themselves. They found an external investor, and the business was restructured as a private company, in which Andrew and Alicia held 16 000 shares each. The third owner (with the balance of the shares) was Marian Borst, who owned a building company and had interests in several other businesses related to real estate. Part of the start-up funds were used to buy a strata-titled office (they regarded this as a smart investment that would give them secure premises), and to provide some of the furnishing stock necessary to equip clients' buildings.

The business has now been trading for two years as a private company, and during this time they have been able to pick up several large contracts with building developers. Work of this nature is often unpredictable. Demand is closely tied to the overall fortunes of the housing and construction industries, which in turn are based on broader economic fundamentals. Tastes for interior fashions change quickly, and clients are not always willing to pay the high prices that Alicia and Andrew charge.

The company operates under a relatively lean structure. The growing demand for their services means that other staff have had to be employed, although most work is outsourced to subcontractors. The only people working in the office are Alicia, Andrew, another architect and a design student from the local technical college who works part time.

Recordkeeping and accounting services are provided by an external accountancy practice. The firm invoices its work, providing generous credit terms. Their work is highly valued, and they operate in a relatively exclusive, specialised market niche. Marian has indicated before that she would be willing to buy out the pair if Andrew finally wanted to fulfil his long-term dream of working with the under-privileged in Africa, and if Alicia decided to move on. Although the office space is shown in the books at purchase (historical) cost, it has actually appreciated in value significantly, and is now worth much more than the $280 000 they originally paid for it — perhaps as much as $400 000.

Business has remained brisk. The two operators are now trying to work out what next to do with their business. Should they expand and take on more staff? This may require borrowing funds. Should they take a 'steady as she goes' approach and continue as they are doing? Or should they sell out while the going is good?

Questions

1. Analyse the attached financial documents. Is the business growing or declining?

2. Are there any financial problems evident in the current figures?

3. What options do you think Alicia and Andrew should pursue: expansion, a continuation of current performance, or sell their interest in the firm?

(*Note:* All figures shown in the financial statements are exclusive of GST.)

House As Art Pty Ltd
PROFIT AND LOSS STATEMENT
for the financial years 1 July to 30 June

	Year 1	Year 2
Sales revenue	$1 000 000	$1 150 000
Less: Sales returns and allowances	35 000	45 000
Net sales	965 000	1 105 000
Less: Cost of goods sold	505 000	630 000
Gross profit	460 000	475 000
Less: Operating expenses		
Salaries	220 000	230 000
Office expenses	95 000	80 000
Less: Financial expenses	2 500	3 000
Net profit	$ 142 500	$ 162 000

House As Art Pty Ltd
BALANCE SHEET
for the financial years 1 July to 30 June

	Year 1	Year 2
Assets		
Current assets:		
Cash	$ 60 000	$ 80 000
Accounts receivable	200 000	280 000
Less: Allowance for doubtful debts	(10 000)	(14 000)
Stock	100 000	80 000
Prepaid expenses	5 000	4 000
Total current assets	355 000	430 000
Non-current assets:		
Office building	280 000	280 000
Less: Accumulated depreciation	(50 000)	(60 000)
Equipment	140 000	140 000
Less: Accumulated depreciation	(60 000)	(80 000)
Total non-current assets	310 000	280 000
Total assets	$665 000	$710 000
Liabilities		
Current liabilities		
Accounts payable	$ 66 000	$ 32 000
Taxes payable	28 000	11 000
Loan instalment	20 000	20 000
Total current liabilities	114 000	63 000
Non-current liabilities		
Bank loan	200 000	180 000
Total liabilities	$314 000	$243 000
Owners' equity		
Ordinary shares (50 000 at $2)	$100 000	$100 000
Retained profits	251 000	367 000
Total owners' equity	$351 000	$467 000

ENDNOTES

1. R.G.P. McMahon, 'Business growth and performance and the financial reporting practices of Australian manufacturing SMEs', *Journal of Small Business Management*, vol. 39, no. 2, April 2001, pp. 152–64.
2. J.C. Brau, 'How do banks price owner–manager agency costs? An examination of small business borrowing', *Journal of Small Business Management*, vol. 40, no. 4, October 2002, pp. 273–86.
3. K. Moores & J. Mula, *Managing and Controlling Family Owned Businesses: A Life Cycle Perspective of Australian Firms*, Research Report, Bond University, Gold Coast, 1993.

4. A.N. Berger & G.F. Udell, 'The economics of small business finance: The roles of private equity and debt markets in the financial growth cycle,' *Journal of Banking and Finance*, no. 22, 1998, pp. 873–97.

5. R.G.P. McMahon & S. Holmes, 'Small business financial management practices in North America: A literature review', *Journal of Small Business Management*, vol. 29, no. 2, April 1991, pp. 19–30.

6. J.W. English, *How to Organise and Operate a Small Business in Australia*, 7th edn, Allen & Unwin, Sydney, 1998.

7. C. James, 'Why it's hard to make a buck', *Australian Financial Review*, 3–4 August 2002, pp. 22–3; Australian Bureau of Statistics, *Business Operations and Industry Performance 2000–2001*, cat. no. 8142.0, ABS, Canberra, 2002, p. 8.

8. B. Brown, 'How to rate a company', *Weekend Australian*, 3–4 August 2002, p. 33.

9. ibid.

10. ibid.

11. J.W. English, *see* note 6.

12. G. Gaujers, J.A. Harper & J. Browne, *Guide to Managing a Successful Small Business in Australia*, McGraw-Hill, Sydney, 1999.

Part 4
Selected topics

Chapter 15

Managing growth and transition

LEARNING OBJECTIVES

After reading this chapter, you should be able to:

- explain the various dimensions of growth in a business enterprise
- discuss the four basic theories that explain how and why organisations grow
- explain the major stages in a typical business life cycle
- outline the changing role of the entrepreneur/small business owner as the business grows
- identify different methods of 'harvesting' a business venture.

M ost small businesses have one of the following goals: to survive; to consolidate and continue to be successful; or to expand and grow. However, on closer inspection, it becomes clear that these three basic activities are often variations on the same theme, and they can be reduced to a focus on expansion and growth in one way or another. After all, growth is a dynamic process and means more than just an increase in size. It also encompasses development and change within an organisation, and it alters the way the organisation interacts with its external environment. The nature of any business organisation is multifaceted, and entrepreneurs and small business owners must constantly view the growth and development of their venture from many different perspectives.

Once a business has grown, what happens next? Entrepreneurship is seen by many as a journey, not a destination. A common sentiment among successful entrepreneurs is that it is the challenge and exhilaration of starting up and building a venture that gives them the greatest kick. Once they have reached this goal, they may seek to enjoy the fruits of their labour through various 'harvest' strategies, such as management buyouts, mergers and acquisitions, public offerings or outright sale.

This chapter outlines the various dimensions of growth, and presents four basic theories on how organisations change. The analysis focuses on the life cycle of the venture and the changing role of the entrepreneur. Finally, several strategies for harvesting and maximising return from the successful business venture are detailed.

The dimensions of business growth

The growth of the venture can be seen from various perspectives, such as: (1) *financial* — growth in income, expenditure and profits; (2) *strategic* — growth in market share and competitive advantages; and (3) *organisational* — growth in organisational form, process and structure.[1]

The various dimensions of business growth must be considered in relation to one another (figure 15.1). Financial growth is a measure of the business's performance in serving the need of its markets, and thus it is a measure of the resources the market has allocated to the firm. The firm must convert those resources into assets. These assets are configured by the organisational structure. Financial growth provides the means by which a business can obtain additional resources (such as staff, equipment, information) to fuel strategic growth and to acquire additional assets. In turn, financial growth is fuelled by the performance of the strategic options taken and by the accumulation of assets within an extended organisational structure.

Figure 15.1: The dimensions of growth

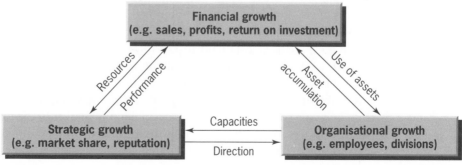

Financial growth

Financial growth relates to the development of the business as a commercial entity. It is concerned with increases in sales, the investment needed to achieve those sales, and the resulting profits. It is also concerned with increases in what the business owns: its assets. These different financial elements help to establish the value of the business — that is, the price a potential buyer would be willing to pay for it.

Analysis of the various financial documents of a business venture, such as its balance sheet and profit and loss statement, can give those interested (the entrepreneur, investors, fiscal authorities and other stakeholders) a general overview of the financial health of the venture. However, there is no absolute measure of performance, and the performance of the firm must be considered relative to its industry and over a period of time. This means that it is important for the firm to compare itself with industry-wide benchmarks in order to assess its own financial performance.

Growth will also bring some financial problems. Some growth will create a need for more spending. If extra stock, larger premises, new tools or additional staff are needed, money has to be found to pay for them. New loans may need to be taken out (in the case of long-term asset purchases), or additional working capital may need to be found for short-term requirements. Although some businesses will already have retained profits that can be drawn on, others may have to set up or extend their overdraft facilities. Businesses that do not have enough cash flow to service debt and to finance current expenses will find themselves in trouble; others may find that they do not have a suitable track record or security to obtain a loan, and so they stagnate from a lack of capital.[2]

Strategic growth

Strategic growth relates to the changes that take place in the way the organisation interacts with its environment as a coherent (or strategic) whole. This is concerned mainly with the way the business develops its capabilities in order to exploit a presence in the marketplace. From a strategic perspective, businesses are able to successfully compete in the market by developing and maintaining a competitive advantage. Growth represents the business's success in drawing in resources from its environment. It is a sign that business has been effective in competing in the marketplace. However, a competitive advantage is not static. Sustaining an advantage simultaneously develops and enhances it. Growth will influence the two basic sources of competitive advantage identified by Porter: cost and differentiation.[3]

The main source of cost advantage is experience effects. As a result of the learning experience, costs tend to fall in an exponential way as output increases linearly. Cost leadership means that the customer can be offered a lower price, leading in turn to an increase in demand and thus an increase in output.

A differentiation strategy stems mainly from knowledge advantages. These arise from knowing something about the customer, the market or the product that competitors do not know, thus enabling the business to offer something of value to the customer. The customer is prepared to pay a premium for the extra value perceived. The development of a knowledge-based advantage depends on two factors: the significance of the knowledge advantage and the rate at which it will be eroded. Clearly, these two factors work against each other. The more valuable the knowledge, the more that competitors will be encouraged to get hold of it for themselves. Knowledge is also difficult to protect. A particular innovation rarely offers more than a transient advantage. If the business aims not just to survive but to grow on the back of a differentiation strategy, then it must stay in a process of constant discovery about what it is offering the market and why the market buys it.

Organisational growth

Organisational growth relates to the changes that take place in the organisational structure, process and culture as it grows and develops. The structure of the organisation and the way that structure develops as the organisation grows are both a response to the circumstances in which the organisation finds itself and a reaction to the opportunities with which it is presented. One well-explored approach to understanding how an organisation defines its structure is provided by contingency theory. In essence, contingency theory regards the structure of an organisation as dependent on contingencies or types of factors[4] such as organisational size, operational technology, strategy, business environment and the role of the entrepreneur.

The choice of not growing

Although market forces may press for quantitative growth, this does not necessarily coincide with the personal interests of the small business owner. The relationships between personal and organisational objectives are important to understand, because they often overlap in the small firm. Thus, for the majority of small business owner–managers, the need to maximise growth, or indeed to grow at all, is not self-evident:

- Growth is rarely seen as an end in itself, and will often be sacrificed in pursuit of other objectives.
- The world of small business owner–managers is unlike that portrayed in economics textbooks, where managerially controlled firms pursue growth objectives.
- In the SME context, a growth-maximising assumption cannot therefore be made; the perceived imperative to grow is often absent.

The first barrier to growth relates to the choice of the owner–manager. Exploiting the growth potential of a firm requires an active commitment to growth on the part of the owner–manager. In many instances a fundamental reluctance to grow, fear of the risks of growth, or a desire to use the business simply to support an established lifestyle rather than to generate maximum capital appreciation constitute the major barriers to growth. The commitment to growth requires a redefinition of the role of the firm's founder. The person who started and initially built up the business is not always the best candidate to take the business forward. There is often a need to bring in professional managers and to reconstitute the firm's initial board of directors as a precondition of growth.

The second inhibitor of growth is the belief on the part of owner–managers that continued growth of the firm will lead to an erosion of their managerial and financial control over the business. The willingness to forgo growth in favour of maintaining financial self-sufficiency and managerial control inevitably sets limits on a small venture's growth.

Conceptualising growth and organisational change

In a review of development and change in organisations, Van de Ven and Poole identified four basic theories about how and why organisations change.[5] These are based on the notions of life cycle, teleology, evolution and dialectic. These four theories represent different sequences of change events that are driven by different conceptual motors and operate at different levels.

Life cycle

The notion of life cycle suggests that the business venture undergoes a pattern of growth and development much as a living organism does. A lifecycle model depicts change in an organisation as progressing through a necessary sequence of stages. Numerous authors have proposed stages of growth or lifecycle models of organisations.[6] These authors vary in the number of stages they propose and the labels they use, but the prevailing themes are clear. Often, the stages follow a pattern of start-up, growth, formalisation and so on. As it is a matter of mathematics and economics that keep rapid growth from continuing indefinitely, growth is typically a 'stage' between struggling inception and relative stability later on.

New venture development

This first stage consists of activities associated with the incubation and initial formation of the venture. At this stage, the budding entrepreneur displays a strong intention to start a business. Intention is a conscious state of mind that directs attention (and therefore experience and action) towards a specific object (goal) or a pathway to achieve it (means).[7] This concept goes beyond that of entrepreneurial propensity: people with the intention of starting a business have not only a propensity to start but also rational behaviour that will allow them to reach their goal. They have already, therefore, taken some steps towards this goal (developed a prototype, gathered some information, conducted a first market research, and saved some money).

Start-up

The second stage encompasses all the foundation work needed to formally launch the business venture. During the start-up stage, a business plan is drafted and presented to the potential key stakeholders in the venture — investors, suppliers and employees. The entrepreneur puts together various resources: financial, human and information. Different measures can be taken to protect any intellectual property owned by the firm, such as registering a patent, a trademark, or a design. The entrepreneur must also decide on a business name and legal form of organisation (sole proprietorship, partnership or company).

At this stage, the founders of the venture are usually technically or entrepreneurially oriented, and they generally disdain management activities; their physical and mental energies are absorbed in making and selling the new product. Another characteristic is the frequent and informal communication among employees. Long hours of work are rewarded by modest salaries and the promise of ownership benefits. Decisions and motivation are highly sensitive to marketplace feedback; management acts as customers react.

Growth

Most business ventures do not experience rapid growth directly after the start-up. Rather, they pass through a vital infancy stage of development.[8] Infancy occurs between the launch of the organisation and its take-off into sustained growth. It occurs typically between the second and the fifth years of operation and is characterised by efforts to achieve technical efficiency and to cope with competitive markets. A poor comprehension of the capital market, resulting in inadequate capital stock is a typical feature of the infancy stage. Owners also concentrate on overcoming technical problems and tend to play down the search for markets.

In contrast to infancy, sustained growth is typically characterised by a strong increase in demand and sales, leading in turn to a growing number of employees. This 'go-go' phase is often accelerated by technological breakthrough, aggressive or ingenious marketing, a hungry market, sluggish competition or some combination of these. Three basic challenges[9] usually confront rapid-growth firms:

- *Instant size.* When firms double or triple in size very quickly, this in turn creates problems of disaffection, inadequate skills and inadequate systems.
- *A sense of infallibility.* By virtue of their success to date, owner–managers often view their strategies and behaviour as infallible and immune from criticism.
- *Internal turmoil.* There is a stream of new faces — people who do not know one another and who do not know the firm. The business founders find themselves burdened with unwanted management responsibilities. They long for the 'good old days' and try to act as they did in the past. Decision making suffers, internal political battles abound and people burn out.

Maturity

The firm enters the maturity or stabilisation stage just after reaching its prime, when everything comes together. During this period, the business is consistently able to meets its customers' changing needs; internal discipline and organisational culture are operating effectively; and production is run with maximum efficiency.

However, this highly desirable state of affairs can quickly be lost. The maturity stage is often characterised by increased competition, consumer indifference to the firm's products and services, and a saturation of the market. Internally, staff welcome new ideas but without the excitement of the growing stages. Financial managers begin to impose controls for short-term results. The emphasis on marketing and research and development wanes. This phase is often a 'swing stage', in that it precedes the period when the firm will either innovate and move back into the growth mode or, alternatively, start to decline.

At this point, a crisis of leadership often occurs. Obviously, a strong manager is needed — one who has the necessary knowledge and skills to introduce new business techniques. But finding that manager is easier said than done. The founders often resist stepping aside, even though they are probably temperamentally unsuited to the job. Those ventures that survive the leadership crisis by installing a capable business manager usually embark on a period of sustained growth.[10]

Rebirth or decline

Several models of lifecycle theory consider that decline is not inevitable for firms reaching maturity. Firms can face a 'rebirth' before they eventually decline. For example, 'continued entrepreneurship' could be the basis of the growth rate of established firms.[11] In any case, expanding the business means expanding the amount of trade it undertakes. Expansion from any base can be achieved in one of three ways:

- *Launching new products or services.* Once a firm has built up a stable customer base and has good relationships, one option is to see what else can be sold to those customers. It may be possible to add other services, offer new products or find ways of doing business that add value to the sale (new processes).
- *Entering new markets.* Finding new customers for present products or services is another solution. For a business in which repeat sales are unlikely, it is essential to keep finding new customers. For example, many of the 'Fast 100' businesses in Australia have grown by expanding geographically, opening new offices and acquiring other businesses.[12] It is also vital to build market share and dominate a market niche. In such situations, the product offering remains the same, but may be tuned to local market conditions.
- *Diversifying.* Finding new products and new customers may be a solution if the business is cash-rich. However, this is a step that should be taken only when staff of the core business possess the requisite knowledge and experience to be successful in handling a new product or market. When this is not the case, many SMEs opt for strategic alliances or acquisitions to pursue a diversification strategy.

If the enterprise fails to implement one of those strategies and to innovate, it will face a decline in its activities. Not making waves becomes a way of life. Outward signs of respectability (dress, office decoration and titles) take on enormous importance. The business institutes witch-hunts to find out *who* did something wrong rather than trying to discover *what* went wrong and how to fix it. A strong bureaucracy is typical within firms at this stage — there are systems for everything, and employees go by the book. Cost reduction takes precedence over efforts to increase revenues.

In all lifecycle models, the development stage of the business determines the importance of different management tasks and leadership styles. Research has focused mainly on differences in internal organisational characteristics (such as leadership and policies, structure and strategy) across theorised stages. Table 15.1 (opposite) provides a summary of these characteristics.

Table 15.1: Lifecycle stage characteristics

Feature	New venture development	Start-up	Growth	Maturity	Rebirth or decline
Size	One or two people, part time	Small	Medium to large	Large	Growing (rebirth) or declining
Sales growth rate	Non-existent	Inconsistent	Rapid and positive	Slow	Bounce back (rebirth) or declining
Business tasks	Evaluate opportunity; build prototype	Set up the organisation; launch product	Capacity expansion; set up operating systems	Expense control; establish management systems	Revitalisation (new products, new markets, diversification) or recrimination (decline)
Organisational structure	Embryonic	Individualistic and entrepreneurial	Directive	Delegative	Participative (rebirth) or autocratic (decline)
Control systems	Embryonic	Market results	Standards and cost centres	Reports and profits centres	Mutual goal setting (rebirth) or red tape (decline)

Teleology

Teleology is the study of design and purpose, and it argues that 'form follows function'. In teleology theory, the purpose or goal of management (such as growth) is the final cause for guiding movement of the organisation. In this perspective, the business venture sets goals, and by adapting its actions it tries to reach its goals. Therefore, a teleological model views development as a cycle of goal formulation, implementation, evaluation and modification of goals based on what was learned by the organisation. Central to this theory is the notion of purpose in organisational change and growth. Entrepreneurs can use their vision of the future to pull the organisation forward. Comparable with the lifecycle theory, teleology theory focuses on a single organisation. However, teleology theory does not prescribe a sequence of events or specify in which direction an organisation must develop to reach its goals. It can only set a possible path and then rely on norms of decisions or actions.

A business venture can pursue different goals; growth can be one of them. Similarly, there are different ways to reach growth objectives. Also, growth is not necessarily a result of accomplishing the goals. Growth can have different meanings — a business can pursue growth in size (employees, sales); in profit (profit before tax, return on investment); in value (shareholder value, stakeholder value); and in quality (image, know-how, innovation).

Evolution

Evolution is a theoretical scheme that explains changes in structural forms of organisations across communities or industries. As in biological evolution, organisational change proceeds through a continuous circle of variation, selection and retention. Variations — the creation of new forms of organisation — are often seen to emerge by chance; they just happen. The selection of organisations occurs through the competition for scarce resources, and the environment selects entities that best fit the resource base of an environmental niche. Retention involves forces (including relative inertia and persistence) that perpetuate and maintain certain organisational forms.

Although one cannot predict which business venture will survive or fail, the overall population persists and evolves through time, according to the specified population dynamics. Birth rates, merge rates and mortality rates influence the characteristics of the population. This process is influenced by competition and legitimation. As a metaphor, evolution reminds entrepreneurs that they are operating in a competitive environment, that they must compete for scarce resources and that the venture must be efficient ('fit') in the tasks it undertakes. As business ventures perform reliably and accountably over time, they demonstrate their fitness and may acquire legitimacy.

Dialectic

The dialectical theory focuses on stability and change based on the collision of power between opposing entities. The dialectical theory begins with the assumption that organisations or members within organisations compete with each other for domination and control. This creates a collision between the entities. Change is the result of the appearance of opposing views (thesis and antithesis) and balance or imbalance of power between entities. Change occurs if an organisation or a stakeholder has sufficient power to confront and engage the status quo (the existing state). If this is not the case, the status quo will remain.

In organisational change and development, the dialectic illuminates conflict and conflict resolution at a number of levels, for example between stakeholder groups such as investors and employees, and within stakeholder groups. The latter would include, for example, political manoeuvring by managerial factions within the business. Accordingly, one of the central tasks of the entrepreneur is to resolve conflicts and bring together stakeholders (whose interests may differ) so that all benefit.

Entrepreneur profile

Li Ka-shing

Some entrepreneurs build new empires; others, like Li Ka-shing, create new eras. Mr Li not only dominates the economy of Hong Kong, he also makes his powers felt all over the world, and even influences the future of whole industries. Li's story resembles that of many successful ethnic Chinese tycoons.

Born in 1928, Li Ka-shing, at the age of 10, moved with his family to Hong Kong from Shantou in southern China. Two years later his father died, leaving him to support his mother and two siblings. For many years Mr Li worked 16-hour days selling plastic belts and watchbands. In 1950, he started Cheung Kong Industries, a plastics manufacturer that later diversified to include a property investment company. Early on, Mr Li avoided the peril of excessive debt that proved the undoing of many other local property companies; by giving landowners a share in future profits, he got around the heavy obligation of paying up-front for land. Since that time Cheung Kong has become a holding company — the investment vehicle of Li Ka-shing — and was listed on the Hong Kong Stock Exchange in 1972.

In 1979, Mr Li bought the property and trading conglomerate Hutchison Whampoa, a Hong Kong based British conglomerate, or *hong*, signalling the beginning of the rise of Chinese entrepreneurs and the beginning of the end of the British business elite. Hutchison Whampoa, which still has many mobile-phone ventures around the world, is the world's largest private port operator, with major operations in Australia, Indonesia, Hong Kong and China.

Today, the Cheung Kong Group's businesses cover a number of areas such as property development, real estate management, hotels, telecommunications, finance, retail, manufacturing, energy, infrastructure, media and biotechnology. For example, most consumers in the region would know the A.S. Watson Group, a subsidiary of Hutchison Whampoa, and a leading retail operator with over 6800 stores. Its portfolio encompasses health and beauty specialist Watson's Your Personal Store, PARKnSHOP supermarkets, Taste food galleria, and Nuance-Watson airport duty-free shops. Watson is also a major producer and distributor of water products and beverages in the region, with Watsons Water the top selling brand in Hong Kong. Cheung Kong is among the top 100 corporations in the world, with businesses in 41 countries and over 175 000 employees. It accounts for about 10 per cent of the total market capitalisation of all Hong Kong publicly quoted companies. Mr Li's net worth, an estimated US$8 billion, makes him one of the richest men in the world.

Dubbed *Chiu Yan*, or Superman, by the local press, Li Ka-shing seems infallible. People rush to buy shares in his new business ventures, as they did in July 2002 when the initial public offering of Mr Li was 120 times oversubscribed. Part of Li Ka-shing's success can be explained by luck — he has been in the right place at the right time. However, he is first and foremost a serial entrepreneur with exceptional business acumen. Not only is Mr Li particularly skilled at identifying new opportunities and launching new business ventures, he also knows how to build a business and when to exit. In 1994, he made a shrewd investment in Orange, a promising mobile-phone operator. Five years later, he sold his stake in Orange for a profit of around US$15 billion. He has always found and hired the best professional managers, many of them foreigners.

Li Ka-shing recently retired from his post as managing director of Cheung Kong but remains as its chairman. He is gradually reducing his workload and letting his eldest son, Victor, take over the reins. Mr Li, however, will still be consulted on major decisions. Now in his seventies, he is determined to challenge the saying that 'wealth does not pass down three generations' in Chinese families. He is trying to systemise the running of his business empire and incorporate his own personal management philosophy so that both his business and his philosophies will live on forever.

From the entrepreneur to the manager

Managing any business venture is a tough job. Managing a rapidly growing enterprise, however, presents a particular challenge because the essential nature of the manager's job changes with growth. As the number of employees increases, and the volume and complexity of work expands, entrepreneurs must change their fundamental approach to managing. To understand this evolution, it is essential to first define the manager's job in a way that explains the pressures being added to the system, the changes that are transpiring as a result, and the responses available to the manager.

Defining the manager's job

In order to frame the management task in a way that allows us to predict and understand the challenges that growth creates, we need to develop a model of the manager's job. Roberts[13] suggested a model that revolves around three key elements that are part of the manager's responsibilities:

- *Strategy and operation. What* task should the enterprise perform? The firm's activities are driven by its goals and its strategy. The strategy is the rationale for a set of operating activities, so the goal-setting and strategic-planning processes are key pieces in the management of the business. Where strategy is an idea or an objective, however, the firm's operations are that idea made real. Thus, the firm's strategy and operation are the set of tasks and activities that the firm is required to execute.
- *Organising. How* should tasks be structured and coordinated? This aspect of the manager's responsibilities includes all the choices about how to accomplish the strategy and operating activities — how these responsibilities are assigned to organisational units; how they are broken down into specific tasks within units; how these tasks are grouped to comprise a job; how those jobs are defined according to performance standards and procedures, tied together with systems, and coordinated to achieve the desired objectives.
- *Staffing. Who* should do the work? This element includes the people who actually fill the jobs and do the work, as well as their selection, training, development and compensation.

These three sets of duties cannot be managed in isolation. There must be some fit between strategy and structure, and between implementation and the skills and capabilities of the people in the organisation.

The manager's tools

As managers execute their responsibilities in a time-related fashion, they need to:

- *anticipate* situations and do as much as possible to prepare to deal with them — this approach includes developing sales and financial forecasts, marketing plans, operating policies and staff allocations
- *act* to carry out plans and, at the same time, deal with unanticipated issues and situations that could not possibly be planned for
- *review* the situation, both to learn everything possible in order to apply it to the next round of events and to reward employees according to their effort.

There are a variety of common tools to help owner–managers in their responsibilities in the anticipating–acting–reviewing cycle. These management tools are detailed in table 15.2. Note that although this cycle makes some intuitive sense, once a business is launched it is difficult to anticipate without first reviewing. That is, in a going concern, the cycle is more likely to begin with a review of past performance, a recasting of plans and objectives in light of this review, and a new round of action.

Note that this cycle does not occur uniformly for all areas of activity. A manager may be simultaneously anticipating bringing a new plant on stream and crafting the action plan for it, working on a new marketing and promotion effort, and reviewing the financial performance of the entire business.

Table 15.2: Tools available to the manager

Manager's responsibilities	Cycle		
	Anticipating	Acting	Reviewing
Strategy and operating	Business plans	Decisions	Plan v. actual
	Budgets	Input	Follow-up audits
	Policies	Revisions	Variance reports
Organising	Job descriptions	Delegating	Job review
	Operating procedures	Coordinating	Work flow analysis
	Workload forecasts	Controlling	Compliance audit
Staffing	Human resource strategy	Recruiting	Performance review
	Job descriptions	Motivating	Feedback
	Staffing plans	Training	Compensation

Source: Adapted from M.J. Roberts, 'Managing transitions in the growing enterprise', Teaching note 9-393-107, Harvard Business School, Boston, 12 February 1993, p. 8. Copyright © 2006 by the Harvard Business School Publishing Corporation; all rights reserved.

The steps towards professional management

Many issues need to be considered when small entrepreneur-driven structures evolve into larger, professionally managed ones. For example, strategic planning in younger and smaller firms tends to be based on personal feel or intuition, or on 'firefighting' approaches. Consequently, such firms will undergo a great deal of pain and distress unless those making the decisions learn to adopt rational and systematic approaches to decision making as their organisations grow.[14] In order to make their businesses grow beyond a certain point, entrepreneurs must be prepared to move from an *entrepreneurial* management style, with centralised decision making and informal control, to a *professional* management style that involves the delegation of decision-making responsibility and the use of formal control mechanisms.

The following four steps[15] have been identified as contributing to any successful transition to professional management:

- *Recognise the need for change.* This is often extremely difficult because it is a by-product of success. Success reinforces beliefs and behaviour that are appropriate to the entrepreneurial mode but inappropriate for the needs of a larger, more complex firm. Often, a crisis will highlight the need for change. However, knowledgeable business advisers can help the entrepreneur avoid a crisis by spotting the warning signs and indicating the need and path for change.
- *Develop human resources.* Given the change of personal role in the organisation, the entrepreneur's next step is to develop the human resources required to implement the growth model chosen. Often, people who can accept and execute responsibility are not present in the entrepreneurial organisation, because the entrepreneur's style has made it difficult for self-sufficient, independent employees to remain with the firm. To develop a competent managerial team, the entrepreneur must overcome personal loyalties that threaten the organisation.
- *Delegate responsibility.* The power of professional management arises from placing decision-making responsibility close to the sources of information. Typically, this means delegating responsibility to managers who are close to customers, suppliers and other partners of the firm. The entrepreneur–CEO must be careful, however, not to give up responsibility on key policy issues that require personal perspective.
- *Develop formal controls.* The final step in the transition process is developing formal control mechanisms. Successful entrepreneurs realise that, with the onset of delegation, they can no longer control the behaviour of individuals in the organisation; the focus of control must shift from behaviour to performance. In establishing these controls, the danger of simply adapting policies and procedures that are used at other firms must be realised.

The evolution of ethnic Chinese family businesses

The need for the entrepreneur's role to change as the business grows applies equally to Western and Asian entrepreneurs. Here again, in order for their companies to continue growing beyond a certain point, entrepreneurs must be prepared either to change their beliefs about organisation to match the life stage of their business, or to face the premature stagnation, decline and even death of their firm.

In a seminal study of Chinese family firms operating in Hong Kong, Indonesia, Singapore and Taiwan, Redding concluded that such companies would not give rise to big multinational corporations comparable to those in the West, owing to incompatible organising values.[16] The owners of such firms typically based their strategic decisions on intuition rather than systematic analysis; preferred simple, functional organisational structures to mechanistic forms; operated by implicit command rather than by means of formal instruction or objective setting; shied away from entrusting significant authority to non-family members; and preferred to use subcontractors rather than directly recruit and select labour.[17]

These practices, which are bound up with Confucian values and traditions, normally lead to small size and limited growth. They would permit growth only if the owner was in a position to concentrate on a single industrial niche (where specialist expertise would compensate for inappropriate organisation) or where the entrepreneur could draw on interpersonal and political connections to protect the organisation against competition.

Asia's top Chinese conglomerates have already embarked on a modernisation program designed to overcome these traditional shortfalls. Many of the basic improvements needed are reasonably clear: better strategy and operations, a structured organisation and more sophisticated human resource management.[18] An important transition is the separation of ownership and control, when the founder accepts outsiders as managers. The evolution from 'ownership control' to 'management control' may often accelerate change. The traditional management style may also be weakened by taking on outsiders as employees; by reassessing the value of service inputs and acquiring them; by hiring Western-trained managers; and by floating some part of the firm on a stock exchange, thereby exposing the firm to outside ownership and to new and more stringent reporting requirements.

The modernisation of Asian family businesses does not always require compromises on ownership and control. Many families are reluctant to fill senior management positions with outsiders, so they send a family member abroad for Western training. Thus, ownership and some management remains in the hands of insiders but, at the same time, formal Western management skills are brought into the organisation.

What would you do?

Softy Fruits Sdn Bhd is a soft drink and fruit juice manufacturer located in Miri, Western Malaysia. The company was established in 1973 by Mr Yap Beng Leong, and currently employs 85 staff. Softy Fruits sells most of its products in eastern Malaysia and nearby Brunei, either to retailers or to restaurants and hotels. The company produces two different flavours of lemonade and four types of fruit juice (mango, pink guava, lychee and pitaya, or dragon fruit). Mr Yap is now over 70 years old and would like his youngest daughter, Stacy, to take over the business in the near future. Mr Yap has two older sons who both studied overseas and have embraced careers in the banking sector in Kuala Lumpur. Stacy obtained her bachelor of commerce degree from Curtin University of Technology in 2005, and she has been working with her father for the past 18 months.

To clearly signal that Stacy is to be his successor, Mr Yap appointed her deputy Managing Director immediately after she started working for Softy Fruits. Stacy is now in charge of the newly created function of business development. They share an office, so that father can teach daughter everything she needs to know about the business. Mr Yap is thrilled to work with his daughter, as it gives him extra motivation to arrive at the office every day for his usual 8 am start. He is still overseeing the daily business activities with Mr Lim, his trusted accountant, who has been with the company from the beginning.

(continued)

Stacy has conducted a lot of research on the beverage industry. After reading a report from Euromonitor, she discovered that Malaysia has a large and increasingly sophisticated soft drinks industry. In 2004, soft drinks in Malaysia continued to post strong growth, and they achieved sales of 931 million litres. Stacy is also aware that, as Malaysians become more health conscious, competitors are embarking on healthier alternatives that will appeal to these consumers. In 2004, most soft drinks enjoyed an off-trade volume growth of at least three per cent. Some of the best performers were bottled water, fruit/vegetable juice and functional drinks. The demand for these soft drinks is growing on the back of higher disposable incomes.

Nevertheless, Stacy is not very happy with her job. She recently clashed with her father about the growth strategies she had informally suggested. 'This is going to cost a lot of money,' said Mr Yap. 'You know that we have always pursued a low-cost niche strategy,' she was told. Another issue of concern is the recent appointment of Mr Lim's son Steve as key account manager for the restaurants in eastern Malaysia. Stacy has known Steve Lim for many years, but she has always disliked him and considers him to be lazy and incompetent. However, Stacy's father is adamant that Steve deserves at least one chance. 'Remember that Softy Fruits is like one big family,' he says.

Questions
1. Identify the current weaknesses of Softy Fruits' leadership style and strategy.
2. What growth strategy would you recommend the company adopts in order to expand its business?

Harvesting

Harvesting:
The process entrepreneurs and investors use to exit a business and realise their investment.

If building and growing a business are the first two steps in creating wealth, **harvesting** can be regarded as the third. The harvesting of a venture is one of the more significant events in the life of an entrepreneurial firm and its owner. After a total immersion in the business, a huge workload, many sacrifices, and quite often burnout, many entrepreneurs want to reap a reward for the effort they have put into launching and nurturing a business venture. Entrepreneurship is often seen as a journey, not a destination, by many people who become 'serial entrepreneurs' — that is, people who build new firms and then exit them to get a maximum profit before starting yet another firm.

This section outlines the key elements to take into consideration when planning an exit. Four exit strategies are presented: sale to a strategic partner or corporate investor, management buyout, strategic alliance and merger, and initial public offering.

Key elements to consider when planning an exit

If the entrepreneur is to take full advantage of an investment opportunity, it is essential not only to evaluate the merits of the opportunity at the outset, but also to anticipate options for exiting the business. If the entrepreneur's goal with the venture is to provide a living, then the exit strategy is of no concern. But if the goal is to create value for the owners and the other stakeholders in the business, a harvest strategy is very important. The exit is more than simply leaving the business; it is the final piece in creating the ultimate value to all participants in the venture, especially the owner, managers and employees.[19] Even if the entrepreneur does not plan to sell the business, there is still a need to prepare a succession plan in the event of retirement, illness or death of the founder. In any case, exit should be an active decision, rather than a passive, externally driven process.

As shown in figure 15.2, there are three main elements to be considered when planning an exit:

- *Strategic elements linked to the business environment.* An exit is attractive for the entrepreneur only if potential buyers are interested in the firm. The business must have a good stream of successful products that are well established in the market. In other words, the entrepreneur must be able to show that the business has a track record and that there is some potential for growth once the entrepreneur has pulled out of the business.

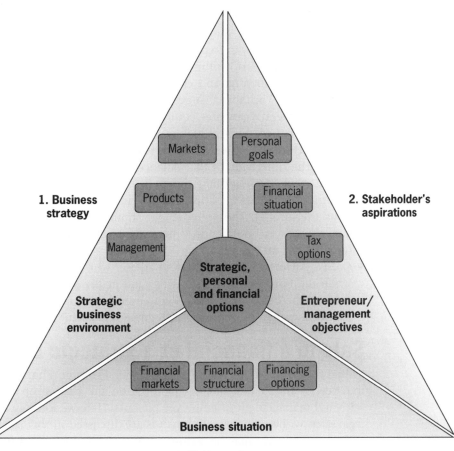

Figure 15.2: Balancing of strategic, personal and financial goals in a harvest strategy

- *Entrepreneur's personal aspirations.* For most entrepreneurs, the business venture is a dominant part of their lives. Thus, the decision to harvest cannot effectively be separated from the entrepreneur's personal goals and objectives. Without an understanding of what is important in life, the entrepreneur is apt to make a bad decision when it comes to harvesting a firm. The view of other stakeholders, such as outside investors and employees, also needs to be considered. Outside investors typically have expectations about their investment that include the firm either going public or being acquired by other investors.

- *Business financial situation*. The business financial situation is another key dimension to consider. For example, it might be difficult to list a business that has a high debt-to-equity ratio (leverage), in which case it may be preferable to sell to a corporate investor who can restructure the balance sheet. Exit strategies offer different financing options for businesses in need of extra funds for pursuing growth. For example, an initial public offering is considered by many business owners as a means of raising growth capital rather than as a tool for facilitating the exit of the founders.

Whatever the final decision by the entrepreneur and others regarding the harvest strategy, opportunities to sell or go public come and go with the condition of the economy and the industry. Entrepreneurs must not only *choose* an exit strategy, but also be aware of *when* they can exit. For example, adverse financial market conditions stopped many entrepreneurs floating their businesses on the stock market during the 2001–03 downturn. Timing is important and entrepreneurs must be sensitive to the opening and closing of a window of opportunity. In shaping a harvest strategy, Timmons[20] suggested the following guidelines and cautions:

- *Patience*. Several years are required to launch and build most successful businesses, so patience is invaluable. A harvest strategy is more sensible if it allows for a timeframe of at least three to five years and as long as seven to ten.
- *Vision*. The other side of the patience coin is not to panic as a result of unexpected events. Selling under duress is usually the worst thing to do.
- *Realistic valuation*. If impatience is the enemy of an attractive harvest, then greed is its executioner. The entrepreneur should value the business from different angles (such as book value, replacement value and discounted cash flows) to obtain a fair market value.
- *Outside advice*. It is best to find an adviser who can help craft a harvest strategy while the business is still growing, and at the same time help determine the value of the firm. Talking to an entrepreneur who has been through the experience of a merger or a sale can also give some useful pointers.

Sale to a financial or a strategic buyer

Selling the business outright is by far the most common harvest method. Sales fall into several broad categories, depending on the buyers: financial sales, strategic sales and management or employee buyouts. Here we focus on financial and strategic sales, while management buyouts are discussed in the next section.

A financial buyer may be a competitor in the industry or a business wishing to achieve 'vertical integration' and diversification by absorbing another business into its core business. In financial sales, buyers look mainly to a firm's stand-alone cash-generating potential as the source of value. Often, this value relates to stimulating future sales growth, reducing costs or both. Financial buyers are in business to make deals, so they may overlook some weaknesses. This has important implications for the seller, because new owners will often make changes to the firm's operations or break up the firm and sell the pieces. They often leave day-to-day operations unchanged, but they buy with a view to selling, which could disrupt the business's life a second time.

Strategic buyers, unlike financial buyers, expect the acquired business to fit in with their other holdings. Generally, these are corporate buyers seeking to effect or further a 'consolidation' strategy. In other words, strategic buyers seek to buy a number of businesses and then cobble them together to eliminate redundant and excess costs and derive economies of scale wherever possible to decrease expenses and, similarly, increase profitability. The best match sometimes comes about if they seek out the potential seller after having determined that the business fits their plans. Consequently, strategic sales often result in the most attractive price for the seller.

An outright sale is often viewed as the ideal route, because up-front cash is usually preferred over shares. However, even this outcome carries some negative consequences: entrepreneurs can find managing money more difficult and less enjoyable than they usually expect, and less rewarding than operating their own business. Often, the disillusionment of selling a firm is particularly evident when the entrepreneur continues in the management of the business but under the supervision of the acquiring owners.

Management buyout

Management buyout (MBO): The purchase of a controlling interest in a business by its management in order to take over assets and operations.

Another harvest strategy, called a **management buyout (MBO)**, is one in which a founder can realise a gain from the business by selling to managers or existing partners in the business. The MBO usually entails high levels of debt (leverage) and, therefore, the new owner–managers must stay clearly focused on the operating performance if they are to meet debt payments and use assets effectively. If the business has both assets and good cash flow, the financing can be arranged via banks or other financial institutions. Even if assets are thin, a healthy cash flow that can service the debt to fund the purchase price may convince lenders to support an MBO.

Three factors are generally considered essential to conducting a successful MBO: (1) the ability to borrow significant sums against the business's assets; (2) the ability to retain or attract a strong management team; and (3) the potential for the participants' (including management's) investment to increase substantially in value. The ability of a business to support significant leverage depends on whether it can service the principal- and interest-payment obligations that accompany that leverage. This in turn requires a business to be capable of generating large sums of cash on a regular basis or to have substantial assets that can be sold to pay off the debt. This usually means a business with a history of operations sufficient to support the borrowing required to fund the deal.

When a management buyout occurs, it often means that the division or business being purchased has a strong management team in place that requires few or no changes to make it complete. It is, after all, the investor's and lender's confidence in management's ability to run the business profitably and to expand its operations that make the buyout possible. Attracting and keeping good management also means cutting them in for a significant portion of the deal. In other words, management usually acquires a healthy percentage of the business's equity. This motivates them to stay with the business and make it grow.

For a company, the potential for increasing the value of its shares comes not only from the ability of strong management to build on an existing base of business but also on the very fact of leverage. The heavy borrowing undertaken to complete a buyout is customarily made directly by the business. This borrowing, because it is large in comparison to the value of the assets of the business, decreases the value of the company's shares, enabling management and outside investors to acquire them at lower prices that reflect the company's value as reduced by the leverage. The leverage reduces the ordinary share value to an amount that is low compared with the underlying market value of the company's assets and its historical level of profit. As the company's debt is paid off, the value of its shares increases, creating wealth for the investors.

Strategic alliance and merger

The entrepreneur can also use the framework of a strategic alliance to sell part of the business to a minority investor. In addition to the cash raised, there are generally wider benefits arising from this cooperation. For example, the investor can induce some economies of scale by pooling common resources or by collaborating in an allied area where the firm needs some expertise. Within a **strategic alliance**, the two allies remain legally independent, although a substantial part of their activities depends on the alliance (economic interdependence).

Strategic alliance:
An ongoing relationship between two businesses, which combine efforts for a specific purpose.

If the strategic alliance takes place between competitors, it can often lead to a **merger** of the two businesses later. In this case, a new legal entity is formed. The newly created enterprise will have a higher profile and an increased ability to continue growing, and may at a later stage be sold or offered to the public.

Initial public offering

Merger:
The combining of two or more entities into one through a purchase acquisition or a pooling of interests.

In the eyes of many entrepreneurs, taking their firm public through an initial public offering (IPO) is the 'holy grail' of harvest strategies. Through the IPO, shares are offered for sale on a public stock exchange. Because the effect of this decision is to change the fundamental financial nature of the business, it must be done with a great deal of care. The merits of going public versus being acquired rest largely on the contention that IPOs provide higher valuations, and therefore better returns, than can be expected from a straight sale. Other advantages to the firm of going public are the negotiability of its securities, the potential use of future issues of its shares to acquire other businesses, and an increase in the stature of the business.

However, there are disadvantages in going public. First, there is the loss of privacy as numerous reports are required by government agencies. Secondly, going public establishes the need for the board of directors to approve certain types of decisions, imposing additional restrictions on management. Thirdly, there is a significant cost associated with going public — not only is there the cost of the IPO itself, but there are also ongoing costs associated with the provision of information required by regulators.

Although IPOs are attractive for several reasons, many privately held firms will never find themselves in a position to go public. They will not qualify because they are too small or they are not in the 'right industry' or they lack the management skills to do so. Therefore, the IPO strategy is appropriate for a very limited set of firms, and even for these it is mainly a way of raising growth capital and is rarely used as a tool for facilitating the exit of the founders. The IPO process is discussed in more detail in chapter 9.

Summary

The growth of the venture can be approached from a number of perspectives: (1) financial — growth in income, expenditure and profits; (2) strategic — growth in market share and competitive advantages; and (3) organisational — growth in organisational form, process and structure. These three dimensions interact with one another and cannot be considered separately in the dynamics of growth. Although market forces may press for quantitative growth, this does not necessarily coincide with the personal interests of the entrepreneur. The relationship between personal and organisational objectives is important to understand, because they often overlap in the small firm. Thus, for the majority of owner–managers the need to maximise growth, or indeed to grow at all, is not self-evident.

Four basic theories can explain how and why organisations change: life cycle, teleology, evolution and dialectic. The notion of life cycle suggests that the business venture undergoes a pattern of growth and development much as a living organism does. Often, the stages follow the pattern of new venture development, start-up, growth, maturity and rebirth or decline. In teleology theory, the purpose or goal of management is the final cause for guiding movement of the organisation. In this perspective, the business venture sets goals and adapts its actions to reach its goals. The third approach, evolution, is a theoretical scheme that explains changes in structural forms of populations of organisations across communities or industries. As in biological evolution, organisational change proceeds through a continuous circle of variation, selection and retention. The fourth theory, dialectics, focuses on stability and change based on the collision of power between opposing entities.

Managing a rapidly growing enterprise presents a particular challenge because the essential nature of the manager's job changes with growth. In order to frame the management task in a way that allows us to predict and understand the challenges that growth creates, a model of the manager's job can be developed. Fundamentally, the key responsibilities of the manager revolve around operating, organising and staffing. Various common tools help owner–managers in the anticipating–acting–reviewing cycle of these responsibilities. In order to make their businesses continue to grow beyond a certain point, entrepreneurs must be prepared to move from an entrepreneurial management style with centralised decision making and informal control towards a professional management style that involves the delegation of decision-making responsibility and the use of formal control mechanisms.

If building and growing a business are the first two steps in creating wealth, harvesting can be regarded as the third. Harvesting is the process entrepreneurs and investors use to exit a business and realise their investment in a firm. Harvesting implies more than simply leaving a business; it is the final piece necessary to create the ultimate value to all participants in the venture, especially the owner, managers and employees. There are four main exit strategies that entrepreneurs can use to harvest a venture: sale to strategic partner or corporate investor, management buyout, strategic alliance and merger, and initial public offering. Whatever the exit strategy chosen, the process must be carefully prepared and special attention should be given to the business environment, stakeholders' interests and corporate finance issues.

REVIEW QUESTIONS

1. What are the different dimensions of business growth?
2. What are the four basic theories that explain how and why organisations change?
3. What are the key responsibilities of a manager and the steps for a successful transition towards professional management?
4. What are the main elements to be considered when planning an exit?
5. What are the standard exit strategies an entrepreneur can use to harvest a business venture?

DISCUSSION QUESTIONS

1. Why are many owner–managers not interested in growing their business?
2. To what extent do the four organisational change theories (life cycle, teleology, dialectics, evolution) differ from the unit of change and mode of change perspective?
3. What are the weaknesses of the lifecycle theory?
4. Why is it generally more difficult to manage growth and transition issues in family businesses?
5. 'Harvesting a business venture is as much about choosing an exit strategy as deciding when to exit.' Explain.

SUGGESTED READING

Collins, J., *Good to Great: Why Some Companies Make the Leap and Others Don't*, HarperCollins, New York, 2001.

Gunther McGrath, R. & MacMillan, I.C., MarketBusters: 40 Moves that Drive Exceptional Business Growth, Harvard Business School Press, Boston, MA, 2005.

Little, S.S., *The 7 Irrefutable Rules of Small Business Growth*, John Wiley & Sons, New York, 2005.

CASE STUDY

Wotif.com

In September 2005, Graeme Wood, co-founder and CEO of Wotif.com, had a lot to rejoice about. The Wotif.com board of directors had just announced its decision to seek a listing on the Australian Stock Exchange. Launched in March 2000, with headquarters in Brisbane, Wotif.com became the leading online accommodation booking service in Australasia, generating more than a third of all online accommodation sales in Australia. Although Mr Wood was very happy with this announcement, he knew there were a lot of issues to deal with in order to ensure a successful flotation.

Company background

Wotif.com is an accommodation booking website. Its easy-to-use website and booking engine advertises vacant rooms at discounted prices up to 28 days in advance. More than 7000 hotels, motels, serviced apartments, resorts, and bed and breakfast establishments in over 35 countries are now listed with Wotif.com. Accommodation can be booked online or through Wotif.com's customer service centre, which operates 24 hours a day, seven days a week.

Consumers were attracted to Wotif.com by cost savings as well as the convenience, simplicity and wide range of available accommodation. The company's customer base was divided between 'unmanaged' business travellers and short-break leisure travellers. Brand awareness in Australia and New Zealand was estimated at 30 per cent and 24 per cent respectively across the population base. This awareness was driven largely by word-of-mouth referrals.

Wotif.com was founded by Graeme Wood, Kevin Fitzpatrick and Andrew Brice in 2000. At the end of 2005, the company employed just over 100 staff, and it had established offices in New Zealand, the United Kingdom, Singapore, Malaysia and Canada.

The inspiration

Prior to the launch of Wotif.com, travel agents were the conventional distribution channel for hotel rooms. Hotels did not utilise yield management, a practice that began in the airline industry during the 1970s. This industry began to maximise efficiency by lowering prices in response to demand — an attempt to ensure all seats were occupied before take-off.

Mr Wood, a marketing and software professional, saw the potential for the short-term accommodation industry to increase profits by selling vacant rooms at reduced rates rather than not selling them at all. Having already founded and established many businesses during the 1980s and 1990s, he came up with the idea of Wotif.com in 1999; just one year later, in March 2000, he and his partners launched the website. The founding partners spent A$200 000 on developing the Wotif.com website. Graeme designed a prototype version that he showed to hotel operators, and then used their feedback to improve and develop the site. Wotif.com also received an AusIndustry grant 10 months after launching the business.

The company business model was straightforward. Suppliers were able to place their accommodation inventory on Wotif.com's website without an up-front cost. Customers selected and booked accommodation from the website and paid Wotif.com by credit card at the time of booking. Wotif.com deducted a 10 per cent margin from the total value of the booking sold through the website and charged a booking fee of A$3.85.

Industry overview

Wotif.com operated within the travel accommodation sector of the travel industry. Traditionally, accommodation sales occurred through travel agents or by customers dealing directly with accommodation suppliers. The emergence of the internet provided customers and accommodation suppliers with a convenient, efficient medium to buy and sell travel products, breaking away from the traditional reliance upon travel agents. This structural change had been demonstrated by the increasing proportion of travel industry products being searched, booked and subsequently paid for online. In Australia, online accommodation sales grew more than sevenfold between 1999 and 2005 to reach A$788 million.

The Australian accommodation sector was very fragmented, with a large number of independent and private owners. There was also a broad range of accommodation options for customers including hotels, motels, serviced apartments, bed and breakfast establishments and holiday resorts. Such a market was considered by Wotif.com to be ideally suited to its business model. Higher fragmentation increased the demand from customers for a service that aggregated the offerings in the market and combined this with real-time booking functionality. In such a market, suppliers also had a greater need to use a service such as Wotif.com that attracted a broad audience of potential customers.

Many different factors contributed to the sustainable growth of the travel accommodation sector. First of all, the positive macroeconomic conditions had been a key driver of activity in the tourism industry and, as a result, the accommodation sector. Secondly, the health of the economy had an impact on business activity and, hence, the aggregate amounts of business travel. Thirdly, the online accommodation booking-services sector benefited from the increasing levels of internet use and accessibility. The emergence of broadband, which provided quicker access to the Internet, would further increase this trend.

The tourism industry is also affected by one-off events that may have a positive or negative short-term impact on activity. In recent years, the threat of terrorism and the outbreak of SARS, for example, have negatively influenced the level of inbound and outbound tourism, whereas events such as the Olympic and Commonwealth Games have had positive impacts on the demand for accommodation.

Competitive landscape

Wotif.com was the leading player in online accommodation with an Australian market share estimated at 36 per cent in 2005. The balance of market was shared between hotel websites and all other online competitors.

In recent years, a range of businesses has emerged to take advantage of the increasing popularity of the internet as a medium for both suppliers and customers.

Wotif.com's competitors range from accommodation-only websites through to those that offer other products and services such as air travel, car rental and package tours. The competitors include both offshore companies that have established their operations in Australia and domestic companies. The main competitors in the Australian market are quickbeds.com (a subsidiary of Flight Centre), ReadyRooms (owned by Qantas), Stayz (owned by Fairfax), and Sensis's GoStay (operated by Australian Online Travel).

Mr Wood remains unfazed by these competitors. 'They're always playing catch-up, they don't know what we're going to do next, and when we do something, they will have to do the same. This is where innovation is so important, to keep the ideas flowing, and for us to keep our first-mover advantage,' he says.

Moving into sustained growth

In just five years, Wotif.com grew to become a niche business with an impressive model and outstanding financial returns (see the tables below and on the following page). Wotif.com's 28 product-team members were charged with the responsibility of maintaining relationships with existing suppliers and sourcing new suppliers worldwide. This effort had secured more than 7000 properties by the end of 2005. At the same time, the website had approximately two million user sessions per month, and converted this traffic into more than 110 000 bookings per month.

Summary of financial performance (year end 30 June, in A$ million)

	Audited		Forecasts	
REVENUE AND PROFIT	2004	2005	2006	2007
Total revenue	**23.4**	**32.1**	**45.3**	**55.8**
Operating expenses	(10.0)	(13.3)	(19.5)	(24.7)
Net profit before depreciation, amortisation and tax	**13.4**	**18.8**	**25.8**	**31.1**
Depreciation	(0.1)	(0.2)	(0.5)	(0.5)
Amortisation of IT development costs	(1.1)	(1.6)	(2.8)	(3.0)
Income tax	(3.5)	(5.0)	(6.8)	(8.5)
Net profit after tax (NPAT)	**8.7**	**12.0**	**15.7**	**19.1**
CASH FLOWS				
Cash flow from operating activities*	17.8	21.6	34.5	35.9
Cash flow from investing activities	(1.2)	(4.2)	(1.1)	(3.5)
Cash flow from financing activities	(3.0)	(7.0)	(19.5)	(9.0)
Net increase in cash	**13.6**	**10.4**	**13.9**	**23.4**

* Cash flow from operating activities = net profit before depreciation, amortisation and taxation + change in working capital − income tax paid. Change in working capital is not provided in this summary table.

Pro-forma consolidated balance sheet (31 December 2005, in A$ million)

Cash	48.3	Payables	44.2
Receivables	1.1	Current tax payable	1.6
Total current assets	**49.4**	Provisions	0.2
Other financial assets	1.0	**Total current liabilities**	**46.0**
Property and equipment	0.7	Contributed equity	1.9
Total non-current assets	**1.7**	Retained profits	3.2
Total assets	**51.1**	**Total equity**	**5.1**

One of the main hurdles that Wotif.com faced during its growth stage was the technical issues that came with the rapid expansion of a 24/7 online business. The company started off with technology that was pretty much knocked together and fairly inexpensive. 'As the business grew, we were playing catch-up all the time to reach the desired reliability and performance levels, and we've always been very keen to deliver high levels of customer service,' says Mr Wood. 'We outsourced the technology early on, for about the first two years, and that was not ideal, so then we hired an experienced chief information officer and brought it in-house,' he explains.

Another challenge was finding the right people to fit into Wotif.com's informal, open-door, flat management structure. You might think that the company would naturally recruit people from the hospitality industry. Not so, says Mr Wood, 'because especially in the early days, the people who came to us from the hospitality industry had their mind set in a certain way, whereas we were doing everything different.'

Another issue encountered during the lead-up to the listing of Wotif.com was getting the right independent directors on the board, and the right chief operating officer to run the day-to-day business. Mr Wood wanted to now focus on managing strategic issues. So in February 2006, Dick McIlwain was appointed as independent non-executive chairman. Mr McIlwain had been Managing Director of UNiTAB since 1999. 'He has a strong track record in business and is very well respected in the financial community. He was ready for a change and he accepted the role,' says Mr Wood. Robbie Cook, his offsider at UNiTAB, also joined Wotif.com as chief operating officer. Mr Wood adds: 'They have experience in running businesses which are not very different to our own.'

The offer

The decision to list had been discussed at board level since mid 2005. However, Wotif.com was prepared for the eventuality long before that time. Its accounts were audited by a large audit company from inception. 'About a year ago we were being approached by all sorts of people to buy us, and a couple of the early shareholders, who are older than I am, wanted to realise some of the assets that had been built up. We all agreed that the fairest way to do that was to list the company,' says Mr Wood.

A prospectus was drafted and circulated amongst the Board of Directors. It was anticipated that 85 984 000 shares would be offered, representing 42 per cent of company shares. Based on the indicative institutional bookbuild price range of A$1.75 to A$2.00, the total offer size would be A$150.5 million to A$172 million.

Sources: Based on author's interview with Graeme Wood and documents provided by Wotif.com.

Questions

1. What theory could be used to conceptualise the development and changes at Wotif.com?

2. How did Mr Wood manage the transition from entrepreneur to manager and the challenges related to this transition?

3. What are the main risk factors, both specific to Wotif.com and of a general nature?

4. What is Wotif.com worth? Would you buy Wotif.com shares?

ENDNOTES

1. P.A. Wickham, *Strategic Entrepreneurship — A Decision Making Approach to New Venture Creation and Management*, Pitman Publishing, London, 1998.
2. M. Schaper, 'Entering the business growth zone', *Inside Business Australia*, 1997, pp. 34–6.
3. M.E. Porter, *Competitive Strategy*, Free Press, New York, 1980.
4. A. Van de Ven & M.S. Poole, 'Explaining development and change in organisations', *Academy of Management Review*, vol. 20, no. 3, 1995, pp. 510–40.
5. ibid.
6. S. Hanks, C. Watson, E. Jansen & G. Chandler, 'Tightening the life-cycle construct: A taxonomic study of growth stage configurations in high-technology organisations', *Entrepreneurship Theory and Practice*, vol. 18, no. 2, 1993, pp. 5–29.
7. B. Bird, *Entrepreneurial Behavior*, Scott Foresman and Company, Glenview, IL, 1989, p. 8.
8. C. Fourcade, 'The 'démarrage' of firms: International comparisons', *International Small Business Journal*, no. 3, 1985, pp. 46–55.
9. D.C. Hambrick & L.M. Crozier, 'Stumblers and stars in the management of rapid growth', *Journal of Business Venturing*, no. 1, 1985, pp. 31–45.
10. L. Grenier, 'Evolution and revolution as organisations grow', *Harvard Business Review*, May–June 1998, pp. 55–67.
11. P. Davidsson, 'Continued entrepreneurship: Ability, need and opportunity as determinants for small firm growth', *Journal of Business Venturing*, vol. 6, 1991, pp. 405–29.
12. C. Benjamin, 'Fast 100 — Three-year hitch', *BRW*, 31 March to 6 April, 2005, p. 40.
13. M.J. Roberts, 'The challenge of growth', Teaching note 9-393-106, Harvard Business School Publishing, Boston, MA, 1993.
14. E. Flamholtz, *Growing Pains: Transitioning from an Entrepreneurship to a Professionally Managed Firm*, Jossey-Bass, San Francisco, 2000.
15. M.J. Roberts, 'Managing rapid growth', Teaching note 9-387-054, Harvard Business School Publishing, Boston, 1989.
16. G. Redding, *The Spirit of Chinese Capitalism*, de Gruyter, Berlin, 1990.
17. A. Lau & R. Snell, 'Structure and growth in small Hong Kong enterprises', *International Journal of Entrepreneurial Behaviour and Research*, vol. 2, no. 3, 1996, pp. 29–47.
18. East Asia Analytical Unit, *Overseas Chinese Business Networks*, AGPS, Canberra, 1995.
19. W. Petty, 'Harvesting', in W.D. Bygrave, *The Portable MBA in Entrepreneurship*, 2nd edn, John Wiley & Sons, New York, 1997, pp. 415–43.
20. J. Timmons, *New Venture Creation: Entrepreneurship for the 21st Century*, 4th edn, Irwin, Chicago, 1997, p. 658.

Chapter 16

Corporate entrepreneurship

LEARNING OBJECTIVES

After reading this chapter, you should be able to:

- define the concept of corporate entrepreneurship and its different forms
- explain the importance of corporate entrepreneurship for established businesses
- discuss the process of new venture development
- identify the key steps in developing entrepreneurial spirit in organisations.

M ost established organisations find it hard to maintain the initial entrepreneurial spirit that helped them to make it through the start-up stage. As businesses grow, they usually become more structured and more rigid. Managers from many organisations across the Pacific Rim region have reported that although they are satisfied with their operating prowess, they are dissatisfied with their ability to implement change. 'How do the excellent innovators do it?' they ask, presuming that excellent innovators exist. 'What drives the development of new promising opportunities?' Others question how to expand an organisation beyond its core business. And most fundamental of all: 'How do we find new ideas?'

The difficulties behind these questions arise from the inherent conflict between the need for organisations to control existing operations and the need to create the kind of environment that will permit new ideas to flourish and old ones to die a timely death. Businesses have traditionally faced many difficulties in identifying opportunities and subsequently turning them into new product and successful product lines.

Faced with this challenge, large organisations have two main strategies for remaining at the forefront of innovation. The first strategy consists of buying young firms with great potential. Some giants, including General Electric and Cisco, have been remarkably successful at snapping up and integrating scores of firms. But many others worry about the prices they have to pay and about hanging on to the talent that dreamed up the idea. The second strategy consists, therefore, of developing more ideas in-house; hence the craze for corporate entrepreneurship — delegating power and setting up internal ideas factories.

This chapter provides a rationale and a definitional framework for corporate entrepreneurship. Successful organisations develop a disciplined, milestone-focused approach to screening and funding new ventures. The five main stages of this new venture development process are presented, and the key steps to follow in instilling an entrepreneurial spirit in organisations are discussed.

Dimensions of and rationale for corporate entrepreneurship

The management structures and processes necessary for routine operations are very different from those required for managing innovation. The pressures of corporate long-range strategic planning on the one hand and short-term financial control on the other combine to produce an environment that favours planned and stable growth based on incremental innovation. Through corporate entrepreneurship, established organisations attempt to exploit their internal resources and provide an environment that is more conducive to radical innovation. This section presents a definition of corporate entrepreneurship and its various underlying dimensions. A rationale for corporate entrepreneurship is outlined, showing that discontinuous opportunities generate disproportionate wealth.

Towards a definition of corporate entrepreneurship

Although organisation creation and innovation are generally regarded as key factors in entrepreneurship, the challenges that entrepreneurs face vary according to whether they are operating independently or as part of an existing organisation. Thus, we need to differentiate between the settings in which entrepreneurship takes place.

Dimensions of corporate entrepreneurship

Today, there is no universally accepted definition of corporate entrepreneurship. Some authors emphasise its analogy to new business creation, and view corporate entrepreneurship as a concept limited to new venture creation within existing organisations. Others argue that the concept of corporate entrepreneurship should encompass the struggle of large firms to renew themselves by carrying out new combinations of resources that alter the relationships between them and their environment. It is possible to combine these different views and to define **corporate entrepreneurship** as the process whereby an individual or a group, in association with an existing organisation, creates a new organisation or initiates renewal or innovation within that organisation.[1]

Within the realm of existing organisations, entrepreneurship encompasses three dimensions that are not necessarily interrelated:

- **Corporate venturing** refers to corporate entrepreneurial efforts that lead to the creation of new business ventures in established organisations.[2] The new ventures — the equivalent of internal start-ups — may reside inside or outside the boundaries of the firm. *Internal corporate venturing* refers to the corporate venturing activities that result in the creation of organisational entities (such as a new division or subsidiary) within an existing firm. *External corporate venturing* refers to corporate venturing activities that result in the creation of semi-autonomous or autonomous organisational entities outside the existing firm (for example spin-offs, joint ventures, venture capital initiatives).

- **Strategic renewal** involves the creation of new wealth through new combinations of resources within the firm. Renewal activities occur within the existing organisation and are not treated as new business by the organisation. This includes actions such as refocusing a business competitively, making major changes in marketing or distribution, redirecting product development and reshaping operations.[3]

- Innovation is also an entrepreneurial activity since it involves new combinations that may dramatically alter the bases of competition in an industry or lead to the creation of a new industry, even though it may not be immediately manifested in organisation creation or renewal. For example, innovation can lead simply to the development of new products, services or processes.

The relationship between the dimensions discussed above is presented in figure 16.1. In light of these manifestations, it is evident that corporate entrepreneurship is not confined to a particular business size or a particular stage of an

Corporate entrepreneurship: The process whereby an individual or a group, in association with an existing organisation, creates a new organisation or initiates renewal or innovation within that organisation.

Corporate venturing: The development of new business ventures inside or at the periphery of an organisation.

Strategic renewal: The new combinations of resources that result in significant changes to an organisation's strategy or structure.

organisation's life cycle, such as the start-up phase. In a competitive environment, entrepreneurship is an essential element in the long-range success of every business organisation, small or large, new or long established.

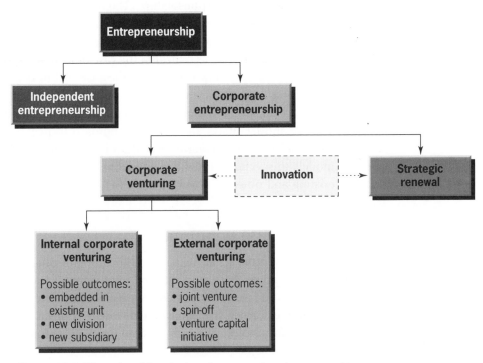

Figure 16.1: Hierarchy of terminology in corporate entrepreneurship

Source: Adapted from P. Sharma & J.J. Chrisman, 'Toward a reconciliation of the definitional issues in the field of corporate entrepreneurship', *Entrepreneurship Theory and Practice*, vol. 23, no. 3, 1999, p. 20.

Internal corporate venturing

Internal corporate venturing activities are located within existing organisations, but they are created in differing ways, involve different levels of innovation, and differ in importance. This suggests that internal corporate ventures may vary in terms of at least three aspects that may affect their development and performance.

The first aspect is structural autonomy — that is, the location of the venture within an organisation. The venture may be completely integrated into an existing division, or a separate new division may be created, or a subsidiary may be set up that is isolated from the rest of the organisation and reports directly to top management. The best place to locate a venture will depend on how much managerial attention it needs, the resources required, and whether it needs to be protected from criticism and opposition from other parts of the organisation.

The second aspect is the extent of innovation or how 'new' it is in the marketplace. This aspect may range from extensions, duplications and synthesis-type innovations to those innovations that 'break the mould' (inventions). If a venture is completely new and even creates new markets, then the innovating firm will face significantly greater challenges.

The third aspect is the nature of sponsorship. What is the degree of formal authorisation for the venture? Corporate ventures may be formally sponsored by top management or they may be informal, independent initiatives of employees without formal organisational sponsorship.[4] The nature of sponsorship has some organisational implications for corporate entrepreneurship. For example, an organisational champion is very important in the case of independent entrepreneurial efforts, but it may not be as critical in the case of formally sponsored efforts.

The three aspects often interact. Consider the case of bricks-and-mortar firms pursuing e-business opportunities. In this situation firms prefer to create a separate subsidiary for several reasons: (1) it demands a clear statement of the new venture's strategy and facilitates an aggressive approach to new business development; (2) it enables greater freedom and flexibility to tailor individual venture business models to specific competitive situations; (3) it facilitates separate valuation by existing and potential investors; and (4) it makes it easier to attract and retain top talent.[5]

External corporate venturing

External corporate venturing can take several forms: **spin-offs**, joint ventures and venture capital initiatives. Both spin-offs and joint ventures lead to the creation of a new business venture outside the existing organisation. The difference between the two is that the former is entirely independent whereas the latter is semi-autonomous (the firm holds an equity stake in the new venture and usually has a say in the management).

> **Spin-off:**
> An individual or organisational unit leaving an existing firm to start as an independent new firm.

Spin-offs have been a particularly popular form of external entrepreneurship over the last decade, giving entrepreneurial-minded employees the chance to take internally spawned projects and create independent concerns. Businesses have always spun off new firms, but what has been different over the past few years is a growing awareness on the part of the parent organisation that new products which do not fit into their strategic plans can sometimes be best developed and marketed by an independent firm. Organisations that are downsizing find that it is easier to maintain an equity position in a spin-off than to develop a venture from within.

Another way to capitalise on clever ideas that fall by the corporate wayside is to develop a corporate venture capital fund. Xerox, for example, set up Technology Ventures in its Palo Alto Research Center (PARC) and elsewhere; this business unit was given US$30 million to exploit ideas that 'didn't fit' within the firm. If researchers are turned down by top management at headquarters, they are free to take their ideas to Xerox Technology Ventures. However, the venture fund insists that corporate entrepreneurs stay at PARC until they perfect a proper working model of their money-making scheme. They are then moved into low-cost commercial premises, with a professional business manager to help them stay on track. In return, the founders get a 20 per cent stake in their new venture.[6]

Macquarie Bank

Macquarie Bank regularly features in the business columns of Australian newspapers, but it made international business headlines in 2006 when it put up a hostile bid for the London Stock Exchange. However, the bank is also well known for its innovative approach and entrepreneurial culture. Founded in 1985, the organisation provides specialist investment banking and financial services worldwide, with a staff of more than 6800 people in 23 countries. Macquarie Bank grew out of the merchant bank Hill Samuel Australia, which began operating in Sydney in January 1970 with only three staff members. Just like CEO Allan Moss, Deputy Managing Director Richard Sheppard joined Hill Samuel in the mid 1970s, when it was a Sydney operation with 50 employees.

Macquarie Bank defies characterisation. Outside its investment banking division, Macquarie is really a private equity firm that makes old economy assets look attractive again. Until recently, it was the only investment bank in the world that invested and managed — on its own and on behalf of clients — ports, toll roads and airports.[7] This is the essence of the Macquarie model. 'This model is distinctive from other organisations because half of our funds under management tend to be listed or unlisted funds which manage real assets, so it's very much a hands-on management approach,' says Mr Sheppard. In addition, the bank uses its own balance sheet to buy assets and to seed new funds. This innovative model of taking real estate and infrastructure assets and then packaging them into funds has achieved worldwide success for assets such as Korean toll roads, British airports and US golf developments. The model is now widely emulated.

Most of the bank's growth has been organic, either through increasing market share in existing markets or by pursuing adjacent opportunities. In fact, the growth strategy of Macquarie is based on two key concepts: adjacency and competency. In pursuing such opportunities, the bank essentially builds on existing skills and knowledge while moving in adjacent market segments; for example, from gold into another metal or commodity, or from property leases into mortgage products. 'Our approach is very much about taking one step at a time. It is rare that we would pursue discontinuous opportunities in areas where we have no expertise at all,' says Mr Sheppard. The concept of competency comes into play when Macquarie enters a new industry in which to apply its model. As it prepares to enter a new field, Macquarie hires experts for advice and to form teams with Macquarie staff who can apply the financial expertise needed to create a new specialist fund.

A key part of Macquarie's success has been its ability to preserve and extend the original Macquarie culture. 'We think of our culture as a small business culture within a larger organisation, and those of us who are in the leadership [group] all remember what it was like to be a part of a smaller business, so we've organised the Macquarie group to maintain that entrepreneurial culture,' adds Mr Sheppard.[8] The bank operates a flat non-hierarchical management structure that allows even the most junior member of staff to interact with senior people in the organisation.

(continued)

The culture of entrepreneurship is driven by a business philosophy that is referred to as 'freedom within boundaries'. This means that the bank seeks centralised control over a small number of key risks — credit risks, market risks, operational standards such as ethics and brand — but leaves as much freedom as possible to the people who are involved in the relevant businesses. Personal development is driven by the individual staff member, who is expected to seek out opportunities and present ideas to the bank. 'We give people all of the incentives that they would have as owners of the business, to grow the business for themselves,' says Mr Sheppard.

Sources: Based on author's interview with Richard Sheppard, Deputy Managing Director Macquarie Bank, and on information from the company website <www.macquarie.com>.

Rationale for corporate entrepreneurship

Existing organisations can introduce two basic types of innovation into the marketplace — incremental or radical innovations. *Incremental innovations* usually come from tweaking existing designs and listening to big customers, who usually just want steady improvements that yield higher margins. Incremental innovations use established technologies and can be implemented easily and rapidly. *Radical innovations*, on the other hand, are based on disruptive technologies and often present teething troubles that spoil the customers' bottom line. As explained below, radical innovations result from the pursuit of **discontinuous opportunities** that have the potential to generate disproportionate wealth.

Discontinuous opportunities: Innovations that move beyond existing business models to create new products and enter new markets.

Identifying and pursuing discontinuous opportunities

In the area of new business development, and especially new business incubation, discontinuous opportunities generate disproportionate wealth. For example, although discontinuous opportunities generally trigger only 14 per cent of new business launches in existing companies, they generate 38 per cent of their revenues and 61 per cent of their profits.[9]

In the Pacific Rim region, firms have traditionally excelled in making things, growing their market share and, at best, exploiting adjacent opportunities. All this, however, is changing. Asian businesses are moving very fast away from providing a manufacturing base for the rest of the world to being providers of products and services for their indigenous markets. The cash cow of the future is creativity and innovation. Discontinuous opportunities occupy a distinct and challenging corner of the new business development arena (see figure 16.2 opposite). These opportunities are challenging because they typically entail both creating new products and entering new markets. Discontinuous business opportunities can be discovered and pursued only if existing organisations have developed adequate corporate entrepreneurship strategies.

Discontinuous opportunities assume two forms:

- *White-space opportunities* involve entering new industries, developing new technologies and marketing new products. Because they are not modifications of existing product lines, pursuit of white-space opportunities often requires knowledge and capabilities that the organisation does not currently possess.

- *Disruptive opportunities* are new technologies or business models that constitute a threat to established business lines. Because these opportunities are often related to the organisation's core business, senior management often considers existing business units the logical home for their stewardship. However, this tendency risks neglect of disruptive opportunities or even 'drowning' by established businesses fearing cannibalisation.[10]

	Existing products/ technology	New products/ technology
New markets	**Adjacent opportunities** Exploit current assets and capabilities	**Discontinuous opportunities** Create new products and enter new markets
Existing markets	**Status quo** Grow market share and profit (considered as business expansion, not new business development)	**Adjacent opportunities** Increase primary market demand

Figure 16.2: The new business development arena

Source: Adapted from *The New Venture Division: Attributes of an Effective New Business Incubation Structure*, Corporate Executive Board, Washington, 2000, p. 4.

Reasons for corporate entrepreneurship

There are several motives for developing corporate entrepreneurship in an organisation:[11]

- *To grow and diversify the business.* Corporate ventures are often formed in an effort to create new businesses in a corporate context, and therefore represent an attempt to grow via diversification. Organisations that merely improve existing products, services and processes in order to grow their market share and their profits face stagnation sooner or later. To grow and counter the threat induced by start-ups in the marketplace, existing organisations must develop new products and enter new market segments.

- *To satisfy and retain bright and motivated staff.* In today's knowledge society, organisations employ better qualified staff to develop increasingly sophisticated products and services. As a consequence, the key to a sustained competitive advantage often resides in the organisational capabilities a business is able to develop. In the war for talent, it is essential that organisations retain their best and brightest staff by giving them enough room to generate new ideas and allowing them to pursue promising new opportunities.

- *To exploit underused resources in new ways.* This includes both technological and human resources. Typically, a business has two choices where existing resources are underused: (1) outsource the process or (2) generate additional contributions from external clients. However, if the business wants to retain direct and in-house control of the technology or personnel, it can form an internal venture to offer the service to external clients.

- *To get rid of non-core activities.* Much has been written of the benefits of strategic focus, 'getting back to basics' and creating the 'lean organisation' — rationalisation which prompts the organisation to divest itself of any activities that can be outsourced. However, this process can threaten the skill diversity required for an ever-changing competitive environment. New ventures can provide a mechanism for releasing peripheral business activities while retaining some management control and financial interest.

The new venture development process

Successful organisations have developed a disciplined, milestone-focused approach to screening and funding new ventures. This process, according to leading management consulting firm Booz Allen & Hamilton,[12] comprises five main stages: idea generation, concept development, business plan development, incubation and commercialisation, and value capture. This section discusses these five stages in detail.

Stage	Idea generation	Concept development	Business plan development	Incubation and commercialisation	Value capture
Objective	Unleash creativity	Refine	Define	Free-standing organisation	Unleash value
Timing	3 hours to 2 days	1 week	3 weeks to 4 months	3 months to 2 years	3 to 4 years
Elements	• Internal development • External sourcing • Idea capture • Idea screening	• Idea evaluation • Concept refinement • Idea becomes a business opportunity	• Business model development • Potential partner identification • Evaluation framework • Target market and customer value proposition validated	• Prototyping, trials • Launch planning • Resource acquisition • Business plan refinement • Technology product development • Management team	• Determination of exit strategy • Preparation for liquidity event • Communication and marketing
Output △ Major decision gates	• High potential ideas	• 2-page elaboration of each idea with recommendation	• Business plan	• Internal start-up	• Value/liquidity event
Decision	• Good idea	• Opportunity • Worth investment in resources to flesh out	• Business economics feasible • Worth investment to launch	• Readiness to launch • Readiness to wean from core	• Timing of liquidity event • Nature of liquidity event

Figure 16.3: New venture development process

Source: G. Neilson, J. Albrinck, J. Hornery et al., *E-Business and Beyond: Organizing for Success in New Ventures*, Booz Allen & Hamilton, New York, 2001, p. 10.

As shown in figure 16.3 (p. 406), this development process evaluates each new venture at predetermined points to decide whether to proceed, refine, accelerate or discontinue the new venture. Using such a time-phased approach, an organisation gradually increases its commitment in line with the availability of more information. As the business venture moves through critical 'decision gates', its performance is measured against pre-established targets, and resource decisions are made. Meanwhile, the process itself 'learns' and becomes 'smarter' as the organisation gathers and assesses more information about the economic and competitive environment and the individual venture's operating history. This is a dynamic screening method that evolves as the venture matures, and it ensures the continuous reliability of the conception at each stage.

Idea generation

The first step of the new venture development process is idea generation. At this stage, quantity, rather than quality, matters. Innovative organisations are those that systematically generate ideas and do not let any idea slip away. Empirical evidence has shown that entrepreneurial businesses need to generate hundreds of ideas to end up with a handful of plausible programs for developing new products. Several large organisations, including 3M, Procter & Gamble, and Rubbermaid, have therefore established 'ideas factories'. Rather than leaving it to chance, these organisations have taken the following steps to help bring out any creative potential in their employees.

- *Allow unofficial activity.* Work conducted without direct official support is what makes it possible for an organisation to go where it never expected to. Unless an organisation makes provision for such activity, relatively few creative acts will occur. Some organisations have established policies that encourage certain employees to devote a certain percentage of their time to unofficial projects. Hewlett Packard's policy is 10 per cent, and Toshiba and 3M allow 15 per cent.
- *Encourage spontaneous discoveries.* An oft-cited example is that of Charles Goodyear, who, after almost two decades of frustration in his search for a useful form of rubber, discovered the answer to his problem — vulcanisation — when he accidentally dropped a mixture of rubber and sulphur on a hot stove. To promote 'fortunate accidents', organisations should encourage tinkering and empirical research work.
- *Create diverse stimuli.* Stimuli are the sparks for creative ideas. Idealab, for example, conducts monthly brainstorming sessions and focuses on those ideas that generate the most passion among staff members. Siemens holds 'idea competitions' in which employees are asked to submit ideas to a cross-functional screening committee. Organisations can influence the set of stimuli employees are exposed to by rotating people in jobs they would not normally do.

Most of the time, corporate entrepreneurship opportunities are conceived because employees have access to unique information through social ties and because they are willing to accept ideas based on subjective criteria.[13] This starting point is important because it provides an explanation for how organisations learn to extend their knowledge in ways that are inconsistent with the dominant belief. Although other objective circumstances, such as industry structure, may determine whether new ideas emerge as market opportunities, the subjective 'opportunity structure' — how the entrepreneur views and interprets the situation — helps the introduction of new ideas.

The question is, then, 'Where does the new information come from?' Based on social network theory, it appears that weak, informal ties provide employees with information to generate ideas and to collect resources in order to engage in the most promising opportunities. Thus it can be assumed that people who maintain relationships not necessarily associated with their formal position are more likely to be a source of entrepreneurial ideas within the business venture. This suggests that the real work in most organisations is done informally through personal contacts.[14] In the dynamic working environment, modern managers perpetually use their personal contacts when they need to meet an impossible deadline, get advice on a strategic decision, or obtain support to back up their ideas.

Concept development

In the concept development phase, a promising one-sentence idea is transformed into a two-page outline of the opportunity, covering such topics as concept description, target market, value for the customer, competition, potential business models and opportunity size. Two or three people who bring the relevant knowledge and skills to the assignment (such as industry and technical expertise or organisational knowledge) flesh out the concept to determine whether it is worth putting resources into.

For an idea to get accepted at 3M, for example, it must first win the personal backing of at least one member of the main board. Only then will an interdisciplinary venture team of researchers, engineers, marketers and accountants be set up to push the idea further. This step is important because evidence suggests that the innovator who first recognises an opportunity may not be the one to champion it for resources within the organisation. Indeed, many innovators are technically minded and find it difficult to explain their ideas in business terms — this may be due to a simple lack of communication skills, but it is more likely to result from the isolation created by the individual's mind set and unique set of social relationships. Conversely, product champions are able to turn a new idea into a concrete new project in which technical and marketing development can begin to take shape.

One of the keys to success at this stage is speed. Concept development should take only weeks, yet many organisations let ideas languish for months, so by the time the idea has formed into a testable business model, the market has changed or competition has usurped the idea. Organisations need to expedite the flow of innovative ideas through this phase and establish an approval 'board' to usher to the next stage those ideas that meet the feasibility test. For example, at Royal Dutch Shell, ideas are submitted to innovations teams by email. Using a screening method devised by an external consultant, six-person 'GameChanger' teams meet weekly to assess ideas. The GameChanger teams assessed 320 proposals during their first two years of operation.

Shell as example for [handwritten annotation]

Business plan development

The new business model is designed and simulated at this stage, which can take up to four months. Management seeks to validate the uniqueness of the business model and the value proposition for its target market. A full-scale business plan is developed and new staff are brought into the venture, since those who are best able to generate ideas are not necessarily the best at translating them into workable business plans.

The need for resources during the process of testing determines which people corporate entrepreneurs will attempt to influence. During this process of validation, corporate entrepreneurs become central figures in an emergent network (for example, a venture team in the 3M case). In addition, corporate venture groups often draw on external resources such as venture capital firms and incubators at this stage. A successful pilot study, for instance, usually leads to more widespread acceptance of the idea's feasibility and desirability. Other forms of empirical support, such as market research or consultant studies, may also be used to lend objective credibility to a proposal and thereby gain more support.

Effective business plans reflect both a strong grasp of technology and a firm understanding of the business and market the new venture is tackling. Moreover, they are 'reality-tested' with key constituencies, such as customers and investors. Ultimately, a document is produced that details such items as market opportunity, competitive evaluation, business model, organisational structure and financial projections.

Incubation and commercialisation

During the incubation phase, it is important that the technological feasibility of the venture is fully tested. Prototypes of the product are built and feedback from potential users is obtained. Resources must also be acquired or borrowed to establish the validity of the business model and test its value proposition. This often takes the form of seed funding, and dedicated advisers or sponsors are assigned to the emergent venture. Partnerships are established both internally and externally (with legal and technology experts, for example) to bring the new venture along. Strict discipline and management skills are needed to recruit and train staff, secure funding, complete the evaluation of the business concept, establish the organisational entity and create contracts with suppliers and potential customers.

This stage of testing may lead to at least three different types of outcome. First, the results may be positive, and the initiative becomes viewed as unequivocally successful. At the other extreme, a test of the idea can be a complete failure, thus ending the entrepreneurial process. Between these two extremes, the testing of new ideas may produce mixed results. Ideas may be seen as meritorious but requiring unacceptable levels of effort to make them practical. On the other hand, initial ideas may prove impractical at first, but the fine-tuning of the first tests may make them viable.

Commercialisation marks the point at which a business plan graduates from theory into practice. At this point, the business model gets its first dose of marketplace experience. As the concept is fully commercialised, it is rapidly tested and scaled up. The venture must prove its ability to produce multiple versions of the products and even start multiple complementary product lines. Although the venture team needs to recognise that the business model will evolve, implementation speed is vital. Learning needs to be rapidly absorbed and incorporated. The duration of this stage is typically between three months and two years.

Value capture

Contrary to the traditional marketing approach of product innovation, which merely focuses on increasing sales or market share, the aim of corporate entrepreneurship is to create value. Several mechanisms exist for capturing value from new businesses once they have been commercialised. These include initial public offerings (IPO), selling to an external bidder, establishing joint ventures, creating separate subsidiaries or divisions and incorporating new ventures back into the parent organisation.

The strategy an organisation chooses depends on a number of factors. For example, if the parent company wants to turn its new venture into cash, it will probably choose an IPO or find a private buyer. This type of strategy is often selected when the new venture does not belong to the core activities of the parent and if it is built on a discontinuous business model that does not fit into the current corporate culture. Alternatively, if the venture can drive growth in the business and if it encompasses a traditional business model, management would be inclined to form a new division or even to incorporate the new venture into an existing division.

Best-practice companies have a clear mechanism for unleashing the value created by new ventures. For example, Xerox takes one of three approaches: (1) if the venture is related to a Xerox core competency but does not fit neatly into an existing business unit, it may become its own separate Xerox company; (2) the venture may be assigned directly to a compatible Xerox business division; (3) the new venture may be spun off to a venture capital firm if it does not strategically fit with Xerox's existing businesses or overall portfolio.

What would you do?

Wong ICT

Wong ICT is based in Hong Kong. The company provides solutions and professional services to help its customers establish their computer information systems and enterprise communication systems. At present, its customers include telecom operators, telecom equipment manufacturers, banks, insurance companies, public utilities, government agencies and IT service providers. Based on technological accumulation in UNIX (an operating system), the company has been moving forward since it was established in 2000. Wong ICT has become a well-known IT service and product provider in the local IT industry. Harry Wong set up the company straight after graduating in computer engineering from a local university. He now has 145 staff on the payroll.

You are an old friend and mentor of Harry, and he has recently approached you to share his concerns. Harry is becoming increasingly worried about retaining the best and brightest employees — what he calls 'the high potentials' — in his company. Five high potentials have resigned from Wong ICT over the past six months. Three out of the five have since joined other IT businesses in Hong Kong, whereas the other two have decided to establish their own businesses to 'realise their dream'. During final discussions, just before these high potentials left the company, they would often blame Harry and Wong ICT management for not letting them pursue new business opportunities.

'I really don't understand why these people are disgruntled,' says Harry. 'In fact, I would consider Wong ICT as a model of an entrepreneurial company.' Harry knows that qualified and motivated staff are a key resource in his company, as well as a source of competitive advantage. He also knows that the IT sector is changing rapidly and that only constant innovation will keep Wong ICT ahead of the pack. Therefore, he has informed his staff that each of them is welcome to submit new ideas. He has also devised a reward system that amounts to 20 per cent of the cost saved by an idea that was submitted. All ideas have to be directly submitted to Harry, and he will evaluate them twice a year. This suggestion system had already led to the company achieving HK$500 000 in cost savings and process optimisation since being introduced.

Questions

1. What are the strengths and weaknesses of Harry's approach to corporate entrepreneurship?
2. What actions would you recommend to Harry in order to improve the entrepreneurial process at Wong ICT?

The key steps in developing entrepreneurial spirit

Developing an entrepreneurial spirit inside an existing organisation requires four steps, as shown in figure 16.4: (1) develop a vision and a strategy, (2) create a culture of innovation, (3) develop organisational support and (4) reward results accordingly. This process requires time and constant effort. Evidence suggests that most firms build up the attributes of corporate entrepreneurship in long-drawn-out processes over many years, not in a one-shot, single event.

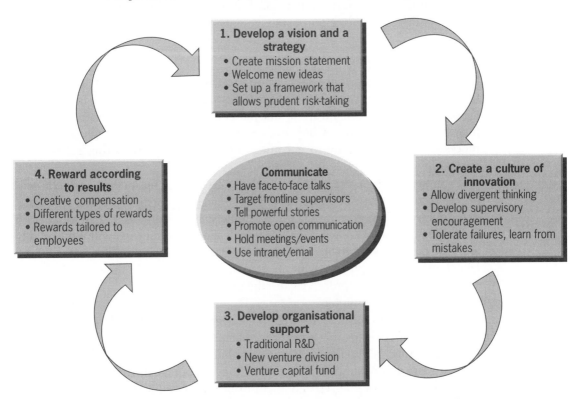

Figure 16.4: Four steps for fostering entrepreneurship in an organisation

Develop a vision and a strategy

The first step towards instilling entrepreneurial spirit in an existing organisation is to develop a clearly understandable vision and a strategy. Leaders of highly innovative organisations welcome new ideas, and by their decisions, actions and communications they demonstrate that innovation propels profitability. Executives, through their words and actions, help people to overcome their fear of failure and, in the process, create a culture of intelligent risk-taking that leads to sustained innovation. These leaders do not just accept failure; they encourage it.

Welcome new ideas

Usually, the vision of the organisation is translated into a mission statement, which states the purpose of an organisation and identifies the scope of its operations in product and market terms, and reflects its values and priorities. Essentially, the mission statement defines the organisation and provides an answer to the question: 'What kind of organisation do we want to be?' It will help an organisation make consistent decisions, motivate employees, build organisational unity, integrate short-term objectives with longer term goals, and enhance communication.

Leaders of highly innovative organisations emphasise developing whole new business concepts and product platforms, and systematically 'destroying one's own'. Continual innovation is their sole business. All other business concerns flow from this single overriding purpose.

Allow prudent risk-taking

IBM's Thomas Watson once said: 'The fastest way to succeed is to double your failure rate'. In recent years, more and more executives have embraced this point of view, coming to understand what innovators have always known: that failure is a prerequisite to invention. A business cannot develop a breakthrough product or process if it is not willing to encourage risk-taking and learn from subsequent mistakes.

The growing acceptance of failure is changing the way businesses approach corporate entrepreneurship. Some build exit strategies into their projects to ensure that doomed efforts do not drag on indefinitely. Some conduct a large number of market experiments, knowing that, although most of their tests will not pay off, even the failures will provide valuable insights into customer preferences. Others launch two or more projects with the goal of sending teams in different directions simultaneously. This approach creates the potential for a healthy cross-fertilisation of new ideas and techniques.

This approach to mistake making is characteristic of 'failure-tolerant leaders' — executives who help people overcome their fear of failure and, in the process, create a culture of intelligent risk-taking that leads to sustained innovation.[15] These leaders do not simply accept failure; they encourage it. They break down the bureaucratic barriers that separate them from their employees and associate with the people they lead.

Create a culture of innovation

Once the vision and the strategy have been established, organisations can work on their corporate culture. An entrepreneurial culture allows divergent thinking, develops supervisory encouragement and tolerates failure.

Allow divergent thinking

Traditional corporate control systems limit creativity through their dependence on convergent thinking. *Convergent thinking* focuses on clear problems and provides well-known solutions quickly. Order, simplicity, routine, clear responsibilities and predictability are the bases of convergent thinking. This is hardly the kind of environment in which discontinuous opportunities can be nurtured.

Conversely, *divergent thinking* focuses on broadening the context of decision making. Essentially, it requires three central skills — conversation, observation and reflection — to identify new business ideas.[16] Managing for divergent thinking means providing plenty of information to stimulate people to ask the right questions. It requires good selection and motivation of employees rather than control of people's actions; ample resources, including time, to achieve results; and genuine respect for other people's capabilities and potential.

Develop supervisory encouragement

Leaders of successful, continually innovative organisations create a sense of community across the whole organisation. In these organisations, everyone identifies with a common purpose, knows why they are working together, and participates in innovation as the basic way the organisation creates and brings new value to customers. Creativity and innovation activities are not delegated to just a few people or functional areas. It is not necessary for a top manager to be the technical inventor or innovator, but to be the innovation leader calling for, recognising and acknowledging innovative results in others.

It is not enough, however, to launch change from the top and hope that communication about change will open like a parachute, blanketing everyone evenly. Entrepreneurial leaders must establish their vision by working with others, especially by finding, empowering and championing 'middle manager entrepreneurs'.[17] These are the frontline supervisors who assume the career risk of pursuing a new idea within the corporation, and who find the necessary resources, deal with problems so an idea can germinate, and bear the brunt of institutional inertia and resistance. In addition, frontline supervisors greatly influence the attitudes and behaviour of others.

Supervisory encouragement by both top managers and middle managers not only creates a vision for innovation, but sustains it, making people feel as if their work matters to the organisation or to some important group of people. Not every idea is worthy of consideration, of course, but in many organisations managers habitually show a lack of enthusiasm that damages creativity. They look for reasons *not* to use a new idea instead of searching for reasons to explore it further. Negativity also shows in the way managers threaten or dismiss people whose ideas do not work.

Tolerate failures

Encouraging employees to innovate invariably implies tolerating failures. Successful innovators know that learning the hard way, through mistakes, is often the best way to create a business with staying power. 3M has one of the most famous cases of this — the glue that would not work because it was too weak became, eventually, the adhesive for Post-it Notes. Consequently, it is important to give employees permission to occasionally fail and to learn from failure. Furthermore, dead ends can sometimes be very enlightening. In many business situations, knowing what does not work can be as useful as knowing what does.

Creating a culture in which people feel comfortable with failure also requires abandoning the traditional approach to personal competition. The idea that achievement is maximised when people compete is not necessarily true — when the road to success requires making others fail, innovation can get left by the wayside. Competition infects co-workers with a desire to win rather than solve problems and move projects forward. In the process, employees inhibit the free flow of information that is vital to innovation. Those who feel they are competing with co-workers will want to protect information rather than share it.

Some future-minded organisations such as Royal Dutch Shell and Monsanto have developed work groups that emphasise collaboration. The main objective of these groups is to exchange information, not to hide it as so often happens in the heat of competition. 3M has encouraged idea sharing for decades, from the informal morning-tea brainstorming sessions years ago to today's more formal Tech Forums and in-house trade shows.

Develop organisational support

The innovation process is enhanced when the whole organisation supports it. Such support is the job of an organisation's leaders, who must put in place appropriate structures and procedures and emphasise values which make it clear that innovative efforts are a top priority. Three main structures can harness the creativity of employees and help incubate new opportunities: traditional research and development departments, new venture divisions, and venture capital funds. Choosing between these structures consists basically of balancing separation and integration of new activities. This section discusses this dilemma and then focuses on the new venture division and venture capital structures.

Should new activities be separated or integrated?

Separation is the model of choice when the new and the old differ greatly, as in the case of an internet start-up launched by an industrial company. Another reason in favour of separation is that planning and resource allocation processes designed for an established business can stifle the prospects of a new one. Established businesses have customers, organisational structures and prejudices that dispose them to stay with the familiar when they decide where to make their investments. In the fight for corporate capital, talent and commitment, new ideas often fail to attract managerial attention, particularly in their early stages; when compared with an existing business, an idea of unproven worth can seem insubstantial. A separate enterprise can also operate under its own resource allocation criteria, performance measurement systems and reward structures.

Although separation can take a business a long way towards achieving the goals of growth and performance, it has several problems, mainly because it pushes the recognition and selection tasks involved in innovation and business building to the higher levels of management. In strictly partitioned organisations, senior executives are responsible for detecting new possibilities and patterns and for bringing new ideas into focus. Top managers, already struggling to maintain contact with existing customers, markets and employees, are faced with a growing information overload. In some cases, new ideas are suppressed too quickly; in others, top managers champion projects whose potential has not been assessed accurately. Moreover, since separation creates new organisational boundaries, it also limits the flow of information and ideas and thereby makes it more likely that they may be lost.[18]

Thus, while ventures do need space to develop, strict separation prevents them from obtaining invaluable resources and robs their parents of the vitality they can generate. A delicate blend of separation and cooperation will help achieve both focused performance and faster growth. In other words, companies have to become 'ambidextrous' in order to develop radical innovations and protect their traditional businesses. Ambidextrous organisations separate their new, exploratory units from their traditional, exploitative ones, allowing for different processes and cultures; at the same time, they maintain tight links across units at the senior executive level. Such companies manage organisational separation through a tightly integrated senior team.[19]

New venture divisions

Many organisations engage in corporate venturing through autonomous new venture divisions (NVDs). NVDs are separate organisational units under the broader corporate umbrella, and they have the task of incubating mainly discontinuous opportunities from concept through to commercialisation and value capture. These in-house venture divisions play the role of corporate incubators, providing emergent businesses with a suite of services in an attempt to leverage the investing corporation's existing assets within the emergent business.

Figure 16.5 (p. 416) shows an NVD model. This NVD model combines traditional corporate business development and venture capital principles. In other words, NVDs provide business ventures with a customised level of corporate sponsorship and support along with the flexibility and autonomy of an entrepreneurial environment.

NVDs manage corporate venturing differently from the way traditional in-house research and development (R&D) does. Venture investments are typically riskier and less subject to rigid management of internal costs than conventional corporate R&D is. Protecting venture investments from such controls is one reason ideas are incubated and start-ups housed under a separate umbrella. In addition, in NVDs' corporate venturing activities, returns are part financial and part strategic, whereas with pure venture capital, investors' expected financial returns are paramount. Clearly, corporate venturing investments should follow the best practices of venture capital firms, but the twin objectives of financial and strategic returns must be balanced in ways that do not concern venture capitalists. Several organisations have established NVDs to build new businesses, including Lucent Technologies, Xerox, Nokia, Nortel and Amway.

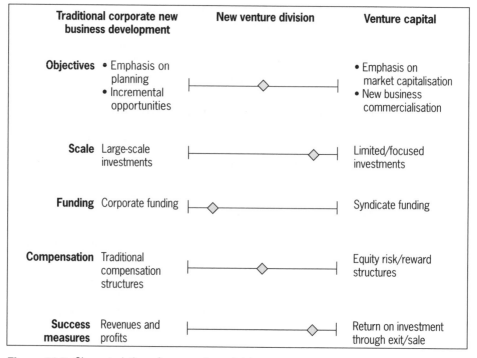

Figure 16.5: Characteristics of new venture divisions

Source: Based on the work of R.A. Burgelman & L.R. Sayles, *Inside Corporate Innovation: Strategy, Structure and Managerial Skills*, The Free Press, New York, 1986.

Venture capital funds

In an attempt to recreate the financial incentives that drive the traditional venture capital (VC) model and gain more direct interaction with early-stage companies, many organisations have set up venture capital funds. Fund managers are often given an interest in the fund to motivate them to produce financial returns in the same manner as a traditional venture fund. The corporate venture fund is therefore good at producing financial returns and, through its independence, is able to avoid some of the internal pressures to invest in businesses where the prospects for financial return are somewhat secondary to other corporate interests.

There are essentially two types of venture capital initiative: internal and external. Internal venture programs replicate all the characteristics of the VC model within the company itself. A venture board of managers is set up to act as an internal VC firm, and employees submit business plans to this board for funding. Internal programs are most appropriate for organisations seeking to increase the volume of ideas they generate, to capture greater value from their ideas, or to increase internal entrepreneurship. But internal programs can run into trouble if few of the required capabilities exist in-house.

External venture funds, on the other hand, involve establishing a VC fund for making investments in the wider start-up community, either directly or via established VC firms. Compared with internal programs, external programs can provide access to a wider variety of new products and technologies and generate better opportunities for technology and skill transfer. They represent a safer financial bet, allowing an organisation both to spread its investments across a more diversified portfolio and to leverage more easily the skills of professional VC firms. External programs are thus the better solution for organisations seeking to import good ideas, play catch-up in a rapidly evolving industry and hedge their bets across a broad array of new technologies.[20]

Reward according to results

Traditional reward systems in organisations are designed for people who enjoy power and status. These systems encourage safe, conservative behaviour. Promotion with broadened responsibilities and higher salaries attracts and motivates employees to become managers. These things, however, are rarely strong motivators for corporate entrepreneurs, whose main focus is achievement. This section suggests that organisations need to compensate creatively by using a mix of financial and non-financial rewards.

Creative compensation

Organisations must compensate creatively. For example, innovative organisations consistently reward creativity, but they avoid using money to 'bribe' people who come up with innovative ideas. Because monetary rewards may make people feel they are being controlled, such a tactic may not work. An organisation's leaders can support creativity by requiring information sharing and collaboration and by ensuring that political problems do not fester. Thus, it is just as important to reward the team as it is to reward the individual, depending on the situation.

Once one moves beyond the idea generation and concept development stages, compensation of the managers who run the corporate venturing function is important. Organisations often tend to stick with the 'outsourced model' (such as an external VC program), even when an internally managed fund would probably be more effective. The problem stems from a fundamental conflict. To ensure that corporations have the best people making their investment decisions, they must offer compensation in line with the market for investment managers/venture capitalists. At the same time, the compensation of their corporate venturing managers should ideally be in line with that of their peers in other parts of the organisation. Consequently, many organisations have implemented schemes they hope will meet the expectations of corporate entrepreneurs, such as bonuses linked to the performance of companies in the investment portfolio or equity in the start-up businesses (or in a side fund that tracks them).

Different types of reward

In the Pacific Rim region, cash is often the favoured motivational tool, followed by travel and promotion.[21] There has been a push to introduce new types of reward over the past few years. The concept of travel-based motivation and rewards is still new, but it is beginning to take hold. Several Asian businesses are influenced by the Japanese, who have used travel as a reward for a number of years. Personal recognition is another important type of reward. At 3M the abundance of rewards and recognition — big, little, weekly or annually — such as the 'Circle of Technical Excellence', reinforces the view that people are the company's most important resource for stimulating innovation.

Companies can also adopt broader compensation schemes such as incentive share options. These are rights to purchase company securities, usually ordinary shares, which are issued to company employees and others the company wants to hire. They are designed to attract new employees and motivate existing employees by giving them the right to purchase company shares in the future at present-day prices. If the company is successful, and its shares increase in value, employees can purchase shares in the future at a price far below the then fair market value of the shares.

Tailor rewards to employees

It is important to tailor compensation to fit the values held by employees, giving each employee the right mix of incentives and rewards (such as monetary bonuses, incentive share options, development opportunities and lifestyle perks). For example, partners and other employees in the Lucent New Venture Group are compensated in much the same way as VC fund partners are, sharing in the performance gains of the whole portfolio. Employees are enticed to each new individual venture with compensation similar to that of an external start-up company — that is, with equity ownership in the business.[22]

Successful organisations clearly communicate how they will treat people and how they will differentiate individual performance and risk-taking in new ventures. This declaration may be prompted by a visionary leader's initiative, the organisation's core culture (whether performance driven or entrepreneurial) or the need to survive. Whatever the case, the declaration encourages employees to take part in a self-selection process if they are willing to innovate and to bear risks in return for the potential upside of a new venture.

Communication

Communication is essential for sharing the vision of top management, for developing an entrepreneurial culture, and for stimulating creativity and innovation throughout the corporate structure. Communication should be about facts and should target frontline supervisors and other key players in the organisation. It is important to promote an open communication to nurture ideas and capabilities.

Communicate facts and target frontline supervisors

Instilling a spirit of entrepreneurship in an organisation entails changing the corporate strategy, culture and administration. The only effective way to communicate a value is to act in accordance with it and give others the incentive to do the same.

For example, creating a risk-friendly environment requires demonstrating that stumbles on the innovation path are forgiven.

Members of senior management must state clearly what they plan to do and set those facts down on paper. Communication should first target frontline supervisors because they are the opinion leaders in the organisation. They greatly influence the attitudes and behaviours of others and are critical to the success of any change in corporate culture. Supervisor briefings are an effective way to gain their acceptance. These are face-to-face meetings between a senior manager working on the development of corporate entrepreneurship and a small group of frontline supervisors.[23]

Promote open communication for sharing ideas

Many things that seem to happen naturally in smaller businesses do not happen so easily in larger ones. One of these is communication within the organisation. If communication occurs only through established channels, employees who do not normally interact with one another will never interact. To promote communication, it is essential to provide opportunities (communal areas, informal gatherings) for employees to meet. The advantage lies in ensuring that every employee can understand the organisation's activities well enough to be able to tap into its resources and expertise.

Communication technologies have also made sharing ideas easier. These now extend well beyond basic email into various kinds of real-time and asynchronous electronic connections — chat rooms and news groups; conferencing systems; technologies for surveys, voting, and joint document preparation and so on. Electronic communications are ideal for involving creative people who might be shunned or perceived as marginal in organisations that rely too heavily on face-to-face idea exchange.

Summary

Most established organisations find it difficult to maintain the initial entrepreneurial spirit that helped them survive the start-up stage. As organisations grow, they usually become more structured and more rigid. Through corporate entrepreneurship, established organisations attempt to exploit their internal resources in order to pursue opportunities that will help the business grow and diversify. Other reasons for developing corporate entrepreneurship include retaining and motivating the brightest staff, exploiting underused resources and getting rid of non-core activities. Corporate entrepreneurship can be defined as the process whereby an individual or a group, in association with an existing organisation, creates a new organisation or initiates renewal or innovation within that organisation.

Successful organisations have developed a disciplined, milestone-focused approach to screening and funding new ventures. Such an approach usually comprises five main stages: idea generation, concept development, business plan development, incubation and commercialisation, and value capture. This development process evaluates each new venture at predetermined milestones to decide whether to proceed, refine, accelerate or discontinue the venture. Using such a time-phased approach, organisations gradually increase their commitment in line with the availability of more information. As the venture moves through critical 'decision gates', its performance is measured against established targets and expectations, and resource decisions are made. To deal effectively with the implementation issues, corporate management must recognise and empower internal entrepreneurs and product champions.

Developing an entrepreneurial spirit inside an existing organisation requires four steps: (1) develop a vision and a strategy, (2) create a culture of innovation, (3) develop organisational support and (4) reward results accordingly. This process requires time and relentless effort. Evidence suggests that most firms build up the attributes of corporate entrepreneurship in long-drawn-out processes over many years, not in a one-shot, single event. This change process must be sustained by appropriate communication. In the initial phase of sharing the vision and initiating the change, communication should focus on facts and target frontline supervisors because they are the opinion leaders in the organisation. It is important to promote open communication in order to nurture ideas and capabilities.

REVIEW QUESTIONS

1. What is the rationale for developing corporate entrepreneurship in an organisation?

2. What are the dimensions of corporate entrepreneurship?

3. What is corporate venturing?

4. What are the stages of the new venture development process inside an organisation?

5. What are the key steps an organisation could follow to develop an entrepreneurial spirit?

DISCUSSION QUESTIONS

1. Why does corporate venturing usually go beyond the new product development often discussed in marketing courses?

2. How is corporate venturing different from traditional business development practices such as takeovers, corporate R&D, and venture capital financing?

3. To what extent do an organisation's social networks play a role in the discovery and pursuit of new business opportunities?

4. What are the arguments in favour of separating new venture development activities from existing operations in the organisation?

5. What is the role of the organisation's executives in developing and sustaining corporate entrepreneurship?

SUGGESTED READING

Elfring, T., *Corporate Entrepreneurship and Venturing*, Springer, New York, 2005.

Sathe, V., *Corporate Entrepreneurship: Top Managers and New Business Creation*, Cambridge University Press, Cambridge, 2003.

Tushman, M.L. & O'Reilly, C.A., *Winning though Innovation: A Practical Guide to Leading Organizational Change and Renewal*, Harvard Business School Press, Boston, MA, 2002.

CASE STUDY

AirAsia

Tony Fernandes founded Tune Air Sdn Bhd in 2001, with a vision of making air travel more affordable for Malaysians. With this vision in mind, Tony and three partners bought AirAsia from DRB-Hicom, a Malaysian conglomerate, for one ringgit. AirAsia was virtually bankrupt at the time, and its fleet consisted of two ageing Boeing jets. Tune Air's initial project was to create a new aviation product in Malaysia by remodelling AirAsia into a low-fare, no-frills carrier. This premise was based on the success of low-fare airlines such as US-based Southwest Airlines and Ireland's Ryanair.

Under the leadership of Mr Fernandes, the fledgling airline has become a thriving business. AirAsia currently operates more than 100 domestic and international flights from its hubs at Kuala Lumpur International Airport (KLIA), Johor Bahru in Malaysia, Bangkok International Airport, and Soekarno-Hatta International Airport in Jakarta. During the 2005–06 financial year, the company transported 5.7 million passengers. Most importantly, AirAsia has generated a profit since its first day of operation. For the financial year ending 30 June 2006, it generated a turnover of RM855 million with a profit of RM127 million.

Tony Fernandes

AirAsia is the brainchild of Tony Fernandes. 'Tony might be the CEO of the company, but he is also the mascot of the company. Because wherever he goes, whatever he does, he represents the company,' says Mohshin Aziz, Head of Investor Relations at AirAsia. There is a cultural symmetry between what Tony Fernandes tries to present and what the company actually represents. 'He doesn't wear fancy millionaire clothes and he doesn't have a driver. He drives a normal Ford SUV, a normal family car, and he wears a normal t-shirt and jeans like any other Malaysian would,' adds Mr Aziz.

Tony Fernandes was born in Kuala Lumpur and studied finance at the London School of Economics. Upon graduation in 1987, he joined the Virgin Group before moving onto Warner Music International in London. Subsequently, he was transferred back to Malaysia. In 1992, at the age of 28, Fernandes became the youngest ever managing director of Warner Music Malaysia. His last serving role at Warner Music was regional Vice President for South-East Asia. He left in order to pursue his dream of starting a budget airline.

Given that the company was founded just after the September 11 terrorist attack in 2001, undoubtedly the worst day in the history of commercial aviation, everyone thought the business was doomed to fail. However, AirAsia has not only survived — it has thrived.[24] The airline has repaid all of its debt and has been profitable since the first day of operation. AirAsia grew from two ageing Boeing jets to 42 aircraft (35 Boeing 737s and five Airbus A320s). Mr Fernandes says his timing was perfect: since September 11, 2001, aircraft leasing costs were down 40 per cent. Also, airline layoffs meant that experienced staff were readily available.[25]

The low cost strategy

AirAsia's fares are significantly lower than those of other operators. This service targets the passenger who can do without frills, such as meals, frequent flyer miles and airport lounges, in exchange for fares up to 80 per cent lower than other airlines. The low-cost strategy is based on reducing cost at all levels by paying attention to detail.

For example, complimentary drinks and meals are not offered. Instead, the airline recently introduced 'Snack Attack', a range of on-board snacks and drinks that are very affordable and prepared exclusively for the airline. Asset utilisation plays an important role too; AirAsia's asset utilisation rate is among the highest in the world. Typically, an aircraft starts its first flight around 7 am, and is in use all day up until 11 pm. The distribution channels are also a great source of cost reduction: 'Because sales from the internet are the cheapest way to devise your sales, to date about 65 per cent of our sales are from internet,' comments Mr Aziz. Wherever possible, AirAsia flies to and from secondary airports rather than from the main congested hubs. This explains why it flies to Johor Bahru rather than Singapore, and to Macau rather than Hong Kong. The airline even operates its own low-cost terminal at KLIA.

Low cost does not equate to a lack of innovation. On the contrary, because of the emergence of new budget airlines in the region (with Qantas recently launching Jetstar and Singapore establishing Tiger Airways), the need for innovation is more pressing than ever. For example, in 2003 AirAsia became the first airline in the world to introduce SMS booking. Passengers can now book their seats, check flight schedules and obtain the latest updates on AirAsia promotions from the convenience of their mobile phones. More recently, AirAsia introduced GO Holiday, the airline's online program through which guests can book holiday packages via the internet in real time.

Midnight sessions

AirAsia's culture is very open and has a flat hierarchy. The headquarters of the company are located in its low-cost terminal at KLIA, and the offices have a view of the planes and runway. This constantly reminds the employees of the company's core business, and helps to keep them focused. If people need help, colleagues will go into the terminal and carry bags. The doors are invariably open, so it is not unusual to see marketing people, engineers, cabin crew and pilots all sharing the same office.

All 2000-plus employees are actively encouraged to make suggestions on how to improve services and processes, and resolve problems. To this effect, 'midnight sessions' (so-called because they take place after working hours) are regularly held throughout the company. During these sessions, top management will brief staff about operational issues, main concerns and the latest financial results; feedback is also sought from employees. Mr Aziz says: 'For example, if we have a recurring problem, it's an opportunity for both parties to actually voice to each other why the problem is arising, how to solve it, what's required of the management and the rest of the staff.' Hierarchy does not exist during these sessions and every employee is considered an equal. Everyone can ask a question and get an answer.

Mobilising staff was one of the key challenges to make AirAsia successful, 'because in the airline industry, it's not the top management, it's not the managers who are interacting with the customers; it's always the cabin crew, the engineers and the ground staff. They are the ones who are key determinants of making the flight enjoyable for customers or not! It's common knowledge that if the employees are not happy, there is no conceivable way that the customers will be happy because the service will be short of one critical ingredient: sincerity!' comments Mr Aziz.

Also, whenever the airline wants to make any major changes or operational changes, it always consult with its employees first. He adds: 'For example, about three years ago, we thought of rebranding the whole image of the company, as we wanted to instil a new fresh and fun image. So we had one of those midnight sessions again and we talked to all the cabin crew, pilots and ground staff, and asked them what they thought of the idea; they gave us a lot of input, and in fact they were instrumental in the change process. They went on to design their own uniforms and the check-in counters.'

The empowerment of staff aims to create passion. Employees are encouraged to use initiative to solve business and operational decisions. This means taking risks and tolerating failures. The example comes from the CEO. 'Never be afraid of failure. You've got to take the risk and go for it. If you are afraid of failure, you aren't ever going to start,' said Mr Fernandes recently.

Rewarding employees

'From a staff point of view, our employees are remunerated better than those of our competitors,' says Mr Aziz. The remuneration system at AirAsia comprises a fixed component and flexible component, dependent on quality requirements. Therefore, the employees have substantial incentives to meet all of the quality requirements. The ratio is fixed or flexible, which varies across the type of employees (cabin crew, pilots, ground staff and engineers). For cabin crew the ratio could be as much as 50:50.

The company is significantly owner-managed. The senior management (CEO, deputy CEO, CFO, and the four directors) own 37 per cent of shares. On top of this figure, the employees own at least 4 per cent of shares. Since the company listed in November 2004, all employees have received share options. 'We believe that's one of the other competitive advantages for the company as well, because when we talk about the health of the company and the need to meet profits, everyone can see how it all translates to our share price,' comments Mr Aziz. This is certainly a clever strategy to align the interests of employees, managers and owners.

Sources: Based on author's interview with Mohshin Aziz, Head of Investor Relations, AirAsia, and on the company website <www.airasia.com>.

Questions

1. What are the ingredients of AirAsia's low-cost strategy?

2. What new opportunities would you advise Mr Fernandes to pursue in order to grow the business?

3. In your opinion, what are the key elements of AirAsia's entrepreneurial approach?

ENDNOTES

1. P. Sharma & J.J. Chrisman, 'Toward a reconciliation of the definitional issues in the field of corporate entrepreneurship', *Entrepreneurship Theory and Practice*, vol. 23, no. 3, 1999, p. 18.
2. ibid.
3. W. Guth & A. Ginsberg, 'Guest editors' introduction: Corporate entrepreneurship', *Strategic Management Journal*, no. 11, 1990, pp. 297–308.
4. S.A. Zahra, 'A conceptual model of entrepreneurship as firm behaviour: A critique and extension', *Entrepreneurship Theory and Practice*, vol. 17, no. 4, 1993, pp. 5–21.
5. J. Albrinck et al., 'Adventures in corporate venturing', *Strategy + Business*, no. 22, 2000, pp. 119–29.
6. 'Adopting orphans', *Economist*, 20 February 1999, pp. 17–18.
7. A. de Ramos, ,The wizard of Oz', *CFO Asia*, April 2006.
8. L. Colquhoun, 'Macquarie boss happy to be part of AGSM Team', *AGSM Magazine*, Issue 2, 1 September 2005.
9. K.W. Chan & R. Mauborgne, 'Value innovation: The strategic logic of high growth', *Harvard Business Review*, January–February 1997, p. 104.
10. S.N. Joni et al., 'Innovations from the inside', *Management Review*, September 1997, p. 50.
11. J. Tidd, J. Bessant & K. Pavitt, *Managing Innovation*, John Wiley & Sons, Chichester, 1999, pp. 277–80.
12. G. Neilson, J. Albrinck, J. Hornery et al., *E-Business and Beyond: Organizing for Success in New Ventures*, Booz Allen & Hamilton, New York, 2001.
13. S.W. Floyd & B. Wooldridge, 'Knowledge creation and social networks in corporate entrepreneurship: The renewal of organizational capability', *Entrepreneurship Theory and Practice*, vol. 23, no. 3, 1999, pp. 123–43.
14. R. Cross & L. Prusak, 'The people who make organisations go — or stop', *Harvard Business Review*, June 2002, pp. 105–12.
15. R. Farson & R. Keyes, 'The failure-tolerant leader', *Harvard Business Review*, Special issue 'The innovation enterprise', August 2002, pp. 64–71.
16. R.N. Foster & S. Kaplan, *Creative Destruction*, Currency, New York, 2001.
17. J. Kao, *Entrepreneurship, Creativity and Innovation*, Prentice Hall, Englewood Cliffs, NJ, 1989, p. 397.
18. J.D. Day, P.Y. Mang, A. Richter & J. Roberts, 'The innovation organisation — why new ventures need more than a room of their own', *The McKinsey Quarterly*, no. 2, 2001, pp. 14–19.
19. C.A. O'Reilly & M.L. Tushman, 'The ambidextrous organization', *Harvard Business Review*, April 2004, pp. 74–81.
20. P. Brody & D. Ehrlich, 'Can big companies become successful venture capitalists?' *The McKinsey Quarterly*, no. 2, 1998, pp. 50–63.
21. 'Revving up Asia's workers', *Asian Business*, February 1996, pp. 41–4.
22. J. Albrinck et al., *see* note 5.
23. T.J. Larkin & S. Larkin, 'Reaching and changing frontline employees', *Harvard Business Review*, May–June 1996, pp. 95–104.
24. 'Tony Fernandes', Special Report: Star of Asia Entrepreneurs, *Business Week Online*, <www.businessweek.com>, 12 July 2004.
25. A. Ranawana, 'This is one guy with no fear of flying', *Asia Week*, 30 November 2001.

Contemporary issues in small business and entrepreneurship

LEARNING OBJECTIVES

After reading this chapter, you should be able to:

- explain the difference between social obligation, social responsiveness and social responsibility

- identify ways in which eco-efficient small firms can reduce or eliminate harmful environmental impacts

- outline the current status of Indigenous entrepreneurship in Australia and New Zealand

- explain the differences between male-owned and female-owned small businesses

- define the concept of social entrepreneurship

- explain how home-based businesses differ from other small firms.

B usinesses do not operate in a vacuum. Small firms are part of the broader community, and to be successful they need to have an understanding of social issues in the societies in which they operate. The hallmark of successful entrepreneurs and small business owners is their ability to identify and respond to new issues long before the impact is understood by competitors. These business owners make a conscious effort to stay ahead of new trends, and take the initiative in dealing with them by keeping in mind the likely impact of such changes when developing their own business strategies. In this chapter, we discuss and analyse some of the contemporary trends in the Pacific Rim region that are affecting entrepreneurs and small firms, or which are likely to affect them in the near future.

The relationship of small firms to society

How small firms relate to social issues can be evaluated in two simple ways: (1) by examining one of the most popular models of firm behaviour in the area of social needs — *social responsibility*, and (2) by looking at the types of financial and other contributions they make to the community — *philanthropic behaviour*.

Social responsibility

Social responsibility refers to the duty of business to contribute towards and improve the welfare and wellbeing of the broader society in which it exists. In other words, it is the obligation of a business to have a positive impact on society.[1]

There are many ways business organisations can adopt socially responsible business practices. These include protecting and improving the natural environment; providing a safe, secure and enjoyable workplace for employees; donating money and materials to charitable activities; and promoting opportunities for groups who have traditionally been excluded from many jobs — people with disabilities, for example.

The argument about whether businesses should be involved in broader community issues is a long-running one. It has traditionally been argued that the responsibility of business lies mainly in conducting its own affairs; in other words, that 'the business of business is business', and anything that prevents a firm from maximising its own profitability is an unnecessary hindrance. According to this perspective, firms that focus on making a profit, rather than on social responsibility, are able to deliver wealth to their owners, which they can then individually use to help society if they wish. Such viewpoints are often accompanied by claims that business owners usually do not have the skills or knowledge, much less the willingness, to become socially responsible. It is the role of government and community groups, not businesses, to determine what constitutes social wellbeing; therefore, it is inappropriate for firms to be involved in such activities.[2]

On the other hand, there are several arguments in favour of greater social responsibility by business. Firstly, it can be argued that firms need to contribute to the society that has supported them. Businesses rely on the community to purchase their products and services, so activities that enrich society and improve its welfare will indirectly help the firm. Another claim is that since business possesses substantial resources (such as money, people and ideas) that can be used to help the community, it should do so. Finally, there is also the suggestion that socially responsible behaviour is a clever strategy. A firm that is seen to be responsible and a 'good citizen' will often generate substantial marketing and goodwill benefits from its activities.[3] Recent evidence suggests that, contrary to the common perception that entrepreneurs are more likely to 'bend the rules' and act irresponsibly, most new venture operators in fact tend to have strong ethical standards.[4]

Sethi has defined the social role of business as a continuum of responses.[5] At one end of the scale, there are those businesses that comply only with their **social obligation** to obey the law. Businesses in the middle of the continuum adopt a position of **social responsiveness**, because they believe there are benefits in doing so, or because of pressure from stakeholders and other parties to do so. At the other end of the continuum, there are firms that adopt a position of **social responsibility**, pursuing long-term goals that benefit society, even though there may be little, if any, business gain.

Social obligation:
The minimum level of socially responsible activity; doing only that which is required by law.

Philanthropic activity

Social responsiveness:
A moderate level of socially responsible activity; engaging in socially beneficial activities, mainly because there is a pragmatic benefit in doing so.

The term **philanthropy** refers to an active effort to improve society, and many businesses provide philanthropic (charitable) support to the community. Studies of small-firm philanthropy in the United States and Canada have shown that social responsibility tends to be essentially a decision made by the business owner–manager and, unlike large firms, few small enterprises have formal policies or guidelines on such activities. Interestingly, although their donations tend to be small in individual amounts, small firms tend to give proportionately more to charitable causes than do larger businesses.[6]

Social responsibility:
The maximum level of socially responsible activity; pursuing long-term goals that benefit society, even if there is no business gain in doing so.

Overall, there has been only limited research into the philanthropic activities of small business in Australia, New Zealand and Asia. However, some recent studies have found that small firms play a major role in business philanthropy by either providing donations, sponsoring charitable activities or entering into partnerships with community organisations. In fact, evidence suggests that small businesses are the largest single donor of money, and the second largest contributor to sponsorship and partnership projects.[7] Two other separate surveys — one in 2000 and one in 2005 — found almost identical results: about two-thirds (67 per cent) of the small businesses surveyed provided support to community organisations and activities.[8] The contribution by SMEs in Australia alone was estimated to be worth about $1.5 billion in 2005.[9]

Philanthropy:
An active effort to improve society.

Data from New Zealand indicate that over half of all business firms in the country contribute to social and community activities, either through sponsorship or donations. The most common reasons for doing so involved a mixture of both altruism and self-interest: firms recognised that it was important to support their local community, but at the same time they realised there were potential marketing benefits for themselves.[10]

Several mechanisms now exist through which small firms can contribute to community development, as shown in table 17.1.

Table 17.1: Information on social responsibility in business

Organisation	Website
Business for Social Responsibility	<www.bsr.org>
Philanthropy Australia	<www.philanthropy.org.au>
NZ Sustainable Business Network	<www.sustainable.org.nz>

It appears likely that, over time, the pressure on firms to adopt more socially aware and responsible practices will increase. However, as the above research shows, small firms are already making a major contribution in this area.

What would you do?

The fin edge of the wedge?

Despite their reputation as fearsome hunters, the world's sharks are in a precarious position. Almost 20 different species are believed to be endangered, and could possibly be facing extinction.

In large part, the demise of some species is due to traditional demand for shark fin soup as a gourmet delicacy. The soup has long been a favourite dish in southern China, and in recent years there has been a strong upsurge in demand for it throughout Asia.

Shark fin fishing can be both wasteful and painful. In many cases, the shark's fin is removed from the animal and the rest of the carcass is thrown back into the sea, thus wasting about 95 to 99 per cent of the animal. Often the fish are not killed in the process, and are left to suffer a slow, painful death.

To help combat this, in recent years organisations such as the Asian Conservation Awareness Program and prominent media stars such as Hong Kong actor Jackie Chan have teamed up to lobby for a ban on shark fishing and protection.

Imagine you are the proprietor of a small upmarket restaurant in Hong Kong. Your market is geared towards affluent local Chinese businessmen and expatriate resident Westerners, and you specialise in local Chinese delicacies. This includes, of course, shark fin soup, which is a popular dish in your restaurant.

Last week you saw a documentary on the plight of shark species in the South China Sea, which made you think about this conservation issue for the first time. Then, two evenings ago, one of your regular American clients quietly raised the issue with you. She asked you to stop offering shark fin soup. 'I entertain a lot of people in this establishment,' she said, 'but I'm reconsidering my position. I really believe that you should not be selling this. When the buying stops, the killing stops.'

For more information on the shark fin debate, visit the website of the Asian Conservation Awareness Program at <www.wildaid.org>.

Questions

1. Would you ban shark fin soup from your menu? Give reasons to justify your answer.
2. What other steps can you take to improve the level of environmental responsibility of your firm?

Environmental issues

Environmental responsibility: The need to protect and enhance the natural environment.

Closely related to the concept of social responsibility is that of **environmental responsibility**, which refers to the need of firms to protect and enhance the natural environment. Environmental issues are becoming increasingly important to all businesses in the twenty-first century; on the one hand, they pose risks (such as the threat of legal action and public disapproval for poor environmental performance), while on the other hand, they provide opportunities (such as a source of niche marketing, reduced waste and costs, and innovation).[11] In addition, increasing population, a declining quality of air and water, biodiversity loss and the need to minimise the use of raw materials are beginning to affect many more communities and the businesses that operate within them.

Small and medium-sized enterprises are often overlooked when the causes of and solutions to environmental problems are examined. This is despite the fact that they account for the majority of the world's business enterprises, about half of all employment, and much of the total level of economic output in each country. Although no definite figures exist, it is also commonly claimed that they are responsible for about 70 per cent of global pollution.[12]

Small firms have only a minor individual impact on the environment, but when taken together they have a substantial collective influence. Moreover, it is often easier to reach key decision makers in such enterprises. This is because management and ownership of the firm are frequently synonymous; indeed, one of the defining features of a small business is that ownership is usually restricted to one or two people who are also the key decision makers in the enterprise.[13] As a result, this provides a unique opportunity for individual owner–managers to put their values into practice in the workplace, and to influence the behaviour of employees, consumers and other stakeholders.[14]

However, the involvement of small firms in measures to protect the natural environment has been one of mixed results so far. Most research in this area has indicated that there is a substantial gap between the environmental views and attitudes of small business owner–managers (which are generally positive and supportive) and the actual practices of their firms (which generally tend to lag behind). Several researchers have shown that although many small business owner–managers have a high awareness of their role in environmental remediation, and have a strong desire to actively do something, their actual performance often falls far short of what is desired.[15] Most owners do not have enough free time or access to the necessary information needed to make their firms greener.[16] This is the so-called SME problem in environmental management.[17] To date, most small-firm responses to environmental issues have focused on 'end-of-pipe' solutions: cleaning up and remedying only the most obvious environmental damage, such as pollution or waste that they directly create. Although this is useful, there is a lot more that can be done.

At a basic level, there is a series of very simple and practical steps that can be taken to improve the day-to-day environmental impact of every small business; these are listed in the box that follows.

Improving environmental outcomes

There are many simple ways in which small firms can contribute to a better environment for the future:

- Recycle newspapers, glassware, obsolete computer monitors, outdated mobile phone batteries and other office waste.
- Recycle office paper — use it for notetaking and phone messages.
- Turn off electrical machinery when not in use.
- Check energy efficiency ratings of all office equipment that the firm purchases.
- Install energy-efficient lightbulbs.
- Install insulation.
- Plant local native vegetation around business premises.
- Conduct an energy audit to identify unnecessary energy consumption and reduce power bills.
- Donate to a local environmental project or organisation.
- Open windows rather than use air-conditioning if possible.
- Conduct a water audit.
- Encourage car pooling by staff.
- Allow staff to telecommute.
- Place long-term investment funds in a socially responsible managed fund (mutual fund).

Source: Adapted from B. Lord, *The Green Workplace*, Schwartz & Wilkinson, Melbourne, 1990.

Eco-efficiency

In the medium to long term, firms and entrepreneurs also need to focus on management systems that are environmentally sustainable and promote innovation and enhanced competitiveness.[18] **Eco-efficiency** is a management strategy that jointly promotes both environmental and economic performance. The World Business Council for Sustainable Development (WBCSD), which first coined the concept, has defined it as:

> ... the delivery of competitively priced goods and services that satisfy human needs and bring quality of life, while progressively reducing ecological impacts and resource intensity throughout the product life-cycle, to a level at least in line with the earth's estimated carrying capacity.[19]

The WBCSD identified seven components of eco-efficiency that, if acted upon properly, can contribute to business growth:

- reduce the material intensity of goods and services
- reduce the energy intensity of goods and services
- reduce toxic dispersion
- enhance material recyclability
- maximise sustainable use of renewable resources
- extend product durability
- increase the service intensity of goods and services.

Eco-efficiency:
A management strategy that focuses on the delivery of competitively priced goods and services which satisfy consumer needs while progressively reducing ecological impacts throughout the product life cycle.

'Ecopreneurship'

In recent years a growing number of business operators have realised that eco-efficiency can also provide a strong long-term competitive advantage for them. Thus, some 'ecopreneurs' have recognised that they can harness consumer concerns about the state of the environment to develop new market niches, and others have identified long-term market changes that they should adapt to.[20] BP, for example, has recently moved to aggressively position itself as a major supplier of renewable energy, rather than just an 'old economy' source of polluting fuels. Ecopreneurs display many of the characteristics of conventional entrepreneurs, including a willingness to take calculated risks, an ability to identify new and emergent business opportunities, and the capacity to 'think outside the box' and use new and innovative business practices (in this case, environmentally friendly ones) to increase profitability and performance. Table 17.2 lists some sources of environmental information for entrepreneurs and small business operators.

Table 17.2: Sources of environmental information

Organisation	Website
APEC Sustainable Development Forum	<www.apecsec.org.sg>
EnviroLink Network	<www.envirolink.org>
Greening of Industry Network	<www.greeningofindustry.org>
World Business Council for Sustainable Development	<www.wbcsd.org>
Business Council for Sustainable Development in Malaysia	<www.bcsdm.com.my>
NZ Business Council for Sustainable Development	<www.nzbcsd.org.nz>

Indigenous entrepreneurs

An area that is often overlooked in the contemporary analysis of entrepreneurship and small business management is the role of Indigenous enterprises. This is an emerging field of study, and is becoming important because small business has the potential to deliver major changes in the economic, political and social status of **Indigenous peoples** in countries such as Australia and New Zealand.

Indigenous peoples: The original inhabitants of a nation, territory or geographical region, and their descendants.

In both of these nations, the original (Indigenous) inhabitants have been displaced by European settlers. These changes often resulted in substantial suffering and disadvantage for Indigenous peoples. As a result, many such groups do not have a strongly developed base of small business ownership and entrepreneurial activity.

In Australia, there are two distinct Indigenous groups: the Aboriginal peoples of the Australian continent and the Torres Strait Islanders who live in the island chain of the Torres Strait, located between Queensland and Papua New Guinea.

Today there are over 400 000 Indigenous people in Australia, accounting for about 2.4 per cent of the country's total population.[21] (At the time of European colonisation in 1788, there were an estimated 750 000 Aboriginal people living throughout Australia.) Yet, although Indigenous communities represent one of the nation's youngest and fastest growing population groups,[22] the proportion of Indigenous people operating their own businesses, either as owner–managers or as self-employed people, is well below the national average. Over the last 20 years, the number of working Indigenous Australians who are small business owners has barely changed, even as self-employment and entrepreneurship has become an increasingly popular career option throughout much of the Australian population as a whole. In 1986, they constituted five per cent of the Indigenous workforce; in 1994, they also accounted for five per cent; and in 2001 represented just seven per cent.[23] Why is this so?

The reasons for this shortfall are complex. Four significant factors that appear to play a role are cultural differences, historical factors, lack of economic resources and geographical considerations.

In the first place, it has sometimes been suggested that certain aspects of traditional Indigenous culture have worked against the notion, common in modern Western economies, of the enterprising individual (see table 17.3, opposite). For example, Indigenous Australian societies have usually placed a strong emphasis on communal ownership of resources, so that property belongs to a group rather than to an individual. Indigenous communities have developed a culture that more frequently emphasises cooperation instead of competition, sharing with family members, and the need for extensive community consultation before making important decisions. This is in stark contrast to the acquisitive, individually focused, monetarised economy of European society.[24] It also sits at odds with the conventional entrepreneurial approach of solo decision making, focusing on private gain and explicit competition with others.

The past treatment of Indigenous Australians by Europeans has also done very little to promote active involvement in a contemporary capitalist economy. For much of the time since European settlement, Indigenous people were economically marginalised and given only the very lowest paid jobs. In many industries, they were remunerated, not with cash, but in kind (paid with food, clothing or other goods) until the 1940s and 1950s. This made it extremely difficult for individuals, or even family and community groups, to accumulate the capital that is needed to start a business venture. It was not until the passage of a constitutional referendum in 1967 that the federal government granted Aboriginal people the right to vote, own land and hold citizenship. Before this, such rights had been provided by state governments to only a very limited number of Indigenous people. Finally, in 1992 the High Court of Australia, in its historic Mabo decision, finally recognised the traditional ownership of land by Indigenous people (and, hence, their right to develop it economically).[25] All this has resulted in an historical legacy of a people who have had very limited opportunity to participate in a capitalist economy, build wealth, or develop the skills needed to manage a modern business organisation. Overcoming such a legacy will take a considerable period of time.

Table 17.3: Differences in business-related values between Indigenous and other Australians

Attitudes towards...	Indigenous Australians	Non-Indigenous Australians
Possessions	Use and share	Accumulate and acquire
Land	Relationship with	Ownership of
Interaction	Cooperation	Competition
Rights	Kin obligations	Individual rights
Basic operating unit	Society	Individual

Source: M. Schaper, 'Australia's Aboriginal entrepreneurs: Challenges for the future', *Journal of Small Business Management*, vol. 37, no. 3, July 1999, p. 89.

Even today, Indigenous communities remain some of the most disadvantaged in the nation, with very high levels of unemployment, poor life expectancy, low household incomes and lower than average educational qualifications.[26] The location of many Indigenous communities also remains a problem for successful venture creation. Many Indigenous people live outside the capital cities of Australia, and it is in the cities that most economic and business opportunities are found. Communities based in small and isolated population centres have limited opportunities to create viable business enterprises,[27] and they face substantial disadvantages in terms of transport and communication costs, market size and access to new ideas and innovations.

Today there are a number of programs designed to remedy these problems, run by Indigenous organisations, state and federal governments and the private sector. There are a number of successful Indigenous enterprises already operating in the pastoral, arts and tourism fields, and there is a small but growing pool of qualified Indigenous professionals, some of whom run their own practices and firms.[28] An example of a community-based Indigenous entrepreneurial project is that of Goolarri Media (see the Entrepreneur Profile on p. 434). However, there is still a long way to go.

Across the Tasman Sea, New Zealand's Maori people represent about 13 per cent of the country's population today. The right of Maori people in New Zealand to own land, earn wages and participate in parliament has long been recognised by government. However, there are still substantial differences in wealth, employment opportunities and entrepreneurial activity between Maori and *pakeha* (European) New Zealanders. The last 20 years has seen a substantial increase in the number of Maori either working for themselves or owning their own businesses. Between 1981 and 1996, their number increased from 6300 to 16 700.[29] However, they are still only half as likely to be self-employed as other New Zealanders. Although almost 22 per cent of all *pakeha* are self-employed or employers of other staff (that is, business owners), the equivalent proportion among the Maori is just under 10 per cent.[30] A recent study of Maori entrepreneurs suggests that most Maori firms in New Zealand have a strong growth orientation, are highly entrepreneurial and frequently face many of the same problems as any other start-up entrepreneur — problems such as difficulty in accessing loan finance, and a shortage of management skills. However, compared to non-Maori entrepreneurs, there is a greater reliance on family and community, and a correspondingly stronger pressure to balance work and family pressures.[31] Table 17.4 lists the URLs for some national Indigenous organisations.

Table 17.4: National Indigenous organisations

Country	Organisation and website
Australia	Indigenous Business Australia <www.iba.gov.au>
New Zealand	Ministry of Maori Development (Te Puni Kokiri) <www.tpk.govt.nz>

Entrepreneur profile

Goolarri Media Enterprises

One form of social entrepreneurship is the creation of community-based businesses, in which an entire group of people creates a commercial venture that has both economic and social benefits. One of the most visible of these is Goolarri, an Indigenous company owned by the Broome Aboriginal Media Association in the north of Western Australia.

The town of Broome has a large and active Aboriginal population, and was once one of the world's leading producers of natural pearls. Today it's a popular tourist location, and the home of many prominent Indigenous musicians and artists. In 1984, several of them got together to form the Broome Musicians Aboriginal Corporation. At that time, the only radio station that reached the town was the ABC, then located in Perth some 2000 kilometres south.

In 1989 Broome Aboriginal Media Association was incorporated and two years later, using the name Radio Goolarri, they broadcast their first radio program from new ABC studios in Broome. These initially began for just one hour a week, but over time Goolarri grew until it was eventually broadcasting for 25 hours per week.

In 1998, the Association obtained a licence to operate its own community, non-profit radio station.

As the station's managing director Kevin Fong explains: 'This is more than just a radio service. Goolarri provides an avenue for Aboriginal people to express social, cultural and political ideas. It supports our traditional language, music and culture, as well as more contemporary artistic expression. It's a place where Indigenous people can tell their own stories in their own way, and somewhere that both non-Indigenous and Indigenous people come together.'

The Association still owns the assets of Goolarri, and elects a board that directly governs the activities. Goolarri Media Enterprises is a registered training organisation and now operates a recording studio, television station and events management service. A survey in 2003 found that Goolarri's 99.7 FM station is the most popular broadcaster in town, reaching out to a population of over 15 000 people living in Broome and the surrounding communities.

For more information on Goolarri, go to <www.gme.com.au>.

Source: Based on author's interview with Kevin Fong, 2006.

Gender differences

In recent years, more and more women have become involved in small businesses, mainly as the owners of their own firms. While most businesses are still run by men, almost one-fifth of all small businesses in Australia are now owned and operated by women, while another fifth are jointly run by men and women.[32] Across the Pacific region, the number of women running their own businesses has grown substantially in recent years. In New Zealand, for example, the number of female employers and female self-employed business operators has doubled over the last 30 years, and they now account for almost a third of all employers and self-employed people in that nation.[33] A similar trend is evident in Singapore, where the number of women entering self-employment has exceeded that of men since the early 1980s.[34] A recent global analysis by the Organisation for Economic Cooperation and Development has indicated that the number of firms created and managed by women is expanding, and usually outstrips the creation rate among men.[35]

There are several reasons for this increase. Many women in large firms find that they are victims of the 'glass ceiling' — the invisible and informal barriers to promotion that often mean women have difficulty in career advancement within established corporations. In addition, the growth of the services economy has meant that there is a greater demand for knowledge-based and personal service industries, sectors in which women have traditionally been employed in large numbers. A further impetus is rising levels of post-secondary education, creating a growth in the number of women with the skills and qualifications needed to operate a business. The rise of the internet and the increasing acceptance of home-based and part-time business operations have also made it easier for women to start their own business at home, operate it with minimal costs, and yet still focus on family and social needs.

But the role and number of women entrepreneurs is significant in more than just a purely numerical sense. Growing numbers of female owner–managers also provide a different perspective on how to create, manage and grow new business ventures. It has often been argued that women begin new businesses with a different set of experiences, opportunities and goals than do men. For example, women and men tend to predominate in different industry sectors, and may therefore have different notions about what makes a successful enterprise, what customers' needs are, and how the firm should be managed. (This difference can also make it harder for females to successfully launch a new venture in a field dominated by men, and vice versa.) There are often greater social expectations placed on women to balance their business activities with household and family needs. This pressure is especially strong in many ethnic Chinese communities across the Pacific Rim.[36] Sometimes the motivation for starting a business is also different. Women, for example, often state that a prime motivation is to meet personal as well as business goals and to reject stereotypes imposed on them by others.[37] There is also evidence that the leadership and managerial styles of women are different from those of men. It has been suggested that women tend to provide a more participative, democratic and consultative style of business management, whereas men tend to be more directive and autocratic in their approach.[38]

Historically, female entrepreneurs have faced different barriers to starting a new firm. A significant barrier is that they have greater difficulty than men do in raising finance for new business ventures. This is often cited in research on women in small business, and appears to arise from a combination of factors. Although gender-based discrimination may be one cause, another possible reason is the fact that women tend to accumulate less capital than men. This condition arises because women are often paid less than men, or suffer career interruptions when they leave the workforce to start and raise a family. Other barriers include a lack of personal business networks and connections, a shortage of mentors and role models, and social typecasting which assumes that women give a higher priority to their family responsibilities than their business activities.[39]

These perceived differences in entrepreneurial intention, opportunities and managerial approach appear to be reflected, at least to some extent, in empirical findings. Men are still more likely to own a business (or work for themselves) than women are, as can be seen in the analysis of working life in New Zealand in figure 17.1.

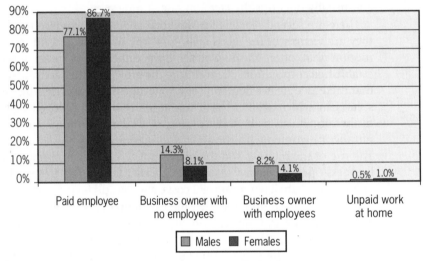

Figure 17.1: Gender differences in work in New Zealand

Source: Data from Ministry of Economic Development, New Zealand, *SMEs in New Zealand: Structure and Dynamics*, Ministry of Economic Development, Wellington, 2006, p. 31.

Likewise, studies of Australian small businesses have found that female-managed firms tend to have lower sales revenue and profits than male-run businesses, suggesting that they may be more risk-averse and more focused on lifestyle considerations.[40] The great majority of businesses run by women tend to be concentrated in the services sector and at the smaller end of the size scale.

Another example of the relative differences between male- and female-managed small businesses is shown in table 17.5 (p. 437). Based on data compiled by the Australian Bureau of Statistics, it provides comparative information on firms run by women, those managed by men, and those jointly run by a male and female pair (such as a husband-and-wife team). The data indicate that males are still clearly predominant in terms of the absolute number of businesses. The table also shows the high concentration of women in self-employment and other micro-businesses compared with their male counterparts.

Table 17.5: Gender differences in Australian small firms

	Female operated	Male operated	Jointly operated	Total*
No staff	174 300 (83.2%)	453 600 (57.7%)	86 500 (31.7%)	714 400
1–4 employees	27 100 (13.0%)	263 700 (33.5%)	125 000 (45.5%)	415 800
5–19 employees	8 100 (3.9%)	69 300 (8.8%)	61 300 (22.5%)	138 700
Total small business	209 500 (100.0%)	786 600 (100.0%)	272 800 (100.0%)	1 268 900

Source: Australian Bureau of Statistics, *Characteristics of Small Business, Australia 2004*, ABS, Canberra, 2005, pp. 50–3.

*Note: total number of businesses does not correspond with figure in table 4.4 due to differences in ABS data sets.

Despite this, small businesses owned by women usually have a higher survival rate than those run by men.[41] This finding is not as surprising as it might at first seem. Firms that are small in scale (such as home-based micro-enterprises), which have low or neglible debt levels (perhaps due to an inability to borrow funds) and which are based on personal skills and services appear to have a greater ability to ride out the inevitable threats and challenges that all business must face from time to time. Table 17.6 lists some regional business organisations for women in the Pacific Rim region.

Table 17.6: Some regional business organisations for women and information links

Country	Organisation and website
Australia	Business and Professional Women Australia <www.bpw.com.au>
Hong Kong	HK Association of Business and Professional Women <www.hkabpw.org>
Malaysia	National Association of Women Entrepreneurs of Malaysia <www.nawem.org.my>
New Zealand	NZ Federation of Business & Professional Women <www.bpw.co.nz>
Singapore	Business and Professional Women's Association <www.sbpwa.org.sg>
Regional	Asian Women in Business <www.awib.org>

Social entrepreneurship

Social entrepreneur: An enterprising person who applies entrepreneurial principles and skills to the resolution of social or community problems.

Traditionally, entrepreneurship has been seen as occurring exclusively in the for-profit (private) sector of an economy. Most textbooks focus either on individual entrepreneurs seeking to start or grow their own businesses or on 'intrapreneurs' working within an existing large firm. However, in recent years there has been a growing awareness of the contribution of entrepreneurial behaviour within the not-for-profit sector, and as a tool of community development.

Social entrepreneurs are agents of social change who apply entrepreneurial principles and skills to the resolution of community problems and for the improvement of society in general. They apply the traditional tools of an entrepreneur to produce more effective solutions to social problems, and display many of the personal attributes found among private-sector entrepreneurs. They take risks and seek innovative approaches in order to help improve the lives of individual people, groups and society, not just for personal gain.[42]

Such entrepreneurs can be found in a variety of settings. Some social entrepreneurs have been advocates of widespread change in society. These are people who have recognised that there are problems or needs which are not being met, and who have attempted to remedy this deficiency. Such social entrepreneurs typically respond by organising resources (such as money and equipment), building and motivating a team of committed people to work with the entrepreneur, developing a customer base, and building awareness of the unmet need among government authorities and the broader community. In this respect, they are not dissimilar to entrepreneurs who launch new business ventures in new or emergent industries.

The other main form of social entrepreneurship is the successful application of sound business principles to not-for-profit and non-government organisations (NGOs) to produce better-managed charities, healthcare organisations, educational institutions and environmental groups. These entrepreneurial managers are people who apply existing management concepts such as business planning, financial accountability, human resource management and marketing to an organisation that traditionally has not operated on such principles. The intention of such work is to produce an NGO which is better able to meet the needs of its clients.

The rise of social entrepreneurship is due to a number of factors. The first form of social entrepreneur (social change entrepreneur) has always existed; however, more researchers have become aware of such enterprising behaviour and its similarity to the conventional notion of entrepreneurship. The second type of social entrepreneur, the entrepreneurial manager, has been driven by an increasing emphasis in many societies on more cost-effective use of welfare and charitable funds; by increasing levels of business education among managers; and by the realisation that business skills can often help produce better outcomes for a community.

Some examples of social entrepreneurs include Maria Montessori (creator of the Montessori educational teaching system in Italy), Florence Nightingale (instigator of many modern nursing techniques) and Muhammed Yunus (originator of the microfinance organisation the Grameen Bank).[43] Two contemporary Australian social entrepreneurs are Kylie Taylor and Valerie Khoo (see the Entrepreneur Profile on p. 439).

Although social entrepreneurs share many attributes with other businesspeople, there are still some significant differences. Many social entrepreneurs lack conventional business skills or have even greater difficulty in accessing venture capital than entrepreneurs do. They also often have to work within the different constraints imposed by not-for-profit organisations. Such entities are usually overseen by management committees (something the self-employed entrepreneur does not have to deal with), and these place a strong focus on measuring performance against a 'triple bottom line' of environmental, social and financial outcomes. In contrast, the private sector conventional entrepreneurs may focus only on monetary returns. Finally, whereas private entrepreneurs usually seek to retain ownership of their intellectual property and ideas, many social entrepreneurs actively seek to share their innovations and to disseminate information to as many interested parties as possible, so as to extend community benefits (see table 17.7).

Table 17.7: Social entrepreneurship organisations

Organisation	Website
Ashoka Foundation	<www.ashoka.org>
Schwab Foundation for Social Entrepreneurship	<www.schwabfound.org>
Social Enterprise Australasia	<www.social-e.org.au>

Entrepreneur profile

Taylor & Khoo

Kylie Taylor and Valerie Khoo are two businesswomen who have put their entrepreneurial skills into a project designed to help orphans in Cambodia.

Working together, they have created Taylor & Khoo, a label that sells clothes and homewares made in Cambodia. Their product range includes cushions, bedspreads, men's ties and women's clothing, all made in handwoven Khmer silk.

Their venture had its genesis in a visit to the town of Siem Reap in 2002.

'Cambodia is one of the poorest countries in the world, and the need is very strong,' explains Valerie. 'When we first visited the Angkor Orphanage it received only AUD $9 a day in government funding, which had to house, feed and clothe sixty orphans. We saw the opportunity to do something.'

The Taylor & Khoo range is available from the firm's central Sydney shop, selected stockists in Australia, online, and through special events in Singapore.

Neither Valerie nor Kylie take any income from the business. They run Taylor & Khoo while both working full-time in their professional careers.

Since inception, about AUD $130 000 has been raised for the Siem Reap orphanage through Taylor & Khoo activities. The orphanage has been able to upgrade its facilities and now houses 140 orphans.

The economic and social impact is much greater than this, however. Taylor & Khoo also have a policy of sourcing their products from numerous individuals and small businesses in Cambodia, so as to help spread income into different groups and to encourage Cambodian entrepreneurs to get started. About 130 local people now generate at least part of their income from the activities of Kylie and Valerie's business.

'Creating job opportunities is a wonderful way to help people help themselves,' says Kylie. 'Not only are people able to break out of the poverty cycle, but the boost to their self-esteem is immeasurable.'

Taylor & Khoo has won awards such as the Australian Humanitarian Award 2005 (business category), Australia Post Small Business Award 2005 (Special Judges' Commendation), Superwoman Award 2005, and Women Who Dare Award 2004. Kylie and Valerie donate all prize money to support the orphanage.

You can find out more about the Taylor & Khoo project, and buy their products online, by visiting <www.taylorandkhoo.com>.

Source: Based on author's interview with Kylie Taylor and Valerie Khoo, 2006.

Home-based businesses

Home-based businesses (HBBs) represent the majority of small businesses operating in Australia, New Zealand and many other countries today, yet their role and impact are often overlooked or poorly understood. Many businesspeople and researchers are often surprised by the size and significance of this sector, which is sometimes also referred to as 'small office, home office' (SOHO).

HBBs consist of two main types of businesses. The first are businesses operated *at home*, where most of the firm's work is carried out at the operator's residence. Typical enterprises in this category include home-based accounting and professional practices. They represent about one-third of all HBBs in Australia. The second (and most numerous) type of home-based enterprise consists of businesses operated *from home*, where owner–operators perform most of their work out in the field or at clients' premises. In this operating model, operators simply use their residence as a base where administration, recordkeeping, raw materials and other resources are maintained. Carpenters, plumbers, bricklayers and other tradespeople typically fall into this category.

Traditionally, HBBs have been regarded as a small-scale phenomenon with limited relevance to the wider economy. In reality, however, HBBs are a major structural force in almost all economies. For example, in 2004 there were an estimated 856 000 home-based businesses in Australia, which accounted for 68 per cent of all small businesses in the nation. These were operated by some 1 040 000 owner–managers.[44] HBBs are equally important to the economy of New Zealand, where it is estimated that there are now over 200 000 such firms, making them the largest single group of businesses in that country.[45] Home-based businesses have been less well known in Singapore, and formal registration of a home office within government-owned residential apartments has been permitted only in recent years. By the end of 2003, there were about 7400 registered home offices in the republic. Most of these, like their Australian and New Zealand counterparts, were concentrated in the services sector, and most operated as either a sole proprietorship or partnership, and with only limited capital (typically under S$10 000).[46] Unfortunately, data about HBBs in other parts of the Pacific Rim region are much harder to come by.

HBBs were once perceived to be highly risky enterprises with low financial returns and only marginal prospects for long-term survival, but many researchers today suggest that the opposite is often true: most HBBs endure for a relatively long period of time (typically more than five years), and are capable of generating significant economic returns for their owner–operators.[47]

A more detailed picture of the characteristics of HBBs is provided by Australian research. The typical HBB in Australia tends to display characteristics that set it apart from other small-, medium- and large-sized enterprises. There is a higher proportion of women who own such businesses, and a higher proportion holding degrees or post-secondary education qualifications. The archetypal HBB operator is usually between 30 and 50 years old, and working only part time in the enterprise. Most operators have had no formal management training, and fund their venture entirely from their own personal finances. Almost 70 per cent have no staff, and their use of technology is much lower than in larger firms.[48]

The emergence of HBBs as a key part of the small business sector has been driven by a number of factors, all of which have served to encourage high levels of growth in this category. At the macroeconomic level, the rapid expansion in the services sector of the Australian economy has opened up numerous opportunities for businesses that can be operated from the owner's home. Unlike manufacturing, wholesaling or retailing, service-based firms rely largely on individual skills, and do not need large storage areas or a location in a retail shopping complex. Not surprisingly, therefore, most HBBs are in the services sector. At the microeconomic level, the expansion of the HBB sector has been encouraged by increasing flexibility in local government zoning and regulations (which permit the use of homes as business premises), and an increased willingness by small-scale entrepreneurs to set up enterprises that are low in capital outlay, allow more time with the family, and can be operated part time if desired.

There are several advantages in working from home. They include the ability to exercise independence and total control over the working environment, thus providing maximum flexibility and versatility in the entrepreneur's worklife. There is usually more free time available to spend with friends and family. Home-based entrepreneurs are also able to save time and money through reduced travelling costs, no rental fees for premises, and use of personal household facilities to double as work tools (such as personal computers).

Working from home, however, is not for everyone. Many small business owners do not have the requisite discipline needed to succeed under the unique conditions that a residential business imposes. These include isolation and loneliness, as the operator does not have ready access to workmates; a weakened professional image, which can arise when customers do not believe that an HBB is a bona fide enterprise; the inability to properly manage one's time so as to prevent personal activities intruding on the working day, and vice versa; and the difficulty of increasing the size of the business. Self-motivation, the ability to effectively manage one's time, and the discipline to ignore non-work distractions are all important ingredients of the successful HBB operator.

There are also some practical administrative and legal decisions that small business owners should bear in mind before opting to work from home (see the box 'HBBs — some questions'). They need to ensure that their financial record-keeping is in order, so that work and personal expenses can be accurately separated and accounted for when preparing financial returns. They also have to bear in mind that local government laws may limit the size and type of firm that can be based at home, the operating hours of the business, customer parking, and the extent to which signage and other advertising can be displayed outside the home. There are also personal security and insurance issues to consider. It may be risky to invite strangers into the home, and a domestic insurance policy usually does not cover losses suffered as a result of operating a business within the house.

It is important to remember the limitations imposed by a home-based business. Although a residential location may be a cost-effective place in which to start an enterprise, in the medium to long term it is usually suitable only for business owners who have limited growth goals, or who wish to remain self-employed. Entrepreneurs who seek to expand in the marketplace, increase their range of product and service offerings, or employ staff to work with them will inevitably find that they need to either outsource such activities or move into commercial premises where greater economies of scale can be instituted.

Table 17.8: Home-based business organisations

Organisation	Website
Micro and HomeBusiness Network, Australia	<www.mbn.com.au>
Home Business New Zealand	<www.homebizbuzz.co.nz>

HBBs — some questions

Premises
- Is the office secure?
- Is the office large enough?
- Is the office separate from the rest of the house, with separate entry for customers?
- If the business grows, how will expansion be accommodated within the house?
- Will there be any outside signage to help clients find their way?

Image
- Do the business stationery and website look professional?
- Is there a separate phone line to deal exclusively with work-related calls?
- Does the office within the house look suitable for entertaining clients?
- Does the outside of the house look suitably well kept?

Management
- Is there someone who can act as a back-up if the owner–operator is incapacitated?
- Does the owner have suitable time-management skills to keep work and play times separate?
- Do other members of the household know that they should not interrupt during working hours?

Finance
- How does the home office affect loan costs (mortgage repayments)?
- How will personal and work-related costs be apportioned for household expenses such as electricity, water and gas?

Legal
- Does the existing insurance policy cover HBB activities?
- Is third-party liability required for visitors to the house?
- Does the local authority allow an HBB to operate here?
- If the house is rented, will the landlord allow an HBB to be based here?

Summary

There are currently a number of trends emerging in society, which entrepreneurs and small business owners need to be aware of. One is the increasing focus on the social responsibility of firms and the role they can play in fostering broad community development. Another is in ensuring that the environmental impact of small firms (waste, pollution and so on) is reduced wherever possible. This may be difficult, since research shows that owner–managers and entrepreneurs may have good intentions but fail to produce positive outcomes; many are not paying enough attention to eco-efficiency. A third trend is the emergence of Indigenous business owners in Australia and New Zealand; nevertheless, the number of Aboriginal and Maori business owners is quite low compared with the rest of the population. The role of another group in the population — women — has become more important in recent years. The number of females running their own firms has increased substantially, and is likely to continue to do so. At the same time, the concept of what constitutes 'entrepreneurship' has been expanded to embrace people working outside the private sector of the economy. It is important to understand that entrepreneurship can be successfully applied to the not-for-profit sector as a tool for community improvement, through the activities of social entrepreneurs. Home-based businesses constitute the largest segment of the small business sector, and have their own special administrative and legal problems that need to be taken into account before an entrepreneur becomes a home-based operator.

REVIEW QUESTIONS

1. What is the difference between social responsiveness and social responsibility?
2. What are the seven components that an eco-efficient firm uses in its activities?
3. How does a social entrepreneur differ from a conventional one?
4. List four significant factors that have contributed to the low rate of entrepreneurial activity among Australian Indigenous communities.
5. List the ways in which women and men differ in the management of a small business.

DISCUSSION QUESTIONS

1. Are the economic needs and concerns of a small business owner always opposed to those of the broader community?
2. What steps could be taken to increase the number of new and small firms owned by Indigenous people in Australia and New Zealand?
3. Is it valid to claim that women are more consultative owner–managers than men?

SUGGESTED READING

Australian Government Department of Family and Community Service, *Giving Australia: Research on Philanthropy in Australia*, Canberra, Commonwealth of Australia, 2005.

Clark, L., *Female Entrepreneurs*, New Holland Publishers, Sydney, 2006.

Foley, D., 'An examination of Indigenous Australian entrepeneurs' *Journal of Developmental Entrepreneurship*, vol. 8, no.2, August 2003, pp. 133–51.

Oppedisano, J. & Fielden, S.L., Special edition: women and entrepreneurship, *Women in Management Review*, vol. 19, no. 3, 2004.

Hannafey, F.T., 'Entrepreneurship and ethics: A literature review', *Journal of Business Ethics*, no. 49, 2003, pp. 99–107.

Schaper, M. (ed.), *Making Ecopreneurs: Developing Sustainable Entrepreneurship*, Ashgate Publishing, Aldershot, UK, 2005.

Zapalska, A., Perry, G. & Dabb, H., 'Maori entrepreneurship in the contemporary business environment' *Journal of Developmental Entrepreneurship*, vol. 8, no. 3, December 2003, pp. 219–36.

CASE STUDY

Instant Jobs

Andrea Jones has run her own business, in partnership with her husband, for the last three years. It specialises in recruiting and placing service-sector personnel (such as secretaries, bookkeepers, retail counter sales staff, call centre staff and administrative personnel) on behalf of large corporations, government departments and non-profit organisations based in and around Darwin. In recent years there has been a strong trend by such employers to outsource the recruitment process, and this has created a niche for firms like Instant Jobs. They place the advertisements in the local newspaper and on the web, screen job applicants, and then draw up a shortlist of recommended candidates for the client corporation or government agency to consider.

Andrea, 42, and Bob, 48, started the business five years ago, using A$400 000 of their own money. For the first three years they ran at a loss, but in the last two years the financial performance has improved. Last year they made a net profit of $85 000 on turnover of $3.6 million dollars, and this year the profit will be $90 000 on a $3.7 million turnover. They are forecasting a similar result for their business the next year.

The firm has been established as a partnership between Andrea and Bob, although there is no written partnership agreement in existence between the two.

Andrea prides herself on the flat organisational structure of the firm. Apart from the CEO position that she occupies, there are no formal management titles. Everyone else is called a 'client services officer'.

People seeking a job placement through Andrea's agency do not need to come into her office; instead she interviews them at a local coffee shop to provide a relaxing environment, and then makes an informal and unwritten judgement as to who she recommends for jobs. She has generally been reluctant to use Indigenous workers. This is unusual, since the Northern Territory has one of the largest Indigenous populations in Australia, and they constitute a significant proportion of the local workforce.

In addition to Andrea and her husband, there are four other staff — one more than the maximum permitted by the local municipal council for home-operated businesses within the area.

Recently Andrea discovered that the national government will provide subsidised grants of up to $100 000, and other forms of financial assistance, to businesses that are owned or part-owned by local Indigenous people; the aim of this is to help encourage Indigenous entrepreneurs.

Last week she approached Merrilyn, a friend whom she has known since they studied at the University of Adelaide 15 years ago. Merrilyn was born and raised in the Tiwi Islands north of Darwin, and now has a bachelor's degree in education and a master of business administration. Armed with these skills, Merrilyn has become a professional trainer, and currently works for a small government agency. It is official government policy that public servants cannot engage in outside work without the express written approval of the government agency's CEO.

'I need to grow the business bigger,' Andrea tells Bob one evening. 'Merrilyn is our key. If we can access financial assistance through employing her, then we can also pick up more government contracts, I'm sure.'

The next morning she rings Merrilyn at work and put an offer to her. 'If you're prepared to come and work part time for me, I can make it worth your while. I won't pay you a wage or put you on my books as an employee, but I will give you ten per cent ownership of the company. What do you think? You can work out of hours and no-one else needs to know.

'In addition, I'll ensure that another ten per cent of our net profits are redirected back into sponsoring local artists and community recreation centres in the Tiwi Islands. We'll provide a free loans scheme to the best young businesspeople in the islands.'

Merrilyn has agreed in principle, but asks for more. She suggests that a separate private company, Bright Insights Pty Ltd, be set up, with Merrilyn and Andrea as the only shareholders and directors, and that the promised part ownership of Instant Jobs and the 10 per cent of its profits be channelled to Bright Insights. She will then take a portion of this for herself, and direct the rest to the envisaged micro-finance scheme in the Tiwi Islands.

Andrea is very pleased with this, and the agreement is put into effect. However, she has not yet told Bob about the outcome of her arrangements with Merrilyn.

Questions

1. Is this a socially responsible business? State your reasons.

2. Would you classify Bright Insights and/or Merrilyn as a social entrepreneur?

3. What current and potential future problems does the business Instant Jobs face?

ENDNOTES

1. T.S. Hatten, *Small Business: Entrepreneurship and Beyond*, Prentice Hall, Upper Saddle River, NJ, 1997.
2. M. Friedman & R. Friedman, *Free to Choose*, Harcourt Brace Jovanovich, New York, 1980.
3. S.P. Robbins, R. Bergman, I. Stagg & M. Coulter, *Management*, 2nd edn, Prentice Hall, Sydney, 2000, pp. 165–6.
4. M.A.K. Hoss, S.L. Christensen & R.G. Schwartz, 'Ethical entrepreneurs: An oxymoron?', Paper presented to the International Council for Small Business, 50th World Conference, Washington DC, June 2005.

5. S.P. Sethi, 'A conceptual framework for environmental analysis of social issues and evaluation of business response patterns', *Academy of Management Review*, vol. 4, no. 1, 1979, pp. 63–74.

6. J.K. Thompson, H.L. Smith & J.N. Hood, 'Charitable contributions by small businesses', *Journal of Small Business Management*, vol. 31, no. 3, July 1993, pp. 35–51.

7. Australian Bureau of Statistics, *Generosity of Australian Businesses 2000–01*, cat. no. 8157.0, ABS, Canberra, 2002.

8. Council of Small Business Organisations of Australia, *The Spirit of Enterprise — National Survey of Small Business Community Involvement*, COSBOA, Canberra, 2000; Australian Government Department of Family and Community Service, *Giving Australia: Research on Philanthropy in Australia*, Commonwealth of Australia, Canberra, October 2005, pp. 13–18.

9. Council of Small Business Organisations of Australia, 'The spirit of enterprise — national survey of small business community involvement', <www.cosboa.com.au>, 2000.

10. S. Knuckey, H. Johnston, C. Campbell-Hunt, K. Carlew, L. Corbett & C. Massey, *Firm Foundations: A Study of New Zealand Business Practices and Performance*, Ministry of Economic Development, Wellington, 2002, p. 51.

11. M.E. Porter & C. van der Linde, 'Green and competitive: Ending the stalemate', *Harvard Business Review*, vol. 73, no. 5, September–October 1995, pp. 120–34.

12. R. Hillary (ed.), *Small and Medium-Sized Enterprises and the Environment: Business Imperatives*, Greenleaf, Sheffield, 2000.

13. Australian Bureau of Statistics, *Small Business in Australia 1999*, cat. no. 1321.0, ABS, Canberra, 2000.

14. D.J. Storey, *Understanding the Small Business Sector*, Routledge, London, 1994.

15. F.J. Tilley, 'The gap between the environmental attitudes and the environmental behaviour of small firms', *Business Strategy and the Environment*, no. 8, 1999, pp. 238–48.

16. M. Schaper, 'Small firms and environmental management: Predictors of green purchasing in Western Australian pharmacies', *International Small Business Journal*, vol. 20, no. 3. August 2002, pp. 235–49.

17. J.Q. Merritt, 'EM into SME won't go? Attitudes, awareness and practices in the London borough of Croydon', *Business Strategy and the Environment*, vol. 7, no. 2, May 1998, pp. 90–100.

18. Asia-Pacific Economic Co-operation Forum, *Eco-Efficiency in Small and Medium Enterprises*, APEC Secretariat, Singapore, 1998.

19. World Business Council for Sustainable Development, *Cleaner Production and Ecoefficiency: Complementary Approaches to Sustainable Development*, WBCSD, Geneva, 1997, p. 3.

20. R. Isaak, *Green Logic: Ecopreneurship, Theory and Ethics*, Greenleaf, London, 1998.

21. M. Saunders, 'Blacks in shift to the cities', *The Australian*, 27 June 2002, p. 4.

22. ibid.

23. L.P. Dana and R. Anderson, *International Handbook of Research on Indigenous Entrepreneurship*, Edward Elgar, London, 2007.

24. W.H. Edwards, *An Introduction to Aboriginal Societies*, Social Science Press, Sydney, 1988.

25. M. Schaper, 'Australia's Aboriginal entrepreneurs: Challenges for the future', *Journal of Small Business Management*, vol. 37, no. 3, July 1999, pp. 88–93.

26. Allen Consulting Group, *Indigenous Communities and Australian Business: A Report to the Business Council of Australia*, Allen Consulting Group, Melbourne, 2001.

27. D. Fuller, S. Gunner & S. Holmes, 'Indigenous small enterprise development: Implications for policy', *Small Enterprise Research*, vol. 10, no. 1, pp. 32–48.

28. F. Carruthers, 'Condition improving', *The Australian*, 7 September 2000, p. 13.

29. Te Puni Kokiri (Ministry of Maori Development), *Fact Sheet 1: Maori Self-Employment*, <www.tpk.govt.nz>, 1999.

30. Ministry of Economic Development New Zealand, *SMEs in New Zealand: Structure and Dynamics*, Ministry of Economic Development, Wellington, 2006, p. 31.

31. A. Zapalska, G. Perry & H. Dabb, 'Maori entrepreneurship in the contemporary business environment', *Journal of Developmental Entrepreneurship*, vol. 8, no. 3, December 2003, pp. 219–36.

32. Australian Bureau of Statistics, *Characteristics of Small Business 2004, Australia*, cat. no. 8127.0, ABS, Canberra, 2005, p. 33; figures exclude agricultural enterprises.

33. Ministry of Economic Development New Zealand, *see* note 30.

34. J. Lee, 'The motivation of women entrepreneurs in Singapore', *International Journal of Entrepreneurial Behaviour and Research*, vol. 3, no. 2, 1997, pp. 93–110.

35. Organisation for Economic Cooperation and Development, *Women Entrepreneurs in Small and Medium Enterprises*, OECD, Paris, 1997, pp. 20–3.

36. P. Chu, 'The characteristics of Chinese female entrepreneurs: Motivation and personality', *Journal of Enterprising Culture*, vol. 8, no. 1, 2000, pp. 67–84.

37. B. Roffey, A. Stanger, D. Forsaith, E. McInnes, F. Petrone, C. Symes & M. Xydias, *Women in Small Business: A Review of Research*, Department of Industry, Science and Tourism, Canberra, 1996, p. xxi.

38. S.P. Robbins, R. Bergman, I. Stagg & M. Coulter, *Management*, 2nd edn, Prentice Hall, Sydney, 2000, p. 623.

39. B. Roffey et al., *see* note 37.

40. J. Watson, 'Examining the impact on performance of demographic differences between male and female controlled SMEs', *Small Enterprise Research*, vol. 9, no. 2, 2001, pp. 55–70.

41. B. Roffey et al., *see* note 37.

42. J.G. Dees, 'The meaning of social entrepreneurship', *Stanford Graduate School of Business*, <www.gsb.stanford.edu >, 1998.

43. Ashoka Foundation, 'What is a social entrepreneur?', <www.ashoka.org>, 2002.

44. Australian Bureau of Statistics, *Characteristics of Small Business 2004, Australia*, cat. no. 8127.0, ABS, Canberra, 2005, pp. 70–3; figures exclude agricultural enterprises.

45. Home Business New Zealand, 'Insights into the home business community in New Zealand', <www.homebizbuzz.co.nz>, 2002.

46. K. Goh & T.W. Chian, 'Profile of home offices in Singapore', *Statistics Singapore Newsletter*, March 2004, pp. 12–15.

47. A.M. Stanger, 'Home-based business marginality: A review of home-based business performance and its determinants', Paper presented to the 45th International Council for Small Business World Conference, 7–10 June 2001, Brisbane, Australia; W. Good & M. Levy, 'Home-based business: A phenomenon of growing importance', *Journal of Small Business and Entrepreneurship*, vol. 10, no. 1, 1992, pp. 34–46.

48. Australian Bureau of Statistics, *Characteristics of Small Business 2004, Australia*, cat. no. 8127.0, ABS, Canberra, 2005, figures exclude agricultural enterprises.

CASE STUDY 1

Les Mills International

On 28 January 2006, Jill Tattersall, Chief Executive Officer at Les Mills International (LMI), world leader in the development of branded fitness programs, heard that the potential distributor for the Western US region had declined the offer to represent LMI. She wondered whether LMI, located in Auckland, New Zealand, should set up its own agency or continue to search for another option.

Les Mills background

After representing New Zealand in the 1960, 1964 and 1968 Olympic Games for the shot-put and discus throw, Les Mills opened his first gym in Auckland in 1968. As the growth of Les Mills Clubs accelerated, Les passed control to his son Phillip, allowing Les to serve as Mayor of Auckland between 1990 and 1998.

In 1980, after winning a track scholarship and completing his studies at the University of California in Los Angeles, Phillip returned to New Zealand. He then pioneered the introduction of freestyle group exercise and developed a series of standardised exercise-to-music classes that were franchised to other gyms, first in New Zealand and later Australia. After focusing on building a chain of local gyms, in 1990 he invented the BODYPUMP class in his own living room.

Within a year of its release in Australia in 2005, an Australian agent had licensed it into about 150 gyms. Soon after, a representative of one of the big American shoe companies saw BODYPUMP in action at a convention and asked to take the program worldwide. Phillip could not come to acceptable terms with them and decided to do it himself.

Les Mills International was incorporated in 1997, funded by Phillip Mills (61 per cent) and a group of private investors. Their plan was to license Les Mills programs worldwide and to separate licensing from the health clubs business in New Zealand. In the beginning of 2006, LMI had grown to 20 overseas distributors, licensing an average of three Les Mills programs per club to 10 000 clubs, serving over 4 million people per week in 55 countries.

Les Mills programs

In January 2006 LMI offered seven programs covering all the main group fitness categories:
- BODYPUMP (weight-lifting)
- BODYCOMBAT (martial arts)
- BODYBALANCE (or BODYFLOW in the USA — yoga, Pilates and tai chi)
- BODYSTEP (high energy cardio)
- BODYJAM (a free flow dance format)
- BODYATTACK (high intensity cardio aerobics)
- RPM (indoor cycling).

All seven programs were designed to make exercise entertaining and motivating through a mixture of music and choreography, often supported by elements of Maori culture, such as the 'Kia Ora' greeting commonly used by instructors. Through these programs, a whole range of activities such as biking and weight-lifting, traditionally conducted solo, were put into class formats. 'With music, entertainment and motivation, people can get two or three times as much exercise in a class as they would on their own and, instead of being a grind, it's fun,' comments Phillip Mills.

The company employed some of the world's best instructors, who trialled and perfected new classes every three months, based on intensive market research to respond to consumer feedback and industry trends. When the class was judged perfect, it was videotaped and dispatched with a licensed music CD and written choreography notes to the 60 000 accredited Les Mills instructors around the world, who then taught it to club members. Instructors also received training at hundreds of quarterly workshops conducted by approximately 500 part-time 'national master' trainers, who also conducted the initial certification training. There was also a management system to support licensed clubs, covering areas such as the recruitment of instructors, studio design and marketing. The company protected its intellectual property through a heavy investment in trademark registration and through the vigilance of its distributors.

Purpose, vision and goal

Phillip Mills says, 'Our purpose is to inspire life-changing fitness experiences, every time, everywhere.' He adds, 'Our long-term vision is that Les Mills International will play a role in reducing obesity and its associated diseases in the Western world and try to make people fitter, healthier and happier worldwide.' Phillip has noted that the global fitness industry association, IHRSA, had a goal of 100 million fitness club members by 2010. LMI planned to contribute to the achievement of that goal by growing the numbers of gyms offering Les Mills classes to 25 000 by 2015.

People

Phillip says, 'If I had to name one single thing that is crucial to our business success, it would be recruiting great people.' He explains further: 'Identifying and recruiting world-class staff for our head office in New Zealand, plus the best agents, master trainers and salespeople in each territory has been a major key to our success. We go about this in many different ways. We network like crazy, trying to find the best recruits via industry associations, trade fairs, trade journals and local contacts. We write inspiring ads and recruit via a sales pitch that includes a world-class video presentation and written materials showing the success of our products. We've received some good help and advice from recruitment companies. We just kept at it and we're still constantly looking for star players.'

The founder adds, 'Our staff defines our spirit as "no boundaries; freedom to succeed" and celebrates our shared values of being "world-class, innovative, gutsy, inspirational and honest". We also encourage productivity through life-changing

staff training, adding to technical training elements of theatre, personal development, motivational psychology and building on cultural rituals. We've made our
team great fun to play on,' he concludes. In 2006, LMI had 35 full-time staff in
New Zealand in addition to a number of contract employees.

Jill Tattersall has been Chief Executive Officer since 2002, after being hired as
General Manager in 1998. She was recruited from City Hall when Les Mills was
Mayor. Phillip Mills passed the daily running of LMI to Jill, but remained actively
involved in major projects.

Program licensing and marketing

Phillip Mills felt it was important to reach as much of the world market as possible, capitalising on his 'first mover advantage.' He therefore believed that a
licensing approach for club owners was the proper way to go, using national or
regional distributors to sell club owners on becoming LMI licensees, distribute
LMI programs, provide training programs, and translate LMI materials into local
languages. Although there was no initial cash payment to LMI for the right to
become a distributor, the distributor was responsible for hiring the appropriate
staff and assuming their adequate training with the help of LMI professionals.
Phillip says, 'What we provide is a quality assurance method for clubs.'

The distributor would collect all monthly licensing fees from club owners and
remit about 25 per cent of this total to LMI. Normally, a distributor starting from
scratch could expect to break even within one and a half to three years, once 250
to 300 clubs had been signed up.

LMI distributors had a variety of backgrounds. However, all of them were
recruited because of their industry contacts. For example, agents could be in the
gym equipment business or offering fitness education. LMI did not insist that the
distributor provide dedicated selling staff for LMI programs, but found this to be
advantageous. Repeated calls were sometimes required to persuade a gym owner
to become an LMI licensee. LMI expected a new distributor to have a team at least
of 18 full-time staff working in sales, marketing, training and accounting, and to
grow at a rate of 150 clubs per year.

LMI spent about NZ$20 million annually to develop new quarterly programs
and promotional material in hard cover and electronic form. Its distributors delivered programs and materials to clubs and provided training, systems and advice
for club owners to help them increase their customer base and improve their
profitability.

The US market

Phillip Mills believed the US market, with at least 20 000 gyms, represented half of
the total world market for LMI programs and that 22 per cent of the US population attended gyms in 2006 — about double the 1993 membership. Attending
gyms had become the most popular 'sport' in the USA. He noted that about
30 per cent of the US population was overweight or obese yet, on the other hand,
the health-, weight- and fitness-conscious segment of the population also continued to grow. He identified the Western world's increasingly sedentary lifestyle

as contributing to the need for exercise, noting that female empowerment and a greater focus on the body by both women and men were additional factors.

LMI had signed an exclusive distribution agreement with an eastern US-based distributor in 1997, which terminated on 1 May 2005.

The move to regional US distributors

Jill Tattersall and Phillip Mills were anxious to assure continued quality service to the 1000 LMI-licensed US clubs after 1 May. Therefore on 1 April 2005, LMI set up an office in Orange County in California to ensure continuity of service. This office was staffed by a group of about 25 LMI employees from around the world, whose tasks included:

- providing the current 5000 instructors around the USA with their necessary training and updated programs
- identifying and signing up prospective distributors for different US regions
- supporting these activities with the appropriate financial and human resources as well as logistics and administrative services.

Jill Tattersall and Phillip Mills spent approximately three months in California, each operating out of this office. Other senior staff were also brought in as required. Six regional distributors, covering the USA east of the Rockies and Canada, were found, and the plan was to have all US agents in place and operating by 1 April 2006.

The western US region

Jill Tattersall and Phillip Mills considered the Western US region a crucial one in the US market. California was seen as the key state in this region, which also included Arizona, Nevada, Washington, Oregon, Utah, Idaho, Montana and Alaska. In April 2005, LMI had 100 licensed clubs in this region. After 1 May 2005, approaches were made to several potential distributors and a number of others initiated contact themselves. For a variety of reasons, including lack of finance, none of these turned out to be suitable. One prospective distributor looked promising, however. First contacted at a Las Vegas trade show in June 2005, this potential distributor seemed to meet LMI's requirements. Over the subsequent months negotiations were carried out and it appeared that an agreement might be reached.

January 2006

On 28 January 2006, Jill Tattersall received the news that the prospective distributor for the Western US region had declined the LMI offer, ending months of expectations. Since no immediate alternative distributor was available, Jill considered the possibility that LMI might set up its own distribution office in this region. The amount of investment required meant that current LMI shareholders would not receive any dividends over the next few years. Finding the appropriate talent to staff the key positions in this office would also be difficult.

Jill Tattersall knew that the next LMI board meeting would take place on 17 February 2006. By that time she would have to inform board members of the lack of progress on the Western US region and her plans for resolving this issue. Certainly by the board meeting she would be expected to have a firm plan in place.

Questions

Put yourself in the position of Jill Tattersall.

1. What would your analysis be of the Western US region distribution decision?
2. What alternatives do you have and what decision criteria are applicable?
3. What action would you take and why?

Supplementary questions

1. What strategy can Les Mills International use to protect its intellectual property?
2. What are the current social trends that can have an impact on Les Mills International?
3. Why would an instructor want to be 'Les Mills certified'?
4. Why would a club owner not be interested in becoming an LMI licensee?

CASE STUDY 2

Neuromonics

In November 2005, Dr Peter Hanley, Chief Executive Officer of Neuromonics Pty Ltd, in Sydney, Australia, reflected on the company's progress to date. Neuromonics, created to commercialise a new treatment for tinnitus, a hearing disorder, had experimented with various distribution approaches in Australia and had commenced exports to the USA. In planning the company's international expansion, particularly in the USA, he faced a key choice: whether to proceed, as the company had done to date, with a conservatively capital-rationed approach, or to seek substantial additional capital in order to fund a more aggressive, accelerated growth trajectory.

Tinnitus

Tinnitus, a hearing disorder involving the perception of ringing, whistling, buzzing or hammering sounds in the ear in the absence of a corresponding external sound, was believed to affect about 15 to 20 per cent of the world's adult population. For one per cent, the effects could be devastating, causing sleep disturbance, an inability to relax or concentrate, sensitivity to loud noise, and generally impacting seriously on quality of life. Exposure to excessive noise was considered the most common preventable cause of hearing loss and tinnitus.

The Neuromonics Tinnitus Treatment

To treat tinnitus, various approaches had been tried in the past — many of them falling into the 'snake oil' category. Other approaches were limited by a lack of consistent clinical efficacy, efficiency and/or user acceptability. Neuromonics identified its major competition as 'no treatment', due to family doctors telling their patients that 'nothing can be done about your condition; you'll just have to learn to live with it'.

The Neuromonics Tinnitus Treatment was discovered and developed over a ten-year period at Western Australia's Curtin University of Technology by Adjunct Associate Professor Paul Davis, himself a tinnitus sufferer. Central to the treatment was a proprietary acoustic stimulus that was customised to suit each individual, thereby accounting for individual differences in the hearing and tinnitus profile. While it was not a cure for tinnitus, and was not suitable for every patient (10 to 20 per cent of tinnitus sufferers had hearing loss too severe to be helped), Paul Davis's clinical trials demonstrated that it was more consistently effective (having a 90 per cent success rate), yielded faster results, and was more acceptable to patients than previous alternatives. Combining the acoustic therapy with about five hours of counselling and support from a specialist clinician over six months, the treatment aimed to provide habituation or desensitisation to the tinnitus signal, thereby reducing awareness, distress and disturbance.

The treatment cost was the equivalent of a pair of mid-range hearing aids, about A\$5500, representing a 100 per cent mark-up on the price paid by the clinician to Neuromonics. Some private insurance policies provided partial to full rebate for the treatment. Neuromonics had developed a money-back trial period for patients, allowing for a full refund to the patient plus \$500 for the healthcare provider. Return rates were very low, at less than ten per cent of patients.

Healthcare professionals

Patients typically go to their family doctor initially to seek assistance with tinnitus. They might then be referred to an ear, nose and throat specialist, and then on to an audiologist. Treatment of tinnitus — including provision of the Neuromonics Tinnitus Treatment — is conducted largely by audiologists. Their education involves an undergraduate degree augmented by a masters' degree or doctorate in audiology. Audiologists are in short supply around the world. In Australia, there are 1300 registered audiologists; in the USA they number about 10 000. They generate most of their income by selling hearing aids, expecting a 70 to 100 per cent mark-up on product sold. Traditionally, they have been conservative in adopting new technologies. Increasingly, audiologists are working in partnership with or being employed by ear, nose and throat specialists; those in private practice are being confronted increasingly by the commercial pressures typical of small business proprietors.

Neuromonics Pty Ltd

Neuromonics aimed to become the number one tinnitus treatment company in the world. It was established in July 2001 by Curtin University of Technology inventor Paul Davis and technology-transfer organisation TechStart Australia. At that time, it secured initial financing from venture capital firm Innovation Capital.

Dr Peter Hanley was appointed Neuromonics Chief Executive Officer early in 2003. He had a bachelor degree in biochemistry and a PhD in immunology. With 15 years of experience in strategy, investment banking, venture capital and healthcare management,

Dr Hanley led a staff of fewer then 20 people, who had various management, technical and clinical skills. Dr Paul Davis was the company's Chief Scientific Officer. The company also had an experienced advisory team, which included healthcare innovators, technologists and business leaders.

Neuromonics' progress

Between August 2001 and November 2005, Neuromonics had made significant progress in a variety of areas. Key achievements included the following:
- *Clinical trials.* Additional randomised, controlled clinical studies were conducted, taking the accumulated patient experience-base to over 200 people with tinnitus. These studies confirmed the superior efficacy, efficiency and user acceptability of Neuromonics' treatment relative to available alternatives. They confirmed the earlier findings of Dr Paul Davis, with 90 per cent of tinnitus sufferers achieving at least a 40 per cent improvement in their condition.

- *Intellectual property.* Neuromonics was granted core patents covering its proprietary technology in the USA, Australia, New Zealand and Singapore, with other jurisdictions pending.
- *Treatment delivery system.* A robust end-to-end delivery system was developed for the treatment, comprising a portable, non-implantable processor for use by the patient, providing patient control and usage data, as well as software tools and clinical protocols for use by the healthcare professional.
- *Regulatory approvals.* Regulatory clearance was secured for market release in Australia, the USA and New Zealand.
- *Global market recognition.* Through presentations by Dr Paul Davis at global conferences and the company's exposure to key opinion leaders in the global tinnitus community, Neuromonics gained increased awareness and appreciation for its tinnitus treatment.
- *Management team and advisers.* The company was able to build a strong management team, complemented by knowledgeable advisers, to take it through its development stages.
- *Australian market acceptance.* The Australian commercial market introduction showed that unaffiliated clinical audiologists could successfully treat paying customers and duplicate results obtained earlier in clinical studies with non-paying patients.
- *Commencement of export sales.* Neuromonics had commenced export sales in modest volumes to the USA and New Zealand, through leading tinnitus clinics in those countries.

Distribution experimentation in Australia

When Neuromonics launched its treatment, the Australian market for tinnitus treatment was undeveloped. Peter Hanley therefore decided on an experimental approach, testing three models of marketing and distribution. In April 2004, Neuromonics opened its own tinnitus clinic in Sydney, followed by another in Perth in January 2005 and Melbourne in March 2005. Also in April 2004, it began selling to independent clinics, training their audiologists to assess and treat patients. The third approach was to send a Neuromonics audiologist to 'visiting sites,' renting a room either fortnightly or for one day a week and providing treatment by appointment.

By November 2005, it had become apparent that owning clinics outright, while attractive from a control and margin perspective, was also capital intensive. The visiting approach also had limitations. Therefore, it became clear that selling to independent clinics provided the most rapidly scaleable and least capital-intensive approach to growth. Thus, by November 2005, 16 independent clinics were offering the Neuromonics treatment. Neuromonics audiologists were providing training assistance and quality assurance, and Neuromonics was fielding interest from many more interested clinicians.

Audiologists Nina Quinn and Sandra Bellekom were hired by Neuromonics in early 2005 as territory managers, responsible for in-house clinic sales as well as with development of sales through independent clinics. Nina and Sandra experimented with various forms of promotion and advertising, including direct-to-consumer promotion using print and radio media, as well as to health-care professionals. In response, a large number of interested patients needing assistance with their tinnitus contacted Neuromonics, and over 500 signed up directly from the campaign.

Funding Neuromonics

Until 2005, Neuromonics had been funded progressively through a series of small funding rounds as it reached key stages in its development. The initial funding, in August 2001, comprised A$1.5 million from Innovation Capital, an Australian- and US-based venture capital firm with a history of successful backing of health sector start-ups. This funding was drawn progressively as the company met pre-agreed operational milestones. Subsequent raisings of A$1.3 million in October 2003 and A$2.9 million in November 2004 were provided by existing share-holders, executives and individuals associated with the existing shareholders.

To recognise the contributions made by Curtin University, by Dr Paul Davis and by TechStart before August 2001, these three parties received ordinary shares amounting to about 25 per cent of the company's fully diluted capital base. Another allocation of shares was set aside for issues of options to key staff.

Funding requirements for international expansion

It was clear to the Neuromonics management team and board of directors that the major growth potential for Neuromonics was in the international market. The company's leadership team also concluded (based on its experiences and achieve-ments in Australia and the market demand for Neuromonics' treatment in the US and Europe) that the company was now ready to embark on international expan-sion. Peter Hanley was now faced with two critical questions that would have a direct bearing on the company's funding requirements:

- What should be the scope of international growth: focus on one key market at a time, or roll out simultaneously in the USA and Europe?
- What should be the pace of the rollout within any one market: take a conser-vative, capital-rationed approach or invest more aggressively in accelerated growth?

Playing on Dr Hanley's mind in relation to both questions was the knowledge that in the dynamic industry of healthcare technology, there is always the threat of another innovation emerging. Dr Hanley was aware of development work being done around the world with drugs, electrical stimulation and other approaches and, although there appeared to be nothing near to market, he wondered how much time Neuromonics had to build the global leadership position to which it aspired.

On the other hand, when it came to the question of scope, Dr Hanley was only too aware of the constraints of 'bandwidth' across the small number of individuals in his management team, and the huge operational challenge that would be associated with a launch into each major market offshore.

On the question of pace, there was a clear relationship between (1) how much the company could invest in sales and clinical support staff and (2) the number of healthcare professionals who could be trained to offer its treatment. Neuromonics could reasonably expect a substantial investment to translate directly into rapid sales growth and, hence, rapid value growth. However, at this stage in the company's development, it was not easy to forecast sales growth accurately. Any delay in sales would result in significant further capital requirements as costs mounted while revenues lagged.

Dr Hanley was also mindful of the investor perspectives on this question. If the company sought to raise funds from the US venture capital community, it seemed likely that incoming investors might prefer the more capital-accelerated approach. This would allow them to put 'more money at work' as well as to more rapidly secure an attractive exit via an initial public offering or trade sale. However, any further capital injections would dilute the holdings of current shareholders unless they contributed to the same level themselves.

Recognising that each of these approaches implied different risks and rewards, it was not immediately clear to Peter Hanley which approach might best suit Neuromonics at this time. Until November 2005, he had strived to manage Neuromonics conservatively, trying to preserve cash and assuring good value for all expenditures. He had attempted to run a lean organisation with minimum staff, hiring outside expertise on a part-time basis and avoiding long term financial commitments. In November 2005, had the time come to change?

Questions

Put yourself in the position of Dr Peter Hanley.

1. What is your assessment of your company's progress to date?

2. What risks do you believe are inherent in a slower growth strategy, and in a higher growth strategy?

3. What growth strategy would you prefer and why?

Supplementary questions

1. Where in the world would you expand after Australia?

2. What production management system would you recommend Neuromonics adopts?

3. Do you think it would be easy for a potential competitor to copy the processor and the Neuromonics treatments?

CASE STUDY 3

Macrokiosk

On 6 April 2006, Henry Goh, Chief Operating Officer of Macrokiosk in Kuala Lumpur, Malaysia, received the quarterly results from its Chinese subsidiary. Macrokiosk, a mobile messaging technology enabler, operates in seven Asian countries, of which China represents by far the largest potential market. About two years after entering this market, Henry was curious to see whether the Chinese venture was getting close to breaking even.

Messaging technology

Although the original invention of short messaging service (SMS) technology took place in the UK around 1986, it did not gain popularity until the advent of the mobile phone. During the 1980s and 1990s, pagers had been messaging devices, primarily in commercial and medical applications. With the arrival of the mobile phone, the opportunity for sending messages was extended to the general population. Because telecommunications companies and other mobile operators were primarily interested in selling and growing voice communications, they deemed the text messaging potential of mobile technology as just another value-added service. Compared to Europe and North America, with their long history of non-mobile technology, Asia was ripe for mobile technology, as 90 per cent of its population could be reached through this medium.

Macrokiosk

In 1995, 17-year-old Kenny Goh decided he would supplement his pocket money by starting a small business with his two younger brothers, Henry and Chee Seng, aged 14 and 11 respectively. The third-generation Chinese brothers convinced their father, a distributor for a Japanese handphone company, to invest RM10 000 in a server to provide miscellaneous services such as website design for school clubs and broadcasts over paging networks for a taxi company. For the next few years, the brothers enjoyed relative success, but completing their studies was their priority; therefore the business, registered as Macrokiosk Sdn Bhd in 1998, took a back seat until term breaks and holidays. They felt indebted to their parents, who both worked hard to pay for their education. Kenny majored in accounting and finance at Australia's Curtin University, and Henry, after an engineering degree, had completed an MBA at Boston University.

Henry explains: 'Dad gave us exposure to Japanese technology but we are really pioneers in the mobile telecommunications industry, providing mobile messaging platform services to companies, helping them build their own business, gain competitive advantage and stay at the forefront of their industry. Our business just evolved very naturally. We are neither inventors nor creators of technology but we find applications for it. We provide connectivity for any mobile device with messaging capability. We're also educating industry as to the potential of SMS technology. We're helping to make businesses more cost effective, convenient and competitive. These are the three Cs at the heart of our value proposition.'

With a staff of nine employees, Macrokiosk was incorporated in July 2000, with the vision of becoming the leading mobile messaging technology enabler in Asia. An early accomplishment of Macrokiosk was the development of etracker, a home-grown global mobile messaging network that allowed the company to build and offer a variety of secure value-added messaging services to the community at large. The etracker provided multiple connections to the SMS centres of the world's major mobile operators. This enabled it to handle a huge volume of bi-directional, multilingual, mass broadcasting, premium, transactional and smart messages.

Initially, Kenny and Henry had problems being taken seriously because of their age. They sent their business plans to a multitude of venture capitalists around the world with no success. In despair, Kenny charged into the office of a local newspaper editor complaining about the lack of local support for small entrepreneurs. Not long after this, Tan & Tan Developments Berhad, a local venture capitalist, approached Kenny and agreed to invest in their business. By 2001 this corporation, later known as Goldis Berhad, a publicly listed Malaysian company, owned 70 per cent of Macrokiosk.

Macrokiosk sales approach

Kenny and Henry knew that the typical Asian manager's attitude to sales representatives was one of fear and avoidance. Therefore, they avoided the term 'sales representative' but used the term 'consultant' instead. After weeks of fruitless attempts to make appointments with certain managers, they tried a simpler 'just walk in' approach. Having studied an industry, and specific companies in it, Kenny and Henry knew what kind of pitch might get a top manager's attention. For example, avoiding any technical jargon, they might say to a bank manager, 'Wouldn't it be great if you could send a message to remind a customer that his loan payment is due shortly?' Kenny and Henry discovered that if they did not get a positive response in the first five minutes of their meeting with a manager, they had lost.

Typically, a first application — a basic one just requiring a one-way message — would represent a new client's first SMS offering. It would be ready for implementation three days to a month later. After this first successful adoption, other possible uses for SMS would be explored with the client. Phase 2 SMS services were bi-directional, requiring a simple response such as 'yes' or 'no'. Phase 3 messaging was also bi-directional, more complicated and required information from the recipient. Once customers were satisfied with one solution, they would tend to return to Macrokiosk for repeat and new services.

Pricing was established on a project by project basis, with recognition given to the number of development hours required by Macrokiosk and the type and number of messages sent.

Henry believes that entrepreneurs must be hands-on. 'Entrepreneurs have to know everything,' agrees his brother. 'They need to know how to get the sales in, how to get the engineers to deliver, making sure employees are taken care of. They are responsible to their employees as well as to their investors. We feel pressure to provide for our staff. Staff are like family as we grow the company together. It is hard work. Our father told us that when you are young, you trade your health for wealth, but when you get older, you spend all your wealth to get back your health. We have learned from our mistakes. We have learned we should not compromise quality and service for additional sales. We also know that nothing is impossible as long as you have the determination, passion and right attitude. We are young and have no interest in leaving the business. We will do our best to make Macrokiosk a reputable global company.'

The China expansion

By 2003, Kenny and Henry Goh realised that if they wanted to become the leading SMS enabler in Asia, then they had to be a major player in the Chinese market. China, with 400 million mobile phones, was a larger market than the rest of Asia combined. After a research trip to China, it became clear to Kenny and Henry that China would represent a major challenge. Chinese government officials had indicated they were not interested in permitting a foreign company to come in, make a quick profit and leave. They indicated that a minimum investment of RM5 million would have to be made to qualify for a licence, and another RM5 million would be required if they were to be considered an acceptable telecommunications provider. Moreover, Macrokiosk would not be allowed to be the sole owner of the Chinese company and would have to find a local partner. Kenny and Henry also believed that adjusting to Chinese culture, customs and language would not be easy.

On the other hand, a number of current clients expressed interest in having Macrokiosk serve their operations and customers in China. Since Macrokiosk's parent company already had various holdings in China, the board of directors approved the China market entry. Using a Malaysian bank loan, its credit line and retained earnings, Macrokiosk found the finances for the first RM5 million. Planning to concentrate on the eastern part of China, Kenny and Henry decided to open their first office in Beijing on 1 March 2004, one year after going through the necessary ground work, registration, funding and incorporation. Revenues in their first full year in operation amounted to RM1 million in 2005.

Macrokiosk in 2006

By April 2006, Macrokiosk had added Hong Kong and Jakarta to their five other major city locations, and there were plans to add Vietnam, Taiwan and the Philippines in the year to come. The company worked with a variety of companies from 18 different industries, ranging from aviation to television. The staff had grown to about 100 employees with an average age of 28. The etracker network provided access to 364 mobile operators in 115 countries, totaling about two billion subscribers around the world. Macrokiosk could process up to 300 messages a second and handled about 10 million messages a month. Pre-tax profit had grown significantly from RM7000 in 2002, RM700 000 in 2003, RM1.2 million in 2004 and RM2.3 million in 2005. Total revenue in 2005 was RM24 million.

China costs and investments

Henry had identified the major costs of operating in China per month as follows:

Rent and utilities	RM 10 000
Licensing fees and taxes	RM 4 000
Salaries:	
Sales consultants	RM 30 000
Engineers	RM 40 000
Others	RM 30 000
Payments to mobile operators	RM 5 000
Advertising and promotion	RM 23 500
Head office charges	RM 5 000
Operational claims	RM 2 500

By April 2006, the following investments had been made in China by Macrokiosk:

Servers, routers, computers, etc	RM 500 000
Office furniture	RM 200 000
Incorporation expenses	RM 200 000
Daily operations	RM 3 600 000

First quarter 2006 results

On 6 April, Henry Goh received China's revenue figures for the first quarter of 2006. The total was RM3 million. Given the importance of the expansion into China to Macrokiosk's own performance, Henry was curious to determine if the Chinese venture was getting close to breaking even. Although the parent company had never requested any dividends from Macrokiosk, it was keenly interested in continuing evidence of Macrokiosk success. Breaking even in China would be good news at the next board meeting at the end of the month.

Questions

Put yourself in the position of Henry Goh.

1. What would be your analysis of Macrokiosk's progress to date?

2. Is China getting close to breaking even?

3. Would it be easy to copy Macrokiosk's business model?

Supplementary questions

1. What is your assessment of the decision to enter the Chinese market in 2003?

2. What are the typical entrepreneurial characteristics displayed by Henry and Kenny Goh?

3. What are the main sources of funding that were used to launch Macrokiosk?

CASE STUDY 4

muvee Technologies

In May 2006, Terence Swee, co-founder and Chief Opportunities Officer of Singapore-based muvee Technologies, the pioneer and leader in automatic video production, was wondering how his company's latest offering, muveeOnline, could generate income from end-consumers.

muvee Technologies Pte Ltd

'We can say we are a 'one idea' company,' quips Terence Swee. muvee (pronounced *mew-vee*, always written in lowercase) was defined as a 'slick video production created in moments, using intelligent, automatic editing technology'. The concept for the muvee autoProducer software, their flagship PC product, originated in 1999 when Terence Swee, a Singaporean electronics engineer, worked with Peter Kellock, a Scotsman with a doctorate in electronic music, at Kent Ridge Digital Labs, a Singapore R&D agency.

They spent hundreds of hours interviewing professional video editors to find out the 'rules' of editing. They then turned these rules into algorithms controlling the software. The research community until then had focused on making computers understand the semantics of video, with two main ambitions: searching and cataloging of large video repositories; and undertaking security and video surveillance. Peter and Terence instead applied video and music analysis techniques to a 'sexier' area — that of automatic video editing. The output from their software was a professional-quality production that cut footage highlights to music with effects and transitions perfectly paced to the tempo. The first version of muvee autoProducer was released in September 2001.

muvee autoProducer enabled users to easily and automatically transform unedited videos and pictures into professional-looking productions. Users simply selected their video clips and/or photos, added in their favorite music, and picked a production style. In minutes, muvee autoProducer intelligently selected key scenes from the video footage, and cut these highlights to the chosen music with effects and transitions synchronised to the beat. 'Many companies provide tools in the video editing space,' said Terence, 'but we are the only ones who do video editing completely automatically and cut the production to the beat of music, and make this technology available on multiple platforms from the PC, camera phones, and digital cameras to the web. We are totally dedicated to the consumer mass-market — the hundreds of millions of people who shoot video or snap photos but never want to master the tedious side of manual video editing.'

muvee Technologies was incorporated as a private company in August 2001. After pitching to more than 70 VCs and other investors from around the world, they secured funding from Temasek Capital, a leading venture capital firm in Singapore.

The executive team

The muvee company is led by an executive team consisting of three key people. Dr Peter Kellock, 51 years old, is the co-founder and Chief Executive Officer. His key role is to lead the creation of new products, build the business and make sure the fast growing company does not lose sight of its vision. He has a passion for 'pushing the envelope wherever media meets technology' and the ability to 'convince a team of people to share a dream and work zealously for years to turn it into a reality'. Terence Swee, 32 years old, is the other co-founder and Chief Opportunities Officer. He has spent a great deal of time in pursuit of new business around the world, diversifying and growing its revenue sources. 'From the start we are a global business,' says Terence. He was instrumental in identifying and negotiating licensing deals with key players in various consumer electronic industries. Philip Morgan, 47 years old, joined the company in 2001 and is muvee's Chief Operating Officer. Philip, who provides the day-to-day support, has an MBA and extensive creative experience in the radio and television industries.

The three leaders feel they complement each other, although they pride themselves on being able to do each other's work at any time if necessary. They admit that they spend a lot of time on strategic debate but consider that this provides a key strength for the company. 'If all three of us agreed all the time, it would mean that maybe two of us were redundant,' comments Terence. 'We leave our egos in the cloakroom when we come to work,' adds Philip.

Staffing muvee Technologies

The executive team has always given recruitment, motivation and staff retention high priority. From eight employees at the end of 2001, by May 2006 the company had grown to over 80 people, with an average age of about 30. The company was hiring at the rate of seven new employees monthly. Its eight vice-presidents were all involved in the process. Each new employee was interviewed up to three or four times, with one of the three executives present in the last interview. 'One of our toughest challenges is to find people with maturity, smarts and passion,' says Philip. 'People smarter than we are,' jokes Terence. Philip continues: 'We are looking for people who possess at least two of three must-haves: technical skills, creativity and commercial drive. The unusual set of skills our people have would be hard to duplicate in other countries and constitutes a considerable barrier to entry for any potential competitor.'

Every new employee is hired on a three-month probationary period. Philip says, 'We give our employees a good rewards package from the start, but we take the three-month probation period very seriously. We rarely hire short-term or contract people. It takes at least three months for someone to become productive with us because of the innovation and specialisation involved in our space. We are building a talented team in a sustainable, scaleable way, and we believe in recognising talent. Our staff are, as a result, highly motivated. They know that what they do will bring joy to millions of lives. Individuals also get recognised for their unique abilities. For instance, when one of our senior engineers visits a key account in the USA, he is recognised as a bit of a guru because of his key involvement and knowledge on one of our flagship products which they ship.'

Philip concludes, 'Unlike many other companies, we don't outsource. All management functions are done within the company. We promote from within and have a very low staff turnover. We are really like a professional football club. Our key strength is in our staff talent. We recognise that if all our employees decided not to come to work for a few days, muvee would not exist!'

Subsequent product development

Between 2001 and 2006, muvee Technologies grew its product line significantly. By the beginning of 2006, the latest generation of autoProducer, version 5.0, was available with over 100 plug-in styles.

Movie Director, developed on the Symbian platform for Nokia camera phones, was the first and only application to allow users to automatically turn video clips captured with their camera phones into personal, MMS-ready 'muvees'.

Early on, muvee achieved sales to original equipment manufacturers (OEMs), who bundled huge volumes of muvee's software. This success propelled muvee into quickly developing the discipline, stringent quality assurance and internal processes required to support these manufacturers. These licensing agreements often required product development cooperation from both parties. muvee's strategy was to charge licensing fees to their OEMs, and also sell product upgrades and additional plug-in styles directly to the end users via the internet.

Another incarnation of the automated video editing process was muveeKiosk. Using this software plug-in, photo-kiosk makers gave customers the option of turning all their pictures and video clips into DVD-ready muvees, instead of just having monotonous slideshows. A revenue-sharing model with the makers of photo-kiosk allowed muvee to collect a royalty on each DVD produced.

Exclusivity and brand

Terence Swee says, 'When you are a small company like us, every large company you sell to wants two things: exclusivity and the chance to brand our software as their own. Both present difficulties for us. We sometimes grant exclusivity for a limited period, like six months or so, if it is framed in a mutually beneficial arrangement. But we always stand firm about our branding. For us, our trademark is very important and we have registered it in many countries. Image is everything to us and we don't compromise on this. We push for consistency in the brand in every instance, like our branding on Nikon's latest Coolpix S Series cameras.'

Patents and intellectual property

The company has four major patents, covering some 50 claims on the techniques and applications of its technology. Terence says, 'As well as our public patents, we do have trade secrets that are guarded carefully. We also believe that running faster than any competition is better protection than a patent. In our business, because the concept and approach is so novel, we need to find a balance between being both market driven and innovative; we are always listening carefully to the unspoken vibes the market is giving out, creating products that fulfil their needs when they may not yet know what those products will look like.'

muveeOnline

Right from the start, the executive team had been trying to find a way to grow the company's revenues on a massive scale. Terence was successful in persuading some of the world's tier-1 consumer electronics companies, such as Hewlett Packard, Sony, Nokia and Nikon, to adopt muvee's technology. It had become obvious by 2005 that selling to such big-name companies on a per licence basis was, while profitable, not going to grow corporate revenues massively. The executive team also realised that gaining future substantial licence fees or royalties from such firms was unlikely, as paying large sums to a small company such as muvee was not especially popular within these big companies.

The direct-to-consumer sales of muvee autoProducer at US$99.95 and style-Packs at US$20 each were generating sound cash flow and growing at about 30 per cent per year. muvee Technologies was thus financially secure but still not meeting the really big growth dreams of its founders and investors. In September 2005, the second round funding muvee received in 2004 remained untouched in the bank, and the company's profit in 2005 was at least six times higher than in 2004. However, the company was still hungry for faster growth prospects. The executive team decided that it was time to enlarge the firm's business model. Instead of selling through intermediaries it would go direct to the consumer, and it would unlock recurring revenues as well. The resulting product was the muveeOnline web service.

When integrated into an online portal, such as a photo- or video-sharing website, muveeOnline would enable consumers anywhere in the world to make and share personalised muvees without the need to download a software application. Users would simply upload their chosen video and pictures, pick a muvee style and submit these choices to muvee's back-end service. A special feature of muveeOnline was its ability to offer an original artist's music video as a style option. Users simply uploaded their own footage and got back a customised, finished muvee that blended users' personal photos and/or videos with the artist's music video. This product could then be viewed online, saved, emailed or burned to DVD.

Terence explains that muveeOnline serves as the glue that binds various parties and their offerings together. The recording artist, for example, gains an enlarged audience and greater exposure, while music label companies such as Sony or Warner Music Group gain an additional sales outlet. An advertiser can also ride on this new user-generated media form. The individual consumer enjoys a novel, simple and fun way of identifying with a favourite artist or band.

In May 2006, muvee Technologies, working with Atlantic Records, developed a muveeOnline contest, inviting consumers to upload their own video and pictures and automatically create muvees that were blended with music video footage from the artist Jason Mraz.

Generating income from muveeOnline

The real attraction of muveeOnline for the company was the opportunity to tap a mass market at relatively low prices while growing the company's revenues massively. The catch was how to collect the money. The company already had a lot of experience with credit card systems for its muvee autoProducer PC software and muvee stylePacks sold to individual consumers online.

Peter Kellock, Philip Morgan and Terence Swee realised that muveeOnline was significantly different, however, in that the charges for a download would have to be so low that a special model for pricing and collection would have to be developed. Therefore, in May 2006, although muveeOnline was ready to make its first appearance on the market, the issue of generating income from it had still not been resolved. Terence knew this would be a continuing topic of discussion with his two co-executives in the weeks to come and wondered what he could suggest as a solution.

Questions

Put yourself in the position of Terence Swee.

1. What would be your analysis of muvee Online as a potential revenue generator?
2. What alternative pricing/collection models would you consider feasible?
3. How would you proceed from here and why?

Supplementary questions

1. What are the key features of muvee's human resource policy?
2. What is the source of muvee's competitive advantage?
3. What is your assessment of this company's use of large brand-name companies as its first customers? Do you see any advantages or disadvantages?

GLOSSARY

100% inspection: When all items produced are inspected (p. 308).

Acceptance (random) sampling: Inspecting random samples of a product to ensure they meet the expected standard; the sample result is generalised to the entire output (p. 308).

Arbitrage: The action of taking advantage of a discrepancy in value that exists in the marketplace. Those who ferret out such discrepancies in value and realise profits by acting on them are called *arbitrageurs* (p. 37).

Assets: Items of worth owned by the business (p. 350).

Attribute inspection: Determining product acceptability on the presence or absence of a key attribute (p. 308).

Attribute listing: The identification and listing of all major characteristics of a product, object or idea (p. 58).

Balance sheet: A document that details the assets, liabilities and net worth (owner's equity) of the business (p. 349).

Blue ocean strategy: A strategy aiming to develop compelling value innovations that create uncontested market space (p. 153).

Bootstrap finance: Creative financing methods of meeting the need for resources without relying on debt or equity finance (p. 237).

Brainstorming: A conference technique by which a group tries to find a solution for a specific problem by amassing spontaneous ideas from its members (p. 59).

Break-even point: The level of sales where all expenses have been met, but no profit has been made (p. 280).

Bridging finance: Financing extended to a firm using existing assets as collateral in order to acquire new assets; bridging finance is usually short term (p. 224).

Business adviser: Someone who works with client businesses to provide specialised skill and knowledge in one or more particular aspects of business operations (p. 247).

Business angels: Wealthy people who invest in entrepreneurial firms and contribute their business skills (p. 231).

Business coach: A person who works with entrepreneurs, business owners or senior managers to help them deal with problems in their work and private life (p. 253).

Business dynamics: Also called business churning; the extent to which firms enter an industry, grow, decline and exit an industry (p. 14).

Business exit: Any situation in which a business ceases to exist, through closure, liquidation, bankruptcy, sale or transfer to another owner, or merger (p. 92).

Business incubator: Dedicated premises provided to help firms get established and become profitable (p. 262).

Business introduction service: A service that arranges or facilitates the meeting of private investors and businesses seeking external capital (p. 231).

Business plan: A written document that explains and analyses an existing or proposed business venture (p. 162).

Business-planning process: A series of logical steps governing the creation, implementation and revision of a business plan (p. 173).

Business system franchise: An arrangement whereby the franchisor supplies the product and gives comprehensive guidelines on how the business is to be run (p. 123).

Cash flow statement (or forecast): A document that shows the movement of all cash into and out of a business during a given time frame (p. 346).

Collateral: Property used as security for a loan. If the debt is not paid, the lender has the right to sell the collateral to recover the value of the loan (p. 41).

Company: A separate legal entity that has an existence independent of its owners and managers (p. 202).

Concurrent control: Control measures performed on work in progress (p. 309).

Contingency plan: How a firm will respond to a threatened risk (p. 311).

Contribution margin: The proportion of money left in each dollar of sales after variable costs have been met, and which is available to cover fixed costs and contribute to profits (p. 281).

Copyright: The exclusive right granted by law to a copyright holder to make and distribute copies of, or otherwise control, their literary, musical, dramatic or artistic work (p. 212).

Corporate entrepreneurship: The process whereby an individual or a group, in association with an existing organisation, creates a new organisation or initiates renewal or innovation within that organisation (p. 400).

Corporate venturing: The development of new business ventures inside or at the periphery of an organisation (p. 400).

Creative destruction: The process of simultaneous emergence and disappearance of technologies, products and firms in the marketplace as a result of innovation (p. 11).

Creativity: The production of new and useful ideas (p. 55).

Depreciation: The diminution of the value of an item through use (p. 348).

Dialogic: A system with a circular causality process (p. 30).

Discontinuous opportunities: Innovations that move beyond existing business models to create new products and enter new markets (p. 404).

Discounting: The selling of a firm's accounts receivable to a financier while the firm keeps responsibility for collecting monies owing (p. 238).

Drawings: The income the business owner takes out of the business (p. 351).

Due diligence: A process of detailed scrutiny aimed at obtaining all the information needed to comprehensively evaluate a business for purchase and to establish whether the projected business is a worthwhile investment (p. 122).

Eco-efficiency: A management strategy that focuses on the delivery of competitively priced goods and services which satisfy consumer needs while progressively reducing ecological impacts throughout the product life cycle (p. 430).

Economic order quantity (EOQ): The amount of goods that minimises the total purchase and storage costs while still being sufficient to meet the production requirements of a business (p. 303).

Entrepreneurship: The process, brought about by individuals, of identifying new opportunities and converting them into marketable products or services (p. 4).

Entry cost: The price of starting up or buying a business enterprise (p. 112).

Environmental responsibility: The need to protect and enhance the natural environment (p. 429).

Environmental scanning: Analysing and understanding the internal and external forces that may affect a company's products, markets or operating systems (p. 140).

Exit cost: The price involved in liquidating or closing a business enterprise (p. 112).

Expert consultant: A business adviser with highly developed skills in a specific area (p. 255).

Facilitator: A business adviser who encourages clients to learn how to diagnose and treat their own business problems (p. 256).

Factoring: The selling of a firm's accounts receivable to a financier who assumes the credit risk and receives cash as the debtors settle their accounts (p. 238).

Feedback control: Control measures instituted after an event has taken place (p. 309).

Feedforward control: Control measures taken in advance of actual performance (p. 308).

Fixed costs: Expenses that remain the same, regardless of the level of activity or sales turnover a business generates (p. 279).

Floor plan: The arrangement of operational activities within a business premises (p. 298).

Focus group: A small group of people with an interviewer trained to solicit their views about a particular issue or product (p. 148).

Forced analogy: Also called forced relationship; the action of making an association between two unlike things in common to obtain new insights (p. 57).

Franchise: An arrangement whereby the originator of a business product or operating system permits another business owner to sell the goods and/or to use the business operating system on the originator's behalf (p. 123).

Franchisee: The business/person given contractual permission by the original owner of a system or product to operate a business franchise system or sell a product (p. 123).

Franchisor: A business or individual who owns the rights to a particular business franchise system or product (p. 123).

Goodwill: An intangible commodity; the extra value ascribed to a business, piece of intellectual property, brand name, or other business-related activity (p. 119).

Harvesting: The process entrepreneurs and investors use to exit a business and realise their investment (p. 386).

Heuristics: Simplifying strategies that can be used to make judgements quickly and efficiently. Heuristics result from cognition, i.e. the intellectual processes through which information is obtained, transformed, stored, retrieved and used (p. 33).

Home-based business (HBB): An enterprise in which all or most of the work is performed at or from the owner–operator's private residence; also known as 'small office, home office' (SOHO) (p. 440).

Human resource management (HRM): A firm's approach to managing its employees (p. 318).

Ill-will: Negative perceptions or attitudes towards a firm; an intangible commodity which detracts from the overall value of a business (p. 122).

In-depth personal interview: An interview that encourages respondents to explain their views, and which probes responses to explore an issue in greater detail (p. 148).

Indigenous peoples: The original inhabitants of a nation, territory or geographical region, and their descendants (p. 431).

Industrial Revolution: The term used to describe the changes brought about by the introduction of technology and methods of mass production in the eighteenth and nineteenth centuries (p. 3).

Initial public offering (IPO): Also called *flotation, going public, listing*; refers to a business's initial offer of shares to the public via a stock exchange (p. 233).

Insurance: A contract to provide compensation for any damage or loss suffered by a firm if a specified act occurs (p. 312).

Job analysis: The process of determining the duties and skill requirements of a job, and the sort of person who might fit these demands (p. 324).

Job description: A written statement of what a job entails, how it is done, and under what conditions (p. 324).

Job specification: The personal traits and experience required from a prospective employee (p. 324).

Just-in-time delivery: An inventory management system where materials are delivered to a firm at the time needed for production (p. 304).

Lease: A written agreement under which a property owner allows a tenant to use the property for a specified period of time and rent (p. 228).

Leverage: The degree to which a business uses borrowed money; what the debt–equity ratio measures (p. 223).

Liabilities: Debts or financial obligations of the business (p. 350).

Locus of control: The extent to which individuals believe that they can control events that affect them (p. 39).

Management buyout (MBO): The purchase of a controlling interest in a business by its management in order to take over assets and operations (p. 389).

Margin: A measure of how much of the final sales price is gross profit (p. 283).

Marketing: The process of planning and executing the conception, pricing, promotion and distribution of ideas, goods or services to create exchanges that satisfy individual and organisational goals (p. 271).

Market research: The use of information to identify and define marketing opportunities and problems (p. 139).

Mark-up: The extent to which the price of a product is increased from its original cost of goods sold to its final selling price (p. 283).

Mentoring: The process of transferring advice and ideas from one businessperson to another on a voluntary no-cost basis (p. 252).

Merger: The combining of two or more entities into one through a purchase acquisition or a pooling of interests (p. 390).

Mind map: A visual method of mapping information to stimulate the generation and analysis of it (p. 59).

Motivation: The willingness of employees to exert effort to achieve business goals (p. 328).

Need for achievement: A person's desire either for excellence or to succeed in competitive situations (p. 39).

Niche market: A narrowly focused target market for goods and/or services (p. 273).

Operations management: The control of the process by which a firm makes a product (p. 295).

Opportunity: A situation in which a new product, service or process can be introduced and sold at greater than its cost of production (p. 6).

Opportunity cost: The cost of passing up one investment in favour of another (p. 35).

Organisational culture: The shared values, attitudes and behaviour of employees in a firm (p. 319).

Organisational structure chart: A diagrammatic representation of the way in which employee work relationships are structured within a business (p. 323).

Overdraft: The amount by which withdrawals exceed deposits or the extension of credit by a lending institution to allow for such a situation (p. 227).

Owner's assets and liabilities: A document that shows the private assets, liabilities and net worth of a business owner (p. 352).

Owner's equity (or net worth): The difference between the assets and liabilities of a business; the value of the business to the owner if all its assets were sold and all liabilities were paid (p. 349).

Pair of hands adviser: A specialist brought into a firm for a set period of time (p. 256).

Partnership: A relationship that exists between people carrying on a business in common with a view to making a profit (p. 201).

Partnership agreement: A written document that covers all matters relating to the partnership (p. 201).

Patent: A legal document giving inventors the exclusive rights to their invention for a number of years (p. 210).

Philanthropy: An active effort to improve society (p. 427).

Placement: The exchange of goods or services between buyers and sellers (p. 287).

Primary data: Information that is collected first-hand for a specific research problem (p. 147).

Problem reversal: The action of viewing a problem from an opposite angle by asking questions such as 'What if we did the opposite?' and 'What is everyone else not doing?' (p. 57).

Product benefit: The advantage that a consumer can receive by purchasing a good or service (p. 275).

Product feature: What a product or service is or does (p. 275).

Product franchise: A franchise to sell a particular product or service (p. 123).

Productivity ratio: A comparison of inputs used with outputs produced (p. 308).

Profit and loss statement: A document that shows business-related revenues and expenses and the resulting profit or loss (p. 348).

Quality assurance system: A set of processes and principles designed to ensure the production of a set of consistent activities, goods or services (p. 309).

Resource: Any thing or quality that is useful (p. 71).

Restraint of trade clause: A contractual restriction on the right of a business vendor to operate a similar business in rivalry with the new purchaser of the firm (p. 122).

Risk: The possibility that a situation may end with a negative outcome for the firm (p. 310).

Risk management: The process of identifying risks in advance, assessing their likely occurrence and taking steps to reduce or eliminate them (p. 310).

Salary: Remuneration in which employees receive a fixed 'total pay' package, regardless of the number of hours worked (p. 325).

Sales mix forecast: An estimate of sales of each major product or service, the revenue generated by each of these, and the resulting cost of goods sold (p. 345).

Scheduling: Setting a time frame and sequence of events to perform an activity (p. 306).

Secondary data: Business research that has been done previously (p. 143).

Security: The protection of equipment and ideas from the risk of theft, loss or unauthorised use (p. 311).

Small business: A small-scale, independent firm usually managed, funded and operated by its owners, and whose staff size, financial resources and assets are comparatively limited in scale (p. 82).

Social entrepreneur: An enterprising person who applies entrepreneurial principles and skills to the resolution of social or community problems (p. 437).

Social network: The sum of relationships that a person maintains with other people as a result of social activity (p. 46).

Social obligation: The minimum level of socially responsible activity; doing only that which is required by law (p. 427).

Social responsibility: The maximum level of socially responsible activity; pursuing long-term goals that benefit society, even if there is no business gain in doing so (p. 427).

Social responsiveness: A moderate level of socially responsible activity; engaging in socially beneficial activities, mainly because there is a pragmatic benefit in doing so (p. 427).

Sole proprietor or **sole trader:** A person who wholly owns and operates a business (p. 199).

Spin-off: An individual or organisational unit leaving an existing firm to start as an independent new firm (p. 402).

Staff turnover: The number of employees who leave the business (p. 331).

Strategic alliance: An ongoing relationship between two businesses, which combine efforts for a specific purpose (p. 390).

Strategic plan: A plan that sets out the long-term focus of the business, its mission and its vision, and attempts to understand the environment in which the business operates (p. 172).

Strategic renewal: The new combinations of resources that result in significant changes to an organisation's strategy or structure (p. 400).

Strategic resources: Resources which provide a sustained competitive advantage to a firm (p. 72).

Survey: A system for collecting information using a questionnaire (p. 148).

Target market: A core group of customers that a business intends to focus its marketing efforts on (p. 273).

Term loan: A loan that is repaid through regular periodic payments, usually over a period of one to ten years (p. 228).

Total quality management (TQM): The adoption of a quality-based philosophy throughout a firm (p. 309).

Trade credit: A form of short-term debt financing whereby goods are received from the suppliers before payment is made (p. 228).

Trademark: A word, phrase, logo, symbol, colour, sound or smell used by a business to identify a product and distinguish it from those of its competitors (p. 211).

Trade secret: Any idea, formula, pattern, device, process or information that provides a business with a competitive advantage (p. 213).

Training needs analysis: An evaluation of the skills and knowledge employees need, what they currently hold, and what gap exists (p. 330).

Trust: An obligation imposed on trustees to deal with the trust property (over which they have control) for the benefit of the beneficiaries (p. 204).

Trust deed: A written document that evidences the creation of the trust. It sets out the terms and conditions on which the trust assets are held by the trustees and outlines the rights of the beneficiaries (p. 204).

Underwriter: An intermediary between an issuer of a security and the investing public, usually an investment bank (p. 235).

Variable costs: Expenditure items that increase or decrease as sales volume changes (p. 279).

Variable inspection: Determining product acceptability by results falling within predetermined boundaries (p. 308).

Venture capital (VC): Independently managed, dedicated pools of capital that focus equity investments in high-growth businesses (p. 231).

Wage: System of remuneration in which employees are paid at a set hourly rate (p. 325).

Working capital: Funds used in operating a business on a daily basis (p. 347).

INDEX